D1684592

AMERICAN DREAMS & REALITY:
A Retelling of the American Story
Volume II, Sixth Edition

AMERICAN DREAMS & REALITY:
A Retelling of the American Story
Volume II, Sixth Edition

John Moretta
Houston Community College System
Houston, Texas

Louise A. Mayo
County College of Morris
Randolph, New Jersey

Anne Kearney
Jefferson Community & Technical College
Louisville, Kentucky

Abigail Press **Wheaton, IL 60189**

Design and Production: Abigail Press
Typesetting: Abigail Press
Typeface: AGaramond
Cover Art: Sam Tolia

AMERICAN DREAMS & REALITY:
A Retelling of the American Story, Volume II

Sixth Edition, 2009
Printed in the United States of America
Translation rights reserved by the authors
ISBN 1-890919-44-6 ISBN 978-1-890919-44-3

Copyright @ by Abigail Press Inc., 2050 Middleton Dr., Wheaton, IL 60187

All rights reserved. No part of the material protected by the copyright notice may be reproduced or utilized in any form or by any means, electronic or mechanical, including photocopy, recording, or any information storage and retrieval system, without permission in writing from the publisher.

ABOUT THE AUTHORS

John A. Moretta earned a B.A. in History from Santa Clara University in CA., an M.A. in History from Portland State University in Oregon, and a Ph.D. in History from Rice University in Houston, Texas. He is currently Professor of History and Chair of the Social Sciences Dept. of Central College, Houston Community College System in Houston, Texas. Dr. Moretta is also an adjunct professor at the University of Houston. Dr. Moretta's first book, *William Pitt Ballinger, Texas Lawyer, Southern Statesman,* won the 2003 San Antonio Conservation Society's award for one of the best books in Texas history. He is also a co-author of *The Western Dream of Civilization* and has completed a biography of William Penn for Addison Wesley Longman's Library of American Biography Series.

Louise Mayo was a professor for twenty-four years at County College of Morris, Randolph, NJ. She is the author of *The Ambivalent Image* (1988), *A House Divided: America in the Era of Civil War and Reconstruction*, and numerous articles and papers in the fields of women and minority history. She has an M.A. from Cornell University in Modern European and Russian History and a Ph.D. from City University of New York in American History, specializing in immigration and minority history. She taught courses in Twentieth Century America, History of American Women, History of Minorities, History of American Cities and Suburbs, and Civil War and Reconstruction.

Anne has a B.A. from Saint Mary's College (Notre Dame, IN), an M.A. and a Ph.D. from the University of Notre Dame in American History, and an M.L.S. in academic librarianship from Indiana University at Bloomington. She presently teaches American History and the History of American Women at Jefferson Community and Technical College - Kentucky Community and Technical College System in Louisville while pursuing a law degree at Brandeis School of Law, University of Louisville. She is listed in *Who's Who in America* and *Who's Who in the World.* She has written articles for the Oxford Biographical Dictionary and Salem Press and presented scholarly papers at the annual meetings of the Catholic Historical Association, Popular Cultural Association, and Community College Humanities Association.

Contents in Brief

Contents

CHAPTER THIRTEEN

THE RISE OF INDUSTRIAL AMERICA & THE POLITICS OF THE NEW ORDER

CHAPTER FOURTEEN

CHAPTER SIXTEEN

CHAPTER SEVENTEEN

APPENDIX

Chapter Twelve

RECONSTRUCTION: The Turning Point That Never Turned

April 14, 1865, was Good Friday. It was the fourth anniversary of the surrender of Fort Sumter. At a ceremony in the remains of the old fortress, Major Robert Anderson, its former commander, hoisted the weather-beaten, ragged old flag he had been forced to pull down in 1861. That evening, a weary President Lincoln and his wife relaxed at Ford's Theater, which was showing a popular comedy, "Our American Cousin," in a benefit performance for disabled Union veterans. The theater was packed, and the cast ad-libbed "many pleasant allusions" to the president, to the delight of Lincoln and the audience.

The nation had come through the greatest threat ever to its existence and now faced further overwhelming challenges. But the leader whose burdens and trials had made him appear to be much older than his fifty-six years seemed to be equal to the task. "I am a tired man," Lincoln said at the end of the war. "Sometimes I think I am the tiredest man on earth." He had overcome his frequent bouts of depression and his personal grief over the death of his lively, inquisitive, and much-loved eleven-year-old son, Willie. (Mary, his wife, never completely regained her stability after a nervous breakdown brought on by her child's death.) Lincoln had also managed to surmount the despair he felt at the death of thousands of Americans in the war. His success in meeting national and personal crises underscored both his greatness and his compassion.

The president was haunted by his dreams. Some, like those about the dead Willie, gave him comfort. Others were alarming, particularly recurring images of assassination. In one such dream, Lincoln was awakened by the loud weeping of mourners surrounding a body lying in state. When he asked a soldier who the corpse was, he was told, "The President. He was killed by an assassin." His friend, Ward Lamon, his self-appointed bodyguard, and Secretary of War Stanton were both alarmed enough about possible dangers to the president's safety to provide cavalry escorts for his carriage and a District of Columbia policeman to accompany him to the theater.

Amidst the joy of surrender celebrations and the merriment of the theater, however, the security precautions had disintegrated. The policeman, who had been charged with guarding the president, carelessly left his post at the door of the president's box to see the play.

Right about the time of the Fort Sumter ceremony, John Wilkes Booth, a young actor, had gone to the theater to pick up his mail. There, he learned about the special performance that the president would attend. As the laughter rose in the theater, Booth made his way to the president's box, derringer pistol and dagger in hand. At the outer door, he was briefly stopped but showed his card and confidently claimed that the president, who was known to enjoy actors, had asked him to come.

Booth was a member of one of America's great acting families. Although overshadowed by his father and his brother, Edwin (who was believed by many to be America's finest actor), John was a fairly successful actor in his own right, earning an impressive $20,000 a year. He was, however, unstable, egotistical, and a fanatical Confederate sympathizer. He obsessed about Lincoln whom he saw as a tyrant responsible for all the nation's problems. Booth had recruited a strange group of malcontents from Washington's underworld, including a Confederate deserter, a Rebel spy, and a mentally handicapped druggist's clerk. Lee's surrender thwarted his original plan to kidnap the president and bring him to Richmond. So, he resolved instead to kill Lincoln, Vice President Johnson, and Secretary of State Seward. The conspirator assigned to kill Johnson lost his nerve. The other accomplice did stab and seriously wound Seward, who eventually recovered.

Meanwhile, Booth, after downing two brandies for courage, stepped into the president's box and fired his pistol into Lincoln's head. After slashing the arm of a major who tried to detain him, Booth vaulted over the box and landed on stage, breaking a leg. He shouted something to the dazed audience. Some said it was "sic temper tyrannis" ("thus be it ever to tyrants"), Virginia's state motto. Then he hobbled off stage out into the alley where he mounted his waiting horse and clattered off into Washington's dark streets. Booth's bullet tore into the president's brain. An army surgeon, who had been sitting in the audience, pronounced the wound to be mortal.

Soldiers carried the unconscious president across the street to a room in a boarding house. There he lingered for the night, surrounded by stricken members of his cabinet, with his wife sobbing uncontrollably in the next room. He died the next morning at 7:22. Tears cascading down his face, Edmund Stanton declared, "Now he belongs to the ages."

John Wilkes Booth assassinated President Abraham Lincoln.

Within minutes, the telegraph carried the tragic news to a stunned nation. No American president had ever been killed before. People openly wept in the streets. Navy Secretary Gideon Welles noted that blacks were especially overwhelmed by Lincoln's death just as victory over slavery occurred: "the hopeless grief (of those poor colored people) affected me more than almost anything else." For fourteen days, millions of Americans stood along the tracks and watched silently as a nine-car train carried Lincoln's body, and the small coffin of his son, Willie, the 1,662 miles from Washington back home to Springfield, Illinois. The president's murder on Good Friday had made him into a Christ-like figure. It gave new meaning to the final verse of the "Battle Hymn of the Republic": "As He died to make men holy, Let us die to make men free."

By April 26, Union troops had trapped John Wilkes Booth in a burning Virginia barn and shot him in the head. As he lay dying, he whispered, "Tell my mother I died for my country . . . I did what I thought was best." Four of his accomplices were hanged and four others were sentenced to hard labor, including the hapless Dr. Samuel Mudd, whose sole crime seemed to be setting Booth's broken leg. The mood of the Northern public after the assassination caused anger, bitterness, and cries for vengeance against Confederate leaders. Yet Lincoln, in his moving second inaugural address, had declared, "With malice toward none; with charity for all; with firmness in the right . . . let us strive . . . to bind up the nation's wounds." With the death of this great man, would it be possible to balance "charity" and "firmness" and create "a just and a lasting peace"?

WARTIME RECONSTRUCTION

The questions that formed the core of Reconstruction surfaced during the war. After the Emancipation Proclamation, Northerners of every political stripe assumed that the South would emerge from the war as a society without slavery. But what system of labor would replace the institution of slavery? Would four million newly freed slaves become citizens? If they did, what rights would they enjoy, and what role would they play in the social and political life of the South? Could the states of the Confederacy rejoin the union? If so, under what terms? Should the president or Congress set these terms?

Military officers, during the war, often had to make decisions about what to do with thousands of ragged freed slaves who flocked to Union armies when they learned about emancipation. Despite his openly expressed contempt for both Radical ideas and freedmen, General Sherman issued a special order reserving confiscated land for the resettlement of freed people on plots of forty acres per family. He also sanctioned lending army mules to the new farmers (leading, perhaps, to the later poignant demand for "forty acres and a mule"). By the end of the war, more than forty thousand people had been resettled in that area of coastal South Carolina and Georgia. By 1865, 20 percent of the farmland under Union control was being worked by independent black farmers. In 1863 General Grant declared that Davis Bend, the estate of Jefferson Davis and his brother, should become a "negro paradise." Davis' former slaves and other black farmers leased its thousands of acres. By 1865 they were raising successful cotton and food crops and earning a profit of nearly $160,000. They formed their own government, including elected judges and sheriffs. Black people desired, above all, to become independent farmers, and some Radical Republicans hoped that the future would see a South of black yeoman farmers working their own land.

Events in Louisiana, however, were more indicative of the labor system that would develop in the South. There, the military commander believed that the army's burden of caring for black refugees could be ended by restoring the plantation system. Former slaves would be coerced into signing yearly contracts with loyal planters and forbidden to leave without permission of the owners. Despite the program's limited success in reviving the state's agricultural system, most army officials operated under the assumption that freed slaves should continue to be plantation laborers.

Northern freedmen's aid societies, founded by abolitionists, attempted to accomplish another Radical vision of the future, that of an educated black population able to fulfill the demands of citizenship. During the war, they sent more than a thousand teachers to the occupied South, precursors of two thousand more who arrived in the early postwar period. Most came from New England, and three-quarters were women. Most were white (although 20 percent were blacks, many of whom were themselves only minimally educated). They strove to instill the Protestant work ethic and the values of self-discipline in the 200,000 or so students they reached. After the war, the freedmen's education program was greatly expanded in a concentrated effort to erase illiteracy. The black scholar and leader, W.E.B. Du Bois, later commented that these missionary teachers were the unsung heroes of the Civil War who "came not to keep the Negroes in their place, but to raise them out of the defilement of the places where slavery had wallowed them . . . . This was the gift of New England to the freed Negro."

Lincoln attempted to deal with the issue of restoration of the Southern states to the Union in December 1863, a year after the Emancipation Proclamation. He issued the Proclamation of Amnesty and Reconstruction, his first extensive program for reconstruction. In it, Lincoln offered the re-establishment of all rights "except as to slaves" to those in conquered areas who took a loyalty oath to the federal constitution. Only high-ranking confederate military and civil officials would be excluded. When 10 percent of the 1860 voting population had taken the oath, a new state government would be established, abolishing slavery. Lincoln based his policy on the theory of the "indissoluble Union." Since states could not legally secede, they were still a part of the Union. The purpose of reconstruction was to enable loyal citizens to regain control of their governments. Lincoln never saw this policy, issued in the midst of war, as an unchangeable blueprint for postwar reconstruction. He hoped to use his "Ten Percent Plan" to weaken the Confederacy by gaining the support of former Southern Whigs, at best hesitant secessionists. He also wanted to get emancipation into as many Southern state constitutions as possible.

Congressman Thaddeus Stevens of Pennsylvania advocated seizing land from Southern planters and distributing it among the freed blacks.

Radical Republicans, led by Charles Sumner and Benjamin Wade in the Senate and Thaddeus Stevens in the House, objected to allowing former rebels back into the Union so easily. They wanted to ensure that committed Unionists controlled Southern governments and that the freedom and civil rights of blacks would be protected. They argued that, by seceding, Southern states had committed "state suicide," reverting to territories that had to apply to Congress for readmission to the Union. When representatives of a Louisiana government that followed Lincoln's plan showed up in 1864, Congress refused to seat them. That same year, Republicans in Congress produced their own view of reconstruction in the Wade-Davis Bill. This law would have required an oath of allegiance from a majority of the voters, rather than 10 percent. Then elections would be held for delegates to a state constitutional convention, with the vote restricted to those who could take an "iron clad oath" that they had never voluntarily aided the Confederacy. This measure would have postponed Reconstruction for a very long period. Lincoln, fearing its consequences for the war effort, pocket-vetoed it.

Although some historians later saw this as evidence of the irreconcilable differences between the moderate, charitable views of the president and the harsh unyielding attitudes of Radicals in Congress, Lincoln himself insisted that he was not "inflexibly committed to any single plan of restoration." Lincoln tended to be flexible and pragmatic, adjusting his ideas to the political circumstances. He worked with his Radical opponents in January 1865 to gain passage of the Thirteenth Amendment, abolishing slavery throughout the nation and ensuring that wartime emancipation measures could never be overturned. He also signed a bill creating the Freedmen's Bureau as a relief agency in the South for refugees of both races. It was empowered to draft and enforce labor contracts, to aid blacks to become independent farmers, and to assist in the operation of freedmen's schools.

Lincoln moved closer to compromise with Congress. He confided to a friend that he "had no plan for reorganization, but must be guided by events." He tried to meet partially the demands of Radical critics and free blacks for black suffrage in the South. He suggested, in his last public speech (April 11, 1865), that the vote be extended to literate blacks and the larger group of those who had served in the Union armies. The *New York Times* noted that Lincoln did not seem to feel the time had yet come for "the statement of a settled reconstruction policy." At a cabinet meeting on the morning of his assassination, Lincoln endorsed a plan to substitute military occupation for civilian government in the Confederate states to ensure the enforcement of black civil rights. The bullets from Booth's gun prevent us from ever knowing whether this gifted and practical politician could have successfully negotiated the contradictions between the competing goals of "charity," "firmness" and "justice."

PRESIDENTIAL RECONSTRUCTION

Andrew Johnson, the man who succeeded Lincoln, seemed to many to have a remarkably similar background to his predecessor. Both rose from rural poverty with little or no formal education to realize their ambitions and achieve success in the public arena. Johnson had been an illiterate tailor whose school teacher wife taught him to write. He acquired a farm and slaves and climbed the political ladder in Tennessee, eventually becoming governor and senator. Johnson resented the snobbery he felt from the old-time plantation Southern leadership. "Some day I will show the stuck-up aristocrats who is running the country," he once vowed. When the Civil War broke out, Johnson was an ardent Unionist, the only senator from a Confederate state who spoke out against secession. As wartime governor of occupied Tennessee, he sternly declared, "Treason must be made odious, and traitors must be punished and impoverished." He promised anxious blacks that he would "be your Moses, and lead you through the Red Sea of war and bondage to a fairer future of liberty and peace." Such comments, coupled with the need to build bisectional support, particularly in the border states, led Lincoln to pick Johnson for vice president in 1864. His thunderous speeches against the "slaveocracy" also led many Radical Republicans to believe that the new president would be more sympathetic to their point of view than Lincoln had been.

Lincoln and the Radicals had misread Johnson, however. The struggle to overcome poverty seemed to have given Lincoln an empathy for others, wit, and the political skills of tact and flexibility. The same struggle embittered Johnson and made him into a suspicious man who, despite personal courage, was intolerant of other views, stubborn, and unable to compromise. Unlike Lincoln, Johnson never viewed slavery as a great moral evil. "Damn the Negroes," he once declared, "I am fighting these traitorous aristocrats, their masters." He believed that nonslaveholding whites were the main victims of slavery, oppressed by the combination of slaves and their masters. He saw no role for the freedmen in a reconstructed South and hoped that they would leave the country. "White men alone must manage the South," he announced. He insisted to Congress that blacks had "less capacity for government than any other race of people . . . . Wherever they have been left to their own devices they have shown a constant tendency to relapse into barbarism." He was a committed Jacksonian in that he favored states' rights and was as suspicious of the "bloated, corrupt aristocracy" of the banks and corporations emerging in the North as he had been of the Southern patricians.

With Congress not due to meet again until December 1865, Johnson was free to implement his own reconstruction policy. Lincoln's tentative reconstruction initiatives based on the wartime theory of indestructible states had become set in stone in Johnson's limited imagination. This was coupled with a rigid view of states' rights that would not allow any real role for the federal government in Reconstruction. Johnson's restoration policy (as he insisted on calling it) became clear in two proclamations he issued in May 1865. One offered amnesty and return of all property, except slaves, to every white man who swore to an oath of future loyalty. Political and military leaders of the Confederacy and those with property valued at more than $20,000 were excluded but given the opportunity to apply to the president for individual pardons. Under the second proclamation, the newly loyal electorate would choose members to a constitutional convention in each state. Despite his stated support for states' rights, Johnson made it clear that he expected each convention to nullify secession, accept the abolition of slavery, and repudiate all Confederate debts. After that, elections would be held for state and federal officials, and Reconstruction would be complete. Under these terms, presidential Reconstruction moved along rapidly. Southern congressmen arrived to claim their seats by the time Congress reconvened in December. But Johnson had

The Freedmen's Bureau established schools attended by ex-slaves. Many of the teachers were white women from the North.

misinterpreted Northern and congressional opinion as completely as the Radicals had misunderstood Johnson's true nature earlier. As a result of the actions of these reconstructed governments, Congress refused to seat the Southern congressmen.

The same president who had spoken sternly about "treason" in April was speaking eloquently of the need to be "forbearing and forgiving" about the past sins of the South by the fall. Despite his often expressed hatred of the old aristocrats, the ego of the former illiterate tailor's apprentice was gratified when members of the proud Southern ruling class came to him to beg humbly for pardons. "I remember the taunts, the jeers, the scowls with which I was treated," the president noted. He was gratified by their confessions of error and their expressions of "sincere respect" for his "desire and intention to sustain Southern rights in the Union." He quickly granted 13,500 pardons to ex-Confederates who were now free to return to power in their states.

Southern Defiance and the Black Codes

When the Confederate armies surrendered, Southerners, as an observer remarked at the time, were "so despondent that if readmission at some future time under whatever conditions had been promised, it would have been looked upon as a favor." But presidential generosity and support led to obstinate overconfidence by Southern leaders. Johnson, now the captive of Southern interests, could not respond to their open defiance. As a result, several states repealed secession instead of repudiating it. Mississippi refused to ratify the Thirteenth Amendment, and Arkansas even appropriated funds for Confederate veterans' pensions. Northerners, who expected some acknowledgment of defeat by the South, were astounded when some states elected the newly pardoned ex-Confederates to local, state, and even national office. In the most publicized example, Georgia chose Alexander Stephens, the former vice president of the Confederacy, as one of its senators.

The inability of Southern whites to accept the free labor ideology of the North was even more disturbing to many Northerners. Southern state legislatures in 1865 and 1866 passed a series of Black Codes, ostensibly to define the legal rights of the newly freed blacks. Most Southern whites were unable or unwilling to accept even minimal notions of legal equality between the races. The codes did concede blacks the rights to have legal marriages, sign contracts, sue and be sued, and obtain property. Southerners claimed that these were substantial advances. However, the codes denied the freed people such basic rights as that of free assembly, bearing arms, serving on juries, testifying against whites in court, voting, or holding office. Although many of these prohibitions existed in the still white supremacist North as well, these open attempts to restrict the Union's most loyal followers in the South irritated many Northerners.

The provisions of the codes that related to labor and vagrancy angered Northerners the most, as they seemed to foreshadow an attempt to bring back plantation slavery. The laws defined vagrancy so broadly that any black who did not have an annual contract to work on a plantation could be arrested, fined, and hired out as an unpaid laborer to any planter who paid the fine. Blacks who wanted to enter any other occupation but agriculture needed special licenses from the state. Children, in homes not deemed to be "adequate," could be sent as "apprentices" to white "guardians," their former owners. Although the army and Freedmen's Bureau suspended enforcement of the worst provisions of the Black Codes, their implications had a deep impact on Northern public opinion. Stories in Northern newspapers bolstered the image of unrepentant, arrogant Confederates. One influential Republican commentator reported, "It is a stubborn fact that our truest friends are threatened and persecuted and that the negro is denied his freedom whenever the population has a chance to act upon its own impulses without immediately being checked."

The Split Between President and Congress

When the representatives of the Johnson governments arrived to take their seats in December 1865, the stage was set for a direct conflict between the president and Congress. Johnson had hoped to create a new centrist Union coalition of Democrats, Southern whites, and moderate Republicans. To do so, however, he would have to compromise on the issue of freedmen's rights. Johnson's friends knew that he would never compromise, preferring a messy struggle. "A fight between the Radicals and the Executive is inevitable," said one. "Let it come. The sooner the better for the whole country."

Many Republicans believed that the future of their party was at stake. An ironic result of the Thirteenth Amendment came out of the elimination of the three-fifths clause in the Constitution. The South would increase its political power by adding 15 to 20 seats, as the entire black population would now count in allotting seats in the House. This hardly seemed fair to Republicans, since these Johnsonian governments were denying the most basic rights to blacks. In addition, rebels whose treason had been ignored by presidential pardons were running those governments. (Ten Confederate generals and nine former Confederate congressmen were in the group of Southern representatives asking to be seated.) It was not surprising that Congress refused to seat the eighty Southern representatives. Congressional Republicans also rejected Johnson's "restoration" plans. Instead, Congress appointed a Joint Committee of Fifteen on Reconstruction.

Moderates, however, dominated the Joint Committee. Compromise still seemed possible. These moderate Republicans conferred with Johnson and believed they had his support for two bills to protect the rights of freed people. The first extended the life of the Freedmen's Bureau, enlarged its legal powers in civil rights cases, and authorized it to build and maintain schools. Johnson dismayed the moderates in February 1866 by vetoing the bill. Democrats organized a mass rally to support the veto. Johnson delivered an extraordinarily unrestrained speech attacking the Radicals as traitors and Judases. He portrayed himself as Christ who would willingly shed his blood to "vindicate the Union and the preservation of this government in its original purity and character." The speech was so intemperate that many Americans wondered if the president was drunk.

Despite their disillusionment over the president's behavior, most moderate Republicans still hoped to avert a complete break. They modified the Freedmen's Bureau bill to meet some of the presidential objections and passed a relatively modest Civil Rights bill. The bill sought to overturn the Dred Scott decision and the Black Codes. It defined blacks as citizens entitled to protection, property, contracts, and equal-

Many African-American families received little help during Reconstruction.

ity under the law. To appease Johnson, the bill did not give blacks the vote or the right to desegregated public facilities. Despite this attempt at compromise, the president shocked the moderates again by vetoing the Civil Rights bill and the second Freedmen's Bureau bill. He made any future reconciliation with Congress virtually impossible by arguing that Reconstruction was already complete under his policies, and only the individual states could deal with the freedmen. Democrats applauded his stand. If Congress had its way, one Democratic paper declared, "how long will it be . . . before it will say the negro shall vote, sit in a jury box, and intermarry with your families? Such are the questions put by the President." But the veto turned potential allies among moderate Republicans into unyielding enemies. "He has broken the faith, betrayed his trust, and must sink from detestation to contempt," declared one disillusioned senator who had tried to work with Johnson. Rather than isolating the Radicals, Johnson's actions pushed the moderates closer to the Radical position. Congress was able to override both presidential vetoes.

The Fourteenth Amendment

The Joint Committee on Reconstruction faced with the break with the president sought to develop a constitutional amendment that would unify Republicans. It would do so by placing the rights of freedmen under national protection where they could not be touched by presidential actions or shifting political currents. Republicans also hoped that the Fourteenth Amendment would provide the terms under which the defeated South could return to the Union. This amendment, which quickly gained the necessary two-thirds vote in Congress, may well be the most important single amendment in the United States Constitution. Much of its significance came from later interpretations. But even at the time, it provided a national guarantee of equality before the law.

The first section of the amendment defined citizenship in the nation as belonging to "all persons born or naturalized in the United States." Thus, any blacks born in America were now automatically citizens, nullifying the Dred Scott decision. No state could abridge "the privileges and immunities" of a citizen of the United States, "deprive any person of life, liberty, or property without due process of law," or deny "equal protection of the laws." In later years this section, the heart of the amendment, was subject to a variety of interpretations. Conservative courts at the end of the century ruled that corporations were "legal persons," and state attempts to regulate them were unconstitutional. In the mid-twentieth century, the "equal protection" provision became the foundation for overturning state mandated segregation of the races.

The second section was a compromise on the issue of black suffrage. It did not grant blacks the right to vote, but it did provide for a reduction in a state's representation, proportional to the number of male citizens denied the vote. If Southern states declined to extend the vote to blacks, at least they would not benefit from the increased representation that derived from the end of the three-fifths clause. The third section was the most controversial at the time, since it barred from national or state office all men who had aided the rebellion after swearing allegiance to the Constitution. This was designed to exclude the pre-war ruling class from power. The fourth section guaranteed the Union debt and repudiated the Confederate debt.

As a whole, the Fourteenth Amendment presented the minimum terms Northern public opinion expected from the defeated South. After all, it did not confiscate land from Confederate supporters or leaders, did not deny them the vote, or even force them to accept black suffrage. It seems likely that Reconstruction would have been over if the South accepted the amendment. Tennessee, controlled by political enemies of Johnson, quickly ratified the amendment in 1866 and was promptly admitted back into the Union. Johnson, however, still totally misunderstanding Northern public opinion, urged the excluded states to reject the amendment. He argued that the amendment was illegal because it kept the Southern states out of the Congress that passed it. The ex-confederate states unwisely followed his advice.

Johnson convinced his Southern admirers that he could rally popular support in the North for his Reconstruction plans and administer a well-deserved whipping to the Radicals in the congressional elections of 1866. The president attempted to launch a National Union movement to support his objectives. This movement, however, failed to get off the ground as a result of basic problems that undermined it in the eyes of the Northern public. Growing violence in the South alarmed Northerners. In May 1866, a quarrel in Memphis between recently discharged black veterans and local whites, led by Irish policemen, erupted into a three-day riot. The white mobs killed forty-six blacks, raped five black women, and burnt or looted hundreds of black homes, schools, and churches. The Memphis riot proved, the *New York Tribune* observed cynically, "that the Freedmen's Bureau ought to be abolished forthwith, and the blacks remitted to the paternal care of their old masters, who 'understand the nigger . . . a great deal better than the Yankees can.'" Three months later, a similar riot rocked New Orleans when a mob attacked delegates to a black suffrage convention, killing thirty-four blacks and three of their white allies, and injuring over one hundred more. Many Northerners agreed with the assessment of one observer that Johnson's lenient policies had caused this "barbarism of the rebellion in its renaissance." The president certainly did not ease these concerns when he delivered a speech in which he blamed the Republicans for inciting the mob and offered no sympathy for the victims.

In fact, the greatest problem faced by the National Union movement may well have been the president himself. Johnson had been an effective speaker in Tennessee, so he decided to take his case to the Northern public. He launched his August-September 1866 "swing around the circle," a campaign tour to influence Northern voters in the upcoming congressional elections. (He was the first president ever to do this.) The trip was an unmitigated disaster. His rough country style, which played so well in Tennessee, turned off Northern voters. He allowed hecklers, planted by Radicals, to draw him into shouted exchanges of insults. "Why not hang Thad Stevens and Wendell Phillips," he exclaimed at one stop. The president had lost all control of himself, and, in doing so, he lost command of the country.

Finally, the Republicans were able to brush the Democrats, by now Johnson's main supporters, with the tar of treason against the Union. This was a tactic later known as "waving the bloody shirt." One Republican speaker declared, "Every unregenerate rebel calls himself a Democrat . . . . Every man who labored for rebellion in the field, who murdered Union prisoners . . . who conspired to bring about civil war in the loyal states . . . calls himself a Democrat." The election had also become a referendum on the Fourteenth Amendment, overwhelmingly favored by Northern public opinion.

All these factors help explain a victory so lopsided that it surprised even the most committed Radical Republican. The Radicals now had a veto-proof majority of more than two-thirds in both Houses of Congress. The Northern electorate had clearly decided that the victory in the war must lead to a fundamental transformation of the South. Republicans even swept Johnson's own state of Tennessee. Its new Republican governor gleefully said, "Give my respects to the dead dog in the White House."

Reconstruction Acts

Led by Thaddeus Stevens, Speaker of the House, and Benjamin Wade, President Pro Tem of the Senate, Radicals believed that they had won a mandate from the public to substitute a congressional reconstruction plan for the president's failing program. Egged on by the president, the Southern states continued to reject the Fourteenth Amendment, the easiest terms they could have reasonably expected. Exasperated moderates then reached a compromise with Radicals on a Reconstruction Act.

The Reconstruction Act of 1867 rejected Johnson's views that the Southern states should be immediately admitted to the Union without qualifications. It also rebuffed Radical demands for an indefinite military occupation, coupled with confiscation and redistribution of plantation lands to provide a foundation for the economic independence of the freedmen. Instead, the act temporarily divided the old Confederacy (except Tennessee) into five military districts. Each would be supervised by an army general who could use the army and the Freedmen's Bureau to register voters and protect lives and property. The act then laid out the steps to create new state governments and admit them to the Union. First, each state would hold a constitutional convention with delegates chosen by all adult males regardless of "race, color, or previous condition." (But not ex-Confederates barred by the Fourteenth Amendment.) The new governments had to allow the same "impartial" suffrage and ratify the Fourteenth Amendment. When these conditions were met, states could send representatives to Congress. The president vetoed the act, protesting that "the people of the South . . . were to be trodden under foot to protect niggers."

Congress rapidly and overwhelmingly overrode the veto. All but three states—Mississippi, Texas, and Virginia—agreed to these requirements by June 1868. The Fourteenth Amendment became part of the Constitution in July. (Those last three states were readmitted in 1870.) The Reconstruction Act, in insisting on black suffrage in the South, combined the idealism of the Radicals with political realism. The black vote might make it possible to establish the Republican Party in the South. Some people felt that it would allow blacks to defend themselves and free the nation of the need for continued federal occupation and intervention.

President Johnson, firm in his belief that Reconstruction was a dangerous revolution, sought to thwart the will of Congress with his appointment powers. Congress, in turn, tried to limit Johnson's ability to do mischief by passing the Tenure of Office Act. This act prevented the president from dismissing any federal official whose appointment had required Senate confirmation until the Senate approved his

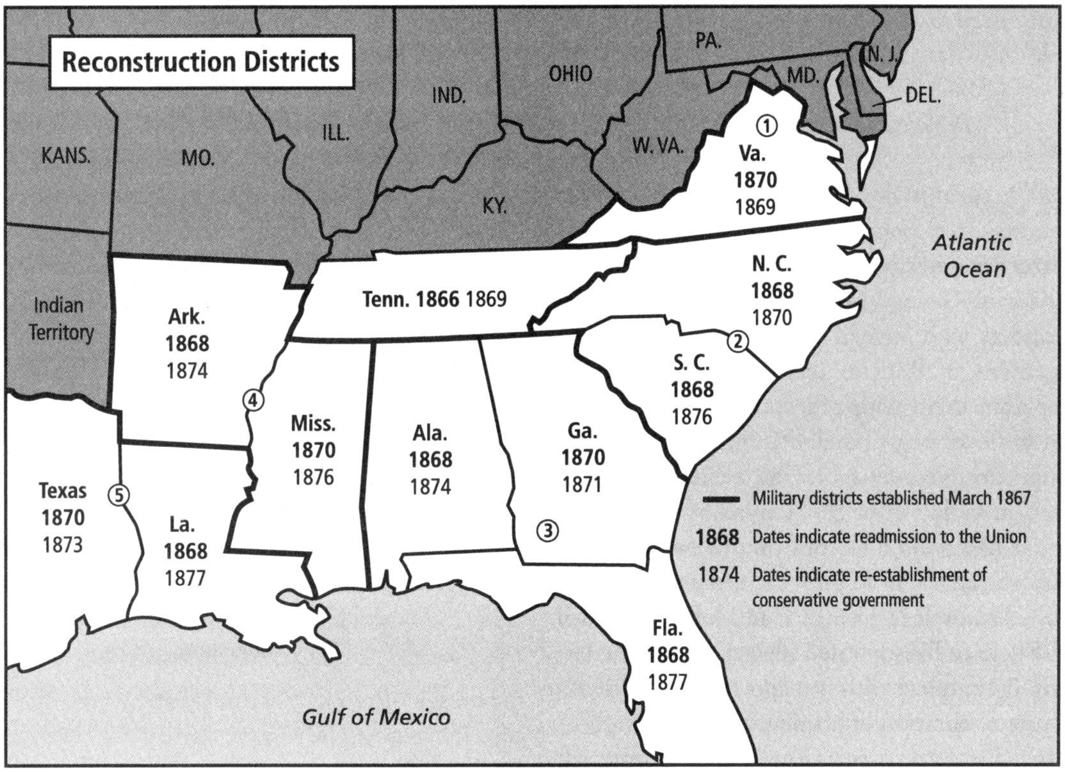

successor. This was designed to prevent Johnson from removing Republican officials who supported congressional reconstruction, particularly Secretary of War Edwin Stanton. Stanton not only supported Radical Reconstruction but he was in a key position to aid in its enforcement and act as an internal cabinet spy for his friends in Congress.

Radical Republicans turned their attentions to reforms at the state level in the North, designed to eliminate obstacles to individual advancement. This was in accord with the party's free-labor ideology that had been at the heart of its opposition to slavery. Michigan expanded state institutions for orphans and the disabled, outlawed racial segregation, and instituted free compulsory public education. Massachusetts' Republicans succeeded in banning racial discrimination in public accommodations and limiting child labor. An ambitious program of reform in New York included a Tenement House Act, Free School Law, Metropolitan Health Act, a Normal School Act that set up eight state teachers' colleges, and the establishment of a State Board of Charities. Despite these undoubted advances, however, most Northern blacks remained in unskilled, low-wage jobs and substandard housing. The arrival of increasing numbers of European immigrants caused many to lose such jobs as barbers and construction workers where they had long predominated. Nevertheless, public life and political rights were now open to them in ways unheard of before the war. The overwhelming majority of blacks, however, continued to live in the South.

The most important effort for Radical reform in the North was the push to extend the vote to blacks. But Northern voters, frightened by the vicious, racist rhetoric of the Democrats and their conservative allies, rejected black suffrage amendments. A French newspaperman noted wryly, "Any Democrat who did not manage to hint in his speech that the negro is a degenerate gorilla, would be considered lacking in enthusiasm." As a result, the Democrats made major gains in the local and state elections of 1867. This emboldened Johnson and his allies. The president treated serenaders at the White House to a "victory speech." One of his aides crowed, "Any party with an abolition head and a nigger tail will soon find itself with nothing left but the head and the tail."

Presidential Impeachment

Johnson, in the mistaken belief that Northern public opinion was now behind him, renewed his efforts to obstruct congressional reconstruction. Ignoring the advice of General Grant, he removed military commanders who seemed too enthusiastic in their enforcement of Radical reconstruction policies and replaced them with officers more sympathetic to Southern whites. Finally, Johnson decided to challenge Congress by removing Secretary of War Stanton, in violation of the Tenure of Office Act. (Congress had refused to confirm Stanton's suspension.) At the advice of Republican senators, Stanton barricaded himself in his office and refused to turn over the keys to his supposed replacement. The latter arrived complete with a major hangover from a premature celebration of his new position.

After this debacle, the House voted to impeach (indict) Johnson by a strictly party-line vote of 126 to 47 even before the actual charges had been listed. Nine of the eventual charges referred to violations of the Tenure of Office Act. The tenth accusation was that Johnson had been "unmindful of the high duties of his office" and had tried to bring Congress into "disgrace, ridicule, hatred, contempt, and reproach."

As the Constitution provides, the Senate acts as jury in cases of impeachment, with the Chief Justice of the Supreme Court serving as presiding judge. A two-thirds vote is required to remove a president. Despite the elaborate legal language, it was clear that the president was really being tried for his unyielding opposition and attempts to sabotage Republican reconstruction, as well as his general incompetence. An influential group of moderate Senate Republicans worried about establishing a precedent by which two-thirds of Congress could remove any president who disagreed with them. This might destroy the constitutional system of checks and balances by creating an all-powerful legislative branch like that of Great Britain. In addition, these moderates distrusted the Radical views and temperament of Benjamin Wade, the president pro tem of the Senate, who would succeed Johnson. (The vice presidency was vacant.) The president's lawyers quietly let these moderates know that, in the future, he would stop denouncing Congress and would enforce the Reconstruction Acts. As a result, thirty-five senators voted for conviction, one short of the necessary two-thirds. Seven Republicans voted with the twelve Democrats to provide the margin of Johnson's "victory." Several others were ready to support the president if their votes were needed. Contrary to later myths, the seven were not "martyrs" who were read out of the party. The crisis that had the potential to shake up the entire constitutional system ended without changing it in any fundamental way.

Andrew Johnson escaped conviction by a single vote.

The Election of 1868

Although Johnson had been humbled by his narrow escape, the acquittal also weakened the position of the Radicals within the Republican Party. General Ulysses S. Grant had emerged from the Civil War as the Union's leading military hero. Although he had supported congressional actions in a bitter split with Johnson, Grant was not known to have any particular ideological convictions. Conservative Northern businessmen, although unenthusiastic about Radical

The Ku Klux Klan was dedicated to preserving white supremacy.

Reconstruction, felt that any attempt to reopen the now settled issue would cause political and economic chaos. They believed a Grant presidency would bring stability and conditions conducive to investment in the South. Grant easily won the Republican nomination on a platform that bragged about "the assured success of the reconstruction policy of Congress."

The Democrats rejected Johnson and his many liabilities and drafted the colorless Governor of New York, Horatio Seymour. Since Seymour had denounced Lincoln during the war as a military despot and had referred to the draft rioters as "my friends," he handed the issue of loyalty and patriotism to the Republicans. As a result, Democrats ran on a platform denouncing Reconstruction as "unconstitutional, revolutionary, and void." Frank Blair of Missouri, the party's vice presidential candidate, had an outstanding record as a Union general during the War. But he frightened many Northern voters by suggesting that the army should be used to break up the unconstitutional Republican governments in the South. He also condemned Republicans for putting the South under the heels of "a semi-barbarous race of blacks who are worshippers of fetishes and polygamists" and want only to "subject white women to their unbridled lust." Racist comments like these made this the last presidential campaign to openly bring up the issue of white supremacy.

Republicans replied by "waving the bloody shirt" even more vigorously. The same Democrats who had betrayed their country during the war, Republicans charged, were now proposing "government by assassination and violence, instead of government by law." Events in the South seemed to confirm Republican warnings. Extra-legal terrorist groups began to wreak havoc on law and order in the South. The Ku Klux Klan was founded as a social club in 1866 in Tennessee. Its members came from all classes within Southern white society. Its leaders included Confederate generals and other officers, headed by the renowned cavalry leader, General Nathan Bedford Forrest. By 1868, it had become an organization of hooded vigilantes, dedicated to preserving white supremacy. In the 1868 election the Klan engaged in an organized reign of terror directed at blacks and white Republican leaders. Assassins murdered a Republican congressman from Arkansas and three members of the South Carolina legislature. In Georgia, threats and beatings kept blacks from the polls. Eleven Georgia counties with black majorities did not tabulate a single Republican vote. In Louisiana more than a thousand people, mostly blacks, were killed by rampaging Klansmen. In one parish (county) alone, the estimated death toll was 200 blacks, leading a local Democratic leader to declare that this taught blacks a "wholesome lesson." On election day, there wasn't even one Republican vote in an area that had cast over 4,700 Republican votes seven months earlier.

These methods enabled the Democrats to carry Georgia and Louisiana and reduce Republican margins elsewhere in the South. By lending credence to Republican charges that the Rebels were trying to regain power through terror, however, the lawlessness in the South probably helped Republicans in the

North. Grant won just about the same percentage of the Northern vote (55 percent) as Lincoln had in 1864 and carried all but three of the Northern states. Grant won an overwhelming electoral majority of 214 to 80. The Republicans retained a substantial margin in the House and Senate. Nevertheless, the great Civil War hero had actually received only about 53 percent of the popular vote against a weak and discredited opponent.

The Fifteenth Amendment

Grant's election assured the continuation of Reconstruction, but it also meant that a new Republican leadership would direct it. House Speaker Thaddeus Stevens, the leading exponent of protecting the rights of freed people and guaranteeing their economic independence, died in August 1868. The mass of mourners that filed past his body as it lay in state in the Capital was eclipsed only by Lincoln. True to his principles, he was buried in a black cemetery so that "I might illustrate in death the principles which I advocated through a long life, Equality of Man before his Creator." His death, followed the next year by that of Edwin Stanton and the loss of his Senate seat by Benjamin Wade, signaled the passing of the old generation of Radicals. The new leadership was more practical than idealistic and driven more by economic concerns.

These Republican leaders worried that a resurgent Democratic Party, bolstered by "rebel" votes, might evict them from power. It seemed to many that it was now crucial to ensure their electoral base by extending black suffrage throughout the country. Blacks still could not vote in eleven of the twenty-one Northern states or the five border states. In addition, the vote in the ten former Confederate states depended on the Reconstruction Acts that could easily be repealed once reconstruction was over. Many Republicans felt a moral obligation to secure the vote for blacks. Naturally, blacks who could vote overwhelmingly favored the party of emancipation, the Republicans. Thus, as one Republican congressman noted, "Party expediency and exact justice coincide for once."

When Congress assembled in December 1868, it moved quickly to pass the Fifteenth Amendment to secure black suffrage. It rejected a Radical proposal to guarantee the right to vote to all male citizens over 21. Such an amendment might be rejected by Northern and Western states who imposed their own limits on voting directed against the foreign born and the Chinese in the Far West. As approved, the amendment prohibited the states from denying the right to vote only "on account of race, color or previous condition of servitude." The warnings of one Radical congressman: "Let it remain possible to still disfranchise the body of the colored race in the late Rebel states and I tell you it will be done," proved to be prophetic. Southern whites were ultimately able to use loopholes that seemed to permit denial of the right to vote on supposedly nonracial grounds. These included literacy and property qualifications. Within thirty years, few Southern blacks were able to vote.

The Fifteenth Amendment was ratified by March 1870. Many relieved Republicans agreed that the passage of the amendment was "the last great point that remained to be settled of the issues of the war." Blacks were already playing a significant role in the newly established Southern governments.

RADICAL RECONSTRUCTION: MYTH AND REALITY

A remarkable period began in Southern history after the passage of the Reconstruction Acts. For the first time ever, governments rested on universal manhood suffrage, without regard to race. All citizens were entitled to "equal protection of the laws." Blacks could now vote, serve on juries, and even hold office. For whites, this was a profoundly disquieting experience, a world "suddenly turned bottom-side up."

The confusion and agitation of the whites led them to characterize Reconstruction as the "tragic era" of an occupied South. Bolstered by later books and films, like *Birth of a Nation* and *Gone With the Wind*, they painted a picture of a society gone mad. In this legend ignorant blacks dominated the governments and ran wild: "It is barbarism overwhelming civilization by physical force. It is the slave rioting in the halls of his master," said one observer. These power mad slaves were aided by villainous Northern "carpetbaggers" who came South "like buzzards" to strip the helpless South of its few pitiful possessions. They, in turn, were abetted by the even more treacherous "scalawags," Southerners who sold out their own people for profit.

This myth, which remained embedded in the American psyche for over a century, bore little resemblance to reality. Blacks did not dominate any of the new governments. (Only South Carolina had a black majority in its legislature.) Military occupation was never widespread and lasted as long as eight years in only three states (South Carolina, Florida, and Louisiana). A small minority of carpetbaggers were the unscrupulous adventurers of the legend. The majority were middle class Union veterans who decided to make their homes in the South. Some of these were entrepreneurs who came for business opportunities. Many were teachers, missionaries, and Freedmen's Bureau agents. Some were idealists like Adelbert Ames, the future Governor of Mississippi, convinced that he "had a Mission with a large M" to help the freed people. Southern supporters of Reconstruction, the so-called "scalawags," also had varied motives. Most had been wartime Unionists in upland counties or pre-war Whigs who had been reluctant secessionists. Some were formerly ardent secessionists who concluded that accommodation would bring economic development to the South. These included General Longstreet, Lee's old lieutenant, who accepted a federal post and campaigned for Grant.

Blacks and Reconstruction

Blacks saw Reconstruction as an opportunity to gain independence and equality. They long remembered the time when "de freedom sun shine out" as the great turning point of their lives. One man recalled, "I felt like a bird out of a cage. Amen. Amen. Amen. I could hardly ask to feel any better . . . ." Now they sought to achieve personal independence and a black community apart from white authority.

Right at the beginning of Reconstruction, blacks tested their new freedom by holding meetings and unsupervised religious services, previously forbidden under slavery. They purchased prohibited items like guns and liquor, flaunted outrageous finery, and even refused to move aside for whites on the sidewalks. Anxious whites complained bitterly about this "insolence" and "insubordination." Many, now free from slavery's restrictions on travel, took to the roads. Between 1865 and 1870 the black population of the ten largest cities in the South doubled. Unfortunately, jobs were scarce, and new segregated neighborhoods arose, consisting largely of broken-down shanties.

The most poignant reason for movement was the attempt to reunite family, the central institution of the black community. One freedman, for example, requested the assistance of the Freedman's Bureau in locating "my own dearest relatives," whom he had not seen in twenty-four years. Slave marriages had not been recognized under Southern law, so couples rushed to make their relationships legal. By 1870, the overwhelming majority of African Americans lived in two-parent households.

Relationships within the family also changed. Under slavery, black men and women had experienced "the rough equality of powerlessness." Now, many hoped to create the type of patriarchal family that was typical in white American households. In the early years of Reconstruction many black women withdrew from field labor, hoping to devote themselves to more domestic responsibilities. Black men were able to play a role in political and public life, while black women, like white women, were not. The Freedman's Bureau reinforced these separate roles by appointing men as heads of household who could sign labor contracts for their families. Black ministers preached that the woman's role was to make the house "a place of peace and comfort" for her husband. The shift from field to home, however, was only temporary. The rise of sharecropping made families responsible for their plots of land. All members had to work this land. In addition, the extreme poverty of most black families, which worsened in the depression of the 1870s, made women's labor a necessity. Thus, a much higher percentage of married black women than white women had to work outside the home. Still, both black men and women struggled to maintain family stability as the cornerstone of the African-American community.

The other key community institution was the black church. Freedmen quickly withdrew from bi-

The schools built by the Freedman's Bureau were segregated but allowed the children in the South to get a formal education.

racial congregations in which they had been required to sit in the back or in the gallery. They pooled their limited resources and built separate black churches. The church was "the first social institution fully controlled by black men in America." Churches became the centers of community life. Ministers were the most respected members of the community, active in political as well as religious life. They fostered a spirit of community self-help that led to the formation of fraternal, charitable, mutual aid, and burial societies.

The freed people's thirst for self-improvement was evident in the push to establish schools, another key institution. In 1860, over 90 percent of the black population in the South was illiterate. Observers have noted, "the almost sacred nature to the Negroes' attitude towards education." Despite all obstacles put in their way, most agreed with Frederick Douglass that, "the pathway from slavery to freedom was literacy." The freed people, themselves, took the initiative to raise money for schools and teachers' salaries. Many of the schools were supported, at least in part, by tuition, generally $1 to $1.50 a month per child. This was a substantial burden to a man who may have earned $10 a month for his labors. The Freedman's Bureau generally came into the picture after schools had been started, offering some modest financial support and supplies of books. This drive for education continued long after the Freedmen's Bureau ended.

The records of the Bureau contained poignant requests for aid: "You must kno that our people are very poor and if we are not helpt we will remain in ignorants a long time." Many of the schools faced active, even violent, hostility from local whites. Particularly in the smaller towns, most of the teachers were freed people, often only semiliterate themselves.

One apologized, "I never had the chance of goen to school for I was a slave until freedom . . . . I am the only teacher because we cannot doe better now." Most of these black teachers earned a modest living, often hardly more than that of a field hand. Some became leaders of the community, even gaining political office.

Surprisingly, many Southern whites taught in the small town and rural schools for blacks. Most were people of limited means who hoped to earn a modest livelihood. One wrote, "I consider myself a pioneer in this laudable cause and being a widow with three children to support, I have undertaken this at the sacrifice of my friends." Northern philanthropic and religious groups also played a part by opening schools in the cities and sending New England "schoolmarms" to inculcate accepted middle class standards of behavior. Eventually, reconstructed state governments began using tax dollars to support separate public schools for children of both races. By 1900, the black illiteracy rate had been cut in half. Even more might have been accomplished had the early valiant efforts been sustained by later white governments. Despite the limitations, W.E.B. Du Bois (a noted African-American scholar and writer) believed that the establishment of a public school system enabled blacks to avoid re-enslavement. It helped them to build an inner culture that withstood the shocks of the outer world.

Blacks, rebuilding their lives and creating their own institutions, realized that true freedom would be achieved solely through economic independence. That, they believed, could only be attained by ownership of land. "What's de use of being free if you don't own land enough to be buried in?" one freedman asked. African Americans also believed that they were entitled to land that had been developed through the sweat of their own and their ancestors' labor over many generations. Some Radicals, like Thaddeus Stevens, favored confiscation of Confederate plantations and their redistribution in 40 acre plots to freedmen. Radicals warned that "to give the slaves only freedom without the land, is to give them only the mockery of freedom which the English or Irish peasant had." But the idea was too extreme for most Republicans. As a result, only a few freedmen gained the economic autonomy for which they had dreamed. Most had to work for white landowners.

Nevertheless, blacks did manage to force basic changes in plantation agriculture. While many worked for wages, more settled for an arrangement under which they would get a share of the crop. Planters divided their estates into small plots that they rented to the freedmen. The sharecropper generally

Most blacks worked as sharecroppers on land owned by whites. In this photograph, black sharecroppers pick cotton. Because the price remained low, sharecroppers often fell into debt and were tied to the land.

could keep one-third of the year's crop after paying for use of the land and necessary supplies, seed, and work animals. Blacks preferred a system that freed them from gang labor and daily white supervision. Poor whites, as well as blacks, became sharecroppers. Planters gained greater stability, as all members of the sharecropping family worked to produce a crop. Eventually, many families were caught up in a web of debt. Even had they been given the small plots of land that they expected, black families, lacking credit or power, would undoubtedly still have suffered economically. But land redistribution would certainly have shaken the foundations of Southern society by creating a group of middle class black farmers.

Despite setbacks, Southern blacks had taken important steps in organizing their own lives. They sponsored newspapers that became a powerful resistance force. They sought to protect these gains by mobilizing and voting in large numbers. At the beginning of Reconstruction, about half of the men qualified to vote were black. Freedmen were the majority of voters in Alabama, Florida, Louisiana, Mississippi, and South Carolina. Despite this, they held only 15 to 20 percent of the government positions. Blacks served as lieutenant governors, secretaries of states, treasurers, and superintendents of education. Sixteen blacks sat in Congress during Reconstruction, including two senators (Hiram Revels and Blanche Bruce of Mississippi). Over 600 were state legislators, and countless more held local positions like sheriff, justice of the peace, and even mayor. Most of these black politicians were young men. Those at the upper levels tended to come from the free black community, largely from the North, and were often college-educated. Many of those at the state and local levels were far less-educated ex-slaves who had held positions of trust within the slave community, particularly drivers and artisans.

Freedmen eagerly joined Union Leagues that mobilized their votes for the Republicans. Black voters were not the ignorant, easily led dupes described by disgruntled whites. The political agenda of freed people included protection of their wages or shares of crops, a tax-supported public school system, assurance of equality before the law, and defense against the violence of white vigilantes. They were, perhaps

Senator Blanche Bruce

surprisingly, uninterested in vengeance against their former masters or in any real push for genuine social integration. The Reconstruction governments, established with their support, now faced the substantial challenge of fulfilling the aspirations of these constituents for a better, more just South. At the same time, they confronted the daunting task of rebuilding a war-torn land in which the average wealth of whites had fallen by one-half.

Republican Rule in the South

Under the rule of the Radical Republicans, both races were able to make considerable social and political progress. The new constitutions ended property qualifications for voting for whites, as well as blacks. They abolished imprisonment for debt and, for the first time, recognized the property rights of married women. Above all, these constitutions established the rights of blacks and whites to public schools.

Still, many white Southerners were deeply disturbed by the support of black schools at public expense. They believed that education would "spoil" blacks, making them discontented and difficult to handle. Despite this, Reconstruction governments increased support for schools, including night schools for adults. Poor white children also, for the first time, were able to take advantage of the new educational system. The Freedman's Bureau and northern philanthropic agencies helped establish black colleges such as Fisk, Hampton, and Tougaloo, initially to train black teachers. Republican governments, for the first time ever in the South, accepted the principle that the state should be responsible for public education.

Also for the first time, Republican state governments built hospitals, orphan asylums, and institutions for the blind, deaf, and mentally ill. Some local governments even provided food, firewood, and free medical care for the poor. State governments attempted to rebuild bridges, public buildings, roads, and other facilities demolished by the war. They provided state aid to railroads destroyed by the war. Most of the investment and construction had to go to rebuilding the railroads. This was accomplished by 1872, and 3300 additional miles were added. Southern Republicans also set up industrial commissions to attract investors to the South, with rather limited success.

Though the achievements of these Reconstruction governments were substantial, they were costly. An entire public school system had to be built. Railroads and rebuilding a war-torn land required substantial funds. As a result, taxes and debts ballooned during Republican rule. Economic problems brought many of the railroads to the verge of bankruptcy. Although no higher than the taxes in the rural Midwest at the time, Southern taxes in 1870 were four times as high as they had been in 1860. Small white landowners had to pay a larger share of taxes than ever before. Their anger at their increased financial burden turned many of these early supporters against the Republicans. In addition, many refused or were unable to pay their taxes. This diminished the services Republican state governments tried to provide, led to economic turmoil, and discredited those governments in northern, as well as southern, eyes.

Corruption in the Reconstruction South further tarnished the image of these governments. One contemporary observer exclaimed, "Such a Saturnalia of robbery and jobbery has seldom been seen in a civilized country . . . greed was unchecked and roguery unabashed." This view became accepted as the key historical truth about Reconstruction. Certainly, profiteering was widespread. The unprecedented sums of money that these new governments were handling led to bribery, kickbacks, and skimming of public funds. Many officials, in fact, saw nothing wrong with helping themselves to a share of the expanding state budgets. This was, however, only a reflection of what was happening throughout the nation. The Tweed Ring (a Democratic machine in New York) probably stole more from the people than all the Southern governments combined. Southern railroad "rings" were only pale imitations of Wall Street "robber barons." Although it may have been unfair, the dishonesty in the Southern governments further damaged Reconstruction in the view of Northern public opinion.

Despite its achievements, Republican Reconstruction government never met its original exalted goals of remaking Southern society in a more egalitarian mold. For example, it was one thing to build schools and quite another to integrate them. White parents did not want their children to share classrooms with blacks. Although New Orleans successfully integrated several thousand students, this bold experiment was not repeated elsewhere. Even black legislators did not seem to believe that interracial schooling was practical and preferred to stress fair division of school funds. Although the system of legalized segregation in public accommodations did not yet exist, discrimination was widespread. Black demands led to laws establishing the right to equal access to public places and transportation. These laws, however, were rarely enforced.

Land ownership presented another fundamental issue that Republican governments failed to confront. Only South Carolina set up a land commission to purchase acreage and resell it to freed people on easy credit terms. After a shaky start, the commission did succeed in establishing 14,000 black families on homesteads. One such community, Promised Land, is still in existence. Outside South Carolina, the hopes of the freed people were disappointed. Most white Republicans, although committed to equality of citizenship, opposed any state attempts to redistribute property. As one paper pointed out at the time, the lack of any land of their own, coupled with the antagonism of the white elite, meant that freedmen "cannot rise . . . . They must be servants to others, with no hope of bettering their condition." In the long run, this proved to be only too true and was, perhaps, the greatest failure of Reconstruction.

THE GRANT ADMINISTRATION AND NORTHERN POLITICS

When they elected Grant president in 1868, most Americans assumed that he would bring the same superb leadership skills to the job that he had demonstrated as a victorious general. But Grant's experiences on the battlefield did not adequately prepare him for the complexities of the presidential office. His lack of any deep ideological convictions, as demonstrated by his slogan, "Let Us Have Peace," further limited his forcefulness in office. Although he had shrewder political instincts than he is generally given credit for, Grant was often naive in choosing his associates. As someone who had consistently failed in business, he particularly admired successful businessmen and turned to them for advice.

Government Corruption

During the Grant years, it seemed as though corruption infected officials in every region and at every level of government. As the economy soared in the North (by 1873 industrial production was 75 percent greater than its 1865 level), opportunities for profiteering also grew. Influence-peddlers crowded state legislatures, seeking advantages for their railroad, mining, or lumber companies. Even relatively honest officials saw nothing wrong in accepting money or favors from businessmen in return for preferential laws or contracts. Local, state, and even federal governments were not well equipped to deal with the demands created by economic growth and increased government services and benefits. This led to alliances between businessmen and politicians that produced the ever expanding corruption of the era.

Although he himself was honest, Grant surrounded himself with people who saw public office as a road to personal profit. During his two terms, his secretary of war, his vice president, many treasury and naval officials, and even his private secretary were involved in public scandals. Government promotion of railroad development offered one prime opportunity. By 1872, the federal government had distributed well over 100 million acres of public land and millions of dollars for railroad construction, particularly to the new transcontinental lines, the Central Pacific and the Union Pacific. This led to the era's most famous scandal, that of the Credit Mobilier. This was a "dummy" corporation created to receive construction contracts from the Union Pacific. It was formed by an inner circle of Union Pacific stockholders. These men made exorbitant profits by awarding themselves contracts at greatly inflated costs. To forestall congressional inquiry, the company distributed stock to important members of Congress and federal government officials. The resulting scandal that broke in 1872 implicated several important Republican leaders, including the vice president.

Other scandals hit the Grant administration even harder. The Secretary of War had to resign or face impeachment when it was revealed that he had taken kickbacks from government-appointed traders in Indian Territory. Another investigation uncovered the widespread Whiskey Ring that looted millions of dollars from federal excise taxes. Investigations revealed that the president's secretary was at the center of the ring. Only Grant's intervention saved him from prison. One observer has noted, "It was the age of the audacious confidence man, and Grant was the incurable sucker. He easily fell victim to their trickery . . . because he could not believe that such people existed."

Foreign Policy in the Grant Years

Grant's best cabinet appointment was, undoubtedly, his Secretary of State, Hamilton Fish, an aristocratic New Yorker. His greatest success resulted from quiet and persistent diplomacy to settle damage claims against the British. These were based on the wartime destruction caused by the *Alabama* and other British-built vessels that had preyed on Union shipping. Eager to maintain American friendship, the British agreed to the 1871 Treaty of Washington, which set up an international arbitration tribunal to settle claims. The tribunal awarded the United States $15.5 million for damages done by the British-made ships. This was not only a victory for American diplomacy, it also established an important precedent for settling international disputes and helped improve relations with Britain.

The biggest foreign policy disaster during the Grant years was the attempt to take over Santo Domingo (the Dominican Republic today). After the victory of nationalism in the Civil War, many Americans again embraced the ideas of Manifest Destiny. In 1867, Secretary of State Seward had negotiated a treaty with Russia to purchase Alaska for $7.2 million. Despite derisive comments about "Seward's Folly," this set a precedent for annexing territory not connected to the continental United States. Various promoters and speculators used their influence with Grant's private secretary to lobby for annexation of Santo Domingo. Although they succeeded in getting Grant to agree to a treaty, the Senate refused to ratify it, leading to further splits within the Republican Party.

Elizabeth Cady Stanton and Susan B. Anthony were a strong team in the suffrage and abolition movements.

Women and Reconstruction

When blacks achieved political rights, women continued to be "the only class of citizens wholly unrepresented in the government." Abolitionists and feminists had long been allied in the American reform movement. When the issues of black male citizenship and suffrage arose in the debates over the Fourteenth and Fifteenth Amendments, women's rights advocates hoped that woman suffrage would be next. They were disappointed when many of their old abolitionist allies deserted them, declaring, "It is the Negro's hour, not the woman's."

The Fourteenth Amendment added the word "male" to the Constitution for the first time (in its description of inhabitants entitled to vote). Militant feminists, led by Elizabeth Cady Stanton and Susan B. Anthony, opposed the Fifteenth Amendment for prohibiting racial but not sexual discrimination in voting. Stanton believed that an extension of the vote that led to universal manhood suffrage only underscored the powerlessness of women and their declining status. Educated and informed women like the reformers, Stanton argued, were far more qualified to make political decisions than immigrants and freedmen "who do not know the difference between the monarchy and the republic." The already small feminist movement split into a radical wing, headed by Stanton and Anthony, and a more moderate group that accepted the reconstruction amendments. Susan B. Anthony actually faced trial for voting in the election of 1872. Both groups continued to fight for women's suffrage, although they were unable to achieve their goals in this era. They were more successful in obtaining property rights for married women. The abolitionist-feminist alliance had totally disintegrated, further weakening supporters of reconstruction.

The Election of 1872

As Grant's renomination became a certainty by 1872, a group of members of his own party, who disagreed

Susan B. Anthony (left) and Lucy Stone (right), feminist leaders whose followers split over support for the Fifteenth Amendment. Anthony headed the more radical wing while the moderate group accepted the Reconstruction Amendments.

with his appointments and policies, launched the Liberal Republican movement. They stressed civil service reform to end the abuses of political corruption and urged amnesty in the South. They hoped to attract candidates of "superior intelligence and superior virtue." As a compromise candidate for the presidency, they nominated Horace Greeley, editor of the *New York Tribune*, the most prominent newspaperman in the country. In his 40 years as a journalist Greeley had supported a wide variety of contradictory positions. Before the Civil War, he had been a staunch abolitionist. After, he moved from advocating tough postwar reconstruction to becoming the leading spokesman for self-government and amnesty in the South. Despite his years of attacks directed at Democrats, the Democratic Party decided to endorse Greeley under the slogan, "Anything to beat Grant."

Greeley's eccentricities, however, made him vulnerable to ridicule. In addition, Greeley's stress on Southern self-government proved to be counterproductive, as many Northern voters still distrusted the white South. Thomas Nast, the *Harper's Weekly* cartoonist who had helped destroy the Tweed Ring, had a similar field day with Greeley. His best known campaign cartoon showed pirate captain Greeley bringing his boat next to the ship of state while armed Confederates waited below to board and demolish it. Another portrayed Greeley stretching a hand over Lincoln's grave to clasp the hand of John Wilkes Booth!

Despite vigorous campaigning, Greeley's candidacy began to lose steam. Grant won 56 percent of the popular vote, the largest margin of any candidate from 1828 to 1904. He carried every Northern state and ten of the sixteen Southern or border states. The Republicans were also able to regain their two-thirds margin in both Houses of Congress. Weary from campaigning, depressed by the results, and mourning the death of his wife, Greeley died three weeks later. The Liberal Republican movement also collapsed. But, when the nation's prosperity dissolved into depression in 1873, Republicans grew more vulnerable to the issues of reform and reconciliation that had been raised unsuccessfully in the election.

RETREAT FROM RECONSTRUCTION

Grant's landslide re-election victory seemed, at least on the surface, to reaffirm the nation's support for continued reconstruction. Many Northerners, however, were becoming increasingly disillusioned with Southern Republicans. Except for the Radical Republicans, few Northerners had ever been deeply committed to racial equality. New issues arising from depression and unemployment led Northern voters, who had never had much real sympathy for the difficulties of Southern blacks, to lose any remaining interest in their plight.

Increase in Terrorism

The waves of terror instituted by the Klan and Klan-like organizations in the South directed against blacks and Republicans continued to grow during the 1870s. The death toll was in the hundreds. Northerners expressed their amazement at the inability of Southern Republicans to maintain order. Attempts by Republican officials to use militia to contain the violence proved to be ineffective. White troops were unreliable because the Klan often infiltrated their ranks. Black militia units increased white anger and led to fears of race warfare. Even when Klansmen were arrested, it was difficult to protect witnesses and find a jury that would convict. One case in Mississippi was dismissed when five key witnesses were murdered. When the governor of North Carolina sought to crush the Klan by declaring marital law, the Democratic-controlled legislature impeached him and discharged him from office in 1871. (He was the first American governor ever to be so removed.)

Congress finally responded to the increasing violence by passing a series of Enforcement Acts, the most extensive of which was the Ku Klux Klan Act of 1871. For the first time, conspiracies to deny citizens equal protection of the law could be prosecuted in federal courts. The president could declare martial law in any community victimized by terror and could even suspend habeas corpus. Led by a new, crusading attorney general, the federal government did intervene in South Carolina and successfully prosecuted several hundred Klansmen elsewhere in the South. By 1872, federal power had broken the back of the Klan and appeared to have returned the rule of law to the South.

Unfortunately, the return to some semblance of order was short-lived. Congressional Republicans began to retreat from their commitment to "carpet-bag governments" in the South. One politician bluntly announced, "The truth is our people are tired out with this worn out cry of 'Southern outrages'!!!" By 1872, Congress had extended amnesty to all but a handful of Confederate leaders and the Freedman's Bureau was allowed to expire. "White Leaguers" in Louisiana killed over one hundred blacks in the town of Colfax. But the entrance of federal troops into the state to end the increasingly bitter conflict provoked cynical complaints in Congress about "federal despotism."

In 1873, the great postwar economic growth suddenly collapsed in a financial panic. Disastrous unemployment and wage cuts led to bitter strikes and protests. Class divisions threatened social harmony. Frightened Republican businessmen became more sympathetic to Southern whites who seemed to be facing the same problems of disorder with lower class blacks. Conservative doctrines, stressing business interests, replaced equal rights for blacks as the Republican Party's central ideology.

As always in hard economic times, the voters turned against the party in power. In the greatest turnaround in the nineteenth century, the huge Republican majority in the House of Representatives became a 60-seat Democratic majority. In New York, where Democrat Samuel Tilden piled up an amazing 50,000 vote majority for governor, a paper declared, "The election is not merely a victory but a revolution." For the first time in a generation, even Massachusetts elected a Democratic governor. Although the depression was the main reason for the Republican defeat, many leaders blamed the party's Southern reconstruction policies for the debacle. *The Prostrate State*, an influential and widely read book by James Pike, a Northern journalist, indicted supposed "Negro rule" in South Carolina. It reinforced the idea that governmental corruption and extravagance were the results of power given to "a mass of black barbarism . . . the most ignorant democracy that mankind ever saw." Some Republican leaders openly spoke of "unloading" the weight of Southern Reconstruction governments.

The Civil Rights Act of 1875

The second Grant administration witnessed a general retreat from Reconstruction. The Supreme Court issued a series of decisions in the 1870s that seriously undercut the protections for blacks, seemingly guaranteed by the Fourteenth Amendment. In one particularly devastating decision, the Court overturned convictions obtained against violent terrorists under the Enforcement Act. The Court ruled that the amendment allowed the federal government to act only against violations of rights by states, rather than individuals. Only local or state authorities could punish individual crimes. This made it almost impossible to prosecute criminals whose violence against blacks was ignored by local officials.

The last of the old Radical "lions," Charles Sumner, senator from Massachusetts, tirelessly labored to secure the passage of the Civil Rights Act to safeguard the fast-fading dream of equality. This measure prohibited racial discrimination in public accommodations, jury selection, cemeteries, and transportation. On his death bed Sumner entreated a visitor, "You must take care of the civil-rights bill, . . . don't let it fail." Its passage was the final tribute of his colleagues to a man whose entire public life had been devoted to ending slavery and achieving civil rights for African Americans. Although the law seemed to call for an unparalleled demonstration of federal powers, in practice it was rarely enforced. It remained a statement of principles, rather than action, until it was declared unconstitutional by the Supreme Court in 1883.

The "Redeemers" Regain Power

The nationwide depression had hit rural white Southerners with particular force. High taxes and a precipitous drop in crop prices combined to undermine the economic position of independent white small farmers. Many joined black farmers in the ranks of the landless. Democrats were able to use racism to rally back country whites whose economic frustrations turned them against Southern Republican governments.

The "Mississippi Plan," which enabled Democrats to regain power in that state in 1875, became the model for "redeemers" throughout the South. The Democrats were trying to "redeem" their states from Republican and carpetbagger control. The first step of the plan was to force the 15 percent of the state's whites who considered themselves Republicans to switch sides through threats and ostracism. The next step was to use violence to intimidate black voters and break up Republican rallies. In broad daylight "Rifle Clubs" marched undisguised and shot down blacks "just the same as birds." In one such incident, mobs murdered thirty-five blacks and two whites in Vicksburg. Democratic newspapers in the state proclaimed the slogan, "Carry the election peacefully if we can, forcibly if we must." The governor of Mississippi, a Civil War Medal of Honor winner and one of the best carpetbag governors, appealed to President Grant for federal troops to control the violence. Northern party leaders, worried that military intervention would cost the Republicans a closely fought contest in Ohio, persuaded the president not to act. In a sentence that summarized the Northern retreat from reconstruction, the attorney general informed the governor, "The whole public are tired out with these annual autumnal outbreaks in the South, and the great majority are now ready to condemn any interference on the part of the Government." As a result, armed men threatened to kill freedmen who voted and openly destroyed ballot boxes with Republican votes. They shot one black state senator in the back. This contempt for federal law and the Constitution of the United States resulted in an overwhelming Democratic victory in Mississippi. It seemed apparent that whatever the results of the presidential election of 1876, Reconstruction itself would not survive.

The Disputed Centennial Election

Millions of Americans flocked to Philadelphia in 1876 to celebrate America's centennial at an enormous Exposition dedicated to the "Progress of the Age." Despite the continuing economic depression and rampant labor conflict, the exhibits extolled new inventions and the possibilities of technological progress. Many groups were left out of the displays. Native Americans were seen only as quaint contrasts to an advanced civilization. A Woman's Pavilion featured women weavers but failed to mention the struggle for women's rights. Susan B. Anthony disrupted the July 4th program at the exposition to read a "Woman's Declaration of Independence." Blacks were not only invisible in the exhibits, they had even been barred from the construction crews that built the display halls.

American politics were nothing to celebrate about either in 1876. Successful intimidation of black voters and the declining courage of white Republicans resulted in Democratic "Redemption" of all Southern states except South Carolina, Louisiana, and Florida. On the national level, the scandals that had overwhelmed the Grant administration burst into public view. This forced the Republicans to find a candidate of unquestioned honesty. They chose a former Civil War general, Governor Rutherford B. Hayes of Ohio, a drab "third-rate nonentity." The Democrats tried to seize the issue of reform by nominating Governor Samuel Tilden of New York, a millionaire corporate lawyer. Tilden had won a national reputation as a reformer when he broke up the infamous Tweed Ring in New York City. Both candidates were conservative men who favored sound money, reform, and limited government. The Democrats hoped to gain Northern swing states by downplaying the "bloody shirt" issues of Civil War and Reconstruction.

Reports of a massacre in Hamburg, South Carolina hampered this Democratic strategy. There, whites murdered five captured black militiamen in cold blood and looted and demolished black shops and homes. This atrocity enabled Republicans to revive Northern fears of Democrats as unreconstructed rebels. Although Hayes did not do as well as Grant had in 1872, he was able to win all but four of the Northern states, giving him 165 electoral votes. Tilden won a 250,000 popular vote plurality. (Although it has been estimated that at least 250,000 Southern Republicans had been terrorized to prevent them from voting, neutralizing that margin of victory.) He carried New York, New Jersey, Connecticut, Indiana, and all the Southern states under Democratic control, a total of 184 electoral votes. With only 185 electoral votes needed for victory, Tilden's triumph seemed evident. Two sets of conflicting returns, however, had arrived from South Carolina, Louisiana, and Florida. On the face of the returns, it appeared that Tilden had carried at least two of the states, but the Republican-controlled election boards certified Hayes as the winner in each state. While this might seem to have been a subversion of honest returns, it was actually impossible to tell what the results of an accurate count of the votes would have been. The Democrats had used fraud and force to keep blacks and Republicans from voting in the first place. For example, one Louisiana parish that had 1688 Republican voters in 1874, recorded only one in 1876.

Congress, lacking any clear guidance in the Constitution, faced an extraordinary predicament in determining who had really won. With a Republican Senate and a Democratic House, Congress decided to turn the problem over to an Electoral Commission consisting of five senators, five representatives, and five Supreme Court justices. The commission was balanced with seven Republicans and seven Democrats. The fifteenth member was to be an impartial Supreme Court justice. But, after some political maneuvering, this final member turned out to be Justice Joseph Bradley, a Republican, who cast the swing vote with the Republicans. By an eight to seven margin, the commission voted to award all 20 disputed electoral votes to Hayes, giving him the 185 electoral votes needed for victory. Many infuriated Democrats felt that they had been robbed and threatened action in the House.

While these proceedings were going on in public, negotiations continued behind the scenes between Republican leaders and "moderate" Southern Democrats. Under this "Compromise of 1877," Southerners agreed to withdraw their opposition to Hayes' inauguration in return for Hayes' assurance that he would remove the remaining federal troops from the South. This was merely the final step in the abandonment of Reconstruction. A month after his inauguration, in April 1877, Hayes ordered the withdrawal of federal troops from Louisiana and South Carolina, causing the collapse of the last two Republican governments in the South. The Republican governor of South Carolina sorrowfully informed his distressed black supporters, "Today, by order of the President whom your votes alone rescued from overwhelming defeat, the Government of the United States abandons you . . . ." Thus, the real losers of the 1876 election were not the Democrats but Southern blacks whose last hopes for equality were crushed.

THE NEW SOUTH

The nation recovered from the depression after 1878. In the 1880s the American economy leaped forward at an astonishing pace. The South shared the buoyant mood that swept the country in the 1880s. The collapse of the last few Radical governments led to the domination of Southern politics by a new class of men. These included merchants, bankers, railroad promoters, and even some industrialists. They allied with the old planter class that, despite a decline of its prewar power, retained considerable influence in rural areas. They called themselves Redeemers, claiming that they had "redeemed" the South from corrupt and extravagant carpetbag rule. They proclaimed the beginning of a "New South" devoted to economic modernization and frugal government. They promised to relieve the North of a burden most Northern-

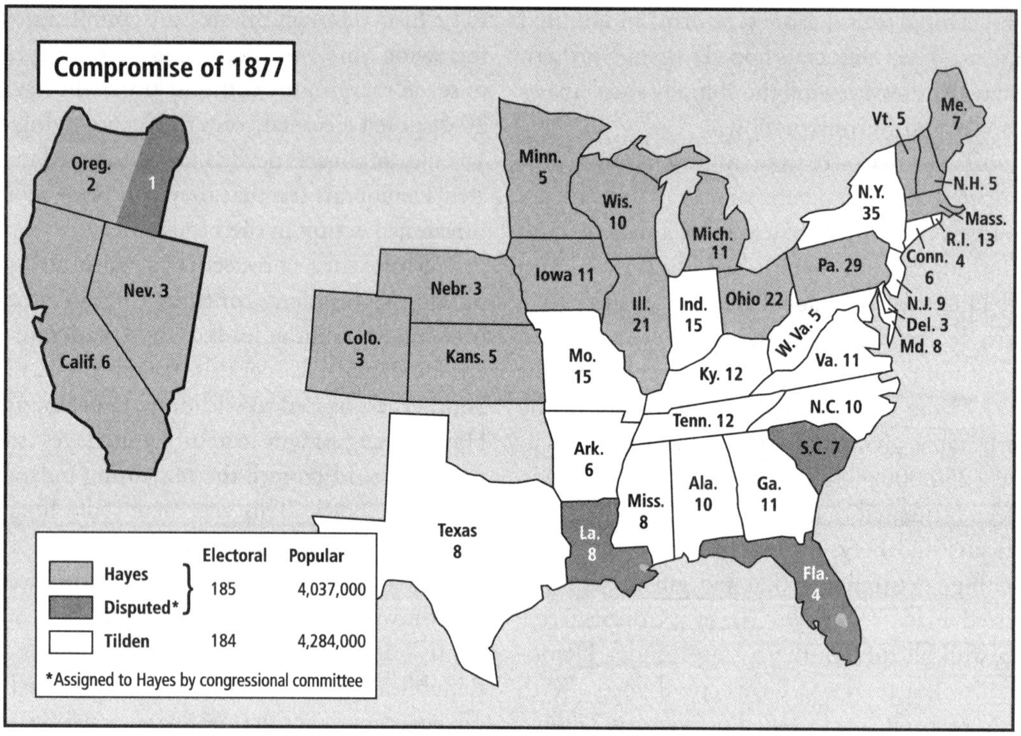

ers did not want: the burden of Reconstruction and the establishment of equal rights for blacks.

Henry Grady, editor of the *Atlanta Constitution*, was the foremost exponent of the expansive New South ideology. He announced that there would be a new stress on the "gospel of work as the South's great need." He assured Northerners that the South had learned its lesson in its defeat and was now willing to embrace Northern economic and social standards. In his famous 1886 speech, he promised that the New South understood "that her emancipation came because through the inscrutable wisdom of God her honest purpose was crossed, and her brave armies beaten." Southerners, he declared, were now glad that "the American Union was saved from the wreck of war."

Booker T. Washington emerged as an African-American exponent of the New South. Washington, who had been born a slave, had worked his way up from poverty after being educated at Virginia's Hampton Institute. He hoped that other blacks would follow in his footsteps in seeking self-improvement. In a famous 1895 speech at the Cotton States Exposition, Washington outlined his "Atlanta Compromise." Blacks would give up agitation for their rights and would concentrate on hard work to make them economically indispensable to whites. This economic importance would eventually lead to white acceptance. His New South institution, Tuskegee in Alabama, emphasized industrial education and improved agricultural methods as the path for black students. George Washington Carver did his pioneer research on the uses of the peanut at Tuskegee.

Despite the widespread publicity given to the ideas of New Southerners, the problem with the image they sought to build was that much of it was not accurate. Far from admitting that the Confederate cause had been wrong, most Southerners believed it had always been right. They were defenders of the "Lost Cause," including even slavery. Every Confederate Memorial Day, they paraded the red Confederate battle flag down the streets of small and large towns. (Even today, that flag remains a source of confrontation between white and black Southerners.)

A more important difficulty with the New South conception was the continuing backwardness of the Southern economic and social system. The new state governments set out to reduce government spending and property taxes. In doing so, they retreated from

Booker T. Washington believed that vocational education was the answer for African Americans.

reconstruction commitments to a state that had responsibilities for the welfare of its citizens. Florida abandoned a nearly completed college, leaving the state without any institution of higher learning. Alabama closed public hospitals. Public schools were the principal victims of the cutbacks. Louisiana spent so little on its system that the percentage of literate whites actually declined between 1880 and 1900. Above all, black schools, so laboriously built and maintained, were hit the hardest as the gap between spending for black and white schools invariably widened.

Agriculture in the New South

This backwardness was nowhere more apparent than in agriculture. Broad new vagrancy laws reinforced planters' control over their labor force. These permitted the arrest of any unemployed person and made it a crime to leave a job before the expiration of a contract. Criminal laws increased the penalty for even the most petty offense. The convict lease system expanded to permit the hiring out of most prisoners. Mines, railroads, lumber companies, and planters vied for these new forced laborers, most of whom were blacks convicted of minor transgressions.

Other laws gave planters control of property and credit, including precedence to their claims for their share of the crops. Even during Reconstruction, sharecropping had perpetuated black economic dependence upon whites. As the system evolved, the sharecropper had to borrow against future crops to pay his debts to the landowner and supply merchant. Inevitably, he became enmeshed in a web of debt from which escape was virtually impossible. The continued reliance on cotton led inescapably to overproduction and declining prices, compounding the misery. The sharecropping system and its labor control worked against any efforts to mechanize Southern agriculture. Most small white farmers succumbed to the same economic forces. In the Deep South, per capita income remained unchanged even in the great era of economic growth in America, 1880 to 1900.

Industry in the New South

Many New South crusaders concentrated on a campaign to develop industry. They achieved some success in the expansion of Southern textile mills. The new fad of cigarette smoking led to the growth of the tobacco industry. Railroad construction continued at a rapid pace. Southern lines were integrated into the national railroad network under the control of Northern capitalists. Despite these advances in industrialization, fueled by promises of low taxes, special concessions, and a docile labor force, the South remained overwhelmingly agricultural. In fact, even by 1900, the New South accounted for a smaller percentage of the nation's industry than the Old South had in 1860. (Industrialization had proceeded at a far more rapid pace in the North.)

While the new upper class continued to prosper, most Southerners, white and black, fell into even deeper poverty. Publicists touted the cotton mills as the salvation of poor whites. But when the poor white farmers gave up their struggle with the land and went to work in the mills, they replaced one life of destitution with another. Men earned wages of about 50 cents a day, and women and children supplemented family income at even lower wages. Companies controlled all aspects of life in company towns and the poor white worker found that, "I owe my soul to the company store." These mill villages did remain all-white and consciousness of racial superiority grew in importance as the century ended.

The Rise of Jim Crow

Illiteracy, lack of adequate nutrition and housing, and a system of social, economic, and political injustice trapped blacks in the "brave" New South. The disillusionment with the end of Reconstruction led more than 50,000 blacks to seek opportunities in Kansas. These "Exodusters" represented only a small percentage of those who would have migrated if opportunities in the North were not still closed to them. Over 90 percent of black Americans in 1900 continued to live in the South.

Despite the end of Reconstruction in 1877 and the continuing intimidation and violence, black voting had not been entirely eliminated in the South. With their economic clout, the conservative upper classes felt that they could effectively manage the black vote. In the late 1880s and early 1890s, however, the growing agricultural unrest led to the formation of the Populist movement. For a while, it seemed that oppressed white and black farmers might get together and challenge conservative rule in the South. The Democratic leadership responded by reviving racist propaganda and returning to warnings about "Negro domination" and "revival of black Reconstruction" to discredit the Populists. The Democrats were successful in maintaining their power and reinforcing a one-party South. A major component of their efforts was the disfranchisement of black voters. Between 1890 and 1910 every Southern state imposed poll taxes, literacy requirements, and property qualifications for voting. Four states even instituted a "grandfather" clause that allowed men to vote only if their ancestors had voted before 1867 (before blacks had been granted the vote). The Supreme Court eventually overturned this obvious violation of the Fifteenth Amendment but not until 1915. These measures succeeded in an almost total elimination of black voting in the South. As late as 1896, 130,000 blacks continued to vote in Louisiana. By 1904, only 1,342 were still able to do so. Although there were loopholes to permit whites to vote, poll taxes and property qualifications did reduce the number of poor illiterate white voters as well.

Southern customs had long separated the races, but in the 1890s a series of Jim Crow laws made segregation into a rigid system. The term Jim Crow came from old blackface minstrel shows. It had come to mean a code for racial segregation in schools, industry, transportation, and all areas of public accommodation. In 1896, the Supreme Court in *Plessy v. Ferguson* ruled that state-mandated separate railroad cars for blacks did not violate equal protection guaranteed by the Fourteenth Amendment if the separate facilities were equal. In an impassioned dissent, Justice John Harlan, a Southerner himself, declared, "The Constitution is colorblind." Later decisions, however, extended this "separate but equal" doctrine to other public facilities, particularly schools. Of course, accommodations were never really equal, and Jim Crow became central to the Southern way of life.

There was also a dramatic increase in white violence in the 1890s, designed to keep blacks more firmly "in their place." The decade averaged 187 lynchings each year. The overwhelming majority of the victims were black. Some were well-planned public events, attracting large audiences and family outings. Some victims were accused of crimes, but the "crime" of many of the victims was "uppityness." Others supposedly made sexual advances to white women. The fear that white women might be attracted to black sexuality, encouraged as a strategy to terrify whites, was one of the underpinnings of rigid segregation. The lack of protection for African Americans in the South made Booker T. Washington's ideas of racial cooperation more popular. Other blacks, however, favored a more militant approach. In 1892, Ida B. Wells, a crusading black journalist in Memphis, launched an international anti-lynching movement. When she investigated the charges of "rape," she found virtually all of them untrue.

Segregation, combined with sharecropping and debt tenancy, stifled the ingenuity and economic potential of a large percentage of the Southern population. The South succeeded in marginalizing itself in the name of white domination. The New South, thus, had very little meaning for most Southerners—white or black. For African Americans, it meant the end of the dream that Reconstruction had encouraged. A black politician, ending his nine-year congressional career, conceded the extravagance of the earlier Reconstruction governments. But, he asked, "can the saving of a few thousand or a few hundred thousands of dollars compensate for the loss of the political heritage of American citizens?"

Ida B. Wells is perhaps best remembered for her antilynching crusade.

CONCLUSION

As the Civil War and Reconstruction faded from view, a romantic haze suffused the era. Organizations staged grand reunions of the "Blue and the Gray." Popular books and plays were devoted to reconciliation (particularly through romances between Southern women and Northern men). Black abolitionist Frederick Douglass struggled unsuccessfully to oppose remembering "with equal admiration . . . those who fought for slavery and those who fought for liberty and justice." Racism even reached the Grand Army of the Republic, which segregated its posts and forced black veterans to march behind whites in Memorial Day parades.

In the early twentieth century, historians, led by William Dunning of Columbia University, rewrote the history of Reconstruction. They believed that blacks were "children," incapable of understanding the freedom that Northerners unwisely thrust upon them. One bestseller even argued that under Reconstruction, Southern whites "literally were put to the torture" by "emissaries of hate" who inspired "lustful assaults" by blacks against white women. The black community understood a different version of Reconstruction. As one 88-year-old former slave told an interviewer in the 1930s, "I know folks think books tell the truth, but they shore don't."

Reconstruction certainly succeeded in bringing the nation along a relatively peaceful path after the ending of the worst war in American history. The victorious and outraged North did not turn on the helpless South in an orgy of revenge through executions or confiscation of property. Except in songs and books, the defeated South did not inaugurate a period of guerrilla warfare. Perhaps most surprisingly, newly freed blacks did not seek revenge against their former masters. They never even attempted to seize the plantations.

In view of the pervasive racism of America of this era, it is less surprising that the constitutional amendments, the Freedmen's Bureau, and the civil rights laws did not bring about permanent change than that they were passed in the first place. In view of deeply held ideas about property rights, limited government, and black inferiority the failure of Reconstruction seems almost inevitable. W.E.B. Du Bois commented, "The slave went free; stood a brief moment in the sun; then moved back again toward slavery." The failure of the experiment in equal rights was a tragedy for blacks and for the whole nation. The issue of race remained a sore on the nation's body for years to come. Nevertheless, the amendments and civil rights laws passed during Reconstruction became the basis of a renewed and more effective struggle for equal rights almost a hundred years later, a struggle that continues to this day.

Chronology

1863 Lincoln issues Proclamation of Amnesty and Reconstruction

1864 Congress passes stringent Wade-Davis Bill

1865 Freedmen's Bureau established
Civil War ends
Lincoln assassinated (April 14)
Black Codes enacted by Southern legislatures
Thirteenth Amendment abolishing slavery added to the Constitution

1866 Congress approves Fourteenth Amendment
Congress passes Civil Rights Act and Freedmen's Bureau Act over Johnson's veto
Ku Klux Klan founded in Tennessee
Republicans triumph in congressional elections despite Johnson's efforts

1867 Congressional Reconstruction Act passed
U. S. purchases Alaska

1868 President Johnson is impeached but acquitted
Fourteenth Amendment ratified
Ulysses S. Grant elected president

1869 Ratification of the Fifteenth Amendment

1870 Last four Southern states admitted to the union

1871 Ku Klux Klan Act passes to end terrorism in the South

1872 Grant re-elected president

1873 Financial panic leads to five-year depression

1875 Whiskey Ring scandal further discredits Grant administration

1876 Disputed presidential election of Hayes vs. Tilden

1877 Electoral commission awards presidency to Rutherford B. Hayes

1890s "Jim Crow" laws passed in the South

1896 *Plessy v. Ferguson* upholds segregation "separate but equal"

SUGGESTED READINGS

Edward L. Ayers, *The Promise of the New South: Life After Reconstruction* (1992).
LaWanda Cox, *Lincoln and Black Freedom* (1981).
Richard Nelson Current, *Those Terrible Carpetbaggers* (1988).
W.E.B. Dubois, *Black Reconstruction* (1935).
Eric Foner, *Reconstruction: America's Unfinished Revolution* (1988).
___, *A Short History of Reconstruction* (1990).
George Frederickson, *The Black Image in the White Mind* (1971).
William Gillette, *Retreat From Reconstruction, 1869-1879* (1980).
Herbert Gutman, *The Black Family in Slavery and Freedom, 1750-1925* (1976).
William Hesseltine, *Lincoln's Plan of Reconstruction* (1960).
Jacqueline Jones, *Labor of Love, Labor of Sorrow: Black Women, Work, and the Family from Slavery to the Present* (1985).
Leon Litwack, *Been in the Storm So Long: The Aftermath of Slavery* (1979).
William S. McFeely, *Grant: A Biography* (1981).
___, *Frederick Douglass* (1990).
Eric McKitrick, *Andrew Johnson and Reconstruction* (1960).
James McPherson, *Ordeal by Fire* (1992).
Michael Perman, *Emancipation and Reconstruction, 1862-1879* (1987).
Willie Lee Rose, *Rehearsal for Reconstruction* (1964).
Theodore Rosengarten, *All God's Dangers: The Life of Nate Shaw* (1974).
Hans L. Trefousse, *Andrew Johnson* (1989).
Joel Williamson, *The Crucible of Race* (1984).
C. Vann Woodward, *Origins of the New South, 1877-1913* (1951).
___, *The Strange Career of Jim Crow* (1974).

Chapter Thirteen

THE RISE OF INDUSTRIAL AMERICA & THE POLITICS OF THE NEW ORDER

It was a cool, clear crisp October morning in the Italian Alpine town of Piantedo—population 650—when fourteen-year-old Aurelia Rossotti awoke at 6 a.m. to catch the train to Milano, which left at 7 a.m. The year was 1903. Aurelia was the third oldest child in a family of ten children—six girls and four boys. Her older brother Pietro and older sister Lena had left for "America" two years earlier. Now it was her turn to leave for the "Promise Land" of the United States. Her siblings had sent her the money for her trip over on a steamer—the same way they had come—that left once a month out of the port city of Genoa. It had taken "Pep"—that is now what Pietro called himself because it was easier for Anglo-Americans to pronounce and sounded "less foreign"—and Lena six months each of work to save enough money to send to their sister, Aurelia. Pep had gotten a job in a lumber mill in northern California, earning about a dollar a day for 12 hours of work. Lena worked as a "domestic" for the mill's owner, a man named Pierce, whose Anglo-American family had been in California since the Gold Rush days of the early 1850s. Indeed, the Pierce family was not only the richest in the area, owning several businesses, including the Eureka Hotel, and thousands of acres of prime land, but also controlled the city government—a Pierce was mayor and another relative was Chief-of-Police. At the time, the most lucrative enterprise was timber, and the Pierce family owned several mills worth millions of dollars. At first, the Pierces used cheap Chinese labor in their mills, but white California nativism raised its ugly head and drove the Chinese out of the area decades earlier. Filling that labor void would be the "new" immigrants, who, beginning in the 1880s on, were primarily from southern and eastern Europe, like "Pep" Rossotti. Pep was just one of several of these new immigrants working in the mill. Working alongside him as he fed raw timber into the cutting saws were other immigrants—a "Bohunk" (the generic WASP pejorative for a Slav or Hungarian) and a Russian, whom the WASP bosses simply called "Ivan," even though that was not his real name. Since these three men did not speak a word of each other's languages, if they wished to communicate with each other, they all had to learn English. None of the Rossotti children had much formal education—the equivalent of the sixth or seventh grade in the United States—so learning a language as difficult as English was not easy. But they all did and were quite proud of that accomplishment until the day they died.

A the time of Aurelia's emigration, a one-way ticket to America cost around $200 (which would be well over

$1,000 in present U.S. value) and that was for space in "steerage"—the bottom of the ship. This was not a luxury liner or cruise ship—no sun decks, no swimming pools, no all-you-can-eat buffets, no exotic shore-leaves, and no shuffle board. This was a ship built for simply packing into its cargo hold as many human beings as possible and transporting them across the Atlantic to the New World, that strange and distant land discovered some five hundred years earlier by another Italian hoping to find fame and fortune. Living conditions on these immigrant steamers were at best barely tolerable and most of the time deplorable. Quarters were cramped with no privacy, rats roamed freely, and the food was usually not worth eating, and so many of the immigrants brought their own familiar fare with them in their packs—salami, cheese, bread, and fruit from the homeland. Despite the rather wretched conditions on board, hundreds of immigrants believed it was worth enduring for the opportunity to have a new and better life in America. This was what Aurelia hoped for. Aurelia was also somewhat of a "rarity"; she was one of only a relative handful of northern Italians on board. The steamer, after picking up Aurelia and some others at Genoa, then steamed south to Naples and then to the island of Sicily, where the majority of the "cargo" got on board. Why were the majority of Italian immigrants who came to America from southern Italy? The answer was simple: southern Italy was by far the poorest region in the country, especially so for the inhabitants of the island of Sicily. Southern Italy was (and still is) overwhelmingly agricultural and rural, its farmers dependent on the cultivation of olives, some wheat, livestock, and that's about it. Land is not that fertile, especially that of Sicily, which is essentially an island of rocks, whose soil and terrain is only conducive to the growing of olives and the making of olive oil. Today, such commodities, especially in the United States, are considered to be "healthy" foods; a hundred years ago, few, if any, WASP Americans even knew what olive oil was. Sicily was also a very violent place, run by very powerful warlord-type of families who were constantly feuding with each other for control of the island. Violence was endemic, part of daily life, which saw murder and assassination become commonplace as gun-battles between the families raged in broad daylight, fought with "luparas"—shotguns used for the killing of wolves, which once roamed the island. All too frequently, innocent bystanders were killed for just being in the wrong place at the wrong time. Thus, one can easily understand why someone would want to leave such a place.

After about two weeks of travel, Aurelia's steamer entered New York City's harbor, where it unloaded its passengers at the newly built "processing" facility at Ellis Island. There, Aurelia and hundreds, if not thousands, of immigrants were put through a battery of different questions, physical examinations, baggage checks, in short, as thorough of a "screening" as was possible to determine whether the individual was physically and mentally healthy enough to enter the United States. Aurelia was. However, her only problem was her first name—none of the Irish or Welsh "processors" could pronounce it correctly. Finally, as her "papers" were approved and had stamped on them "WOP"—which meant "without passport" but has since come to be one of the pejoratives for Italians—a Welsh immigration official looked at Aurelia, noticed her red hair and rosey-red cheeks, and decided that henceforth her "new" American name would be "Rosie." From that moment on, Aurelia Rossotti became "Rosie" Rossotti.

After spending a few days in New York City in an Italian-owned boarding house, "Rosie" boarded the train at Penn Station in NYC and headed west for California to join her brother and sister. It only took about seven days for the train to reach San Francisco, as it stopped only twice along the way to take on more passengers. To travel 3,000 miles in that short of time was remarkable testimony to the speed and facility of the American railway system, which had only finished its transcontinental lines a decade and a half earlier. When Aurelia arrived at the station in San Francisco, her brother and sister were there to meet her. She was so excited and relieved to see them, especially since she could "speak" again. Ever since she left Italy, Aurelia had spoken hardly at all for there were very few people with whom she could converse! Even on board the steamer with fellow Italians, Aurelia had difficulty speaking with them because of their different "dialects." Aurelia spoke "Lombardia," a northern Italian dialect very different from the "Italian" spoken by a "Siciliano," "Napolitano," or "Calabrese." There was no "official" Italian language yet; the Italian government was still trying to create one when Aurelia left Italy. She spoke not a word of English but did speak surprisingly a little German, which she had been taught in school. The region of Italy, Lombardia, where Aurelia was from had once been part of the Austro-Hungarian empire and while under Habsburg rule, all Italians were forced to learn German. Along the way to California, Aurelia met some "tdeschi"—the Italian word for Germans—and had brief but pleasant conversations with them. She was amazed by how quickly they were able to switch from German to English and English to German. She someday wanted to be able to do that as well.

After spending the day in San Francisco with her siblings and other Italians (many of whom were also from Lombardia and other areas of northern Italy, with whom she very much enjoyed the company of, especially their cooking!) in the North Beach area of that city, the Rossottis boarded a train for Eureka, arriving there late the next day. No sooner was "Rosie" in her "new home," a flat that Lena and Pep rented near the town's hospital, than Aurelia got a job at the hospital as a "cleaning woman" for about 80 cents a day. It obviously was very little money for such hard work, but it helped Lena and Pep pay the rent. Aurelia stayed with her brother and sister for two years, all the while working in the hospital. One day a local "lumberjack" came in with a badly cut hand. His name was Amadeo Acquistapace, was also from Piantedo, and whom Aurelia knew by name only. The Acquistapaces were legendary in the area for their passionate support of socialism. They were outspoken critics of the constitutional monarchy that ruled Italy at the time and vociferously urged its overthrow by revolutionary means, if necessary. Such public advocacy got young Amadeo into trouble with the law, and thus to escape possible imprisonment, he fled to the United States in 1900. By the time Aurelia met him, he was known as "Andy" and spoke "perfect English," at least according to Aurelia. He was twenty-six when they met; Aurelia was sixteen. They married in 1906 and went to San Francisco for their honeymoon, which turned into the most frightful event of their lives. The young couple experienced one of the worst natural disasters in United States history: the 1906 San Francisco earthquake. The quake itself did not destroy the city; it was the ensuing fires that did the most damage to life and property. The newlyweds escaped the calamity, returning to Eureka as soon as they could get out of the city. Andy and Rosie remained in Eureka until 1931. In those years, they worked hard, saved their money, and in 1920, they bought the Eureka Hotel from the Pierce family. They prospered as hotel owners. During the 1920s Californians discovered the "north Coast" of the state—coming there to vacation. Also, beginning in that decade, Italians began buying land in the area to start vineyards, and today, as a result of Italian entrepreneurship, many California wines are recognized as some of the best in the world.

Andy and Rosie had six children—four girls and two boys. In 1931, as a result of the Great Depression, Andy and Rosie were forced to sell their hotel. The tourists weren't coming anymore—they had no money to spend on vacations and other amenities—and so for many small business owners like Andy and Rosie, dependent on tourism for survival, the depression meant the end of their dream. They swept up their children and moved Auburn, California, a small town of about 2,000 people, nestled in the foothills of the Sierra Nevada Mountains. Andy and Rosie moved there because it reminded them of Piantedo. They briefly thought about going back to Italy but quickly dismissed that idea for Andy was still a hardcore socialist. The fascist Mussolini had been in power since 1922, and since that time, had declared "open season" on all opposition, especially targeting socialists and communists for his reign of terror. Moreover, they were Americans now; proud of their citizenship, which they both attained in 1914. Rosie was proud of her English, though spoken with a noticeable accent. Rosie got a job in the post office, "the lady who gave you your stamps," while Andy opened a hardware store. They made it even through the darkest days of the Great Depression. All six of their children became "one hundred percent American"—that is, they refused to speak Italian, especially in public, refused to eat or cook Italian food, went to public schools, and some even married non-Italians!! However, I am proud of my "one hundred percent Italian heritage," for I am one of Andy's and Rosie's ten grandchildren. My mother is Anna Acquistapace, who married an "Italian boy," John Anthony Moretta, from Brooklyn, New York in 1946. John and Anna named one of their five sons, John Anthony Moretta, Jr., co-author of ***American Dreams and Reality****.*

In the decades following the Civil War, the United States underwent one of the most rapid and profound economic transformations of any nation in world history. Perhaps only Japan's equally rapid rise at the same time, from a feudal, agrarian society to a modern, industrial one, rivaled that of the United States in historical importance. Slavery and sectionalism, the two dominant forces of antebellum America, gave way to industry and the various social and political issues that were associated with it. Although industrial development began in the Northeast before the Civil War, it speeded to a fever pitch from 1865-1890. By the end of the nineteenth century the United States led the world in manufacturing, far surpassing Great Britain, the undisputed leader in production throughout most of the nineteenth century. In the years between 1865 and the 1890s, the country was transformed from an overwhelming agrarian and rural society to a nation of factories and cities. Industrial progress, however, caused unprecedented socioeconomic and political upheaval, as cycles of boom and bust dominated the economic landscape. Panics, sharp economic downturns usually precipitated by stock market crashes and accompanied by bank failures and unemployment, occurred more often than not and caused two major depressions, one following the Panic of 1873 and a deeper depression after the Panic of 1893. Industrialization was an exclusively Northeastern phenomenon, while the South and the West remained predominantly rural and agricultural. Outside of the Northeast, only the cities/states bordering the Great Lakes, such as Chicago, Illinois, or Cleveland, Ohio, experienced industrial expansion. In those places busy ports witnessed an influx of cheap labor and a correspondingly impressive outflow of American industrial, finished, or processed goods.

Post-Civil War industrialization created a new class in the United States, men whose wealth and concomitant political power were derived from the new industrial order. These "plutocrats" as they came to be called, represented only a handful of individuals, but their dominance of the economy and politics of the Gilded Age was so complete that they have had few rivals since. Their names are legendary still: Andrew Carnegie, Jay Gould,

Immigrants from Antwerp, Belgium, sit on the deck while bound for Ellis Island. The wave of immigration had a major impact on the way America developed. New customs, manners, languages, food, religious practices, and cultures flooded the country.

John D. Rockefeller, and J. P. Morgan, to name but a few, were larger-than-life figures who controlled not only the economy and politics but the popular imagination as the heroes and villains in the high drama of industrialization.

Bound closer by a network of railroads and telegraphs, with the fate of small towns linked as never before to the fortunes of big cities, the United States was finally becoming the vision of Alexander Hamilton and Henry Clay: an integrated, national, self-sufficient economy, a nation united in fact as well as in name. Perhaps ideologically as important as the realization of the Hamiltonian vision or of Henry Clay's American system was the fact that industrialization meant the end of Jeffersonian agrarianism as the nation's ethos. By the 1890s, the businessman had replaced the yeoman farmer as the new symbol of America; upon his shoulders now rested the future of the democratic republican experiment begun one hundred years earlier. Not until the 1930s, with the Great Depression and the New Deal, would Americans reject the values of big business. During that decade they would find a new value system based on justice, compassion, and cooperation—values totally antithetical to the principles of the amoral market place of laissez faire capitalism, of which the plutocrats of the Gilded Age were the progenitors.

OLD INDUSTRIES TRANSFORMED, NEW INDUSTRIES BORN

In the aftermath of the Civil War the magnitude of American industrial development was unprecedented and dramatic. Old industries evolved into the nation's first corporations or "big businesses," while discovery and invention stimulated a whole host of new industries, such as oil and electricity. However, without question the most important and dominant post-war industry was the railroad, without which virtually none of the others would have existed. The rise of the railroad played the key role in the transformation of the American economy, helping to create a more consolidated, unified economy and network that enabled a variety of businesses to become truly national in scope and scale.

THE RAILROADS: THE UNITED STATES' FIRST BIG BUSINESS

From the end of the Civil War to 1900, the United States embarked on one of the most ambitious infrastructure undertakings in world history: the building of one of the largest railroad networks. In the process, the railroad builders also created the nation's first big business. The Republic's first transcontinental rail system was completed in 1869 when the Union Pacific and Central Pacific lines met at Promontory Point, Utah and drove the famous golden spike into the ground commemorating the occasion. Over the course of the next thirty years, the amount of track laid quadrupled, totaling over 193,000 miles by 1900. That total was greater than all of the track laid in all of Europe and Russia combined. The impressive amount of track belied the fact that most of the nation's system was haphazard at best with poor organization and very few integrated networks. Most of the early lines, except for the first transcontinental, did not connect with one another and trains ran on tracks of varying gauges. During the 1870s, more than one thousand roads appeared, often built for financial speculation rather than for viable transportation. Speculation in railroad stock became notorious and an easy way to make fortunes (or lose them as the case was more often than not) by "watering stock"—that is stock issued in excess of the actual assets of the railroads. Unfortunately, this practice carried over into the twenty-first century—witness the rise and fall of the Enron Corporation in Houston, Texas, which resurrected this practice first "developed" by railroad speculators. As with Enron, as long as investors remained optimistic about the future, a boom mentality prevailed. Buyers could be found for the overvalued stock, and a handful of individuals turned huge profits.

Perhaps the most interesting and personal way to gain an understanding of the rise of the railroad industry is to look at the career of Jay Gould, one of the nation's most legendary plutocrats and railroad developers par excellence. Gould bought his first rail line before he was twenty-five. It was only sixty-two miles long, in bad repair, and on the brink of failure. Within two years, however, Gould refurbished it and sold it at a profit of $130,000. Thus began the ascendancy of the individual who would pioneer the development of the nation's railway system and become the era's most notorious and ruthless speculator.

Gould admitted he knew little about railroads and cared less about their operation. Nevertheless he came "to write the book" on the concept of corporate expansion, the architect of the vast railroad system that developed in the 1870s. In short, Gould bought and sold, or controlled, railroads only as a means to make money: immediate profit. He had no intention of owning any lines forever, or of even controlling the network for an indefinite period of time. He was simply a stock market "player" who looked for vulnerable lines to buy, purchasing enough of its stock to give him controlling interest and then threatened to undercut his competitors until they bought him out at a high profit. The railroads that fell into his hands fared badly and often went bankrupt. Gould's genius and wealth was the result of his shrewd buying and selling of railroad stock, not in providing transportation.

The ease with which Gould was able to manipulate railroad stock and control lines illustrates the haphazard nature of the early rail industry. Partly responsible for this was the federal government, which was so anxious to develop the West in the post-war years that it gave vast amounts of the public domain to the railroad builders for free. The railroads not only received land for rights-of-way but were granted liberal sections on alternating sides of the track (sometimes up to twenty square miles on both sides of the track!) to do with as they pleased, most often to sell to settlers who followed the lines west. Between 1870 and 1900, the federal government granted the lines a total of 180 million acres, an area larger than the state of Texas. But the lion's share of the capital for the roads came from private investors, a good portion of whom were foreigners, mostly Englishmen.

Lack of planning led to over-expansion of lines. Already by the 1870s, the railroads competed fiercely for business on the eastern seaboard. A manufacturer who needed to ship goods to market and who was fortunate enough to be in an area inundated by competing lines could get a greatly reduced shipping rate in return for promising to use that particular road exclusively. This type of cutthroat competition between the lines caused many to lose money and go under. Those that survived realized that such competition was ruinous to all and thus set up agreements or "pools" to divide up territory more equitably and set uniform rates. But these informal combinations invariable failed because they were never legally formalized and because "corsairs" like Gould were determined to destroy all competitors by undercutting whatever rates they offered their customers.

In the 1880s, Gould attempted to put together from existing lines, and from the construction of new ones, a second transcontinental system to compete with the Union and Central Pacific. His decision meant that other railroads had no choice but to defend their interests by adopting his strategy of expansion and consolidation. Beginning in that decade and stretching into the next, the other railroad titans went to war with Gould, resulting ultimately in his defeat, but in the process, by the 1890s, the lines west of the Mississippi had been consolidated into three major roads that controlled all rail travel—the Southern Pacific, the Northern Pacific, and the Atchison, Topeka, and Santa Fe.

One of the most important by-products of the emerging railroad industry was the introduction of new, more efficient business practices such as new cost accounting methods and new business structures that enabled the railroads to run at a profit and give new meaning to the term "big business." In the antebellum period, even the largest Northern textile mill employed only 800 workers, most often working in one town or even one factory. By 1874, the Pennsylvania Railroad, the largest line in the East, and for awhile in the country, employed more than 55,000 workers and managers and controlled more than 6,000 miles of track spanning half of the nation. Capitalized at over $400 million, the Pennsylvania could boast that it was the largest private enterprise in the world. The Pennsylvania could rightly be called one of the nation's first corporations, and its organization, size, and profitability pointed the way toward the future for all other businesses wanting to become as powerful and profitable. Consolidation became the key to such status, and thus the transformation began from small partnerships to huge "incorporated" entities.

An equally important revolution in communications coincided with the growth of the railroads. In the 1840s Samuel F. B. Morse developed a code to send messages across electrical wire. Morse's intricate series of dots and dashes, tapped out on a single key, allowed telegraphers to send messages virtually instantaneously over the wires, thus giving the country its first national communication system. The telegraph marched across the continent with the railroads, on rights-of-way furnished by the lines themselves. The telegraph system became the nerve center for the railroads, providing the companies with the instantaneous communication they needed to control their far-flung rail empires. Here again, Gould played a crucial role. In 1878, through his mastery of stock manipulation, the robber baron gained control of Western Union, the company that monopolized the telegraph industry. With control of Western Union, Gould could thus dictate to the other roads the price they had to pay for such services. Needless to say, Gould's acquisition of Western Union only made him that much more powerful and that much more hated by his competitors, such as they were.

Not all of the early railroad magnates were as ruthless as Gould. James J. Hill, owner of the Great Northern (Minneapolis, Minnesota to Seattle, Washington), built his line well and without the benefit of federal largesse. Hill had to plan carefully and calculate which areas would best be served by the line to maximize returns to his investors. As a result, the Great Northern was one of the few major roads able to remain solvent and running during the 1890s, when depression hit the country in 1893. In contrast, speculators like Daniel Drew and Jim Fisk, Gould's partners at the Erie Railroad, could more accurately be described as wreckers than as builders. They ruined the Erie, one of the East's most important early lines, by gambling with its stock to line their own pockets. In the West, the Big Four railroad moguls—Collis P. Huntington, Richard Crocker, Leland Stanford, and Mark Hopkins—became so powerful that critics claimed the Southern Pacific held California in the grip of an "octopus."

The public's increasing alarm at the railroad tycoons' control of the economy provided a barometer of attitudes toward big business itself. When Jay Gould died in 1892, the press described him as "the world's richest man," estimating his fortune at over $100 million. His competitor for that title, the "Commodore," Cornelius Vanderbilt, who built the New York Central Railroad, judged Gould "the smartest man in America." But to the public who found in Gould a symbol of all that most troubled them about the rise of big business, he was, as he himself admitted shortly before his death, "the most hated man in America." Why? Many, no doubt, remembered Gould's attempt to corner the gold market in 1869. Anti-Semitism also was a factor since many mistakenly believed Gould to be Jewish. Finally, many Americans had long hated men who earned great wealth by "shuffling paper" and speculation with other people's money rather than by their own physical exertions or producing goods. Since Gould did neither, his image was further tarnished. However, by the time of his death, more than 150,000 miles of track stretched across the country, and no one could claim to have had a greater hand in its building than Jay Gould.

The Panic of 1873

The nefarious, speculative activities of railroad barons such as Gould, Fisk, Drew, and others helped to precipitate one of the worst and most prolonged economic contractions in United States history: the Panic of 1873. As noted above, the exhilarating yet frenzied railroad expansion of the immediate postwar years came to a wrenching halt in the fall of 1873. In September, Jay Cooke and Company, the cornerstone of the nation's banking system, went under after being unable to market millions of dollars of bonds of the Northern Pacific Railroad, a line that was to provide the country's second transcontinental system. The failure of Cooke's company precipitated a national financial panic as hundreds of banks and brokerage houses failed as well. So intertwined was the stock market with railroad speculation that it temporarily suspended operation while investors attempted to recoup losses and rally the market back to health.

Factories throughout the land laid off thousands of workers as a result of the railroad industry's collapse. Of the nation's 364 railroads, 89 went into bankruptcy by the end of the panic's first year. Eighteen thousand related businesses failed in two years. Unemployment rose to 14 percent by 1876, as hard times settled across the land like a pall. The downturn lasted for over ten years; not until the mid-1880s did the economy recover and stabilize, and then, as will be seen, "good times" lasted for only a few years as yet another depression hit the nation in 1893.

ANDREW CARNEGIE AND THE RISE OF THE STEEL INDUSTRY

Railroad construction stimulated the development of a second major industry—steel. The first railroads ran on iron rails, which cracked and broke with alarming regularity. Steel, stronger and more flexible than iron, remained too expensive for use in rail until an Englishman named Henry Bessemer developed a way to make steel from pig iron, which the United States had vast quantities of near the Great Lakes. With such an abundance of iron ore, the Bessemer process found its most enthusiastic employers among American steel manufacturers. Andrew Carnegie was one of the first steel producers to use the Bessemer process and the first champion of the new "King Steel." Within a decade, Carnegie monopolized the steel industry.

Unlike Jay Gould, who by the time of his death was despised, almost from the beginning of his rise to industrial preeminence, Andrew Carnegie became an American icon. The hatred toward Gould and the affection for Carnegie testified to the country's divided reaction to industrialism. Carnegie, a barely literate Scots immigrant, came to personify the American dream (or myth!) of rags-to-riches. He rose from a job in a textile factory cleaning bobbins at age twelve for a $1.20 a week to become one of the richest men in America. Before he died, he gave away more than $300 million of his fortune, most notably to public libraries. His alleged generosity or philanthropy, combined with his own rise from poverty, went far to promote a popular image with the public. In reality, Carnegie was a shrewd, often ruthless, manipulative

Andrew Carnegie

businessman, in many respects no different than Gould. He simply atoned for his callousness and greed in his twilight years by becoming a philanthropist.

Carnegie's swift rise to plutocrat coincided with the propagation of the popular myth promoted by the writer Horatio Alger, whose novels, such as *Ragged Dick, Mark the Matchboy, and Pluck and Luck,* filled Americans' heads with the notion that if one just worked hard, led a clean, sober life, like Carnegie allegedly did, they too could become millionaires. To a certain degree, such was possible in the immediate aftermath of the Civil War, which allowed a few men, such as Carnegie, to take advantage of such a wide-open economic system in a state of constant flux and change. In many ways, Carnegie did embody an Algeresque quality: pluck and luck to be in the right place at the right time. After he left the textile factory, while still a teenager, he got a job as a telegraph operator for the Pennsylvania Railroad.

Under the auspices of Tom Scott, the line's superintendent, Carnegie rose through the ranks, all the while maintaining Scott's friendship. It was Scott who loaned Carnegie the money for his first investments in the stock market that netted him enough money to plunge into the steel business. Carnegie's twelve years with the railroad also provided him with a great education in business management that he put to good use when he struck out on his own to reshape the iron and steel industries.

In 1872 Carnegie began his rise in the steel industry. By applying the lessons of cost accounting and efficiency he had learned at the Pennsylvania Railroad, Carnegie turned steel into the nation's first manufacturing big business. In the town of Braddock, on the outskirts of Pittsburgh, Pa., he built the most modern Bessemer steel plant in the world and began turning out steel at an unprecedented rate. By the 1890s, Carnegie's blast furnaces poured out an incredible ten thousand tons of steel a week. Using railroad accounting methods, he cut the cost of making rails in half, from $58 to $25 a ton. Carnegie's formula for success was simple: "Cut the prices, scoop the market, run the mills full; watch the costs and profits will take care of themselves." Indeed, by 1900, Carnegie Steel earned more than $40 million in a single year. But at what human costs? "Cut the prices" meant, like for Gould, you simply destroy all competitors by having lower prices than anyone else. Lower prices meant lowering the costs of production, which meant cutting potentially the most expensive production cost—labor. Carnegie's workers were grossly overworked and underpaid—exploited callously by a man who had become a hero known for his supposed humanity and compassion, for he himself had "once been there." Workers toiled at least twelve hours a day in most of his plants, and when the shift changed every other week, they worked twenty-four hours at a stretch in the hazardous steel mills. Carnegie held an absolute majority of stock in his company and rarely paid dividends to his shareholders. Instead, he poured the profits back into new plants and new machinery—not into higher wages, safer working conditions, nor shorter hours for his workers. Obviously, the richer Carnegie became the more he forgot "where he came from."

Carnegie's steel monopoly was the result of a system of business organization or incorporation called vertical integration. Vertical integration simply means that all facets of a given manufacturing enterprise, from the procuring of essential raw materials to the finished product, including transportation, are under the control of one business or ownership. In Carnegie's case, as one contemporary observer noted, "from the moment these crude stuffs were dug out of the earth until they flowed in a stream of liquid steel in the ladles, there was never a price, profit, or royalty paid to any outsider." Between 1875 and 1900, Carnegie sought to control every aspect of the steel making process, from the mining of iron ore on the Great Lakes to its transport to his mills, to the production of crude steel and rails.

Carnegie dominated the steel industry for three decades, building Carnegie Steel into an industrial giant, the largest steel producer in the world. Carnegie's steel built the nation's first skyscraper, formed the skeleton of the Washington Monument, supported the elevated trains in Chicago and New York, and provided the superstructure for the Brooklyn Bridge. By 1900, Andrew Carnegie was world famous, and steel had replaced iron as the most important heavy construction material.

JOHN D. ROCKEFELLER, STANDARD OIL AND THE TRUST

Edwin Drake's oil discovery in Pennsylvania in 1859 sent thousands rushing to that state's oil fields searching for "black gold." In the days before electricity, the automobile, and gasoline, crude oil was refined for lubrication oil for machinery and kerosene for lamps to light homes and streets. Observing the difference between the price of crude oil gushing from wells at fifty cents a barrel (forty-two gallons) and the kerosene sold in the East at fifty cents a gallon, smart entrepreneurs turned to oil refining as the key to making a potential fortune from this particular resource. The amount of capital required to buy or build an oil refinery in the 1860s and 1870s was relatively low, about $25,000, the cost of laying one mile of railroad track. Since investment cost was low, the story of the new petroleum industry was one of

John D. Rockefeller

riotous, cutthroat competition among the plethora of small refineries. Inspired by both Gould's and Carnegie's ruthlessness and single-mindedness, one man, John D. Rockefeller, came to dominate oil refining through the use of yet another new business organizational strategy called the trust. By the 1890s, Rockefeller controlled nine-tenths of the oil refining business through his Standard Oil Company.

John D. Rockefeller grew up the son of a shrewd Yankee doctor who peddled quack cures for cancer. Under his father's tutelage, he learned early some of the more invidious skills that would help him establish his oil empire. "I cheat my boys every time I get a chance," Bill Rockefeller boasted. "I want to make'em sharp." John D. started out rather humbly, a bookkeeper in Cleveland, but owned his own business by the time he was twenty-one. One of the secrets of his success lay in his ability to obtain loans. He borrowed constantly to build up his profits, making other people's money work for him. A taciturn young man with an all-consuming passion for business, Rockefeller, like his cohorts, Gould and Carnegie, hired a substitute to fight for him during the Civil War, so he could remain on the homefront, profiting from the war while others fought and died to keep him safe and making money. Like many other shirkers, Rockefeller became wealthy during the war years. In 1865, he bought out his partner with borrowed money and took over the largest oil refinery in Cleveland. Like a growing number of his fellow plutocrats, Rockefeller realized that a partnership was no way to maximize profit and minimize personal liability; a corporation was. Thus, in 1870, he incorporated his oil business, founding the Standard Oil Company, the precursor of today's Exxon Corporation.

As the largest refiner in Cleveland, Rockefeller demanded rebates or "kickbacks" from the railroads, which they gave. Indeed, his volume of shipping was so great that the railroads not only gave him the rebates on his fares but also slipped him "under the table" a portion of the fares paid by his competitors. Such wheeling and dealing allowed Rockefeller to undercut his competitors. He not only could ship his oil at a dollar a barrel cheaper but he also received a dollar a barrel "rake-off" on every barrel his competitors shipped. Using this kind of leverage, Rockefeller soon pressured competing refiners to sell out to him or face ruin. By 1871 Standard Oil had "cornered" the petroleum business in Cleveland, and now John D. set his sights on the national market.

The cities of Cleveland, Pittsburgh, Philadelphia, and New York City competed to become the center of the nation's petroleum business. By combining railroad rebates with efficient production, Standard Oil strengthened its position. Major refiners began to sell out. In a series of secret mergers, or combinations, they received stock in Rockefeller's company and continued to run their refineries as before under their own names. Stubborn independents who refused to capitulate to Rockefeller's often menacing demands to sell, either unwittingly sold to companies that were secretly controlled by Standard Oil or somehow mysteriously blew up!! Rockefeller was infamous for doing whatever it took to eliminate his competition; in that sense he may have been more shameless and ruthless than either Gould or Carnegie. Not until 1879, when a New York legislative committee investigated railroad practices did the American people learn the extent of Standard Oil's hidden empire.

Rockefeller's clandestine activities were necessary because such combinations were illegal. Laws forbade one corporation from controlling another. Rockefeller, however, circumvented the laws by shrewdly developing yet another new organizational structure that came to be called a trust. Such an entity was a form of horizontal integration, which differed from Carnegie's vertical approach in steel. In a trust, several "trustees" hold stock in the various companies doing the same business in "trust" for the parent company's stockholders. In the case of Standard Oil, trustees held stock in the various refineries "in trust" for Standard's stockholders. Initially, Rockefeller did not attempt to control every facet of the oil business from crude oil at the well to the final product. Rather, he opted to move horizontally to control only the refining process by taking over all the refineries he could. He used the trust to increase profits by controlling output, thus raising prices consumers had to pay. Because Standard Oil monopolized the market and controlled the output of an essential commodity, "heating oil," and in effect "lighting" for homes, schools, hospitals, businesses, and street lights, the public soon cried out against the company, accusing it of conspiring against the public for private profit. When the federal government threatened to outlaw the trust as a violation of free trade, Rockefeller simply changed his tactics and organized Standard Oil into a holding company, which operated in much the same way as a trust but was legal. Instead of competing companies agreeing to set prices and determine territories, such as the railroads did for awhile, the holding company simply combined competing companies under one central administration. The state of New Jersey helped to promote this new form of consolidation and monopoly by passing laws that allowed state-chartered corporations to hold stock in out-of-state enterprises. Suffice it to say, very quickly conglomerates such as Standard Oil company and a host of other large combinations transferred their company "headquarters" to New Jersey, which by the end of the century was "home" to some of the nation's largest corporations.

As Rockefeller's empire grew, central control became essential. Interestingly, Rockefeller personally did not move to New Jersey but to neighboring New York City, where from his office at 26 Broadway, he began to vertically integrate á la Carnegie steel, Standard Oil. In reality, Standard Oil became unique: it was both horizontally and vertically integrated, allowing it to ultimately control the entire petroleum industry from crude oil sources in the ground (which at this time were exclusively located east of the Mississippi in the states of Pennsylvania, Ohio, and parts of West Virginia) to home and business delivery of the final product.

Rockefeller enjoyed unprecedented business success. Before he died in 1937 at the age of ninety-eight, he had become the nation's first billionaire. For most of his adult life, he was undeniably the richest man in the Republic. Despite his modest habits, his pious Baptist habits, and his many philanthropic acts, the American people never embraced him the way they had Carnegie. The individual most responsible for Rockefeller's negative public image was journalist/muckraker Ida M. Tarbell, whose classic magazine expose, *History of the Standard Oil Company*, published in *McClure's Magazine* beginning in 1902, revealed to the American people that Rockefeller was perhaps the most ruthless and callous of all the plutocrats. Tarbell's devastatingly thorough history showed an individual so determined in his business pursuit that he willingly and unashamedly used whatever tactics—threats, assassination, sabotage—that would bring the desired result: complete control of the petroleum industry of the United States. By the time Tarbell finished her story, Rockefeller had become such a demon in the public's eye that he literally slept with a loaded revolver by his bed to defend himself against possible assassins.

Even though Andrew Carnegie was at times as cold and ruthless, it was Rockefeller who aroused the people's fear of industrial concentration. Americans vilified him because they feared the vast power of one company to so completely control the production and supply of so vital a resource such as oil. At any time, Standard Oil could shut the nation down if its unscrupulous, greedy owner thought he could make more money by doing so! However, plutocrats such as Rockefeller, despite having their own personal fears for their safety, were secure for years to come from

Alexander Graham Bell, inventor of the telephone, made the first successful call on March 10, 1876.

any laws being passed by the federal government that curtailed their power or ability to do as they pleased, regardless of the harm done to the public welfare.

Although Americans may have feared and despised the plutocrats such as Rockefeller, they warmly embraced the inventors, even though many of them were closely tied to the plutocracy. At the turn of the century, Alexander Graham Bell and Thomas Alva Edison had become folk heroes. However, regardless of how profound or revolutionary the invention, the inventor and his "creation" ultimately came under the plutocrats' control. Such was the case for two of the most important innovations in technological history—the telephone and electricity—both of which were the brain child of American genius.

Alexander Graham Bell, like Carnegie, a Scots immigrant, developed a way to transmit voice over wires—the telephone. The emperor of Brazil, Dom Pedro II, who attended the 1876 Philadelphia Centennial Exposition was dumfounded by a telephone on display and cried out, "My God, it talks!" Bell's demonstration of his new device immediately caught the attention of Western Union, which wanted to buy Bell's patent but was distracted from doing so because it was involved in its own battle for survival against Jay Gould. Bell, seeing the possibility of losing control of his own invention, wisely formed his own company, American Bell, with himself as owner. But Bell was an inventor, not a business man, and thus wisely deferred such matters to his brilliant professional manager, Theodore N. Vail, who over the course of two decades built Bell America and its subsidiary, American Telephone and Telegraph (AT&T) into one of the nation's largest communications corporations. In 1900, AT&T became the parent company of the entire "Bell system." Taking a page from Rockefeller's book, Vail organized first Bell America and then AT&T both vertically and horizontally, which meant that AT&T had a complete monopoly of the new telephone industry and would remain in control of it until the late twentieth century. Via Western Electric, which AT&T also owned, the company manufactured and installed its own equipment as well as controlling long-distance telephone service. In practical terms, AT&T meant that Americans could communicate not only locally in their towns and cities but across the country. Unlike a telegraph message, which had to be written out and taken to a telegraph office, sent over the wire, and then delivered by hand to the recipient, the telephone connected both parties immediately and privately. Bell's invention proved a boon to business, contributing greatly to speed and efficiency.

However, since AT&T monopolized this new communication industry, it, like any of the other big businesses discussed so far, dictated supply, service, and prices. If one wanted "phone service," then it would be provided but at AT&T's convenience and price. Many rural folk, for example, would not have a telephone in their homes for decades after it became a household item for most urban dwellers. Why? It simply was not "profitable" for AT&T to supply service to people living in the country. It would cost the company too much money to build lines for such

Edison not only invented the light bulb but designed power plants and generators to make the entire system work. Before the electric light bulb, homes were lit by candles, kerosene lanterns, and gaslights.

limited use. However, if one lived in the country and wanted to be "connected," then rates would be exorbitant compared to those paid by city folk. Thus, ironically, the telephone, which could have brought Americans closer together (which it did for urban residents), only served to further separate country folk from city folk, creating over time a serious socioeconomic and cultural chasm that grew ever wider in the twentieth century.

In the eyes of Americans, Thomas Edison came to personify the virtues of rugged individualism and Yankee ingenuity, working twenty hours a day in his laboratory in Menlo Park, New Jersey, vowing to turn out "a minor invention every ten days and a big thing every six months or so." Edison almost fulfilled his pledge. At the height of his career, he averaged a patent every eleven days and invented such "big things" as the phonograph, the motion picture camera, and the electric light bulb. No industry that developed in the post-Civil War period faced more obstacles than electric light and power. Edison's invention of a filament for the electric light bulb in 1879 ushered in the age of electricity. But perplexing Edison was the way to sell this most important product. Before he could begin marketing electric light and power, he had to develop an integrated system of conductors, power stations, generators, lamps, and electrical machines. Because electricity was so technically complex and so potentially dangerous, it demanded an entirely new system of marketing, one that relied on skilled engineers. Initially, the new industry depended on private generators. Financier J.P. Morgan had electricity installed in his New York City mansion on Madison Avenue in 1882, making it the first private home in the country with electric lighting. An engineer visited the house daily to start the generator. When the lamp

Edison's incandescent light bulb.

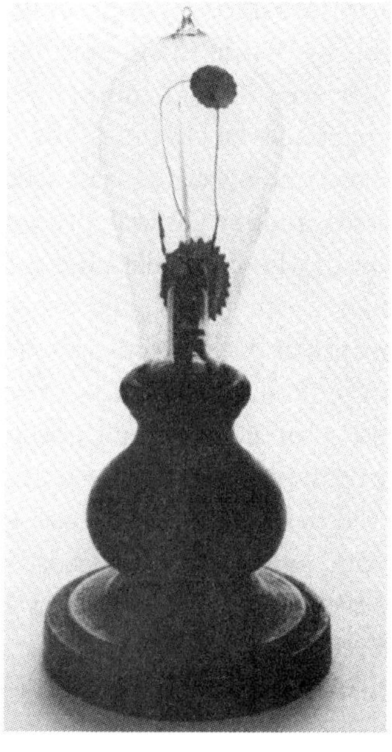

in Morgan's library short-circuited and set fire to his desk, the engineer promptly fixed the problem and restored Morgan's faith in electricity, so much so that he invested heavily in the Edison General Electric Company.

Edison worked diligently to build power stations and provide electric current. But his system had one serious drawback: it relied on direct current, which meant that he could only supply electricity for up to two miles from a power station. George Westinghouse, a contemporary of Edison's and inventor of the air brake for trains, solved the problem by "inventing" alternating current, which could travel much greater distances. Westinghouse saw great—profitable—potential in supplying people with this new product and created his own company to compete with Edison General Electric. Both companies created large, complex, vertically integrated enterprises to meet their unique marketing and distribution needs. They staffed sales offices with technicians trained to advise consumers, safely install and operate equipment, and provide repair services. Despite Edison's protests, Westinghouse's superior alternating current became the accepted standard for electric power.

By 1900 electricity had become, like the telephone, part of American urban life. It powered trolley cars, subways, and factory machinery. It lighted homes, apartments, factories, and office buildings. Indeed, electricity became so exclusively associated with urban life that it became one of the most visibly symbolic manifestations of the increasing gap between city and country. As will be seen in a later chapter, as late as the 1930s, only 10 percent of rural America enjoyed or had access to this most important product. As was the case with the telephone, those who controlled the electrical power business, like Westinghouse and others, hoped to personally profit and thus only provided to markets where money could be made—the cities. Poor farmers and other rural folk could not afford the rates charged because to provide such a desultory population with electricity would have "cost" too much for the electric companies to profit. Thus, rural Americans would have to wait until the New Deal to have what had become a necessity of life for urban Americans some forty years earlier.

While Americans thrilled to the new electric cities, the day of the inventor quietly yielded to the heyday of the corporation. In 1892, J.P. Morgan consolidated the electric industry, selling Edison General Electric, of which he had become its major investor and shareholder, out from under its inventor and dropping Edison's name from the corporate title. The new General Electric Company, which was four times the size of its closest competitor, Westinghouse, soon dominated the market.

The Emergence of Mass Marketing

By the 1880s, thanks largely to the railroads, a national mass market emerged for producers of consumer goods. Indeed, the United States was one of the first industrial nations to produce simultaneously capital and consumer goods, the latter often in greater quantities than the former. Manufacturers of consumer goods integrated methods of mass production with those of mass distribution via the railroads to establish some of the first major consumer-oriented enterprises in America. Some of the first and most important of the new consumer industries to emerge were in the meatpacking and food processing industries, where innovative ownership allowed producers to reap huge profits from hot dogs and ketchup.

What Carnegie did for steel, Gustavus Swift did for meatpacking. Until well after the Civil War, cattle were transported out of the West (mainly Texas until the 1880s) on the hoof (actual live steers) to be slaughtered by local butchers. To feed an expanding Northern and Eastern population, Texas cowboys would drive large herds to the closest railheads, and then from there the live steers would be shipped to the meatpacking plants where they would be slaughtered. The problem was that much of the cattle had already lost weight from long drives out of south Texas and thus would not be of very good quality once they reached the packing house and were slaughtered. Swift believed it would be more efficient and produce a better quality of beef if the cattle were slaughtered in the Midwest, such as in cities like Kansas City, Missouri, and then transported North or East in refrigerated railcars while still fresh. To accomplish this, Swift created a vertically integrated meatpacking

Cattle are forced up the chute into a railroad boxcar. Scenes like this were common before the 1870s.

business headquartered in Chicago that controlled the entire process—from the purchase of cattle for slaughter to the mass distribution of initially fresh then processed meat to retailers and consumers. Swift was the first to use the refrigerated railcars, and through high quality, low prices, and effective advertising, he won over consumers who worried about buying meat not butchered locally. Swift's success led the older meatpackers, such as Philip Armour, to build similarly integrated businesses to compete with Swift. Armour, for example, was able to initially "corner the market" on processed meat in the form of bologna and hot dogs. By the 1890s, the city of Chicago had become, thanks to Swift and Armour, the center of the nation's meatpacking industry. From the Windy City, all manner of fresh and processed meat found its way into homes all across the nation. Though the quality of processed and even fresh meat was often questionable, the innovative ideas of Swift and Armour provided American consumers with a quantity and variety of food that was envied by the rest of the world.

Just as Swift combined mass production with mass distribution to revolutionize meatpacking, Henry John Heinz transformed the processed food industry. In 1880 Heinz was a local producer of pickles, sauces, and condiments. Operating on the outskirts of Pittsburgh, Heinz was still recovering from the Panic of 1873, which caused him to go bankrupt, when he adopted new, more efficient methods of canning and bottling and built a network of sales offices to advertise his fifty-seven varieties of condiments and sell them across the nation. To ensure the necessary and continuous flow of vegetables and other foodstuffs into his factories, he created a large buying and storing organization to contract with local farmers. By 1888 Heinz had become one of Pittsburgh's wealthiest citizens, and ketchup had become a household staple. Using similar methods, the owners of other processed food companies, such as Quaker Oats, Campbell Soup, and Borden Condensed Milk, coordinated mass production with mass distribution to produce inexpensive, canned, and easily prepared foods for a national market. Companies producing other commodities such as tobacco, grain, matches, and soap integrated manufacturing and distribution to dominate their respective markets. American Tobacco, Procter & Gamble, Quaker Oats, and Pillsbury

Flour all started during the Gilded Age, becoming giants in that time and are still flourishing today.

To boost and sustain sales in a nationally expanding market of consumers, businesses realized the importance of promoting their goods by advertising. Just as the railroads made possible a national market, newspapers made possible advertising on a national scale. Gilded Age advertising bore little resemblance to the slick, sophisticated industry of today. Nineteenth-century advertising agents neither wrote the copy nor selected the illustrative materials. All of that was done by the advertiser, "the client" or business wishing to display its products, primarily in newspapers and later in magazines. What the agent did do was buy and sell space in the newspapers and magazines. With more than 8,000 papers printed in the United States by 1876, few business owners could afford the time away from their companies to learn the names and locations of the papers, let alone check the circulation figures and bargain for advertising space. That became the agent's job, taking the client's prepared copy and placing it in specified papers. The ad agent earned his livelihood by being paid a commission, not by the advertiser but the newspaper publishers.

Gilded Age advertising was tainted by its frequent association with all manner of questionable products, ranging from quack medicine cure-alls to rotten canned or processed meats. Products like Lydia Pinkham's Vegetable Compound, a "sure cure for female complaints," pioneered early advertising and made Lydia Pinkham a household name. Reputable firms eschewed advertising because of its dubious, unethical practices. Organizations like the American Medical Association, which emerged in the late Gilded Age to try to purge the medical profession of quacks and phony medicines, prohibited its members from plying their trade in print. By the turn of the century, however, advertising and attitudes toward it began to change. As companies pursued a larger share of the national market, they turned to advertising to boost sales by extolling the virtues of their products. Ivory Soap—"99.44% pure—so pure it floats;" Quaker Oats—"the easy food;" and Coca Cola—"The ideal brain tonic"—cashed in on the growing trend toward national advertising. As companies competed for the national market, advertising became more professionalized, as ad agents began increasingly to not just place ads but actually write them as well. By the end of the century full-service advertising agencies started appearing in the larger urban areas such as New York City, soon to become the home to the burgeoning advertising industry. In short, advertising became an integral part of the product package.

FROM COMPETITION TO CONSOLIDATION: THE RISE OF THE CORPORATION

Even as plutocrats like Rockefeller and Carnegie built their empires, their days of independent ownership and autonomy were numbered. Once privately-owned and operated companies were selling out to impersonal, anonymous entities called corporations, which by the beginning of twentieth century were becoming the dominant form of business organization. Soon corporations, managed by faceless boards of directors—supposedly educated, professional business "experts"—replaced the great business titans of the previous decades. Already by the end of the nineteenth century, the corporation had begun to eclipse the partnership and sole proprietorship as the major business enterprise. Corporations had the advantage of limited liability, which protected investors from losing their own assets should the company go under. A corporation could "outlive" its owners and was not susceptible to the vagaries that frequently destroyed family businesses, as one generation could ruin a company painstakingly created by its predecessors. Corporations also separated ownership and management, placing the company's daily operations in the hands of professional managers. Since the corporation could raise money by issuing stocks and bonds, the owners in most instances were individual investors, a consortium of the majority stockholders, who were more than glad to leave management to elected or chosen boards of directors and the daily operations to trained experts. Also, because the law—the Fourteenth Amendment—recognized the corporation as a "person" and granted it protection under that legislation's due process clause, it was difficult to regulate or redress corporate abuse through legislation. Finally, corporations could buy out and control other corporate entities, and it was this power that came to dominate in the early twentieth century as businesses consolidated into ever larger corporate giants.

The merger trend that resulted in the formation of Standard Oil and General Electric intensified in the years between 1890 and 1903. When trusts came under scrutiny, businesses consolidated into holding companies, as Standard Oil had done, to avoid prosecution. As many companies went under as a result of the depression of the 1890s, many went into bankruptcy courts where they were restructured, reorganized, and consolidated by court-appointed receivers. Banks and financiers played a key role in this consolidation, so much so that the era of the individual entrepreneur gave way to the dominance of the financial capitalist. No one better defined this role than J.P. Morgan, the great New York banker, who single-handedly reshaped American business at the turn of the century, consolidating several major industries, including the railroads and steel, into large corporate entities. During these years, a new social philosophy, based on Darwinian theory, helped to justify consolidation and to prevent state or federal intervention to regulate or control the excesses or corporate capitalism. The Supreme Court, a bastion of conservatism during this time, further promoted consolidation by "strictly" interpreting the Constitution and thus declaring unconstitutional legislation designed to regulate railroad rates and to outlaw trusts and monopolies.

J.P. MORGAN AND FINANCE CAPITALISM

The new consolidationists loathed competition and whenever possible pursued a policy of incorporation and central control. No one was a more zealous promoter of consolidation than J. Pierpont Morgan, whose life seemed circumscribed by three things: the pursuit of order, predictability, and profit. Morgan was one of the most dominant Wall Street financiers and "players" of all time. A large man (over six feet tall, which was several inches more than Carnegie or Gould, both of whom were under five feet five, the average height for an adult male) with a prominent acne-scarred nose and a cold, aloof demeanor, with eyes that seemed to pierce right through you, Morgan disdained the climbers and speculators with a haughtiness that led his enemies to call him "Jupiter" after the Roman god. The son of a successful banker, J.P. Morgan inherited along with his wealth the stern business code of the old-fashioned merchant bankers, men who valued character and reputation. From his own age, Morgan embraced the new business ethos and believed that investment banking could play a decisive role in reorganizing business and transforming the stock market.

Morgan acted as a power broker in the reorganization of the railroads and in the creation of corporations like General Electric and United States Steel. When depression engulfed the nation in the early 1890s, once again the railroad industry was hit hard. Morgan, with his passion for order and his access to capital, decided it was time to restructure the entire industry, consolidating as many of the lines as possible to prevent the industry's future collapse when hard times hit. He had already restructured the Baltimore and Ohio, the Reading, and the Chesapeake and Ohio Railroads in the 1880s. After the panic of 1893, he added the Santa Fe, the Erie, and the Northern Pacific and Southern Railroads to his list. In 1901, Morgan's railroad empire reached its zenith when he created the Northern Securities Company, a supersystem designed to bring peace between the feuding Great Northern and Northern Pacific Railroads. Other investment bankers did the same as Morgan for other lines but none did it on the scale of J.P. Morgan.

Morgan's purpose for creating the Northern Securities Company was to establish a "community of interest" among the new entities managers, men he handpicked. Often, Morgan partners sat on the boards of competing firms, forming interlocking directorates. By the time Morgan was finished reorganizing the railroad industry, seven major groups, all under his auspices, controlled two-thirds of the nation's rail lines.

Banker-control of the railroads rationalized or coordinated the industry. But such cooperation and harmony among the lines belied the fact that Morgan heavily watered the stock of the railroads, issuing new stock lavishly to keep old investors happy and to guarantee large profits. Morgan's firm made millions from commissions and from blocks of stock acquired in the reorganization process. The blatant overcapitalization caused by the watered stock negatively affected the railroads, saddling them with enormous debts. Equally detrimental was the management style of the Morgan directors, who were not railroad men but essentially "cost analysts" whose background was banking and accounting, and thus their conservative policies discouraged the continued technological and organizational innovation necessary to run the line effectively.

In 1898 Morgan believed it was time to consolidate the steel industry. The story of his acquisition of Carnegie Steel is not only legendary but symbolic of the passing of an old era and the coming of a new one. The heyday of the individual entrepreneur was ending by the late nineteenth century, and in its wake came the rise of the corporation. Carnegie represented the old order—Morgan the new. As he began to challenge Carnegie's empire, Morgan wisely first merged all the smaller steel companies, thus eliminating the last remnant of competition in the steel industry. In the merger process, Morgan also vertically integrated his new cartel by having his companies move from the manufacture of finished steel products into actual steel production. Carnegie, who for decades had monopolized crude steel production, countered this obvious move by creating a new plant for the manufacturing of finished steel products such as tubing, nails, wire, and hoops.

The press covered the impending war between the feisty Scot and the arrogant Wall Street broker as if it were a major sporting event, but the battle of the titans proved in the end to be little more than the wily maneuvering of two shrewd businessmen so adept that even today it is hard to discern who won. The sixty-six-year-old Carnegie, for all his obstinacy, longed to retire to his castle in Scotland and may well have invited Morgan's bid for power. Surely Carnegie knew that Morgan was probably the only individual who had enough money to buy him out. When an intermediary sought Carnegie out on the golf course and asked him to name his price, Carnegie scrawled a number on his score card, and the go-between scurried back to Morgan's office and handed him the card. Morgan, who disdained haggling, accepted the price; he agreed to pay $480 million for Carnegie Steel. Carnegie's personal "take" was more than $250 million. According to legend, when Carnegie later teased Morgan that he should have asked for a $100 million more, Morgan had the last laugh, telling the Scotsman, "You would have got it if you had."

Morgan quickly merged Carnegie Steel with his other steel companies, forming one of the largest conglomerates in United States history and in the world at the time: United States Steel, known today as USX. Created in March 1901, U.S. Steel became the country's first billion dollar corporation. Yet despite its monolithic size and despite Morgan's attempt to gain a monopoly on steel production, he could not. There remained enough smaller, independent producers, such as Bethlehem Steel, to create a competitive system know as oligopoly, in which several large combinations, not one alone, controlled production. Other industries, such as meatpacking and electricity, were also oligopolies. Businesses in this new arrangement did not compete with each other by cutting prices; rather they simply followed the lead of giants like U.S. Steel in setting prices and dividing the market so that each business held a comfortable, profitable share. Although oligopoly did not eliminate competition all together, it definitely limited the competitors to a handful of companies.

When J.P. Morgan died in 1913, he estate was worth $68 million, not counting an additional $50 million in art treasures. Andrew Carnegie, who gave away more than $300 million before he died six years later, is said to have quipped, "And to think he was not a rich man!" But Carnegie's remark missed the point. Morgan was driven by the pursuit of personal power and order, which he believed consolidation of businesses into corporations would achieve. Morgan's imprint on the Gilded Age, and even down to today, was far greater than that of either Carnegie or Rockefeller. When the country faced bankruptcy in 1895, it was Morgan to whom the president turned. And as the reorganizer of American's railroads and the creator of U.S. Steel, General Electric, and other large combinations, Morgan ushered in the era of oligopoly that has continued to be an integral feature of the nation's business scene to the present.

SOCIAL DARWINISM AND THE GOSPEL OF WEALTH

As the plutocrats made their fortunes, many worried how they would be publicly perceived. Would the people embrace them as the epitome of rugged individualism, the realization of the American dream that hard work and a clean, sober life brings material success and rewards? Or, would they be viewed as ruthless, self-serving scoundrels who made their money by callously exploiting others? Even those who cared less about their public image, nonetheless, believed it essential to find justification or rationalization for how and why they "made it" while the majority of people suffered in miserable poverty, despair, and hopelessness. As already noted, the plutocrats often engaged in cutthroat competition from which fewer and fewer winners emerged. The road to wealth and power taken by these "robber barons" was strewn with ruined competitors and brutally exploited labor. Such ruthlessness not only seemed to become increasingly necessary for personal aggrandizement, it was also transformed into a "virtue" by the twin ideologies of Social Darwinism and the "gospel of wealth."

For men like Andrew Carnegie, the writings of Social Darwinists Herbert Spencer and William Graham Sumner helped expiate feelings of personal guilt. "I remember that light came as in a flood and all was clear," Carnegie remarked after reading Spencer's work. Spencer and his disciples believed that the same natural forces or laws that determined evolution and survival in the animal world were applicable to the human condition as well. As in the animal world, Darwin's concept of natural selection meant that in human society, the "fittest" individuals survived and flourished in the marketplace while those less "endowed" were destined or predetermined to be swept away by obviously superior individuals. Survival of the fittest supposedly enriched not only the winners but also society as a whole. Human evolution would produce what Spencer called "the ultimate and inevitable development of the ideal man" through a culling process of eliminating supposedly weaker, inferior human beings.

According to the Social Darwinists, poverty and slums were as inevitable as the concentration of wealth. Spencer argued that "there should not be a forcible burdening of the superior for the support of the inferior." His protégé, Sumner, asserted "If we do not like the survival of the fittest, we have only one possible alternative, and that is the survival of the unfittest." Both men believed that government or charitable intervention to improve the conditions of the poor interfered with the functioning of supposed "natural law" and prolonged the life of "defective gene pools" to the detriment of society as a whole. In short, Social Darwinists propagated a perverted Darwinism designed to bolster or justify not just the plutocrats' ruthless rise to power and wealth but to denigrate and keep oppressed as well the masses, whom they regarded as the "unfit." The Social Darwinist theory was imbued with overt racism and ethnocentrism, for the "fit" or superior individuals were clearly Anglo-Saxon or white Northern Europeans (excluding the "degenerate" Irish, of course!), while the unfit or inferior were the rest of humanity who were not of that "stock" and were thus to be either subordinate at all times to the superior race or ultimately "extinguished." As will be seen shortly, Social Darwinism became very popular among the nation's WASP (White, Anglo-Saxon Protestants) elite, especially from the 1890s on because of the massive influx of Southern and Eastern European immigrants whom they regarded as the "unfit."

Suffice it to say, plutocrats like Carnegie and Rockefeller enthusiastically embraced this theory. Rockefeller told his Baptist Sunday school class, "The growth of large business is merely the survival of the fittest. This is not an evil tendency in Business. It is merely the working out of nature and a law of God." Some who found the callousness of Social Darwinism unpalatable sought religious justification instead. Since colonial times, the Protestant work ethic had informed the American creed, denouncing idleness and viewing material success as evidence of being among the "elect"—God's chosen people for whom salvation was a certainty. Expanding on this assumption, the more religiously affected plutocrats constructed the "gospel of wealth."

In this context, some were simple and direct in their certainty, like Rockefeller, that their rise to industrial preeminence and wealth was ordained by

God: "God gave my riches," Rockefeller sanctimoniously declared as a "reward" for having led a most clean, sober, diligent and righteous life. Carnegie produced a written, logically argued rationale for his success: "Not evil but good, has come to the race," he wrote, "from the accumulation of wealth by those who have the ability and energy that produces it." To justify his exploitation of labor, Carnegie was certain that the masses would waste any extra income "on the indulgence of appetite." "Wealth, passing through the hands of the few," Carnegie wrote, "can be a much more potent force for the elevation of our race than if it had been distributed in small sums to the people themselves," whom the steel magnate was convinced would only spend it on the pleasures derived from vice and dissipation. In short, Carnegie believed that individuals like himself who have clearly demonstrated their "fitness," or superiority, should decide what other people needed. In Carnegie's case, he took that responsibility seriously, distributing over $300 million to such philanthropic causes as the founding of libraries and the Carnegie Foundation.

Among the most effective apologists for the wealthy were religious leaders such as the Episcopal Bishop William Lawrence, who proclaimed that "Godliness is in league with riches." Not only did the elite deserve their wealth, but the poor were responsible for their low status because of their obvious personal flaws and defectiveness. God was punishing them for their alleged "sins" of depravity and laziness. The eminent preacher Henry Ward Beecher reaffirmed this belief when he announced that "no man suffers from poverty unless it be more than his fault—unless it be his sin."

Thus, according to supposed scientific and religious thought, the maldistribution of wealth was not only inevitable but desirable, for it ultimately would "cleanse" society of all the "unfit" and leave only those "worthy" of continued existence. Probably more important was the support and propagation of such perversion by popular culture. *McGuffey Readers* stressed the virtue of hard work and its inevitable rewards. Popular literature reinforced the idea that success always came to those who deserved it in America, the land of opportunity.

INTERNAL MIGRATION AND EUROPEAN IMMIGRATION

The appeal of Social Darwinism among WASP America intensified during the last decade of the nineteenth century and into the early twentieth century because of unprecedented European immigration. Never before or since had so many human beings come to the United States seeking a new and better life. Indeed, between 1880 and 1920, some 23 million people arrived in the United States, mainly from Europe but from Canada, Mexico and Latin America, and Japan as well. Europe, however, provided over 80 percent of the total, and in that context, after 1880 and until 1914, the majority of immigrants came from southern and eastern Europe. Among them were 4 million Italians, 2 million Russian and Polish Jews, 2 million Hungarians, 4 million Slavs, and 1 million from Lithuania, Greece, and Portugal. Hundreds of thousands came as well from Turkey, Armenia, Lebanon, Syria, and other Near Eastern lands abutting the European continent.

It was this particular phase of immigration that resurrected the nativism, prejudice, and discrimination WASP America had previously displayed in the antebellum period toward the Irish and Germans. The same fears WASP America had about the Irish and Germans they now simply transferred to the Italians, Hungarians, eastern European Jews, Turks, Armenians, Poles, Russians, and other Slavic peoples. Not only did WASP America fear the Catholicism and supposed ethnic/racial inferiority of the new arrivals (the same "anxieties" they felt about the Irish in the 1840s), but compounding those trepidations was the fact that many of the new people weren't even Christian—they were Jewish or Muslim, two faiths the majority of white Americans had no understanding or knowledge of in any capacity and had always viewed with suspicion, contempt, and hostility. Up to this time, except for the momentary "fear" the influx of Irish and Germans created in the 1840s, WASP America's supremacy was unchallenged. Now, that was about to potentially change with the massive "invasion" of Europe's unwanted and "unfittest." Indeed, as the popular journal *Public Opinion* editorialized, "they are the very scum and offal of Europe."

This is a scene in one of New York's immigrant ghettos. People were forced to live in small apartments with little or no sanitation facilities.

Though a very high percentage of these immigrant groups were indeed illiterate peasants from some of the most impoverished areas of southern and eastern Europe who were "coming to America" to escape such despair, they were nonetheless all castigated for being uneducated, backward, and outlandish in appearance. Terence Powderly, head of the labor organization the Knights of Labor, complained—with a degree of accuracy because they were discriminated against and segregated into the city's most wretched areas—that the newcomers "herded together like animals and lived like beasts."

Old-stock WASP elites like Henry Cabot Lodge of Massachusetts, formed an unlikely alliance with organized labor (which was also at this time WASP-dominated and feared that the influx of unskilled labor, which the immigrants represented, would adversely affect their jobs and status) to press for immigration restriction. A precedent for keeping out "undesirables" had been established in 1882, when labor agitation and racism in California led to passage of the Chinese Exclusion Act, which stopped the legal immigration of Chinese nationals. On the east coast Lodge and his nativist followers championed a literacy test, a device designed to limit immigration from Italy and eastern Europe by requiring immigrants to demonstrate the ability to read and write in their own language. As mentioned above, since the vast majority of Italian and Slavic peasants had little to no formal education, it was assumed few would be able to pass the test. In 1896, Congress approved a literacy test for immigrants, but President Grover Cleveland promptly vetoed it. "It is said," the president reminded Congress, "that the quality of recent immigration is undesirable. The time is quite within recent memory when the same thing was said of immigrants, who, with their descendants, are now numbered among our best citizens." Cleveland's veto forestalled immigration restriction but did not stop the forces seeking to build such a "moat" around the United States. Hard-core nativist like Lodge would continue to press for restriction until they achieved their goal in the 1920s.

Why They Came

The new wave of immigration that brought southern and eastern Europeans to the United States beginning in the 1880s resulted from a number of factors. Improved economic conditions in northwestern Europe, as well as immigration to Australia, Canada, and Argentina, curtailed the flow of "old" immigrants to the United States. Prior to the 1880s, the overwhelming majority of new arrivals—the "old" immigrants— came from Germany, Ireland, Great Britain, Scandinavia, the Low Countries, and France. At the same time, a protracted economic depression in southern Italy, the religious persecution of Jews in eastern Europe, especially in Russia, with the infamous "pogroms," and a general desire to avoid conscription into the Russian army (which affected both Slavs and Poles) led many in southern and eastern Europe to come to the United States.

Economic factors in the United States also played a role, the most important of which was American industries' insatiable demand for cheap, unskilled labor, especially during good times. So important was immigrant labor in the rise of American industrial preeminence that without it the United States would not have become the leading industrial power in the world, at least not as rapidly. Had the millions of Europeans remained in their respective homelands or migrated instead to Germany, England, or France, then it was possible that one of those nations, not the United States, would have been the greatest industrial power by 1900. Nor would the plutocrats' profits and wealth been as great or as legendary had it not been for such cheap labor costs. Although the U.S. government did not offer direct inducements to immigrate (despite some pressure to do so by big business), the steamship companies solicited immigrants who provided a highly profitable self-loading cargo. Agents from large lines traveled throughout Europe drumming up business. Colorful pamphlets and posters mingled fact with fantasy to promote America as the land of promise and opportunity.

Though socioeconomic factors played a key role in European migration, in the final analysis, the decision whether to leave the Old Country and come to the United States, remained an individual or family choice. Immigrants were neither the "huddled masses" nor the bold adventurers determined at any cost to enter the "golden door." Nevertheless, immigration fever affected whole villages, as the entire population of a rural hamlet in southern Italy or in the Balkans would collectively decide to come to America or at least pool resources and send its most able-bodied. Would-be immigrants eager for information about America relied on letters, advertisements, and word of mouth—sources not always reliable or truthful. Promotional pamphlets all too frequently exaggerated the United States' economic opportunities, especially those that advertised "free land" or other such wild notions. Such falsehoods helped to create an image in the peasant/immigrant mind of an America whose "streets were paved with gold." Glowing letters from immigrants to friends and relatives back home boasted of how wonderful and better life was in America. In most cases, it was all fabrication, for those who left certainly did not want to appear failures when so many were counting on them to succeed and either be able to bring more over or return with the promised riches. As one Italian immigrant recalled, "Everything emanating from America reached [Italy] as a distortion. News was colored, success magnified, comforts and advantages exaggerated beyond all proportions." No wonder immigrants left for America believing "that if they were ever fortunate enough to reach America, they would fall into a pile of manure and get up brushing the diamonds out of their hair."

In at least one respect, life in the New World differed markedly from that in the old. In their home countries the majority of immigrants were farmer/peasants living in often very isolated rural villages. In America they became reluctant urbanites and industrial/manufacturing workers. Once they arrived and reality set in—there was no free land for them to have, even in the West—they were forced to stay and work in the urban, industrial centers where their wages were so low that their dream of ever moving out of such an environment and owning land was an illusion. The concentration of immigrants in the nation's industrial cities became symbiotic with urbanization. By 1900, almost two-thirds of the country's immigrants resided in cities. Although nowhere yet did the foreign-born population outnumber old-stock Anglo-Saxon inhabitants, the immigrants and their American-born children did makeup a majority in many of the nation's cities. By 1900, 50 percent of Philadelphia's population was foreign-born or the progeny of such parents, and the percentages were even higher in other cities: 66 percent in Boston, 75 percent in Chicago, and an amazing 80 percent in New York City.

Not all newcomers came to stay. Over the time period 1880-1910, perhaps eight million, mostly young men, came to the U.S., worked for a year or a season, trying to earn as much money as they could, and then went home. American immigration officers referred to such individuals as "birds of passage" because they followed a regular pattern of migration to and from the United States. By 1900, almost 75 percent of the new immigrants were single young men. Intent on making money as quickly as possible, they were willing to accept jobs and conditions others, especially native white workers, would not. They showed little interest in labor unions, which initially did not welcome them anyway because of the early union's often virulent nativism. Only later, when they realized that they were not going to return home, that America was now their permanent home, did they join unions.

Jews from eastern Europe most often came as family units and came to stay. In the 1880s, a wave of violent persecutions, or pogroms, in the Russian empire led to the departure of more than a million Jews in the next two decades. They settled mostly in the port cities of the East coast. New York City's Lower East Side replicated the Jewish ghettoes of eastern Europe, teeming with street peddlers and push carts. Hester Street, at the heart of New York's Jewish section, rang with the calls of vendors hawking their wares from pickles to feather beds. Jews were not the only immigrants to have their own "neighborhoods" in American cities. Soon after their arrival, virtually all the immigrant groups were segregated into their own enclaves by a WASP America fearful of their possible "mixing" or integration. Thus, springing up in New York City or Boston were the "Little Italys," or "Little Polands," and a whole host of other such communities in the inner city of the nation's major urban centers. In such enclaves the immigrants would remain (some forever) for several generations. As will be seen in subsequent chapters, as their numbers swelled and their affect on the city landscape became more pronounced, WASP America realized that no matter how deplorable their existence, the "new" Americans were here to stay. Once old-stock Americans accepted this reality, they then stopped running and wisely realized that if the immigrants intended to make the United States their permanent home, then the best policy to pursue was the newcomers' acculturation and assimilation. As will be seen, such a new attitude proved successful in transforming the once "unwanted" into "acceptable" citizens.

Pushcart peddlers on Hester Street on New York's Lower East Side. Hester Street was the place to live for newly arrived Jewish immigrants.

Working in the underground mine shafts was extremely dangerous. Poor working conditions also caused illnesses, such as black lung disease. Explosions and cave-ins were a constant danger.

Immigrant Labor

How important were the immigrants to the industrial work force? In the first decade of the twentieth century, immigrant men and their sons constituted 70 percent of the workforce in 15 of the 19 leading U.S. industries. Their concentration was highest in industries where the work was most exploitive and dangerous: railroad construction and tunnels; in the coal, iron ore, and other mineral mines; in the steel mills, and in the putrid, disease-infested meatpacking houses. Within this context, certain ethnic groups predominated. For example, after 1900, Slovaks and Poles overwhelmingly worked the coal mines and steel mills of western Pennsylvania, Buffalo, and Cleveland, while Poles, Lithuanians, and Italians were the rank and file in the meatpacking and food processing industries. Italians also exceeded all other groups in the heavy construction business, such as the building of New York City's subway system. In the "lighter" but no less arduous work of garment manufacturing, Jews and Italians predominated. Most egregious, however, was the preponderance of immigrant children in the garment industry "sweat shops." Here, hunched over sewing machines, twelve to fourteen hours a day, with tiny, nimble fingers often getting torn to shreds by the rapidly-moving needles, could be found young immigrant women and boys and girls as young as ten-years old, earning pennies per piece of clothing. Not only did these sweat shops callously exploit immigrant youth, they also were physically some of the most deplorable, hazardous, and sometimes fatal workplaces.

Immigrant labor workweeks averaged 60 hours—10 hours per day except Sunday. Workers who were granted Saturday afternoons off—thus reducing their workweek to 55 hours—considered themselves fortunate. Steel workers were not so lucky. They labored from 72 to 89 hours a week and were required to work one 24-hour shift every two weeks.

Women and children earned additional income in the home by doing "piece work." Employers paid for each finished item.

Immigrants were forced to work long hours just to barely make ends meet. In 1900 the annual earnings of American industrial workers averaged between $400 and $500 a year, although there were substantial variations from region to region and level of skill. Southern workers only earned on average $300 annually, while Northern counterparts earned $460. The better paying jobs by the late nineteenth century went to the "older immigrants"—Yankees, Germans, Irish, and Welsh. Through their unions, workers of Northern European extraction also controlled access to new jobs that opened up and usually managed to fill them with a son, a relative, or fellow countrymen. Consequently, relatively few of the new immigrants rose into the prosperous ranks of skilled labor. Ironically, though old immigrant skilled workers earned more than the recent arrivals, as the nineteenth century progressed, the old immigrants found themselves increasingly unemployed as the captains of industry replaced them with machines, easily operated by the unskilled new immigrants.

From the Farm to the City

Certainly not all of urban America's newcomers were foreign-born immigrants. Indeed, until the 1880s, the majority of a city's new inhabitants came from within the country, the result of an internal migration that brought hundreds of thousands of farm boys and girls looking for jobs in the burgeoning urban industrial centers and hoping to make their fortunes. The lure of the bright lights and the promise of wages, coupled with the theaters, the dance halls, the great amusement parks like Coney Island in New York City, and the cultural and educational advantages offered by the city, the likes of which they never dreamed existed, all served as a powerful magnet for many young folk.

For at least one group of Americans, the city promised something more. African Americans came north, not just looking for jobs, but to escape as well violence and oppression. Beginning in the 1880s, ex-Confederate states one by one put in place a series of laws called Jim Crow, that completely segregated black folk and white folk in the South. Further, by the 1890s, black voters were completely disfranchised in the South and with such laws, apartheid became complete. Worse, the 1890s marked the high point of a vicious racism against black folk, which saw the lynching of African Americans living in the south reach an all-time high. Southern white supremacy and segregation were further buttressed by the Supreme Court of the United States, which ruled in its 1896 landmark decision in *Plessy v. Ferguson,* that segregated facilities were legal under the doctrine of "separate but equal." With such an endorsement by the highest court in the land, white Southerners felt free to use whatever intimidation and violence necessary to "keep the Negro in his place." These indignities combined with the lack of economic choices to impel many southern blacks to leave their homes and seek a safer and materially better life in the North. "To die from the bite of frost is far more glorious than at the hands of a mob," proclaimed the *Defender,* Chicago's largest African-American newspaper. By the 1890s, many southern black folk agreed. Black migrants, nearly all of them from the rural South, headed to northern cities, either in the Midwest or the Northeast. There they found jobs, usually at the bottom of the occupational ladder, as janitors, cooks, common unskilled laborers, or domestic servants. Unfortunately, racism in the North was as commonplace as it was in the South, though often not as overt. In the North, Jim Crow's slick cousin, James Crow, was alive and well, covertly, insidiously, oppressing black folk, keeping them a segregated, subordinate class. Despite the existence of James Crow, the urban North continued to attract African Americans. By 1900, New York, Philadelphia, and Chicago contained the largest black communities in the nation. Although the greatest black exodus out of the South would occur during and after World War I, 185,000 African Americans had already moved north by 1890. The great migration was underway.

LAISSEZ FAIRE IN THEORY AND PRACTICE

Prevailing economic theory also bolstered greed, exploitation, and opposition to any government or private intervention to alter the "natural" laws of the free marketplace and the forces of unbridled capitalism. Since the nation's founding, Adam Smith's theory had informed the nation's economic system. Smith asserted that the market was directed and controlled by an "invisible hand" composed of a multitude of individual choices. If government did not meddle, competition would naturally lead to production of desired goods and services at reasonable prices—the natural laws of supply and demand. In short, Smith believed that since all humanity was motivated by self-interest, no individual or group of individuals would willingly succumb to greed or avarice, for to do so would only hurt their realization of personal—material— happiness. Thus, individuals must be left alone to act according to self-interest and in the process, the resulting economy would be best suited to meet society's demands.

Acceptance of Smith's theory led to a policy called laissez-faire. Government was to leave the economy alone and not disrupt the operation of these natural forces. Business leaders naturally endorsed the theory's rejection of governmental intervention and regulation, yet they saw no contradiction in asking government for aid and subsidies to further promote industrialization and modernization. To a large extent, Gilded Age capitalists got what they wanted: a laissez-faire policy that left them alone to pursue their objectives, free from all government interference, and government assistance whenever they asked to further expand and protect their enterprises, regardless of the harm their pursuit of "self-interest" had on people and the environment. Ironically, this distortion of Smith's theory helped produce an economy where business consolidation wreaked havoc on the very competition needed for natural regulation of the economy.

Unfettered industrial capitalism boggles the modern mind. Yet, as will be seen in a later chapter, such a possibility did not occur until the Progressive period, and really not until the 1930s and the New Deal. Until then, no laws protected the consumer from adulterated foods, spurious claims for ineffective or even dangerous patent medicines, the sale of stock in non-existent companies, any sort of regulation of the stock market, no laws abolishing child labor or establishing a forty-hour work week, or unsafe and overpriced transportation services. No national regulating agency of any kind existed before the establishment of the Interstate Commerce Commission in 1887. The proclamation, "Let the buyer beware," asked people to make decisions and choices without enough information to protect their interests.

While denying support and protection to consumers and workers, government at all levels willingly aided the plutocrats. Alexander Hamilton's vision of an industrializing nation promoted and protected by government participation had never entirely died. Indeed, it was resurrected by the Republican Party by 1860. In that year, the party pledged to enact higher tariffs to protect domestic northern industry, to subsidize the completion of a transcontinental railroad, and to establish a stable national banking system—all Hamiltonian ideas first introduced in the 1790s. As will be seen shortly, the Republican victory in that year and for the next several decades undoubtedly boded well for the emerging business and industrial elite, as the party evolved into the strongest supporter and promoter of big business and their interests.

Big business not only found a strong ally in the Republican Party but in the U.S. Supreme Court as well. During the 1880s and 1890s, the Court increasingly reinterpreted the Constitution to protect business from taxation, regulation, labor organization, and antitrust legislation. In a series of landmark decisions, the Court used the Fourteenth Amendment, originally intended to protect freed slaves from state laws violating their rights, to protect corporations. The Fourteenth Amendment declares that no state can "deprive any person of life, liberty, or property, without due process of law." By defining corporations as "persons" under the law, the Court determined that legislation designed to regulate corporations deprived them of "due process." Using this rationale, the Court struck down state laws regulating railroad rates, declared income tax unconstitutional, and judged labor unions as a "conspiracy in restraint of trade." As the plutocrats and their enterprises destroyed the environment, exploited labor, and generally ran roughshod over anyone or anything they felt not worth their time or energy, the Court insisted on elevating the "rights of property"—the capitalist interests—over the rights of people. According to Justice Stephen J. Field, the Constitution "allows no impediments to the acquisition of property." Field, born to a wealthy family and educated at the best schools of his day, spoke with the bias of the privileged class to whom property rights were sacrosanct. Imbued with this ideology, the Court refused to restrain corporate consolidation and did nothing to curb the excesses of industrial capitalism.

Labor Strife

With such attitudes shared by the government and plutocrats toward the working class, it was inevitable that sooner than later, the nation's working classes would rise up in protest against the plutocracy's exploitation and oppression. Perhaps the violent confrontations between labor and the industrial capitalists could have been avoided had the government been more concerned with the workers' plight. Since it was not, workers, finding no redress of their grievances through either the established political or legal system, decided to take matters into their own hands and through their own efforts, try to win the rights and respect they were entitled to as citizens.

Several factors drove workers toward protest and organizing and joining unions. Workplace safety, for example was one such cause. The drive for greater speed and productivity on railroads and in factories gave the United States the unfortunate distinction of having the world's highest rate of industrial accidents. Another factor was the erosion of worker autonomy in factories, as increasingly machinery replaced skilled workers and managers made operational decisions about pace and procedure rather than the workers. In short, as the Gilded Age progressed, once proud, skilled craftsmen became commodities to be bought for wages rather than a mastery whereby the worker sold the product of his labor rather than the labor itself. For skilled artisans this was an alarming trend. Their efforts to preserve or recapture independence from "bosses" and robber barons fired much of the era's labor unrest, which often escalated into violent, bloody confrontations between workers and owners.

The Great Railroad Strike of 1877

Because railroads were the nation's first, most important, industrial corporations it would only be natural that they would become the focal points of early labor strife. Citing declining revenues during the depression of the 1870s, several railroads cut wages by as much as 35 percent between 1874 and 1877. When the Baltimore and Ohio Railroad announced its third 10 percent cut on July 16, 1877, workers struck and prevented the line's trains from running. The strike spread rapidly to other roads and within weeks all rail traffic from St. Louis to the East coast was brought to a standstill. Ten states called out their militias to try to force strikers back to work but workers would not succumb to such intimidation and fought back, not only firing on the troops but setting fire to rolling stock and roundhouses as well. By the time federal troops restored order in the first week of August, at least one hundred railroad workers, militia, and bystanders had been killed and hundreds more injured, as well as millions of dollars of railroad property razed. It was the worst episode of labor violence in U.S. history to that time; the specter of class conflict frightened many upper and middle class Americans who believed that the nation was headed for social revolution.

As a result of the Great Railroad Strike, many workers hoped that through better organization they could win a redress of grievances without having to resort to striking, which they just witnessed would be brutally suppressed by the plutocrats and the government. Thus emerged the Knights of Labor, initially a secret fraternal society founded in 1869 in Philadelphia. However, in 1879, under the leadership of Terence Powderly, a skilled machinist by trade, the Knights "came out" and declared themselves a federation of unions, or "assemblies," as they were officially known. Powderly organized the Knights' assemblies by industry rather than by craft, giving many unskilled and semiskilled workers union representation for the first time. Some assemblies admitted women and black workers as well but despite this inclusiveness, tendencies toward exclusivity of craft, gender, and race divided and weakened many assemblies.

A paradox of purpose also handicapped the Knights. The goal of most the union's members was to improve their situation within the system through higher wages, shorter hours, better working conditions, and job security—the nuts and bolts objectives of working class Americans from this time forward. This meant collective bargaining with employers; it also meant striking if such concessions were not granted. The assemblies won some strikes and lost some. Powderly and Knights' leadership, however, discouraged the calls for strikes for they believed that in the end, strikes only weakened assemblies because workers, more often than not, lost to management who replaced the striking workers with strikebreakers or scabs, if not breaking the strike all together with the use of force. Powderly also opposed strikes for ideological reasons. Powderly was a "closet" socialist, who believed that strikes constituted a tacit recognition of the legitimacy of the wage system, which siphoned off to capital a part of the wealth created by labor. Like a good but visionary socialist, Powderly believed capitalism would ultimately give way to worker's cooperatives, which would own the means of production. But if workers continued to strike and alienate especially the middle class, which he believed would become sympathetic to the work-

Terence Powderly was president of the Knights of Labor for more than ten years. Powderly detested strikes.

Women delegates at a national meeting of the Knights of Labor. Women belonged to separate associations affiliated with local all-male unions.

ers' plight and support them, then there was no hope for workers to someday through cooperatives to own and operate mines, factories, and railroads to the benefit of all Americans. Despite Powderly's pleas for workers to avoid strikes, the Knights gained their greatest triumphs by striking. In 1884 and 1885 successful Knight-led strikes against the Union Pacific and Missouri Pacific railroads won enormous prestige and a rush of new members, which by 1886 totaled 700,000. But defeat in a second strike against the lines in 1886 was a serious blow. Then came the Haymarket bombing in Chicago.

Haymarket Square

Since the late 1870s, Chicago had become the center of labor radicalism, home to not only the Socialist Labor Party but to anarchism as well. The majority of anarchists were foreign-born, mostly Germans, and by 1886 they had gained significant influence within the Windy City's Socialist Party. The anarchists called for the violent destruction of the capitalist system so that a new socialist order could be built on its ashes. Anarchist had also infiltrated some of the city's unions, and from such bases of operation they led the call for a general strike on May 1, 1886, to achieve the eight-hour workday. Compounding an already nervous environment was the fact that Chicago police were notoriously hostile to labor organizers and strikers, so the scene was ripe for an inevitable violent confrontation between workers and police.

The object of the strike was the McCormick farm machinery plant in Chicago. A fight broke out between striking workers and "scabs," which resulted in a police attack on the strikers in which four people were killed. Anarchist used the incident to call for a massive protest rally at Haymarket Square on May 4. Toward the end of the meeting, as the rain-soaked crowd dispersed, the police suddenly arrived in force. When someone threw a bomb into their midst, the

The Haymarket meeting in Chicago in 1886 breaks into violence.

police opened fire indiscriminately. When the melee was over, 50 people lay wounded and 10 dead, 6 of them policemen.

The alleged "riot" unleashed a wave of anti-labor hysteria throughout the city and even the nation. Chicago police rounded up hundreds of labor leaders, including eight German-born anarchists they believed responsible for the bombing incident. They were tried for conspiracy to commit murder, though not a shred of evidence ever surfaced to prove that any of them had thrown the bomb. Nonetheless, all eight were convicted, and seven were sentenced to be hanged, of which only four ended up swinging from the gallows. One committed suicide and two others' sentences were commuted to life imprisonment. The affair became a cause celebre that bitterly divided the country; some Americans believed it a blatant act of repression of civil rights and judicial murder; others, the majority of citizens, applauded the court's actions and hoped it would send a warning signal to labor radicals that their ideas and actions faced "zero tolerance."

In the aftermath of the Haymarket affair, the Knights of Labor soon dissolved. However, a new national labor organization emerged to take its place: the American Federation of Labor founded in 1886 by immigrant cigar-maker Samuel Gompers. Gompers organized the new union not by industry as Powderly had done but by trade or craft, which in effect made the new union for skilled workers only. Under Gompers' leadership the AFL shunned radical crusades, accepted capitalism and the wage system, and worked for better conditions, higher wages, shorter hours, and job security—"pure and simple unionism" as Gompers called his organization's agenda. The AFL's endorsing of the capitalist order, his condemning of militancy and radicalism, and its not too outlandish demands for workers' rights allowed the AFL to not only survive but to prosper in a difficult climate. In short, Gomper's call for "working within the system" did not alienate or arouse the hostility of the capitalist plutocrats. As a result, the union's membership grew from 140,000 in 1886 to nearly one million by 1900. Though Gompers was able to calm the fears of capitalists and the anxieties of Americans in general that labor was not going to plunge the nation into social revolution if its demands were not met, labor militancy did not die. Two best-selling books helped to keep it alive, especially the call for a more egalitarian social order. Although neither of the two works had the impact of an *Uncle Tom's Cabin,* they nevertheless affected the millions who read them.

Henry George

Progress and Poverty, written by the self-educated author, Henry George, in 1879, seemed an unlikely candidate for best-seller status. Prior to becoming a newspaper editor in California, George had spent fifteen years traveling and working in various occupations. In his travels across the nation, he was appalled by the contrast between wealth and poverty. He came to believe that "land monopoly" was the cause: the control of land and resources by the few at the expense of the majority of citizens. His solution was 100 percent taxation on the "unearned increment" in the value of land—that is, on the difference between the initial purchase price and the eventual market value (minus improvements), or what today we would call capital gains. Such gains were created by society, he insisted, and thus should be confiscated by taxation for the benefit of society. This would eliminate the need for all other taxes, George argued, and help narrow the gap between rich and poor by either giving all the unused land to the landless or using the money to provide work for all.

Though not an easy book to read, by 1905, *Progress and Poverty* had sold over 2 million copies and had been translated into several languages. A single-tax movement emerged to propagate George's ideas, but they mostly fell on deaf ears. The book's real impact came from George's descriptions of grinding, abject poverty and despair in the midst of plenty. George became a hero to labor. He joined the Knights, moved to New York City, and ran for mayor in 1886 and narrowly lost. His campaign dramatized labors' grievances and alerted the major parties to the power of that constituency. George's legacy lasted well into the next century. As will be seen in a later chapter, many Progressive reformers were first sensitized to social issues by their reading of *Progress and Poverty.*

Edward Bellamy

The other Gilded Age work that had mass appeal was Edward Bellamy's *Looking Backward.* A devout Christian reformer, Bellamy wrote a utopian romance that took place in the year 2000 and contrasted the America of that year with the America of his time, 1887. In 2000, all industry is controlled by the government; everyone works for equal pay; there are no rich and no poor, no strikes, and no class conflict. *Looking Backward* had obviously a socialist "leaning," even though Bellamy preferred to call his collectivist order "nationalism," not socialism. He definitely was not a Marxist socialist for he condemned the idea of class conflict as the only means to achieve the cooperative state. His vision of a world without social strife appealed to many middle class Americans, who bought 500,000 copies of his book every year for several years in the early 1890s. So inspired by Bellamy's work, that Nationalist clubs sprang up throughout the nation, advocating government or public ownership if not of all industries at least public utilities—"gas and water socialism."

An offshoot of Bellamy's Nationalist movement and inspired by his work was the Social Gospel movement that emerged in the 1890s in American cities, and significantly affected mainstream Protestantism and many Catholic leaders as well. Appalled by the poverty and overcrowding in the sprawling tenement districts of urban America, clergymen and laypeople associated with the movement embraced a new theology of social activism: helping to ameliorate the plight of the poor was just as important, or should be, to religious leaders as saving souls. They were willing to go into the bowels of the immigrant tenement slums and not only help "save" the inhabitants from engaging in "sinful" activities but help to deliver them as well from poverty. Social Gospelites pressed for legislation to curb the immigrant worker exploitation and provide them with opportunities for betterment.

The Homestead Steel Strike

By the 1890s, there was plenty of evidence to feed the fears of many middle class Americans that the nation was unraveling. Strikes occurred with a frequency and fierceness that made 1877 and 1886 look like mere preludes to Armageddon. The most dramatic confrontation took place in 1892 at the Homestead plant of the Carnegie Steel Company. Carnegie and his plant manager, Henry Clay Frick, were determined to break the power of the country's strongest union, the Amalgamated Association of Iron, Steel, and Tin Workers. Frick used a dispute over wages and work rules as his opening salvo in his war with the union. He staged a "lockout" to reopen the plant with nonunion workers. Union workers, however, called for a strike and refused to leave the plant. Frick then called in 300 Pinkerton guards to oust them. The Pinkerton detective agency had evolved since the Civil War era into a "big business" private security force that specialized in "union busting." A full-scale gun battle erupted between workers and Pinkertons on July 6, leaving nine workers and seven detectives dead and scores wounded. Frick persuaded the Pennsylvania governor to send in 8,000 militia to protect the strikebreakers or "scabs, and the plant reopened. Public sympathy, much of it pro-union at first, shifted when an anarchist tried to murder Frick in his office. Frick was severely wounded but lived. The result, however, was the turning of the public against the union, which allowed the militia to brutally crush the union and the strike with popular support.

The Pullman Strike

Even more alarming than the Homestead strike, which remained local from start to finish, was the Pullman Strike of 1894, which had national repercussions. In 1880 George Pullman, manufacturer of elegant dining, parlor, and sleeping cars for the nation's railroads, had constructed a factory town, called Pullman, ten miles south of Chicago. The "planned" community provided solid brick homes for workers, beautiful parks and playgrounds, and even its own sewage-treatment plant. Pullman also closely watched his workers' activities, outlawing saloons, and insisting that his properties turn a profit. When the 1893 depression hit, Pullman slashed his workers' wages without reducing rents. In response, thousands of workers joined the newly formed American Railway Union, led by the fiery young organizer Eugene V. Debs. The union called for a strike, which Pullman's workers willingly joined. Union members working for the nation's largest railroads refused to switch Pullman cars, paralyzing rail traffic in and out of Chicago, one of the nation's most important rail hubs. In response, the General Manager's Association, an organization of top railroad executives, set out to break the union. The managers imported jobless "scabs" from the East coast and asked U.S. Attorney General Richard Olney, a former railroad attorney, for a federal injunction (court order) against the strikers for allegedly refusing to move railroad cars carrying U.S. mail. In truth, the strikers volunteered to switch mail cars onto any trains not pulling Pullman cars, and it was the railroad's managers who were delaying the mail by refusing to send their trains without the full complement of cars. Nevertheless, Olney, bolstered by President Cleveland and citing the Sherman Antitrust Act, secured an injunction against the union's leaders for restraint of commerce. Despite the government's crackdown, union leaders refused to back down and return to work. But the government was determined to break the union. Debs was arrested and federal troops were sent to Pullman to crush the strike, which they eventually did but not after the loss of thirteen lives, fifty-three wounded and the burning of seven hundred freight cars. By exploiting and fabricating middle class fears that strikers and unions in general were hotbeds of labor radicalism, crafty corporate leaders persuaded state and federal officials to help them squash organized labor's desire to negotiate with business for basic worker rights. When the Supreme Court in the 1895 case, *In re Debs,* upheld Deb's prison sentence and legalized the use of injunctions against labor unions, the judicial system made its blatant support of big business clear and that in the future, the plutocrats could count on that body to help preserve the status quo and their hegemony over it. By the beginning of the new century, it was painfully clear that the United States and its middle class citizenry had no intention of embracing unions or even the idea that its industrial workers were entitled to basic rights. Working class America was viewed with suspicion and hostility, and even its slightest attempt at a redress of grievances was regarded as "radical." The Pullman strike made it clear that from this point on, federal and state officials would side with the plutocrats against its working class citizenry. Ineffective in the political arena, blocked by state officials, and frustrated by

On July 3, 1894, President Cleveland ordered federal troops to Chicago to end the Pullman strike. By July 20, the federal troops had been withdrawn, and military guards were operating the trains. The union had been defeated.

court decisions, American unions failed to expand their base of support. Post-Civil War labor turmoil had drained the vitality of organized labor and given it a negative public image that it would not shed until the 1930s, when a change in middle class values and attitudes would find common cause with that of the working classes.

GILDED AGE POLITICS

As can be easily discerned from reading this chapter so far, the most dominant and interesting, if not dramatic individuals of the era, were not politicians but the businessmen-entrepreneurs and financiers who so dominated the time period. Indeed, political leadership, especially at the national level, is marked by some of the most uninspiring, complacent, and outright lackluster men ever to sit in the Oval Office. While men like Carnegie, Rockefeller, and Morgan jump vividly from the pages of the past, the presidents lie pallid on those same pages. Though many Americans today complain about the lack of strong, vibrant, and purposeful presidential leadership, if they had lived in the Gilded Age with those same expectations and hopes, they would feel even more depressed and disassociated. The weakness of the presidency and the federal government in general in the years between Abraham Lincoln (1861-65) and Theodore Roosevelt (1901-1909) was one of the most pronounced and prolonged periods in the nation's history. Beginning with Reconstruction and the pathetic, tumultuous presidency of Andrew Johnson, presidential leadership seemed to plummet to an all-time low. Concomitantly, the lack of quality men in the White House allowed Congress to gain ascendancy, and it was that body the plutocrats manipulated and controlled to ensure that there would be no governmental interference in their affairs. During the Gilded Age, a good portion of both the House and Senate membership were on the plutocrat's "payroll." This waning of federal power, especially in the executive branch, became a persistent pattern in American government, interrupted only by the activism of the progressive movement under the leadership of Theodore Roosevelt, and later, during the Great Depression of the 1930s, when Franklin Roosevelt assumed the Oval Office.

The presidents from Rutherford B. Hayes (1877-1881) to Grover Cleveland (1885-1889, 1893-97), are indeed forgotten men. All too frequently when

Americans are asked "who were these men?" rarely does anyone say, "Oh, wasn't he a president?" More often than not, the responses range from, "Oh, wasn't he a major league pitcher?" or "Didn't he invent something?" Or, most revealing, when someone is told he was a president of the United States, a look of complete surprise crosses his or her face and out comes "I didn't know that—I never heard of the guy!" Sad but understandable because so little was expected of these presidents and the federal government in general. Until the 1890s, when the excesses of industrial capitalism became apparent, few Americans believed that the president or the national government should have any role in addressing the problems accompanying the industrial transformation. The dominant creed of laissez-faire coupled with the tenets of Social Darwinism warned government to leave business alone; intervention to ameliorate even the most vile effects of industrialization would only retard the natural "evolutionary" progress allegedly taking place in the United States, led by those best "fit" to do so—the plutocrats. This belief in non-government intervention in the economy and society reduced the role of the federal government to something of a sideshow. The real energy and action took place elsewhere—in party politics on the local and state levels and in the centers of business and industry. Nevertheless, important changes transformed American political life in the decades following the Civil War, as industrialism replaced sectionalism as the driving force in national politics. The corruption and abuses associated with party politics produced civil service reform. By the 1880s, important economic issues such as the protective tariff, the currency, and federal regulation of the trusts and railroads moved to the forefront.

The Political Culture of the Gilded Age

Looking back on Gilded Age politics, there is some irony in the fact that voters of that time turned out in record numbers to elect those lackluster presidents. Voter turnout in the Gilded Age averaged a hefty 80 percent, compared with a turnout of only 51 percent in 2000. Why were voters in a supposed politically apathetic and complacent period so eager to cast their ballots?

The answer lies in the "political culture" of the late nineteenth century. Since the Jacksonian Period, political parties had used patronage or the "spoils system" to reward voters for their support. Many voters owed their livelihood to party bosses—the local party leader or "hack" responsible for sustaining the spoils system. Often these local politicos were involved in all manner of graft and corruption in order to maintain party loyalty and control of local politics. During the Gilded Age, "machine politics," particularly at the municipal level, became the order of the day. In essence, machine politics meant the control of every level of city government by either of the dominant parties, Republican or Democrat, depending upon the city involved. Under the guiding hand and sharp eye of the boss, political power was organized vertically within the machine in a hierarchical system of patrons and clients. The style of the Gilded Age boss was new and coarse, more personalized and direct than that of his eighteenth-century gentleman predecessor. The urban political machine's stock and trade was jobs and appointments, transit franchises, paving contracts, public construction bids, licenses, permits, and hundreds of other saleable items needed to conduct city business.

The impulse motivating the city boss was essentially conservative: the need to bring a semblance of order to his district. From at least mid-century, bosses like New York City's William Marcy Tweed and Philadelphia's James McManes had watched the aimless spreading of their cities and understood the problem of managing them. Tweed frankly admitted that New York's population was "too hopelessly split into races and factions to govern under universal suffrage, except by bribery of patronage and corruption." Their domains, the bosses realized, were fragmented like giant jigsaw puzzles. Only a professional could provide the liberal application of patronage to glue them together, even though his workmanship might be both slipshod and expensive. In New York City immediately after the Civil War, Boss Tweed secured a grip on the city government, built a mammoth new county courthouse, completed plans for Central Park, and began work on a city-wide transit system. All of these achievements came at the cost of widespread corruption and an astronomical increase in the city's debt.

Bosses seldom achieved the efficiency they sought. At best they surrounded themselves with oligarchies that presided over loose federations of wards and precincts. In the 1890s the bosses' failings in efficiency and accountability would give progressive reformers much ammunition in attacking the urban machines. But in the absence of a genuine science of public administration and of a corps of professional managers to apply it, the bosses at least provided a minimum of order and services—however lavishly and corruptly they improvised with the materials at hand. It also must be remembered that the bosses and their machines provided one of the chief forms of entertainment for voters and nonvoters alike in an age before mass recreation and amusement. The local machine sponsored parades, rallies, speeches, picnics, torchlight processions, and Fourth of July fireworks, attracting thousands of city dwellers, all for the purpose of ensuring machine support and keeping machine candidates elected.

William Marcy Tweed

Patronage Politics in the States

In the 1870s such state bosses as Roscoe Conkling in New York and James G. Blaine, the "Plumed Knight" from Maine, were highly visible, colorful characters who were masters of the art of demagoguery and personal leadership. By the 1880s, however, a new generation was taking over, achieving political control in many states and building loyal machines. The new bosses of the 1880s were quieter, behind-the-scenes operators who were much cleverer and more cautious than their more raucous predecessors. They were determined to avoid the constant feuding among placemen, which helped to contribute to their forerunner's demise. Matt Quay in Pennsylvania, Tom Platt in New York, Nelson Aldrich in Maine, William Vilas in Wisconsin, and George Hearst in California were typical of a new breed of party chieftains who conducted national business in Washington while keeping a vigilant eye on their cronies back home, solving patronage quarrels, settling factional disputes, and smoothing discontent.

The key device for harmonizing party interests at the state level was the caucus, where local bosses, county chairmen, and state legislators gathered to approve the state's boss choice of candidates for various offices. Here was the real power-base of the men mentioned above, and their ability to more or less force subordinates to accept their "men" was what kept them in power. Naturally, the process involved bribery, even extortion if necessary, to ensure the "system's" survival. Democratic Party bosses won control over their states more slowly than Republicans and, particularly in the one-party South, kept a looser grip on the party reins. Yet, southern Democratic, or "Bourbon," conservatism soon became the model for long-time Democrats who continued to invoke the name of Jefferson in deploring the "spirit of centralization" while quietly employing just that concept in staffing and strengthening their organizations. In both parties, as in the business world after 1880, consolidation was the order of the day.

Increasingly in the 1890s, politics became limited to white males only. Although black men voted during Reconstruction, the abandonment by the Republican Party of southern black folk after the Compromise of 1877, greatly affected black voting thereafter. One of the main goals of the Redeemers was to wrest political power from the freedmen and that was accomplished by the 1890s. Through the use of terror and intimidation, white Southerners denied black men their right to vote, and those who attempted or asserted their right usually ended up swinging from a tree at the end of a rope! White supremacy and rule was entrenched by the 1890s and so was one-party rule, that of the Democracy. From the end of Reconstruction and for the next seventy years, the old Confederate South voted Democratic in every election. Labeling the Republican Party the agent of "Negro rule," white southern Democrats engaged in all manner of race-bating and white-line bombast to keep southern voters (white, of course) voting straight Democrat—the party of white supremacy.

Opposing the "Solid South" was the Republican Northeast, with nearly enough electoral votes to guarantee its control of the White House. To preserve Republican ascendancy at the national level, the party had to carry key states such as Ohio, Indiana, and New York and had to prevent an alliance from developing between the agricultural South and the West. Northern Republican politicians, like their southern Democratic counterparts, continued to fan the flames of sectionalism with emotional appeals to the Civil War, a tactic known as "waving the bloody shirt," which was used effectively by the party in the 1868 election to get U.S. Grant into the Oval Office. Strong Unionist states in the Midwest responded by voting consistently Republican. "Iowa will go Democratic," one observer joked, "when Hell goes Methodist." Veterans of the Grand Army of the Republic formed an important base of Republican Party support, which rewarded their loyalty with generous pensions. By 1886, an astounding one-quarter of the federal budget went to pensions, not a penny of that to ex-Confederates.

Despite being left out of pension benefits and being labeled as "traitors," ex-Confederates and southern whites, in general, were fine with Republican hegemony at the national level. This was true because as long as the Republicans did not interfere with their "Negro problem" and allowed southern whites to oppress black folk, then the "trade-off" was more than acceptable. Southern white priority was not seeing one of their "own" in the White House but control of the region's black majority. As long as the Republicans turned a blind eye toward Jim Crow and other forms of southern apartheid, then southern whites willingly accepted Republican hegemony at the national level, including the White House.

Religion and ethnicity also played a significant role in politics. In the North, Protestants, from the old-line denominations, particularly Presbyterians and Methodists, were drawn to the Republican Party, which championed a series of moral reforms such as temperance. The Democratic Party courted immigrants and attracted Catholic and Jewish voters by consistently opposing laws to close taverns and other businesses on Sunday and by charging that crusades against liquor only masked the real intention of temperance crusaders: a blatant, ethnocentric attack on immigrant culture.

The power of the two major parties remained about equally divided throughout the 1870s and 1880s and into the 1890s. Although the Republicans dominated the White House, they rarely controlled Congress. The Democrats, noted more for their local control and appeal than for their national unity, for the most part, dominated the House of Representatives. Not until the Seventeenth Amendment was passed were senators directly elected by voters. Until then, (1912), the state legislatures selected senators. In an era legendary for its tolerance of all but the most flagrant bribery and corruption, state legislatures rather easily and all too frequently came under the control of the powerful capitalist-industrialist interests. In *Wealth Against Commonwealth* (1894), his book on the Standard Oil Company, journalist Henry Demarest Lloyd wrote, "The Standard has done everything with the Pennsylvania legislature except to refine it." Senators were often closely allied with business interests, as in the case of Nelson Aldrich, the powerful Republican from Rhode Island, whose daughter married John D. Rockefeller, Jr. and who didn't mind being called "the senator from Standard Oil."

The Shadow Presidents

Since real political power at the national level resided in Congress during the Gilded Age, the principal task given by party managers to the era's presidents was to get themselves elected without compromising their reputations by saying anything provocative and then to dispense patronage to party worthies. Winning the presidency was not easy, especially when neither party's platforms differed to any noticeable degree. James Bryce, the British minister in Washington who observed the 1884 presidential election, between Republican James G. Blaine and the Democratic nominee, Grover Cleveland, was amazed that neither party had a distinctive agenda. "Neither party has any principles, any distinctive tenets. Both have traditions. Both claim to have tendencies. . . .All has been lost, except office or the hope of it."

President Rutherford B. Hayes, whose disputed 1876 election marked the end of Reconstruction, proved to be a hard-working, well-informed executive who wanted peace, prosperity, and an end to party strife. Although ridiculed by the Democratic press as "Rutherfraud," and "His Fraudulency," Hayes was a man of integrity and honesty, who seemed well-suited for his role as a national leader. But Hayes faced a formidable task in attempting to end party strife, which greatly handicapped his implementation of any national agenda or vision he might have had. Unfortunately for Hayes and his Republican successors, his party remained wracked by internal factionalism and was controlled by party bosses who boasted that they could make or break a president.

The three Republican factions bore the colorful names Stalwarts, Half-Breeds, and Mugwumps. The Stalwarts, led by New Yorker Roscoe Conkling, were Grant supporters and thus were associated with the scandals of his administration and consequently were perceived to be willing to continue that legacy. Opposing them were the Half-Breeds, led by Senator James G. Blaine of Maine, a group that was only slightly less corrupt than Conkling's bunch in its pursuit of party dominance and spoils. Against both factions was a small but noteworthy group of liberal Republican reformers, mostly from Massachusetts and New York, whose critics dubbed them the Mugwumps, the name of an Algonquian Indian chief, but was used derisively by the faction's opponents who asserted that the Mugwumps were fence-straddlers when it came to the most important issue of party loyalty. The Mugwumps were determined to purge the Republican Party of all those who had so tarnished its image as the party of the Union and the Grand Army of the Republic. They were determined to drive the other factions out of the party and institute badly needed governmental reforms to ensure that competent, honest men like themselves were in control. In their pursuit of reform, they evaded the complex and divisive economics issues, such as tariff reform and monopolies, and instead focused on government reform through civil service reforms designed to set standards for office holders and put an end to the spoils system.

Hayes, despite his virtues, soon managed to alienate powerful party members. A realist, he used federal patronage to build Republican strength by selecting for government jobs if not the best men, the best—most qualified and honest—Republicans he could find. To the Stalwarts, he was a traitor; to the Mugwumps, his appointments still smacked of the spoils system. Hayes soon found himself without a party and thus, come election time, announced that he would not pursue his party's nomination in 1880.

Party bosses like Blaine and Conkling easily overpowered and destroyed Hayes' modest though sincere attempts at party reform. Fiery, dynamic, shrewd, manipulative, petty, and vindictive, as well as tied to corporate interests, Blaine and Conkling dominated national politics at this time. The imperious Conkling had nothing but contempt for the Mugwumps. He lambasted "snivel service" reform. "Parties," he declared, "are not built up by deportment, or by ladies' magazines, or gush." His archrival, the "plumed Knight," James G. Blaine, was a charismatic Irish-American, with a devoted following so fanatical in their support that they were dubbed "Blaniacs." Blaine condemned blatant Stalwart corruption but was himself tarnished by questionable dealings in railroad bonds. More careless than criminal in his business relations, Blaine, typical of so many of his cohorts, drew no fine distinction between public service and private gain; indeed they were symbiotic to men of Blaine and Conkling's ilk. Yet, Blaine's shady dealings caused enough public disaffection to cost him the Republican nomination in 1880 and the presidency four years later.

In 1880, the Mugwumps had just enough influence to block a Stalwart attempt to bring U.S. Grant out of retirement and run again for the presidency. Blaine, too, was passed over, and instead a dark-horse candidate, Representative James A. Garfield of Ohio, a virtual "nobody," was nominated. Conkling, however, insisted that one of his "boys," Chester Alan Arthur, a fellow Stalwart from New York, be put on the ticket as vice-president. The Democrats, still trying to unite a sectionalized party, nominated ex-Union general (the Republicans had had great success with such nominees—Grant, Hayes, and now Garfield), Winfield S. Hancock. But such a choice was not going to endear southern Democrats even though the "Solid South" voted for Hancock over Garfield. As one observer noted, "It is a peculiarly constituted party which sends rebel brigadiers to Congress because of their rebellion, and which nominated a Union General as its candidate for president because of his loyalty." Although the popular vote was close, Garfield won 214 electoral votes to Hancock's 155.

"My God," Garfield cried out after only a few months in the Oval Office, "what is there in this place that a man should ever want to get into?" Garfield, like Hayes, confronted the difficult task of remaining independent while attempting to placate the screaming bosses for "jobs" and the howling reformers for a massive overhaul of the federal bureaucracy. To an indecisive and easily overwhelmed man like Garfield, the presidency was a nightmare. He found the job of dispensing federal patronage grueling and distasteful, especially as he was forced to award positions to individuals whom he knew were not only completely unqualified for the job but venal and corrupt as well. More than 140,000 federal civil service jobs needed filling. Thousands of office seekers swarmed into Washington, each clamoring for a place. In an era before constant Secret Service protection for the president was established, the White House door was literally wide open. Garfield took a fatalistic view: "Assassination," he told a friend, "can no more be guarded against than death by lightning, and it is best not to worry about either."

On July 2, 1881, less than four months after taking office, Garfield was indeed assassinated, waiting for a train at a Washington, D.C. railroad station. His assassin, Charles Guiteau, though clearly insane, was a disgruntled office seeker who claimed to be motivated by political partisanship. He told the police officer who arrested him, "I did it; I will go to jail for it; Arthur is president, and I am a Stalwart. Garfield did not die instantly or in a few days; he lingered on through the summer, finally succumbing in September 1881. The press was outraged, holding the Stalwarts responsible for the president's tragic, violent death. Even though the Stalwarts were not responsible for Guiteau's actions, they nonetheless helped to create the hostile political environment that produced such individuals and violence. Stalwart leader Roscoe Conkling, who came under heavy attack for his partisanship in the wake of the assassination, had to give up his presidential ambitions and retire from politics and assumed a career as a corporate lawyer. Assaults on the spoils system increased, as did public demand for civil service reform. Though Garfield's death galvanized support for civil service reform, the ensuing congressional, as well as public, debate was long and hard. Those opposing reform cried out that it was class and ethnically biased. When Mugwumps spoke of government run by the "best men," they meant men of their own class and ethnic stock—WASPs. Reform would be particularly detrimental to Irish-Americans, who by this time were attaining increasing numbers of positions of political power in Northeastern cities. They would not want to see government once again in the hands of an educated Yankee elite. At a time when few men had more than an elementary school level of education, office seekers would not want to take a written civil service examination. One opponent argued, "George Washington would not have passed examination for a clerkship," noting that "in his will written by his own hand, he spells clothes, cloathes."

Despite acrimonious debate, civil service reform at the national level was instituted with the passage of the Pendleton Act in 1883. Both parties claimed credit for the act, which established a permanent Civil Service Commission of three members, appointed by the president. Some 14,000 jobs were placed under a merit system that required examinations for office and made it impossible to remove individuals for political reasons. Half of the postal jobs and most of the customhouse jobs—long two of the most "rewarded" jobs under the spoils system—passed to the control of the Civil Service Commission. The new law prohibited federal officeholders from contributing to political campaigns, thus helping to dissolve a major portion of the party bosses' revenue. Soon business interests replaced officeholders as the nation's chief political "fund-raisers." Ironically, civil service reform thus gave the plutocracy an even greater influence in political life than it already had.

"Chet Arthur, president of the United States! Good God!" exclaimed many Americans upon hearing of Garfield's death. Such foreboding was not unwarranted, for there was little in Arthur's background that qualified him for the highest office in the land. Only four years earlier he had been dismissed from his customhouse position in New York on charges of corruption. But a sort of metamorphosis took place as Arthur, now free of Conkling's grasp, quickly dispelled the nation's fears and acted independently, signing the Pendleton Act that his fellow Stalwarts had so long opposed. Arthur himself had little "faith in reform" but was politically savvy enough not to stand in the path of public sentiment. Beyond signing the Pendleton Act, Arthur's presidency was one of the most lackluster in history, doing nothing else of consequence except to refurbish the White House with his own money and in keeping with his bachelor taste. He put a billiard table in the basement. As long-time Mugwump Carl Schurz observed, "whenever Arthur did a creditable thing, people would say, 'He is after all a better man than we thought he was.'" Arthur surprised his critics by turning out to be a competent president, but his was a boring, mundane administration. As election year 1884 approached, Republicans were excited that their most charismatic standard bearer, James G. Blaine, would breathe new, more exciting life into the party and carry them to victory once again.

This cartoon pictures Winfield Scott Hancock as the biblical Samson against the "Republican Philistines." Hancock lost to the favored James A. Garfield by less than 10,000 popular votes but Garfield won the electoral votes.

1884: THE DEMOCRATS FINALLY WIN THE BIG ONE

Grover Cleveland in the White House

At their tumultuous Chicago convention, the Republicans, as predicted, turned to their "Plumed Knight," James G. Blaine, to lead them to victory in 1884. Blaine represented the younger, more dynamic wing of the Republican Party that was now eager to shed the taint of Grantism with Conkling out of the way. Blaine and his supporters also promoted continued economic development and a more assertive foreign policy. Unfortunately for Blaine, however, his charisma could not overcome the stigma of being involved in the tawdry politics of the Gilded Age. It was "leaked" that in 1876, while serving as Speaker of the House, Blaine had offered political favors to a railroad company in exchange for stock. Blaine also supported the spoils system, though not as rabidly as Conkling. Nonetheless, in the eyes of staunch Mugwumps like E. L. Godkin, editor of the respected magazine, *The Nation,* Blaine "wallowed in spoils like a rhinoceros in an African pool."

Sensing Blaine's vulnerability, the Democrats chose an individual who politically represented a sharp contrast to Blaine: Grover Cleveland of New York. Cleveland's rather meteoric rise from reform mayor of Buffalo to governor was noteworthy because along the way he fought the bosses and spoilsmen and won. He was short, rotund, and resembled a bull dog, but he was his own man. The savvy of the Democrats' choice became readily apparent when reform stalwarts such as Godkin and Carl Schurz bolted the Republican Party and supported Cleveland. But Cleveland was not without liabilities, the most notorious of which was his admission that he had fathered an illegitimate child as a young man. The Republicans naturally exploited this, jeering at rallies, "Ma, Ma, where's my pa?" Cleveland also had to overcome the powerful influence of New York City's Tammany Hall who hated Cleveland for his attempts while governor to destroy their machine. Tammany still controlled the immigrant vote of the city, which was increasingly more important as that population grew. If immigrant voters "stayed home" come election day, Cleveland could lose his own state. But in October a rabid Protestant Republican clergyman denounced the Democrats as the party of "Rum, Romanism, and Rebellion." Blaine failed to immediately repudiate the remark, which allowed Cleveland's supporters to claim that such a statement only showed that the Republicans were anti-Catholic, anti-drink, and were insulting patriotic Democrats tired of the "bloody shirt." This blunder and the Mugwumps' defection allowed Cleveland to carry New York state by 1200 votes and with it the election. Cleveland won the popular vote by only 25, 685 votes and in the electoral college the margin of victory was 37 votes.

Tariffs and Pensions

Though he had established himself as his own man when it came to dealing with machine politicians, Cleveland showed no such boldness or courage when it came to challenging the business elite. Indeed, in most respects Cleveland demonstrated that he was the plutocrats' friend, embracing the belief that government must not meddle in the economy. In the Jacksonian period, laissez faire had been a radical "liberal" idea endorsed by ambitious small entrepreneurs who wanted business conditions favorable to competition; by the 1880s it had become the plutocrat's rallying cry against any form of government intervention in their affairs. Approving of this ethos, Cleveland asserted presidential power mostly through his vetoes and displayed a limited understanding of industrialization's impact. For example, he vetoed a bill that would have provided seeds to drought-stricken Texas farmers, admonishing that people should not expect the government to solve their problems.

One public issue did arouse Cleveland from his legislative slumber: the tariff, a matter involving a tangle of conflicting economic and political interests. Tariff duties were a major source of federal revenue in the era before an income tax, so the tariff was really a form of taxation. But which imported goods should be subject to duties, and how much? Opinions differed radically. The producers of such commodities as coal, hides, timber, and wool demanded tariff protection against foreign competition, and industries that prospered behind tariff walls—iron and steel, textiles, machine tools—wanted protection to continue. Workers in these industries agreed, convinced that protection meant higher wages and secure jobs. Other manufacturers, however, while seeking protection for their finished goods, wanted low tariffs on the raw materials they required but had to import. Massachusetts shoe makers, for example, urged high duties on imported shoes but low duties on imported hides. Most farmers, by contrast, hated the protective tariff, charging that it inflated farm-equipment prices (because large farm machinery companies such as John Deere and International Harvester had monopolies because tariffs had locked out foreign farm equipment makers), and by impeding trade, made it hard to sell American farm products abroad.

Cleveland's call for the lowering of tariffs arose initially from the fact that in the 1880s the high tariff, generating millions of dollars in federal revenue, was feeding a growing budget surplus. Since government expenditures were negligible during this time, a huge surplus of money had accrued in the treasury, largely from tariff and land sales revenue. This surplus tempted many legislators, especially those from the low-income and undeveloped South and West, to demand that the money be distributed in the form of veterans' pensions or expensive public works projects in their home districts. Believing paternalistic government an anathema, Cleveland viewed the budget surplus as a corrupting influence. In his annual congressional message in 1887, Cleveland argued that lower tariffs would not only cut the federal surplus but would also reduce prices and slow down mergers and consolidations by introducing a degree of competition (foreign) in many markets. Although the 1888 Democratic campaign gave little attention to the issue, Cleveland's talk of lowering the tariff alienated many once-supportive plutocrats.

Cleveland stirred up another hornet's nest when he took on the Grand Army of the Republic. Veterans' disability pensions cost the government millions of dollars annually. No one opposed pensions for the deserving, but by the 1880s fraudulent claims had become a public scandal. Unlike his predecessors—who were all Republicans and who did not want to lose this most important voting bloc—Cleveland investigated these claims and rejected many of them. In 1887 he vetoed a bill that would have pensioned the disabled veterans (even if their disability had nothing to do with military service) and their dependents. The pension list should be an honor roll, he declared, not a boondoggle.

THE 1888 ELECTION

The Plutocrats and the GAR Strike Back

By 1888, many disaffected Democrats, and even Republicans who had defected, concluded that Cleveland was not the man they had hoped for and thus must go. "The Plumed Knight," Blaine, decided he was through seeking the big prize and bowed out of seeking the Republican nomination. Party chieftains, especially those tied to the plutocracy, believed it necessary to find someone who could win but whom they could control as well. They turned to Benjamin Harrison of Indiana, the grandson of old "Tip," former president William Henry Harrison. A corporation lawyer and former senator, Harrison was so void of personality and aloof that some ridiculed him as the human iceberg. His campaign managers learned to scurry him away after speeches before anyone could engage him in conversation or experience his effete handshake.

Soon after the hustings began, the issues quickly distilled down to two: the tariff and veterans' pensions, which Harrison hit hard. Cleveland was falsely accused of "free trade"—the elimination of all tariffs. Harrison asserted that the high protective tariff ensured prosperity, decent wages for industrial workers, and a healthy home market for farmers. Thanks to donations from big business, the Republicans amassed a campaign chest of $4 million. Such a war chest went far, not only for posters and buttons but also votes. Despite Republican chicanery, Cleveland beat Harrison in the popular vote by over 100,000 but unfortunately for the Democrat, the popular vote doesn't matter in the end; the electoral vote does and Harrison carried the key states of Indiana and New York and triumphed in the electoral college by winning 233 votes to Cleveland's 167. The Republicans held the Senate and regained the House. When Harrison righteously stated that Providence aided the

Republican cause, his campaign chairman retorted that "Providence hadn't a damn thing to do with it. . . . A number of men approached the gates of the penitentiary to make him president."

Harrison quickly rewarded his supporters via the spoils system, handing out hundreds of jobs to individuals whom the plutocrats and other Republican power brokers "recommended." He appointed as commissioner of pensions a GAR official, who on taking office declared, "God help the surplus!" The pensions soon ballooned from 676,000 to nearly a million. This massive pension system, coupled with medical care in a network of veterans' hospitals, became the nation's first large-scale public welfare program. In 1890 the triumphant Republicans also enacted the McKinley Tariff, which raised the rates on many imported manufactured goods to an all-time high of over 40 percent ad valorem. This new tariff stirred a hornet's nest of protest. The people had elected Harrison to preserve protection not to enact a higher tariff. The McKinley Tariff helped deplete that "vexing" surplus by raising duties so high that many foreign producers simply stopped selling their goods in the United States. Democrats naturally seized on the unpopularity of the tariff, labeling the Republican Congress that passed it as "The Billion Dollar Congress," as it unleashed an unprecedented spending frenzy of the entire surplus. Most of the money was spent on "pork-barrel" programs, that is, legislation passed for no real benefit other than to bring federal largesse to a congressman's or senator's "favorite" constituents. So upset were voters with such programs and spending that in the off-year election of 1890, they swept the hapless Republicans, including McKinley, out of office. Two years later, in a rather remarkable come back, Cleveland defeated Harrison for the presidency, promising to lower the tariff.

THE RAILROADS, THE TRUSTS, AND THE FEDERAL GOVERNMENT

American voters may have disagreed on the tariff, but increasingly they concurred on the need for federal regulation of the railroads and federal legislation against the trusts. As early as the 1870s, farmers had organized to combat the railroads and their exploitive, discriminatory policies toward especially small farmers. One of the first such organizations was the Grange, founded in 1867, initially as a social and educational association for farmers. However, by the 1870s, the Grange became politicized because of railroad abuse and launched an independent political party for a redress of their grievances against the railroads. Surprisingly, at the local and state level, the Grangers elected a number of officials that made it possible for several Midwestern states to pass laws regulating the railroads. At first, the Supreme Court upheld their right to do so. In *Munn v. Illinois* (1877), the Court ruled in favor of regulation. But in 1886, the Supreme Court reversed itself in the *Wabash* case (*Wabash, St. Louis, and Pacific Railway Co. v. Illinois*) and ruled that because railroads crossed state lines, they fell outside state jurisdiction. With more than three-fourths of railroads crossing state lines, the Supreme Court's decision effectively stopped regulation.

Public outcry was so great over the Court's ruling that the first Cleveland administration passed the first federal law to regulate the railroads, the Interstate Commerce Act of 1887. The act established the nation's first federal regulatory agency, the Interstate Commerce Commission, which was charged with the power to investigate and oversee railroad activities. In its early years, the ICC was never strong enough or sure enough of its role to pose a serious threat to the railroads' continued monopolistic practices. In the end, the act and the commission proved more important as a precedent than as an effective watchdog.

Concern over the growing power of the trusts led the federal government during the Harrison administration to pass the Sherman Antitrust Act in 1890. By then enough Democrats and disaffected reform Republicans coalesced in Congress to pass such a law if it could be accomplished without hurting the economy, which whether one liked it or not, was inextricably tied to the vagaries of consolidated enterprises, whether they were trusts, holding companies, or whatever "bigness" implied. The Sherman Act allowed for corporations but struck at the trusts. Businesses could no longer enter into agreements to restrict competition. The law outlawed pools and

The National Grange, founded in the 1870s, originally was a social and community-service association for farmers. Angry with the government's failure to alleviate their problems, the Grangers became politically active in the 1880s.

trusts but did nothing to prohibit huge holding companies like Standard Oil, since a holding company, no matter how big, was one entity and not an agreement among separate businesses to set prices or restrict trade.

The Sherman Act proved to be a weaker, more feeble attempt at government regulation than the Interstate Commerce Act. In the decade after its passage, the government successfully mandated the break up of only six trusts. However, the law was used four times against labor by outlawing unions as a "conspiracy in restraint of trade." In 1895, the Supreme Court dealt the law a crippling blow in the *E.C. Knight* case. The Court drastically narrowed the law by allowing the American Sugar Refining Company, which controlled 98 percent of the nation's sugar production, to continue its monopoly on the grounds that manufacture did not constitute trade. Both the Sherman Act and the Interstate Commerce Act testified to the nation's growing concern about the excesses of corporate capitalism and an increasing willingness to turn to the federal government as a source of redress for such abuses. Not until the twentieth century would more reform-minded activist presidents be willing to engage the corporations and use the full power of the federal government to protect the public welfare.

The Fight for Free Silver

Though many Americans wanted the government to curtail the power of the trusts, the most important issue of the 1880s and 1890s had to do with the currency. During the Civil War, the Union printed greenbacks (paper money), which provided funds for the war effort and simultaneously created inflation because the dollars were not backed by gold or silver. Debtors, who could pay back their loans with the devalued dollars, liked inflation; creditors, of course, opposed it. Because most debtors were Southern and Western farmers and most creditors and investors were Northeastern bankers, the controversy assumed intense sectional partisanship and overtones, as the issues of inflation versus deflation, of greenbacks versus hard money, and later gold versus silver, pitted the Northeast against an allied South and West.

In the 1870s, supporters of cheap money (paper) organized a third-party movement, the Greenback Labor Party, whose platform argued that the nation needed an expanding monetary system to keep up with population growth and commercial expansion. Greenbackers insisted the paper money was "the people's currency, elastic, cheap, and exportable, based on the entire wealth of the country." But in 1879, Congress voted to resume the gold standard, thus siding with creditors as opposed to debtors by tying the nation's currency to its gold reserves. Greenbackers responded by running General James B. Weaver for president in 1880. Despite the appeal of inflation among Southerners and Westerners, especially the farmers of those regions, voters below the Mason-Dixon line could not bring themselves to cast their ballot for a former Union general, and the party soon dissolved after the election. Despite Congresses' resolve with the gold standard, the currency issue would not go away. As a result of the return to the gold standard, money became even tighter. By the 1890s, the call for easier money and credit reappeared, with debtors calling not for the reissuing of greenbacks but for backing the dollar with silver.

The silver controversy stirred passions like no other issue of the day. On one side stood the "gold bugs"—mainly Northeastern creditors who believed that gold constituted the only honest money and who did not want to be paid in devalued dollars, which they asserted silver would do. On the opposite side, stood the "silverites"—led by the Western silver mining interests, whose stake in the battle was obvious. In the 1860s and 1870s, the West exploded in a silver bonanza, producing far more silver than gold. However, there was so much silver on the market that the price of silver plummeted. Mining states like Colorado and Nevada wanted the government to buy silver and mint silver dollars to help raise the price. Allied with the silver mining companies for very different reasons were Southern and Western farmers who had fallen on hard times during the 1870s and 1880s and who saw in silver a panacea for their problems. A grinding cycle of debt and deflation had left farmers in those regions in need of relief. Farmers hoped that increasing the money supply—inflation—with silver dollars would give them some relief.

Silverites pointed out that until 1873, the country had enjoyed a system of bimetallism, with both silver and gold coins minted. In that year, Congress demonetized (stopped buying and minting) silver, an act bimetallist denounced as the "crime of '73." They accused the domenetizers of a conspiracy to limit the money in circulation and place the West and the South at the mercy of Northeastern financiers. In 1878 Congress took steps to appease the silverites by passing the Bland-Allison Act over Hayes' veto. The measure required the government to buy silver and issue silver certificates. The act also helped mine owners, who now had a buyer for their ore, but it had little inflationary impact. Pressure for inflation continued, but the silverites were unable to make any progress until 1890, when in return for their support of the McKinley Tariff, Congress passed the Sherman Silver Purchase Act, increasing the amount of silver the government bought. Once again, the measure fell far short of generating inflation, and advocates began to call for "the free and unlimited coinage of silver," a plan whereby virtually all the silver that was mined would be minted into silver coins and circulated at the rate of sixteen ounces of silver to one ounce of gold.

The silver issue crossed party lines, but the Democrats hoped to use it to achieve an alliance between Western and Southern voters. Though the Democrats recaptured the White House in 1892 with Grover Cleveland's second administration, the president was still as economically conservative as he was during his first term. Cleveland supported the gold standard unequivocally; so much so that in 1893 he called a special session of Congress and brow-beat that body into repealing the Sherman Silver Purchase Act. Repeal only further divided the country, making the Mississippi River for a time as potent a political boundary as the Mason-Dixon line. Angry farmers warned Cleveland not to travel west of the river if he valued his life.

Compounding the silver controversy was the Panic of 1893, which the silver-gold issue helped to cause. As was the case in the Panic of 1873, the railroad industry once again was responsible for initiating this most recent downturn. As was true with industry in the 1870s, investment in the railroad boom of the 1880s triggered speculation among investors. Typical of the previous decade, railroad companies fed the speculative mania by issuing more stock (and enticing investors with higher dividends) than the soundness of the line warranted. Weakened by agricultural stagnation, railroad expansion halted in the early 1890s, affecting many related industries, including iron and steel. The first hint that this most vital industry was faltering came with the failure of one of the East's most important roads, the Philadelphia and Reading Railroad.

The line's failure occurred at the same time as the silver-gold controversy was intensifying, especially as the public's confidence in the gold standard waned. This diminished faith had several sources. First, when a leading London investment bank collapsed in 1890, hard-pressed British investors sold millions of dollars worth of stock in American railroads and other corporations and converted their dollars to gold, draining U.S. gold reserves. Second, as noted earlier, was the Harrison administration's lavish pork-barreling and veteran payouts, which drained government resources at a time when tariff revenue was declining because of the high McKinley Tariff. Third, the 1890 Sherman Silver Purchase Act further strained the gold reserve by requiring the government to pay for its monthly silver purchases with treasury certificates redeemable in either gold or silver; naturally certificate holders chose gold over silver. Between January 1892 and March 1893, when Cleveland took office, the gold reserve had plummeted to around $100 million, the minimum considered necessary to support the dollar. This decline alarmed those who viewed the gold standard as the only sure evidence of the government's solvency.

As typical in financial panics, fear fed on itself as fearful investors converted their stock holdings to gold. Stock prices plunged in May and June 1893; gold reserves sank; by the end of the year, seventy-four railroads had gone under as well as more than 15,000 commercial institutions, including 600 banks. After the Panic of 1893 came four years of depression.

The Depression of 1893-1897

By 1897, about a third of the nation's railroads were in bankruptcy. Just as the railroad boom had stimulated the industrial prosperity of the 1880s, so had its collapse caused the entire economy to be adversely affected. The Depression of 1893 took a heavy human toll, more so than that of 1873. Industrial unemployment soared to almost 25 percent, leaving millions of factory workers with no money to feed their families and heat their homes. Recent immigrants faced disaster. Jobless men tramped the streets and rode freight trains from city to city, region to region, looking for work. The unusually harsh winters of 1893 and 1894 only made things worse. In New York City, where the crisis quickly overwhelmed local relief agencies, a minister reported actual starvation. Amid the suffering, a rich New Yorker named Bradley Martin threw a lavish costume ball costing several hundred thousand dollars. When news of such foppish frivolity and insensitivity reached the city's masses, the outrage was so great that Martin, fearing for his life (and rightly so!), wisely moved his family abroad.

Rural America, already hard-hit by declining agricultural prices, faced ruin. Farm prices dropped by more than 20 percent between 1890 and 1896. Corn plummeted from fifty cents to twenty-one cents a bushel and wheat from eighty-four cents to fifty-one cents. Cotton sold for five cents a pound in 1894. Some desperate Americans turned to protest. In Massillon, Ohio, a self-taught monetary expert, Jacob Coxey, proposed as a solution to unemployment a $500 million public-works program funded with paper money not backed by gold or silver, simply designated "legal tender" (just as it is today). A man of action as well as ideas, Coxey organized the first serious "march on Washington," to lobby for his scheme. Thousands joined him en route, and several hundred actually reached the Capital in late April 1894. Police arrested Coxey and other leaders when they attempted to enter the Capitol grounds, and his "army" disbanded. Although some considered Coxey an eccentric, his proposal closely resembled programs the New Deal implemented during the 1930s to help relieve the unemployed.

In the harsh winter of 1894-95, Cleveland aggravated an already highly charged political climate by his deal with J.P. Morgan to save the country's gold reserves by having the financier lend the government $62 million in exchange for U.S. bonds at

A picture of the Brooklyn Bridge under construction. The separation of the Brooklyn residents from Manhattan by the East River demanded the building of the Brooklyn Bridge between the boroughs. It had the longest span of any bridge previously built and was the first to use suspension cables. Construction began in 1869 and was not completed until May 24, 1883.

a special discount. With this loan from "the House of Morgan," the government purchased enough gold to replenish its reserve, which had dwindled to $41 million by 1895. Naturally, Morgan and his partner, August Belmont, resold the bonds for a substantial profit. Cleveland saved the gold standard but at a high price. His dealings with Morgan and Belmont and the bankers' handsome profits on the deal only underscored many people's suspicions of an unholy alliance between Washington and Wall Street. Cleveland's policies split the Democratic Party. Farm leaders and silver Democrats condemned his repeal of the Sherman Silver Purchase Act. South Carolina's Ben Tilman, running for the Senate in 1894, announced that Cleveland was a "scoundrel" and an "old bag of beef and I am going to Washington with a pitch-fork and prod him in his fat old ribs." This split in Democratic ranks affected the 1894 and 1896 elections and reshaped politics as the century ended.

The 1893 depression also helped change social thought. Middle-class charitable workers and reformers, long convinced that individual character flaws caused poverty, now realized—as socialists had long argued and as the poor well knew—that even sober, hardworking people could succumb to economic forces beyond their control. As the social work profession developed in the early twentieth century, its disciples spent less time preaching to the poor and more time investigating the social and environmental sources of poverty. Many Americans also began to question the sanctity and validity of the laissez-faire ethos as many depression-worn citizens began embracing the idea of government intervention on behalf of the public welfare to ameliorate the more egregious social consequences of industrialization. In the early twentieth century, this new view would energize powerful political forces. The depression, in short, not only brought suffering; it also taught lessons.

CONCLUSION

Mark Twain, one of America's greatest writers, humorists, and shrewdest social critics, called the period following Reconstruction the "Gilded Age." He chose that term to ridicule the ugliness, crass materialism, and sham of a time when glitter on the outside masked what lay beneath. Twain's label has stood for more than a century as a fair representation of an era when political corruption strutted with the haughty arrogance of a Conkling and industrialists like William Vanderbilt cried, "The public be damned!" But if the age spawned greed, corruption, and vulgarity on a grand scale, it was not without its share of solid achievements. In the three decades after the Civil War, America made the leap into the industrial age. Indeed, by 1900 it was the leading industrial/manufacturing nation in the world, whose standard of living was fast becoming the envy of other nations. Where dusty roads and cattle once sprawled across the continent, steel rails now bound together a nation. Cities grew from the ground into the sky. In New York City, the Brooklyn Bridge spanned the East River with steel and stone, more strikingly beautiful than all the showy mansions on Fifth Avenue. In the offices and business boardrooms, men like Rockefeller, Carnegie, and Morgan consolidated American industry. By the end of the century, the country had achieved industrial maturity. No other era in the nation's history witnessed such a rapid transformation. However, it remained to be seen whether the nation could curb the plutocrats' vast and overwhelming power and work to solve the social and economic problems accompanying industrialization.

Chronology

1869 Completion of first transcontinental railroad
Knights of Labor founded.

1870 John D. Rockefeller incorporates Standard Oil Company in Cleveland, Ohio.

1873 "Crime of 1873" demonetizes silver
Panic on Wall Street leads to major economic depression.

1874 Pennsylvania Railroad capitalized at $400 million and employing 55,000; largest private enterprise in the world.

1876 Alexander Graham Bell demonstrates telephone at Philadelphia Centennial Exposition.

1877 Rutherford B. Hayes sworn in as president after disputed election
Great Railroad Strike cost 100 lives and millions of dollars in damage
U.S. Supreme Court upholds right of states to regulate railroads in *Munn v. Illinois.*

1878 Bland-Allison Act to remonetize silver passed over Hayes' veto.

1879 Henry George publishes *Progress and Poverty*
Congress votes to resume gold standard
Thomas Alva Edison perfects filament for incandescent lightbulb.

1880s Jay Gould attempts to build a second transcontinental railway system
Gustavus Swift revolutionizes meatpacking with refrigerated rail cars to transport fresh meat to the east
H.J. Heinz pioneers mass production and distribution of his fifty-seven varieties of condiments.

1880 Greenback Labor Party runs General James B. Weaver for president
Dark horse Republican candidate James A. Garfield elected president.

1881 Garfield assassinated by Charles Guiteau
Vice-President Chester A. Arthur becomes president.

1882 Standard Oil develops the trust

1883 Railroads establish four standard time zones
Congress passes Pendleton Act establishing civil service reform

1884 Grover Cleveland elected president; first Democrat to serve since before the Civil War
Mark Twain's *Huckleberry Finn* published and subsequently banned in Boston

1886 Knights of Labor membership peaks at 700,000
Haymarket riot causes antilabor backlash
American Federation of Labor founded
In *Wabash* case, U.S. Supreme Court reverses itself and disallows state regulation of railroads that cross state lines

1887 Edward Bellamy publishes *Looking Backward*
Interstate Commerce Act creates first federal regulatory agency.

1888 Benjamin Harrison elected president of the United States.

1889 Standard Oil reorganizes into a holding company

1890 Congress passes the McKinley Tariff, Sherman Antitrust Act and Sherman Silver Purchase Act

1892 Grover Cleveland elected to second term as president
J.P. Morgan consolidates electric industry, creating the General Electric Company
Homestead steel strike erupts into violence and bloodshed and eventually suppressed

1893 Financial panic begins economic depression
Congress repeals Sherman Silver Purchase Act

1894 Coxey's Army of the unemployed marches on Washington
Pullman strike paralyzes the railroads and provokes federal intervention

1895 J.P. Morgan bails out U.S. Treasury and saves nation's gold reserves

1901 J.P. Morgan buys out Carnegie Steel and creates U.S. Steel, first billion dollar corporation in the United States.

SUGGESTED READINGS

Paul Avrich, *The Haymarket Tragedy* (1984).

David H. Bain, *Empire Express: Building the First Transcontinental Railroad* (1999).

Robert V. Bruce, *Alexander Graham Bell and the Conquest of Solitude* (1973).

Sean Dennis Cashman, *America in the Gilded Age* (1984).

Alfred D. Chandler, *The Visible Hand: The Managerial Revolution in American Business* (1977).

Alfred D. Chandler Jr., *The Railroads: The Nation's First Big Business* (1965).

____,*Scale and Scope: The Dynamics Of Industrial Capitalism* (1990).

Dino Cinel, *From Italy to San Francisco: The Immigrant Experience* (1982).

Peter Collier and David Horowitz, *The Rockefellers: An American Dynasty* (1976).

Vincent P. DeSantis, *The Shaping of Modern America, 1877-1920* (2nd. Ed., 1989).

Melvyn Dubofsky, *Industrialism and the American Worker, 1865-1920* (1975).

Richard Ellis, *American Political Cultures* (1993).

Saul Engelbourg, *Power and Morality: American Business Ethics, 1840-1914* (1980).

Philip S. Foner, *The Great Labor Uprising of 1877* (1977).

Donna Gabaccia, *From the Other Side: Women, Gender, and Immigrant Life in the U.S., 1820-1990* (1994).

John A. Garraty, *The New Commonwealth, 1877-1890* (1968).

Ray Ginger, *Age of* Excess (1963).

Julius Grodinsky, *Jay Gould, 1867-1892* (1957).

Herbert C. Gutman, *Work, Culture, and Society in Industrializing America: Essays in American Working-Class and History* (1976).

Robert Higgs, *The Transformation of the American Economy, 1865-1914* (1971).

John Higham, *Strangers in the Land* (1955).

Richard Hofstadter, *The Age of Reform* (1955).

Ari Hoogenboom, *Outlawing the Spoils: The Civil Service Reform Movement, 1865-1883* (1961).

____, *The Presidency of Rutherford B. Hayes* (1988).

Irving Howe, *World of Our Fathers* (1976).

Jacqueline Jones, *The Dispossessed: America's Underclass from the Civil War to the Present* (1992).

Mathew Josephson, *The Robber Barons: The Great American Capitalists, 1861-1901* (1934).

Thomas Kessner, *The Golden Door: Italian and Jewish Mobility in New York City, 1880-1915*(1977).

Maury Klein, *The Life & Legend of Jay Gould* (1987).

Sidney Lens, *The Labor War: From the Molly Maguires to the Sitdowns* (1974).

Andre Millard, *Edison and the Business of Innovation* (1990).

Gwendolyn Mink, *Old Labor and New Immigrants in American Political Development* (1986).

David Montgomery, *The Fall of the House of Labor: The Workplace, the State, and American Labor Activism, 1865-1925* (1987).

Humbert Nelli, *Italians of Chicago, 1880-1920* (1970).

James D. Norris, *Advertising and the Transformation of American Society, 1865-1920* (1990).

Nell Irvin Painter, *Standing at Armageddon: the United States, 1877-1919* (1987).

Glen Porter, *The Rise of Big Business, 1860-1910* (1973).

Andrew Sinclair, *Corsair: The Life of J. Pierpont Morgan* (1980).

John Sproat, *The Best Men: Liberal Reformers in the Gilded Age* (1968).

David J. Rothman, *Politics and Power: The United States Senate, 1869-1901* (1966).

Ronald Takaki, *Stringers From A Different Shore: A History of Asian Americans* (1989).

George R. Taylor and Irene D. Neu, *The American Railroad Network, 1861-1890* (1956).

Peter Temin, *Iron and Steel in Nineteenth-Century America* (1964).

Irwin Unger, *The Greenback Era: A Social and Political History of American Finance* (1964).

James A. Ward, *Railroads and the Character of America, 1820-1887* (1986).

Allen Weinstein, *Prelude to Populism: Origins of the Silver Issue, 1867-1878* (1970).

Robert H. Wiebe, *The Search for Order, 1877-1920* (1967).

Virginia Yans-McLaughlin, *Family and Community: Italian Immigrants in Buffalo, 1880-1930* (1977).

Chapter Fourteen

THE TRANS-MISSOURI WEST: The Last Frontier

The Nez Percé Indians were a small tribe living peacefully in the beautiful Wallowa Valley of Oregon, a fertile area of mountain forests, meadows, winding rivers, and a pure blue lake. Earlier in their history, when the half-starved and illness-weakened Lewis and Clark expedition entered their territory, they had welcomed the whites, supplied them with food, and looked after their horses. In seventy years of contact, they had never killed a white settler. In the 1850s, the Christian, "progressive" branch of the tribe agreed to turn over large tracts of mineral-rich land to the federal government. They accepted the white man's offer to live on a large reservation set aside for them in Idaho. In 1863, the discovery of gold greatly diminished this reservation. But the larger group under its leader, the dignified and statesman-like Chief Joseph, refused to sign any treaty giving up more land. Joseph reflected the views of most Native Americans when he declared: "The earth was created by the assistance of the sun, and it should be left as it was.... The country was made without lines of demarcation, and it is no man's business to divide it." While most whites saw the land and its resources as there to be exploited, Native Americans believed that people were a part of nature, not its master. Chief Joseph affirmed, "The earth and myself are of one mind. The measure of the land and the measure of our bodies are the same." Like other Indians, he felt that land could be used but could no more be owned than the air all people breathed.

An advocate of peaceful coexistence with whites, Joseph and his tribe were able to survive on their little piece of paradise until the 1870s. White settlers began to covet this prime area. They pressured the government into forcing the rest of the Nez Percés onto the Idaho reservation in 1877. With a heavy heart, Joseph convinced his people that resistance was futile, and they began their long journey from the land they loved to the reservation. On the way, however, some of the younger hot-heads in the tribe, fortified by alcohol and angry at their plight, killed four white settlers.

Joseph understood that retribution would be swift and terrible. He persuaded his people to flee with him, hoping to gain sanctuary in Canada where many Sioux Indians had received refuge. At the battle of White Bird Canyon, he was able to drive off the pursuing American troops. Then the Nez Percés scattered in many directions. Joseph led the largest group of 200 men and 350 women, children, and old people. A remarkable chase followed through Idaho and Montana. The Nez Percés traveled east through Yellowstone Park where they frightened some of the astonished tourists and almost encountered General Sherman fishing in the area. Then they headed north. The weary band of Indians covered 1,321 miles in 75 days, hunted by some 5,000 embarrassed government troops. Fascinated readers of Eastern newspapers, uniformly sympathetic to the underdog Indians, eagerly followed each day's story. (Native Americans had long since been eliminated there, so Easterners could far more easily feel tolerance toward the Indian.) The embarrassed generals explained their ineptitude by dubbing Joseph, "the red Napoleon."

The army regiments finally caught up with the Nez Percés within sight of the Canadian border. Some bands of resolute warriors were able to slip across the border where Sitting Bull in his Sioux Canadian village welcomed them. But Joseph and most of his tribe surrendered, exhausted, freezing, and broken hearted. Of the four hundred Nez Percés left, only eighty-seven were fighting men. General Nelson Miles, who greatly admired Joseph's efforts for his people, agreed to allow the band to return to the Idaho reservation. After meeting with the general, Joseph declared, "Hear me, my chiefs. I am tired; my heart is sick and sad. From where the sun now stands, I will fight no more forever." Then, the chief swept his blanket across his face as a symbol of mourning and surrendered. It had cost almost $2 million to vanquish Joseph and his followers.

The American government reneged on the promise General Miles had made to the Nez Percés. Rather than sending them to the Idaho reservation, it moved them from one desolate place to another, finally settling them in a flatlands reservation in Oklahoma. Many died from malnutrition and disease, including Joseph's six children. In 1885, the government transferred the survivors to a reservation near Spokane, Washington, where their descendants remain to this day. Chief Joseph puzzled Buffalo Bill Cody when he joined the "Wild West" shows. The chief was willing to repeat his famous speeches, but he always refused to don war paint and re-enact the end of his people's quest. He died in 1904. The Indian agency physician listed the cause of death as "a broken heart."

THE STRUGGLE OF NATIVE AMERICANS

On the eve of the Civil War, there were approximately 250,000 Indians who shared the Great Plains and mountains of the West with wild animals such as the wolf, coyote, wild horse, jack rabbit, and, above all, the buffalo. These constituted about two-thirds of the Native Americans remaining in the United States (compared to approximately 2.5 million who lived here at the time of Columbus). There were many different languages, customs, and tribes among these Indians. Some, such as the Zuni, Navaho, and Hopi, were fairly well settled farmers, sheep herders, and gardeners. Most, like the Sioux, Apache, and Cheyenne, were nomads and hunters who followed the vast buffalo herds (numbering anywhere from 13 to 25 million) over immense distances.

The buffalo was central to the existence of most of the Plains tribes. Bands (smaller groups of about 500 within the tribe) would pursue the herds through the grasslands, riding powerful small horses descended from those introduced to the New World by the Spaniards. When they stopped, they constructed temporary dwellings (teepees). When they left, the land was virtually undisturbed as a result of the deep respect for nature that was characteristic of Indian religion and culture. The buffalo provided virtually all the basic necessities for these Native Americans. The meat was their main food source. Buffalo hides could be turned into clothing, blankets, robes, shoes, and teepees. The bones became arrow tips, knives, hoes, and even children's sleds. The tendons were used as thread or strings for bows. Fats became cosmetics, and bladders turned into water bags. Even the buffalo droppings—"buffalo chips"—were burned for fuel!

Native Societies

Despite the tribal differences, there were some basic similarities among these Native Americans. Their societies rested upon extended family networks. Unlike the individualism emphasized by white American capitalist competition, Indians stressed cooperation and the welfare of the group. Their religion focused

Joseph, Chief of Nez Percé

on the intimate interrelationship between human beings and nature. Most agreed with Chief Joseph that land could never be owned by man. To some, this reverence for the land meant that farming was a sacrilege. One chief explained, "You ask me to plow the ground! Shall I take a knife and tear my mother's bosom?...You ask me to cut the grass and make hay....But how dare I cut my mother's hair?" Many tribes had special pieces of land or water that they considered particularly sacred. Often, these were burial grounds where ancestral spirits lived. Whites tended to ignore or even desecrate these holy lands, leading to bitter conflicts.

Most tribes had loose governmental structures in which authority was shared. Although the chiefs were ceremonial leaders, they had relatively limited power. This led to misunderstandings with whites who thought treaties and agreements with an individual chief would automatically be accepted by the whole tribe. Many bands followed a method of decision-making in which most members took part. As in white society, gender tended to determine responsibilities. Women's work consisted of cooking, raising children, gathering food, sewing, and tanning hides. If a band remained settled for any length of time, women tended the farms. They also created most of the beautiful works of art produced by Native American culture. Women had rights respected by their husbands and often participated in ceremonial dances and tribal councils. Men were the hunters, traders, warriors, and religious leaders.

To whites, the most important attribute of Plains Indian tribes like the Sioux and Cheyenne was their prowess as mounted warriors resisting white advances. Their nomadic lifestyle clashed with the interests of the oncoming railroads, miners, ranchers, and farmers. Their herds of buffalo interfered with westward expansion by knocking over telegraph poles, overturning construction, and even derailing trains when they stampeded. Worst of all, the military skills of the Plains Indians made them the fiercest enemies the whites had ever met. As early as the 1850s, a "scientific" discourse explained, "The *Barbarous* races of America...although nearly as low in intelligence as the Negro races, are essentially untamable....Our Indian tribes submit to extermination, rather than wear the yoke under which our negro slaves fatten and multiply." Thus, while black labor could be valuable under suitable controls, the only solution to the Indian problem was elimination. Most settlers agreed with Theodore Roosevelt that the West was not destined to be "kept as nothing but a game reserve for squalid savages."

When Americans believed that much of the trans-Missouri West was the "Great American Desert," of little value and virtually uninhabitable, the tribes had been largely free to roam its vast spaces. In fact, the federal government considered the area west of the Missouri River "one big reservation." It had even relocated the Five Civilized Tribes of the Old Southwest to the "permanent Indian territory" in the area. By the 1850s, traders, explorers, and settlers advanced into Indian lands and demanded protection. The government began to adopt a new policy of "concentration" under which each tribe would be dealt with separately and confined to smaller reservations. Treaties, often obtained through dishonest means, divided land between Indians and settlers and limited the rights of each on the lands of the other. Whites lived up to these treaties only when the lands in question were undesirable for farming or mining.

As threats to their way of life grew, Indians began to mount a formidable resistance. Warriors, traveling in raiding parties of twenty or thirty, attacked isolated farms and ranches, wagon trains, and stagecoaches. The United States Army intervened, and battles with the tribes broke out. Despite their considerable military abilities, the Plains Indian fighters had many limitations that, in the long run, would make their defeat inevitable. They were unable to centralize, either politically or militarily, to resist white aggression. In fact, they frequently became involved in battles with each other. Many Native Americans were particularly vulnerable to the white man's contagious diseases, such as smallpox that killed thousands. Of course, the most obvious difficulty was that they faced a numerically and technologically superior force.

Destruction of the Buffalo

The destruction of the buffalo herds may well have been the most significant factor in the ultimate defeat of the Plains tribes. After the Civil War, a nationwide craze developed for buffalo robes from the fabled West. This was followed by a brief period in which buffalo tongue became a highly sought delicacy in posh restaurants in the East. In 1871 a tannery in Pennsylvania discovered that buffalo hides could be turned into valuable leather. Groups of professional hunters armed with repeating rifles flooded the area, shooting vast numbers of the huge beasts. Amateurs, sometimes firing from the windows of passing railroad trains, often joined in the "sport" of shooting down the slow-moving animals. Sometimes hundreds of carcasses were left to rot on the open plains (either with only their tongues removed or for no apparent reason at all). Railroad companies hired hunters like Buffalo Bill Cody to mount shooting junkets to remove impediments to railroad traffic. Cody claimed that he killed four thousand buffalo in eighteen months. Even a few Indian tribes, such as the Blackfeet, joined in the kill to make profits from the new demand. Much of the slaughter was not very profitable as the supply of buffalo robes glutted the market, driving down prices. One hunter reported, "I saw buffaloes lying dead on the prairie so thick that one could hardly see the ground. A man could have walked for twenty miles upon their carcasses." Eventually, scavengers created a minor occupation gathering the tons of buffalo bones strewn over the plains for five dollars a ton.

The army and Bureau of Indian Affairs agents encouraged the destruction of the buffalo herds to lessen Indian resistance. "Kill every buffalo you can" one army officer suggested. "Every buffalo dead is an Indian gone." In 1872, the Indian commissioner accurately predicted that before long the "most powerful and hostile bands of today" would be "reduced to the condition of supplicants for charity." By 1883, there were few of the huge beasts left on the plains. The designer of the famous "buffalo nickel" had to go to the Bronx Zoo in New York to find a model. Just as modern Americans are totally dependent upon the oil supply, Native American society on the plains could not survive this decimation of the buffalo.

Indian Wars

Despite this inevitable result, however, small scale skirmishes began to escalate into full scale battles. The first of these conflicts took place during the Civil War when regular army units went to fight the Confederacy and raw recruits replaced them. Led by Little Crow, the eastern Sioux in Minnesota rebelled against conditions in a cramped reservation where corruption by white Indian agents ran rampant. Before being defeated, they killed seven hundred whites. A court martial condemned three hundred to death, but President Lincoln commuted all but thirty-nine of the sentences. Thirty-eight of the Sioux were hanged in a public ceremony, and the rest of the tribe was shipped to the Dakotas. Little Crow, who had managed to escape the noose, left his hiding place to pick raspberries. Deer-hunting settlers spotted him and, motivated by the $25 bounty Minnesota had placed on Sioux scalps, shot him. The state awarded them a $500 bonus and displayed Little Crow's preserved skull and scalp at an exhibition in St. Paul.

Meanwhile, warfare raged in Colorado when miners grabbed lands that the government had guaranteed to the Cheyenne and Arapaho only ten years earlier. In 1864, in response to attacks on settlements and stagecoaches, the army threatened to launch a campaign of retribution. The territorial governor promised that friendly Indians who exhibited the American flag and camped at army posts would be under official protection. In response, one band gathered near an army post in Sand Creek. Colonel Chivington, the "Fighting Parson," declaring, "I believe it is right and honorable to use any means under God's heaven to kill Indians," led a volunteer militia against the unsuspecting, unguarded camp. Despite attempts by the Indians to show peaceful intentions by hoisting a white flag, the militia butchered hundreds of innocent men, women, and children. The bodies were mutilated. The "heroes" of Sand Creek brought over 100 scalps, some of them women's pubic hair, back to Denver. There, they were stretched across the stage of a local theater for public approval. "Colorado soldiers have again covered themselves with glory," a local paper exulted. The massacre destroyed the lives or influence of every

Cheyenne and Arapaho chief who favored peace with the whites, and Indian hostility greatly intensified as a result.

A congressional committee investigated the causes of strife in the West. It recommended an Indian Peace Commission to negotiate agreements. In 1867 and 1868, there were conferences to persuade tribes to relocate to reservations in the Black Hills of the Dakotas and to undesirable land in "Indian Territory"—Oklahoma. In return, the government promised supplies and assistance. While some tribes acquiesced in the inevitable, many resisted. Between 1869 and 1875, over two hundred battles erupted between the army and the Indians. The army commander in the West, General S. R. Curtis, was clear about his intentions: "I want no peace until the Indians suffer more."

In 1868 a band of Cheyenne was caught at the Washita River in Oklahoma by an army unit led by the "fair-haired boy" of the military, Colonel George Armstrong Custer. Custer was undoubtedly the most picturesque and charismatic army officer of the era. He was over six feet tall, slim, and broad shouldered. He swaggered when he walked and wore his golden hair past his shoulders. His entire life was a reckless pursuit of glory. With his long blond hair flying behind him as he rode, Custer supervised the slaughter of the chief and his tribe at the Washita. His fame for this encounter came from a widely publicized exaggerated report he wrote that failed to mention that, of the 103 Cheyenne killed, only eleven were warriors. The rest were women and children. Many whites justified such actions by dehumanizing Native Americans. Oregon whites who hanged a seven-year-old Indian child echoed a widely held view that, "nits breed lice."

A new Board of Indian Commissioners, created in 1869, attempted to undermine the collective nature of Indian life, weaken tribal structure, and force the people to assimilate into white culture by becoming farmers. President Grant favored a policy of pacifying the natives through peace overtures rather than battles. This was known as "Quaker Policy," because of the number of Quakers (and other church people)

Custer first distinguished himself during the Civil War. At the Battle of Washita, Custer defeated Black Kettle's Cheyennes. The battle marked the culmination of the campaign against the Indians of the southern Great Plains.

involved in its implementation. The poor quality of the land on reservations and the Indians' view of farming as "women's work" undercut their efforts. Another problem lay in the management of Indian concerns by the Bureau of Indian Affairs. The agents, who gained their jobs through political patronage, were often corrupt and incompetent. Even the best of them had little understanding of tribal culture. The Indians, in effect on welfare and totally dependent on the government, received rotten meat, spoiled flour, and threadbare blankets. It became harder and harder to keep them on the reservations.

The Northern plains were the domain of the Sioux, the one tribe that had never suffered a major defeat at the hands of whites. Poor conditions on their Dakota reservation became even more intolerable when miners invaded sacred lands in the Black Hills. The miners were drawn by rumors that there was "gold in the grass roots." One Indian lamented, "The white man is in the Black Hills just like maggots." As the Sioux resisted the trespassers, the whites demanded government protection. The government, following its customary policy of resorting to force, ordered all hostile Sioux back to their reservation or face punishment. Bands of warriors, under the leadership of Crazy Horse and Sitting Bull, gathered in Montana. Numbering between 2,500 and 4,000, it was one of the largest Indian armies ever formed in North America. Three army columns arrived to round them up. The glory-seeking Custer led the Seventh Cavalry. He firmly believed that his men could beat any Plains Indians and that this might be his "lucky turn" to achieve renown. Custer's attitude towards Native Americans was apparent in his *My Life on the Plains*. He described the Indian as "a savage in every sense of the word...one whose cruel and ferocious nature far exceeds any wild beast of the desert."

Although his scouts reported large numbers of hostile Indians in the area, Custer believed that he could strike a quick and decisive blow as he had at Washita. Perhaps fearful that he might have to share some of the accolades, Custer did not wait for the other parts of the expected three-prong attack. His grandiosity led him to deny his troops any reasonable rest and to fail to order the most basic reconnaissance. On June 25, 1876, Custer ordered a charge at the Little Big Horn River against an Indian force that outnumbered his by more than eight to one. The Sioux benefitted from the superior generalship of Crazy Horse, rallying to the cry, "It's a good day to die!" Taking no prisoners, all 260 soldiers were annihilated. Word of "Custer's Last Stand," burst into headlines to an astounded public on July 5, 1876, the day after the nation's great centennial celebration. The defeat, described as a "massacre," led to a general cry for revenge against the Indians. The *New York Times* reported, "It is agreed on all hands that there must now be an Indian war till the hostile Indians of the Northwest have been chastised and subjugated." Despite the sensation, this famous Indian victory was short-lived. The Indians discovered, as one historian has commented, that "the slaying of a big white chief could spell the doom of a people." Within a few months, lacking food, supplies, and unity, the hostile bands of Sioux and Cheyenne were broken up, surrounded, and defeated. Most moved into reservations where disease, starvation, and alcohol succeeded in diminishing their numbers and destroying their spirit. Sitting Bull and a handful of his followers escaped into Canada. But, in 1881, he chose to return to his people on the reservation.

In the Southwest, tribesmen known as hunters and warriors resisted the narrow confinements of windswept desert reservations. For seventeen years there was almost continuous warfare with the Apaches whom Westerners saw as particularly tricky, fierce, and slippery. In 1871, a group of angry ranchers slaughtered over a hundred sleeping Apaches and captured twenty-nine children who they sold as slaves to rival tribes. These murders horrified Easterners. President Grant threatened to place Arizona under martial law if the murderers were not brought to trial. Local authorities arrested the leaders of the group and quickly acquitted them.

Meanwhile, leading generals attempted to persuade the Apaches to surrender peacefully. One tough-minded old warrior, Cochise, agreed to peace in exchange for a reservation that included some traditional tribal land. After his death, however, his tribe found themselves increasingly frustrated by pressures to assimilate and by the famine that resulted from inadequate rations. One leader of the Chiricahua Apaches, Geronimo, established mountain bases in Arizona and Mexico and led raids against white outposts for more than a decade. By 1886, Geronimo's tiny band numbered no more than thirty-six, even though they had kept more than five thousand soldiers occupied with their lightening-fast tactics. The government spent about $1 million for every Apache killed. Finally, Apache scouts talked Geronimo into surrendering. He and his followers were sent to a Florida reservation. Later, he was transferred to Fort Sill, Oklahoma, where he became quite a celebrity. Described by one observer as "half clown and half monster," he enjoyed riding in Wild West shows and parades, wearing a high silk hat. He made a living selling souvenir bows and arrows to impressionable tourists. He died in 1909. A legend arose that his bones were secretly removed and taken to the mountains he loved. His fame was revived in World War II when American parachuters shouted his name as they jumped from their planes. Geronimo's surrender marked the end of formal warfare between whites and Native Americans.

Wounded Knee: The Final "Battle"

The success of the government in forcing Indians onto reservations meant that the old economic system and, with it, the traditional culture were in danger of extinction. Civilizations facing such crises often turn in hope to a messiah. The prophet many turned to was a Paiute Indian named Wovoka. While living with the family of a white rancher, Wovoka had studied the Bible and learned of the miraculous powers of the white medicine man, Jesus. During an eclipse of the sun in 1889, he experienced a vision in which God told him that he was the Indian messiah. When pilgrims from Western reservations journeyed to his lodge for inspiration, Wovoka showed them scars on his hand where whites had nailed him to a cross many centuries ago. He preached a spiritual reawakening in which the mystical "Ghost Dance," performed by ecstatic masses of Indians, would hasten the return of dead relatives. These ghosts would drive out the whites, bring back the buffalo, and restore the old way of life. Participants also wore "ghost shirts," decorated with mystical designs and conferring invulnerability to the white man's bullets. The proud Sioux, their

Wovoka, the Paiute prophet

glories fading and close to starvation, were particularly committed followers of Wovoka. Dancing was so widespread on Sioux reservations that virtually all other activities were halted.

Alarmed settlers and Indian agents, believing that the rapturous dancing might lead to renewed conflict, sought to suppress it by calling in troops. In the melees that followed, an Indian policeman killed the old chief, Sitting Bull. Worried that this might result in Indian resistance, the Seventh Cavalry (Custer's old regiment) tried to round up more than three hundred cold and hungry Sioux. The group had left the reservation and camped at Wounded Knee, South Dakota, December 29, 1890. The troops surrounded the band, two-thirds of whom were women and children, and disarmed the Indians. When one hidden gun was fired by an Indian (It is not clear whether accidentally or on purpose.), the nervous soldiers turned their new Hotchkiss machine guns at point-blank range on the Indians. They mowed the Indians down in the snow, where an approaching blizzard froze the bodies. The next day they were thrown into a mass grave. The wounded, four men and forty-seven women and children, were carried to a local missionary church where they lay beneath a banner declaring, "Peace on Earth; Good Will to Men." Three days later, the cleanup troops found a baby beneath the snow, wrapped in a blanket and wearing a buckskin cap with a beadwork embroidery of the American flag. Incredibly, she was still alive. General L. W. Colby, commander of the troops at Wounded Knee, adopted her and named her Marguerite. The Indians dubbed her Lost Bird.

The cavalry believed that Custer was finally avenged. Congress gave special medals to the soldiers for their roles in this last "military engagement." Frank Baum, who ten years later wrote *The Wizard of Oz*, noted approvingly that whites were now "masters of the American continent." He proposed that the few "miserable wretches" who remained among the Indians would be better off with "total annihilation." Forty years later, Black Elk, a Sioux holy man, recalled Wounded Knee: "I can still see the butchered women

Brigadier General L. W. Colby, commander of the troops at Wounded Knee, holds his adopted Indian daughter, Marguerite, whose parents had been killed in the massacre.

and children lying heaped and scattered....And I can see that something else died there in the bloody mud, and was buried in the blizzard. A people's dream died there." On December 29, 1890, one historian commented, "the Indian frontier of the American West vanished in the smoke of Hotchkiss shells bursting over the valley of Wounded Knee Creek."

The Reformers and Their Vision

Some Americans were appalled by the consequences of the army's "victories" over the Indians. Public sympathy had been aroused by such events as Chief Joseph's dramatic plea to be allowed to return to his homeland in the Northwest and the tragic attempt by Dull Knife's Cheyennes to escape from Indian Territory and return to their old home in Montana, only to be gunned down by soldiers. Native Americans appeared to be on the brink of extinction, their population declining rapidly, their game gone, their land taken. Arapaho dancers mournfully sang:

> My Father have pity on me!
> I have nothing to eat,
> I am dying of thirst—
> Everything is gone.

The destruction of independence, traditional authority, and culture led many Indians to turn to alcohol to escape bleak reality. Others followed peyotism in using the powerful drug to experience sensational dreams and a heightened feeling of personal worth. Some turned to a revival of the Sun Dance, which involved days of fasting, dancing, and self-mutilation through skewers in the skin of the chest to achieve oneness with the Great Spirit.

The end of any real danger from the Indians allowed some people to demonstrate greater tolerance and sympathy. Prominent whites were alarmed by the catastrophe they believed stemmed from humiliating dependency and pagan practices. They formed reform organizations like the Indian Rights Association. Helen Hunt Jackson was a particularly passionate crusader for Indian rights. She hoped that her 1881 book, *A Century of Dishonor*, would awaken the public to the hardships of Indians in the same way that *Uncle Tom's Cabin* had done thirty years earlier to the plight of slaves. Her book, while not as huge a best seller as that earlier novel, was widely read and did arouse the public conscience. Three years later, her romanticized novel, *Ramona*, about the tragic annihilation of the California Indians, also was enormously popular. Despite being dismissed by

Slaughtered frozen bodies of the Sioux at Wounded Knee were piled like cordwood.

The Hampton Institute in Virginia took these before and after photographs of three young Crow Indian girls who had been sent East from their reservation. They had been "civilized" with a book, new dresses, a doll, and checkers.

Theodore Roosevelt as "foolish sentimentalists," the reformers were gaining influence.

The paternalistic vision of these white liberals rested on the desire to Americanize the Indians by stripping them of their cultural heritage, converting them to Christianity, educating them in English, and preparing them to function in a white capitalist economy. Then, these reformers were confident, white hostility would disappear. The first step would be to "individualize" or "detribalize" Native Americans. They would be taught individual responsibility and labor, according to the Protestant work ethic. Then, they could break free of the tribe that held them back and jump into the mainstream of American life.

The first step in this process would be to hasten the breakup of the reservations and of tribal lands by allotting small farms to individual Indians. Sensing the possibilities of great profit, land speculators supported the reformers. After all, as one Indian Commissioner observed, it seemed a shame that public lands, rich in resources and waiting to be farmed "in obedience to the divine command, can long be kept simply as a park, in which wild beasts are hunted by wilder men." Jubilant reformers hailed the passage of the Dawes Act in 1887 that envisioned the creation of Indian yeoman farmers. One reformer compared the act to the Magna Charta, the Declaration of Independence, and the Emancipation Proclamation, all in one! Under this law, the president could divide tribal lands, giving 160 acres to each head of family and smaller allotments to single Indians. To protect the Indians from being fleeced, the Bureau of Indian Affairs would hold the land in trust for twenty-five years. After allotments, "surplus" reservation lands could be sold to whites.

What reformers failed to understand was that even though reservation policy had been a failure, its original purpose, at least, had been to set up boundaries that not only limited Indians but also restricted white access. They did not foresee the consequences of the Dawes Act. The disastrous result was the loss of more than 60 million "surplus" acres by Indian tribes. The 2,000 Sisseton Sioux of South Dakota, for instance, lived on a reservation of 918,000 acres of rich farmland. After allotment, more than 600,000 surplus acres remained and were opened to white farmers. The settlers rapidly moved in among these Sioux and destroyed any remaining tribal culture. Later laws enabled greedy speculators to buy allotted land, often at ridiculously low prices. Some forty years after the passage of the Dawes Act, Indians retained only one-third of the land they had held in 1887, much of it of poor quality.

Education went side by side with individual land ownership as a key element of reformers' ideology. They believed it would provide the transition from savagery to civilization. Schools provided instruction in English, manual and agricultural skills, American patriotism, and Christianity. An Indian pupil in one of the schools clearly described its goals. "I believe in education," he said, "because I believe it will kill the Indian that is in me and leave the man and the citizen." As a result of reformist pressures, the federal government appropriated more than a million dollars for Indian education by 1887. When schools on reservations did not seem to be effective in assimilating Indians, nonreservation boarding schools were set up to remove Indian children, sometimes forcibly, from the tribal environment. Navaho children were chained to rusty pipes to discourage them from using their native language. These schools were patterned on the Carlisle Indian School in Pennsylvania. This school followed a policy of "total immersion" in white civilization and ruthless assimilation. While the Carlisle school displayed its most successful graduates at world's fairs and exhibitions, most found themselves misfits in dress and attitudes when they returned to their old reservations. Some left the reservation, but most returned to their old way of life. (During World War II, the American military was grateful that Navahos had clung to their native language. The Japanese were never able to break the "code" broadcast by Navaho radiomen.) Reformers, who had naively expected the rapid obliteration of Native American culture, were astonished at its tenacity. Despite the poverty, disease, and unemployment endemic on the reservations, Indians remained stubbornly loyal to old tribal ways.

One historian commented, "Except for the internment of the...Japanese during World War II, Indian removal is the only example of large-scale government-enforced migration in American history. For the Japanese, the move was temporary; for the Indians it was not." Even as their lives became increasingly difficult, Indians became part of the romantic folklore of the West. Dime novels recounted tales of Indian fighting on the Plains. Wild West shows, started by Buffalo Bill Cody in 1883, featured Plains Indians attacking innocent whites and their inevitable and well-deserved defeats. The shows began with Wild Bill Hickok galloping on stage, shooting Indians who menaced beautiful heroines while declaiming, "Fear not, fair maid; by heavens you are safe at last with Wild Bill, who is ever ready to risk his life...in defense of weak and helpless womanhood." Thus, the story of the Indian wars was rewritten to make

A Navajo Indian before and after his "assimilation" into the Carlisle Indian School in Pennsylvania

the whites blameless victims of Indian aggression. In 1885, Cody prevailed on Sitting Bull to join his show. The chief drew tremendous crowds, many of whom gave him money for copies of his signed photograph. He returned to his reservation with two gifts from Buffalo Bill—an enormous white sombrero and a performing horse. It is said that when Sitting Bull was killed the old show horse went through his tricks, seeming to onlookers to be performing the Ghost Dance, and then galloped off into the hills, never to be seen again.

MIGRATION TO THE WEST

Waves of new settlers poured into the West from other parts of the United States and from overseas. They came on the heels of earlier migration that had brought California and Oregon into the Union as states before 1860. While these settlers had arrived by the thousands before the Civil War, after the war they numbered in the millions. They spread rapidly over the immense western territories. With the same kind of thoroughness they had demonstrated in the annihilation of both buffalo and Indians, they systematically exploited the natural resources of the West. The mountains and plains, they discovered, were rich in minerals such as gold, silver, lead, zinc, iron, coal, and copper. There were pasture lands suitable for grazing cattle and sheep and some of the world's most productive farm lands. Most of these migrants were white Anglo-Americans who left established communities in the older sections of the country, but other people came as well. Between 1870 and 1900 over two million foreign-born immigrants also made their way to the West. Many of these were German, British, or Scandinavian farmers. Others came from Ireland, China, and Eastern Europe to find work. African Americans also sought a better life in the land of seemingly boundless opportunities.

Chinese Immigrants

At the same period in which millions of Europeans crossed the Atlantic in search of new opportunities in the East, thousands of Chinese left their impoverished homeland to cross the Pacific for a better life on the "Golden Mountain" in the West. The first group had come in the 1840s and 1850s to look for gold after the California gold discovery. Discriminatory laws and the hostility of white miners drove most of them away from prospecting. Some worked sites abandoned by white miners. The shift to hydraulic extraction, financed by large eastern corporations, led many Chinese to accept jobs as hired laborers in the mines. Others became servants, laundry workers, and restaurant owners.

After the Civil War, as jobs in mining declined, railroad work became the largest source of employment. Over twelve thousand found jobs building the first transcontinental railroad. These Chinese laborers made up 90 percent of the workforce on the Central Pacific Railroad, building the line from San Francisco to Utah. The railroad company, like many businesses, preferred Chinese laborers because they worked for very modest wages and made few demands. One employer testified before a California Senate committee: "I find this difference: the Chinaman will stay and work, but the white man, as soon as he gets a few dollars, will leave and go elsewhere." Many had been recruited for railroad work in China. When they arrived, they were organized into work gangs under Chinese supervisors. The greatest challenge was the climb up the Pacific slope of the Sierras where tunnels had to be cut through granite cliffs and 40 miles of snowsheds were constructed. The Central Pacific did little to protect its workers from dangerous conditions or from the elements. In the winter, many workers dug shelters in snow banks to find some warmth. These makeshift refuges often collapsed and smothered those trapped inside, but the work continued.

When the first transcontinental railroad was finished in 1869, Chinese workers found jobs on the Southern Pacific Railroad, building dams and irrigation systems, and as the first migratory workers on the large wheat and fruit farms of California. Others established modest farms or set up fishing villages along the Pacific coast. Even more migrated to "Chinatowns" in Western cities, the largest of which was in San Francisco. By 1880, there were 200,000 Chinese in America. Almost all of them lived in the Far West, three-quarters in California.

The specter of "hordes" of Chinese entering the United States rapidly became a heated issue. The New York *World* announced that, "Asiatics are cunning, treacherous and vicious, possessing no conception of American civilization." The paper worried that the western states were "degenerating into Chinese colonies," making any further Chinese immigration "disastrous" to the American way of life.

These fears were increased by the life style of these "exotic" immigrants. Most saw their move to America as a temporary step to secure some wealth and return to their villages in China where they would gain respect and wives. As a result, they brought few women with them (Only 1 in 20 Chinese immigrants was female.), and some of those were prostitutes. Their "bachelor" communities were self-contained. Lives revolved around clan organizations led by wealthy merchants. These groups, like the "Six Companies" of San Francisco, helped meet the social and welfare needs of the poorer immigrants. The *tongs* were independent secret societies that were sometimes involved in criminal activities, particularly prostitution and the opium trade.

Many Americans were frightened by the presence of these nonwhite, nonChristian males. They believed that Chinese men had sexual designs on white women. Chinese "opium dens" seemed far more sinister than the bars popular with white American workingmen. The depression of the 1870s added to the hostility. California was hit particularly hard as land values slumped, gold output from the mines continued to decline, and a lull in railroad construction brought thousands of unemployed Chinese workers back to the state. "Anti-coolie" clubs attacked Chinese workers in the streets. Mobs in Los Angeles lynched fifteen Chinese men and burned homes. Vigilantes in Chico, California murdered Chinese, and a San Francisco riot burned down many Chinese laundries. The worst incident occurred in Rock Springs, Wyoming when frenzied white miners massacred fifty-one Chinese and expelled hundreds more. The Workingmen's Party was formed in San

The joining of the Union Pacific and Central Pacific Railroads on May 10, 1869 at Promontory, Utah changed life in America. Coast-to-coast travel was possible for the first time.

Francisco in 1878 by Denis Kearney, an Irish immigrant. The party charged that the Chinese were stealing all the available jobs. Its manifesto proclaimed, "Treason is better than to labor beside a Chinese slave." Other groups, arguing that the Chinese were "unassimilable," demanded that they be excluded from the country.

Congress responded to this western pressure by passing the Chinese Exclusion Act in 1882, banning future Chinese immigration. In the next forty years, Chinese population in America declined by 40 percent. Western corporations were forced to look elsewhere for cheap labor.

Hispanics in the West

For three centuries most of the Far West had been a part of the Spanish Empire in the New World and then of the Mexican Republic. As a result of the Mexican War, the United States in 1848 had acquired not only a vast additional territory but also almost eighty thousand new citizens. These Mexican Americans were now seen as a "colored," Spanish-speaking, Catholic minority group in a society overwhelmingly white, Protestant, and English-speaking. Spanish-speaking communities, scattered throughout the Southwest, were rapidly altered by the migration of Anglo-Americans and the expansion of the capitalist economy into their areas.

The old Spanish elite quickly lost both their influence and their land. Mexican residents of California once owned 15 million acres of land. Vast numbers of English-speaking immigrants poured into the region, occupying their lands. The completion of the Southern Pacific Railroad in 1876 brought thousands more. The outnumbered Mexican Americans were unable to counter endless litigation and fraud that stripped them of their property. By the 1880s few still owned their own land. In New Mexico, the Santa Fe Ring, a clique of white bankers and merchants, used heavy property taxes to force Mexican-American landowners to sell their land at bargain prices. The ring quickly gained control of several million acres of land. In Texas, increasing white claims on grazing and farming land to meet world demand for beef, sheep, and cotton led to a similar pattern of fraud and intimidation. The southern Protestants who settled Texas were particularly prejudiced against the "colored" *tejanos* (Mexicans). The famed Texas Rangers helped enforce white control and land claims. Historians have estimated that the Rangers killed almost five thousand Mexican Americans in the 1800s. Some of these may have been criminals, others revolutionary *banditos*, but many were simply tejanos whom whites wanted to "dislodge" from the land.

Mexican Americans increasingly became part of the working class in city *barrios* (ghettos) or as migrant farm workers. By 1900, the growth of large commercial farms with heavy investments in sophisticated equipment and irrigation systems priced most of the remaining small Mexican-American farmers out of the business. The use of irrigation and fertilizers caused a threefold increase in farm acreage in the Southwest between 1870 and 1900. At the same time, the dynamic economy, bolstered by the railroads, attracted new waves of Mexican immigrants. They poured across the unregulated border by the thousands in search of new opportunities. The passage of the Chinese Exclusion Act led many growers and businessmen to recruit Mexican laborers.

The new migrants, like the old Hispanic residents, came to a society in which they were subordinate to whites and restricted to the lowest paying jobs. In some places, particularly in Texas, they faced the literacy tests and poll taxes that had already denied voting rights to blacks in the South. They often attended segregated schools. The paternalistic, extended family that had once been part of Hispanic culture faced serious challenges in the new society. The weakened Mexican-American community was not well prepared to confront a western society dominated by the push for progress and modernization.

Other Minorities in the West

The perception of greater opportunities and a more open society in the West attracted many migrants from other groups. Irish workmen came to lay railroad track. Most of the laborers on the Union Pacific, running West from Omaha, Nebraska to Utah, were Irish. Many, more adventurous Irishmen headed west to seek their fortunes as miners or ranchers. Richard

King, the son of poor Irish immigrants, founded the King Ranch in south Texas. He bought his original holding of 15,000 acres for two cents an acre. With the help of obliging Texas Rangers, who enforced his often fraudulent land claims, he was able to increase his holding to 600,000 acres. Marcus Daly, a formerly penniless Irish immigrant, established the Anaconda copper mines in Montana and filled his work force with Irish miners. He socialized with his workmen and was popular as a fair employer. Most Irish who came west, however, remained in working class jobs and concentrated in cities.

Just as German Jews had done before them, some Eastern European Jews came west, ready to take risks for better opportunities. A few attempted to found agricultural colonies in North Dakota or in the cooperative community of New Odessa, Oregon, with minimal success. Others took up peddling or ran small businesses. Jews experienced greater social mobility in the West than in the older sections of America. One example was the Madanic family that came from Russia in 1889. After toiling in the sweatshops, they saved enough money to open a reasonably successful clothing store in Illinois. By 1908, they moved to the boomtown of Tulsa, Oklahoma. Their business was so successful there that they were able to open branches in nearby towns. Eventually, they changed their name to the May Brothers, and their stores spread throughout the country. The record of most European pioneer immigrant groups demonstrated that economic success was attainable and social integration possible, particularly in their children's generation.

African Americans, disillusioned by the failure of Reconstruction, hoped to find the opportunities to farm their own land that they had been denied in the South. Some three hundred of these "Exodusters" were attracted to Nicodemus in northwest Kansas by handbills that read, "All Colored People that want to GO TO KANSAS, on September 5th, 1877, Can do so for $5.00." By 1879, "Kansas Fever" had even spread to desperately poor black families in the lower South. These black settlers had fewer resources than whites and got little or no support from the institutions of local society in the West. Even when their communities survived, they rarely prospered. In the 1880s, a substantial minority of the cowboys working in Texas and Oklahoma, perhaps as many as 25 percent, were African Americans. Some of the famous gunfighters of Western legend were black, including "Deadeye Dick" and "Isom Dart." The peacetime American army, much of it stationed in the West, attracted a large number of black Civil War veterans. Many of these became part of the regiments known as "Buffalo Soldiers," which played a significant role in the Indian wars. San Francisco was the home of the black leaders of the Pacific Coast area. They led an eventually successful 20-year struggle to open the schools to their children and held equal rights conventions. Most of the substantial number of African Americans in the West, however, were laborers seeking work. A household in Tombstone, Arizona, in 1880 was typical. It consisted of a 30-year-old South Carolinian laborer and his younger wife, and eight black men in their 30s and 40s who were blacksmiths, cooks, waiters, and laborers.

Western workers tended to be single, highly mobile, men. Single women often worked in dance halls or as prostitutes. Although Americans perceived of the West as the section of boundless opportunity, real social mobility was no greater than that of the older sections of the country. Those who most rapidly succeeded generally were people who were well off before they arrived. The Western labor force was amazingly multiracial. Even more than in the East, white Anglo-Saxon Americans worked alongside blacks, Chinese, Mexicans, Indians, and immigrants from eastern and southern Europe. But this work force was also racially stratified. Those who did the unskilled and most strenuous jobs in the mines, farms, and on the railroads usually were nonwhites. The limited mobility into more skilled or supervisory jobs was reserved for white workers. An Irish unskilled laborer might expect, over the years, to move up to slightly better work. A Mexican, African-American, or Chinese worker could not look forward to the same opportunity.

THE MINING FRONTIER

The first great economic boom in the Far West occurred in mining, and miners were generally among the advance guard in the frontier. The mining boom had a relatively brief life-span, but its impact was enormous. It encouraged settlement, caused the creation of governments and laws, stimulated transportation, and enticed both capital and labor to the West.

The mining rushes followed the pattern of the 1849 California Gold Rush. A prospector would discover nuggets or dust that had been washed into streams or rivers by the forces of erosion. The news spread quickly to other miners who stampeded into the area searching for a bonanza. The early arrivals found easy pickings, using large metal pans. A handful of prospectors might find as much as $8,000 in gold a day, but most were lucky to end up with an ounce of gold ($16). The initial discoveries played out quickly. Within a few years, as surface yields dwindled, corporations entered the picture to find the veins of gold hidden in rocks and hills. They could pay for the costly heavy machinery and hydraulic mining that brought up the ore hidden beneath the surface. Some disillusioned prospectors took jobs as miners for the big companies, but thousands of others surged to the next strike and the continuing dream of instant wealth.

The first great mineral rush after the California Gold Rush occurred in Colorado just before the Civil War (1859). Thousands poured into the region with the slogan, "Pike's Peak or Bust," painted on the canvas of their wagons. The boom helped make cities out of mining camps, particularly Denver. The placer (surface) boom rapidly fell on hard times. Soon disappointed miners trekked back home with a new slogan, "Busted by Gosh!" Others stayed on and took jobs in shaft mining or tried their hands at farming or grazing. Later, gold was found at Cripple Creek, and a rich bed of silver was discovered at Leadville. The "Mile High City" of Denver became the prosperous center for smelting ore from throughout the Rockies and for the production of mining equipment. By 1876, Colorado gained admission to the union as the Centennial State.

Even before the first Colorado boom ended, news of another strike in Nevada sent miners swarming into the treeless and waterless Washoe Mountains. Two Irishmen found the Ophir silver vein, the richest in history. (The find was called the Comstock Lode after the lackadaisical Henry Comstock who claimed a share of the profits based on his supposed ownership of the stream where the silver was found.) The boomtown of Virginia City quickly emerged at this forlorn site. Although there were no railroads and no means to produce supplies, entrepreneurs rapidly organized to ship everything from equipment

African-American cavalrymen were not treated as well as white soldiers.

and food to prostitutes and liquor from California. The silver in this fabulous strike was embedded in quartz, so crushing machinery was required to reach the treasure.

The big mines needed blasting, drilling, and timbering (building huge wooden bunkers to prevent the mountain from caving in). After twelve substantial strikes, the greatest of all, the "Big Bonanza," took place in 1873. One company, excavating 1,167 feet, found a 54-feet wide vein filled with gold and silver. The $200 million this vein produced created the "Kings of the Comstock." George Hearst from California, father of the newspaper mogul, William Randolph Hearst, was one of these. He and his partners took their huge profits with them back to San Francisco where they built spectacular mansions.

The merchants, bankers, and mine owners erected lavish homes that looked down on the flashy town of Virginia City, which had grown to twenty thousand. They sat on their porches sipping champagne, as Irish, Welsh, Cornish, German, and Mexican miners toiled in the tunnels far below. In the depth of these mines, the working conditions were horrible. The intense heat of over 100 degrees made it difficult to work for more than a few minutes at a time. Cooling stations had tubs of ice and towels that were dipped in ice water and thrown on the miners' bodies. The tunnels filled with the stench of unwashed bodies, blasting powder, rotting timber, and human waste. (There were no toilets.) Tunnel floods, cave-ins, explosions, and accidents were commonplace. In view of the great risk involved, the miners earned $4 a day, decent pay for a workingman. Eventually, even this fabulous source of ore played out, and the price of silver suffered sharp declines. The great mines of the Comstock Lode closed. By the 1890s, Virginia City was a ghost town.

This pattern was repeated in every subsequent strike. Gold was discovered in 1874 in the Black Hills on the Sioux reservation. By 1876, the army gave up any effort to keep the prospectors out. Before long, there were 25,000 people in Deadwood, South Dakota, a town that rivaled Tombstone, Arizona as the toughest in the West. As in other booms, the surface resources quickly disappeared, and a big corporation took over. After ore worth $287 million had been extracted in a remarkably short time, the population rapidly declined, and Deadwood passed into the realm of legend. The Dakotas eventually developed into an agricultural economy.

Other, less exciting, resources ultimately proved to be even more important in the development of the West. Marcus Daly was disappointed when he found out that his Anaconda silver mine contained copper and only small amounts of silver. But his mood turned to joy when he realized that it was one of the largest and purest copper deposits ever discovered. "The Richest Hill on Earth" made millionaires out of Daly and several other investors. Access to railroads enabled Anaconda to market its vast deposits. Copper from Montana played an important role in the miles of electric wiring that were powering factories and lighting cities in both America and Europe. The "Copper Kings" of Montana were involved in continuous conflicts to win control of the state's economy and government, along with its copper output. Eventually, as greater and greater investments were needed to build huge electric generating plants and smelting facilities, Eastern investors with ties to Standard Oil took control. In other places, lead, tin, quartz, and zinc mining proved to be profitable. In 1901, just before the advent of the automobile, Black Gold gushed from the Spindletop fields in Texas, creating the most lucrative industry of all, the oil industry.

The constant danger, lack of safety devices, and terrible discomfort in the mines created a sense of beleaguered brotherhood among many of the miners. They began to form unions to aid the injured and demand better working conditions. In an 1892 Idaho miners' strike, state and federal troops were called in to break up the strike. Seven miners were killed in the resulting melee. The Western Federation of Miners (WFM) had its headquarters in the copper town of Butte, Montana, the "Gibraltar of Unionism." Within a decade, the WFM had over 50,000 members in the region. It became the base for the far more militant Industrial Workers of the World (IWW). The unwillingness of the mining corporations to even discuss issues with their workers and their tendency to call for troops to end strikes led to escalating violence. Despite these labor problems, however, mining created the wealth that laid the grounds for an expanding economy.

THE CATTLE KINGDOM

As prospectors rushed westward to seek their fortunes, cattlemen began moving into the Great Plains. They were attracted by the open range, the expansive grasslands in the public domain where herds could graze without charge, unfettered by the boundaries of private property. The rapid growth of population in northern markets increased the prices offered for steers. Even before the Civil War, there were five million head of wild Texas longhorn roaming the Texas range. These were descendants of stock imported by Spanish colonists. Steers valued at $4 a head in Texas, where they attracted few buyers, sold for $30 to $50 in Chicago. Fortunes, equal to those attainable by miners, could be made by those who could bring the cattle to market. The only issue was how to get them there.

Long before America annexed Texas, the Mexican *vaquero*, the predecessor of the American cowboy, had developed techniques and equipment to capture and herd cattle. These included roundups and ropings and much of the distinctive cowboy gear, including lariats, saddles, spurs, chaps, and even the five-gallon hat. The coming of the railroad inspired cattlemen to risk a cross-country drive of their stock to the railroad town of Sedalia, Missouri in 1866. In this first "long drive," 260,000 steers were driven north. They were beset by cattle rustlers, Indians, gun-totting farmers trying to protect their crops, and stampedes. Only a fraction of the herd ever arrived in Sedalia, but those that did sold for $35 a head. This inspired other ranchers to try their luck.

A shrewd young Illinois meat dealer, Joseph McCoy, realized that he could make his fortune by providing a place where buyers and breeders could do business. He picked the insignificant little town of Abilene, Kansas. Its main advantage was that it lay on the Kansas Pacific railroad line that ultimately connected to Chicago. There, he built stock pens, stables, railroad loading facilities, and a hotel. By 1868, 75,000 head of cattle arrived in Abilene, and, within a few years, the numbers increased enormously. The arrival of cowboys soon led to the construction of saloons, gambling parlors, and houses of prostitution. Wild Bill Hickok became famous as a fast shooting marshal in this cow town.

As railroads expanded, other cattle towns developed. The most famous was Dodge City on the Santa Fe Railroad. It was called the "Cowboy Capital," particularly in the decade from 1875-85. At its height, 250,000 cattle arrived each year. It also supported the usual assortment of drunks and reckless adventurers, many of whom ended up in the celebrated Boot Hill Cemetery.

The long drive was an amazing sight, so it is understandable that it became the most romanticized sector of western life. In the spring, cattlemen rounded up their herds from the open range. Calves were branded and turned loose with their mothers to pasture. Year-old steers were combined with those of other herds. Then, accompanied by a dozen or so cowboys, the herd of three thousand was moved north at a rate of 300 to 500 miles a month. The cattle wore furrows on the trail so deep that they continued to be visible for years. Despite the myths that grew up about picturesque cowboys, the work, in the words of a veteran of the drive, was a "tiresome, grimy business for the attendant punchers, who traveled ever in a cloud of dust," with the "constant chorus... from the bellows, lows and bleats of the trudging animals." Despite his romantic image that captured the imagination of Easterners, the cowboy was, in reality, a poorly paid ($25 to $40 a month) worker whose life was hard and monotonous. Few were good shots. Many (at least a third) were Mexicans or blacks, even though they were invariably portrayed in popular legend as white. When Texas cowboys struck for higher wages, the cattlemen crushed their strike. The cattle companies began replacing Anglo cowboys with Mexicans who were given only one-half to two-thirds of the pay.

A successful drive could produce very substantial profits of 40 percent or more. Despite the risks of "Texas fever," a deadly cattle disease, rustlers, Indians, and natural disasters, Eastern and European investors were tempted by dreams of amazing profits. (British investors alone poured some $45 million into the cattle industry in the 1870s and 80s, owning some 20

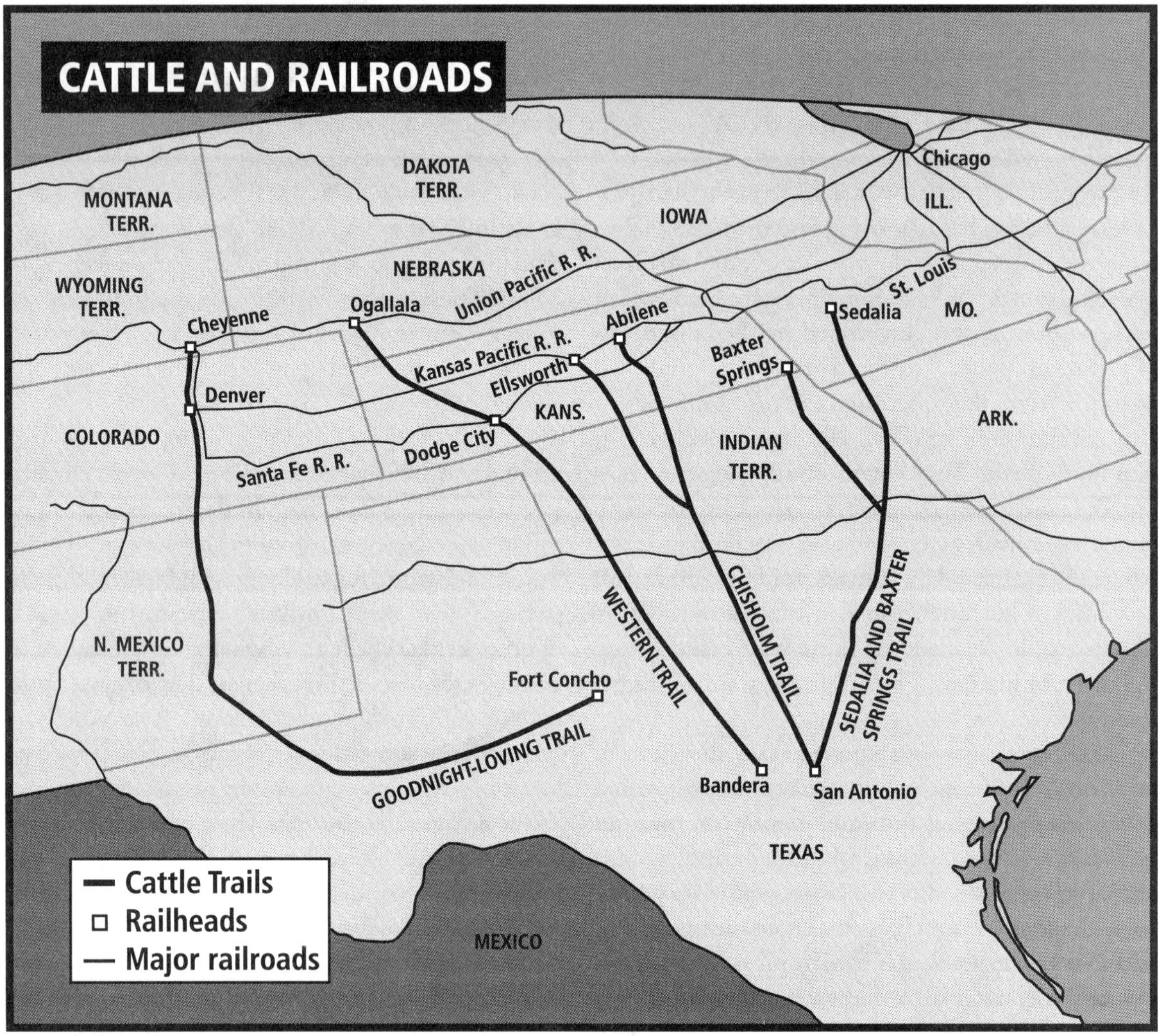

million acres of grazing land.) The old free-wheeling stockman was rapidly being replaced by large corporations. Businessmen realized that the tough, scrawny longhorns, derided as "8 pounds of hamburger on 800 pounds of bone and horn," were perfect for enduring the long drive but not as suitable to producing tender, juicy steaks. And the long trip did not improve the quality of the meat. Ranchers began to breed longhorns with better quality imported stock in permanent and fenced ranches.

The long drive was also doomed by the same railroads that had made the drive possible in the first place. They brought thousands of farmers to the plains. These permanent settlers objected to cattle breaking down their fences and trampling their crops. They retaliated by enclosing their homesteads with barbed wire that was deadly to onrushing cattle and by persuading state legislatures to pass laws designed to limit the entrance of the herds. Sheepherders also came to the range in large numbers. Contemptuous cattlemen wrongly argued that sheep spoiled the water and destroyed the grass by eating its roots as well. The sheep owners were often immigrants or nonwhites. Cattlemen believed sheep were "inferior animals herded by inferior men." Eventually, the sheep outnumbered the cattle. Bloody, armed conflicts erupted between sheepmen and cattlemen, between farmers and ranchers, and among arrogant cattle barons for control of an area. In one such episode, the 1892 Johnson County War, the Wyoming Stock Growers

Association hired gunmen to eliminate small ranchers they accused of rustling.

Other forces were even more devastating. The feverish, speculative expansion led to overcrowding on ranges reduced by actions of farmers and government. President Cleveland, for example, evicted herds of cattle trespassing on land in the Indian Territory. By 1884, 20 million cattle grazed the American West. Supply was greatly outpacing demand, and the price of beef began a precipitous decline. Nature then delivered the final crushing blow. Two terrible winters of blizzards in 1885-6 and 1886-7, with a blistering, scorching summer between them, devastated the plains. Thousands of cattle piled up and died. Grass and streams dried up. Cattle raisers rushed their weakened and often emaciated steers into the declining market to salvage what they could from the disaster. In Chicago, the price of beef plummeted from $9.35 per hundred pounds in 1882 to $1 in 1887. The old Cattle Kingdom died. But the better run companies that had centralized and modernized survived the bad times. They had fenced in grazing land, raised hay for winter feed, and upgraded their stock. Their cowboys increasingly became workers who were just as liable to build fences, dig irrigation ditches, and cut hay as to ride herd. Eventually, the ranchers produced more beef than ever, although they continued to depend on public lands for grazing and federal projects to bring them irrigation.

Boom Towns, Cities and Lawlessness

Both the mining and cattle booms, as well as the railroads, produced towns that followed similar patterns of overnight development. Virginia City, for example, began its existence as a shantytown, but the mining bonanza turned it into a metropolis containing mansions, an opera house, a six-story hotel, 131 saloons, four banks, and numerous houses of prostitution. Men outnumbered women by more than three to one. The same was true of the cow town of Abilene. There, amidst the streets ankle-deep in mud, the crude wooden sidewalks, and the dilapidated store fronts, a cowboy could find many ways to spend the several months' pay burning a hole in his pocket. Bright lights beckoned from saloons like the Bull's Head and from gambling parlors featuring roulette or poker games. The Novelty Theater presented sleazy entertainment, and the "Devil's Half Acre" featured world-weary prostitutes. Other boom towns exhibited a similar flashy, tawdry picture.

Many Western men were adherents of the "Code of the West," which stressed that a real man never retreated from confrontation; people must redress their own grievances. This popular attitude could be seen in an old folk song:

> Wake up, wake up darlin' Corrie
> And go and get my gun
> I ain't no hand for trouble
> But I'll die before I run.

The code placed great value on personal courage, often leading, in the words of one historian, to "reckless bravado." In a televised address to the nation in 1953, President Dwight Eisenhower admiringly described the old code of Abilene (his hometown) and of its marshal, "Wild Bill" Hickok: "Meet anyone face to face with whom you disagree" and "if you met him face to face and took the same risk as he did, you could get away with almost anything (killing included), as long as the bullet was in front." Westerners were, at the same time, the most heavily armed group of civilians in the world.

Cattle and mining towns presented particular opportunities for men whose guns were their means of livelihood. Some of the gun wielders were outlaws, recast by myth into Robin Hood-like figures. One historian has called them "social bandits," expressing the grievances of many others who would never have dared to commit criminal acts. There were approximately three hundred "glorified gunfighters" whose exploits became Western legend. Some, like Jesse James, whose daring was admired as that of "strong men who could protect and avenge themselves," robbed the banks and railroads that were resented by peaceful ordinary citizens for their unfair charges. When the Southern Pacific Railroad successfully used hired gunslingers to clear out dissident farmers with conflicting land claims, its actions aroused resentment. One result was popular admiration for two holdup men—Chris Evans and John Sontag—who specialized in Southern Pacific Railroad trains and dramatic shoot-outs with railroad detectives.

The famous Lincoln County War, which struck New Mexico in 1878, involved two factions struggling to dominate local commerce. The "War" provided the training ground for at least nineteen gunfighters, including the legendary Billy the Kid. In reality, the "Kid" was neither the mythical hero portrayed at the time nor the "mentally inferior" psychopath depicted by later revisionists. Instead, he was a typical young gunfighter involved in the conflicts of the era and unsuccessful in his attempts to turn to a more peaceful civilian life. In his "short and violent life" of only 21 years, he was probably responsible for ten deaths. Many of the outlaws, like the James and Younger brothers and the terrifying John Wesley Hardin (responsible for at least twenty deaths), learned outlaw tactics of raiding and shooting as Confederate guerrillas during the Civil War.

Some of these gun fighters became law enforcement officers like Wyatt Earp and his brother Virgil. Cowboy outlaws, who frequently rode into Tombstone, Arizona, to have a rambunctious good time, angered the elite Republican mine owners who ran the booming town. The town leaders turned to Wyatt and his brothers to use their gunfighting skills to end the killings in Tombstone and restore some order. In addition to coming from a strong unionist Republican family, the Earps were ardent speculators in area mines and real estate. In the famous showdown at the O.K. Corral in 1881 the Earps and their ally, Doc Holiday, were able to defeat the cowboy-rustler-outlaw faction headed by the Clantons and McLaurys.

Sometimes the line between lawful and unlawful killer was rather blurred. Wild Bill Hickok, a professional gambler, often found himself on the wrong side of the law. Yet, he also served as an effective law officer at various times. McCoy, the businessman who built Abilene, hired Hickok, a Union veteran from an abolitionist Illinois family, to subdue the violence-prone Texas cowboys who swept into town. His face-to-face shooting of a well-known Texas gunfighter and gambler helped Hickok fulfill his goal of bringing order to Abilene. (Contrary to legend, Hickok killed only one more person in his tenure in Abilene and that one by mistake.) Hickok eventually moved to Deadwood where he was shot in the back while playing poker, assuring his place in Western myth.

Many historians feel that later romantic legends greatly exaggerated accounts of Western gun fighting. Despite their unruly character, homicide rates in the boom towns were not particularly high. The five main Kansas cattle towns, for example, had a total of forty-five homicides over a 15 year period. Western violence, however, was more complex than official homicides. The lack of effective law enforcement institutions to protect life and property resulted in the creation of vigilante bands, usually led by the wealthy elite in the Western towns. Men like California railroad magnate and senator Leland Stanford, engaged in vigilante violence. There were over two hundred vigilante movements west of the Mississippi. In one year, in California alone, mobs executed forty-seven people. They justified their challenge to legal authority by emphasizing the right of self-preservation of the community. Since the Virginia City police force was too small and dishonest to keep order, vigilantes took over the town in 1871 and hanged two infamous outlaws. A Denver newspaper approved of a nearby vigilante hanging in 1879, noting that it was not only "well merited but a positive gain to the county, saving at least five or six thousand dollars."

Other aspects of Western violence involved racial and ethnic tensions that culminated in brutality directed against Indians, Mexicans, Chinese, or blacks. Within the majority white community, tensions exploded when the new forces of industrialization clashed with the old combative Code of the West. Miners, loggers, and mill workers struggled against the new corporate elite. Sometimes the state militia crushed strikes, leading to bitter conflicts. In one shocking incident in Ludlow, Colorado, in 1914, a "Thirty Years War" between miners and a Rockefeller-owned company culminated in the suffocation death of thirteen women and children and the shooting of many other people.

The pattern of violence gradually changed, for the most part, as the boom towns faded. Either they disintegrated into "ghost towns," or they were reformed by the efforts of stable and permanent settlers. As the

West urbanized as a result of the advances of technology, the criminal justice system responded to public demands for a more tranquil society. The production and exchange of goods and services requiring an urban setting increased in the West. Theodore Roosevelt, in his *Winning of the West* (1896), noted that when Kentucky became a state in the 1790s, only 1 percent of its population resided in Lexington, its largest city. But when Colorado entered the union in 1876, one-third of its people lived in Denver. "Nowadays," the future president proudly noted, "when new states are formed the urban population in them tends to grow as rapidly as in the old."

Denver, the "Queen City of the Rockies," vividly demonstrated these changes in Western life. Until 1870, the city existed to fulfill the needs and desires of miners, and to outfit and equip them. Visiting observers noted, "Drunkenness and rioting...existed everywhere." Saloons, brothels, and gaming houses were omnipresent and, "in these horrible dens a man's life is worth no more than a dog's." The completion of railroad connections in 1870, however, enabled the city to diversify its economy. The 1870 population of 4,759 grew to 10,500 by 1890. By then, visitors could travel on cable cars. (The electric trolley was introduced the following year.) Observers marveled at the spread out character of the handsome new city and noted, "a general absence of frontier ruggedness." The houses and shops remarked one, "would do credit to Broadway."

San Francisco was, undoubtedly, the paramount city of the nineteenth-century West. By 1890, it had close to 300,000 inhabitants and ranked eighth in population among the nation's cities. The city collected raw materials and produced foodstuffs, shoes, clothing, and equipment distributed throughout the Far West. A British observer compared it to "a New York that has no Boston on one side of it and no shrewd and orderly rural population on the other to keep it in order."

THE WESTERN FARMER

Farmers had begun moving west of the Mississippi and even the Missouri before the Civil War. After the war, however, what had been a trickle became a flood. Between 1870 and 1900, farmers doubled the land under cultivation from 407 to 841 million acres. This newly farmed acreage was greater than the amount of land that had been cultivated in the entire country from its beginning. Many of these new farms were on the Great Plains.

Farmers Settle the Plains

For many years, farmers feared moving into the Great Plains. Besides coarse grass, the area had little vegetation. There were few animals suitable for hunting. The lack of water and wood was even more important. No wonder Americans had dubbed this area the "Great American Desert."

Before the Civil War, the forbidding Great Plains had been reachable only after an obstacle-filled journey by wagon. The building of the transcontinental railroads created an immense railroad network that made access to the Great Plains much easier. To gain customers and to increase the value of their enormous land holdings granted by generous governments, the railroad companies energetically promoted land settlement. Their land bureaus and agents in the East and Europe offered long term loans and low cost transportation to prospective buyers. One promoter assured young men that "this vast region...with its boundless, undeveloped resources," was beckoning. "They will be nobodies where they are—they can be somebodies in building up a new society."

These campaigns were amazingly successful. Along with millions of Americans, mostly from nearby states, over two million foreigners settled in the West. More than two-thirds of the people in the Dakotas in 1880 were of foreign parentage. By 1905, the Santa Fe Railroad alone had moved sixty thousand Mennonites from the Ukraine to Kansas.

Federal government land policy was another key factor in pulling settlers to the West. The Homestead Act of 1862 attempted to make the long-cherished ideal of a nation of independent farmers into a reality. Under the act, public lands in the West were opened to free settlement by citizens and those who declared that they would become citizens. Settlers, who paid a modest $10 fee, could get plots of 160 acres if they occupied the land for five years and improved it.

Although 400,000 families gained title to homesteads under the act, the law hardly functioned as Congress had presumably envisioned.

One problem was the 160-acre limit. While 160 acres was more than enough in the fertile soil of older sections, it was not adequate for the drier land of the plains. A second problem was the prevalence of fraud. Dishonest speculators and cattle and mining interests were able to file false claims and grab the choicest locations. Undermanned government land offices were unable to provide the kind of supervision that would have assured that land went to legitimate settlers. Later acts that attempted to rectify the shortcomings of the Homestead Act, by increasing the size of land grants and shortening the period of residence, only seemed to encourage even more extensive fraud. Many more settlers bought their land at prices from $2 to $10 an acre from railroads, land companies, and state governments that had been given federal land for educational purposes. It has been estimated that less than 15 percent of Great Plains' farmers actually got their land from the Homestead Act. Nevertheless, the idea of ample free land available from the government helped keep the dream alive of the West as a land of opportunity.

A temporary climate change was another factor that contributed to the surge of settlement. For several years, particularly after 1877, rainfall in the plains far exceeded the normal totals. Watching their abundant crops grow, many settlers wondered why the area had ever been called the "Great American Desert." Some went as far as to argue that the cultivation of the plains had caused permanent climate change, particularly increased rainfall!

Farming on the Plains: Overcoming Problems

Those who came to farm on the plains had to confront and overcome daunting obstacles. The lack of trees in the area presented the first challenge. This made it prohibitively expensive to build even rough log cabin homes and to put up fencing to enclose property and protect crops from range cattle. The development of inexpensive barbed wire in 1874, and its rapid availability to farmers, solved the latter problem. The first dwelling the pioneer set up might be a cave, a lean-to, or even a canvas-topped cart. Eventually, settlers hit on the idea of using the tough matted sod, like oversized bricks, to build houses. These homes were invariably dark, dirty, and subject to mud falling down on the furniture when it rained. While these dwellings seemed picturesque to visitors, homes of imported wood or local stone replaced them as soon as improved circumstances permitted. The shortage of wood made it difficult to heat houses in some of the coldest sections of America. Early settlers used dried buffalo "chips" or hay in special slow-burning stoves. But the predicament persisted until the railroads began to bring in coal.

Nature presented a variety of other problems. Prairie fires were a menace to homes and crops. On the northern plains, blizzards were particularly dangerous. Among the pests that plagued the settlers, the grasshoppers were the worst. At times, they were as thick as a heavy snowstorm, and they ate everything in sight, including clothes hanging out to dry. Masses of grasshoppers, making the tracks dangerously slippery, even held up the railroads. The prairie sod was so tough that it required a special steel plow pulled by several oxen to break up one to two acres a day.

The lack of an adequate water supply was the most serious difficulty of all. Some farmers turned to digging wells to reach water as far down as 500 feet. Well-digging crews with expertise and expensive equipment toured the region, charging a dollar a foot. Windmills, harnessing the powerful winds of the area, raised the water from the deep wells. These windmills, however, were limited to supplying household needs and, perhaps, a vegetable garden. Experts developed special varieties of wheat, barley, and other crops requiring less water. Many farmers turned to "dry farming" cultivation techniques. After each rainfall, farmers plowed the field, enabling the turned over mud to serve as a mulch to store water. Irrigation might have been the most effective solution in some areas, but it required capital investment on a scale that only the federal government could provide. In the 1870s and 80s, it was unable or unwilling to fund such projects.

After 1887, climate conditions returned to normal. The dry seasons turned the once fertile lands into a semi-desert. In the earlier booming years farmers were able to obtain easy credit to expand. Crop failures and conflicts in Europe had greatly increased the demand for American grain. As one Kansas farmer noted, "Haste to get rich has made us borrowers, and the borrowing has made booms, and the booms made men wild, and Kansas became a vast insane asylum...." When the droughts came, many farmers found themselves unable to repay their debts. In the drought year of 1888, thousands of wagons of the "defeated legion" rolled eastward, some bearing despondent signs, "In God We Trusted; In Kansas We Busted."

At the same time, farmers, both the successful and the unsuccessful, were deeply affected by the commercialization of farming, especially after the mid 1890s. The open plains country lent itself to large scale farms that specialized in one crop and mechanized almost as much as contemporary factories. Such inventions as cord binders, rotary plows, seeders, mowers, and combines brought economies of scale. By the end of the 1880s, two men and a team of horses could harvest 20 acres of wheat a day. (Earlier farmers had been happy if they managed eight acres of wheat a **season.**) The hours required to farm one acre of wheat dropped from sixty-one to an astonishing three. Farmers learned about "scientific agriculture" from the land-grant colleges established by the 1862 Morrill Act. The result was soaring production. At first, the growing cities and foreign countries bought up these crops. Eventually, Russian wheat production recovered, Australia entered the world market, and a worldwide overproduction caused a precipitous drop in prices. Farmers began steadily to lose ground. In 1860 they received 30 percent of the national income; by 1910 their share fell to 18 percent. The new economic order did not seem nearly as attractive to them as it once had.

The Role of Women

Frontier farms were family enterprises. As in earlier eras, the responsibilities of the farmer's wife could be overwhelming. She carried out the then common household tasks of cleaning, cooking, washing dishes and clothes, mending, and ironing. These were far more difficult on the plains where they might involve washing clothes in the hardest water, keeping a dirt house clean, and giving birth to a succession of children with little or no help. She probably also fed extra men at harvesting time, preserved food, worked in the garden, took care of the barnyard poultry, milked and churned the butter, and sewed the family's clothing on her new, indispensable treadle sewing machine. Accidents, often resulting in tetanus, and diseases like malaria were commonplace. Doctors were a rarity. Generally, women provided the rudimentary medical treatment. "Out here," wrote one, "we have to dope ourselves." Few of these women had the luxury of running water or an indoor toilet.

The worst problem for many women (as it was for many men) was the loneliness and isolation of life on the prairie. This remained true despite community and church building and such social events as quilting bees. Even the wife of a successful farmer later wrote of her Kansas homestead, "In all the years we spent there we never could see a neighbor's light in the evening. I did wish so much we could, to relieve the loneliness." An empty cabin in the Texas panhandle displayed a more bitter view, "250 miles to the nearest post office; 100 miles to wood; 20 miles to water; 6 inches to hell...Gone to live with the wife's folks."

The fatiguing labor, the hard water, winter blizzards, burning summer heat, and continual winds made many of these pioneer women look old by thirty. Hamlin Garland, a fine American writer, returned to visit his Iowa hometown in 1887. He was taken by the "sordid struggle and half-hidden despair" he found in every house. The sight of a woman he remembered "in the days of her radiant girlhood," particularly moved him. The burdens of wifehood and motherhood had led to "lovely girlhood wasting away into thin and hopeless age."

While women's lives remained difficult and women's roles largely traditional, Western states were more supportive of women's rights. Perhaps as a result of the important part women played in Western settlement or in hopes of attracting the stabilizing influence of more women, Western states were the first to grant women the vote. In the 1890s, Wyoming, Utah, Colorado, and Idaho were the only states to approve of women's suffrage. By 1914, Washington,

A wagonload of sod bricks stands ready for roof repairs on this sod house.

California, Oregon, Arizona, Kansas, Nevada, and Montana had enfranchised women. All of these states were in the trans-Missouri West.

Farmers' Grievances and Politics

Western farmers were keenly aware that something was seriously wrong in their world. The main cause of farmers' problems was, probably, declining prices for their crops, a result of overproduction. But overproduction and dependence on world markets seemed distant and abstract to most farmers. They sought more comprehensible and tangible explanations for their woes. One writer summed up the views of many when he declared that something was radically wrong with the system: "The railroads have never been so prosperous, and yet agriculture languishes. The banks have never done a better...business and yet agriculture languishes. Manufacturing enterprises never made more money,...and yet agriculture languishes."

The farmers' greatest grievance was against the railroads. They were totally dependent on noncompetitive railroads to ship their products. It seemed to them that the railroads were charging higher rates for farm products than other products and for goods in the West and South than for those in the Northeast. (Railroad officials argued that the sparser population made this differential necessary.) Railroads also ran elevator and warehouse facilities that charged high storage rates. In many western states, railroads controlled the government. As one Oregon senator said about the owner of the Oregon Central Railroad, "Ben Holladay's politics are my politics and what Ben Holladay wants I want."

Farmers also blamed their plight on banks and loan companies that controlled credit. Farmers had taken out loans to expand or buy machinery when farm prices were high. Interest rates ranged from 10 to 25 percent. Many had to pay these loans back at a time when farm prices were declining and currency was scarce. Many agrarian leaders favored increasing the monetary supply to make repayments easier.

Another vital issue involved prices. Farmers had no control over the prices for their crops, which often rose or declined as a result of unpredictable external forces. Usually, they harvested all the crops in one region at the same time. All the farmers had to sell immediately to pay their loans. "Middlemen"—

speculators and local or regional agents—seized the opportunity to get the crops at artificially low prices. Then, they sold when the prices rose. Often, their profit margins exceeded that of the farmer who had labored long and hard hours to produce the product. In addition, while farm prices fluctuated, the prices of manufactured goods the farmer bought remained high as a result of tariffs and eastern monopolies.

Many farmers saw the railroad owners, the bankers, and the monopolists as the villains who had conspired to oppress them. "It is," one declared, "a struggle between the robbers and the robbed."

Some farmers realized that, in an era of economic consolidation, they needed to organize. The first effort to create a national farm organization was the Grange or "Patrons of Husbandry" founded in 1867 to provide education, fellowship, and social interaction. By the 1870s, membership had grown to more than a million. Grangers began to address the economic grievances of the farmers by emphasizing railroad regulation and cooperatives. Grangers successfully lobbied several state legislatures to establish railroad commissions to regulate railroad operations and even fix maximum rates for freight shipments. Cooperative stores purchased directly from manufacturers to eliminate the middleman. Some granges even set up cooperative banks and grain storage elevators.

Granger successes, unfortunately, were not permanent. Lacking adequate capital and management skills, the cooperatives began to fail. Some members supported the Greenback movement, which favored inflation and easier credit by increasing the amount of paper money in circulation. When farm prices experienced a temporary revival after 1878, thousands of farmers deserted the Grange and lost interest in government reform. (The Grange did continue as a social and educational institution that helped to ease the burden of social isolation.)

In an early case, the Supreme Court had upheld "Granger laws," regulating grain elevators and their rates. But in the *Wabash* case of 1886, the Court weakened those laws by prohibiting states from regulating interstate railroad rates. Although Congress responded to this by creating the Interstate Commerce Commission in 1887 to provide federal regulation of railroads, the commission did little to limit the monopolistic practices of railroads. Despite these limitations, the Grange movement laid the groundwork for the more militant agrarian protest movement of the 1890s.

The Populist Movement

In the 1880s farmers' Alliances arose to replace the Grange. At first, these organizations existed largely on paper and devoted their energies to educational and social programs. As the decade wore on, the repeating cycles of declining prices, indebtedness, and limited money supply severely rocketed the chronically poor South and the Great Plains. In the South regional groups joined in the Southern Alliance with a membership variously estimated at 1.5 to 3 million. An affiliated Colored Alliance claimed another million members. The blizzards and droughts that hit the Great Plains in the late 1880s spurred the growth of the Northwestern Alliance.

Years of resentment brought forth impassioned leaders who articulated agrarian grievances. In the South, Alliance leaders like Tom Watson of Georgia urged cooperation between black and white farmers to achieve common goals. In the West, fiery orators advocated radical solutions. These included women like Mary E. Lease, a Kansas lawyer and homesteader. "Wall Street owns the country," she declared. "The West and South are bound and prostrate before the manufacturing East." She implored farmers to "raise less corn and more hell."

In the elections of 1890 the Alliances endorsed candidates who supported their objectives, whether Democrats in the South or independents in the West. They were remarkably successful. In the South, Alliance-endorsed candidates captured four governorships, eight state legislatures, forty-four congressmen, and several senators. On the Great Plains, Alliancemen were able to gain control of four legislatures and elect a governor in Kansas and two senators. In 1892, flushed with their new-found respectability, Alliance leaders from the South and West joined hands in a convention in St. Louis to form the People's or Populist Party. As the party's presidential nominee, they chose James B. Weaver, a former Union general and Greenback nominee for president. As a balance, they picked a former Confederate officer for vice president. The Populists conducted a lively and colorful campaign, described by one observer as a blend of "the French Revolution and a western religious revival."

The party's platform reflected a radical agrarian agenda, derided by some as "hayseed socialism." Populist farmers, as landowners, did not consider themselves socialists. They did believe that "natural monopolies," like the railroads, telegraph, and telephone, should be government-owned and operated to benefit all the people. They favored a more activist federal government that would pay for its programs by instituting a graduated income tax under which the rich would pay a larger percentage of their income. They wanted a flexible currency based on free coinage of silver that would increase the money supply. This would enable farmers to repay their debts, while aiding silver miners. The platform also advocated the "subtreasury plan" to help maintain farm prices. Under this proposal, farmers could borrow government funds at modest interest secured by crops stored in government warehouses. The platform proposed that "excess" land in the hands of railroads be reclaimed to benefit legitimate settlers. Government would be restored "to the hands of the people" by direct election of senators (still elected by state legislatures), the secret ballot, and the initiative and referendum. (These enabled the people directly to propose and enact laws.) To broaden support to the urban worker, the party also favored an eight-hour day and immigration restriction. The preamble to the platform announced: "We seek to restore the government of the Republic to the hands of the 'plain people' with which class it originated."

In the 1892 presidential election, Weaver became the first third-party candidate to garner over a million votes. He carried Kansas, Colorado, Idaho, and Nevada and gained respectable totals in most of the Great Plains. He did not do nearly as well in the older agricultural states or in the East. In the South, Democratic Party leaders successfully appealed to racism and intimidated black voters to lessen Populist support. In the future, Southern politicians, like Tom Watson, who hoped to appeal to poor whites,

Mary E. Lease advised farmers to "raise less corn and more hell."

stayed within the Democratic Party and combined their populism with extreme racism. The following year, however, brought the Panic of 1893, followed by a major depression. The resulting disruptions and discontent made the Populists seem far more dangerous to conservative leaders and gave the party serious expectations for the election of 1896.

As the impact of the depression deepened in both urban and rural areas, public anger at Grover Cleveland and his government reached the boiling point. In the midterm elections of 1894, most voters turned to the Republicans, but Populist votes also increased by more than 40 percent. A book backed by Western silver-mine owners, *Coin's Financial School*, aided their cause. This best-seller argued that "the conspiracy of Goldbugs" caused the misery of the depression. The complicated issue of money was reduced to the simplest of terms: the farmers and the nation could be saved only by the free coinage of silver. Then, property values would increase, the debtor could repay his debts, and the country would revive. Unfortunately, this obsession with silver overshadowed the genuine issues once stressed by the Populists.

The Election of 1896

In 1896, the Republicans nominated William McKinley for president. He was a supporter of big business, high tariffs, and continuation of the gold standard. The silverites won control of the

Democratic Party and nominated a dynamic, young (36-year old), congressman from Nebraska, William Jennings Bryan. Bryan, a fiery orator whose booming voice could be easily heard in the back of the gallery of the huge hall in Chicago, electrified the delegates. In his famous "Cross of Gold" speech, Bryan declared that American prosperity rested upon "our broad and fertile prairies." He scornfully rejected the gold standard, concluding to wildly enthusiastic applause, "You shall not press down upon the brow of labor this crown of thorns, you shall not crucify mankind upon a cross of gold."

Bryan's nomination presented the Populists with a painful dilemma. If they endorsed him, they would lose their identity as a third party. Free silver was only one plank in their extensive platform of reform. But if they ran their own candidate, the reformist vote would split and a conservative Republican would inevitably be elected president. With obvious reluctance, the Populists endorsed Bryan and attempted to show some independence by picking their own candidate for vice president.

The campaign of 1896 was one of the most important and dramatic in American history, offering the voters a clear choice of vastly different platforms. Bryan crisscrossed the nation, traveling over 18,000 miles, and delivering more than 600 free-silver speeches. The dignified McKinley stayed on his front porch in Canton, Ohio. He issued carefully crafted statements while his campaign operated like a well-oiled machine. Republicans successfully pictured Bryan as a dangerous radical whose ideas would bring inflation, raise food prices, and destroy jobs and industry. Employers went as far as to threaten their workers with pink slips if they didn't vote for the Republicans. McKinley won the popular vote by a margin of over 600,000 and the electoral vote by 271 to 176. Bryan carried the South and most of the Great Plains but lost the settled family farmers of the Midwest, as well as the urban centers of the Northeast.

"God's in his heaven, all's right with the world," the Republican campaign manager wired McKinley when he learned of the victory. Bryan's crushing defeat led to a Republican domination of national politics for all but eight of the next thirty-six years. New discoveries of gold ironically caused the very inflation that farmers had expected from silver. Farm prices rose again. In the election of 1900, McKinley, boasting of prosperity and "The Full Dinner Pail," defeated Bryan again, even more decisively.

The election of 1896 destroyed the Populist movement. The more inclusive progressive movement, however, adopted many of its ideas. Some of its "radical" proposals eventually became law, including direct election of senators, a graduated income tax, and farm price supports.

THE WEST IN CULTURE, MYTH AND IMAGINATION

The image of an unsettled and boundless West had long held a special place in the imaginations of both Americans and Europeans. As early as the seventeenth century, the vast interior areas seemed to many to represent both opportunity and refuge. The trans-Missouri West, with its Great Plains, magnificent mountains, incredible deserts, and other wonders, seemed even more spectacular than anything Americans had seen before. Artists of the new "Rocky Mountain School" painted enormous landscapes that were often sent on tours of the country. The new landscape photographers, some of whom accompanied government geological surveys, matched the grandiose visions of the artists. Viewing these magnificent landscapes helped produce a torrent of public support for the creation of national parks. In 1872 Congress responded by creating Yellowstone National Park to preserve for all time, "wonders within said park...in their natural condition."

The romance of the West's natural beauty led to the development of an organized conservation movement to counter the greedy exploitation and destruction of the environment. The most effective publicist for wilderness protection was John Muir, a Scottish immigrant who fell in love with the redwood forests of the Yosemite Valley. He lyrically advised city people to climb mountains: "Nature's peace will flow into you as the sunshine into the trees...cares will drop off like autumn leaves." His efforts brought about the creation of Yosemite National Park in 1890 and the formation in 1892 of the Sierra Club. That organization committed itself to wilderness protection in the Pacific mountain region.

In many ways, the romanticized, individualistic lifestyle they associated with the West enthralled more Americans than its unequaled landscape. The cowboy, ignoring his reality as a low-paid worker, was transformed into a mythical hero, "the knight of the plains." Cheap paperbacks, known as "dime novels," flooded the country from the 1860s to the 1880s. The most popular were "westerns" that emphasized noble, self-reliant heroes who inevitably defeated the forces of evil, whether "savage" Indians or no-good cattle rustlers. They were often written by men who had never left the East. *Buffalo Bill: King of the Border Men* (1869), very loosely based on the experiences of "Buffalo Bill" Cody, was one of the most successful of the dime novels. Over 121 "Buffalo Bill" books followed.

The success of his fictional counterpart led the real Cody to launch his Wild West show in 1883. The show was an enormous popular hit, seen by millions of Americans. Cody promised his enthralled audiences that he was presenting "actual scenes, genuine characters" from the West. He depicted history as a modern morality pageant in which the Western hero repelled Indian attacks. Whites became victims of Indian aggression in the show. Cody's claim that his myth was reality was reinforced by the presence of real Indians, including the most famous of all, Sitting Bull. The shows also presented such glamorous western skills as bronco riding, roping and shooting. (The most admired shooter was Annie Oakley, an Eastern woman, billed as a perfect frontierswoman.) Cody became an international superstar. One bronco rider, who stayed with the cast for seven years, traveled around the world three and a half times on tours. There were two command performances for Queen Victoria of England. Prince Albert of Monaco journeyed all the way to Wyoming for a chance to "kill a grizzly bear or two" with the help of the great Buffalo Bill. Eventually, the demand for the Wild West Show faded. The rodeo developed as replacement entertainment for Americans who still longed for evidence of the courage and pioneer spirit of the West.

The works of three young men, who left their eastern upper class homes to find fulfillment in the part of the country where life was as simple and heroic as the dime novels, supported the legend of the West. Theodore Roosevelt, Frederick Remington, and Owen Wister found what they were looking for in the West. Roosevelt extolled the glories of the frontier in his four volume, *The Winning of the West* (1889-96). Remington, in his paintings and sculptures, depicted heroic white cowboys and Indian-fighters. Wister, a Harvard-educated lawyer, refined the dime novel image of the romantic, manly cowboy in numerous short stories and books. The most famous was *The Virginian*, a gigantic best-seller that sold 50,000 copies in its first two months. The hero, an honest, brave cowboy (who never does any hard physical cowboy work), easily defeats the forces of evil, wins the beautiful school teacher, and becomes a successful businessman.

Even Mark Twain, one of America's greatest authors, reinforced the romantic image of the West as the last escape from the bonds of modern civilization. His 1872 memoir, *Roughing It*, describes his entertaining experiences as a reporter during the Nevada mining boom. His great novel, *The Adventures of Huckleberry Finn* (1882), deals with boyhood on an earlier frontier, a Missouri River town. But the characters' attempts to break away from the repressive forces of order, represent the vision of the West as the last possibility for real freedom.

Probably the clearest statement of this romantic view of the West and the first interpretation of the frontier's importance came in 1893 from Frederick Jackson Turner, a Wisconsin scholar who would become the most eminent historian of his generation. Four years after the Oklahoma land rush had overrun the Indian Territory, the last major tract of Indian land, Turner delivered a paper entitled, "The Significance of the Frontier in American History." In it, he declared that, "the advance of American settlement westward," by white men was the central event of American history. This expansion had brought about opportunities, individualism, and democracy. It had created the distinctive American character. He cited the 1890 census that declared that a continuous frontier line no longer existed. "Now," Turner

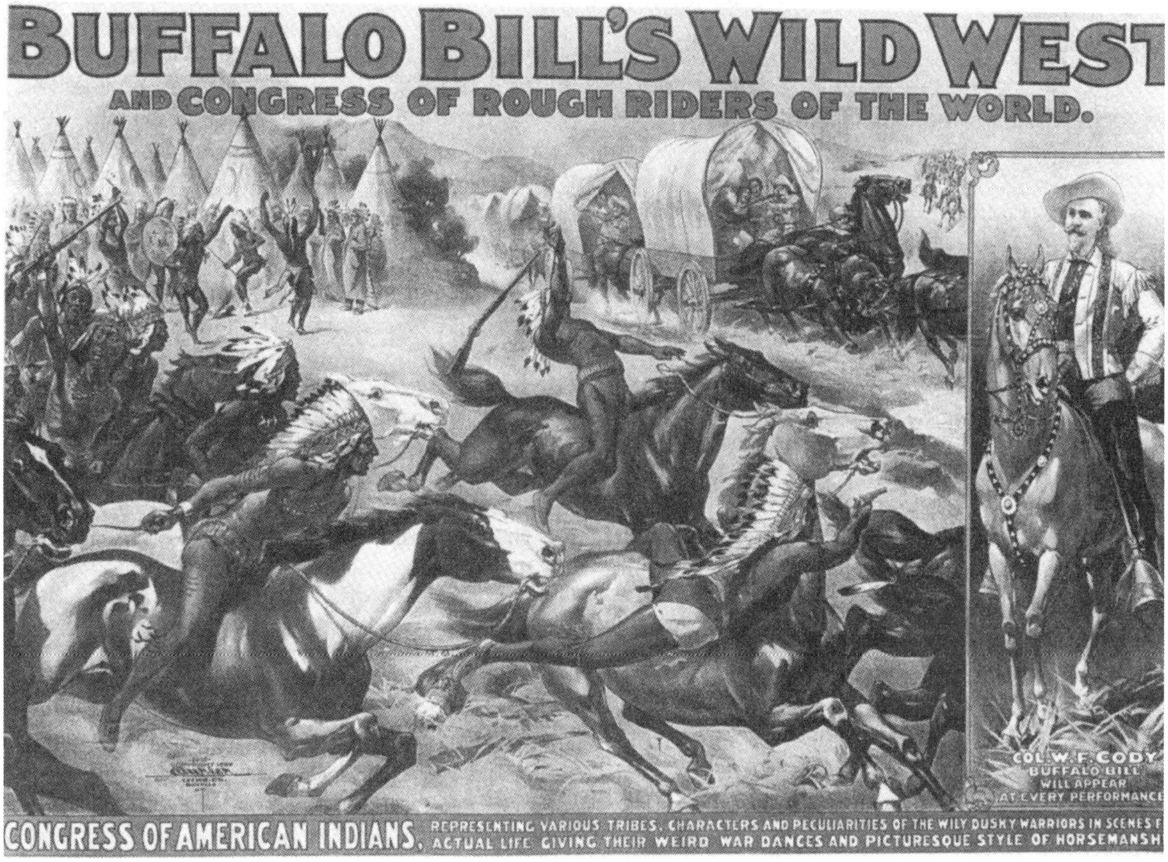

concluded sadly, "the frontier has gone and with its going has closed the first period of American history."

Later historians argued that Turner's "frontier thesis" was inaccurate. It ignores the civilizations of Native Americans and Hispanics that already existed in the supposedly empty spaces of the West. Its emphasis on the feats of brave white men neglects the contributions of women, African Americans, Asians, and others. One historian, who studied the lives of prostitutes in Helena, Montana, found that they were their own bosses, saving and investing their earnings, in the early years. Then, men came in and took control of them and their money. This extremely non-Turnerian view of the marker of the closing of the frontier suggests that, "the frontier ends when the pimps come to town." Triumph and individualism in the real West coexisted with failure, greed, exploitation of resources, and, above all, modern industrial capitalism. There were vast areas of unoccupied land in the West still to be settled Nevertheless, the myth endured. Americans felt a real sense of loss at "the passing of the frontier." Where would opportunities arise in the future? What would happen to America's "Manifest Destiny" now that it had completed the conquest of the continent? Would the eyes of American expansionists now be focused overseas?

CONCLUSION

The myth of the individualistic Westerner continued well past the "closing of the frontier." Later popular writers, such as Zane Grey, continued in the tradition of Owen Wister. With the arrival of motion pictures, the "western" gained renewed popularity. One of the first films was a 1903 western, *The Great Train Robbery*. Movie serials and successful films, as well as radio shows, featured such Western heroes as the Lone Ranger, Tom Mix, Hopalong Cassidy, and

Roy Rogers. "The Virginian" was later made into a popular Gary Cooper movie and a 1960s television series. The great director, John Ford, relied on the works of Frederick Remington for his lighting, costumes, and color. The brave, self-reliant hero who single handedly destroys the forces of evil was reborn in such excellent movies as *Shane* and *High Noon*. Some of the most popular programs in early television were such westerns as "Gunsmoke," "Wyatt Earp," and "Bonanza." The remarkably successful Marlboro Man advertising campaign depicted a rugged cowboy who rode free and was "not about to take advice from Washington bureaucrats like the surgeon general." More recently, the image has shifted from the old West to the new frontier of space where heroes perform feats of equal daring in such epics as *Star Wars*.

Modern historians have painted a more realistic picture of the West. This includes a variety of peoples of both genders and many nationalities and races. Great mining booms often ended as ghost towns. The farmer faced real problems of weather, water, indebtedness, and uncontrollable market forces. They organized in very non-individualistic movements of protest. Native Americans were more often the victims of aggression than the wild savage aggressors of the Wild West show.

Perhaps the children who for generations dressed as cowboys and Indians were the closest to the real West. They were Catholics, Jews and Protestants, black and white, male and female, and from every conceivable ethnic group. Their imaginary West was an amazingly diverse place. But so was the real West of the nineteenth century.

Chronology

1862	Homestead Act Sioux War erupts in Minnesota
1864	Sand Creek massacre of Cheyennes
1867	The Grangers founded—first national farmers' organization Joseph McCoy organizes cattle drives to Abilene, Kansas
1869	First transcontinental railroad completed
1872	Yellowstone National Park established
1873	Giant silver strike discovered at Nevada's Comstock Lode
1874	Gold found in Black Hills of South Dakota Barbed wire invented
1876	Custer and his troops annihilated at Little Big Horn Colorado, the "Centennial State," admitted to the Union
1881	Helen Hunt Jackson writes *A Century of Dishonor*
1880s	Buffalo herds decimated
1883	Buffalo Bill Cody introduces his Wild West show
1886	Droughts and blizzards on the Plains devastate cattle ranching and wheat farming
1887	Dawes Act passed
1889	Indian territory in Oklahoma opened to settlement Ghost Dance religion rises among western Indians
1890	Massacre of Sioux at Wounded Knee, South Dakota
1892	Populist Party formed and receives over a million votes in presidential election
1893	Frederick Jackson Turner, "The Significance of the Frontier in American History" Major economic depression begins
1896	McKinley defeats Bryan

SUGGESTED READINGS

Stephen Ambrose, *Nothing Like it in the World: The Men Who Built the Transcontinental Railroad* (2000).

Susan Armitage and Elizabeth Jameson, eds., *The Woman's West* (1987).

Dee Brown, *Bury My Heart At Wounded Knee* (1970).

William Cronon, et. al., eds, *Under the Open Sky: Rethinking America's Western Past* (1992).

William F. Holmes, *American Populism* (1994).

Julie Jeffrey, *Frontier Women* (1979).

Patricia Nelson Limerick, *The Legacy of Conquest: The Unbroken Past of the American West* (1987).

Robert D. McGrath, *Gunfighters, Highwaymen, and Vigilantes* (1984).

Robert C. McMath, *American Populism: A Social History* (1993).

Clyde Milner, et. al., eds., *The Oxford History of the American West* (1994).

Nell Irvin Painter, *The Exodusters* (1977).

Rodman W. Paul, *The Far West and the Great Plains in Transition, 1859-1900* (1988).

Robert E. Riegel and Robert G. Athearn, *America Moves West* (1971).

David Roberts, *Once They Moved Like the Wind: Cochise, Geronimo, and the Apache Wars* (1993).

William R. Savage, *The Cowboy Hero* (1986).

Fred A. Shannon, *The Farmer's Last Frontier, 1860-1897* (1945).

Henry Nash Smith, *Virgin Land: The West as Symbol and Myth* (1978).

T.J. Stiles, *Jesse James: Last Rebel of the Civil War* (2002).

Robert Utley, *The Indian Frontier of the American West, 1846-1890* (1984).

___, *The Lance and the Shield: The Life and Times of Sitting Bull* (1993).

Richard White and Patricia N. Limerick, *The Frontier in American Culture (1994).*

Teddy Roosevelt, San Juan Hill in Cuba

Chapter Fifteen

THE IMPERIAL REPUBLIC

In January 1899, the United States Senate was locked in an intense, often acrimonious debate, over whether to ratify the Treaty of Paris, officially ending the recent war with Spain, allegedly fought for the liberation of Cuba. While the politicians argued, thousands of United States soldiers, half-way around the world, were engaged in a vicious, brutal guerrilla war against Filipino rebels, wanting the same thing their Cuban counterparts had longed for—independence. Unfortunately for both groups, neither would receive their independence for decades to come. Both countries became the victims of eventual U.S. colonialism. Ironically, only a few weeks before, Americans and Filipinos had been allies, together defeating the Spanish to liberate the Philippines. The American fleet under Admiral George Dewey had destroyed the Spanish naval squadron in Manila Bay on May 1, 1898. Three weeks later, a U.S. warship brought from exile the Filipino insurrectionary Emilio Aguinaldo to lead rebel forces on land while the United States' gunboats patrolled the seas.

At first, the Filipinos believed the Americans to be their liberators. Although U.S. intentions were never clear, Aguinaldo believed, like his Cuban counterparts, that the Americans had no imperial ambitions; their purpose was pure and altruistic—to help liberate an oppressed people. They would simply drive the Spanish out and then leave the Philippines to the self-determination of the Filipino people. In June, Aguinaldo declared Philippine independence and began setting up a constitutional government. U.S. officials completely discounted the independence ceremonies. When an armistice ended the war in August, American troops denied Aguinaldo's Filipino soldiers an opportunity to liberate their own capital city and shunted them off to the suburbs. The armistice agreement recognized American rights to the "harbor, city, and bay of manila," while the proposed Treaty of Paris gave the United States the entire Philippine Islands archipelago.

When news of the U.S. "acquisition" of the islands reached Filipinos, they protested in the streets of Manila and elsewhere. This was not what they believed would happen. They now viewed Americans, especially the troops stationed there, as an army of occupation, which, in effect, it was. Tensions between American and Filipino soldiers escalated to the point that the streets of Manila became a war zone as both sides dug into trenches span-

ning 14 miles through the city. Taunts, obscenities, and racial epithets were shouted across the neutral zone. Barroom skirmishes and knife fights between the soldiers became "normal" occurrences and "pastimes." American soldiers wantonly searched houses without warrants and looted stores. Their behavior was completely unjustified and deplorable.

On the night of February 4, 1899, Privates William Grayson and William Miller of Company B, 1st Nebraska Volunteers, were on patrol in Santa Mesa, a Manila suburb surrounded on three sides by insurgent trenches. The Americans had orders to shoot any Filipino soldiers who were in the neutral area. As the two Americans cautiously worked their way to a bridge over the San Juan River, they heard a Filipino signal whistle, answered by another. Then a red lantern flashed from a nearby blockhouse. The two froze as four Filipinos emerged from the darkness on the road ahead. "Halt!" Grayson shouted. The native lieutenant in charge answered "Halto!"— either mockingly or because he had similar orders. Standing less than fifteen feet apart, the two men repeated their commands. After a moment's hesitation, Grayson fired, killing his Filipino "ally" with one bullet. As the other Filipinos jumped out at them, Grayson and Miller "opened up" and shot two more. As they fired at the Filipinos, Grayson exulted that he shot "my first nigger." While three Filipino soldiers laid dying in the streets of their own city, killed by men supposedly their friends and comrades-in-arms, Grayson and Miller ran back to their own lines shouting warnings of attack. Within minutes of Grayson's and Miller's return, the Filipinos retaliated, launching a full-scale attack in revenge for the murder of their cohorts.

The next day, Commodore Dewey cabled Washington that the "insurgents have inaugurated general engagement" and promised a quick and decisive suppression of the insurrection. The outbreak of hostilities ended the Senate debates, which had up to this point favored the rejection of the treaty for its obvious imperialist ramifications. But now, with the beginning of a full-fledged revolt against U.S. subjugations, those senators who were wavering voted to support the treaty for they could not vote against it while American soldiers were so engaged. On February 6, 1899, the Senate ratified the Treaty of Paris, thus formally annexing the Philippines and sparking a war between the United States and Aguinaldo's Filipino revolutionaries who represented a small percentage of the population.

In a guerrilla war similar to those fought in the twentieth century in Eastern Asia, Filipino nationalists tried to undermine the American will by hit-and-run attacks. American soldiers, meanwhile, remained in heavily garrisoned cities and undertook search-and-destroy missions to root out rebels and pacify the countryside. The Filipino-American War lasted until 1902, three years longer than the Spanish-American War that caused it and involving far more troops, casualties, and monetary and moral costs. The United States won its first encounter with a nationalist uprising fought by guerrillas. However, the nation would not be as lucky in its next foray, some sixty years later. In that conflict, against a similarly motivated adversary, the United States would ultimately be defeated. In the aftermath of that "shock," Americans confronted a new reality that forced them to accept the fact that American might and righteousness no longer automatically guaranteed victory, even against an alleged "inferior" foe. In the end, the Vietnam conflict proved that a people's desire for the right of self-determination regardless of the power arrayed against them, if they persevered, they would triumph. Ironically, both the Filipinos and the Vietnamese borrowed a page from the history of the United States, a nation born in a war of national liberation but a nation that forgot its own history somewhere along the way.

AMERICA'S QUEST FOR EMPIRE 1880-1900

The United States had been an expansionist nation since its inception. Throughout the first half of the nineteenth-century, as the nation's population grew and pressed westward, the national government accommodated the movement by continually acquiring, either by purchase or by force, new territory: the trans-Appalachian West, the Louisiana Purchase, Florida, Texas, Oregon, the former Mexican Borderlands of California, Nevada, New Mexico, Arizona, Colorado, and, after the Civil War, Alaska. After the Louisiana Purchase, the second largest territory acquired was that taken from Mexico in the nation's first imperialist war justified by the rhetoric of "Manifest Destiny," which has since become a label for the whole complex of attitudes, concepts, and actions that swept American dominion to the shores of the Pacific Ocean. At the heart of this impulse was an exuberant faith in the democratic creed: Anglo-Americans were a chosen race, and their appointed mission was to extend the area of "freedom." As will be seen later in this chapter, late nineteenth-century imperialists resurrected Manifest Destiny and applied its basic tenets to justify the United States' need to expand beyond the confines of the North American continent in pursuit of an empire. By the end of the century, American hegemony was established in the Western Hemisphere as well as in the Pacific rim. Motivating many Americans to engage in an aggressive, acquisitive foreign policy was the desire to see the United States take its rightful place among the world's great powers, many of whom were themselves intensely involved in drives for empire (most notably England, France, Germany, and Japan) to either expand their existing dominions or, as in the case of Germany and the United States, to "join the imperialist club." By the end of the century, the drive for empire among the great powers, which will include the United States, will bring much of the underdeveloped world under the control of the Western industrial nations.

Voices for Expansion

Several different groups helped to promote American imperialism. One of the earliest and most vociferous were Protestant missionaries. Integration of the world economy made evangelical Protestants, like most Americans, more conscious of the diversity of the world's peoples. Overseas missionary activity intensified between 1870 and 1900, most of it directed toward China, which saw increasing numbers of Western, including American missionaries, penetrate that nation in an attempt to convert the Chinese to Christianity. Convinced of their superiority, Anglo-Saxon Americans and Englishmen considered it their Christian duty to teach the Gospel to the "ignorant" Asian masses and save their souls. Missionaries also believed that their proselytizing would help to "civilize" and "uplift" an inferior people, who resembled the immigrant masses at home whom they were also trying to "redeem." Thus, American imperialism—as well England's—will be imbued with a sense of righteous duty incumbent upon civilized Christian nations to bring "enlightenment" and "freedom" to the "heathen" and supposedly save them from themselves.

American industrial capitalists and investors also played key roles in promoting overseas expansion, hoping to increase business profits and their personal fortunes in foreign lands. The Asian market was especially alluring to such men, who believed that China, with its 400 million people, was a potential "gold mine" of opportunity. By the late 1880s, James B. Duke, head of American Tobacco, was selling one billion cigarettes a year in East Asian markets. Looking for ways to fill boxcars for his Northern Pacific Railroad, heading west from Minnesota to Tacoma, Washington, J. J. Hill wanted to load them with wheat and steel destined for China and Japan. He actually published and distributed wheat cookbooks throughout East Asia, trying to convince the people there to change their diets and eat less rice and more bread, which he believed would make them "healthier!" Although export trade with East Asia during this period never fulfilled Hill's or others' expectations, their promotion of Asia as a source of great potential markets for the United States convinced many politicians and imperialists that this part of the world was important to the national well-being.

The economic crises of the 1890s also intensified the clamor for foreign markets. The capitalists' agitation for material expansion was reinforced ideologically by one of the most original and important historical theories ever promulgated within the confines of American academic and intellectual circles: Frederick Jackson Turner's "frontier thesis." By 1890, which that year's census revealed, the United States had completed the task of internal westward movement. In 1893, Turner, an assistant professor of history at the University of Wisconsin, published his seminal essay, "The Significance of the Frontier in American History," that articulated what many of Turner's fellow citizens feared: that the frontier had been essential to the nation's economic growth and to the cultivation of democracy. It had provided (white) Americans, filled with wanderlust, an opportunity to own land, which was once in abundance. The fact that land was in such plentiful supply helped to relieve the nation of potential social unrest born of class tensions created by economic inequities. Simply put, as long as there was the frontier, Americans could escape the congested cities and wretched factories and start anew somewhere in the West on their own land. It was in the wilderness, Turner argued, that the American identity was born because that environment forced Europeans coming to the New World to transform themselves into different human beings if they hoped to survive and "make it." As they adapted to the wilderness, the Europeans slowly but steadily shed all their Old World customs, habits, and beliefs and over the decades acquired uniquely "American" characteristics—rugged individualism, egalitarianism, and a democratic faith. Now that the frontier was allegedly "closed," Turner and others wondered could the United States continue to prosper and provide its citizens with the stability and security that had long been the hallmarks of its historical development?

In recent years, historians of the American West have disavowed Turner's thesis, arguing that the very idea of the frontier as uninhabited wilderness negates the fact that already living in the West for thousands of years were tens of thousands of Native Americans. They also assert, and rightly so, that today and even in Turner's time, much of what Americans believed about the West had been highly romanticized and distorted: more myth than reality. Contrary to what Turner claimed, the West was still a very undeveloped region by the 1890s and thus provided Americans with ample opportunity to exploit for their own aggrandizement. Indeed, as will be seen in a later chapter, it was not until the 1930s and after World War II that Western resources were fully exploited and the region developed.

Even though modern historians' assessments of Western development are accurate, they would have meant very little to Turner's contemporaries. For them, as for Turner, concern about the disappearing frontier expressed a fear that the increasingly urbanized and industrialized nation had lost its way. Turner's essay appeared just as the country was entering the deepest, longest, and most conflict-ridden depression and decade in its history. What could the republic do to regain its economic prosperity and political stability? Where would it find its new "safety valve" frontiers that would save the nation from upheaval and renew the people's faith in the great democratic republican experiment? One answer to these questions came from the proponents of overseas expansion. As Senator Albert J. Beveridge of Indiana declared in 1899: "We are raising more than we can consume. . . .We are making more than we can use. Therefore, we must find new markets for our produce, we must find new occupation for our capital, new work for our labor."

Whatever the effect of such physical phenomena as the expansion of the American frontier to the Pacific Ocean and the enrichment of the nation's economy, much of the impetus for overseas expansion in the last third of the nineteenth century was mental. Old political ideas like the Monroe Doctrine were imbued with more expansionist overtones, and newer ones like manifest destiny offered spiritual sustenance for aggressive behavior. Proliferating theories of racial superiority, buttressed by science or pseudoscience, became accepted "wisdom." Regardless of class or education, the majority of WASP Americans believed their country had a special mission, sanctified by geography and race, to lead and dominate the "unfit" and the "uncivilized" peoples of the world.

The Imperialists

Eager to assist the expansionist capitalists who believed that the acquisition of overseas markets would be the panacea for the nation's economic woes were a group of politicians, intellectuals, and military strategists who viewed such expansion (the acquisition of territory) as essential for great power status. They wanted the nation to take its place alongside Britain, France, Germany, and Russia as a great imperial nation. They believed that the United States should join the intensifying competition among the major European powers for colonies; it should build a strong navy, solidify a sphere of influence in the Caribbean, and extend markets into Asia, just as the Europeans were doing, not only in that region of the world but in Africa and the Middle East as well. Indeed, by the late nineteenth century only one independent nation existed in Africa—Ethiopia. The rest of the continent had been carved up by the European powers. Even tiny Belgium had a "piece of the action," controlling the resource-rich present-day nation, the Congo, while France possessed geographically the largest empire in Africa, even though most of it was desert. Watching the European superpowers carve up the world were the envious American imperialists who began agitating for the United States to get into the race for empire while "the gittin' was still good."

The imperialists, to justify their new outlook, resurrected the pre-Civil War rhetoric of manifest destiny that now became consonant with imperialism; indeed, they were now one-in-the-same. John Fiske, noted American anthropologist and imperialist, as well as a popular lecturer, toured the country giving a set-piece presentation entitled "Manifest Destiny." Fiske asserted that "The work the English race began when it colonized North America is destined to go on until every land on the earth's surface that is not already the seat of an old civilization shall become English in its language, in its religion, in its political habits and traditions, and to a predominant extent in the blood of its people."

As noted in the previous chapter, Darwinian theory was distorted to reinforce the cult of capitalism, allowing plutocrats like Rockefeller and Carnegie a way to justify their ruthless acquisitiveness and their brutal exploitation of their workers. The imperialists also found ideological succor from Social Darwinism to bolster their expansionist assertions. Implicit in Social Darwinism was the claim of Anglo-Saxon racial superiority. The imperialists were overwhelming of such ethnic/racial stock and thus held that America's democratic institutions—i.e., the New England town meeting—came not from ancient Greece but from early German tribes via England. They quickly incorporated Darwinism into their new approach to imperialism. The peripatetic Fiske argued that Anglo-Saxon expansion, based on Teutonic theories of democracy, justified any conquest.

The most popular propagator of Anglo-Saxonism/imperialism was the Protestant evangelical, Josiah Strong, whose paean to Anglo-Saxonism, *Our Country*, was a national bestseller in the late 1880s. In his book, Strong asserted that "the wonderful progress of the United States as well as the character of its people, are the results of natural selection." For Strong and his disciples, the Anglo-Saxon race represented civil liberty and "pure spiritual Christianity." North America was to be "the great home of the Anglo-Saxon, the principal seat of his power, the center of his life and influence." With its obvious genetic and biological superiority, the Anglo-Saxon race "will spread itself over the earth" to Mexico, to Central and South America, and "out upon the islands of the sea" to Africa and beyond. Feeling no remorse for the "inferior races" doomed by the Anglo-Saxon advance, Strong asked rhetorically, "Is there room for reasonable doubt that his race, unless devitalized by alcohol and tobacco, is destined to dispossess many weaker races, assimilate others, and mold the remainder, until, in a very true and important sense, it has Anglo-Saxonized mankind?"

Strong's sanctimonious boosterism and racism would be easy to dismiss as rubbish if it had not been so popular with the nation's increasingly anxious (because of immigration) Anglo-Saxon masses or if his rantings had not been embraced and articulated in the classrooms and lecture halls of some of the nation's best universities. Unfortunately, late nineteenth century American academic institutions lacked today's student diversity, and thus those sitting in the classrooms were overwhelming young WASP males, who wholeheartedly concurred with their professors who preached white, Anglo-Saxon supremacy and the need for their race to dominate all others to prevent the "mongrelization" of humanity. Darwin, to his chagrin, set scholars scrambling to determine racial superiority by measuring facial angles, skull size, brain weight, and even human hair. There was hardly a major university in the United States that did not include racially based courses in its core curriculum. To the imperialists/Social Darwinists, success in international competition and conquest reflected the laws of nature. America's destiny required that it prove itself the military equal of the strongest European nations and the master of the "lesser" peoples of the world.

Thus, as the nineteenth century came to a close, the United States was a restless and racist society. Those who believed the myth of Anglo-Saxonism could ascribe inferiority to masses of people at home and abroad: African Americans, Native Americans, workers, immigrants, and most foreigners. Such a cultural atmosphere was extremely conducive to imperialist initiatives, because imperialism—like Anglo-Saxonism, Social Darwinism, and manifest destiny—was also based on the principle of racial inequality.

ADMIRAL ALFRED THAYER MAHAN AND THE RISE OF AMERICAN MILITARISM

Perhaps the most influential imperialist was Admiral Alfred Thayer Mahan, whose seminal work, *The Influence of Sea Power on History, 1660-1783* (1890), laid out the blue-print for the nation's first, most significant peacetime military buildup. In his book, Mahan argued that all the world's great empires, beginning with Rome, sustained their hegemony by controlling the seas. If the United States hoped to attain great power status, it was imperative that it embark immediately on an aggressive expansion and modernization of its navy, with enough ships and fire-power to make its presence felt everywhere in the world. Ironically, during the Civil War, the United States possessed one of the world's largest navies; by the 1880s the United States ranked twelfth behind sleeping China, decrepit Turkey, and tiny Chile. To be effective, that global fleet would require a canal across Central America through which U.S. warships could pass swiftly from the Atlantic to the Pacific Oceans. It would also demand a string of far-flung service bases from the Caribbean to the southwestern Pacific. Mahan thus urged the United States government to take possession of Hawaii and other strategically located Pacific islands with superior harbor facilities.

As will be seen, Presidents William McKinley and Theodore Roosevelt would eventually make almost all of Mahan's vision a reality. In the early 1890s, however, Mahan believed his ideas and exhortations were falling on deaf ears, for he was certain that few Americans were willing to bear the costs and responsibilities of empire. Although the imperialists counted in their ranks prominent individuals like Theodore Roosevelt and Senator Henry Cabot Lodge of Massachusetts, there were still too many Americans who insisted that the United States should not aspire to world power by emulating the Europeans by using military might and force to acquire bases and colonies. Such an approach, they believed, would not only "degrade" the United States, putting the nation on the same "level" as the Europeans, but tarnish, as well, the revered image of a country whose people were known for their sense of justice, decency, and humanity.

Mahan's skepticism quickly dissipated as the government's alarm over the Europeans' expansionist policies moved both Congress and the presidents to action. Every administration from the 1880s on committed itself to a "big navy" policy. By 1898 the U.S. navy had moved from twelfth to fifth in the world; by 1900 it ranked third, behind only England and Germany. Already in 1878, under the farsighted auspices of the "Plumed Knight," James G. Blaine, who was serving as Secretary of State for Rutherford B. Hayes, the United States secured rights to Pago Pago, a superb deepwater harbor in Samoa (a collection of islands in the southwest Pacific inhabited by Polynesians).

These attempts to project U.S. power overseas had already deepened the government's involvement in the affairs of foreign lands. For example, four years after securing harbor rights to Pago Pago, in 1889, the United States established a protectorate (the "uniquely" American term for "colony") over part of Samoa, a move intended to block German and British attempts to weaken American presence and influence on the islands.

In the early 1890s, Grover Cleveland was increasingly drawn into Hawaiian affairs, as tensions between American sugar planters and native Hawaiians upset the islands' economic and political stability. In other words, by that decade, a small but powerful coterie of American sugar planters had pretty much gained economic and thus political control of the islands, relegating the native population to an underclass of subservient lackeys. Tensions between native Hawaiians and whites began as early as the 1820s when American missionaries arrived to try to convert the islanders to Christianity. In the process they began buying up huge parcels of land and to subvert the existing feudal system of landholding. They simultaneously encouraged American businesses to buy into sugar plantations, and by 1875 U.S. corporations dominated the sugar trade. American capitalists, in effect, turned the islands into one vast sugar-producing economy, which they completely controlled. By this time Hawaii appeared in James G. Blaine's opinion to be "an outlying district of the state of California," and he began to push for annexation. In 1887 a new treaty allowed the United States to build a naval base at Pearl Harbor on the island of Oahu. Now, together with Pago Pago, the United States had two Pacific fueling stations for its growing naval fleet.

Emboldened by the Pearl Harbor treaty, American sugar planters took a step further toward hopeful annexation by overthrowing a weak king, Kalakaua, and replacing him with the more pliant Queen Liliuokalani, whom they believed would be their puppet. Queen "Lili," however, chose not to become their lackey and tried to assert her independence. The planters were determined to control the islands, and under the leadership of pineapple magnate, Sanford B. Dole, and with the help of U.S. sailors, the planters overthrew the queen in 1893. The planters then put pressure on Cleveland to make Hawaii a protectorate, which he did in that same year. Congressional imperialists wanted the president to outright annex the islands, but Cleveland refused to acquiesce to their demands. In 1900, however, during the presidency of William McKinley, Hawaii was officially annexed as a territory of the United States. The native Hawaiians were not consulted about this momentous change in their national identity.

By this time, imperialist sentiment in Congress and throughout the nation was being energized by "jingoism." Jingoists—the word was originally coined in Great Britain in the 1870s and quickly entered American foreign policy parlance—were supernationalists (hardcore Social Darwinists as well) who believed that an aggressive, arrogant foreign policy with a willingness to go to war would enhance the nation's glory. They were constantly on the alert for insults to their country's honor and prestige and swift to call for military retaliation if so affronted. This predatory brand of nationalism emerged not only in Britain and in the United States, but in France, Germany, and Japan as well. The anti-imperialist editor, E.L. Godkin, of *The Nation* exclaimed in 1894, "The number of men and officials in this country who are now mad to fight somebody is appalling." Spain's behavior in Cuba in the 1890s gave the imperialists the war they sought. The imperialists had grown up in a period of weak presidents, an exploding economy, escalating military power, rising expectations, and disappointing performance. Now the time for action was fast approaching, and they would seize it.

President William McKinley

THE SPANISH-AMERICAN WAR

By the 1890s the islands of Cuba and Puerto Rico were virtually all that remained of Spain's once vast New World empire. Ever since the late 1860s the Cubans had been in a constant state of revolt against Spanish rule. Though ultimately suppressing the early uprisings, by the late 1890s, the Spanish were finding it increasingly more difficult to subdue the Cuban rebels, whose numbers were growing each year. Interestingly, helping to ignite the 1895 insurrection was a tariff passed by the United States a year earlier that made sugar, Cuba's main export, too expensive for the

U.S. market. The tariff caused economic contraction, which in turn only intensified Cubans' resentment toward their Spanish rulers, even though they had not caused the depression. The fighting between Spanish soldiers and Cuban rebels was brutal, as both sides often committed unspeakable atrocities. The rebels razed large areas of the island, not only destroying tobacco and sugar crops but making it uninhabitable as well. The Spanish army retaliated, responding in kind on the orders of General Valeriano Weyler, who rounded up thousands of Cubans and "relocated" them into concentration camps where they were horribly mistreated, causing thousands to die. Indeed, an estimated 200,000 Cubans—one-eighth of the island's population—died of starvation and disease.

Such reprisals, especially those attributed to "Butcher" Weyler (as he was now being labeled in the U.S. press), inflamed American public opinion. Many Americans sympathized with the Cubans, whom they believed were fighting the same anti-colonial war they themselves had waged against another "effete" European power over 100 years earlier. The American public was kept well-apprised of events in Cuba, especially in the newspapers published by either William Randolph Hearst or Joseph Pulitzer, who together owned the majority of the nation's largest dailies. Pulitzer and Hearst were revolutionizing American journalism in the late nineteenth century by creating a new kind of newspaper, which catered openly to a readership of lower socioeconomic status than those citizens who read the more traditional press. In short, they created the first tabloids, which today can be seen in every supermarket check-out stand around the nation. Like today's *National Enquirer*, and other such publications, Hearst's and Pulitzer's papers specialized in lurid, sensational news; when such news did not exist, editors were not above making it up. All such presentation was designed to boost circulation, which meant more money for Hearst and Pulitzer. By the 1890s, both men were engaged in a ruthless circulation war, and they saw the struggle in Cuba as a great opportunity. Both sent hordes of reporters and illustrators to the island with orders to provide accounts of Spanish atrocities committed on innocent Cubans. All too frequently Hearst and Pulitzer reporters greatly exaggerated or distorted what was actually taking place in Cuba, if not blatantly fabricating stories to please their greedy publishers. They were accused by the legitimate press of engaging in "yellow journalism"—embellishing stories with titillating details when the true reports did not seem dramatic enough. "You furnish the pictures," Hearst supposedly told an overly scrupulous artist, "and I'll furnish the war."

Helping the jingoists and interventionists agitate the American public were the thousands of Cuban émigrés in the United States living primarily in the cities of Miami, Philadelphia, New York, and Trenton, New Jersey. These folk gave extensive support to the Cuban Revolutionary Party, headquartered in New York, and helped to make its slain leader, Jose Marti, a "freedom-fighting" hero and martyr in the eyes of many sympathetic but duped Americans. With the financial backing of prominent American capitalists, Cuban Americans formed other clubs and associations to support the cause of *Cuba Libre.* In some areas of the country, the émigrés' activities and solicitations were more important in garnering popular support for U.S. intervention in Cuba than the falsehoods circulated by the yellow journalists.

The increasing public outcry against alleged Spanish brutality and imperialist agitation for U.S. intervention in Cuba failed to move President Grover Cleveland to action. He proclaimed American neutrality and urged New York City officials to muzzle Cuban émigrés there who were trying to rally New Yorkers to the cause of Cuban independence. Cleveland's Republican successor, William McKinley, elected in 1896, appeared more amenable to the jingoists' and imperialists' cries for intervention in Cuba. Soon after taking office, McKinley formally protested Spain's "uncivilized and inhuman" behavior, causing the Spanish government (which was growing more fearful of American intervention) to recall Weyler, significantly modify its "relocation" policy, and grant Cubans limited autonomy. At the end of 1897, because of the concessions granted by the Spanish, the insurrection abated and for the moment it seemed that U.S. intervention might be averted. The jingoists and imperialists naturally believed that it was their "saber-rattling" that had caused Spain to capitulate and modify their Cuban policy. To a degree they were correct; the Spanish government, as will be seen shortly, wanted to avoid a war with the United States at all costs—a war Spain knew it could not win.

Unfortunately, the events of February 1898 mitigated the chances for a peaceful settlement. The first crisis occurred with the publication in U.S. papers of the de Lome letter, a communiqué written by the Spanish minister in Washington, Dupuy de Lome, that had been stolen by a Cuban agent in Havana and "somehow" found its way into American dailies. In this private correspondence, de Lome described McKinley as a weak man and "a bidder for the admiration of the crowd." Interestingly, many Americans felt the same way about McKinley, including fellow Republican Theodore Roosevelt, who declared the president as having "no more backbone than a chocolate éclair." Americans accepted as part of partisan politics the right of citizens to openly criticize their president. But no "foreigner" was allowed such freedom, and if one had the audacity to do so, they would quickly incur the wrath of the American public. Such was the situation for Dupuy de Lome, who promptly resigned after reading his comments in American newspapers.

While anger over the de Lome letter was still high, the U.S. battleship *Maine* blew up in Havana harbor, causing the death of 260 sailors. McKinley had sent the *Maine* into Havana harbor in late 1897 to protect U.S. citizens and property from supposed Spanish loyalists' attacks. No sooner did the ship explode, than the jingoists and imperialists screamed "retribution" and agitated for war. They were certain that the Spanish had sunk the ship, particularly after a hastily assembled naval court of inquiry declared (inaccurately) that an external explosion by a submarine mine had caused the disaster. Later evidence established that the incident occurred as a result of an accidental explosion in the engine rooms. Regardless of the true cause, at the time, sufficient numbers of Americans were convinced it was the dastardly act of the evil Spanish, and thus war hysteria swept the land and Congress, responding to the public clamor for retaliation, unanimously appropriated $50 mil-

The U. S. battleship, *Maine*, exploded in Havana harbor. The ship was destroyed and all of the crew still aboard were killed. "Remember the Maine" became the battle cry.

lion for military preparations. Echoing the rallying cry used in Texas by Anglo-Americans some sixty years earlier—"Remember the Alamo"— to defeat an equally perfidious "Latin" people, the Mexicans, "Remember the *Maine*" became the new Anglo-American mantra for revenge against the Spanish.

McKinley still hoped to avoid a conflict; others in his administration, including Assistant Secretary of the Navy, Theodore Roosevelt, clamored for war. In March 1898, the president notified the Spanish government of his conditions for avoiding war: Spain would pay an indemnity for the *Maine,* abandon its concentration camp policy, end the fighting with the rebels, and commit itself to Cuban independence. On April 9, Spain agreed to all the demands but one—Cuban independence. Though McKinley was inclined to accept Spain's bid for peace, the jingoist/imperialist pressure from within his administration and from the public was too great for him to withstand. Jingoist and imperialist propaganda had been successful in whipping the American public into a war frenzy; nothing short of a violent display of new American power would satisfy the American people. Moreover, the nation's new war machines, especially the navy, had been modernized at great expense and now the opportunity presented itself to see whether it was sufficient enough to earn the United States the respect it deserved as a great power. In short, the imperialists believed it was essential for the U.S. to go to war; if Spain simply acquiesced to American demands then the nation would not have the opportunity to demonstrate its awesome military power nor the "virility," "masculinity," and martial spirit of its people. There was no better way to show the other great powers that the United States had "arrived" militarily and economically than to unleash upon another country its new war machines and in a brief, decisive war earn an empire. Thus, on April 11, 1898, McKinley asked Congress for authority to go to war. Three days later Congress approved a war resolution, which included a declaration (spelled out in the Teller Amendment) that the United States would not use the war as an opportunity to acquire Cuba. On April 24, Spain responded with a formal declaration of war against the United States.

"A Splendid Little War"

Secretary of State John Hay called the Spanish-American conflict "a splendid little war," a view most Americans—with the exception of the actual combatants—seemed to share. Declared in April 1898, it was over by August of that year. The war was so brief largely because the Cuban rebels, after years of fighting, had significantly weakened Spanish forces on the island, thus making U.S. intervention in many respects nothing more than a "mopping up" operation. Out of the one million men who volunteered to fight, only 460 were killed in battle or died from wounds. However, 5,200 others perished from diseases such as malaria, dysentery, and typhoid, to name just a few. Casualties among the Cuban rebel forces who continued to bear the brunt of the fighting were much higher.

Another factor contributing to the relatively easy American victory was U.S. naval superiority. In the war's first major battle, a naval engagement in Manila harbor on May 1, 1898, in the Philippines, Spain's strategic Pacific possession, a U. S. fleet commanded

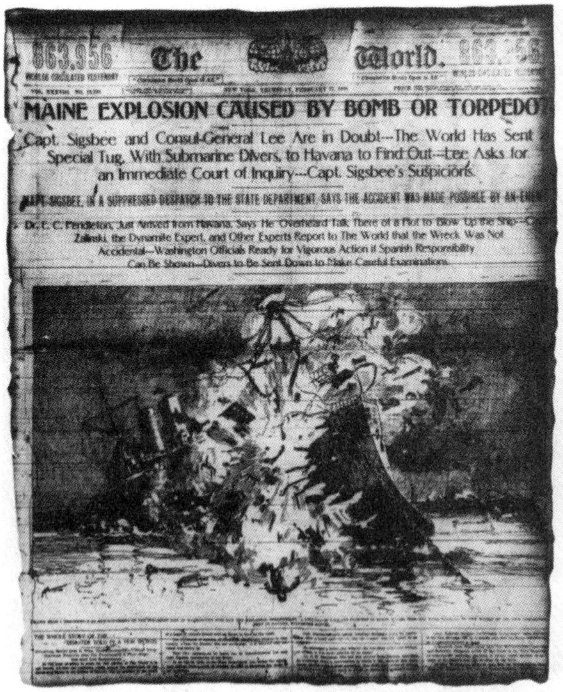
863,956 The World.

MAINE EXPLOSION CAUSED BY BOMB OR TORPEDO

Capt. Sigsbee and Consul-General Lee Are in Doubt--The World Has Sent Special Tug, With Submarine Divers, to Havana to Find Out--Lee Asks for an Immediate Court of Inquiry--Capt. Sigsbee's Suspicions.

Newspapers printed sensational headline stories, stirring up the public to go to war with Spain as pictured in here in Joseph Pulitzer's *New York World.*

by Commodore George Dewey, destroyed an entire Spanish fleet while losing only a sailor (to heat stroke). In mid-August, U.S. troops occupied the capital, Manila. On land the story was different as the nation went to war with a standing U.S. Army of only 26,000 troops, which were scattered throughout the western United States, whose only combat experience had been skirmishing with Indians and chasing down bandits and other desperadoes. In short, the army was ill-equipped and ill-prepared to fight an all-out war. Even though Spain was not a great power, nor even remotely close to even pretending to be one, it nonetheless was going to fight to try to keep the last vestiges of its once vast empire, and thus greeting American forces on Cuba was a Spanish army of 80,000 regulars. Congress immediately increased the Army to 62,000 and called for an additional 125,000 volunteers. The response to this call was astounding but outfitting, training, and transporting the new recruits overwhelmed the Army's capacities. United States soldiers endured serious supply problems: a shortage of modern rifles and ammunition, having to wear blue flannel uniforms, totally inappropriate attire for the hot, humid Caribbean weather, inadequate medical services, and food rations so bad that many soldiers died from food poisoning! It took more than five days in June to ship an invasion force of 16,000 men the short distance from Tampa, Florida to Daiquiri, Cuba.

There were also racial conflicts. A significant number of the combatants, whether they were volunteers or regular army, were African Americans. In the regular army there were black regiments who had been stationed in the West to defend white settlements from Indian raids and were now transferred east to fight in Cuba. As the "Buffalo Soldiers" trav-

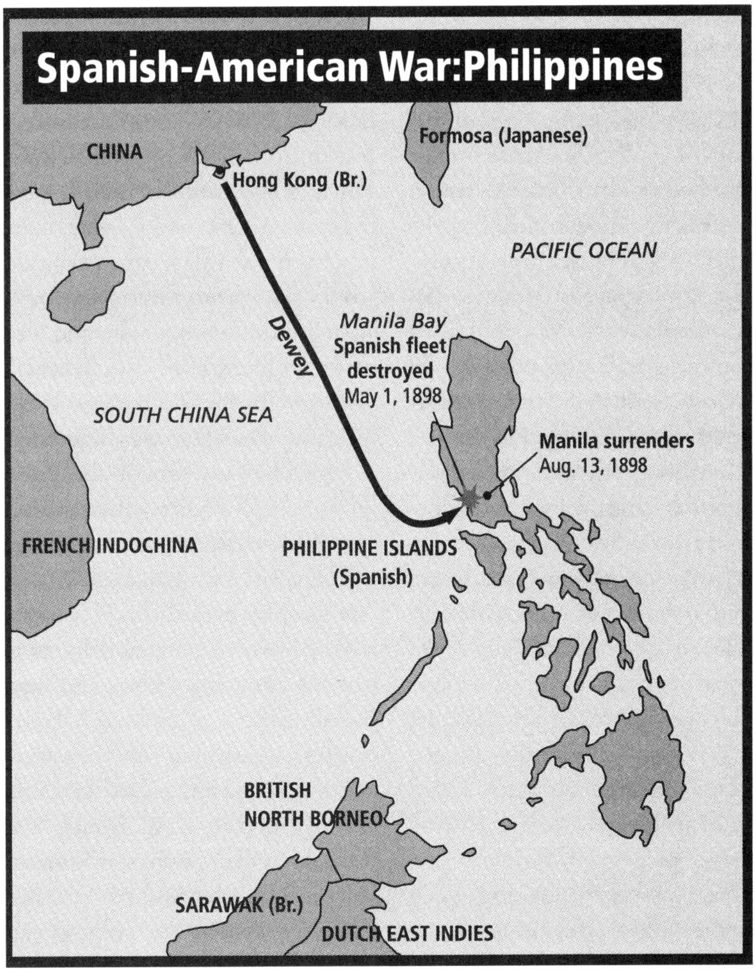

eled through the South toward the training camps, they resented the rigid segregation and name-calling they were subjected to and occasionally fought back. Black soldiers in Georgia deliberately camped out in a "whites-only" park; in Florida, they beat a white soda-fountain worker who refused to serve them; in Tampa, attempted white intimidations provoked a black retaliation that resulted in a nightlong black-white confrontation that left thirty white civilians wounded.

Another interesting and ironic racist taint to the war was the fact that the majority of the Cuban guerrilla fighters were black. This shocked U.S. forces because they believed the Cuban "freedom-fighters, fully nine-tenths of them," were white because U.S. newspaper reports had described them as "intelligent, civilized, and democratic, possessing an Anglo-Saxon tenacity of purpose." The Spanish oppressors, by contrast, were portrayed as dark complexioned—"dark, cruel eyes, dark swaggering men," is how the writer Sherwood Anderson depicted them—and possessing the characteristics of their "dark race": barbarism, cruelty, and indolence. The U.S. troops' first encounters with Cuban and Spanish forces dispelled these myths. Their Cuban allies appeared poorly outfitted, rough in their manners, and primarily dark-skinned. By contrast, the Spanish soldiers were light-complexioned, appeared well-disciplined, and tougher in battle than was expected. The Cuban rebels were actually skilled guerrilla fighters but racial prejudice prevented U.S. soldiers and reporters from crediting their contributions to eventual victory. Instead, they judged the Cubans harshly, asserting that they were primitive, savage, and incapable of self-control or self-government. As will be seen, such ascriptions went far in helping the imperialists persuade the American people that Cuba must become an American protectorate, if for no other reason than to "save" the Cubans from themselves! During the actual fighting, U.S. troops (the majority of the white troops) refused to associate with their black Cuban allies. They refused to fight alongside the Cubans, and increasingly they denied their "allies" information about Spanish movements and other strategy.

Despite the U.S. Army's ineptitude and racial prejudice, its soldiers were filled with the appropriate martial spirit, as all of them—both black and white—were eager for combat. No one was more excited about that prospect than Theodore Roosevelt, who, along with Colonel Leonard Wood, led a volunteer cavalry unit comprised of an interesting and somewhat motley crew of Ivy League gentlemen (Roosevelt's Harvard cronies), western cowboys, sheriffs, prospectors, Indians, and small numbers of Hispanics and ethnic European Americans. Roosevelt's "Rough Riders," as the battalion came to be known, landed with the invasion force and played an active role in the three battles fought in the hills surrounding Santiago de Cuba, the main theater of action on the island's southeastern coast. Their most famous action, the one on which TR would build his lifelong reputation as a warrior/hero, was a furious charge on foot, not on horse, up Kettle Hill into the heart of Spanish defenses. Roosevelt's bravery was remarkable though his judgment was faulty. Nearly 100 men were killed or wounded in the charge. Accounts of TR's bravery overshadowed the equally, if not more courageous, performance of other troops, most notably the 9th and 10th Negro Cavalries, which played a key role in clearing away Spanish fortifications on Kettle Hill and allowing Roosevelt's Rough Riders to make the charge. One of TR's men commented: "If it had not been for the Negro cavalry, the Rough Riders would have been exterminated." Another added, "I am a Southerner by birth, and I never thought much of the colored man. But I never saw such fighting as those Tenth Cavalry men did. They didn't seem to know what fear was, and their battle hymn was 'There'll be a hot time in the old town tonight.'" The 24th and 25th Negro Infantry Regiments performed equally important tasks in the U.S. Army's taking of the adjacent San Juan Hill.

Despite prejudice, discrimination, and segregation, African-American soldiers risked their lives in proving their patriotism and courage. At the time, Roosevelt and others publicly lauded their contributions to ultimate victory. He praised his black comrades-in-arms as "an excellent breed of Yankee," and declared that no "Rough Rider will ever forget the tie that binds us to the Ninth and Tenth Cavalry." But soon after returning home, he began diminishing their role, even to the point of calling their behavior

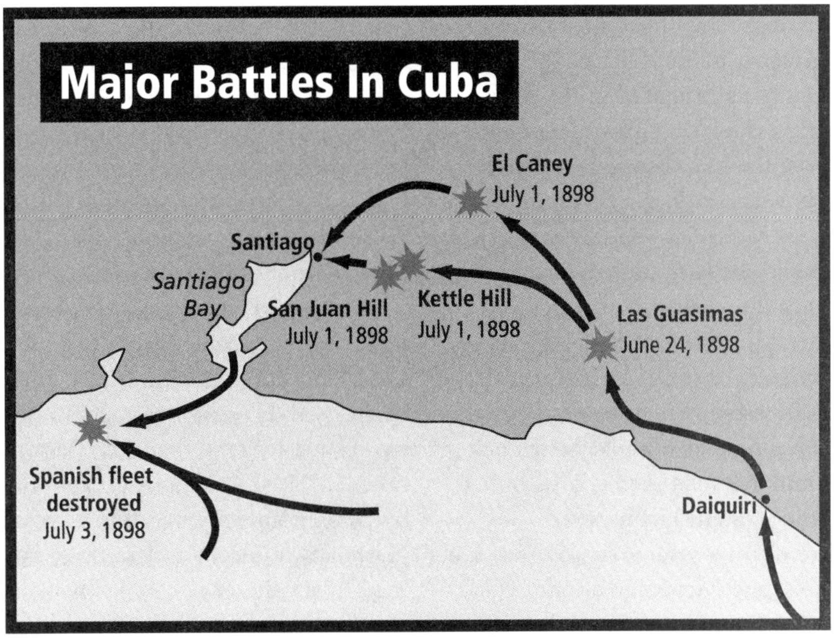

cowardly. Like most white American officers and enlisted men of the time, TR had difficulty believing blacks could fight well. By the time of U.S. entry into the Great War in 1917, the U.S. military had adopted a policy of excluding black troops from combat roles altogether. Moreover, it must be remembered that if African-American soldiers' bravery and contributions to victory were too exalted by white America, such acclaim could go far toward helping African Americans achieve equality at home—something few white Americans were ready to embrace.

Though victorious on the battlefield, by mid-July 1898, American troops were short of food, ammunition, and medical facilities. Their ranks were so decimated by malaria, typhoid, and dysentery that Roosevelt despaired, "We are within measurable distance of a terrible military disaster." Fortunately, the Spanish had lost the will to fight, realizing that to do so would cause even greater humiliation and death. As Spain's Atlantic fleet tried to retreat from Santiago harbor, the U.S. navy raked and sank their archaic fleet, killing 474 Spanish sailors. The Spanish army in Santiago surrendered on July 16; and on July 18 the Spanish government asked for peace. While Spanish and U.S. officials negotiated an armistice, American forces took Puerto Rico. On August 12 the U.S. and Spanish government agreed to an armistice, but before the news reached the Philippines, the U.S. captured Manila and took prisoner 13,000 Spanish soldiers. In the ensuing formal peace settlement, finalized in the Treaty of Paris in December 1898, Spain recognized Cuban independence, ceded Puerto Rico and the Pacific island of Guam to the United States, and after receiving a payment of $20 million, the Spanish agreed to give the Philippines, as well, to the victorious United States. Americans now possessed an island empire stretching from the Caribbean to the Pacific.

THE UNITED STATES BECOMES A WORLD POWER

The United States' acquisition of the Philippines, Guam, and Puerto Rico had little, if not nothing, to do with the reasons the nation had gone to war. Initially, the U.S. proclaimed to the world and to its own citizens that the Republic was going to war to help liberate the Cuban people from their brutal Spanish oppressors, and in that context, the country would be upholding its democratic creed of self-determination. For the imperialists such rhetoric was simply a ruse to disguise their real intention, which was to incorporate Cuba into a new American empire. Naïve anti-imperialists, who supported the war, believed it was to liberate the Cubans from the last decadent "remnant" of the Old World, Spain. Naturally the imperialists delighted in the Treaty of Paris, which ceded to the U.S. Guam, Puerto Rico, and the Philippines, the last viewed as essential for the projection of U.S. power in the Pacific and Asia. In the end, President McKinley was just as much an imperialist as the men who surrounded him and who were the architects of the expansionist policy and the war. As noted earlier, McKinley annexed Hawaii, giving the U.S. permanent control of its first-rate deep-water port at Pearl Harbor. Then, he set his sights on setting up a naval base at Manila. Never before had the United States pursued such a large military presence outside the Western Hemisphere.

In a departure of even greater significance and future ramifications, the McKinley administration announced that the newly acquired territories would be regarded as colonies and governed as such. Virtually all the territory previously acquired by the United States had been settled by Americans, who eventually petitioned for statehood and were admitted to the Union with the same rights as existing states. In the case of the new possessions, only Hawaii would be allowed to follow the traditional path toward statehood. That occurred largely because of the influence of the powerful American sugar planters, who controlled the island and believed it best for their economic interests if Hawaii was made a "territory" in the traditional sense so that it could someday become a state. In 1900, Congress obliged the sugar planters by passing an act extending U.S. citizenship to all Hawaiian residents and putting the islands on the road to statehood in 1959. The story of the Philip-

Colonel Roosevelt and his Rough Riders at the top of San Juan Hill

pines, as will be seen shortly, was quite different. There, no powerful American clique resided who desired eventual statehood status. The U.S. had little interest in the Philippines beyond controlling Manila harbor. The decision to make the whole country an American colony was proclaimed to prevent other powers, such as Japan and Germany, from gaining a foothold somewhere in the 400-island archipelago and launching attacks on the American naval base at Manila.

The McKinley administration might have taken a different approach toward the Philippines had it not been for the racism that informed much of American imperialist policy and attitudes at this time. Helping U.S. forces to defeat the Spanish in the Philippines was a broad-based indigenous rebel movement led by Emilio Aguinaldo, who, like his Cuban counterparts, looked to the United States as the liberator of his country. However, much to Aguinaldo's eventual disappointment and betrayal, the U.S. never had any intention of granting the islands their independence, which they could have done by simply brokering a deal with Aguinaldo, giving the Philippines independence in exchange for a naval base at Manila. An American fleet stationed there would have protected the islands from other aggressive imperialists, such as Japan or Germany, serving the larger interests of both the U.S. and Filipinos. Outright annexation was also an alternative, granting the Filipinos the same status as the Hawaiians and putting them on the road toward statehood. However, McKinley chose none of these possibilities. He believed, like most other imperialists, that the Filipinos were an "inferior" people incapable of self-government and the right of self-determination. In short, McKinley believed that American rule would enormously benefit the Filipinos, whom he called "our little brown brothers." A devout Methodist, he explained that America's mission was "to educate the Filipinos and to uplift and civilize and Christianize them, and by God's grace do the very best we could by them." In reality, the majority of Filipinos were already Christianized, Catholic in fact, a legacy of centuries of Spanish rule. Indeed, a substantial percentage of the islanders not only had assumed Spanish names but were bilingual as well, able to speak both Spanish and their native tongue. They were hardly a people bereft of "civilization." Nonetheless, the U.S. would undertake a solemn mission to "civilize" the Filipinos and help to prepare them for independence. Until the U.S. deemed they were sufficiently "civilized," the island would be ruled by American governors appointed by the president. As will be seen shortly, the Filipinos believed they were "civilized" enough and ready for their independence and if it was not given freely, then they would take it from the United States by fighting a second war of national liberation.

Critics of Empire: The Anti-Imperialists

Even before the ink was dry on the Treaty of Paris, strong voices of opposition to empire had emerged, led by the recently organized Anti-Imperialist League. The association's membership was an impressive list of noted Americans, ranging from former president Grover Cleveland to the plutocrat Andrew Carnegie, to the labor leader Samuel Gompers, and to some of the nation's foremost men of letters and intellectuals such as Mark Twain, William James, and William Dean Howells. Disturbing them most was the acquisition of the Philippines, which they believed was a blatant contradiction and violation of the nation's most precious principle: the right of all people to independence and self-government. Moreover, they feared that the large military and diplomatic establishment that would be required to administer the colony would threaten political liberties at home. Though capitalists like Carnegie could be found among the more righteous and altruistic anti-imperialists, the majority of Carnegie's plutocratic cohorts joined the cause out of self-interest. U.S. sugar producers feared competition from Filipino producers. Trade unionists, like Gompers, worried that cheap Filipino labor would stream across the Pacific and flood the U.S. labor market and reduce wage rates. Some businessmen warned that the cost of maintaining an "imperial" outpost in the Philippines would far exceed any economic benefits the colony would provide to the nation. Many Democratic anti-imperialists typically used the acquisition of the islands for partisan purposes, as an entrée to criticize Republican foreign policy in general. Finally, many anti-imperialists were hardcore social Darwinists, who already were anxious about the massive influx of southern and eastern Europeans and their "breeding" potential for mongrelization. They now feared the contaminating effects of contact with "inferior" Asian races.

In February 1899, the anti-imperialist coalition in the Senate failed by one vote to prevent that body's ratification of the expansionist Treaty of Paris. Helping to deliver the imperialist victory was the news on the eve of the vote that the Filipinos had risen in revolt against the U.S. army of occupation. With another war looming and the lives of American soldiers imperiled, a few senators who had been reluctant to vote for the treaty may have felt obligated to support the president. McKinley's overwhelming reelection victory in 1900 and the defeat of the expansionist critic William Jennings Bryan eroded the anti-imperialist cause. Nevertheless, at a time of jingoistic rhetoric and militaristic posturing, many of them had upheld an older and finer vision of the United States.

GUERRILLA WAR IN THE PHILIPPINES, 1898-1902

A Prelude to Vietnam

Unfortunately for both Americans and Filipinos, "uplifting" the latter embroiled the United States in a bloody struggle that lasted for nearly five years and cost the lives of over 4,000 American soldiers and as many as 20,000 Filipino resistance fighters. By the time the fighting ended in the summer of 1902, more than 120,000 U.S. soldiers had served in the Philippines. The conflict cost $160 million, or eight times what the U.S. paid Spain for the archipelago. The war brought Americans face-to-face with a disturbing reality: American actions on the islands were all too often no different than those of the Spanish on Cuba. Like Spain, the United States was refusing to recognize a people's desire for self-rule. Like "Butcher" Weyler, American generals turned a blind eye as their soldiers used savage tactics to "search and destroy" rebel encampments, units, and any civilian hamlets believed to be harboring rebels or their supplies. In the process, whole communities suspected of supporting the rebels were "relocated" into concentration camps, while their entire village was razed. American soldiers executed so many insurrectionists (whom they called "goo-goos") that the ratio of Filipino dead to wounded reached 15 to 1, a statistic that made the U.S. Civil War, in which one soldier had died for every five wounded, seem relatively humane. One New Yorker wrote home that his unit had killed 1,000 Filipinos—men, women, and children—in retaliation for the killing of a single American soldier. Reflecting the racist attitude of most Americans, whether civilian or military, toward the Filipinos, the infantryman wrote home that "I am in my glory when I can sight my gun on some dark skin and pull the trigger." Estimates of total Filipino deaths from American bullets, starvation, and disease range from 50,000 to 200,000.

The United States finally gained the upper hand after General Arthur MacArthur (father of Douglas) was appointed commander of the islands in 1900. MacArthur did not seek an immediate peace settlement; indeed, the fighting's ferocity continued unabated. He realized, however, that peace could not be won by guns alone and thus initiated an amnesty program for all Filipino rebels who laid down their arms. He also cultivated close relations with the island's wealthy elites. McKinley supported this effort to build a Filipino constituency accepting of U.S. presence. To that end, he sent William Howard Taft to the islands in 1900 to establish a civilian government. A year later, Taft became the colony's first "governor-general" and declared that he intended to prepare the Filipinos for independence. Taking a page from British imperialism, Taft and subsequent American governor-generals, to create the façade that the "colonists" were governing themselves, ruled through puppet local elites. Everyone knew, however, that the United States still controlled the islands and that whatever autonomy had been granted was the result of American "munificent" self-interest. Nonetheless, many governmental functions were transferred to Filipino control, and Taft initiated a vigorous program of public works (roads, bridges, schools) that would give the Philippines the infrastructure necessary for economic development and political independence. Naturally, few such projects were undertaken without an eye toward usefulness to the United States as well.

After all, it was an American colony from which benefits were expected. By 1902, the combination of ruthless suppression and concessions ended the revolt. Though sporadic fighting continued until 1913, American control of the Philippines was secure. In 1946, nearly half a century after Admiral Dewey's guns had boomed in Manila Bay, independence finally came to the Philippines.

Controlling Cuba and Puerto Rico

Helping the Cubans free themselves from Spanish oppression and then allowing for their independence had allegedly been the main purpose for war against Spain. However, as in the case of the Philippines, American altruism quickly changed as the McKinley administration made it clear that the United States was not about to relinquish control of the island. At the president's urging, Congress attached the Platt Amendment to a 1901 army appropriations bill that abrogated the earlier Teller Amendment, that in effect had disavowed any American intention of acquiring Cuba. Despite its obfuscating verbiage, the Platt Amendment made Cuba another American colony by stipulating that Cuba would not be permitted to make treaties with foreign powers; that the United States would have broad authority to intervene in Cuban political and economic affairs; and that Cuba would sell or lease land to the United States for naval stations. Suffice it to say, Cuban nationalists felt betrayed and outraged by such American duplicity but, unlike the Filipinos, did not rise in revolt. The dependence of Cuba's vital sugar industry on the U.S. market and the presence of a substantial U.S. army of occupation rendered resistance futile. In short, the Cubans had no choice but to write the Platt Amendment into their constitution if they hoped to have even a modicum of self-rule. Unfortunately for the Cubans, their economic dependence on the United States allowed for their constant political subjugation. Between 1989 and 1914, American trade with Cuba increased more than tenfold—from $27 million to $300 million—while investments more than quadrupled—from $50 million to $220 million. The United States intervened in Cuban political affairs a total of five times between 1906 and 1921 to protect its capitalist interests. As in the Philippines, the United States ruled through a pro-U.S. business indigenous elite that remained in power until 1959, when Cuban rebels, led by Fidel Castro, overthrew the last of such puppet regimes. Until then, the Cubans endured a half century of internal suppression and external exploitation of their country. Needless to say, the economic, military, and political control the United States imposed on Cuba would fuel anti-American sentiment there for years to come and help prepare the way for Castro's victory in 1959.

Puerto Rico received somewhat different treatment. The United States was not going to grant the Puerto Ricans independence, even though ironically under Spanish rule the islanders enjoyed a large measure of political autonomy. Nor did the United States impose Puerto Rico any sort of Platt Amendment that made the island a "colony" like its Caribbean neighbor, Cuba. Instead, the U.S. annexed the island outright via the Foraker Act (1900). This act was unprecedented in U.S. history for unlike all previous annexations, this measure made no provision for making the inhabitants citizens of the United States. Puerto Rico was designated an "unincorporated" territory, which meant that Congress would dictate the island's government and specify its inhabitants' rights. In short, with the Foraker Act, Congress had invented a new imperial mechanism for ensuring sovereignty over lands deemed vital to U.S. economic and military security. Though in effect another U.S. colony, Puerto Rico fared better than allegedly "independent" Cuba. Puerto Ricans were granted U.S. citizenship in 1917 and won the right to elect their own governor in 1947. Still Puerto Ricans did not have the same rights as other Americans in the 48 states. Moreover, as "citizens," Puerto Ricans' standard of living was still far below that of the mainlanders. Indeed, as late as 1998, one-fourth of Puerto Rican households subsisted on $1,000 or less annually, a figure thousands of dollars below the U.S. poverty line. In its skewed distribution of wealth and its lack of industrial development, Puerto Rico resembles the poorly developed nations of Central and South America more than it does the affluent country that took over its government in 1900.

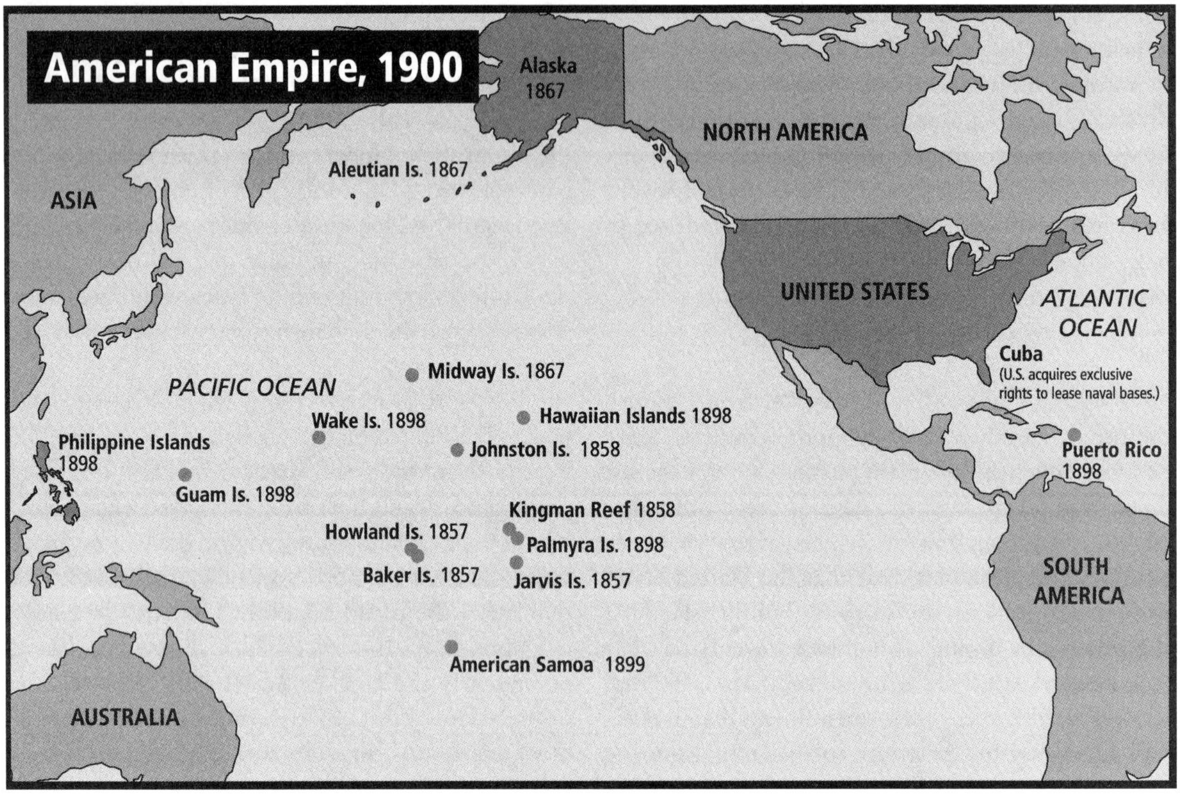

Unlike the Philippines, very few Americans were disturbed by the subjugation of Cuba and annexation of Puerto Rico. Since the promulgation of the 1823 Monroe Doctrine, the United States, had, in effect, claimed the Western Hemisphere as its sphere of influence. With that sphere, many Americans believed, the United States possessed the right to act unilaterally to protect its interests, as well as those of the hemisphere in general, from foreign interlopers and aggressors. Before 1900, most U.S. international actions (with the exception of the Mexican War) focused on keeping the European powers out of the hemisphere—Britain, France, Russia, and Spain. After 1900, however, the U.S. assumed a more aggressive role, seizing land, overturning governments not "favorably disposed" to American interests and exploitation—in short, forcing its economic and political policies on weaker neighbors to turn the Caribbean Sea into what policymakers called an "American Mediterranean."

THE UNITED STATES AND CHINA: THE OPEN DOOR POLICY

In the aftermath of the Philippines debacle, the imperialists wisely made no further attempts to subjugate other Asian territory, which might well have precipitated a conflict with the other great powers already established in the region. Moreover, the American public, weary of the bloodshed and cost of suppressing the Filipino rebellion, rejected any further, overly-ambitious and financially burdensome engagements in the area. Much to the disappointment of some of the more bellicose imperialists within the McKinley administration, diplomacy rather than militarism prevailed when it came to achieving other foreign policy initiatives relative to Asia. Of the greatest interest and concern for policy makers was the nation's relationship with China, a country representing vast commercial potential for American capitalists, and, for the geopolitical imperialists, a prospective ally and countervailing force against rival powers, most notably the Russians, Japanese, British, French, and Germans, all who were seeking to increase their hegemony over China. Indeed, by 1900, these powers had succeeded in carving a prostrate China into "spheres of influence," seizing by force large chunks of Chinese territory, which they then occupied and exploited for their own economic aggrandizement.

In effect, via their respective spheres of influence, these nations dominated China, either by exacting economic and territorial concessions from the weak Chinese government or by taking outright the land and trading privileges they desired. Once in control of such areas, the foreign powers closed off all outside access to their sphere of influence, especially forbidding trade relations with other countries. Thus, much to the dismay of American capitalists and their imperialist allies, the United States was shut out of the lucrative China market.

Leading the effort to get the other powers to open up their spheres of influence to outside trade was McKinley's Secretary of State and noted imperialist, John Hay. Hay's objective was twofold: to prevent China's further balkanization if not dissolution, while simultaneously gaining American commercial access to the whole of China. For this purpose, Hay sent "Open Door" notes to the major powers, asking each of the nations with spheres of influence in China to open up their respective territories to the trade of other countries. Hay also asked for reasonable harbor fees, railroad rates, and, most important, for the other powers to respect Chinese sovereignty by enforcing Chinese tariff duties and to cease any further designs they may have on increasing their spheres at China's expense.

This last stipulation reflected Hay's, as well as the desire of the other imperialists within Congress and the McKinley administration, to begin to cultivate China as a potential U.S. Asian ally by championing Chinese sovereignty and independence from foreign hegemony. If the United States could begin now by presenting itself as China's protector and savior from foreign interventionists, then, once China had liberated itself from the other imperial powers, it would look favorably upon the United States for having supported their independence movement. As a thank you, China undoubtedly would grant the United States increased trade and other concessions and privileges. This is what Hay and other American imperialists hoped would be the long-run effect of the Open Door initiative. By the 1920s Hay's vision came to fruition as the United States had become China's most important Western protector and benefactor while American goods flooded the China market.

Although impressed by Hay's diplomacy (or audacity), the secretary's Open Door overture engendered little enthusiasm among the other powers. Hay should have expected at best a lukewarm response or "theoretical" acceptance, for there was absolutely nothing for the other powers to gain by supporting Hay's proposal other than not wanting to irritate the United States, an emerging world power but not yet really tested. Crushing a hapless country like Spain in six weeks might have been a great ego boost for American imperialists and militarists, but the U.S. victory hardly impressed the great European powers. For the major powers, Hay's attempt to persuade them to relinquish valuable territory because their stranglehold on Chinese resources and trade was "unfair" seemed pretentious righteous indignation, if not ridiculous, coming from a nation that had just recently modernized its armed forces. To the Europeans, hardened by centuries of warfare, only the prospect of a clash of arms would motivate them to seriously ponder the Hay proposal. Knowing neither the American people nor their government representatives would be willing to militarily engage them over China, the great powers did not have to fear a military reprisal from the United States if they did not agree to Hay's mandates. Doing what was decent or moral to promote goodwill had little stock in the competitive, self-interested world of real politik by which the European powers operated.

Interestingly, Hay, not wanting the United States to appear weak by being unable to convince others to heed its requests, declared to the American public that China's occupiers had agreed to observe his Open Door principles and that he regarded their "assent" as "final and definitive" acceptance of his initiative. A naïve American people, flushed with nationalist pride after displaying their supposed military and moral superiority over a corrupt and decadent European nation (Spain), bought Hay's braggadocio. Suffice it to say, the other powers were taken aback by Hay's effrontery.

Boxer Rebellion

No sooner was the Open Door policy allegedly promulgated than it was challenged; not by the Europeans but by Chinese nationalists, who naively misinterpreted the initiative, believing its real intent was to protect Chinese sovereignty as well as a declaration of U.S. assistance when the Chinese attempted to liberate themselves from foreign occupation. Such a scenario occurred in May 1900, when a nationalist movement, colloquially known as the "Boxers," rose in armed rebellion in order to "cleanse" China of all "foreign devils" and influences. The Boxers, who considered themselves the protectors of traditional Chinese culture and society, rightly claimed that European occupation had destroyed centuries of security and stability, leaving China divided, prostrate, and bleeding. The Boxers killed hundreds of European "devils" as well as many Chinese men and women who had converted to Christianity. The insurrection caught the foreign community by surprise, and thus the Boxers initially appeared to be winning their war for national liberation.

For 55 days the Boxers laid siege to the foreign legations in Beijing, cutting off communication between the city and the outside world. In order to raise the siege, the imperial powers momentarily put aside their own rivalries and formed a coalition force to rescue the diplomats and punish the rebels. At this juncture the United States found itself in a dilemma: although sympathetic to the Chinese nationalist movement, which if successful could economically benefit the United States, if they did not join the coalition they would alienate the very powers they were attempting to woo into accepting the Open Door initiative. In the end, the U.S. opted to side with the other imperialist powers. After all, they were all members (except the Japanese) of the allegedly same superior white race, and thus, in the name of white (although not Anglo-Saxon) solidarity, the United States joined the coalition to help put down the "mongrel" uprising. The McKinley administration ordered 5,000 troops to be rushed from the Philippines to help the other powers break the Beijing siege and crush the Boxer insurrection, which was accomplished by October 1900.

Hay feared the Boxer Rebellion spelled the end of any hope his Open Door proposal might have had, for he believed the uprising would prompt the other major powers to demand even greater suzerainty over China. Hay, however, was not to be deterred. He sent out another round of circulars, in which he not only reiterated his original Open Door proposal but also warned the other powers that it had been their refusal to respect China's political independence and territorial integrity that had provided the impetus for the Boxers to rally their countrymen to their cause. Hay believed that the only way to prevent future insurrections was for the other powers to accept his Open Door agenda. Impressed by America's show of military prowess in helping to suppress the Boxers, and worried that the Chinese rebels might strike again, the key imperialists rivals—Great Britain, France, and Germany—endorsed Hay's policy outright. With such powerful support behind him, Hay was able to check the designs on Chinese territory of the more recalcitrant Russians and Japanese, who eventually capitulated to the Open Door program as well once they saw the forces arrayed against them. Significantly, when the powers demanded that the Chinese government pay them reparations for the damages done by the Boxers to their property and personnel, Hay convinced them to accept cash payments rather than taking more Chinese territory as compensation. Thanks to Hay, what was left of China was kept in tact, and now all of China was open to free trade. The United States had achieved, largely by Hay's persistent diplomacy, a major foreign policy victory. Perhaps most important for the future, Americans began to see themselves as China's savior and protector.

THEODORE ROOSEVELT AND THE FOUNDATION OF AMERICAN FOREIGN POLICY

Rarely in the history of the United States has one individual left as indelible a mark on both domestic and foreign policy as did Theodore Roosevelt. "TR's" legacy is perhaps more significant in the area of foreign policy, for it was during his presidency, and mostly because of his personal initiatives that the United States became the respected (and feared) world power Roosevelt and other imperialists envisioned during the 1890s. It was during that decade that Roosevelt emerged as one of the most outspoken, often bellicose, champions of utilizing the nation's industrial might into making the United States one of the world's great powers—a destiny, TR believed, ordained by God and the superiority of the Anglo-American character. Roosevelt and his imperialist cohorts had worked assiduously, both publicly and privately and often clandestinely, to convince their fellow Americans to embrace their vision for the nation. Roosevelt believed perhaps more passionately than others that the chains of isolationism had to be forever broken and that the United States must muster all its resources, both human and material, for the purpose of realizing its destiny as a great power. In that status also laid true greatness, for to TR it was incumbent on the United States to exercise its power for the preservation of peace while simultaneously serving as an example to the world of the virtues of democratic republican government. Only by playing an active role in world affairs could the United States realize its ultimate responsibility to humanity, which was to lead the rest of the world down the righteous and glorious path toward democracy and freedom.

Roosevelt's conception of the United States' role in world affairs not only resonated with many of his contemporaries but, perhaps more significantly, with future presidents and foreign policy makers as well. In many ways, Roosevelt laid the essential foundations of modern American foreign policy upon which his successors added new dimensions in order to deal with exigencies that did not exist in TR's time. Roosevelt established this fundamental premise, captured in his quip, "Speak softly but carry a big stick." In effect, what TR implied in his now famous line, and the image of the United States he wanted to project to the world (and which the United States still does), was that of a nation above all dedicated to the preservation of peace, stability, and freedom in the world, yet a country, if provoked or violated, not afraid to unleash upon its adversary its overwhelming industrial/military strength. It has been this image of American power and presence in the world, first outlined and articulated by Theodore Roosevelt that still defines the essence of United States foreign policy.

For all his exuberance, bluster, and arrogance, Roosevelt understood the dynamics of real politik; he never for a second assumed that because of Americans' supposed ethnic/racial (Anglo-Saxon) superiority and righteousness that the other nations of the world would simply acquiesce to United States' dictums. A nation, like an individual, had to strive for and earn respect and greatness. It had to demand of its citizens physical and mental toughness, the essential components of military preparedness, for in the history of all great nations war was an unfortunate but inextricable part of a country's rise to preeminence. In short, TR believed that the United States must train and develop a skilled and dedicated warrior class capable of not only defending the nation but of projecting American power abroad as well. Potential adversaries must live in fear that if provoked, the United States possessed the armed forces—army and navy—capable of annihilating enemies as well as protecting American interests and citizens around the globe.

TR's passion for the good fight caused many to worry about the ascension of this "cowboy" to the White House after McKinley's assassination in 1901. However, as noted above, Roosevelt was no saber-rattling war monger. Indeed, he understood, better than most, all the complexities, machinations, and historical imperatives of international relations and power politics. As much as he craved power for himself and the nation, he knew the United States could not dominate every portion of the globe through military or economic means. Consequently, taking a page out of English history, TR pursued a policy of bringing about a balance of power among the great industrial nations (much as the United States does today via the yearly "G-8" summits) through negotiation rather than war. Since all the great powers had mutual interests and concerns—that of maintaining their preeminence—then all should be willing to peacefully resolve tensions among them and pursue an agenda of collective security in order to preserve their status. Such a rapprochement would enable each imperial power to safeguard its key interests while helping to maintain world peace and progress.

Unfortunately, absent from TR's geopolitical thinking was concern for the world's lesser nations and their peoples. Reflecting not only his own inherent racism and ethnocentrism but that of the great powers as well, Roosevelt turned a deaf ear to the cries of sovereignty and human rights emanating from small countries, whose people TR believed weak and inferior. In his eyes, Latin Americans, Asians (except the Japanese), and Africans fell into the Social Darwinian category of inferior humans, incapable of self-government and material progress without being under the "tutelage and care" (subservience) of the superior Anglo-Saxon and Teutonic peoples of Europe and the United States. Suffice it to say, Roosevelt wholeheartedly embraced the "white man's burden" rhetoric of his time.

The Corollary

Perhaps no initiative better reflected Roosevelt's mentality and his desire to establish American hegemony in a vital region of the world than his 1904 "corollary" to the Monroe Doctrine. The original 1823 Doctrine's purpose had been to promote a degree of hemispheric solidarity against any further European intrusions in New World affairs. Most important, the United States declared itself the hemisphere's spokesman and guardian by asserting its right to use force if necessary to keep the European powers from meddling in the hemisphere's business, especially in matters relating to Latin America. However, at the time, the United States lacked the military might to prevent European intervention, and thus throughout most of the nineteenth century the European powers violated the doctrine with impunity.

However, by the time of Roosevelt's presidency, the economic and military condition of the United States had changed dramatically; America was no longer a second-rate power; quite the opposite, the United States possessed the third largest navy in the world, fully capable of defending the hemisphere from European encroachment. Thus in his corollary TR declared that the United States had the right to intervene in the domestic affairs of hemispheric nations to quell disorder and prevent European intrusion. In many ways, Roosevelt's "addendum" simply formalized the United States' previous military occupation of a "troubled" Cuba and Puerto Rico in 1900 and 1901. However, it was events in Venezuela and the Dominican Republic that hardened TR's resolve to establish intervention as a necessary component of United States hemispheric policy. To Roosevelt, his corollary not only helped to preserve hemispheric stability but also reflected his determination to establish in the eyes of the European powers that the New World, particularly the Caribbean, was an "American lake" and that Central America as well was under United States suzerainty.

Theodore Roosevelt's "Big Stick" diplomacy toward Latin America.

Helping TR to further justify U.S. intervention was the fact that both the governments of Venezuela and the Dominican Republic were controlled by corrupt, brutal dictators who had defaulted on loans owed to German and British banking houses. Their reneging prompted a German-led European naval blockade and bombardment of Caracas, Venezuela in 1902 and a potential invasion of the Dominican Republic by Italy and France in 1903. In response, TR issued a bellicose statement to Germany, threatening military action if they did not withdraw from the Venezuelan coast, which they did in 1903. In the Dominican Republic, after an insurrection overthrew the dictator, the U.S. assumed control of the nation's customs collections in 1905 and refinanced the Dominican national debt through U.S. financiers.

Unfortunately for the Latin American people of the Caribbean and Central America, the first several decades of the twentieth century saw the coming to power of corrupt, dictatorial regimes and the willingness of European bankers to loan these governments money. Within a few years, such relationships ended in bankruptcy, social unrest and, ultimately, to foreign intervention. To prevent further European invasion and occupation of Latin American countries, Roosevelt now made it clear that henceforth the United States would assume the responsibility of "policing" the hemisphere and that all future issues between the Europeans and Latin American nations would be "arbitrated" by the United States. In effect, TR declared American hegemony over the entire hemisphere and that any attempt by the European powers to ignore or violate such "sovereignty" would be met by a military reprisal.

As far as the Latin Americans suffering under such endemic oppression and violence were concerned, TR dismissed their plight as simply confirmation of their inferiority—their "inherent" incapacity for democratic government and socioeconomic progress. Roosevelt's only interest was maintaining hemispheric order and, in the process, asserting and sustaining U.S. hegemony. Thus, when the Cubans revolted in 1906 in an attempt to liberate themselves from a repressive U.S.-backed puppet government, TR sent in the Marines to crush the uprising and maintain the status quo. American troops remained in Cuba for three years to ensure there would be no further populist insurrections against the American capitalist-supported-regime. Interestingly, as will be seen in a later chapter, when Fidel Castro led a revolution in 1958 against the corrupt, U.S.-bolstered Batista government and succeeded in overthrowing that dictatorship, he had the overwhelming support of the Cuban people, who by that time had not only come to hate the lackey "presidents" installed by the United States but the U.S. government as well, which had since TR's days controlled and exploited the Cuban people for its own aggrandizement.

The Panama Canal

Without question the acquisition and construction of the Panama Canal marked the high point of Roosevelt's agenda in establishing the United States as a recognized world power. Roosevelt, influenced by his reading of Alfred T. Mahan's seminal works on sea power, believed more passionately than ever that since the United States had become a naval power, it needed a way of moving its ships swiftly from the Pacific Ocean to the Atlantic Ocean. The United States could no longer afford to traverse the great oceans by going around the tip of South America. Such a journey of several months could result in the nation not being able to protect its far-flung possessions. Thus, Roosevelt concluded that for reasons of "national security," the United States must find a way to reduce the travel time within its empire; the Imperial Republic needed a canal and the logical place to build one was across Central America at its narrowest width: the Colombian province of Panama. In the 1880s, a French company had attempted such an undertaking. However, technological difficulties and the financial costs of literally moving mountains stymied their effort. Moreover, French doctors could not control the spread of malaria and yellow fever, which incapacitated or caused the death of hundreds of workers. By the time TR became president, the French Panama Company had gone under.

Roosevelt was not deterred by the French failure. Indeed, he was as confident as ever that superior American ingenuity, skills, and perseverance could overcome any natural obstacle and build a canal across Central America. However, before he could move boldly ahead, TR did have to overcome a few, "minor" diplomatic niceties. First, he had to get the British to approve the United States building a canal on its own; since 1850, the two nations had agreed that any canal project in the region would be a joint undertaking. The 1901 Hay-Pauncefote Treaty with Great Britain released the United States from such an arrangement. Although initially intending to build the canal across Nicaragua, TR changed his mind when he realized that the Panamanian route was shorter and that the canal begun by the French was 40 percent complete. However, the French company, Compagnie Universelle du Canal Interoceanique, initially wanted $109 million for a "buy out," but after some tough bargaining by Hay, the company was willing to accept $40 million, which Congress readily approved. Not to lose momentum, Hay then quickly negotiated an agreement with the Colombian charge d'affaires in Washington, Tomas Herran, (the Hay-Herran Treaty), which gave the United States the right to build a canal along a six mile wide strip across the province of Panama. For this "privilege," the United States was to pay Colombia a one-time payment of $10 million and annual rent of $250,000.

Much to TR's subsequent chagrin and rage, the Colombian legislature reneged on the arrangement, demanding instead a onetime payment of $20 million and a share of the $40 million paid to the French government. The Colombians hoped to stall negotiations until 1904 when the French company's contract expired. When that occurred, the Colombian government not only would regain the right to the canal zone but to the $40 million sale priced promised as well to the French. Roosevelt felt "hoodwinked" by the Colombians even though they were acting within their rights as a sovereign nation. Infuriated by such a "betrayal," TR decided that he would use military action to get what he believed was a "deal" between the French company and the United States government. Behind closed doors, TR, in conjunction with Philippe Bunau-Varilla, the director of the French company, and Panamanian "freedom fighters" (for 25 years the Panamanians had sought independence, rebelling several times against the Colombian government), planned another uprising. Roosevelt promised the Panamanians that they would succeed in securing their independence this time because he would offer "assistance"—the United States navy and troops. With such an assurance, the Panamanians revolted in 1903, and true to his word, TR sent the *U.S.S. Nashville* to prevent Colombian troops from entering Panama. U.S. Marines then came ashore to help the new "nation" retain its freedom. The United States formally recognized the sovereign state of Panama only two days after the revolt against Colombia began.

Further questionable arrangements followed between the United States and Panama, reflecting TR's determination to build and own a canal regardless of his actions' legitimacy. Bunau-Varilla declared himself Panama's diplomatic representative, even though he was a French citizen and member of a Wall Street law firm and had not been in the country for fifteen years. TR accepted Bunau-Varilla as Panama's bona fide ambassador and ordered Hay to quickly sign a treaty with him that would give the United States its desired objective. Thus in 1903, the Hay-Bunau-Varilla Treaty formalized the United States' right to a ten-mile wide canal zone in return for the package Colombia had rejected—$10 million down and $250,000 annually. Thus, by rather dubious means the United States (Theodore Roosevelt) secured its canal. Interestingly, when the legitimate Panamanian delegation arrived in Washington to discuss and negotiate a treaty, the United States handed the officials a *fait accompli,* which infuriated the Panamanians, but there was nothing they could do to change the conditions. Nonetheless, one member of the delegation, upon seeing Bunau-Varilla, became so enraged that he knocked the Frenchman out cold. Despite such a betrayal, Panama was stuck with the treaty. If it refused to acknowledge the arrangement, the U.S. might withdraw its troops, leaving Panama vulnerable to a Colombian invasion force and loss of independence. Suffice it to say "the treaty which no Panamanian signed" embittered relations between Panama and the United States for the rest of the twentieth century.

Roosevelt's high-handedness infuriated many Americans, including, ironically, the one-time imperialist, William Randolph Hearst, whose newspapers labeled the Panama foray as "nefarious" and "a quite unexampled instance of foul play in American politics. Typically, TR was not intimated nor worried by such criticism of his actions. Moreover, TR had his cabinet's full support, as reflected in a comment by Elihu Root, his new Secretary of State, after a meeting with the president. Root told TR that, "You have shown that you were accused of seduction and you have conclusively proved that you were guilty of rape." With his customary bravado, TR later gloated, "I took the Canal Zone and let Congress debate!"

Typically, TR turned the building of the canal into a showcase of superior American technology, ingenuity, and perseverance. Engineers overcame every physical or natural obstacle; doctors developed drugs to combat malaria and yellow fever; and some 30,000 West Indian "coolie" workers labored for a 10-year period, for 10 hours a day, for six days a week, for ten cents an hour, making "the dirt fly." Roosevelt visited "his project" in 1906, the first American president to travel outside the United States while in office.

When the canal opened with great fanfare in 1914, the British ambassador to the United States, James Bryce, described the waterway as "the greatest liberty Man has ever taken with Nature." The canal shortened the voyage from the West Coast to the East Coast by some 8,000 miles and as TR hoped, the undertaking greatly enhanced the United States' international prestige. Indeed, from the beginning, driving TR to acquire the territory on which to build the canal was his obsession to demonstrate to the great powers that the United States possessed all the essential material, technological, and human will power to engage in such an enterprise. Prior to the construction of the Panama Canal, the only other nation to have performed such an engineering feat and human endeavor was Great Britain with the construction of the Suez Canal and its completion in 1869. Thus, out of an interesting dichotomy of personal admiration and envy of Great Britain's perceived status as the most powerful nation in the world, TR believed it imperative for the United States to build and own a waterway as important to the world and the United States as the Suez was to Great Britain. The Panama Canal became the perfect venue for TR to impress the great powers (especially England) that the United States had not only "arrived" industrially and technologically, but that the American people possessed as well the moral and physical character essential to accomplish such an undertaking. In short, Roosevelt was not about to let any nation outdo the United States, no matter what the adventure or struggle. Finally, the canal's strategic location further bolstered TR's corollary, making the sending of U.S. troops for intervention or occupation purposes to Central America or the Caribbean that much easier.

In 1921 the United States paid the Colombian government $25 million as compensation (atonement) for having, in effect, stolen Panama. However, sincere restitution was made over 70 years later when President Jimmy Carter signed a treaty with Panama in 1977 for turning the Canal Zone over to Panamanian sovereignty and the transfer of the canal itself to Panama by the year 2000. With some minor "modifications" the Bill Clinton administration honored the Carter accord.

Interestingly, TR's aggressive policy of asserting United States hegemony with military force in the Caribbean and Latin America abated in his Asian initiatives. No doubt the fact that a more militaristic and bellicose posture would not "fly" with the great powers heavily involved in the region—Russia, Japan, and the United Kingdom—affected Roosevelt's attitude. Thus, TR pursued a policy of maintaining acceptance of the Open Door Policy relative to China and of playing the balance of power game relative to the rest of the area. However, the thwarting of particularly Russian and Japanese aggression in China proved more difficult than initially reckoned. Both nations coveted Manchuria and Korea. For Russia having a warm water port on the Pacific was necessary, and Japan, in the throes of industrialization, desired access if not complete control of the rich ore deposits of Manchuria. For Japan, Korea had no value other than giving Japan a foothold on the Asian continent from which it could launch a future invasion of China proper.

Competition for the territory escalated into a full-blown war between Russia and Japan in 1904. Much to the surprise of the European powers, who still regarded the Japanese as an "inferior yellow people" incapable of defeating a great, white European power such as Russia, the Japanese routed the Russians on both land and sea with superior naval and land forces. The conflict quickly became a war Russia should never had engaged. Much to the shock of the other great powers, the conflict revealed that Russia was still essentially an industrially backward nineteenth century country, incapable of fighting, let alone winning, a modern (industrial) war. Moreover, the Russo-Japanese conflict unleashed the 1905 Russian revolution, as the Russian people, particularly those in urban areas, suffered from all manner of exploitation and deprivation, much of it caused by the demands of war. Popular uprisings, street demonstrations, and strikes by workers and leftist groups opposed to czarist autocracy and the war began in earnest on Easter Sunday 1905 in St. Petersburg after government troops opened fire on peaceful marchers, slaughtering hundreds who had come to plead with Nicholas II for relief. Although ultimately put down by the czarist regime, the 1905 Revolution marked the beginning of the end of 300 years of Romanov autocracy. As will be seen in a subsequent chapter, the 1917 Russian Revolution, especially after the Bolsheviks came to power, had a significant impact on American foreign policy and diplomacy at the time.

Geopolitically, a Russian defeat in Asia would end Russian presence in the region, thus ending the precarious Asian balance of power, allowing the Japanese to gain ascendancy, especially in China, over the other great powers. Sensing such an outcome, Roosevelt entered into secret negotiations with both belligerents, seeking to end the war before Russian annihilation became complete. If that occurred, Japanese preeminence would prevail in the area, establishing Japan as a potential threat to United States' interests in Asia and the Pacific.

TR thus invited to the United States (Portsmouth, New Hampshire) representatives from both countries, hoping to secure a negotiated comprise that would preserve the balance of power. Despite all of Roosevelt's cajoling, brow-beating, and admonishing, the Japanese came out "winners," refusing to relinquish the territory its forces had won on the battlefields and sea. Korea became a Japanese protectorate while the southern part of Sakhalin Island, Port Arthur (China), and the South Manchurian Railroad, also came under Japanese control. However, thanks to TR's intercession, Russia did not have to pay Japan a huge indemnity, and it retained Siberia (a "wasteland" in Japanese eyes), thus preserving its image (albeit a significantly diminished one) as an East Asian power. TR's only coup at Portsmouth was his persuading of both Russia and Japan to leave Manchuria, thus maintaining China's territorial integrity and simultaneously the United State's Open Door agenda. For his "peace" initiative, Roosevelt became the first American to win the Nobel Peace Prize in 1906.

Typically, TR had little interest in protecting or upholding the sovereignty of smaller, weaker Asian nations. Roosevelt's main objectives were simple and straightforward: to preserve the Asian balance of power among the great powers while simultaneously securing respect for American interests in the region. Such a priority was reflected in the secretly negotiated Taft-Katsura Agreement of 1905, whereby the United States recognized Japanese suzerainty over the Korean peninsula in exchange for a Japanese promise to respect U.S. hegemony over the Philippines and never attempt to take by force the U.S. possession. In the 1908 Root-Takahira Agreement, the U.S. reversed its earlier stand on the inviolability of Chinese sovereignty by allowing the Japanese to expand into southern Manchuria. In short, TR recognized that Japan's power was on the rise in Asia and that in the future Japan, not China or Korea, or any other Asian country, would dictate Asia's future. Interestingly, although allegedly not possessing the "character" and "qualities" of superiority ascribed to the Anglo-Saxon or Teutonic races, TR nonetheless respected and admired Japanese industrial and military might. Indeed, he viewed Japanese imperialism and expansion into East Asia as the assertion of a naturally superior people's dominion over supposedly inferior humans—the Chinese and other East Asian folk. Based on this perception, Roosevelt even promoted the idea of allowing Japan the "right" to create spheres of influence throughout all of East Asia, similar to what the U.S. had established in Central America. Hopefully, such recognition of Japan as an equal power with the United States and the Europeans would establish peaceful relations between the United States and Japan.

Implementing such an accord with Japan was a delicate diplomatic task, requiring TR's utmost skills and acumen in international relations, especially when simultaneously in California another outbreak of anti-Japanese hysteria engulfed the state. White Californians had long resented Asians in their state, and for several decades the federal government capitulated to such nativism. In 1882 Congress passed the Chinese Exclusion Act, which ended most Chinese immigration to the United States. By the early twentieth century Japanese immigration had replaced the Chinese influx; by 1906, the Japanese population in California had reached 24,000. Reflecting a blatant racism, in that year the San Francisco school board ordered the removal of all Asian schoolchildren from the city's public school system so they would not "contaminate" the white children. In 1907 the California legislature seriously considered passing a law that would stop all future Japanese immigration into the state. Violent anti-Asian riots erupted in San Francisco and Los Angeles. Most of the outbreaks were caused by the press, whose editorials about the "Yellow Peril" whipped white Californians into such a frenzy.

Suffice it to say, the Japanese government was outraged by the treatment of its citizens. Japanese militarists began talking about a possible war with the United States. TR, putting his own racism aside, assured the Japanese government that he too was appalled by white Californians' behavior. In 1907, TR reached a "gentleman's agreement" with Japanese officials by which the Japanese government agreed to halt the further immigration of Japanese adult male laborers to the United States in return for Roosevelt's pledge to bring an end to anti-Japanese discrimination in California. TR upheld his word; he forced the San Francisco school board to retract its segregation ordinance. However, de facto segregation of Japanese citizens, both children and adults, continued, as did violent assaults on the Japanese people and their property.

Not wanting to appear weak to the other major powers or to Japan for acquiescing to Japan's demands that he protect its citizens from white reprisals, TR ordered the main part of the United States fleet—16 battleships of the line—to embark on a 45,000 mile world tour with stops at every major port-of-call, including Tokyo Bay. There was no doubt TR wanted to display to the world (particularly Japan) U.S. military and industrial might, and at this time, there was no better way of showing off such prowess than for a large navy made of steel ships, with guns that could shoot for miles, to steam around the world and "visit" all the major powers. Interestingly, TR was criticized for such bravado, as many congressmen not only deplored the cost of the tour but worried as well that such a display of U.S. power, especially in a Japanese port, would provoke the Japanese into a military response. Typically, TR ignored his critics, and true to his prediction, the Japanese were not provoked; rather, they were impressed by America's industrial and military strength embodied in the showcasing of the "Great White Fleet." In many ways TR's various negotiations with Japan marked the highpoint of his foreign policy initiatives. Unlike most Americans, he did not allow his racist attitudes to dictate his agenda. He knew when to make concessions and when to stand firm. His policies lessened the prospect of war with Japan (at least for the time being) while preserving a strong U.S. presence in East Asia.

Although TR pursued a conciliatory policy toward Japan, especially on the issue of accepting Japanese imperialism, one nonetheless cannot help but wonder if the seeds of future tensions between the U.S. and Japan were not sown by Roosevelt, particularly by such initiatives as the "gentlemen's agreement," an obvious sop to white racism. Moreover, by condoning Japan's "right" to assert its hegemony over the rest of Asia, TR confirmed the growing belief among Japanese militarists that it was Japan's "destiny" to dominate all of Asia because of Japanese superiority, sentiments TR promoted. As will be seen in a later chapter, by the 1920s and certainly by the early 1930s, this mindset came to dictate Japanese foreign policy, and thus it would be only a matter of time before the delicate balance of power in East Asia, constructed by TR, would become completely "imbalanced" by Japanese aggression—a belligerence that not only led to the Japanese conquest of most of East Asia but to a devastating attack on the United

States possession of Hawaii and inevitable war with the United States in 1941.

WILLIAM HOWARD TAFT AND DOLLAR DIPLOMACY

TR's hand-picked successor, the three-hundred pound, jovial William Howard Taft, brought valuable foreign policy experience to the presidency. He was the first governor-general of the Philippines and as Roosevelt's Secretary of War, he served as chief negotiator of the delicate 1905 Taft-Katsura Agreement. Under TR's auspices, Taft learned a great deal about international real politik and how to deal with the United States' imperialist rivals. Yet, although an educated, intelligent man, Taft lacked Roosevelt's perspicacity in the area of balance-of-power politics and the charisma for leadership in foreign affairs. Moreover, Taft proved to be much less personally involved and interested in foreign policy issues, preferring instead to delegate this most crucial area of executive activism to supposed experts, such as his Secretary of State, the one-time corporate lawyer from Pittsburg, PA. Philander C. Knox proved to be no John Hay or Elihu Root when it came to formulating and implementing American imperialist policies. Indeed, Knox's grasp of the often complex dynamics and exigencies of the international power politics scene was at times wholly lacking. Reflecting his years of defending the excesses of American corporate capitalism and the plutocracy responsible for such wantonness, Knox believed that at this point in American foreign policy, the main focus should be on expanding American corporate investment abroad—a disposition that prompted critics to deride his agenda as "dollar diplomacy."

Taft and Knox, however, were not deterred by such carping. Both men believed that U.S. investments would not only reap great rewards for the U.S. economy but offer a more peaceful, less bellicose and coercive way of winning new international friends for the United States while simultaneously maintaining order and stability, especially in the Western Hemisphere without the use of military action. Chiding TR's "big stick policy," Taft announced that in his view, "modern diplomacy is commercial."

Taft's and Knox's inabilities to grasp the complexities of power politics led to diplomatic reversals in East Asia, upsetting the delicate balance of power rapprochement TR had established with Japan. Knox, prodded by his Wall Street friends, sought to expand American investment in China, even into Manchuria, an area Roosevelt had previously declared to be a Japanese sphere of influence. In 1911 Knox put together a consortium of European bankers to buy the South Manchurian Railroad (then under Japanese control) for the purpose of opening up North China to international trade. The Japanese naturally viewed Knox's scheme as an U.S. attempt to deprive them of a sphere of influence that Roosevelt had recognized.

In response, the Japanese signed a friendship treaty with their former adversary, Russia, allowing that country's goods into Manchurian markets while preventing the penetration of American, French, and British products into the region. The Japanese knew they could not stand alone against such a powerful Western syndicate. They were thus willing to engage in détente with Russia, which desperately needed markets for its industrializing economy. If Russia joined with Japan in such an arrangement, perhaps the Western powers would back off, for they would not want to alienate future potential allies, as tensions between Britain/France and Germany/Austro-Hungarian empire mounted. As a result of the Russo-Japanese rapprochement, Knox's syndicate idea collapsed, dealing America's Open Door Policy a serious blow in the process. Most important, in 1912, the foreign-controlled puppet government of China fell, precipitating ten years of revolution and civil war, resulting in the loss of millions of U.S. investment dollars. It appeared that Taft's and Knox's over zealous devotion to the value of the U.S. dollar in determining foreign policy initiatives had backfired.

Dollar diplomacy fared somewhat better in the Caribbean and Central America, where U.S. hegemony was unchallenged. Knox thus encouraged American investment in the hemisphere, both to provide corporations with opportunities for profit and to supplant the European investors already there or to beat them to the punch in acquiring new ventures. During the Taft administration, over half of all U.S. dollars invested abroad were found in various Latin

American enterprises, ranging from oil to public utilities to railroads and agriculture. Most important, U.S. conglomerates became such powerful economic entities in these host countries, especially in the more vulnerable countries of Central America, that they not only controlled the country's economy but politics as well. Such was the power of the United Fruit Company of Boston, Massachusetts, founded by Minor Keith. By controlling the majority of the banana plantations of Costa Rica and Honduras, (bananas were the main staple/export of both countries), the company virtually owned both nations. So driven by their devotion to dollar diplomacy were Taft and Knox that they assured U.S. corporations that if at any time their enterprises were threatened by political opposition or turmoil in the countries they had such a presence, the U.S. would simply send troops to protect their interests.

Such a provocation occurred in 1910 when the Nicaraguan dictator, Jose Santos Zelaya, allegedly began negotiating with a European country to build a second trans-Isthmian canal. Upon hearing of such supposed double-dealing, Taft sent a force of U.S. Marines to overthrow his regime. Marines landed again in 1912 when Zelaya's successor, Adolfo Diaz, a U.S. puppet, alienated his own people by his pro-American policies. Nicaraguans rose in rebellion against Diaz but Taft sent Marines to keep the Diaz government in power. Except for a brief period in 1925, U.S. troops would remain in Nicaragua continuously from 1912 to 1933. Interestingly, in his willingness to send troops to safeguard his dollar diplomacy approach, Taft engaged in the same militarism his predecessor readily employed in order to sustain puppet governments friendly to the United States and maintain order in Latin America.

CONCLUSION

America's rise to a global power by the eve of World War I can be assessed from two perspectives: either in relation to the imperialist agendas of the great powers or in the context of the fulfillment or realization of the American mission to export to the world its democratic ideals. In the realm of real politik, America's emergence in a relatively short time to great power status is impressive, for the nation achieved its major objectives: the U.S. established its undisputed hegemony over the Western Hemisphere and projected its military and economic power into Asia. Such was accomplished with minimal loss of American lives while muffling the jingoistic impulse for more aggressive military adventure and conquest. The U.S. added only 125,000 square miles to its empire in the years 1870-1914, while Great Britain, France, and Germany enlarged their respective dominions by 4.7, 3.5, and 1.0 million square miles. Comparatively few foreigners were subjected to American colonial rule. By contrast, in 1900, the British empire extended over 12 million square miles and embraced one-fourth of the world's population.

Nonetheless American suzerainty could be harsh; witness the brutal suppression of the Filipino insurrection of soldiers and civilians alike. Yet, on the whole, American dominion was no more severe than British rule and significantly less oppressive than that of the French, German, Belgian, or Japanese imperialists. Perhaps most important, until 1917, America's imperialist presidents—McKinley, Roosevelt, and Taft—all placed limits on American expansion and worked assiduously to prevent becoming so entangled in international power politics that war would be the end result.

If American foreign policy is assessed in the context of the nation's own democratic ideals, then U.S. initiatives must be judged more harshly. American policy was racist, exploitive, bellicose, and militaristic; in many ways not any different in attitude and behavior than the European imperialists, to whom we proclaimed we were different. The Cubans, Puerto Ricans, Filipinos, and Nicaraguans would beg to differ, for American subjugation, whether economic or military, of those peoples' countries confirmed that the U.S. was similar in every capacity. Like their European counterparts, American imperialists regarded the peoples they subjugated as inferior, primitive, and barbaric, and thus not "worthy" of self-government. In the eyes of Latin Americans, Filipinos, Hawaiians, and Asians, Americans were hypocrites, declaring to value liberty more than power. The Open Door Policy, the Platt Amendment, the Roosevelt Corollary, the Panama Canal, the "Gentlemen's Agreement, and

Dollar Diplomacy, to name but some of the initiatives of the early 20th century, substantiated the belief held by many that the United States had become a full-fledged member of the European imperialist club.

Many Americans of the time judged their nation by both standards and thus faced a dilemma that would affect the nation throughout the 20th century. On the one hand, they agreed with TR that the size, economic strength, and honor of the United States required the nation to accept its destiny as a world power and policeman, whose most important mandate, bequeathed by Providence, was to use its superior power and character to preserve world peace. On the other hand, many Americans believed that the principal mission of United States presence in world affairs was to spread the values of 1776 to the farthest reaches of the earth. Interestingly, we are still debating these same issues today; we are still trying to decide what should be America's principal role in world affairs.

Chronology

1868-78 Cubans revolt against Spanish rule in Ten Years' War

1875 U.S. agrees to allow Hawaii to export sugar to America duty-free

1878 U.S. gains treaty rights for base at Pago Pago in Samoa

1887 U. S. gains treaty rights for base at Pearl Harbor in Hawaii.

1889 First Pan-American Congress meets

1890 Alfred Thayer Mahan publishes *The Influence of Sea Power on History*, exhorting the government to modernize the nation's navy and through it assert American power world-wide. Also, U.S. ends favored status of Hawaii in sugar trade, damaging Hawaii

1893 U.S. sugar planters in Hawaii foment rebellion against weak native king
Harrison signs annexation agreement with Hawaii but new president Grover Cleveland rejects it.

1894 Wilson-Gorman tariff on Cuban sugar plunges island economy into depression, exacerbating political tensions between Cubans and Spanish officials.

1895 Invoking Monroe Doctrine and asserting hemispheric hegemony, Cleveland administration intervenes in boundary dispute between Venezuela and Great Britain, demanding U.S. right to arbitrate the issue. Cuban insurrection against Spanish renews.

1898 Jingoist/imperialist newspaper magnate, William Randolph Hearst, publishes deLome letter
U.S. battleship *Maine* explodes in Havana harbor
Congress declares war on Spain, April 25
Spanish army in Cuban retreats
Dewey captures Philippines
U.S. and Spain sign armistice August 12
Treaty of Paris (December) cedes Puerto Rico, Philippines, and other Spanish possessions to U.S. and recognizes Cuban independence
U.S. formally annexes Hawaii
Anti-Imperialist League formed.

1898-1902 Philippines revolt against American rule

1899 Senate ratifies Treaty of Paris
Hay releases "Open Door notes" on China

1900 Foraker Act establishes civil government in Puerto Rico
Hawaii granted territorial status
Boxer rebellion breaks out in China
McKinley reelected president

1901 American forces capture Filipino rebel leader Emilio Aguinaldo
U.S. establishes civil government in Philippines
Congress passes Platt Amendment making Cuba a U.S. colony/protectorate

SUGGESTED READINGS

Robert L. Beisner, *From the Old Diplomacy to the New, 1865-1900.* (1986).

___, *Twelve Against Empire: The Anti-Imperialists, 1898-1900* (1968).

James E. Bradford, *Crucible of Empire: The Spanish American War and Its Aftermath* (1993).

Michael Blow, *A Ship to Remember: The Maine and the Spanish-American War.*

Paul Carano and Pedro Sanchez, *A Complete History of Guam* (1964).

Raymond Carr, *Puerto Rico: A Colonial Experiment* (1984).

Warren J. Cohen, *America's Response to China* (1971).

Graham A. Cosmas, *An Army for Empire: The United States Army in the Spanish-American War* (1971).

John Dobson, *America's Ascent: The United States Becomes a Great Power, 1880-1914* (1978).

Philip S. Foner, *The Spanish-Cuban-American War and the Birth of American Imperialism,* 2 volumes (1972).

William B. Gatewood Jr., *"Smoked Yankees; Letters From Negro Soldiers 1898-1902* (1971).

David F. Healy, *U.S. Expansionism: Imperialist Urge in the 1890s.* (1970).

Walter R. Herrick, *The American Naval Revolution* (1966).

James H. Hitchman, *Leonard Wood and Cuban Independence, 1898-1902* (1971).

Paul M. Kennedy, *The Samoan Tangle* (1974).

Walter LaFeber, *The Cambridge History of Foreign Relations: The Search for Opportunity, 1865-1913* (1993).

Patricia Nelson Limerick, *The Legacy of Conquest: The Unbroken Past of the American West* (1987).

Gerald F. Linderman, *The Mirror of War: American Society and the Spanish-American War* (1974).

William E. Livezey, *Mahan on Sea Power* (1981).

Thomas J. McCormick, *China Market: America's Quest for Informal Empire, 1890-1915* (1971).

Ernest R. May, *Imperial Democracy: The Emergence of America as a Great Power* (1961).

Stuart Creighton Miller, *"Benevolent Assimilation:" The American Conquest of the Philippines, 1899-1903* (1982).

Joyce Milton, *The Yellow Journalists* (1989).

H. Wayne Morgan, *America's Road to Empire* (1965).

Edmund Morris, *The Rise of Theodore Roosevelt* (1979).

Louis A. Perez, *Cuba Under the Platt Amendment, 1902-1934* (1986).

Julius W. Pratt, *Expansionists of 1898* (1936).

___, *America's Colonial Empire* (1950).

Emily Rosenberg, *Spreading the American Dream: American Economic and Cultural Expansion, 18909-1945* (1982).

William A. Russ Jr., *The Hawaiian Republic, 1894-1898 and Its Struggle to Win Annexation* (1961).

Daniel B. Schirmer, *Republic or Empire? American Resistance to the Philippine War* (1972).

Peter Stanley, *A Nation in the Making: The Philippines and the United States, 1899-1921* (1974).

Merze Tate, *The United States and the Hawaiian Kingdom* (1965).

E. Berkeley Tomkins, *Anti-Imperialism in the United States,1890-1920: The Great Debate* (1970).

David F. Trask, *The War With Spain,* (1981).

Richard E. Welch, Jr. *Response to Imperialism: The United States and the Philippine War, 1899-1902* (1979).

William Appleman Williams, *The Tragedy of American Diplomacy*

Marilyn B. Young, *The Rhetoric of Empire: American China Policy, 1895-1901* (1968).

N THE NAME OF GO
AND
UMANITY
TEMPERANCE
LEAGUE
WINE &
LIQUORS
RUM
WHISKY
GIN
BRAND

Chapter Sixteen

PROGRESSIVE ERA

A beautiful young teenager from the slums of Chicago was thrilled to get her first job working in the local match factory. She was sure that she would not have to work there for too long; she would either get married or get a job working on the new machine, the typewriter. She would never get "phossy jaw," a degenerative disease caused by the phosphorus on the heads of the matches. No! She would not look like other girls who were old women at nineteen.

In another part of Chicago, a young immigrant boy was pleased that he had gotten a job at a meat packing plant not far from his tenement home. True, the smell was horrible; the work was dangerous. His next door neighbor had been seriously injured by an enraged bull not killed by the mallet blow to his head, and the pay was not good. But it was a start to the American dream. He was strong and young and sure that he would not have to work there so long that he would be permanently bent over like an old man by age twenty-five.

A middle-class family in Chicago looked forward to a delicious breakfast of that new deviled ham product produced locally. Then the calm of the early morning was punctuated by a scream from the kitchen. When the mistress of the house went to investigate, she found the cook lying on the floor. She had fainted after finding three bloody human fingers in the canned meat!

When the mistress went to her meeting of the Women's Christian Temperance Union, she heard first-hand reports of spousal and child abuse at the hand of a drunken husband. She decided that she, too, would join the movement for women's suffrage. How else could wives and children be protected?

Her husband's day was not much better. On the way to his office he encountered filth flowing down the streets, resulting from the lack of garbage pick-up. Political corruption prevented an efficient and clean city. Meanwhile, the newspaper that he read on the way to work reported the latest doings of the new upper class: a party where the guests rode their horses onto the expensive carpeting of one of New York's best hotels. At dinner guests ate oysters that contained perfect black pearls. After dinner they lit cigarettes rolled in one hundred dollar bills. When he got to work, he found that his company had been bought out by a huge trust, and his job was one of many to be eliminated.

It was such abuses that fueled the desire of many to join the reform movement that spanned the last years of the nineteenth century and the first twenty years of the twentieth, the Progressive Era. While often given the dates from 1900-1917, the administration of Theodore Roosevelt to the United States' involvement in World War I, the roots of the Progressive Era go back much further, and its accomplishments continued past the end of World War I.

PROGRESSIVE IDEOLOGY AND GOALS

Progressivism was founded on the notion that social progress was possible, indeed necessary. Progressives differed in their approaches, but most of them had the same goals: to make economic life fairer and more competitive, to make political life more democratic, and to make social life more moral and more just. Some hoped to broaden opportunities for the common man, whether he was a farmer, skilled or unskilled worker, or recent immigrant. At the same time they wanted to eliminate special privileges and favoritism for the wealthy.

Their motives were not completely unselfish. Most reformers were from middle-class backgrounds and had no love for immigrants or the nouveau riche, whose over-indulgence in all things led Mark Twain to dub an earlier period the Gilded Age. Progressives believed changes were necessary to prevent democracy from moving toward either a **plutocracy**, a government of the rich, or to the socialism that seemed ready to infect the working class as a result of horrendous working conditions.

Progressives realized that, although society appeared healthy and prosperous, many problems were festering beneath the surface. The working class had more comforts, but the wealth of the nation was unequally distributed. The poorest Americans lived at a shameful level of existence.

TRUSTS AND FINANCIAL CAPITALISM

The Second Industrial Revolution contributed to many conditions that brought the rise of heavy industries: oil, steel, and transcontinental railroads. Although the theory of capitalism is competition, the nineteenth century reality was monopoly and concentration of wealth. With the advantages brought by these new industries came problems of price-gouging, industrial poverty, greater swings in the business cycle that created periods of large unemployment, and bank failures. The amazing growth of capitalism would have been impossible without laws that favored corporations. Although joint stock companies had existed in the United States since the founding of the first colony, the Civil War and the Supreme Court's interpretation of the Fourteenth Amendment, as defining corporations as "persons," enabled corporations to grow and prosper until they were the dominant form of business organization. For example, in 1899 corporations made 66 percent of all manufactured goods; ten years later, it was 79 percent.

As the huge steel, oil, mining, and manufacturing concerns grew, so did the need for a domestic investment market where the savings of Americans could be solicited for stocks. By 1900, tens of thousands of Americans owned corporate securities; at the close of the Progressive Era in 1917, it was hundreds of thousands.

The large corporations meant that investors no longer managed their own capital; they simply owned stock in large corporations over which they had little control. Corporation officials were subject to the extraordinary temptations that arose from handling other people's money. Shrewd operators used reorganizations, mergers, and other devices, though often planned for sound business reasons, to manipulate funds for their own purposes and to eliminate competitors.

To the person of modest means, the potential investor, and the ambitious new entrepreneur, big corporations seemed to be obstacles that shut down the most profitable avenues of enterprise and confronted one with overwhelming competition. To the employee, the corporation represented a world of impersonal, mechanized, bureaucratized, and standardized relationships, rather than a world of personal employer-employee relations. Although corporations could offer employees many advantages that the small business could not, these were not yet part of the economic scene in the Progressive Era.

From 1893 to 1903 corporate consolidation increased rapidly because of the growing change from entrepreneurial capitalism to financial capitalism. Rather than an individual founding a corporation, it was the banker who provided the financing. The best-known instance of this process was in railroading. In 1893, two leading Wall Street investment houses, J. P. Morgan & Co. and Kuhn Loeb & Co. (a Rockefeller Company), concluded that lack of organization and excessive competition had caused much of the chaos

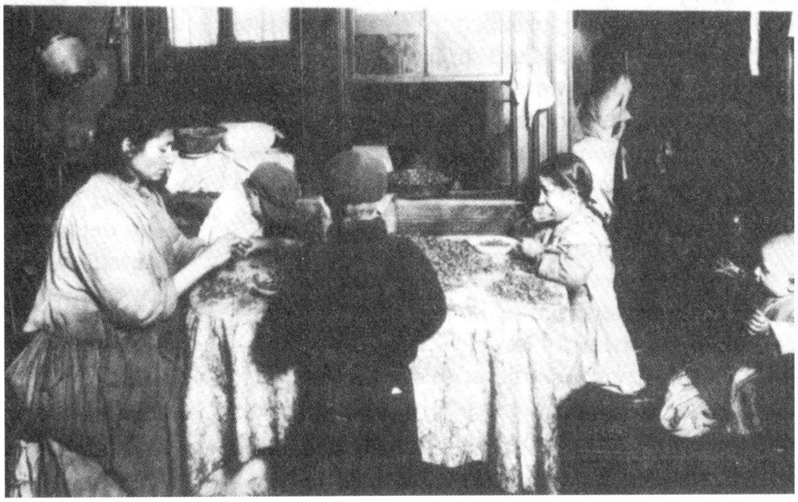

These pictures show the sharp contrast between the nouveau riche and the working class.

in railroading. They began to consolidate railroads. This worked so well that Morgan next turned his attention to the steel industry. When rivalry between Carnegie and the other steel men threatened to precipitate a price war, Morgan stepped in and formed the first billion dollar corporation, United States Steel Corporation. Morgan continued to look for other fields where he might use his expertise. He acquired new industries and secured positions for his partners and representatives on many of the boards of directors.

Morgan's opportunities for consolidation arose because of cutthroat competition in some industries that he thought endangered the industrial base of the United States. The Depression of 1893 made this kind of competition all the more severe. When prosperity returned in 1897, banks easily floated the new issues of securities needed to finance consolidations. Between 1898 and 1904 the number of consolidations reached a peak not to be equalled until the 1920s.

In John Moody's 1904 book, *The Truth About The Trusts*, he listed 318 great corporations that had been organized or were in the process of being organized that year. Such trusts included United States Steel, Standard Oil, Consolidated Tobacco, Amalgamated Copper, International Mercantile Marine Co., American Smelting and Refining Company, International Harvester, General Electric, New York Life, Mutual Life, and Equitable Life. Insurance companies were considered particular plums for financial capitalists since they represented good markets for securities. Consolidations were also taking place in the utilities: telephone, telegraph, and gas.

The public learned of the activities of financial capitalists when a fight broke out in the railroad industries over control of the Chicago, Burlington and Quincy Railroads, which would provide a Chicago link to one of the transcontinental railroads. Two major banking interests, the House of Morgan and Kuhn, Loeb and Company, backed the two top contenders. One of the results was a market crash that wiped out thousands of stockholders and brokers. It did not, however, harm either the Rockefeller or Morgan interests who compromised and emerged wealthier than ever.

The masters of the great combinations thought unity was preferable to competition. This lesson was reinforced when the two banking groups had to act together to stem a stock-market panic in 1907. After that, the two groups tended to merge through interlocking directorates and the purchase of stock in each other's companies.

For the economy as a whole, large corporations had sweeping significance for they meant that men who controlled a few strategic businesses could create vast economic empires. An investment banker like J. P. Morgan could extend his bank's control by lending money to a corporation or by selling its securities if the corporation made room for a Morgan man on its board of directors. Since the banker-director could control what new money the corporation might borrow, he played a decisive role in the corporation's decisions.

In 1913 the Pujo Committee of the House of Representatives, which had worked for two years to untangle their financial affairs, showed that persons belonging to either the Morgan or Rockefeller interests controlled more than three times the assessed value of all property in the thirteen Southern states and more than the assessed property values of the twenty-two states west of the Mississippi.

MUCKRAKERS

While congressional committees played a small role in exposing the inequities of the era, most people's source of information was a group of investigative reporters whom Teddy Roosevelt nicknamed "**muckrakers.**" Roosevelt devised the term from a character in John Bunyon's *Pilgrim's Progress,* who could not look anywhere but at the filth he was raking up. Although Roosevelt agreed with many of the muckrakers' charges, he condemned them because he feared that their widely read exposes of the "muck" or underside of the business world, government, and society to the general public would arouse dangerous discontent. The muckrakers responded that the facts they exposed would make the American people indignant enough to fight for necessary reforms.

The digging up of dirt didn't begin with the muckrakers but was aided by the growth of popular magazines and newspapers as well as an increase in the number of readers who could buy such publications. Magazines such as *McClure's*, *Cosmopolitan*, *Everybody's*, *Collier's*, and *American Magazine* financed the muckrakers' investigations and provided them with a built-in audience. The public wanted the inside dirt, and the publishers were willing to give it to them. With this monetary backing, reporters could dig into court records, locate witnesses, and dig up mountains of facts. The new muckrakers named names and recounted misdeeds in sensational detail, and the new national magazines gave them national influence. Nothing escaped their pens.

Often cited as the first muckraker, Henry Demarest Lloyd examined monopolies including Standard Oil and published his finding in 1894, *Wealth Against Commonwealth*. Lloyd showed how the heads of the huge corporations and trusts answered to no one and were able to exert considerable control over the government by assiduous use of their wealth to support their friends and punish those they saw as enemies. Another early muckraker was Jacob Riis, who wrote extensively on the life of immigrants in the city and exposed the disease, vice, and desperation of its residents. His expose was published in book form in 1890, *How the Other Half Lives*; in 1902 he published *The Battle With the Slum*.

What is considered the golden era of muckraking began with Lincoln Steffens who wrote on political conditions in American cities. These articles were republished in 1903 as *The Shame of the Cities*. With $2,000 from *McClure's* available for research, Steffens investigated city government in Philadelphia, Pittsburgh, Minneapolis, St. Louis, and other cities.

McClures magazine was at the front of the crusade for reform. Ida Tarbell wrote an expose on the Standard Oil Company.

They all suffered from the same ills: bribery by businessmen, corrupt and shrewd party bosses, political collusion, special privileges, organized vice, venal police, and apathetic citizens.

Ida Tarbell's expose of Standard Oil, also financed by *McClure's* for $4,000, was eventually published in 1904 as the *History of Standard Oil Company*. Tarbell, whose father had been driven out of business by Rockefeller, retold the story of the pitiless methods by which that huge combine bent other companies to its will. Her three years of research resulted in a more detailed analysis than Lloyd's and was even more damaging.

Another woman who reported on societal ills was Marie Van Vorst, a socialite-turned-muckraker, who described the life of working women in a Massachusetts' shoe factory and went undercover as a mill worker in a South Carolina textile mill where she exposed the abuses of child labor. Van Vorst's collected articles were published in 1903 as *The Woman Who Toils*. Even worse conditions of child labor abuses existed in the industrial Northern states. In 1900 in Pennsylvania 120,000 children under fifteen worked in mines and mills while in New York in that year 92,000 children worked ten to twelve hours a day, often seven days a week, in dangerous and unhealthy conditions.

Muckrakers wrote on a variety of social problems. David Graham Phillips, a *Cosmopolitan* reporter, wrote a series about the United States Senate, a private club of millionaires who put personal interests first. These articles were also republished in 1906 as the *Treason of the Senate*. It was in response to this publication that Roosevelt had coined the term "muckraker." Gustavus Myers drew upon old court records and other forgotten materials to show the extent to which American enterprise had thrived on exploitation, dishonesty, and unearned profits. Other muckrakers included Charles Edward Russell, who exposed the beef trust, Thomas Lawson, who wrote about Amalgamated Copper, and Upton Sinclair's expose of the Chicago meatpacking industry in his novel *The Jungle* (1906).

While Ida Bell Wells Barnett, a prominent African-American woman, is not often included in the standard listing of muckraking reporters, her expose of lynching in the South was of that genre. Wells Barnett was already well known as an advocate of integration of trains and schools before she began her campaign to eliminate lynching in the South. She wrote articles in the *Memphis Free Speech* that showed how African-American males were murdered for being "sassy" or for supposed rape even when a victim testified that the rapist was a white man. These articles infuriated the white power base in Memphis who destroyed the newspaper and told her that her life would be worthless if she remained in Memphis. Wells Barnett moved to Chicago and, in 1909, co-founded the National Association for the Advancement of Colored People.

In some cities children like these boys worked in the garment industry instead of playing with their friends.

Some muckrakers' efforts did produce results. Upton Sinclair's novel, *The Jungle,* exposed conditions in the Chicago meat-packing industry that helped lead to the passage of the Meat Inspection Act and the Pure Food and Drug Act. Burton Hendrick's expose of insurance companies in *The Story of Life Insurance* resulted in the governor of New York pushing for regulation of the great insurance companies in New York State. The life of innocence was over for the American citizen.

PROGRESSIVISM ON THE LOCAL AND STATE LEVELS

The same pervasive influence of giant corporations applied at the local and state levels. The progressive movement, like the Populist Movement, began at the local level, spreading from cities to states and, ultimately, to the federal level. On the urban scene the movement for municipal reform began in New York City in 1894, when reformers overthrew Tammany Hall, and in Chicago, as an aftermath of the attention drawn to the corruption of the city during the Columbian Exposition. In 1901 a reformer was elected mayor of Cleveland. He secured tax reforms and made Cleveland one of the best run cities and a model for other reformers.

Because the state legislatures controlled the cities, political bosses often went to them in an attempt to thwart the reformers. This is how the progressives started moving into the state level of politics. One of the greatest of the state reformers was Robert La Follette who was elected governor of Wisconsin in 1900. He ousted the strong Republican state machine, established his own, made advances in the regulation of railroads and public utilities, and reformed the tax system of the state. Hiram Johnson did a similar job in California. In New York Charles Hughes fought for the regulation of railroads and utilities. Woodrow Wilson did the same in New Jersey.

Their goals were to cripple the power of the political machines, to put the control of affairs more directly into the hands of the citizens, and to increase the efficiency of government. To improve municipal government, reformers insisted that a commission of administrators without party affiliations replace the mayor and council. This advanced the idea of a city manager. There was a tidal wave in Galveston, and the city council proved completely incompetent to handle this emergency so the legislature set up a five-man commission to govern the city. This worked, and soon other cities adopted it. The final modification happened as a result of a flood in Dayton, Ohio. Here the board of commissioners hired a city manager, who was someone especially trained for the job. By 1923 over 300 cities had this form of local government.

Besides concern for economic justice as consumers, there was also a concern for economic justice for those who worked for big business whether it was the oil, railroad, or the steel industries. Nor was industry itself free from the same exploitations that the trust used on the individual. As Ida Tarbell detailed it, those railroads that served Standard Oil, which was synonymous with the oil industry, might be held up for rebates, money returned to them under the table so that they paid cheaper rates than those published. Large trusts like Standard Oil also demanded drawbacks, by which the railroad would raise the published rates to all oil companies and return to Standard Oil its regular rebate and most of the increased rates charged to its competitors. Thus, its competitors would be subsidizing Standard Oil.

Social Evils

The progressives also addressed problems women faced. Recognizing that many women and children suffered when the men in the family drank, there was a movement to prohibit the making, selling, and consuming of alcoholic beverages. The movement is most closely identified with the Women's Christian Temperance Union. It was a movement for prohibition not temperance. Although Frances Willard was the founder of the WCTU, Carrie Nation was its best-known advocate. An imposing woman six feet tall and 175 pounds, Carrie Nation was arrested thirty times for breaking up saloons with her axe. The WCTU was also involved in many other projects: members ran a hotel for working women, provided classes in stenographic skills, and campaigned for kindergartens, prison reform, and woman suffrage.

To combat the social evils of the day, the Social Gospel developed within the Protestant tradition. The idea was that Christians should conduct themselves as if Christ were alive and living in the tenements of the cities. While the Social Gospel occurred only in some Protestant churches, the majority of the inhabitants of the slums were recent immigrants from southern or eastern Europe who were primarily Roman Catholic, Russian or Greek Orthodox, or Jewish. Thus, it had little effect.

HULL HOUSE

The settlement house movement that began in Europe was a different attempt to improve life in the slums. Operating much like a latter-day Peace Corps, the volunteers lived in the worst sections of the cities. Rather than telling the residents what was wrong, settlement house workers sought to work with their neighbors to solve the problems that the community identified.

The most famous of the settlement houses was Jane Addams' Hull House in Chicago. Jane Addams was typical of the new generation of middle-class college-educated women. Financially secure, Addams did not have to work and, in fact, her family expected her to stay at home and live the passive life of the stereotypical nineteenth century woman. Her reaction to this was also typical of many women. Like the writer, Charlotte Perkins Gilman, she suffered a bout of "nervous" prostration. Her physician was Dr. S. Weir Mitchell, the same "alienist," a nineteenth century term for psychiatrists, who had also treated Gilman. Weir prescribed a rest cure of total seclusion, soft food, darkened rooms, and massages from the physician. While many women responded positively to this common prescription, it was equally ineffective for both of these active women. Gilman was eventually cured by becoming a popular author and lecturer and Addams by her involvement in the settlement house movement.

During a trip to Europe with her best friend, artist Ellen Starr, Addams visited the original settlement house, Toynbee Hall in London, and saw young college graduates living among the poor to aid them. When they returned to Chicago, Addams and Starr bought an abandoned mansion from Charles J. Hull, and thus the most famous settlement house in the United States was begun.

Although Addams began as a naive do-good-er, she was able to overcome this and learn from the immigrants who lived near Hull House what their basic needs were. Soon Hull House was offering classes in English, hosting union meetings, providing kindergartens, and other services. Although Hull House had many successes, workers also met defeats. One occasion was the attempt to get the city government of Chicago to correct the problem of raw sewage running down the streets of the Hull House neighborhood. The greatest success of Hull House and settlement houses was that it involved many upper-class women in a world outside their own and thus educated them to the inequalities of society. They also led to a new profession, that of social worker.

Over the years a host of important women came to Hull House and changed Addams' goals. Doctor Alice Hamilton, a volunteer who also was a physician, took on the match girls' problem of "phossy jaw," a disintegration of the jaw bone caused by the phosphorous used on the heads of matches. She solved the problem and saved the girls' jaws by finding a substitute for the dangerous phosphorous. Another Hull House volunteer, Julia Lathrop, was instrumental in the founding of the juvenile court system.

One of the most important residents was Florence Kelley. Like Addams, Kelley came from an upper middle-class home and was college-educated. A graduate of Cornell University, she was denied admission to law schools in the United States. As a result, she studied law in Zurich, Switzerland where she became a Socialist. When Kelley's marriage to a Polish-German Socialist broke up, she moved to Illinois where it was easier to obtain a divorce than in New York.

Kelley provided a contrast to Addams. While Addams was unmarried and may have been a lesbian, Kelley was a divorced mother. Addams was proper and reserved while Kelley was hot tempered and explosive. While Addams liked evening prayers, art lessons, and scholarly meetings, Kelley was an activist. In 1892 she was appointed to the State Bureau of Labor Statistics where she was asked to inspect factories in Chicago. Later, she was appointed the first factory inspector for the state of Illinois. Kelley's influence has been credited with turning Addams from a philanthropist to a reformer.

Jane Addams founded Chicago's Hull House in 1889. The settlement house brought hope to poverty-stricken slum dwellers.

Addams' work as a reformer made her one of the first native-born Americans to recognize the importance of environment in explaining the problems of the immigrants. Addams, however, was more interested in solving the immediate problems of the poor than in a philosophical examination of the nature of capitalism. Her beliefs led her to become a leader of the Progressive Party that, in 1912, called for an eight-hour day, six-day week; abolition of tenement manufacture; improvement of housing; prohibition of child labor under sixteen; regulation of employment for women; a federal system of accident, old-age, and unemployment insurance; and woman suffrage.

WOMAN SUFFRAGE

During the Progressive Era, a new generation was coming of age in the woman suffrage movement. Members were less ideological and more focused than Elizabeth Cady Stanton and Susan B. Anthony had been. These new leaders like Carrie Chapman Catt and Anna Howard Shaw sought to win the support of middle-class women. To do that, they purged the movement of unconventional leaders and radical positions. Catt succeeded Anthony as the president of the National American Woman Suffrage Association (NAWSA). Her strategy was first to pursue suffrage on a state by state basis to get the grass roots support that would be necessary to get a federal amendment passed. She wanted the suffrage message carried into every town meeting, caucus, and primary to influence the ordinary voters who would never come to NAWSA meetings. When Catt resigned the presidency due to the illness of her husband, she was succeeded by Anna Howard Shaw, a woman of great organizational ability but a leader who lacked the people skills necessary to build unity and to secure victory. During her tenure the movement was at a standstill.

On the local level the new generation was changing the strategy from the demand for full equality to the argument that women deserved the vote because they were morally superior, an argument that fit in comfortably with Victorian notions. They truly believed that when women got the vote, they would support candidates who would solve the social and moral problems of the era. The arguments used were undemocratic but appealed to the racist and anti-immigrant feelings of the middle class: women could counteract the votes of ignorant males whether black or immigrant. By 1903 the woman suffrage movement was completely separated from the black movement, a discarding of the movement's roots in the pre-Civil War abolitionist movement.

The final push for woman suffrage began in 1910 as several states gave women the right to vote. It was accelerated when several American women, Harriot Stanton Blatch, Elizabeth Cady Stanton's daughter; Alice Paul; Lucy Burns; and others returned from England where they had learned the militant tactics of the radical wing of the British suffrage movement. Emmeline Pankhurst and her daughters who led the British movement believed in civil disobedience and confrontation with the government. Their activities included chaining themselves to buildings, burning down buildings, battling with the police, and mass marches. When they were arrested, they went on hunger strikes.

By 1915, those who were more radical grouped under the leadership of Alice Paul, who organized the Congressional Union to take advantage of the political power of four million women who already had the vote. Paul's strategy was to hold the party in power, the Democrats, responsible for women's lack of the vote. She proposed harassing the Democrats and their leader, President Woodrow Wilson, until they ceased their opposition. The NAWSA leaders disliked Paul's plan as it ran counter to their non-partisan policy. Many in NAWSA also considered Paul's tactic of mass marches and picketing improper. When Carrie Chapman Catt returned to power as president of NAWSA, Paul was expelled. After that, Paul and other members of the Congressional Union organized the Woman's Party that had one plank: winning the vote for all women. While Catt was working for a state by state strategy, Paul took more direct action.

In 1916, Paul's Woman's Party campaigned against Wilson's re-election bid. Although Wilson won, the Woman's Party had forced politicians to take note of the suffrage issue. Members began to picket the White House standing in silent vigil in all types of weather holding banners that referred to Wilson as "Kaiser Wilson" or that demanded "Democracy should begin at home." After several months, police began making arrests. When the pickets returned, they were charged with obstructing traffic, found guilty, and sent to Occaquan workhouse in Virginia, a notorious hellhole. Those sentenced included Alice Paul. Like their British counterparts, they demanded to be treated as political prisoners and went on hunger strikes. The result was that they were force-fed. This turned out to be a mistake for it aroused sympathy for the women and their cause. Their convictions were overturned, and when they were released from prison, they began picketing again!

A 1911 women's suffrage parade

The combination of the tactics of the Woman's Party and the NAWSA worked and the Rules Committee of the House, after many years of bottling up the suffrage amendment, brought it to the floor for debate. By the war's end, it was clear that women's suffrage would eventually pass; the question was when. The antisuffrage forces had gathered strength for the final battle. They included conservatives who painted woman suffrage as a radical plot; racists who claimed enfranchising black women would mark the end of white supremacy; liquor interests who opposed it because they feared it would lead to prohibition; and northern political bosses who feared women's reformist impulses might drive them out of power. Antisuffragists had no hesitation about bribing politicians, lying about the nature of the women's movement, and producing scurrilous propaganda. One group, the National Women's Organization to Oppose Suffrage, said the vote would be a burden that woman did not want.

Finally on January 10, 1918, Jeannette Rankin of Montana, the first woman elected to Congress, introduced the suffrage amendment onto the floor of the House where it passed. It took another year and a half for the amendment to pass in the Senate. The final battle was to secure ratification by thirty-six states. The battle was won in August 26, 1920, when Tennessee ratified the Nineteenth Amendment by one vote, ensuring its addition to the Constitution. NAWSA evolved into the League of Women Voters, and the Women's Party began working on an Equal Rights Amendment.

ECONOMIC AND SOCIAL PROBLEMS

At the bottom of the economic ladder was a class of workers who were plagued by unemployment, huddled into hideous slums, and vulnerable to all sorts of diseases. Some worked 72 hours a week. Industrial accidents brought tragedy and then poverty to a large portion of the working class. Even by 1913 when numerous industries had adopted safety measures, many workers were killed on their jobs and thousands gravely injured. Women and children worked long hours in factories without any protection of laws or unions. Immigrants lived in the cities under the most trying and dangerous conditions. African Americans, victimized by a heritage of slavery, were terrorized and voteless in the South.

The newly minted millionaires were a concern of the progressives. During the 1840s there were approximately twenty millionaires; by 1892 the New York *Tribune* listed 4,047. The distribution of wealth was also a concern since in 1893, 71 percent of the wealth was owned by 9 percent of the families! The new millionaires were extraordinary rich, numerous, and often uncultivated and crude. They were the new barbarians who came from above. The mere existence of "robber barons" was provocative to the rest of society. Their swollen fortunes made men of more modest means feel insignificant. Their lack of scruples put men of principle at a disadvantage.

Even their charities and philanthropies seemed overly conspicuous and threw other men's generosity into the shade. The follies they and their families indulged in were in keeping with their means: ostentatious houses, squads of retainers and mistresses, and extravagances of all kinds.

The new rich were firm believers in Social Darwinism, Charles Darwin's concept of survival of the fittest applied to economic life. They also believed in laissez faire capitalism where the government kept hands off of the economy except for the enforcement of contracts. Those who had large fortunes increasingly determined public economic, social, and political philosophy through the members of Congress whom they figuratively and often literally owned. They planned to use their wealth to buy whatever was needed politically to keep it! Political leaders like Teddy Roosevelt were afraid that the life style and activities of the rich would provoke the public into dangerous political extremes. After 1900 progressives became involved in politics to see their ideas put into action.

Social Legislation

The progressives had their greatest success with social legislation, particularly in state legislatures. State laws were now passed against child labor. By 1914 every state but one had a minimum age for child labor. Other prohibitions prevented night work and employment in dangerous occupations. Efforts at the federal level were not so successful. In 1918 the United States Supreme Court declared the Keating-Owen Act, which prohibited the interstate shipment of goods made in factories, mines, or quarries employing children under specified ages, unconstitutional. The Court declared the act a violation of the police powers of the state and an attempt to use the interstate commerce clause to achieve other ends.

The campaign to protect women in industry also resulted in state laws limiting the number of hours of female labor: New York and Massachusetts had a limit of 60 hours per week. In 1908 the Supreme Court decided the case of *Muller v Oregon* in which an employer challenged the Oregon law limiting the hours women worked to 10 a day. The law was declared constitutional. By 1917 some thirty-nine states enacted new legislation governing women's work. Minimum wages were also set. The Supreme Court, however, declared a law regulating the wages of women in the District of Columbia unconstitutional because it deprived them of the freedom of contract. This effectively ended the reform movement.

After 1909, a number of states adopted the accident insurance systems we call workmen's compensation. By 1920, all but five of the states and territories had fallen into line with some kind of insurance. Before that, workers and their families had to sue the company, a risky and costly business.

In 1911 states began to accept the idea that it would be better to aid dependent children in their own homes rather than putting them in institutions. States began to pass mother assistance acts that set up public agencies to grant relief or financial help to working mothers with dependent children. In 1914 some of the states began to pass legislation to help the aged poor in their own homes. Arizona began the practice although its Supreme Court found the law

On March 25, 1911, a fire broke out on the eighth floor of the Triangle Company's building. Exit doors had been locked by the company to prevent theft and to shut out union organizers. Many terrified seamstresses jumped to their deaths on the street below. In all, 3 men and 143 women and girls died.

unconstitutional. In the 1920s, thirty states passed such legislation.

Progressives in Political Life

In the political sphere, the progressives sought greater involvement in the political life of the state and federal governments. One way to break the power of the political machines, they thought, was to institute the direct primary as the source for nominations to office. This proposal enabled the ordinary members of political parties to vote for their party's candidates rather than a political boss choosing the nominees. Progressives hoped that this would insure the selection of abler and more independent candidates. By 1916, some form of direct primary had been adopted by all states except Rhode Island, Connecticut, and New Mexico. To involve the citizens more directly in their government, referendums were added to state constitutions. Here an issue, proposed by the legislative body at a city or state level, would require the approval of the citizenry at the next election. In some states this was followed by the idea of the initiative whereby citizens can propose legislation by securing signatures on petitions. Such devices were particularly popular in the Western states.

The next task was what to do about people who were not performing in their elective offices. This led to the movement for recall in which an elective official can be recalled after sufficient signatures have been collected on a recall petition. The official then has to stand for election again. To the conservatives, the most radical and objectionable proposal of all was the recall of judges. This measure gained strength because many judges were invalidating the social reforms. Several states adopted judicial recall, although it was never invoked. Another plan was to push for a constitutional amendment for the direct elections of United States senators who were still chosen by the state legislatures.

The Square Deal of Teddy Roosevelt and the New Freedom of Woodrow Wilson came out of this reform impulse, as well as a host of other reforms that were, strictly speaking, not part of either program but that won the support of men in both major parties.

PRESIDENTIAL PROGRESSIVISM

When Theodore Roosevelt succeeded to the office of president in 1901, at the age of 42, he was the youngest man to hold that office. He was also one of the most interesting with his unconventional family. "Teddy" was the sickly, asthmatic son of an aristocratic New York family that traced its ancestry back to the original Dutch settlers. The Harvard

Fire nets did not help the Triangle workers who jumped from the upper stories to escape the flames. Labor organizer Rose Schneiderman spoke out against a system that treated human beings as expendable commodities.

graduate became an ardent advocate of physical fitness, working hard on a ranch in the Dakotas where he experienced "the strenuous life" firsthand.

The Spanish-American War made Roosevelt a national hero. He parlayed his fame as a "Rough Rider" into election as governor of New York in 1898. As a moderate reformer, he quickly clashed with the local political bosses who used their influence to "kick him upstairs" to the vice presidency, a job that buried most of its occupants. In fact, Roosevelt himself wrote, "I would a great deal rather be anything, say a history professor, than Vice President." A worried presidential adviser, Mark Hanna, implored McKinley to survive, since only he stood "between that madman and the White House." But in September 1901, McKinley was suddenly dead, the victim of an assassin. "I told McKinley that it was a mistake to nominate that wild man," Hanna reportedly declared ruefully, "Now that damned cowboy is President."

Roosevelt did not look like a president. He was short, wore thick glasses, had buck teeth, and spoke in a high-pitched voice. He did not act like a president either. Nor did his family. His sons rode their ponies into the White House. Reporters spotted Teddy and the Japanese ambassador on their knees searching for young Quentin's missing frog. His daughter, Alice, was equally unconventional and indulged her taste in smoking and making cutting remarks. At one point someone asked Roosevelt if he couldn't do something about Alice's behavior. He responded that he could control Alice or he could run the United States, but he could not do both!

His views were mostly conventional: the government should interfere in the economy only to make competition more humane; blacks and, by extension, all non-Anglo-Saxons were inferior; foreign trade was seen as beneficial because it made America strong; and Anglo-Saxons were being outbred by fecund immigrants. He deplored the social callowness of men of great wealth while at the same time fearing radicalism and agitation. He was an ardent nationalist who saw in devotion to the nation and to the public welfare an answer to the extremes of both big business dominance and radical agitation. He was shrewd in practical politics and had an ability to deal with other politicians. He also had a remarkable intuitive sense for the workings of the popular mind. He was quick to grasp concerns of the ordinary person and to express them. Few presidents have projected their personalities so vividly and with such success to the American public particularly in an era before mass media and have remained so popular for so long as Theodore Roosevelt.

Conservation

Roosevelt was dedicated to the conservation movement that then meant that natural resources be efficiently developed. Forests, for example, should be preserved because they protected watersheds, and timber production should be balanced against other uses. While forests could be exploited, it was only under the guidelines established by the Forest

Service, headed under Roosevelt by Gifford Pinchot. In accordance with the Forest Reserve Act of 1891, Roosevelt set aside almost 150 million acres of unsold government timber lands in various parts of the country as forest reserve and closed about 85 million additional acres in Alaska and the Northwest to public access so that the mineral and water resources of the area could be studied. The result was that the land under Pinchot's control tripled in size. Because the Forest Service believed in efficiency, it often favored large timber companies over small ones and cattle ranchers over sheep ranchers and farmers. A significant split existed between those like Pinchot who wanted to conserve resources for continuous human use and those like John Muir who wanted to set aside wilderness areas. Muir never forgave Pinchot for endorsing a water reservoir in the wild Hetch Hetchy Valley of Yosemite National Park to supply water to San Francisco.

Trust Buster

Roosevelt thought that there was a difference between bad trusts and good trusts. Good trusts were a result of efficiency and evolution; bad trusts, like Standard Oil, became rich from illicit practices. While good trusts could be tolerated, bad ones should be broken up. Roosevelt's reputation as a trust buster rested on the actions he took in 1902 when he ordered his attorney general to bring suit to dissolve the Northern Securities Company organized by the Morgan and Rockefeller interests after their fight over the Chicago, Burlington and Quincy Railroads. It was an excellent way of dramatizing the vigor of the new administration. The announcement suggested that Roosevelt was going to battle with the mightiest of financial giants. The suit dragged on for almost two years. In 1904 the Supreme Court handed down a decision that seemed a great triumph for the president and the anti-trust principle. By a 5-4 decision the Court ruled that the combination must be broken up. This reversed a previous decision and opened the way to further prosecution. Roosevelt thought that this was the greatest achievement of his administration. "The most powerful men in this country were held accountable before the law."

Roosevelt soon ordered more prosecutions. One suit was brought against the "Beef trust," a combination of packing companies and others against Standard Oil and the American Tobacco Co. These cases dragged on and had rather indecisive results. While they did not halt the wave of business consolidation, they did keep alive the possibility that a particularly ruthless firm might find itself confronted with a costly prosecution. In 1903 Roosevelt set up a Bureau of Corporations under the new Department of Commerce to investigate corporations, and it provided valuable information on several industries that were in time made subject to prosecution.

In 1902 Roosevelt intervened in a labor dispute. In May John Mitchell of the United Mine Workers called a bitter strike in the anthracite fields. The workers got much sympathy because of a statement made by George F. Baer, president of the Reading Railroad and spokesman of the mine operators. He announced that the miners would be protected "not by the labor agitators but by the Christian men to whom God in His infinite wisdom, has given control of the property interests of this country."

As the strike wore on and it looked as if there would be real coal shortages in the cities in the winter, Roosevelt took action. In October he called Mitchell and the operators to the White House for a meeting. Mitchell agreed to arbitration, but the owners refused. Roosevelt made plans to have the United States Army take over and operate the mines on behalf of the government. He also asked J. P. Morgan to try to get the operators to arbitrate before the impending seizure became necessary. The mine operators agreed with one condition: that no labor officials be appointed to the commission on arbitration. Roosevelt did not argue the point; instead, he appointed a former president of one of the railroad unions to the board as an "eminent sociologist." Ultimately, the mine workers won a 9 hour day, a 10 cent wage increase, a permanent board of conciliation, and the right to select check-weighmen. It was the most decisive, most impartial, and most satisfactory intervention that an American president had ever undertaken in a labor dispute. It added greatly to Roosevelt's prestige and strengthened the public's perception that, at last, a man occupied the White House who could deal successfully and in the public's interest with the great masters of capital.

In 1904 Roosevelt was nominated for president in his own right and won handily. During the next four years his major achievements involved railroad regulation, protection of consumers, and the conservation of natural resources.

The Interstate Commerce Act had been a disappointment partly because previous administrations had neglected to make much use of it but also because the Supreme Court's narrow interpretation of the powers of the commission rendered it almost helpless. In 1903 Congress passed the Elkins Act, making it illegal for railroads to depart in practice from their published freight rates and making shippers, as well as railroads, liable for infractions. This measure struck at rebating fees to bigger customers, which the railroads themselves began to see as a nuisance. However, the Elkins Act failed to give the Interstate Commerce Commission any power to fix rates, which was what farmers and businessmen wanted most.

The Hepburn Act passed in 1906 was the first really effective regulation of railroads by the federal government. It failed to go as far as most reformers wanted, but it did authorize the commission, when a complaint was received, to set maximum rates and to order railroads to comply after 30 days. The Courts were instructed to assume the Interstate Commerce Commission's rulings sound until evidence was massed to the contrary. This threw the burden of proof on the railroads and its lawyers and reduced judicial setbacks for the Interstate Commerce Commission.

The Hepburn Act also extended the Interstate Commerce Commission's powers to include regulation of storage, refrigeration, and terminal facilities, sleeping cars, express, and pipe-line companies. In 1910 it was expanded to include telephone and telegraph companies.

The next businesses to be regulated were the food and drug industries to prevent undesirable additives and preservatives from being added to the nation's food supply. The *Ladies Home Journal* and *Colliers* published articles on patent medicine and their misleading and exaggerated claims. One of the most notorious was Lydia Pinkham's Vegetable Compound, which was 18 percent alcohol. In 1906 Congress responded by passing the Pure Food and Drug Act and the Meat Inspection Act, which struck at some of the worst abuses.

In 1907 a financial panic occurred. While J. P. Morgan was busy serving in the unofficial role as the nation's central banker, he advised Roosevelt that the panic could be stemmed if United States Steel was allowed to acquire control of Tennessee Iron and Coal Company. Whether this was true or not, Roosevelt gave his consent. His secretary of the treasury also released Panama Canal bonds on terms both generous and reassuring to bankers. The panic was stemmed, and prosperity returned. One result of this was the desire of financial authorities to search for ways to strengthen national finance that eventually led to the establishment of the Federal Reserve Act of 1913. Roosevelt's actions demonstrate that he was not an opponent of capitalism but rather believed that government must regulate its excesses.

WILLIAM HOWARD TAFT

At the end of his second term Teddy Roosevelt bowed to the two-term tradition and threw his support to his secretary of war, William Howard Taft of Cincinnati, Ohio. He had been a circuit court judge, governor of the Philippines, and administrator of the Canal Zone. Although Taft was not a man bitten by the presidential bug, his wife Nellie wanted to be First Lady, and so he accepted Roosevelt's support and the Republican Party's nomination. The Democrats again ran William Jennings Bryan. The progressive reforms that Roosevelt had pushed undercut Bryan, and he lost for the third and final time.

It would have been difficult for anyone to follow the flamboyant and popular Teddy. Taft, a genial man who lacked political instincts, was cautious, slow-moving, and passive. Already obese, his weight ballooned to over 350 pounds. A special oversized tub was installed for his use lending credence to the rumor that he once was stuck in a too snug tub.

Roosevelt and Taft thought their views were alike, but they were wrong. Taft was much more conservative than Roosevelt. Taft did not want to tussle with the Old Guard in the Senate with whom

Roosevelt had had to bargain for every reform. His notion of the presidency was much more passive than anything Roosevelt had ever envisioned. As a result, the Republicans gradually returned to their conservative ideology.

Although Roosevelt was known as the trust buster, it was Taft who instituted twice as many antitrust actions under the Sherman Antitrust Act in one administration than Roosevelt had done in two. Taft concluded the prosecutions of Standard Oil and American Tobacco begun under Roosevelt. Taft also proceeded with antitrust cases against International Harvester and United States Steel for acquiring Tennessee Iron and Coal Company. Both were unsuccessful.

Progressives, rather than Taft, must be credited with what was accomplished in railroad regulation. The Mann-Elkins Act of 1910 represented a victory by empowering the Interstate Commerce Commission to suspend general rate increases and to take the initiative in revising rates. A Commerce Court was established to speed up the judicial process by hearing appeals directly from the commission. Railroads were also prohibited from acquiring competing lines. The Physical Evaluation Act enabled the Interstate Commerce Commission to do a physical evaluation of railroad property as a basis for rate making. Now the Interstate Commerce Commission could fix rates on the true value of operating properties rather than the watered stock that the railroads had been in the habit of issuing since the time of Daniel Drew and Jay Gould at the Erie Railroad.

Except for his antitrust policies, President Taft was not closely identified with the progressive measures that Congress enacted during his administration. He split with the progressive members of his party, known as the insurgents, over the tariff. Taft called Congress into special session in March of 1909 to lower the tariff, but when these proposals for a downward revision met with strong opposition from Senator Nelson Aldrich, who was the spokesman for special interests, Taft acquiesced in raising the tariff. When the Payne-Aldrich Bill passed, Taft signed it. He further alienated the progressives by calling it the best tariff the Republicans had ever passed.

Taft also irritated the progressives by helping to quash a rebellion of insurgents against the Speaker of the House, Joseph G. Cannon of Illinois. The progressives and a number of Democrats were trying to replace Cannon, who was a virtual dictator, but Cannon appealed to Taft, who supported him in order to get his vote. Nevertheless, early in 1910, Cannon was removed from the Rules Committee, which meant that he no longer could appoint members to standing committees thus weakening his power.

The Pinchot-Ballinger affair was the last straw for Republican unity. Chief Forester of the Department of Agriculture, Gifford Pinchot, heard from an investigator that Secretary of the Interior Richard A. Ballinger had agreed to sell to the Guggenheim mining interests several million acres of reserved coal lands in Alaska. Pinchot encouraged the investigator to appeal to Taft while he issued a statement denouncing Ballinger. Taft chose to believe Ballinger's denials rather than the investigator's charges and authorized the investigator's dismissal. Pinchot carried on with the attack until he, too, was removed. Congress now investigated and found Ballinger not guilty. However, it was obvious that he was no conservationist. Taft was a conservationist, but after his support of Ballinger, it was easy to persuade people that he wasn't.

After March 1910, open warfare erupted between Taft and the insurgents as Taft used presidential patronage to build up conservative Republicans in the Midwest, the insurgents' power base. The congressional elections that year showed that the Republicans could not succeed without the progressives. The House went Democratic for the first time since 1893, and many Democratic governors were elected. It seemed that the Democrats might even capture the White House. It also seemed that the insurgents would capture the Republican Party and repudiate Taft.

The obvious man to lead the insurgents was Robert La Follette of Wisconsin, who had been active in Republican politics since 1880. He was the first leader in American history to make use of a brain trust, most of whom were his old school friends from the University of Wisconsin. He made good use of professors at the university, and he did careful research into economic and social programs before he gave speeches. Some of the most ardent progressives wanted him to be the Republican candidate for president. Others, who felt La Follette could not be elected, supported Taft.

Election of 1912

Taft's break with the insurgents also included a break with Theodore Roosevelt, who now proceeded with caution. When Roosevelt returned to New York in 1910 from his year-long trip to Africa and Europe, he was dismayed at how Taft had allowed the party to go to pieces. At first, he refrained from making comments, but by August 1910 he gave a famous address in Kansas in which he came out for a number of progressive anti-administration reforms, including more federal regulation of business and judicial recall. His accusation that the federal judiciary was obstructing the popular will shocked conservatives throughout the nation. La Follette thought Roosevelt was going to support him, but when La Follette, tired, ill and troubled by the illness of one of his daughters, collapsed while delivering a major speech, the more formidable progressive Republicans deserted La Follette. In February of 1912, at Roosevelt's instigation, seven Republican governors wrote him, urging him to announce his candidacy. Two weeks later, his hat was in the ring.

A savage fight followed between Roosevelt and Taft for the Republican nomination. At the convention, there were 254 contested seats; the Taft forces carried all of them, and Roosevelt's delegates stormed out of the hall, leaving Taft to be renominated by a now split party.

The Roosevelt Republicans quickly organized the Bull Moose Party, which took its name from Teddy Roosevelt's statement after an assassination attempt that he was as fit as a Bull Moose. The Bull Moose Party met in Chicago, nominated Roosevelt, and adopted a platform calling for the adoption of almost all the long-proposed social reforms: initiative, referendum, recall, popular overturning of judges, workmen's compensation and social insurance, minimum wages for women, women's suffrage, child-labor laws, and federal trade and tariff commissions to regulate business. Roosevelt's followers said, "Roosevelt bit me and I went mad."

Meanwhile the Democrats had gotten the good news that Bryan would not run again. Among the leading aspirants was Woodrow Wilson, the progressive Democrat from New Jersey. Because the Democratic Party required a two-thirds vote for nominees, it took forty-six ballots for Woodrow Wilson to receive the nod. Their platform also called for a number of reforms and was particularly outspoken in demanding business and tariff reform.

Wilson combined a flair for politics and a high respect for statesmanship. He had been educated for law but swiftly turned to academic life. He attended graduate school at Johns Hopkins University and wrote a book on congressional government, receiving a Ph.D. in 1886. In 1902 he became president of Princeton University where he began to make reforms. He was seen as a democratic spokesman at a time when people were looking for vigorous leaders. In 1910 the party bosses offered Wilson the nomination for governor of New Jersey. Once elected, he repudiated their backing, which surprised them. He then espoused a variety of reforms that brought him the ardent support of the New Jersey progressives. In the first legislative session he won a primary and election law, corrupt practices act, workmen's compensation, utilities regulation, school reforms, and an enabling act giving New Jersey cities the right to adopt the commission form of government.

As a person, Wilson was a bundle of paradoxes. Although his political career was in the North, he was the son of a Virginia minister. Outwardly cold and forbidding, he was extraordinarily intense. Despite his substantial achievements as a reformer, he also displayed a deep sense of tradition and a great reverence for the past, particularly when it involved race relations. He sought to restore a social and economic order long dead. That Wilson was successful in politics was remarkable. He was an excellent speaker with rhythmic speech, clear and dignified, an impressive campaigner. But offstage he was ill-suited to the give and take of American politics. His personality expressed itself in terms of ideals and principles, not personal loyalties. He was too rigid to compromise. To continue to be so high-principled and yet to engage in practical politics meant that Wilson had to deceive himself, a self deception that some of his critics called hypocrisy. As president, he left patronage to his Postmaster-General. Like Roosevelt his goals were those of moderation. He disliked both the plutocracy and distrusted radicals of the extreme left.

In 1912 his greatest asset was the split in the Republican ranks. The three-way fight soon narrowed down to Wilson versus Roosevelt. Since both campaigned as progressives, the issue turned on the question of how to deal with the trusts. Wilson favored regulated competition; Roosevelt favored regulated monopoly. Wilson said the trusts were too big to be regulated for they would soon control the government itself. He pointed to big businessmen who were among Roosevelt's financial backers. To Wilson, the only possible answer was to restore true competition to business and for the government to take vigorous action to suppress unfair and illicit competition.

Teddy Roosevelt countered with the claim that Wilson's ideas were archaic. To restore competition as it had once existed would be undesirable. It would deny the nation the benefits of large-scale operations, which were seen as more efficient (although that was far from always being accurate). Roosevelt claimed that Wilson was attempting to reverse the natural progress of economic evolution. For Roosevelt, trusts were regulated for the best interests of the nation.

Wilson got 6,296,547 votes, 41.9 percent of the popular vote and 435 electoral votes; Roosevelt was second with 4,118,571, 27.4 percent of the popular vote and 88 electoral votes; Taft received 3,486,720 votes, 23.2 percent of the popular vote and 8 electoral votes. The Democrats captured the House and won a working majority in the Senate, so Wilson had the prospects for a constructive administration with a united party and a large bloc of Republican progressives behind him.

WILSON'S ADMINISTRATION

The years of the Wilson administration, 1913-1921, were years of extraordinary fruitfulness in significant reform legislation. The first item on Wilson's agenda was a revision of the tariff. The Underwood Tariff, which lowered the tariff to 29 percent, passed the House with no problem but encountered problems in the Senate where special interests began their work. Wilson reacted with a public statement denouncing the lobbyists working to defeat the bill. La Follette and other progressives inquired of the senators what properties they had that the tariff would affect. The Underwood Tariff was the first downward revision since the Civil War. It also included an income tax of 1 percent on incomes over $4,000 with a graduated surtax from 1-6 percent to make up the revenues lost. This was possible because the Sixteenth Amendment added to the Constitution in 1913 provided for a federal income tax. A second progressive amendment adopted in the same year was the Seventeenth that provided for the direct election of United States senators.

Wilson's second item was banking reform. The need for a federal central bank had been made obvious in the Panic of 1907. A lender of last resort was needed for the banking system. The nation no longer could depend on having a J. P. Morgan to come to the rescue. A bill was finally developed that included twelve Federal Reserve Banks representing twelve regions of the country. These were owned by member banks of the Federal Reserve system who subscribed part of their capital to the banks. The regional banks acted as agents and servants of the member banks. The Federal Reserve system was under the direction of the Federal Reserve Board, consisting of the secretary of the treasury, comptroller, and seven others appointed by the president for fourteen-year terms. A new currency was issued known as federal reserve notes. All national banks had to join the system, and state banks were also eligible. By 1923, 70 percent of the banking resources were in the system. The Federal Reserve system created a currency that was both flexible and sound.

Corporate, Labor, and Farm Legislation

Wilson pushed two regulatory acts through Congress that reflected his philosophy regarding trusts. The Federal Trade Commission Act, passed in 1914, was designed to prevent rather than to punish unfair trade practices. It set up a five-member "watch dog" agency, the Federal Trade Commission (FTC), with the power to investigate corporations engaged in interstate commerce, to look into alleged violations of anti-trust laws, and to issue cease and desist orders. The commission could also sue corporations. Under Wilson the commission issued 379 cease and desist orders.

The second act was the Clayton Antitrust Act of 1914, which described a list of illegal activities such as price discrimination, contracts that forced purchasers to refrain from buying the products of competitors; and corporate acquisition of stock in competing concerns, interlocking directorates connecting corporations with capital of more than $1 million or banks with capital of more than $5 million. Officers of corporations were made individually liable for prosecution and victims of price discrimination could sue for compensation three times the amount of damages suffered. Labor unions were not to be construed as illegal combinations and labor injunctions were forbidden except when necessary to prevent irreparable injury to property or property rights. Wilson's appointments to the Federal Trade Commission weakened many of its provisions. In the 1920s most of its provisions were nullified under Republican administrations.

Four important acts met the needs of farmers. In 1916 the Federal Farm Loan Act created a Federal Farm Loan Board patterned after the Federal Reserve Board. Twelve Federal Land Banks were established with a minimum capital of $750,000 and could offer farmers loans of five to forty years at 6 percent interest rates. Farm lands, buildings, and improvements for up to 70 percent of the assets secured the loans. Profits were to be distributed to the members of the association. Within fourteen years over four thousand loans were made.

The second act was the Warehouse Act of 1916, which like the old Populist sub-treasury plan authorized licensed warehouse operators to issue warehouse receipts against farm products deposited with them. The third act was the Smith-Lever Act of 1914, which provided millions in federal grants-in-aid for farm demonstration agents working under the land-grant colleges, and the fourth act in 1917 was the Smith-Hughes Act, which subsidized vocational and agricultural education and rounded out the program begun in the Civil War with the land grant colleges. Although not strictly an act for farmers, those that had cars were very interested in the Federal Highways Act of 1916, which provided dollar-matching contributions to state highway departments that met federal standards.

The inaction on labor legislation was also overcome in the Wilson administration with the passage of the Kern-McGillicuddy Bill, which provided workmen's compensation for federal employees. This was followed by the Keating-Owen Child Labor Act. The last act was the Adamson Act, which required an eight-hour day with time and a half for overtime for workers on interstate railways and appointed a commission to study the problems of railroad labor.

It was under Wilson's administration that the last two of the four progressive amendments to the Constitution were passed: the Eighteenth Amendment that prohibited the manufacture, sale or transportation of intoxicating liquors within the United States and the Nineteenth Amendment that gave women the right to vote.

MINORITY RIGHTS IN THE PROGRESSIVE ERA

Although many things were accomplished during the Progressive Era, it did not extend to minority Americans.

As mentioned earlier in the discussion of the women's suffrage movement, the suffrage movement and its divisions represented one example of problems related to race. Suffrage leaders ignored black women who had worked in the movement and appealed to Southern whites that the vote should be given to women so that they could join with their WASP (White Anglo-Saxon Protestant) husbands to counteract the votes of black men and ignorant immigrants. Of course, since black men had already been effectively disenfranchised in the South, there was no danger of black women joining their husbands in voting. The Nineteenth Amendment would, in reality, only enfranchise white women.

There were other examples of racism seen in this period besides the lynching in the South and the treatment of Japanese in the West. Roosevelt had been considered a friend of African Americans when he invited Booker T. Washington to lunch at the White House to consult on distributing minor federal jobs to black Republicans in the South. A storm of racist criticism ensued, including a complaint that the White House Republicans "had been painted black." It took more than thirty years before a president (Franklin Roosevelt) dared to invite a black to dine at the White House.

Teddy Roosevelt's African-American supporters were disappointed at his handling of a 1906 incident in Brownsville, Texas, which seemed to demonstrate his true feeling towards blacks. After a shoot-out between black troops and white townsmen, Roosevelt ordered the entire black regiment to be dishonorably discharged without any trial or even any investigation. Roosevelt's action was even more incomprehensible when you consider that it was black regiments known as Buffalo Soldiers who had rescued Roosevelt at San Juan Hill during the Spanish-American War. The 25th Regiment that had been stationed in Brownsville had an interesting history. At one point the Army considered replacing horses with bicycles and to test the idea, the 25th Regiment, known as the Black Bicycle Brigade, rode bicycles for 2,000 miles from Montana to St. Louis. Their acts of courage and endurance were for naught. It was 1972 before Congress removed the "dishonorable" from the military records of these black soldiers.

While the Taft administration began segregation in the federal department buildings, it was accelerated under Woodrow Wilson, the first Southerner to be president since the Civil War. Although the leaders seemed to have been the Secretary of the Treasury and the Postmaster General, Wilson was well aware of their policies. An additional innovation was the requirement that applicants for civil service positions include a photograph with their applications. Despite this executive action, Congress refused to adopt legislation to segregate the races in the federal departments. Nor did they enact any legislation that curtailed black rights. In response to criticism, Wilson declared that segregation was "in the interest of the Negro."

Neither in foreign affairs nor in domestic affairs did the progressive presidents extend the basic tenets of progressivism to non-whites.

CONCLUSION

Wilson's New Freedom Program represented the apex of the Progressive Movement and with it reform came to a halt. The movement was nullified by the war and the conservative reaction of the 1920s. Although many reforms were enacted, the results were not always what the reformers had wanted. Party machines found ways to manipulate the political processes despite the direct primary. Initiatives and referendums were cumbersome and often misfired. Recall was used only rarely. Money still continued to influence politics although there were more punishments for corruption. Too often the reforms lasted for only a short term and often depended upon the personality and drive of only one person. The bosses eventually came filtering back, more careful but still powerful. Reformers had to console themselves that without their efforts things might have been worse.

Chronology

1889 Jane Addams founds Hull House in Chicago

1901 U. S. Steel Corporation founded first billion dollar corporation.
Jacob Riis, *How the Other Half Lives*

1894 Henry Demarest Lloyd, *Wealth Against Commonwealth;* Tammany Hall overthrown

1896 *Wabash vs Illinois*—U. S. Supreme Court outlawed state regulation of interstate commerce

1898 Spanish-American War

1899 Thorstein Veblen, *The Theory of the Leisure Class*

1900 International Ladies Garment Workers Union (ILGWU) founded; Carrie Chapman Catt becomes president of National American Woman Suffrage Movement

1901 McKinley assassinated; Theodore Roosevelt becomes president; Colonial war fought in Philippines

1902 Roosevelt mediates coal strike; Roosevelt orders attorney general to bring suit to dissolve Northern Securities; Jane Addams, *Democracy and Social Ethics*

1903 Maria Van Vorst, *The Woman Who Toils;* W. E. B. DuBois, *Souls of Black Folks;* Revolution organized in Panama

1904 Roosevelt elected president; *Northern Securities Case* resolved; Lincoln Steffens, *The Shame of the Cities;* Ida Tarbell, *History the Standard Oil Company;* John Moody, *The Truth About Trusts;* Roosevelt Corollary to the Monroe Doctrine

1905 International Workers of the World (IWW) organized; Pinchot head of the U. S. Forest Service; Roosevelt mediates Russo-Japanese War settlement; At Roosevelt's urging San Francisco desegregates schools

1906 David Graham Phillips, *The Treason of the Senate;* Hepburn Act to regulate railroads; Upton Sinclair, *The Jungle;* Pure Food and Drug Act; Meat Inspection Act; Roosevelt wins Nobel Peace Prize

1908 William Howard Taft elected president

1909 National Association for the Advancement of Colored People (NAACP) founded; Ballinger controversy

1910 Push for woman suffrage increases with several new states granting women the right to vote; Mann-Elkins Act empowered; Interstate Commerce Commission

1911 Triangle Shirtwaist Company fire; Standard Oil dissolved

1912 Three way election - GOP (Taft), Progressives (T. Roosevelt), and Democrats (Wilson). Wilson elected; U. S. troops in Mexico

1913 Pujo Committee; Federal Reserve Act; Sixteenth Amendment—income tax Seventeenth Amendment—direct election of senators; 30,000 march in New York for woman's suffrage

1914 Clayton Anti-trust Act; Completion of Panama Canal; Federal Trade Commission Act

1915 Congressional Union founded to push for woman suffrage

1916 Federal Farm Loan Act; Wilson re-elected; Margaret Higgins Sanger opens birth control clinic

1918 Jeanette Rankin introduced suffrage amendment that passed the House

1919 Eighteenth Amendment—prohibition

1920 Nineteenth Amendment—woman's suffrage

SUGGESTED READINGS

John Milton Cooper Jr., *The Warrior and the Priest: Woodrow Wilson and Theodore* (1983).

Robert Morse Crunden, *Ministers of Reform; The Progressives' Achievement in American Civilization, 1889-1920* (1984).

David B. Danbom, *"The World of Hope":Progressives and the Struggle for an Ethical Public Life.* (1987).

Noralee Frankel and Nancy F. Dye, (eds.), *Gender, Class, Race and Reform in the Progressive Era* (1991).

Elizabeth Frost and Kathryn Cullen-DuPont, *Women's Suffrage in America, An Eyewitness Report* (1995).

Richard Hofstadter, *The Age of Reform: From Bryan to F.D.R.* (1955).

Harold Howland, *Theodore Roosevelt (1921).*

William O'Neill, *The Progressive Years: America Comes of Age* (1975).

John Lugton Safford, *Pragmatism and the Progressive Movement in the United States: The Origins of the New Social Sciences* (1987).

Dorothy Schneider and Carl J. Schneider, *American Women in the Progressive Era, 1900-1920* (1994).

Mildred I. Thompson, *Ida B. Wells-Barnett: An Exploratory Study of an American Black Woman, 1893-1930* (1990).

Ida B. Wells-Barnett, *On Lynching: Southern Horrors, A Red Record Mob Rule in New Orleans* (1991).

Marjorie Spruill Wheeler (ed)., *One Woman, One Vote: Rediscovering the Woman Suffrage Movement* (1995).

Robert H. Wiebe, *Businessmen and Reform* (1962).

SURE!
We'll
Finish
the Job
Gerrit A. Beneker 1918
VICTORY LIBERTY LOAN

Chapter Seventeen

THE "GREAT" WAR: World War I

We Lost Everything But What We Had On

As this chapter will recount, the war years and their immediate aftermath, witnessed some of the most brutally violent and destructive moments of racial tension and discrimination in this nation's history. Interestingly only a handful of the riots occurred in the South; rather it was in Northern cities such as Chicago and St. Louis where the most serious outrages took place. In the summer of 1919 both cities exploded into what became the two worse episodes of racial violence in the United States until the 1960s. As this letter from an African American caught in the middle of the terror in East St. Louis, Illinois confirms, the rage exhibited by whites toward black citizens bordered on the psychopathic. Over the course of several days, rabid white mobs attacked African Americans, many of whom, to the surprise of their attackers, did not hide or flee their homes; they fought back instead. Although refusing to "go quietly in the night," when the smoke cleared, 39 African Americans had been killed, most of whom were unarmed, innocent by-standers who simply found themselves in the path of the white fury. Prompting such rage among primarily working class whites was their fear of losing their jobs to African-American migrants in the war industries. In many ways the plutocrats who owned the factories were initially responsible for the outbursts. They willingly employed (and exploited) in their plants the "cheaper" African-American workers at the expense and anger of their more costly white counterparts. Suffice it to say, wartime profiteering took precedent over maintaining racial harmony in many Northern urban/industrial centers.

Dearest Louise:
Was very glad to hear from you. Your letter was forwarded from what used to be my house. Louise, it was awful. I hardly know where to begin telling you about it. First, I will say we lost everything but what we had on and that was very little.

It started early in the afternoon. We kept receiving calls over the phone to pack our trunks and leave, because it was going to be awful. We did not heed the calls but sent grandma & the baby on to St. Louis & said we would stick no matter what happened. At first, when they first started, we stood on Broadway & watched it. As they [the white mob] neared our house, we went in & went to the basement. It was too late to run then. They shot & yelled something awful, finally they reached our house. At first they did not bother us (we watched from the basement window), they remarked that "white people live in that house, this is not a nigger house." Later someone must have tipped them that it was a "nigger" house, because, after leaving us for about 20 minutes, they returned & yelling like mad, "kill the niggers, burn that house."

It seemed the whole house was falling in on us. Then some one said, they must not be there, if they are they are certainly dead. Then some one shouted, "they are in the basement. Surround them and burn it down." Then they ran down our steps. Only prayer saved us, we under tubs & anything we could find praying and keeping as quiet as possible because if they had seen one face, we would have been shot or burned to death. When they were about to surround the house and burn it, we heard an awful noise & thought they were dynamiting the house. (The Broadway Theater fell in we learned later). Sister tipped the door to see if the house was on fire. She saw the reflection of a soldier on the front door—pulled it open quickly & called for help. All of us ran out then & was taken to the city hall for the night—just as we were. The next morning we were sent on to St. Louis. Had to walk across the bridge with a line of soldiers on each side in the hot sun, no hats & scarcely no clothing.

On Tuesday evening our house was burned with two soldiers on guard. We were told that the crowd looted the house before burning it.

WILSONIAN "MISSIONARY DIPLOMACY"

Historians often contrast the diplomatic philosophy of Franklin Delano Roosevelt (U.S. president during World War II) and Woodrow Wilson (U.S. president during World War I). Roosevelt was a realist, seeing the world as it was, not as he wished it to be. He was perfectly willing to support Latin American dictators provided that those dictators also supported the United States. Wilson, however, was an idealist, seeing the world as it should be, not as it was. He believed that the U.S. had a special destiny to spread democracy, capitalism, and American religious (Protestant) tenets all over the globe. For Wilson, foreign policy was missionary work.

Wilson generally upheld the idea that people should be ultimately responsible for creating and maintaining the governments of their choosing, or to what Wilson called the right of every nation to self-determination. Wilson, however, did not have such regard for non-Western peoples. He believed, similar to Theodore Roosevelt and other imperialists, that the more advanced, "civilized" (white) nations should assume the role of mentor to the non-Western (non-white) nations or people of Africa, the Middle East, and Asia. Wilson also believed that people's rights, liberties, and freedoms were best guaranteed when promulgated in written constitutions. Ironically, when non-Western people tried to gain Wilson's support in writing their constitutions, such as in the case of a young Vietnamese nationalist named Ho Chi Minh, Wilson refused to help. Instead, he supported continued French occupation until the Vietnamese people were deemed "ready" by their French "tutors" to embrace democratic ideals.

Wilson also believed in universal disarmament; without a prevalence of advanced arms and weapons among the great powers the chance of future wars would dwindle. Finally, Wilson saw the U.S. as a redeemer nation. He believed God had mandated the U.S. to spread America's enlightened, humanitarian, and democratic blessings throughout the whole world. Initially Wilson believed this particular U.S. role could best be accomplished by the United States remaining neutral throughout the European conflagration. However, as will be seen, in the early spring of 1917, Wilson had changed his mind, believing that the U.S. could only help fix the world's ills by joining the crusade to make the Great War "the war to end all wars." Interestingly, prior to the outbreak of war in Europe in the summer of 1914, Wilsonian idealism was tested repeatedly in the nation's own backyard.

Woodrow Wilson, despite having campaigned on a non-interventionist platform, became as intimately involved in Latin American affairs as his predecessors. Indeed, Wilson's intervention in the affairs of many Latin American nations was disingenuous and hypocritical; prior to becoming president, Wilson had lambasted Theodore Roosevelt's and the Taft's administrations' heavy-handed imperialism and interventionist policies in the Western Hemisphere and pledged he would eschew such an approach. Within months of his inauguration, Wilson sent Marines into Nicaragua, ostensibly to protect American interests. Such a move reflected a policy no different than Taft's Dollar Diplomacy or TR's interventionist pursuits. In fact, Wilson invoked the Roosevelt Corollary to justify U.S. occupation of Nicaragua. The Marines remained in Nicaragua until President Franklin Roosevelt ordered their removal in 1933.

Wilson sent William Jennings Bryan to negotiate a treaty with that nation's most powerful controlling family, Chamorro, led by General (and future dictator) Emiliano Chamorro. The Bryan-Chamorro Treaty gave the U.S. sole right to build and maintain a canal through Nicaragua. The U.S. Senate passed the Nicaraguan Canal Treaty in 1916. It appeared that when it came to canal building Wilson wanted to leave a legacy equal to that of his rival Theodore Roosevelt.

Wilson also sent the U.S. Marines into Haiti in 1915 and the following year into the Dominican Republic. In both instances, Wilson believed the Marines were necessary to bring stability to the hemisphere by ending the civil war and endemic violence that seemed to plague both of those countries. Naturally Wilson hoped that with U.S. assistance both Haiti and the Dominican Republic would be transformed into pro-U.S. democratic governments. United States' policies failed in both countries as Haitians and Dominicans until recently lived under corrupt and brutally oppressive dictatorships, suffering through decades of constant civil war. The U.S. has rarely succeeded in creating democratic-capitalist pro-U.S. regimes as a result of military intervention and occupation (As will be seen in a later chapter, post-World War II Japan and Germany proved to be the exceptions).

Throughout most of its history the United States traditionally expanded its frontiers and spread its political and economic values through territorial acquisition by purchase or negotiation: the Louisiana Purchase (1803); Florida (1819), the Oregon country (1846), southern Arizona and New Mexico—the Gadsden Purchase (1853), Alaska (1867), and Guam (1899), to name a few. Thus in 1917 Wilson, with the consent of Congress, purchased the Virgin Islands from Denmark.

Closer to home, and much more problematic for Wilson, was the issue of the Mexican Revolution, which erupted in 1910 when lawfully elected presidential candidate Francisco Madero triumphed at the polls over one of Mexico's longest-standing dictators, Porfirio Diaz. Although Diaz had agreed to the election and had promised to step down if defeated, he reneged, largely because he succumbed to foreign capitalist pressure led by the United States to remain in power. Foreign investors were wary of Madero, who had pledged during the campaign that he would nationalize all foreign-owned enterprises, which by 1910 controlled most if not all of Mexico's most important industries—railroads, telegraph, telephone, mining, and oil. Foreigners also controlled either directly or indirectly the bulk of Mexico's land. American newspaper magnate, William Randolph Hearst, owned ten million acres in the northern state of Chihuahua. As a result of Diaz's close ties with foreign capitalists, if Madero wanted to become Mexico's president, he unfortunately had to take office by force. Thus began the Mexican Revolution, a ten-year-long bloodbath in which thousands of Mexicans died or fled across the Rio Grande to the United States for safety.

Rallying to Madero were other anti-Diaz and anti-*gringo* leaders, whose names have become legendary on both sides of the Rio Grande: Pancho Villa, Emiliano Zapata, Alvaro Obregon, Plutarco Calles, and Venustiano Carranza. Although many of these *caudillos* joined with Madero for personal reasons and frequently engaged in outright banditry and murder in "the name of the Revolution," they nonetheless were united in their cause to drive both Diaz, who they regarded as a *gringo* lackey, and all foreigners out of Mexico. In 1911, Madero, with the help of such individuals, defeated Diaz's forces and the former president fled to Cuba and eventually to Spain, where he lived the remainder of his life.

However, no sooner did Madero take office than counter-revolutionary, right-wing military leaders in collusion with foreign capitalists conspired to over-

U.S. Marines standing along railroad tracks in Vera Cruz, with Hotel Terminal in the background, during the Carranza revolution against Huerta's government. May 16, 1914

throw his government. In 1913 General Victoriano Huerta succeeded in toppling via a coup d'etat the Madero regime. Madero was held prisoner for a few days then along with his entire family and cabinet brutally executed by Huerta henchmen. Madero's murder had the full-fledged support of the foreign capitalists and their respective legations. With Huerta in power European and American businesses could now continue their exploitation of Mexico's resources and industries and its people for their own private profit. Despite the backing of United States and European capitalists, Huerta could not quell the fires of revolution. Villa, Zapata, and the other pro-Madero chieftains formed uneasy alliances to overthrow the Huerta regime.

Much to the chagrin of American and foreign capitalists, Wilson considered Huerta a "brute," and allowed American arms to flow across the Rio Grande to Huerta's principal rivals, Carranza and Villa. It was only a matter of time before a showdown would occur between the Huerta regime and the Wilson administration. The volcano erupted at the Gulf of Mexico seaport city of Tampico, when Mexican authorities arrested a small group of American sailors for "disorderly conduct." The sailors were indeed unruly, engaging in unprovoked fisticuffs and barroom brawling and assaulting innocent Mexicans. However, local police, realizing that their action could cause further rancor between the U.S. and Mexico, promptly released the seamen and apologized to the American legation. They refused, however, to comply with the U.S. admiral's demand for a twenty-one-gun salute as an act of contrition. Wilson unwisely and precipitously used this "insult" as an excuse to eliminate Huerta, asking Congress for authority to use force against Mexico. Before Congress could act Wilson retaliated, ordering the navy to seize the Mexican port of Vera Cruz until Huerta "formally" apologized for "insulting" the United States. The American navy bombarded the city and when the smoked cleared, the Marines assaulted and declared Vera Cruz under United States "occupation." Much to Wilson's surprise, the Mexican people and even Carranza and Villa rallied to the Huerta regime in defiance of this high-handed Yankee maneuver. Critics in the United States, Europe, and Latin America branded the capture of Vera Cruz a reckless act that could escalate to a general war between the United States and Mexico at a most inopportune time. Fortunately, a shooting conflict was avoided when Argentina, Brazil, and Chile interceded, offering to mediate the dispute.

The situation defused when the Huerta government collapsed in July 1914, the result, interestingly, from pressure from the very European powers that had helped him come to power in the first place.

Apparently they no longer considered him to be as reliable a puppet as they previously thought. Seizing power in the wake of Huerta's collapse was Venustiano Carranza, who Wilson officially recognized as Mexico's "legitimate" president.

By the time Carranza had seized power, he and Villa had become estranged. Carranza no longer considered Villa to be a fellow revolutionary but a brigand out for personal plunder. For Carranza, the revolution was over, confirmed by Wilson's de facto recognition of his seizure of power. Thus all opposition to Carranza's "legitimacy" was to be crushed. Wilson's support for Carranza resulted in Villa launching attacks against U.S. interests on the Mexican side of the U.S.-Mexican border. In January 1916, Villa hauled 16 young American mining engineers off a train traveling in northern Mexico and executed them. Villa, who had now come to despise Carranza as a "gringo sell-out," hoped to provoke a war between Wilson and "el presidente." In March 1916, Villa with five hundred men blazed across the border and raided the New Mexican town of Columbus, killing another twenty innocent Americans. In retaliation, Wilson ordered the U.S. Army to invade Mexico.

Under the leadership of the grim-faced, ramrod-erect General John "Blackjack" Pershing, a veteran of the Cuban and Philippine campaigns, the U.S. contingent of 15,000 was to find Villa, bring the outlaw to justice, and destroy his "bandit" army. Pershing's troops penetrated deep into the rugged terrain of the northern Mexican state of Chihuahua, Villa's home. They engaged both Carranza and Villa forces, defeating them handily in all encounters but failed to locate and apprehend Villa. In retrospect, Wilson should have known there was no way Pershing would ever find Villa, for no Chihuahuan would have ever cooperated with the gringos in the seizure of their region's and one of their country's most celebrated revolutionaries. After a year of aimlessly wandering the mountains and deserts of northern Mexico, searching in vain for Villa, Wilson in January 1917 recalled Pershing and his army. Tensions with Germany had reached the breaking point and Wilson realized that potential war with that country represented a more urgent crisis than having the United States Army senselessly roaming northern Mexico trying to find a "bandit."

THE OUTBREAK OF THE GREAT WAR

To the majority of Americans, the European powers had been engaged in constant warfare for centuries, and thus when the Great War began in the summer of 1914, few were surprised that they "were at it again." George Washington and Thomas Jefferson, in their respective farewell addresses, had warned fellow citizens to remain as detached from European affairs as was possible and to maintain a policy of isolationism to prevent from becoming entangled in European machinations, intrigue, and power politics, which invariably led to conflict among the great powers. Although by 1914 the majority of Americans took great pride in their nation's world power status, they nonetheless remained committed to avoiding involvement in any capacity in a general European conflagration. In effect, Americans still embraced a semi-isolationist mentality, and thus when war erupted in Europe in 1914, they were determined to have the United States maintain a neutral position.

Causes for the War

Although several long-standing issues ultimately caused Europe to convulse in war in 1914, four in particular seemed to have had the most significant impact: militarism (arms race), nationalism, secret alliances, and imperialism. Since the 1880s and the Second Industrial Revolution in Europe, France, Great Britain, and Germany had become embroiled in an intensely competitive and potentially dangerous arms race. The rivalry between Great Britain and Germany had become especially keen in the race for empire and in the building of war ships. They increasingly used their technology and resources to produce the most advanced war machines their respective military-industrial complexes could deliver. Interestingly, the impetus for such militarism had been the United States' Civil War, which the great powers found "fascinating," not only for the conflict's brutality and carnage but also by the new and impressive weaponry the Americans unleashed upon each other.

During that bloodbath, the Great Powers' military observers witnessed first-hand the devastating effects of modern, total war, with mass armies engaged in pitched battles, some of which, such as Gettysburg, lasted for three days and resulted in 50,000 casualties. Even more shocking to the Europeans were the Yankee sieges of Confederate cities inhabited mostly by civilians, such as Vicksburg and Petersburg, with artillery barrages that lasted for several hours each day from canons placed on railroad flatcars that could shoot for several miles.

If that was not enough of the horrors of modern war to satisfy the Europeans morbid curiosity, they could have then accompanied Union General William Tecumseh Sherman on his "march to the sea" (Chattanooga, TN, to Savannah, GA) in which he engaged in one of the most vicious scorched-earth campaigns in military history, including the burning to the ground of Atlanta, Georgia. Along the way, his troops pillaged Rebel homes and shot with impunity all "secessionist traitors" to the Republic who resisted Federal occupation. Such events not only appalled many of these European observers, but perhaps more importantly, gave them a glimpse of their own future, in which they would slaughter each other in similar madness with even greater numbers of troops and with even more sophisticated weaponry. In short, the United States Civil War, in many ways, became the precursor to the Great War of 1914-1918.

Even many of the weapons the Europeans would use to kill each other to the tune of 9 million soldiers dead, made their first appearance in the Civil War. From the Gatling gun (which the British transformed into the machine gun), to the repeating rifle, hand grenade, and to even the submarine, which made a "cameo" during the Civil War, the Europeans would develop these weapons into even more precise killing apparatuses. Of all the modern weaponry first introduced during the American Civil War, it was perhaps the submarine that proved to be the most devastating. The Confederacy developed a crude but fairly effective version of this particularly important device (and one the Germans would perfect and use with deadly precision on Allied shipping in the Atlantic) to try to break the Union blockade of its seaports. As will be seen shortly, it was the issue of submarine warfare that ultimately led Woodrow Wilson to declare war on the German Empire in April 1917.

Also causing tension among the Great Powers was imperial rivalry, and again this particular problem was most serious between Great Britain and Germany. Since unification in 1870, Germany aspired to become the most powerful country in Europe and believed the only nation that could block such pretension was Great Britain. Ironically, those German leaders pushing Germany toward such a "destiny" believed one of the prerequisites for supremacy was the possession of a colonial empire, which the British had proven over the centuries to have been the key to their prolonged wealth, power, and global hegemony. Thus beginning in the 1880s and over the course of the next several decades, Germany embarked on one of the most aggressive territorial acquisition campaigns in European history, gobbling up as many colonies and "spheres of influence in Africa, Asia, and the Pacific as it possibly could. Since Germany (and the United States) joined the race for empire "late in the game," the Germans often found their ambitions stymied, especially by the British, who certainly did not welcome such a challenge to their suzerainty.

Compounding the Anglo-German imperial rivalry was the Franco-German tension over the same issue, and frequently this led to France and Great Britain allying against Germany in certain areas of the world to block German expansionism. Needless to say, Germany did not "take kindly" to such obstruction to its quest for power, and consequently the German, French, and British governments found themselves often perilously close to war wherever in the world they competed for colonies.

Without question, the greatest "tinderbox" in Europe was the Balkan states, which for decades witnessed constant unrest and fighting as the Slavic Christian majorities engaged in wars of national liberation from the Muslim Ottoman Empire. However, no sooner did these Slavic peoples free themselves from the Turks than they found a new potential oppressor in the form of the Austro-Hungarian empire, whose Habsburg rulers had long wanted to expand the empire into southeastern Europe but for centuries had been blocked by the Ottomans. Now that Turkey had become "the sick man of Europe," the Habsburgs believed the Serbs, Bosnians, and Montenegrans would be easy prey for their imperial ambitions. However, the Slavic peoples of those countries were acutely aware of Habsburg designs and for protection turned to Holy Mother Russia, a fellow Slavic country. The Romanovs were more than willing to offer the Balkan Slavs "security," for the Romanovs were just as territorially ambitious in this region as their rival the Habsburgs. Thus, by 1914, the tensions between the Habsburg and Russian empires in this most volatile part of Europe had reached the point where both sides anticipated a showdown; they were simply waiting for the "right" crisis to occur.

Finally, and perhaps what in retrospect was one of the more absurd causes for the Great War, was the long list of countries who promised to mobilize their forces in support of other allies if they found themselves at war with another coalition. By 1914, the major powers had divided into two binding alliance systems: the Triple Entente of Russia, Great Britain, France, and the Central Powers, consisting of Germany, Austria-Hungary, Turkey and Italy, which wisely opted to remain neutral when the war began in 1914. However, the Italians' sagacity was momentary; in 1915 they joined with the Triple Entente, believing that their affiliation with the members of that alliance would prove more beneficial in the war's aftermath. As will be seen later in this chapter, they were sorely disappointed.

Compounding this senseless obligatory military union was the interesting relationship among three of the major powers' heads of state: Alexandra, the Czarina of Russia, Kaiser Wilhelm II of Germany, and King George V of England were first-cousins, a kinship arranged in the nineteenth century by the "matriarch" of Europe, Queen Victoria of Great Britain. Victoria believed she could ensure peace in Europe for generations to come by uniting via marriage the major ruling households of Europe by blood, then they would never go to war, for to "behave" in such a manner would upset "Grand-Mama" Victoria. Interestingly, as long as Victoria reigned in England, her "grandchildren" did indeed comport themselves according to Her Majesty's wishes. However, no sooner did Victoria die than the arrangement quickly dissipated. "Cousin Willie" of Germany in particular had been waiting for the "old lady" to pass, for he never had any intention of restraining himself in the name of family and European peace. Within a few years of Victoria's death, a war among the "cousins" became a certainty. All that was needed was an episode that would give them the excuse to plunge headlong into Armageddon.

The incident that lit the fuse of the powder keg on which the major powers had been sitting on for several years was the assassination of the Archduke Franz Ferdinand of Austria, nephew of Emperor Franz Josef II of the Austro-Hungarian Empire and heir to the throne, and his wife Sophia by a Serbian nationalist (Gavrilo Princip) in late June 1914. In many ways the Austrians purposely provoked the crisis by insisting on the Archduke's "goodwill visit," which they secretly hoped would end in such a calamity. They could then use the assassination as pretext for war against Serbia. The Serbian government had warned the Austrians that they could not guarantee the Archduke's safety, for their people detested the Austrians, whom they knew wanted to annex their country. With Germany as an ally, Serbia's defeat would be a given and Serbia would then be absorbed into the Austro-Hungarian empire. The Serbians were keenly aware of Austrian intentions and thus turned to their protector, Holy Mother Russia, who vowed to come to the Serbs aide if threatened by Austria.

Interestingly enough, Ferdinand was so unpopular at home in general, and with his family in particular, that his uncle went on vacation rather than attend his nephew's funeral. Nevertheless, Austria demanded that Serb officials hand over the assassins. The Serbian government refused, prompting an ultimatum from Austria, which if not complied would result in a declaration of war by Austria, which was the intention all along. While the clock ticked, Germany mobilized its forces in preparation for war against Serbia.

Meanwhile the Russians mobilized their army in preparation for war against Austria but not Germany. "Cousin Niki" (Czar Nicholas II of Russia)

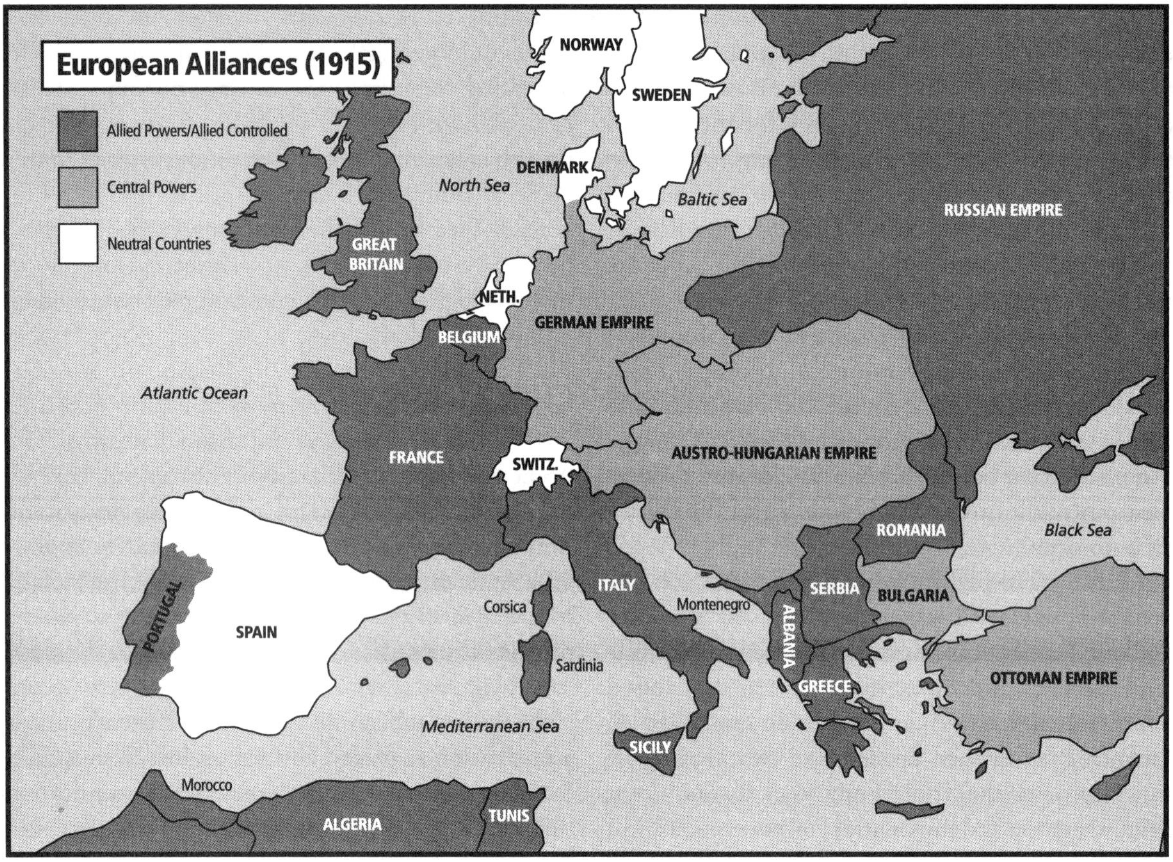

pledged that although he was preparing his forces for a possible conflict with Austria, he was not about to declare war on his "Cousin Willie"—Kaiser Wilhelm II of Germany. Much to Nicholas' chagrin, the Kaiser, a megalomaniac, declared war on Russia. That shock precipitated a French declaration of war on Germany for France was obligated by an array of treaty agreements with Russia to come to Russia's aide if war erupted between Russia and any member of the Central Power alliance. Before the French could mobilize, the Germans implemented the Schlieffen Plan, which called for a quick knockout of the French before the British could come to their rescue. In order for the strategy to be effective, the Germans had to reach Paris as quickly as possible and that meant invading through neutral Belgium, which they did. Much to the Germans' surprise, the Belgians resisted, allowing time for the French to mobilize and for the English to come to their assistance. The invasion of Belgium was the official reason that Britain entered the conflict, but in reality, the British worried that a German victory would upset the balance of power on the continent and thus threaten Great Britain itself.

All diplomatic attempts to stop the madness failed, and war came, again, to the Europeans in the summer of 1914. Unlike previous wars, this one proved to be horrific in the sheer number of causalities. For example, at the conclusion of the First Battle of the Marne (September 1914) over 500,000 German, French, and British had been killed. Europe would eventually lose an entire generation of young men before the guns fell silent on the eleventh hour, of the eleventh day, of the eleventh month of 1918.

American Neutrality

No sooner did "the Guns of August" begin to fire, than Woodrow Wilson asked his fellow citizens to remain neutral. He asked Americans to be dispassionate in thought, word, and action. Wilson's reasons for such an extreme approach were multiple. First, Wilson worried that a protracted European conflict could negatively impact the American economy. To prevent such a possibility, and not unlike his Founding Father predecessors, Wilson believed that Americans should be allowed to trade with all combatants provided that the U.S. was not a belligerent itself.

Second, on the home front, WASP nativism reemerged toward German Americans, whom many feared would become a fifth-column and manipulate the United States into the war on the Fatherland's side. German populations were especially significant in the states of Wisconsin, Illinois, Michigan, Minnesota, and South and North Dakota. It was in these states that WASP xenophobia and anti-German nativism was most evident, with Anglo-Americans wondering if their German neighbors would support their newly-adopted land or their homeland.

Also suspect were Irish-Americans. Because of their strong Catholicism and equally passionate support for Irish independence, which saw many Irish-Americans donate money to such ultra-nationalist and quasi-terrorist organizations as the Irish Republican Army and Sinn Fein, many Anglo-Americans still disdained the Irish and questioned their loyalty to the United States. To a certain degree Anglo-American leeriness was somewhat justified. For many Irish-Americans the liberation of their homeland from centuries of English oppression and exploitation became their principal motivation in their support for U.S. neutrality. They were confident that if America refrained from participation, a German victory would be the result and with such a triumph would come the end of British rule, for in the war's aftermath a humiliated and indebted British government would no longer want or be able to sustain such a rebellious colony. Moreover, U.S. neutrality and British preoccupation on the continent would create the perfect scenario for a massive Irish uprising during the war, which, it was hoped, would lead to Irish independence at that time. Such a prospect occurred on Easter Sunday, 1916, but unfortunately for the Irish rebels, the British had enough force already stationed in Ireland to put down the insurrection, thus crushing Irish (and Irish-American) hopes for independent Ireland during the war.

In short, for many Irish-Americans the key to their homeland's liberation was American neutrality, and thus during the Great War, and especially after the United States entered the conflict, Irish-Americans became some of the Wilson administration's most vociferous critics for having abandoned neutrality in favor of war on the Allied side. Much to the outrage of the Irish-American community and other progressive civil libertarians, many of their fellow citizens were charged with sedition and incarcerated for speaking out against Wilson's wartime policies. Such harsh reprisals especially against Irish-Americans reflected the Wilson administration's desire to not offend in any way its British allies.

Third, why should the U.S. pick a side? There was no reason to believe that this war would be any different from other European conflicts. Regardless if it was the Balkan War, Franco-Prussian War, or the Crimean War, the U.S. had sat on the sidelines, the best and safest seat in the house to watch the Europeans engage in senseless slaughter. Thus to Wilson and to the majority of Americans there was no good, tangible, beneficial reason to join this latest European madness.

Finally, Woodrow Wilson dreamed about creating what he called the "New World Order" and this could only come about if the United States remained dispassionately objective regarding both the war's causes and its outcome. Only by remaining neutral would the U.S. be in the best position (economically, militarily, politically, and diplomatically) to remake the world (in a Wilsonian image) in the war's aftermath. All that would be required for establishing a lasting peace would be for all the belligerents, whether they ended up on the winning or losing side, to construct a postwar peace based on Wilson's impartial "Fourteen Point" assessment, which Wilson had drafted months before the United States entered the war on the Allied side. In fact, Wilson had been formulating in his mind his postwar agenda almost from the war's outset. Initially, he had hoped he could implement his vision without the United States having to enter the conflict. Unfortunately the Germans left him no choice but to fight if he hoped to see his New World Order come to fruition.

Naval and Submarine Warfare

Wilson ultimately used German submarine warfare to justify, on moral grounds, U.S. entry into the conflict. In speeches denouncing the German employment of such a "weapon," Wilson referred to submarine attacks on Allied shipping as a "cruel and unmanly business." Although Wilson ultimately declared war on Germany because of its policy of unrestricted submarine warfare, which saw the killing of hundreds of American citizens traveling on belligerent luxury liners, at the war's outset the United Kingdom and France were the more egregious violators of American neutral trading rights. For example, the Royal Navy threw up an undeclared blockade and mined the North Sea. Both of these actions flew in the face of international agreements, such as those mandated at the 1899 and 1907 Hague Conventions. In addition, the United Kingdom armed merchant ships. Through World War I, ships were either designated as military or for civilian use. The latter had special protections and were defined as civilian, in large measure because they were prohibited from being armed. Military ships did have the right to stop and search civilian ships for contraband. However, military ships did so without fear of being attacked, such as when German submarines would surface in order to board English merchant ships. When those submarines, which Germany called *Unterseeboot*, or U-boat, surfaced, they lacked the ability to launch torpedoes, thus making themselves proverbial sitting ducks. The armed British merchant ships then opened fire on the German military ships, contravening international agreements.

The United Kingdom unilaterally expanded products it considered to be contraband, stopped U.S. ships, and confiscated U.S. property that appeared on its list of items that they would not allow to be sold or traded during war. The United Kingdom blacklisted American companies that traded with neutral countries suspected of trading with Germany or its allies. The United Kingdom routinely stopped U.S. mail ships, confiscated letters and packages, opened the U.S. mail, and then censured or destroyed what the United Kingdom decided "jeopardized" their war efforts.

Finally, English ships flew an array of flags of neutral countries, hoping to confuse the German U-boats lying in wait in the Atlantic ready to torpedo British ships carrying munitions and other war

A German U-boat in New York. Photo credit: Library of Congress

materiel from countries such as the United States. British audacity in this capacity knew no bounds as British merchant ships often flew the U.S. flag, hoping to scare Germany into steering clear, or else risk unleashing the full force of the American war effort if Germany dared to attack a U.S. ship.

Compared to the United Kingdom's actions, Germany was restrained. They did have a public relations problem, especially when it came to German naval attacks in the Atlantic. After numerous English violations of international agreements, Germany declared that they would alter their tactics to include firing on suspected merchant ships that were armed or English ships trying to evade attack by flying the flags of neutral countries. Ultimately, Germany warned all ships flying neutral flags to stay away from English waters. Shortly thereafter, President Wilson gave his first speech on the issue of torpedoes on the high seas:

> If the commanders of German vessels of war should act upon the presumption that the flag of the United States was not being used in good faith and should destroy on the high seas an American vessel or the lives of American citizens, it would be difficult for the Government of the United States to view the act in any other light than as an indefensible violation of neutral rights, which it would be very hard, indeed, to reconcile with the friendly relations now happily subsisting between the two governments.

This piece of diplomatic ambiguity was intended as a thinly-veiled threat to Germany yet one that would not propel the U.S. into a war that Wilson believed the nation was unprepared to fully fight. Wilson's first threat would be tested on the war's first anniversary. In August of 1915 a German U-boat attacked a British ship and when a nearby merchant ship (the *Arabic*) flying the English flag came to rescue the survivors, that vessel was torpedoed as well. The dead included two Americans. The German government quickly apologized, promising the U.S. that their nation's U-boats would never fire on passenger ships without offering sufficient warnings and only after securing the safety of non-combatants. Within a month the German government issued a report to Secretary of State Robert Lansing (and uncle to John Foster and Alan Dulles who will play pivotal roles in the early Cold War administration of Dwight David Eisenhower). According to their investigation, the German U-boat commander fired on the *Arabic* because he feared that the ship was going to ram his submarine, a tactic often employed by English merchant ships after they surrendered to a surfaced U-boat. In 1916 German officials authorized their naval commanders to attack armed merchant ships but not passenger ships. A French passenger ferry, the *Sussex*, was torpedoed by a German U-boat, resulting in the deaths of many French but no American citizens. Wilson once again waved his diplomatic finger in the face of the German government, demanding that they cease these attacks. Despite Wilson's constant public proclamations that his administration remained committed to neutrality, the Germans believed his announcements were disingenuous and that it was only a matter of time before Wilson's inherent Anglophilia would get the better of him and the United States would enter the war on the Allied side. Thus, to forestall the inevitable as long as possible, the German government issued the "Sussex Pledge," in which they declared that their U-boats would no longer attack any civilian ship without first securing the safety of its non-combatants.

Interestingly enough, these attacks, promises, threats, and pledges all followed on the heels of the greatest loss of civilian life on the high seas. In the early spring of 1915, carrying nearly 2,000 passengers from the U.S. to England, the British luxury liner *Lusitania* was hit by a single torpedo from a German submarine. The ship sunk in less than ten minutes with the loss of nearly 1200 of its passengers, including many Americans.

Prompting the German U-boat to sink the *Lusitania* was the Germans' long-held suspicion that American arms manufacturers were secretly loading all manner of war materiel on Allied passenger liners. Such an assertion was true because the *Lusitania* was carrying contraband. De-classified government documents confirmed that this clandestine activity did indeed occur on a regular basis. Moreover, from the moment the war began, U.S. plutocrats, especially munitions manufacturers, were keenly aware of the immense profit to be made selling their "wares" to the belligerents. Initially they played no favorites, but as the war dragged on, it became apparent that the Allies were in greater need of weapons than the Germans. By 1915 U.S. munitions manufacturers were almost exclusively selling their products to the Allies, and thus it became clear to the Germans that the U.S. was no longer "impartial." The Germans doubted the sincerity of Wilson's repeated assurances that his administration and his fellow citizens were faithful to neutrality in both sentiment and action. Consequently, the Germans no longer felt morally obligated to respect American neutrality if American capitalists had no intention of honoring that position. The German government thus ordered its U-boats to sink all Allied ships regardless of the "cargo" they were carrying.

Historians still debate what degree of complicity or knowledge of this activity Wilson had, and if he was aware of the plutocrats' surreptitious activity, why did he not publicly and formally condemn such underhanded behavior. Some believe that by 1915 Wilson personally was ready for war against Germany but needed to convince the American public of the "moral imperative" of becoming involved against such an "immoral" country as Germany—a nation that did not hesitate to kill innocent civilians. Moreover, if Wilson was genuinely committed to neutrality, he also should have forbidden Americans from traveling on any belligerent luxury liners. No doubt any current president would have issued such a decree in a similar situation unless they too needed to prod Americans into accepting a "moral justification" for war. Despite Wilson's outrage and condemnation of the Germans for their "immoral actions," the sinking of the largest, fastest, luxury ship in the world did not propel the U.S. to officially enter the war. Wilson would have to wait until there was a direct threat to American sovereignty.

By the beginning of 1917, the tide of war had shifted in Germany's favor. In February of that year the Russian Revolution began, largely as a result of the Russian army's devastating defeats at the hands of the Germans on the Eastern front. The Germans were hopeful that it would only be a matter of time before Russia would be defeated and out of the war. If that became reality, the Germans could then transfer men and materiel from the Eastern front to the Western front and launch a massive offensive that would overwhelm and defeat the Allies before the U.S. could enter the war. In order for such a plan to work, the Germans had to prevent the Allies from getting American military hardware. Despite Wilson's repeated warnings that a declaration of unrestricted submarine warfare would have "dire consequences" relative to U.S.-German relations, the Germans announced in early 1917 that their U-boats would sink *all* Allied ships, regardless of type, crossing the Atlantic.

The Germans knew their manifesto would more than likely be the final straw for Wilson and that the United States would soon thereafter enter the war on the Allied side. The Germans thus decided that if U.S. entry was inevitable, then they needed to somehow find a way of preventing the Americans from coming to Britain's and France's aide before they could launch their massive, knock-out, spring offensives. In short, the Germans needed to find a way of keeping the Americans "pinned down" in their own backyard long enough for them to finish off the Allies. To put their plan into operation they needed to find a potential New World ally willing to go to war against "the colossus of the North." The Germans concluded that Mexico was the "logical" choice for a new comrade-in-arms.

Why Mexico? The Germans were aware of how strained U.S.-Mexican relations had become during Wilson's tenure. They were confident they could entice the Mexican government with a generous alliance proposal, which included helping Mexico get back territory lost to the "gringos" during the Mexican-American War of 1846. Although there was certainly no great love lost between the U.S. and Mexico, the Germans underestimated the wily and opportunistic Mexican President Carranza, whose regime Wilson had recognized over a year earlier as "legitimate." Carranza knew any German alliance proposal would not only be disingenuous but absurd as well. Carranza had long reconciled that the Southwest was U.S. territory and that any attempt to retake the region whether by invasion or by negotiation was lunacy. The German promise of money and troops was equally preposterous; how could the Germans afford to spread themselves so thin when their objective was to knock-out the Allies. Moreover, whether he liked it or not, Carranza knew he had to "live" with the gringos; the two countries shared a two thousand mile border and the Mexican economy remained dependent on U.S. investment. Carranza thus concluded that the Germans' offer was all "gas," and that if he helped to expose this latest German conspiracy to violate United States sovereignty, such a gesture would go far toward currying even greater favor with the Wilson administration. Thus, the German attempt to prevent U.S. entry into the war failed, making their ultimate defeat a certainty.

Arthur Zimmermann, German Foreign Secretary, sent an encoded telegram to Heinrich von Eckardt, German Ambassador to Mexico in January of 1917. The telegram was intercepted by British intelligence on Galveston Island (located about 30 miles south of Houston, Texas), decoded, and handed over to President Wilson a month later:

> We intend to begin on the 1st of February unrestricted submarine warfare. We shall endeavor in spite of this to keep the United States of America neutral. In the event of this not succeeding, we make Mexico a proposal of alliance on the following basis: make war together, make peace together, generous financial support and an understanding on our part that Mexico is to reconquer the lost territory in Texas, New Mexico and Arizona."

Although the telegram was widely published in American newspapers beginning on March 1, 1917, over a month's time passed before Wilson asked Congress for a declaration of war. In the intercession, Wilson gave his second inaugural address. He talked about the economic soundness of the country and only in the most cursory, oblique way did he touch upon the storm clouds on the horizon. He called for peace and for everyone who loved liberty and justice to continue to be impartial in thought and action relative to the European conflict. Wilson debated with himself, with his friends, and with his cabinet over what the U.S. should do next. Wilson did not choose the path to war lightly, because, as Wilson confided to the editor of *The World*, Frank Cobb, "Once lead these people into war . . . they'll forget there ever was such a thing as tolerance . . . the spirit of ruthless brutality will enter into the very fiber of our national life . . . every man who refused to conform would have to pay the penalty." In other words, Wilson feared that American entry into the war would forever change this nation. He was correct.

DECLARATION OF WAR

On April 2, 1917, Wilson asked, and 48 hours later received, a declaration of war against Germany –not Austria, the Ottoman Empire, or any of the other several countries aligned with the German Empire. The Senate voted 82 to 6 to declare war on April 4,

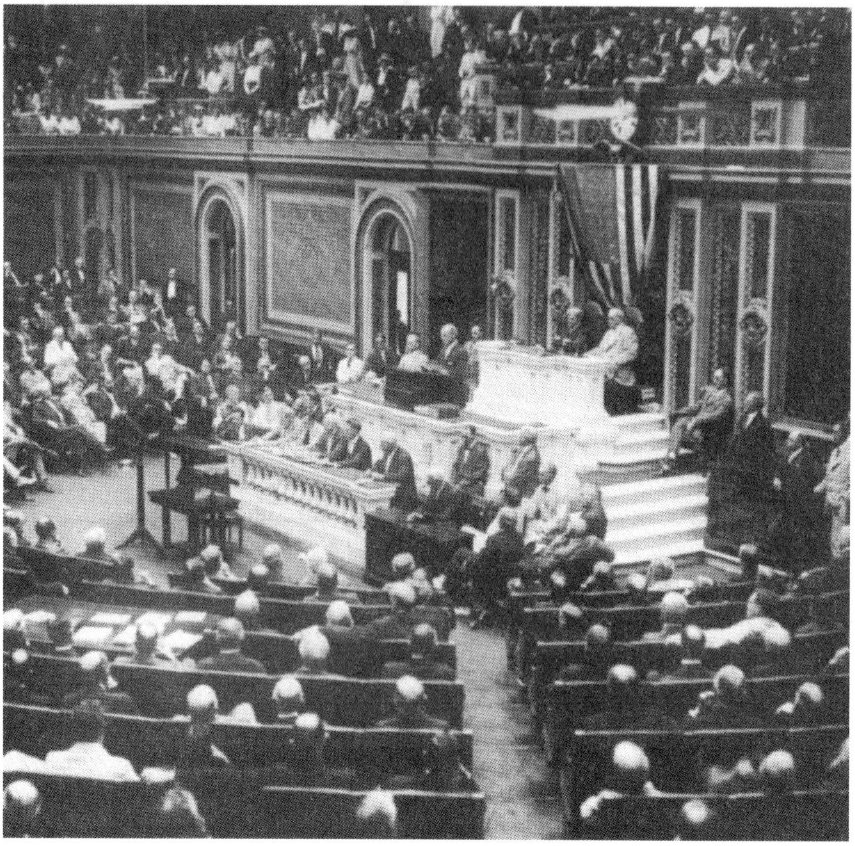

President Woodrow Wilson addressed Congress on Februry 3, 1917. Wilson announced that the United States was breaking diplomatic relations with Germany.

1917; the House concurred on April 6 by a vote of 373 to 50. Jeannette Rankin of Montana, the first woman to serve in the House of Representatives, was among those who voted against the war. "I want to stand by my country, but I cannot vote for war," declared Rankin. Later on, she clarified her decision to vote against going to war on the grounds that "I knew that we were asked to vote for a commercial war [and] that none of the idealistic hopes would be carried out." The war's aftermath would prove Rankin to have been a most prescient individual.

Over fifty members of the House agreed with Rankin, including the Chairman of the House Ways and Means Committee, Claude Kitchin (D-NC). Kitchin rejected the decision for war, believing that those who will be called to fight and die will not be the ones who declared the war to begin with: "Let me once remind the House that it takes neither moral nor physical courage to declare a war for others to fight."

General Leonard Wood, the one-time U.S. military commander/governor of Cuba, was Wilson's Chief of Staff until 1914. Wilson and Wood disagreed on their interpretations of how prepared the U.S. was for war. Wilson feared that preparing for war would necessarily lead to war, while Wood believed that creating and maintaining a ready standing army should be a matter of general policy. No matter how one interpreted the situation, the U.S. was undeniably woefully unprepared for war. Much of the U.S. Navy's front-line ships had not been updated since Teddy Roosevelt had sent the fleet on its round-the-world tour. Not only was the U.S. Navy unprepared to transport American soldiers and equipment to Europe but most of this country's military was engaged in the Mexican civil war. Relative to military equipment, where was the U.S. going to get all the guns, bullets, and other war material? What about food and fuel? Did the U.S. grow and produce enough food and fuel for the needs of its citizens as well as for U.S. troops fighting abroad?

Propaganda and Hysteria

Once committed to war, Wilson made a priority the boosting of American morale on the home front. To accomplish that objective, Wilson created the Committee on Public Information (CPI), headed by George Creel. Creel's and his agency's main task was to affirm to both our allies and our enemies, and to the American people, that the nation's citizens unequivocally favored U.S. intervention on the Allied side as well as supporting a possible protracted conflict.

The CPI found Hollywood to be a most useful medium through which to promote the theme of a united America, determined to "make the world safe for Democracy." CPI had Hollywood produce a series of uber-patriotic movies depicting clear and explicit differences between the liberty-loving Americans and the German animals, such as "The Claws of the Hun" and "The Kaiser: The Beast of Berlin" (insert trilogy of mock-horror, minor chords here).

Creel created a special pool of amateur speakers whose main audience was to be those immigrant communities that he and the Wilson administration believed could be wavering in their support for the U.S. war effort because of possible lingering sentimental attachment to the homeland. Wilson and Creel were determined to convey to the Allies that when the United States goes to war, *all Americans,* regardless of place of origin, whether native born or naturalized, wholeheartedly embraced the cause and that the virtues and qualities of American life had transformed all into one-hundred percent "Americans." The speakers were to deliver their propaganda message in no more than four minutes. In homage to the American Revolution and to further promote patriotism, Creel named these on-call orators the "Four-Minute Men." According to Creel, over 75,000 individuals gave an estimated 7.5 million speeches. Major ethnic groups such as Jews, Germans, and even Native Americans were targeted to ensure their support for the war. Rabbi A.G. Robinson of New York reported that Jewish speakers reached "about 25,000 people per week. We expect soon to have every Jewish audience in a motion-picture house or a Jewish playhouse addressed by a Jewish speaker."

German-American communities were asked to take "The Pledge" (an oath in support of the U.S. war effort against the Huns). Progressive era groups, such as the American Protective Association, focused on homes with German sounding names to ensure that there were no pictures of the Kaiser on their walls. American flags blossomed all over the country, like tulips and daffodils in the spring. A new group, the Boy Scouts of America, sold war bonds and collected money, rubber, and tin in support of the war effort. German groups and clubs were banned, closed, and at times burned by those liberty and justice-loving Americans willing to use whatever means necessary to promote one-hundred percent Americanism. Such violent reprisals against suspect groups such as the Germans were of course all for the purpose of "national security."

Robert Prager, a German-born American refused to sign the Pledge. One evening members of the local "Council of Defense" (a self-appointed ultrapatriotic group charged with routing out all anti-Americanism as they defined anti-Americanism) knocked on Prager's front door. They gave him one final chance to sign the Pledge. When Prager refused, someone in the crowd shouted, "Get the rope!" According to Prager, "The first I knew was when the rope was about my neck and around my body under my arms." Fortunately Prager was not lynched as some members of the Council believed that by giving him a good "scare" he would now take the Pledge, which Prager promptly did on the spot. Although Prager barely escaped with his life, many other German-Americans and other "suspect" ethnics did not.

Women and the War

Women also joined in the preparation efforts. Women took jobs in U.S. weapons factories (a precursor of things to come in the 1940s); they sold Liberty Bonds at church, school, and social functions; they led clothing drives for soldiers and immigrants; they ran canteens for American service men in England; and over 10,000 American women volunteered as Red Cross nurses in France. Women's organizations put their work on the back burner in order to help in the total war effort. For example, the National American

Women's Suffrage Association (NAWSA) sponsored mobile field hospitals in France and England and urged their female workers and supporters to go to other western European nations affected by the war and help to staff those hospitals as well. Interestingly, some NAWSA leaders were concerned that Jeannette Rankin's "no vote" would taint their organization. Rankin had been one of the movement's stalwarts for years. However, much to NAWSA's relief, their efforts assuaged any reservations other citizens may have had about the association's devotion to the war effort. Indeed, even Rankin participated in some of the more humanitarian programs sponsored by NAWSA.

The first meaningful step undertaken by the federal government after declaring war was to create a capable military and in order to make that a reality Congress believed it necessary to pass the Selective Service Act on May 15, 1917. The "draft" as the act became popularly called soon after its passage (and forever more), required all men between the ages of 18 and 30 to register with the federal government for possible conscription into the nation's armed services. Ten months later, and fearing that the U.S. military had not secured a sufficient amount of men to fight in the war, the U.S. Senate debated a bill that would have created mandatory and universal military training for all male U.S. citizens between 19 and 21. The Senate defeated the measure by a vote of 36 to 26. Approximately 24 million men registered for the draft and nearly three million American males were inducted into military service by the end of the Great War.

The federal government also blitzed the American public with one of the most ubiquitous and visually overwhelming advertising campaigns in American history. In effect, the Wilson administration "sold" the war to the American public. Posters became the most important medium used; radio was in its infant stages of development and of course television was nonexistent.

Many of the posters simply tried to remind Americans of their duty to support the war by purchasing war bonds. One poster showed a grandmother figure with out-stretched arms standing in front of a U.S. flag. Peaking from behind the flag one could see bodies, sinking boats amidst tumultuous waves with a caption that read "Women! Help America's Sons Win the War! Buy U.S. Government Bonds!"

As noted earlier, the Wilson administration readily turned to Hollywood to make propaganda movies designed to not only boost American morale but to promote the righteousness and moral necessity of the United States' involvement. Of course, historical parallels with past heroic Americans at war became a major theme. One motion picture that conveyed such a message was *The Spirit of '76.* Set during the American Revolution, the idea behind the movie was that the colonists were unprepared to battle, let alone win in a war, against the largest, best military in the world: Great Britain. Of course the unprepared and outmatched but relentlessly determined and virtuous Americans triumphed, which was the movie's message. If American patriots could overcome their unpreparedness for battle in 1776, surely the Americans of 1917 could do the same. The director of the movie, Robert Goldstein (a Jewish American of German descent), portrayed the British in the movie as not only the enemy (which they were) but also as brutes who inflicted all manner of cruelties on the Americans. Goldstein's presentation of the British in such a light proved to have been a rather foolish act, for when the movie came out (1917) the British were American allies and thus they did not take too kindly to being portrayed in American cinema as barbarians. The British and American press lambasted Goldstein, who eventually was arrested and found guilty of violating the 1918 Sedition Act for having shown the two war-time allies (Great Britain and the U.S.) fighting against one another. However, Wilson understood Goldstein's intent with his picture and thus reduced Goldstein's sentence from ten years to 18 months in prison.

Dissenters and the Suppression of Civil Liberties

One of the first "victims" of nearly every U.S. war is the First Amendment, and World War I proved no exception. The Alien Act (1917) and the Sedition Act temporarily trumped Americans' rights to religious freedom, to speak freely, to publish freely, and to freely petition their government. The Espionage Act made it a crime to pass information with the intent of harming the success of American armed forces. Eugene Debs (labor leader, Socialist, and perennial presidential candidate) was arrested for making an anti-American speech. He was tried and found guilty under the Espionage Act, even though the act did not specifically prohibit speaking against the government. Thus, to shore up the Espionage Act, Congress passed the Sedition Act which expressly prohibited anyone from speaking, writing, or publishing anything against the federal government, the U.S. war effort, or its allies or "incite insubordination, disloyalty, mutiny, or refusal of duty, in the military or naval forces of the United States," which included interfering with recruitment operations.

The Attorney General, Thomas Gregory, wanted to do more and thus instructed the Postmaster General, Albert Burleson, to censure and if necessary discontinue delivering any anti-American or pro-German mail (letters, magazines, and newspapers). Gregory also enthusiastically supported the work of the American Protective League (APL). The APL curbed dissent at home by compelling German-Americans to sign a pledge of allegiance. The APL also conducted extra-governmental surveillance on pro-German activities and organizations (such as unions). Created by the native-born Chicago millionaire, A.M. Briggs, the APL's real purpose was to end all union activities in the country, which of course plutocrats like Briggs believed handicapped

Eugene Debs leaving the White House, December 26, 1921. Photo credit: Library of Congress

the war effort. The most targeted union on the APL's list was the radical International Workers of the World (IWW or "Wobblies"), formed in 1905 in an attempt by more left-leaning labor leaders to bring together in one organization socialists, communists, anarchists, and all other leftist groups who opposed the anti-strike position of the American Federation of Labor.

Gregory and Burleson targeted thousands of suspected enemies of the state to include such prominent Socialists as Eugene Debs, Mary Harris Jones (aka "Mother Jones"), Emma Goldman, and Max Eastman because of their use of the U.S. mail to distribute what Gregory and Burleson considered to be un-American literature. Besides Socialist newspapers such as *The Call*, Burleson prohibited the delivery of what he considered to be anti-British publications such as *The Irish World* and *The Gaelic American.*

Anti-German fervor during the Great War at times bordered on the ridiculous and the extreme, resulting even in the renaming of German (or German-sounding) food. Sauerkraut became "liberty cabbage," frankfurters became "hot dogs," and Salisbury steak transformed into meat loaf. Extralegal organizations, such as the Wisconsin Loyalty League sought to control their relatively large German population as well as their own elected officials who questioned the war. Wisconsin Senator Robert LaFollette, a Progressive Democrat, decried American entry into the war on the basis that the U.S. had indeed been breaking international law by shipping explosives on civilian ships (such as the *Lusitania*) and thus going to war to protect neutral rights was absurd to the Wisconsin solon. Ex-president Teddy Roosevelt called LaFollette a "shadow Hun" and "the most sinister enemy of democracy in the United States." LaFollette was certainly no traitor nor enemy of the state, and Wisconsin voters rallied to their popular senator, reelecting him every time he ran for the Senate until his death. Wisconsinites also sent to the House of Representatives this nation's first Socialist party member, Victor Berger (1910-1912, 1918-1920, and 1922-1928).

In 1919, in *Schenck v. United States,* the U.S. Supreme Court upheld the constitutionality of the Espionage and Sedition Acts. In 1918, Charles Schenck, one of the Socialist Party of America's leaders, who oversaw his party's anti-war pamphleteering campaign, which urged tens of thousands of young men of draft age not to serve if drafted, for the act violated the Thirteenth Amendment, was charged with sedition, found guilty, and imprisoned. In a unanimous decision, the thrice-wounded Civil War veteran Chief Justice Oliver Wendell Holmes, Jr., stated "[w]hen a nation is at war many things that might be said in time of peace are such a hindrance to its effort that their utterance will not be endured so long as men fight, and that no Court could regard them as protected by any constitutional right." In other words, according to Holmes and his fellow justices, the needs of the state, especially in times of crises, superseded those of the individual and thus dissent of any stripe or form was illegal.

African Americans in the Military

For the second time since the end of slavery, African Americans served this country during a time of foreign war not only for traditional patriotic reasons but also to prove to white Americans that black folk were as intelligent, honorable, dedicated, courageous, and as loyal to the Republic as their fellow white citizens. As noted in a previous chapter, although slavery had long since been abolished, a de facto apartheid existed in the American South, popularly known as Jim Crow. Creating a completely segregated black and white America was deemed not only appropriate by the majority of white Americans but constitutional as well, evidenced by the 1896 Supreme Court decision in *Plessy v. Ferguson.*

Despite their oppression, over 400,000 African-American males entered the ranks of the U.S. military during World War I. Most African Americans in the armed services had been drafted and the number of black draftees accounted for 13 percent of all American males conscripted. Yet, African Americans represented only 10.7 percent of the total U.S. population in 1910 and 9.9 percent in 1920. Moreover, only a small percentage of African-American soldiers saw combat. Indeed, the overwhelming majority worked mainly as mess-boys (mealtime aides), laborers, and stevedores (ship cargo handlers). Although relegated to often menial tasks, some jobs such as that of a stevedore, proved indispensable to the war effort. Sometimes working 24 hours non-stop, black stevedores unloaded vital supply ships with incredible speed and efficiency. Surprisingly, especially to their white counterparts, black AEF soldiers, regardless of assignment or task, were welcomed by the French military and people and treated with respect; indeed, as equal human beings. Suffice it to say, such displays of humanity initially shocked African-American troops, but as they interacted with the French people, they came to realize that not all white societies were like that of the United States. There were predominantly white countries in which they could live free from prejudice and discrimination. Thus, it was no surprise that after the war hundreds of black veterans chose to remain in France for the rest of their lives, enjoying a quality of life as an expatriate that they sadly could only dream about having back home in the United States.

The American military at the time of the Great War reflected the segregated nature of American society. All branches of the armed services were separated into all-white and all-black units, with white officers in charge of African-American enlistees and draftees. Moreover, the relegation of the majority of black soldiers and sailors to menial, often demeaning, work reflected the white military establishment's belief that African-American men were incapable of holding up in combat, certain they would run at the first sign of a fight or danger because of their supposed "inherent" character defects such as cowardice. Although we know today that such an assessment of African Americans in combat is ridiculous, at the time such beliefs were widespread among white officers and their superiors in the chain of command. However, when given the opportunity to fight, black soldiers distinguished themselves above and beyond the call of duty. Such was true of the famous and highly decorated all-black 369th Infantry known as the "Harlem Hell Fighters," the 803rd Pioneer Infantry Band, No. 16, and the 370th Regiment, Illinois National Guard, to name a few. The Harlem Hell Fighters, under the command of Colonel William Hayward, became one of the most decorated U.S. military units of the war. They were the first U.S. outfit to be awarded the French Croix de Guerre. The commander of the American Expeditionary Force, General John "Blackjack" Pershing, "loaned" the 369th to France and thus this nearly-all-black (save for the officers), brigade saw some of the war's most vicious and brutal fighting long before any other American soldiers, such as that witnessed at Chateau-Thierry and Belleau Wood, where nearly 10,000 Allied troops were killed or wounded. The Hell Fighters spent 191 days in the trenches (longer than any unit from either side), and they were the first Allied contingent to cross the Rhine. The 369th also had its own popular band led by James Reese Europe. Europe was promoted to lieutenant and became, as a band leader, the highest ranking black soldier in the unit.

The federal government created a new officer training school in Iowa where over 1,000 African-American men received commissions as officers for the war. However, only a handful ever commanded fellow black soldiers. Even the country's first black graduate of the U.S. Military Academy at West Point, Charles Young, who saw combat in Cuba, the Philippines, Haiti, and Mexico, was not allowed to command troops in Europe.

Many prominent African Americans joined the military such as Napoleon Marshall, Spotswood Poles, and James Reese Europe. Poles was the popular and talented centerfielder for the New York Lincoln Giants of the Negro Leagues. Reese was probably the most nationally-known African American to serve in the military. Reese was a Harlem bandleader and possibly the most popular song writer of the early twentieth century. His music inspired new dance steps, led to the creation of new, dance-oriented night clubs, and in the process, helped to transform dancing into one of the most popular forms of entertainment among young people. In 1914, Europe's orchestra (usually known as Europe's Society Orchestra) became the first black band to record commercially in the United States.

When the men of the 369th mustered out of the service in early 1919, Europe began writing and recording popular songs that capitalized on his war-time experiences. Songs such as "On Patrol In No Man's Land" evoked feelings of patriotism while under fire from a German mortar barrage and "All Of No Man's Land Is Ours" is a love song in which a returning combat veteran calls his fiancé upon arriving back in the U.S.

Europe did not live long enough to profit from his post-war fame. During a live performance in Boston in early May 1919, a heated argument developed between Europe and one of his drummers, Herbert Wright. Wright whipped out a knife and stabbed Europe in the neck. Europe died en route to the hospital. Newspapers reported the loss with the banner "Jazz King is Dead." James Reese Europe was buried at Arlington National Cemetery.

Given the nature of African-American oppression at home, why any black men, let alone someone of Reese's stature, would enlist in the New York National Guard. Perhaps motivating Reese and others was a true patriotism, which even for a moment more militant black leaders such as W.E.B. Du Bois, promoted as well. Du Bois believed that despite their oppression, African Americans had a duty to serve in the military as a way of demonstrating their intelligence, bravery, and loyalty to country and to white Americans. Du Bois publicly called upon his brothers to enlist, to fight and if necessary to lay down their lives for the United States. "If this is our country," declared Du Bois "then this is our war. We must fight it with every ounce of blood and treasure." Like many black leaders before him, Du Bois hoped that the patriotism and courage demonstrated by black soldiers in battle would prove yet again that African Americans deserved to sit as full participants at the table of equality. However, as will be seen later in this chapter and in the next, such was not to be the case for either returning African-American soldiers or for the larger black community at home. Indeed, life for the majority of African Americans in the war's aftermath remained tragically as oppressive, brutal, and short as it was before the Great War.

Nonetheless, African Americans supported the war effort either by enlisting or as civilian activists for the cause at home. One such homefront booster was Emmett J. Scott. Scott spent most of his career working for the NAACP, which included eighteen years as Booker T. Washington's private secretary. When the U.S. declared war on Germany, President Wilson wanted a spokesman for Black troops in the War Department and thus Scott became a special assistant to Newton Baker, the Secretary of War, overseeing the recruitment, training, and overall morale of Africa-American troops.

However, no amount of African-American displays of patriotism could mitigate the brutality of Jim Crow. Without question one of the most infamous episodes of white resistance and shame occurred in Houston, Texas, in the summer of 1917, the now legendary "Camp Logan Riots." The incident involved African-American troops from California and Wyoming sent to Houston for training at a camp set up just outside the city for such purposes, Camp Logan, which today is the site of the city of Houston's premier recreational park, Memorial Park. Like their counterparts throughout the South, white Houstonians were not terribly happy to see the influx of black people, especially potentially "uppity" black soldiers. Although more progressive than most Southern cities in black-white race relations, Houston nonetheless had its own version of Jim Crow—just as restricting, just as blatantly discriminatory; and just as harsh in enforcement as elsewhere in the South. Black folk could not ride on certain trolleys, eat at certain restaurants, or congregate in groups of more than five people in most public places. Suffice it to say, Houston's all-white law enforcement establishment was especially leery of having such a large contingent of black soldiers on the city's outskirts, fearing that when they came to town on leave there could be "trouble," which they were ready to suppress at the slightest provocation and with the harshest reprisals.

One hot, sticky August day a young African-American recruit tried to stop a Houston cop's beating of an Africa-American woman for allegedly "resisting arrest," for having called the officer "vile names." The cop, Lee Sparks, turned his club against the recruit, who overcame Sparks, but to no avail as several other officers came to Sparks' rescue, wielding their night-sticks furiously at the young soldier, beating him unconscious and literally dragging him to jail. Upon hearing the news of the arrest of one of his men, non-commissioned officer Corporal Charles Baltimore went to Houston to inquire about what had happened. No sooner did he arrive at the police station than he was arrested as well. When the news of Baltimore's incarceration reached Camp Logan, the rest of the outfit became enraged, determined to not only set their comrades free but to resist with force any further insult or degradation. They marched with their weapons to the police station and demanded their brothers' release, which initially the police refused to do. That proved to be the final straw; the soldiers attacked in full fury those police at the station. In the ensuing melee, which lasted for several hours and saw the city's white and black civilian population become involved, fifteen people died, including five policemen and six blacks, four of whom were African-American soldiers.

The fracas would officially be called "The Camp Logan Riots." In the ensuing investigation by United States Army officials, sixty-three African-American troops would be arrested and charged with mutiny. At the first of several courts martial, thirteen African-American soldiers were found guilty and sentenced to death, including Corporal Baltimore. Seven more troops would be executed at the close of the second trial, and dozens imprisoned with sentences raging from 24 months to life at the final court martial proceedings. Race riots were not limited to war-time America. The century opened with violent bloodbaths in New Orleans 1900; Atlanta 1902 and 1906, and in Springfield, Illinois in 1908. In each of those cities whites, not black folk, initiated the outburst, and every incident ended with African Americans having paid the highest price in numbers murdered and property destroyed. Tragically, the race riots that occurred before the war paled in comparison with those that erupted between 1916 and 1923. Indeed the riots that exploded in East St. Louis, Illinois, Tulsa, Oklahoma, and Rosewood, Florida in the war's aftermath were some of the bloodiest in the nation's history. However, until the 1960s, the city of Chicago had the "distinction" of being home to the worst manifestation of post-war repression and racial violence. In July 1919, while a white police officer stood by, whites stoned to death a black youth who swum or drifted accidentally into the "wrong" white area of a lakeshore beach. Incensed by what they saw, African Americans, many of whom were ex-veterans, mobbed the police officer and killed him. The next day, in retaliation, gangs of white thugs, some with machine guns, attacked black neighborhoods in south Chicago, killing indiscriminately any black person—men, women, children—they came across. However, unlike in the past, and led by black veterans, the African-American community fought back. The killing, looting, and burning of both white and black areas raged for five days, leaving more than 500 injured by beating or gunfire and 38 people dead. Most important, African Americans had armed themselves and fought back, no doubt inspired by retuning black soldiers urging their fellow black citizens to resist white racist reprisals against African Americans for simply demanding their Constitutional rights as equal citizens under the law. As will be seen in the next chapter, the decade of the 1920s witnessed the emergence in Northern cities, such as New York, the emergence of the "New Negro," whose community will not only reject and resist white supremacy but also display for the first time a sense of black pride and identity distinct from white America.

In the aftermath of the 1919 riots, NAACP Executive Secretary Walter White, explained to a stunned white America the unprecedented black armed resistance they had recently witnessed. In many instances African American veterans had encouraged and led the black counterattack. "These men [black veterans] with their new outlook on life, injected the same spirit into their companions, a thing that is true of many other sections of America. One of the greatest surprises to many of those who came down to "clean out the niggers," is that these same "niggers" fought back. Colored men saw their own being killed, heard of many more and believed that their lives and liberty were at stake. In such a spirit most of the fighting was done."

Although few and far between, there were instances where black folk successfully resisted and triumphed over Jim Crow oppression. Such occurred in Rocky Mount, North Carolina, where black female workers in a textile factory walked off their jobs to protest the verbal abuse of their white floor manager. According to the *Norfolk Journal and Guide*, "when the superintendent learned of the trouble later in the day he immediately began to visit the homes of the operatives asking them to return to work. The offending white manager was discharged and the girls returned to their work with no loss of time." Apparently, the last thing the Wilson administration needed was a strike at an important wartime industry such as textiles, for any stoppage in production could adversely affect the overall war effort. After all, soldiers needed uniforms on a regular basis.

Finally, and perhaps most important, the war years saw the first major emigration of African Americans out of the South to the North. Prompting many black Southerners to move North during the war years was the potential for jobs in Northern industrial cities, many of whose factories were intimately involved in wartime production. As a result of this internal exodus, between 1910 and 1920, the African American population of manufacturing cities such as Gary, Indiana and Detroit, Michigan witnessed an increase of 1300 percent and 611 percent respectively. New York, which already had a well-established African-American community (over 90,000 in 1910), saw its black population increase by 66 percent (to over 150,000 by 1920). Many of these black migrants became the first members of their family since the end of slavery to not only have left the South but to have earned a livelihood other than as a sharecropper or agricultural laborer. Equally significant for the future demographics of post-Great War America, the majority of these mostly young men would not return to the South after the war. Although Jim Crow's slick cousin "James Crow" existed in Northern cities, relegating blacks to segregated neighborhoods, menial jobs, and other manifestations of discrimination and prejudice, life in the urban North was nonetheless more exciting, less circumscribed, less emotionally and psychologically oppressing, and potentially more materially rewarding. Indeed, thanks to the money earned during the war years, a legitimate and viable black middle class emerged and flourished during the 1920s in many Northern cities. Unfortunately the Great Depression ended for many urban middle class African Americans their first taste of economic independence, solvency, and freedom.

The American "Doughboys"

In 1918, a Yankee of Irish roots named George M. Cohan, penned what became one of the most popular, patriotic ditties ever written in the history of war-time America, *Over There.* It was if Woodrow Wilson had Cohan's song in mind when he asked young men to drop their plow shears, leave their factory jobs or the universities, and enter the ranks of the U.S. military to prevent Germany from running roughshod over Europe. So inspirational was Cohan's song for the nation's warriors and the home front, that on the eve the U.S. entry into World War II, Congress presented Cohan with a Congressional Medal of Honor in recognition of his prolific patriotic song-writing career as well as for his having written what became the unofficial U.S. anthem during the Great War, *Over There*:

However, in the end, neither uplifting lyrics nor impassioned calls to arms could alleviate the emotional and psychological distress experienced by thousands of American soldiers after witnessing the greatest human slaughter in the history of mankind.

No sooner did the United States enter the Great War than Wilson appointed as commander of American troops General John "Black Jack" Pershing, whom he had recently recalled from Mexico. Pershing, a career soldier and combat veteran, was well aware of the Army's lack of preparedness, especially for the type of warfare American soldiers would be called upon to fight. Pershing knew that if not trained properly, American soldiers would be invited to the slaughter, for they would be encountering on the Western front a battle-hardened German soldier supported by one of the most advanced war machines the world had seen. Realizing the horrible reality of modern warfare American lads were about to confront, Pershing insisted that his troops undergo at least six months of rigorous training, with basic preparation in the United States and with more focused, intense, combat-readiness training upon arrival in Europe. Despite Pershing's pleas for such preparedness, the Wilson administration buckled to the Allies' insistence that the Americans forego training in the United States and get to Europe as quickly as possible before it was too late. Thus, by the time of their first engagement, relatively few "doughboys" had been properly trained in the "art" of modern, total warfare.

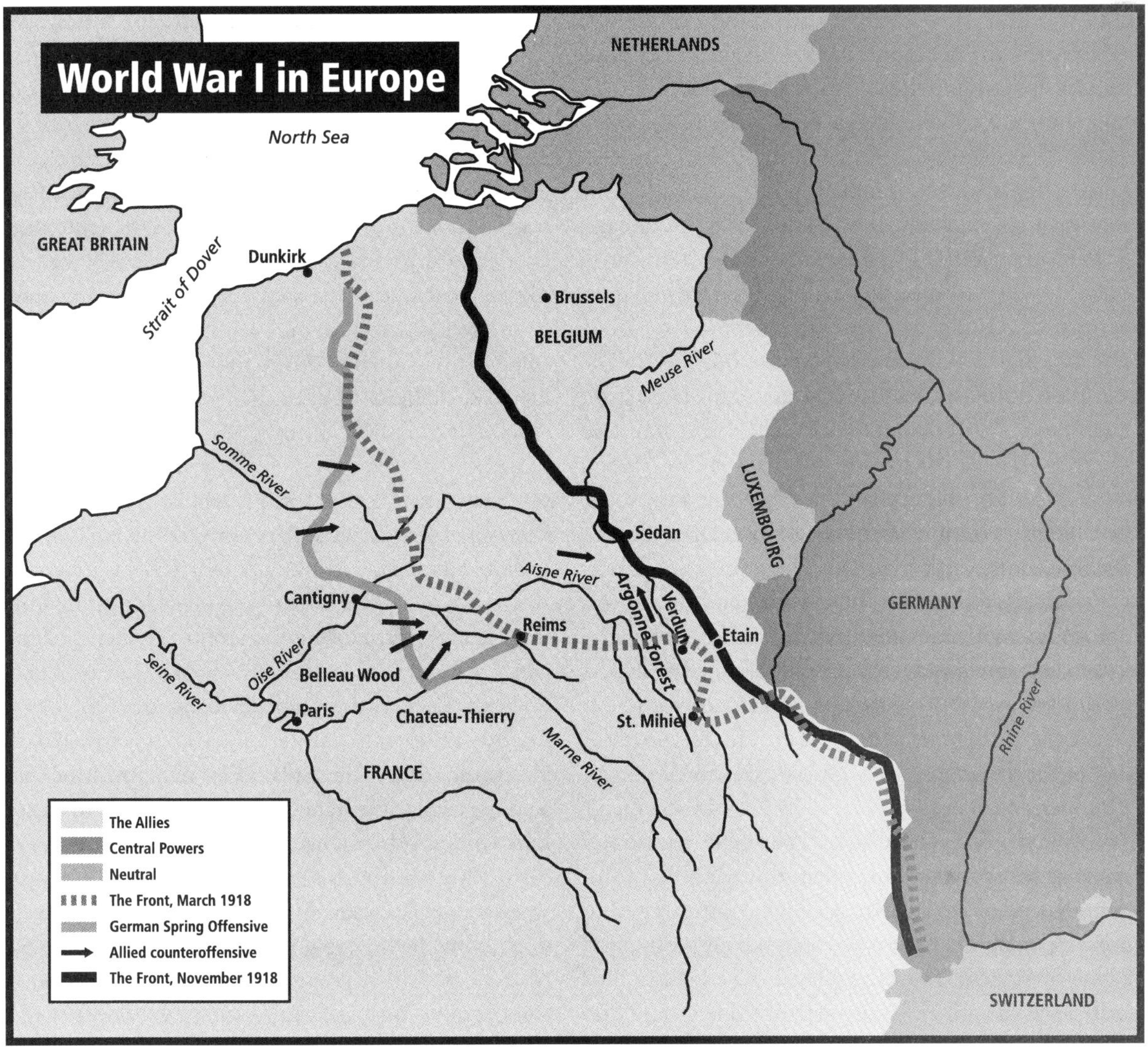

The AEF in France

The first U.S. troops arrived in France in October 1917. Eventually about 2 million American soldiers served in France as members of the American Expeditionary Force (AEF). Although arriving in the fall of 1917, American troops did not see combat until the spring of 1918 when in March of that year, Germany launched a major offensive along the Somme. A few American battalions (about 3,000 U.S. soldiers) participated in the fighting around Amiens and Armentieres, helping to stem the German advance. In May 1918 the Germans launched their second assault along the Aisne River, driving the Allies back to the Marne, giving the Germans a nearly open road to Paris, fifty miles away. However, as the French government prepared to evacuate the "City of Lights,' American forces arrived in strength, with parts of three U.S. Army divisions (about 27,000 men) and a Marine brigade (about 4,000 soldiers), helping to stop the Germans at the town of Chateau-Thierry and nearby Belleau Wood.

These two German offensives had punched deep holes (salients) in the Allied line. A German drive intended to capture the cathedral city of Rheims between these two salients was stopped with the help of some 85,000 American troops. Allied/American victories at Chateau-Thierry and Belleau Wood proved to be the war's turning point; from this point on the Germans would be on the defensive; indeed they would be desperately trying to stave off defeat, which now appeared imminent with the presence of tens of thousands of fresh American troops and plentiful amounts of U.S. military hardware and money at the Allies disposal. Contributing to the Germans' failed offensives as well as to their ultimate vanquishing was the fact that many German soldiers, already weakened by battle fatigue and poor diet, fell victim to influenza, an infectious disease that would soon emerge as a deadly worldwide pandemic.

Some 270,000 American soldiers fought in the last Allied offensive to push the Germans back from the Marne. The counterattack, the Second Battle of the Marne, began on a rainy July 18, 1918 and lasted until August 6, of that year. The rain turned the roads into bogs, making it difficult for the Americans to transport men and materiel. However, the Americans persevered, and by August they and the British could claim another Allied victory, having driven the Germans almost back to the Belgian frontier. Thanks to the Americans, Parisians no longer worried about having to evacuate their beloved city, for by the fall of 1918, the Germans were at a "safe" distance of over 100 miles east of Paris.

Pershing's first fully independent command came in September 1918, when supreme allied commander, Marshal Ferdinand Foch, authorized an AEF campaign to close a German salient around the town of St. Mihiel on the Meuse River, about 150 miles east of Paris. Pershing assembled over 500,000 American and 100,000 French soldiers for his massive offensive. Shelling of German positions began at 1:00 a.m. on September 11, and as an American recorded in his diary, "In one instant the entire front was a sheet of flame, while the heavy artillery made the earth quake." Within four days the salient was closed, in part because some German units had already withdrawn. Even so, St. Mihiel cost 7,000 U.S. casualties.

The war's last battle, the Meuse-Argonne Forest campaign, began on September 26 and lasted until November 1918. The assault represented the most protracted period U.S. soldiers were to be involved in constant combat and the first time they had to endure the filth, vermin, and dysentery that had become part and parcel of the trench warfare their Allied and German counterparts had suffered for four years. The stench of poison gas (first used by the Germans in 1915) hung in the air, and bloated rats scurried in the mud, gorging on human remains. Few of the American doughboys who fought in this particular offensive would forget what they experienced for several months in the fall of 1918. As shells streaked over head at night, one American recalled, "We simply lay and trembled from sheer nervous tension." Many welcomed injuries, even inflicting them upon themselves as a ticket out of the trenches. Many others collapsed emotionally and were hospitalized for "shell shock." The fighting for the Americans was particularly ferocious in the Argonne Forest, which saw many instances of vicious hand-to-hand combat between German and American soldiers. "We are not men anymore, just savage beasts," wrote a young American after three days of such fighting along three long, heavily fortified German trenches called Stellungen. Even the hardened Pershing could not hold back emotion after witnessing such slaughter. One day as he rode in his staff car past the site of a particularly gruesome scene, where dead German and American soldiers were still entangled from having engaged and killed one another in hand-to-hand combat, Pershing buried his head in his hands and moaned his dead wife's name: "Frankie, Frankie, my God, sometimes I don't know how I can go on with this madness." But the AEF prevailed, overrunning the dreaded German trenches and pushing the Germans ever deeper into Belgium and Alsace-Lorraine by early November 1918. By that date it had become apparent to the German High Command that with the American presence, which they had hoped to prevent, the Allies were poised for victory. If an invasion of Germany proper was to be avoided then it was time to surrender before such a calamity could unfold.

The war came to an end on November 11, 1918 at 11a.m. Although over 200,000 Americans had been wounded and 113,000 troops died (around 52,000 in battle and 60,000 from non-combat issues such as disease), the comparatively short presence of the U.S. in the war saved American soldiers from experiencing the horrors of trench warfare and the massive loss of lives which were the reality for the Russian, German, French, and English people.

Military and civilian deaths for Great Britain topped one million, 1.7 million for France, 2.3 million for Russia, and 2.5 million for Germany. About 500,000 combatants alone were killed or wounded during the First Battle of Marne (1914), 230,000 at the Battle of Ypres (1914), and 700,000 at Verdun (1916). As can be readily seen from just these few statistics, compared to the loss of life and property suffered by the Europeans after four years of slaughter, Americans escaped the madness relatively *physically* unscathed. However, the psychological and emotional impact on both the American people and the nation's warriors was surprisingly deep and profound; there laid the greatest scars and most searing memories of the war's awfulness, and it would be the trauma and anguish suffered at that level that would prove to be some of the most important factors in defeating Woodrow Wilson's post-war vision for the United States and the world.

THE HOME FRONT

Once the U.S. openly joined the war, Congress worked to ensure that Americans at home and the soldiers fighting in Europe had sufficient resources with which to sustain such an unprecedented human and material effort. Congress thus adopted the Fuel and Food Control Act in 1917. The Fuel Administration controlled the production, distribution, and price of the nation's main fuel sources, such as oil, gas, and coal. Directing the agency was Dr. Harry A. Garfield—son of and witness to the assassination of President James B. Garfield in 1881. Like many of the men with whom Wilson surrounded himself, Garfield was a fellow academic, president of Williams College in Massachusetts at the time of his appointment. Although a Republican, Garfield, like Wilson, was first and foremost a Progressive, who believed in the transformative nature of the human spirit. According to Garfield, academia was the place of "cultivated men, earnest and seeking by all ways to advance the cause of civilization." Garfield's progressivism set him apart from the rest of Wilson's wartime cabinet. For unlike the majority, he did not believe the war effort demanded greater government control of the economy. At a meeting of the Academy of Political Scientists, Garfield offered a justification for the Fuel Administration's existence as well as assurances that under his watch the Fuel Administration would not nationalize the fuel industry. In his speech entitled "Task of the Fuel Administration," the gap between the fuel needs of a country at war compared to the needs of the U.S. in 1916 would be largely met through conservation, he argued, not a government takeover of the industry in order to ensure energy efficiency and proper use for the war effort. Forecasting the government-academic cooperation that would become common place in the decades after World War II, Garfield turned to university scientists and mathematicians to resolve some of the issues pertaining to fuel conservation in wartime America.

Food production and consumption also worried the Wilson administration, and thus the president issued Executive Order (2679A) creating the U.S. Food Administration. Headed by future president Herbert Hoover, Wilson charged the agency with assuring the supply, distribution, and conservation of food during the war, facilitating commodities transportation, preventing monopolies and hoarding, and maintaining governmental power over foods by using voluntary agreements and a licensing system.

In trying to get Americans to conserve what they had and to use less of what they grew or made, Hoover promoted "Meatless Mondays" and "Wheatless Wednesdays." Hoover also targeted the new immigrant populations, inundating their communities with all manner of visuals such as posters to remind them that they were in America now, and that one of the ways they could demonstrate their loyalty to their new homeland was to support the food conservation program. One such poster portrayed a well-lit, golden-colored, Oz-like New York in the far background with the Statue of Liberty in the near-background and a halo rainbow of red, white, and blue that seemed to hang in the sky as a physical divider between light and dark, new and old, progressive and regressive. In the foreground you saw numerous immigrants dressed in Old World clothes including babushkas on the elderly women. "FOOD WILL WIN THE WAR," the poster proclaimed, "WHEAT is needed for the Allies – Waste Nothing. You came here seeking Freedom. You must now help to preserve it." Another

Hoover slogan urged Americans to "Serve Beans by all Means," which suggested that people could find equally nutritious substitutes for those food commodities needed to feed the troops overseas. Even president Wilson did his part by pasturing a flock of sheep on the White House lawn.

The Food Administration asked Americans to grow their own vegetables (called "Victory Gardens") and to pledge to follow the call to preserve, consume less, and grow more in order to ensure that sufficient meat, wheat, fats, and sugars made it to the U.S. troops and American allies. The *Milwaukee Journal*, the largest daily in Wisconsin, proclaimed that 100 percent of their citizens took the pledge to eat less and conserve more. Wisconsin had more German immigrants than any other state as well as an active Socialist movement and thus it was important for the newspaper's publisher to ensure his readers locally and nationally, that *all* Wisconsinites, regardless of ethnicity or ideology, were one hundred percent behind the "war to end all wars," and the war "to make the world safe for democracy." The publishers of *Good Housekeeping* urged its readers to support the government efforts believing that:

> its large circle of earnest, patriotic women readers will respond gladly to a call to service at home. It is a tremendous task—this one of conservation and elimination of waste. Every woman is urged to do her part. It can best be done through close cooperation with the government. Enlist now and pledge yourself to do your share.

Finally, the War Industries Board (WIB), created in mid-summer of 1917, was another federal agency tasked with ensuring that Americans at home and abroad had access to acceptably priced merchandise and equipment. Wilson appointed Wall Street financier Bernard Baruch to head this particular agency. In addition to being a close friend and political ally of Wilson, Baruch had also been a major financial donor as well as unpaid adviser to the Democratic Party for most of his adult life. As part of Wilson's "War Cabinet," Baruch worked closely with Hoover. While Hoover's emphasis was on agriculture, Baruch focused on transforming American industry into an efficient, prolific producer of every essential for a country at war. In short, Baruch wanted American soldiers to not only have the best weaponry U.S. manufacturers could produce but all other supplies as well, from boots to uniforms, to blankets, to medical supplies, and in conjunction with Hoover's agency, more than adequate nourishment.

The WIB's main purpose was to ensure that all of the nation's key productive industries were producing at maximum output for the war. It was thus vital that the nation's raw materials were not squandered on superfluous products or were withheld for the purpose of profiteering. Thus the WIB set production quotas for war-related industries and oversaw the allocation of raw resources. In short, the WIB controlled all aspects of war procurement and production, from the distribution of raw resources to the placing of price controls on finished goods, which included chemical, steel, textile, rubber, and leather products. The standardization of bicycle manufacturing, for example, saved tons of steel. Perhaps most important, the establishment of the WIB marked the first time in U.S. history that the federal government participated in such a capacity in the private sector.

These two agencies represented the tip of the regulatory iceberg. Nearly 5,000 government-created agencies supervised home front activities. Some others of note were the Shipping Board, which regulated the transport of goods by water; the National War Labor Board, which worked assiduously to resolve labor-management disputes that if not ameliorated, could have led to striking workers that would have jeopardized production; and the Railroad Administration, headed by treasury secretary William McAdoo. When lines refused to allow their competitors to use their tracks to transport goods, a stoppage occurred in the flow of supplies to Europe in the winter of 1917-1918. McAdoo's agency intervened and soon transformed (consolidated) the thousands of miles of track owned by the competing companies into an efficient national rail system under his board's "direction" (control). In effect, McAdoo (with Wilson's and Congress' approval) "semi-nationalized" the nation's rail system, bringing all of the major carriers under direct government regulation for the war's duration. Although tightly monitoring the railroads' shipments of goods, the federal government did not take the revenue for such services; significant profits from such enterprise continued to flow into the coffers of the railroad magnates. Indeed, the railroad remained the king of mass transportation, and the lines' owners, like their Gilded Age plutocratic counterparts, had become some of the most notorious robber barons of the early twentieth century.

American businesses, much maligned by Progressives before the conflict, saw the war emergency as an opportunity to revamp their public image. Corporate executives such as Baruch ran regulatory agencies; factory owners distributed pro-war propaganda to workers; and trade associations coordinated war production. Unfortunately much of the patriotic ballyhoo was disingenuous, a plutocratic ruse to get the federal government and reformers out of their businesses, not only during the war but also more importantly after the conflict was over. By presenting a more solicitous, public-spirited face during the war, both the American public and the federal government would look kindlier upon them, thanking them for their significant wartime contributions by allowing them to once again reign supreme. As will be seen in the next chapter, that precise scenario unfolded in the aftermath of the Great War. Indeed, the 1920s in many ways marked the heyday of American big business, and the plutocrats of that era owed much of their power to their predecessors' shrewd manipulation and exploitation of wartime sentimentality.

Even before the war ended and government restraints removed, big business was on the march as witnessed by the ongoing process of corporate consolidation and economic integration. Wilson's track record of progressive trust-busting before the war was at best mediocre. During the war his administration stopped all such endeavors and instead encouraged private sector cooperation in the name of the war effort. Businesses "cooperated" all right, seizing a rare, government-sanctioned opportunity to further consolidate their enterprises. As a result, the number of corporate mergers jumped sharply. Commenting on the epidemic of "mergeritis," the Progressive magazine, *Harper's Weekly* observed, "The war has accelerated a tendency that was already irresistible. Instead of punishing companies for acting in concert, the government is now in some cases forcing them to unite. If this trend continues, the years after this war are over could come to represent some of the worst abuses of the commonweal by the corporations. The war has opened a Pandora's Box of business consolidation, the likes of which the country has not seen in years. It may be impossible to put these companies back into the box after the war."

Suffice it to say, the nineteen months in which the United States participated in the Great War was good for American businesses. Despite added business taxes imposed by Congress, wartime profits soared. After-tax profits in the copper industry, for example, jumped from 12 percent in 1913 to 24 percent in 1917.

Wartime Diplomacy

Woodrow Wilson envisioned a quick war, and to that end, Wilson believed it essential that the Allies coordinate as expeditiously as possible, through a Supreme War Council, all food production, equipment needs, and communication to produce victory. Representing the United States on the council was Army Chief of Staff Tasker H. Bliss. Initially, the council focused on mobilizing resources and securing an Allied military victory, but as triumphed neared, the Council turned its attention to the equally pressing issue of the post-war peace settlement.

To Woodrow Wilson if the Great War just completed was to be "the war to end all wars," then it was imperative that the United States not only participate fully in the peace process but also provide the blueprint as well for an end to international conflict. Thus in a speech given on January 8, 1918, Wilson outlined his goals, a "fourteen-point" program for not only how the war should end but a vision as well that he believed would ensure lasting peace for the post-war world.

Many of the ideas Wilson expressed before Congress were the initiatives of an assemblage of academics Wilson had called together soon after the United States entered the conflict in 1917. Nicknamed the "Inquiry," these members of the nation's intelligentsia met in secret at the offices of the American Geographic Society in New York City. Wilson charged the group to develop proposals, based on their knowledge and research of European and world history, which he could then formulate into an agenda and present to the European belligerents as the basis for a just and permanent peace settlement. Wilson had great confidence in the "Inquiry's" ability to provide him with the right ideas, for as the 28-year old Harvard graduate, Walter Lippmann, who recruited the scholars and managed the Inquiry in its formative phase, declared, "We are skimming the cream of the younger and more imaginative scholars. What we are on the lookout for is genius—sheer, startling genius, and nothing else will do." Wilson formalized the Inquiry's "genius" into The Fourteen Points, which the president unveiled in his January speech before Congress.

In his address, Wilson reminded the joint session of Congress that the U.S. entered the Great War not only to protect American liberties at home but also to propagate as well American ideals throughout the world. Wilson envisioned a world "made fit and safe to live in and particularly that it be made safe for every peace-loving nation, which, like our own, wishes to live its own life, determine its own institutions, and be assured of justice and fair dealing by other peoples of the world as against force and selfish aggression." Thus among some of the "points" Wilson called for were international trade unrestricted by law or tariffs, an end to secret treaties and military alliances, and an end to colonialism. However, to Wilson, none of his thirteen points could be established and enforced without the creation of a vigilant world organization for international cooperation. As Wilson described such a body in the final of his fourteen points, "A general association of nations must be formed under specific covenants for the purpose of affording mutual guarantees of political independence and territorial integrity to great and small states alike."

Much to Wilson's feigned "surprise," American and European leaders accused the president of wanting to remake the post-war world in an American image. Wilson quickly dismissed such allegations, reassuring both his American and European listeners that, "the United States has no desire to interfere in European affairs or to act as arbiter in European territorial disputes." In other words, Wilson wanted to convey to the European belligerents that his January 8 speech was nothing more than an intellectual exercise and not any sort of plan to rebuild the world along American dictates.

England and France were the most wary of Wilson's Fourteen Points agenda, for of all the allies (excluding Russia, now the Soviet Union) they had fought the longest and sacrificed the most in both material and human lives. In short, they did not greet Wilson's ideas for a new world order with open arms. Arthur Balfour, the British Foreign Secretary and one-time Prime Minister, seemed to be uninterested in any sort of negotiated settlement, instead calling for Germany to provide England and France with "unconditional restoration and reparation" of all taken, plundered, and destroyed lands. Neither did the Belgian Prime Minister accept Wilson's extensive plan. Baron Charles de Broqueville demanded "reparation for damages and guarantees against repetition of the aggression." Earlier, Wilson had called for "peace without victory," which meant that the Allies did not need to crush and then humiliate Germany with unrealistically harsh reparations and demands. However, that was precisely the Anglo-French position and thus the Inquiry and Wilson underestimated the Allies' desire to punish Germany not only as the vanquished but for having allegedly caused the war as well. To the British and French, the old cliché was still relevant: "to the victor(s) go the spoils of war." Sensing hostility to his proposals and determined to see his ideas prevail, Wilson believed it essential that he go to France, to Paris, in order to secure future peace. Wilson thus became the first president to ever leave the United States and travel abroad while in office. Wilson's journey also reflected his desire to continue to personally direct American foreign policy and his determination to see the United States assume a greater international role, a status previously confined to a hegemonic position in the Western Hemisphere.

THE END OF THE WAR AND THE SEARCH FOR PEACE

Thirty-six nations gathered from January to June 1919 at the famous Versailles palace just outside Paris. However, excluded from the gathering were both Bolshevik Russia and Germany, nation's considered persona non grata by the Allies, including the United States, although Wilson did somewhat half-heartedly support Germany's presence but passionately opposed granting the Soviet Union a seat. Indeed, Wilson was as anti-Bolshevik as his English and French counterparts, who prodded him in August 1918, even before the Great War had ended, to send 15,000 American troops into Russia to help defeat the Bolsheviks, who at the time were engaged in a bloody civil war against various Russian anti-Bolshevik factions, known collectively as the "Whites."

The second phase of the Russian Revolution had begun in November 1917 when the Marxist Bolshevik Party overthrew via coup d'etat, the quasi-democratic/parliamentary Provisional Government headed by Alexander Kerensky, who came to power during the revolution's first phase in February 1917. It was Kerensky and his followers who had forced the disastrous Czar Nicholas II to abdicate. However, from the moment Kerensky and his tenuous coalition of anti- Bolshevik socialists (Mensheviks), Kadets, SR's (Social Revolutionaries), constitutional monarchists, and an assortment of other ideologically disparate factions seized power, their tenure was destined to be short-lived. Although Kerensky's government faced a multitude of domestic issues and crises, it was his government's refusal to withdraw Russia from the war and to fight on instead that ultimately toppled his regime. By the time Kerensky became de-facto executive of the Provisional Government, the Russian people, especially the nation's soldiers, had grown sick of the war. The conflict had brought them nothing but untold miseries, ranging from starvation to never-ending strikes, to the slaughter of hundreds of thousands of poorly-clad and equipped peasant conscripts on the battlefronts. By succumbing to the Allies relentless pressure to have Russia remain in the war (largely for Allies own selfish reasons), Kerensky sealed the fate of Russia's brief experiment in parliamentary government.

When the Bolshevik Party, led by the ruthlessly brilliant V. I. Lenin, proclaimed that his party offered "peace, land, and bread"—manna from heaven to the vast majority of war-weary Russians—Kerensky's days were numbered. No sooner did Lenin seize control of Russia, than he quickly initiated peace talks with Germany (who had helped to smuggle him back into Russia so he could overthrow the Provisional Government) while urging workers in Europe and the United States to rise in revolt against the "capitalist-imperialist war," for which they had become lackeys and fodder. To further discredit the supposed righteousness of the Allied cause, Lenin published the secret treaties the Allies had made amongst themselves to carve up the territory and colonies of the Central Powers at war's end. Such revelations were especially embarrassing for Woodrow Wilson's claims that the United States had entered the conflict to help establish the right of all people to self-determination. Finally, the Bolsheviks' calls for a revolution that would bring about far-reaching social transformations, ending the corrupt and bankrupt notions of bourgeois-capitalist liberalism, had great appeal among the downtrodden around the world. For some, the fiery revolutionary

Lenin, not the intellectual reformist Wilson, seemed the towering figure of the age.

Although supporting liberal-capitalist reform movements throughout the world, Wilson vehemently opposed anti-capitalist revolutions, not only in Russia but in China and Mexico as well. Wilson wanted to reform capitalism; the Bolshevik leader Lenin wanted to destroy it. Thus the Wilson administration used a variety of means—diplomatic, economic, and military—to isolate and hopefully destroy Lenin and the Bolsheviks. Despite massive aid, all of Wilson's as well as the other Allies' (including Japan) efforts failed. By 1920 the Red Army, under the brilliant and ruthless leadership of Leon Trotsky, had crushed the Whites and with their defeat, all foreign "imperialist mercenaries" left the country. The Bolshevik revolution (and terror) could not proceed without the fear of being externally overthrown.

Despite Wilson's insistence in his Fourteen Points address that nations should engage in "open covenants, openly arrived at," all major discussions and decisions at Versailles were made not only behind closed doors but became the handiwork of essentially the four individuals representing the victorious Allies: Woodrow Wilson of the United States; David Lloyd George, prime minister of Great Britain; Vittorio Orlando, prime minister of Italy, and "Le Tigre," Georges Clemenceau, president of France, who proved to be the most insistent in demanding revenge and security for France.

Accompanying Wilson to France were nearly all of the members of the Inquiry as well as his closest friend and unofficial adviser, Colonel Edmund House. Suffice it to say, Wilson's entourage of perceived diplomatic "novices" and neophytes not only irritated the State Department's sense of protocol but insulted as well many of its members professionalism, expertise, and years of experience. Although greeted everywhere in Europe he went—France, England, and Italy—with the greatest fanfare—close to two million Frenchmen lined the boulevard des Champs-Elysees and screamed his name while throwing flowers in his path—not all diplomats shared in the popular adulation. Not even remotely impressed was the bitter and vindictive Clemenceau, who complained that "Wilson thinks he is another Jesus Christ come upon earth to reform men." In the end, however, it would not be Clemenceau's vengeful obstructionism to Wilson's agenda but rather the president's own arrogance, high-mindedness, and inattention to other developments at home that made it a certainty the American people would reject the Versailles Treaty. Before leaving, Wilson did not engage public or congressional opinion. Perhaps most damaging, he failed to build bipartisan support for his program: his handpicked delegation included only one Republican of marginal influence. The wise choice would have been the powerful Senate Foreign Relations Committee chairman, Henry Cabot Lodge. Wilson's snubbing of such stalwarts as Lodge was especially remiss considering that the 1918 off-year congressional elections saw the Republicans sweep to majority control of both houses of Congress.

Despite Wilson's shunning of diplomatic niceties and shortsightedness in picking the right entourage, his overarching problem at Versailles was his allies. France and England had no interest in discussing, analyzing or negotiating anything but how they were going to dismantle the German empire, both in Europe and in those areas around the world where Germany had colonies. Despite vehement opposition to such a policy by Wilson, the Allies successfully carved up the German empire. The Rhineland, one of Germany's most vital natural resource areas, was demilitarized and designated a French "protectorate" for fifteen years. The treaty also allowed the French to occupy the coal-rich Saar region for a similar period. The treaty also returned to France the province of Alsace-Lorraine taken by Germany in 1871 at the conclusion of the Franco-Prussian War, which saw Prussia defeat France in six weeks time and then humiliate France by dictating the peace terms at Versailles. It was now France's turn to humble a defeated Germany. To add further insult to injury, the treaty cut eastern Germany into two parts by giving the newly independent Poland access to the Baltic by way of the east Prussian city of Danzig, which now became a Polish city in which close to one million Germans lived. Another 500,000 Germans of the Sudetenland became Czech "citizens." In the end, the treaty stripped Germany of one-eighth of its territory, one-tenth of its population, and all of its

colonies and saddled the nation with a reparations bill of $33 billion to be paid to France and Great Britain. Suffice it to say, the treaty humiliated and enraged the Germans without crushing them and fueled their desire for revenge. To his credit Wilson tried to prevent such reprisals, all the while warning the British and French that if they imposed such a harsh and dishonorable settlement upon the Germans they would be sealing their own future fate: that of ensuring another European conflagration of retribution. In 1939 Woodrow Wilson's prediction came true, as Europe and the world convulsed in the greatest, most destructive human conflict in the history of humankind.

Wilson also could not prevent the Allies from grabbing territory they had promised each other in secret treaties mentioned above. For example, for abandoning neutrality and joining the Allies in 1915, Italy received the promised seaport on the Adriatic (Trieste) and the South Tyrol from Austria. The Ottoman empire was also dismembered, with Great Britain acquiring Palestine, Jordan, and most important oil-rich Mesopotamia (present-day Iraq). Great Britain also received all of Germany's African colonies. From the Ottomans France received Syria and Lebanon. Japan obtained all of Germany's islands in the Pacific and its sphere of influence in China, Shantung province. Also ignored by the Allies was Wilson's call for freedom of the seas and tariff reductions. Wilson did not push for these "points" because he feared that if he did Clemenceau would have used the mandates as negotiating points to impose an even harsher treaty on Germany, one that would have made the Rhineland, for example, permanently French.

Not all of Wilson's entreaties fell on deaf ears. The Allies accepted and implemented Wilson's call for self-determination, especially for Eastern Europe, by creating an independent Poland and recognizing as sovereign nations the Baltic states of Estonia, Latvia, and Lithuania (territories Germany had seized from Bolshevik Russia in 1918 at the treaty of Brest-Litovsk). Also created by the concept of self-determination were the nations of Czechoslovakia and Yugoslavia, the latter a uniting of the various Slavic peoples of the previously independent entities of Serbia, Bosnia, Herzegovina, and Montenegro. As noted earlier, although the Czechs and Slovaks received a homeland, in the process the Allies foolishly placed hundreds of thousands of Germans under Czech/Slovak rule, a move for which the Allies and the Czechs/Slovaks would suffer future dire consequences.

It should also be noted that Poland's creation reflected the Allies ulterior motives when it came to their supposed embracing of the Wilsonian idea of self-determination. Poland not only served as a zone of occupation for about a million east Germans (the city of Danzig) but also as a buffer between the West and the Soviet Union, which the Allies perceived as the greatest threat to their present security. They hoped that by creating a large Polish state, the Poles could serve as a bulwark against the spread of Bolshevism. In the Great War's aftermath, the Allies wanted to put the greatest distance between them and the Bolsheviks, and a large Polish state would go far toward that end. However, as will be seen later, by the 1930s, fascism not communism posed the greatest threat to European peace and stability, and thus one of the reasons for creating a large Poland was no longer valid. Indeed, Poland will become one of Adolph Hitler's rallying cries for reuniting all German-speaking people under his Third Reich, and the one million Germans living under Polish rule, placed under such occupation by the Allies at Versailles, will ultimately lead Hitler to invade Poland to "liberate" his people, thus igniting World War II.

Although in the end forced to accept Allied dictates, especially when it came to Germany, Wilson hoped such shortsightedness would be ameliorated through the work of the League of Nations. Wilson insisted the League be made part of the peace treaty. The covenant for the new international organization called for a small but powerful executive council to be comprised of the alleged "superpower" nations of the moment: France, Italy, Great Britain, Japan, and the United States. In reality, only three could claim any legitimate superpower status: the United States, Great Britain, and Japan. The League would have a large assembly in which every independent nation in the world would be represented and have one vote. The League's headquarters would be Geneva, Switzerland. The most important component of the League's charter was Article 10, which established the concept of collective security, whereby each member nation would pledge to respect and preserve each other's independence and territorial integrity against aggressors, and to use whatever means appropriate or necessary—economic or military sanctions—to stop the invader and restore peace. In an attempt to avoid future wars, members agreed to submit for arbitration all disputes that created tensions between countries that could lead to war. They also agreed to address the arms race issue and to create a permanent court of international justice, popularly known as the World Court.

Wilson believed that all the shortcomings of the Versailles Treaty would ultimately be rectified by the League of Nations, led by the moral persuasion and strong presence of the United States. To Wilson the League with the United States as its most active participant was the world's best hope for peace and security. As Wilson exclaimed to the Senate when he presented the treaty in July 1919 for ratification, "The stage is set, the destiny disclosed. It has come about by no plan of our conceiving, but by the hand of God who led us this way. We cannot turn back. America shall in truth show the way."

The Fight for the League

Unfortunately for Woodrow Wilson, the United States, and the world the president's vision of a liberal, harmonious, and peaceful world order would soon lie in ruins. Even before Wilson returned from Europe with the treaty, opposition to the document had emerged, led by the powerful isolationist Republican senator from Massachusetts, Henry Cabot Lodge. Instigated by Lodge, thirty-nine Republican senators sent a letter to Wilson in February 1919 rejecting the League in its present form. Irritating the senators most was Article 10, the collective security clause, which the solons interpreted as an obligation by the United States to enter into every "peace-keeping" endeavor

Railroad car in which was signed the armistice, November 11, 1918.

(war) that involved an act of aggression upon one of the League's member nations. To many of these legislators, the Senate's authority under Article I, Section VIII of the U.S. Constitution to "To declare war, grant letters of marque and reprisal, and make rules concerning captures on land and water" would be trumped by any tyrant, king, or madman who invaded a member state. Although Lodge and many of his Republican cohorts took exception with Article 10, they did not reject the whole treaty, and thus Lodge and his followers, which included Democrats such as William Jennings Bryan, became known as the "Reservationists." They accepted the treaty but wanted to amend the United States' role relative to the League of Nations and until Wilson agreed to such a modification, Lodge kept the treaty bottled up in the Foreign Relations Committee after Wilson had sent the document to the Senate for ratification in July 1919.

Lodge and his contingent were the least of Wilson's political worries. An even more powerful group of Republican senators led by William Borah of Idaho were determined to torpedo both the treaty and the League of Nations and have the United States return to the "proven" security of isolationism. Much to Wilson's surprise and eventual dismay, even left-leaning senators rejected U.S. membership in the League and a return to isolationism because they feared the League of Nations would be a body controlled by Europe's imperial powers created to further entrench European colonialism and imperialism throughout the world. These senators became known as the "Irreconcilables." Together both groups presented Wilson with an unanticipated battle for ratification. Furious at both Lodge and Borah for their obstructionism and convinced that he could rally public support for the treaty, Wilson left Washington on September 3, 1919 on a barnstorming western speaking tour. Speaking before large and enthusiastic crowds in every western state he visited, Wilson covered 9,000 miles by train and gave 37 speeches in 22 days arguing for the necessity for the United States to join the League of Nations. People wept as Wilson graphically described his visits to American war cemeteries in France and cheered his vision of a new world order to be led by the United States.

Wilson appeared on the brink of victory of rallying public support for the League when tragedy befell him. While speaking in Colorado on September 25, Wilson collapsed from exhaustion. His train sped back to Washington where the president suffered a devastating stroke on October 2. For a time he lay near death. Despite a partial recovery, Wilson spent the rest of his term a reclusive invalid, his mind clouded, his fragile emotions fluctuating between vindictive actions and tearful outbursts. He broke with close advisers, refused to see foreign ambassadors, and dismissed his Secretary of State, Robert Lansing, for "disloyalty." In January 1920, his physician advised him to resign, but Wilson refused and since the Twenty-fifth Amendment, dealing with issues of presidential disability, was not adopted until 1967, Wilson, despite his debilitations, could legally remain in office.

Unfortunately for Wilson, his vision, and the United States, stepping into the leadership void was Wilson's imperious second wife, Edith Galt, whom he married in 1915. Edith fiercely guarded her husband's incapacity, as would another future First Lady, Nancy Reagan, in a very similar scenario. Mrs. Wilson hid her husband's condition from the public, controlled his access to information, and decided who could see him. Regardless of their stature—Cabinet members, foreign diplomats, congressional leaders, even the vice-president—all were screened first by Mrs. Wilson for she wanted no one or no issue to upset her husband. As she told one political leader who desperately needed to talk to the president, she did not care about "the welfare of the country. I am not thinking of the country now, I am thinking about my husband." Although Mrs. Wilson's single-minded devotion to her husband's well-being could be lauded, politically her actions proved disastrous, for they doomed to defeat what her husband most cherished: ratification of the Treaty of Versailles and U.S. membership in the League of Nations.

Indeed, with Wilson "out of the way," the treaty's defeat was almost a certainty. Led by Borah, Hiram Johnson of California, and Robert LaFollette of Wisconsin, the isolationist Irreconcilables had a field day carving up the treaty, claiming that every one of Wilson's Fourteen Points would somehow lead the United States into another world calamity in which the United States would get nothing in return but debt, thousands of dead fellow citizens, and the violation of many Americans' civil liberties. Despite the Irreconcilables persuasive hyperbole, there was still a chance for a Wilsonian victory had the president been willing to compromise by embracing some of the Lodge-led Reservationists amendments to U.S. membership in the League. Indeed, the consensus among historians of this time period is that had Wilson accepted accommodation, the Senate would probably have ratified the treaty, bringing the United States into the League of Nations. Wilson's illness however, exacerbated his already non-conciliatory nature. From his isolation in the White House he instructed Senate Democrats to vote against even the slightest modification of the treaty as it stood. To Wilson, any altering of the document and any weakening of U.S. participation in the League represented "a knife thrust into the heart of the treaty."

Interestingly, the treaty's death knell came in many ways from the American people, who despite giving Wilson enthusiastic receptions on his speaking tour did not rally behind the League. Two factors contributed to the peoples' rejection of the treaty and League. First, by 1919, the full, terrible impact of the war had reached the American public as they watched the "doughboys" return from Europe, either in coffins, or maimed and scared for life, both physically and emotionally. Many Americans felt ashamed, guilty, for having sent overseas so many young men to die or come home missing limbs, or with bodies scarred or flesh burned, in order to "make the world safe for democracy." To the post-war American public, the price had been too high and thus not worth the sacrifice of so many. Many Americans thus felt duped and betrayed by Wilson and vowed to those who had died and to those who had returned that they were not only sorry for having supported such an ignoble war but that they would never call upon another generation of young Americans to make such a worthless sacrifice. Thus, the Irreconcilables found much public support for their position and with such popular endorsement felt confident they could defeat the treaty in the Senate.

The second factor that contributed to the treaty's defeat was the Wilson administration's reactionary and proscriptive policies during the war years, especially toward the conflict's opponents. As noted earlier, Wilson's desire to create the image of an American people one-hundred percent committed to the war effort witnessed some of the most egregious violations of many citizens' civil liberties in the history of the United States. Wilson's actions were now coming back to haunt him. As the editor of the liberal *The Nation* magazine opined, "If Wilson loses his great fight for humanity, it be because he was deliberately silent when freedom of speech and the right of conscience were struck down in America." With such distaste and opposition arrayed against Wilson, few Americans were surprised that the Senate rejected the Treaty of Versailles and thus United States' membership in the League of Nations. A president elected amid grand expectations in 1912, hailed when he called for war in 1917, and adulated when he arrived in Europe in 1918 lay isolated and debilitated, his leadership repudiated. What might have been Wilson's crowning triumph had turned to ashes.

Postwar Racism and the Red Scare

With the fighting in Europe over and the issue of U.S. membership in the League finally put to rest, white Americans returned to a more familiar type of "fighting": against other races and against foreign ideas. The wartime spirit of "100 percent Americanism" left a bitter aftertaste, especially when it came to black-white relations. The years 1919-1920 saw new racial violence and fresh antiradical hysteria. As noted earlier, violence toward African Americans, especially in Northern cities, was particularly violent and appalling. White mobs in various parts of the country lynched seventy-six blacks in 1919, the worst toll in fifteen years. The victims included ten veterans, several still in uniform. Some of these killings were incredibly brutal, such as the episode in Omaha, Nebraska, where a mob shot a black prisoner more than a thousand times, mutilated him, and hung his body in a busy intersection as a warning to other African Americans that the war had changed nothing relative to race relations. African Americans had better know that their "place" was still that of second class citizens and that any attempts to rise above that status would be dealt with the harshest reprisals.

As discussed earlier in this chapter, the city of Chicago witnessed the most devastating race riot of the immediate post-war years. However, other cities exploded as well such Washington, D.C. and Tulsa, Oklahoma. Why such white hostility toward African Americans in the post-war years? According to the NAACP, which investigated the various riots, it appeared that many whites perceived the "New Negro" as potential radical subversives in which somehow black folk during the war years had become "infected" with communism and other radical un-American ideas. To many whites post-war African-American demands for equality reflected not the simple desire to be treated fairly and decently but rather the influence of subversive radicals and the propagation among the black community of their ideas, which allegedly got normally docile "Negroes all agitated and uppity." In short, many whites believed there was a supposed conspiracy among African Americans and radical groups such as the Wobblies (members of the labor union, the International Workers of the World, which did allow both African American and female membership) and other "reds" to overthrow the established order of white supremacy. Although even at the time such assertions were fantastical and absurd, sadly many white Americans believed such collusion existed and thus not only must "the Negro" be kept in his place but a similar repression must be put into effect against all radical organizations as well. Thus the wartime antiradical panic crested in a postwar Red Scare as Anglo-Americans in particular went after all whom they considered a threat "to the American way of life," which meant adherence to White, Anglo-Saxon, and Protestant values, ideals, and beliefs. Anything else was to be considered "un-American" and had to be extirpated.

Fears of "bolshevism" intensified when a rash of strikes broke out in 1919. Anti-union sentiment had always been strong in the United States, largely because of unionism's collective nature, which many Americans believed to be antithetical to one of the nation's most cherished notions: rugged individualism. The majority of Americans had disdained unions since their inception in the latter part of the nineteenth-century. Unions seemed unnecessary because of the supposed inherent quality of unfettered American capitalism to ensure all citizens a decent standard of living by allowing workers to individually negotiate with their employers for wages and benefits free from the artificial and "unnatural" restraints and dictates of unions. To the laissez faire, free-marketeers of the post-Great War era, the booming prosperity the war brought made unions not only unwarranted but impediments as well to an individual's right, via personal initiative, to gain for himself his supposed fair share of the American pie of prosperity and security. In reality, such an interpretation of American capitalism at the beginning of the decade of the 1920s could not have been more inaccurate. It was all plutocratic propaganda designed to justify, with government assistance if necessary, the crushing of unions as dangerous, subversive, and self-serving entities determined to overthrow the most "beneficent" economic order in the world: American capitalism. Thus, when labor leaders in Seattle, Washington in February 1919 united in a general strike for higher wages, the politically ambitious conservative mayor of the city, Ole Hanson, contrary to all evidence, immediately colored the striking workers "red," ensuring that he would have universal support in crushing the strike, because it "duplicated the anarchy of Russia." The mayor had no problem requesting federal troops to maintain public order, even though there was no need for such heavy-handedness. Indeed, the striking workers had created a General Strike Committee, which had set up milk delivery for children and laundry service for hospitals and organized some five hundred uniformed war veterans to patrol the streets.

In Boston, even the police struck, walking off their beats when the police commissioner suspended nineteen officers for attempting to establish a patrolmen's union affiliated with the AFL. Unfortunately for the striking officers, a wave of rowdyism, theft, and violence hit the city, which in turn enraged Massachusetts governor Calvin Coolidge, who denounced the policemen for their dereliction of duty to protect the commonweal and declared that none of the strikers would be rehired. To restore law and order in Boston, Coolidge mobilized state troops while he recruited unemployed veterans for an entirely new police force. Mayors, governors, and the general public applauded Coolidge's stand.

Anxiety engulfed Washington, D.C. when various public officials received packages containing bombs. One blew off the hands of a senator's maid. Another damaged the home of Attorney General A. Mitchell Palmer. When 350,000 steel workers went on strike in September 1919, they virtually shut down the industry in ten states. The steel plutocracy responded with a reign of terror on the striking workers and their supporters as company "goons" beat, arrested, shot, and drove out of steel towns "the troublemakers." In Clairton and Glassport, Pennsylvania, club-wielding state troopers wantonly attacked peaceful worker gatherings. If violent reprisals failed to get the workers off strike, company owners then resorted to splitting the strikers along ethnic and racial lines by bringing in African American and Mexican American strikebreakers. Of course throughout the walkout's duration, newspapers and company propaganda constantly labeled the strike a Bolshevik plot engineered by "Red agitators." Unfortunately, the fact that the majority of the striking workers were of immigrant backgrounds (primarily eastern Europeans with a smattering of Italians) helped to further the public's fear that the conflict was an attempted revolution by foreign-born radicals. With such overwhelming forces arrayed against the walkout, the workers' resolve weakened; in January 1920, the unions threw in the towel and workers returned to the mills. The immigrant steelworkers had demonstrated a capacity for sustained militancy and discipline but because the steel barons had overwhelming government and popular support, they were able to crush even the most massive of walkouts.

The strikes gave the federal government and state governments the excuse to politicize the antiradical paranoia. In November the House of Representatives refused to seat the legally elected Socialist Victor Berger of Wisconsin because of his earlier indictment under the Espionage Act. The New York legislature expelled several socialist members, and the federal government via the Justice Department ordered the arrest of hundreds of suspected "communists" and radicals. In December 1919, the government deported 249 Russian-born aliens, including the radical Emma Goldman, a leader of the birth-control movement. The government's anti-radical crusade won enthusiastic support from the American Legion, a newly founded veteran's organization as well as from the National Association of Manufacturers. The worst however was yet to come.

In January 1920, in one of the most intense dragnets ever initiated by the federal government in conjunction with local police, Attorney General A. Mitchell Palmer authorized the Justice Department to raid the homes of suspected radicals and radical organizations in thirty-three cities without search or arrest warrants. Law enforcement officials took more than 5,000 persons into custody, with some 550 eventually deported. Many of the apprehended were humiliated as police paraded them through the streets handcuffed or in chains and then confined them in crowded and unsanitary cells with hardened criminals without formal charges or the right to post bail. One of the more perverse ironies of this most disquieting episode in American history was that the individual most responsible for these egregious violations of thousands of Americans civil liberties was a Quaker!

A report prepared by a group of distinguished lawyers questioned the legality of Palmer's high-handed tactics. The Attorney General's popularity had waned by the spring of 1920, when it became clear to most Americans that his earlier forecast that revolutionary uprisings were imminent were wildly exaggerated. Nonetheless, the Red Scare left an ugly legacy: wholesale violations of thousands of citizens' civil liberties, deportations of hundreds of innocent people, and fuel for the fires of nativism and intolerance. Plutocratic organizations such as the National Association of Manufacturers found "red-baiting" to be a most effective post-war tool in squashing unionization in their factories. Indeed, as will be seen in a later chapter, another government-sanctioned "witch-hunt" emerged in the aftermath of World War II with even more devastating consequences for thousands of American citizens than that experienced by many of their compatriots in 1919. In many ways, the Red Scare of 1919 helped to pave the way for that future dark moment called "McCarthyism."

In reaction to these attacks on Americans' civil rights, progressive reformers such as Helen Gurley Flynn helped to organize the American Civil Liberties Union, which would come to the future assistance of those Americans finding their Constitutional rights being violated by federal, state, or other public (and eventually even private) agencies and institutions. Fortunately for potentially thousands of other "suspected" American citizens as the nation entered the new decade of the Roaring Twenties, the majority of Americans wanted to put all associated with the war years behind them and thus the country's first "Red Scare" faded away.

Doughboys returning from western Europe brought back stories, medals, souvenirs, and tragically one of the most deadly influenza viruses to ever hit the continental shores of the United States. Called the "Spanish flu," the virus infected approximately 28 percent of the nation's population. Worldwide the pandemic killed close to 30 million people; ten times as many human beings died from influenza than were killed during the Great War. Before the first anniversary of the armistice, 675,000 Americans had died from the disease. One of the thousands of Americans affected by the virus was Franklin Delano Roosevelt, who fortunately survived the epidemic only to be stricken and crippled for life three yeas later by polio. By 1920 the pandemic had run its course, and as with all episodes associated with the war years, Americans soon forgot that they had just endured one of the most deadly contagions to ever affect the United States. It was time to put so many of those painful memories behind and embrace full-force all of the glamour, excitement, and new technology of one of the most exhilarating, fun-filled, carefree, and self-absorbed decades in American history, the "Roaring Twenties." Within a few years of that decade's opening all the misery, suffering, fear, uncertainty, and trauma of the Great War era and all that had occurred before that event became distant memories for the majority of Americans, who looked happily forward to a time of peace, stability, and prosperity.

CONCLUSION

Compared to the casualties and socio-political upheavals that swept across Europe in the aftermath of the Great War, the United States largely escaped such trauma and dislocation. However, upon closer scrutiny, it is readily apparent that the war years unleashed powerful socio-economic and political forces that reshaped much of American life long after Armistice Day. Post-war Republican administrations resurrected the pre-progressive alliance between big business and the government, as this particular complex reached the zenith of its power during the 1920s. Indeed, the post-war plutocracy became even more powerful and entrenched, as their ethos came to define in so many capacities the United States in the 1920s. Ironically, it was the Progressive Wilson administration that opened this Pandora's Box, the result of wartime production needs, which big business was more than glad to supply but at a future cost.

Patriotic fervor and the exaggerated specter of Bolshevism were used to suppress and extirpate from the body politic all manifestations of supposed radicalism, organized labor, and the last remnants of progressive reform. Indeed, the war years undermined the best aspects of the progressive reform impulse—its openness to new ideas, its commitment to social justice, and its humanitarian concern for the downtrodden and oppressed. Government war propaganda fostered an intolerance of dissent, ideological conformity, and a fear of radicalism, all of which coalesced to smother prewar progressivism. The climate of reaction intensified in 1919-1920, as the nation repudiated Wilsonian idealism. The nation that celebrated the armistice in November 1918 was very different from the one that Woodrow Wilson had solemnly taken into battle only nineteen months earlier.

The wartime measure of national prohibition evolved into one of the most contentious social issues in United States history. Sophisticated sales techniques, psychology, and propaganda used to promote the war effort at home transformed into the new mega-industries of advertising and public relations, both of which made millions by telling Americans forever more what they should buy, eat, wear, and even who and what they needed to see. The growing visibility of immigrants and African Americans in the nation's burgeoning cities provoked a xenophobic and racist backlash in the decade's politics. More than anything else, the desire for "normalcy' reflected the deep anxieties evoked by the United States' wartime experience.

Chronology

1914 Wilson sends U.S. troops to occupy Vera Cruz, Mexico
Archduke Franz Ferdinand assassinated by Serbian nationalist
World War I begins in Europe; Wilson declares American neutrality

1915 U.S. marines occupy Haiti and the Dominican Republic
German submarine sinks British liner, *Lusitania*, killing 1200 (128 Americans)
Jane Addams and others form Women's Peace Party
Wilson begins preparedness program

1916 After sinking the *Sussex*, Germany promises to cease unannounced U-boat attacks
General Pershing leads military expedition into Mexico in pursuit of Pancho Villa
Wilson wins re-election

1917 Germany resumes unrestricted submarine warfare
British inform Wilson of Zimmermann telegram, proposing Mexican alliance with Germany
United State enters war (April 6)
Selective Service Act sets up military draft
Wilson creates War Industries Board and Committee on Public Information
Espionage Act limits rights of freedom of speech, press, and assembly
Bolshevik revolution leads Russia to leave the war

1918 Wilson outlines his Fourteen Points
Armistice ends World War I (Nov. 11)
Worldwide influenza epidemic claims more than 20 million lives

1919 18th Amendment added to the Constitution
Treaty of Versailles signed
Racial violence erupts in Chicago and elsewhere
Wilson launches speaking tour to support Versailles Treaty, but suffers paralyzing stroke.
Versailles treaty rejected by Senate
Wave of labor strikes hits nation

1920 Justice Department launches "Palmer Raids;" "Red Scare" hits nation
Nineteenth Amendment (Women's Suffrage) added to Constitution
Senate again rejects Treaty of Versailles
Warren G. Harding elected president

1924 Woodrow Wilson dies

SUGGESTED READINGS

Arthur E. Barbeau and Florette Henri, *The Unknown Soldiers: Black American Troops in World War I* (1947).
Robert H. Ferrell, *Woodrow Wilson and World War I, 1917-1921* (1983).
Frank Freidel, *Over There* (1964).
Martin Gilbert, *The First World War: A Complete History* (1994).
Maurine W. Greenwald, *Women, War and Work* (1980).
Ellis W. Hawley, *The Great War and the Search for a Modern Order: A History of the American People and Their Institutions* (1992).
David M. Kennedy, *Over Here: The First World War and American Society* (1980).
Arthur S. Link, *Woodrow Wilson: Revolution, War, and Peace* (1979).
Carole Marks, *Farewell—We're Good and Gone: The Great Black Migration* (1989).
Barbara Tuchman, *The Guns of August* (1962).
William Tuttle Jr., *Race Riot: Chicago and the Red Summer of 1919* (1970).

Chapter Eighteen

THE ROARING TWENTIES

In 1926 a young midwestern son of a radical Progressive politician, Charles Lindbergh Jr., was earning a modest living as an air mail pilot on the St. Louis-Chicago route. Commercial aviation was a new and still hazardous occupation in which pilots were often forced to land in emergency fields, lit only by an occasional kerosene lantern (when they could find any field). "Slim," as his friends called him, supplemented his income by stunt flying at county fairs.

One night, while flying his mail route, Lindbergh formulated a plan to try for a long-standing $25,000 prize offered for the first successful non-stop flight from New York to Paris. Several famous and well-financed aviators were vying for the reward. Their plans required elaborate designs of three-engine planes with crews of at least two men. Lindbergh believed that a single-engine plane of lighter aluminum construction with a larger fuel reserve would be better able to cross the ocean successfully. And he proposed to fly the plane by himself! He persuaded some St. Louis businessmen to back him financially and supervised the building of a monoplane to his own specifications. He named it The Spirit of St. Louis. On the morning of May 20, 1927, the little plane took off a rain-soaked runway in Roosevelt Field, New York, ahead of his highly publicized competitors.

Struggling against sleep and dreadful weather, and without a radio that he felt would add too much weight, Lindbergh crossed the lonely ocean in 33 and a half hours. "In flying I tasted the wine of the gods," he said many years later. Lindbergh, who understood the benefits of good publicity, had notified reporters of his takeoff. Both sides of the Atlantic featured the news, including photographs of the youthful (25-year-old) daredevil who was bravely defying the elements alone in a single-engine plane. When he landed at Le Bourget airport in Paris, he found 100,000 delirious French people waiting. It was the wildest demonstration since the Great War had ended.

Lindbergh, with unassuming manners and innocent good looks, was a press agent's dream. His references to himself and his plane as "we" also fascinated Americans. (That was the title of the quickie book he completed three weeks after his flight.) The concept of the unity of man and machine was entrancing to a public mesmerized by the wonders of the new age of transportation. Lindbergh's reception in America eclipsed anything he had experienced in Europe. The normally taciturn President Coolidge effusively praised "this wholesome, earnest, fearless, courageous product of America" whose plane represented "American genius and industry." Before a wildly approving crowd, Coolidge awarded him the Distinguished Flying Cross and a promotion to colonel in the Officers Reserve Corps.

The greatest show of all was a ticker tape parade down Fifth Avenue in New York City. Four million people lined the streets to cheer and shower the hero with more than 1800 tons of shredded paper. Song writers wrote about "Lucky Lindy" and a new dance, the Lindy Hop, was named for him. He received 3,500,000 letters, including 14,000 gifts and 7,000 job offers. Vaudeville circuits and movie companies offered him huge contracts that he modestly declined.

The nation was truly in the grip of a Lindbergh cult. In an age of cynicism, political scandals, anxiety about morals, racial and religious prejudices, the ascendancy of gangsters, and deep divisions in society, the public longed for a genuine, pure hero. At a time of mass production and growing anonymity, he was a "Lone Eagle" who represented the best of American individualism. As stated by F. Scott Fitzgerald, "In the spring of 1927, something bright and alien flashed across the sky. A young Minnesotan who seemed to have nothing to do with his generation did a heroic thing, and for a moment people set down their glasses in country clubs and speakeasies and thought of their old best dreams."

"Lucky Lindy" did not remain the unscathed hero after the era of the 1920s. When one has the world at his feet at the age of 25, what can one do to top that at age 35 or 45? Perhaps, as a reporter shrewdly remarked at the time, "Too much supermanning can hardly help one." When Lindbergh's first born child was kidnapped and murdered in 1932, the public was appalled. But the ghoulish fascination and overwhelming publicity drove the Lindberghs from America. In Europe Lindbergh became enthralled by the "new order" in Nazi Germany. He returned to America as the poster boy for isolationist and anti-Semitic forces. In the 1920s, however, Lindbergh remained the greatest symbol of the yearning for individual heroism.

DIVISIONS IN AMERICAN LIFE

The American obsession with Lindbergh and his exploits also illustrated the duality of American life in the Twenties. On the one hand, his achievement represented the triumph of American technology in the new field of aviation. On the other, it exemplified the supposed virtues of a simpler, more innocent, small-town America. Many historians portray the Twenties as the beginning of modern America—"the first decade of the twentieth century." The Great War, they argue, provided the final blow to the nineteenth century. Yet, there were still many areas of American life firmly in the grasp of that presumably dead Victorian past. The tensions between the "two Americas"—the one exhilarated at the possibilities of a limitless future, the other longing for "traditional values"—typified the Twenties.

The Scopes Trial

Protestant fundamentalists believed in the divine inspiration and literal truth of every word in the Bible. Their numbers had grown, particularly in small towns and rural America, in reaction to the skepticism and irreverence they felt resulted from America's infatuation with scientific theory. The growth of the big bad cities, with their hordes of Catholic and Jewish immigrants, reminded them of the Biblical Sodom and Gomorrah, destroyed by God for their evil ways. By the early 1920s fundamentalists decided that the increasing acceptance of the theory of evolution (first propounded by Charles Darwin in 1859) symbolized an alarming rejection of Christian ideas and Biblical truth. They worked for the passage of legislation prohibiting the teaching of evolution in several southern states.

One such state was Tennessee. A new law, passed in 1925, made it a crime to "teach any theory that denies the story of the Divine creation of man as taught in the Bible." A 24-year-old science teacher in the drowsy little town of Dayton agreed to test the law by reading a sentence from a biology textbook to his class. He was promptly prosecuted. A team of American Civil Liberties Union (ACLU) lawyers, headed by the noted Chicago criminal defense lawyer,

Clarence Darrow, arrived to defend Scopes. William Jennings Bryan, three-time presidential candidate, populist reformer, and defender of the true faith, rushed to the scene as a volunteer prosecutor.

The "Monkey Trial" became a media sensation, attracting throngs of reporters and interested bystanders and live coverage from the new medium of radio. In the resulting carnival atmosphere, banners were strung across the streets declaring: PREPARE TO MEET THY MAKER, WHERE WILL YOU SPEND ETERNITY? and READ YOUR BIBLE DAILY. Below them hot-dog vendors, Bible salesmen, lemonade stands and stores featuring little cotton apes and pins reading "Your Old Man's a Monkey" competed for business with street evangelists.

The judge opened each session with a prayer over the objection of "the greatest infidel of his age," Darrow. He moved the proceeding to the lawn to accommodate the hordes of curious people and mitigate the oppressive heat and humidity. The greatest drama lay in the confrontation between Bryan, the defender of "revealed religion," Darrow, the urban intellectual, and the two Americas they represented. Stymied in his attempt to summon scientific experts to testify, Darrow, in a brilliant stroke, called upon Bryan to take the stand as a "Biblical expert." In answering a series of remorseless questions, Bryan affirmed his beliefs that a big fish had swallowed Jonah and Joshua had made the sun "stand still." He added that when, "The Bible states it; it must be so." Bryan protested that the questions had "no other purpose than ridiculing every Christian who believes in the Bible." Darrow replied, "We have the purpose of preventing bigots and ignoramuses from controlling the education of the United States." While Darrow had easily held Bryan's "fool ideas" up to ridicule and scorn, it took the local jury only a few minutes to find Scopes guilty. (The State Supreme Court later threw out the case.) Scopes subsequently went on to graduate school, became an eminent geologist, and never returned to Tennessee.

Although the prosecution had officially won, a tired and ill Bryan retreated to a friend's house to read the derision heaped upon him by the nation's press. "Do they have a law to keep a man from making a jackass of himself?" Will Rogers mockingly inquired. One reporter more sympathetically wrote, "To see this wonderful man . . . whose silver voice and majestic mien had stirred millions . . . humbled and humiliated before the vast crowd which had come to adore him, was sheer tragedy, nothing less." Less than a week after the trial, Bryan died. They buried him at Arlington National Cemetery where his tombstone read, "He kept the faith." The issues raised by the Scopes trial have endured. They have resurfaced in recent years in fundamentalist attacks on "secular humanism" and demands to teach "creationism" in public schools. Bryan was dead, but fundamentalism survived.

New denominations, independent churches, and roving evangelists took up the cause. They had their roots in the long American tradition of revivalism that dated back to the colonial Great Awakening. Billy Sunday, a former professional baseball player who threatened to close down Chicago, was, perhaps, the most successful. Father Divine attracted urban blacks. His large following of "children," with such names as Glorious Illumination and Heavenly Dove, went into ecstatic trances and "holy rolling" on the floor. The Reverend Bob Shuler, "the Lord's avenger," gained fame by surprising the Los Angeles police chief in bed with a woman who had married into an infamous crime family.

Aimee Semple McPherson was the most spectacular of all. In her flowing white satin robes, she

Aimee Semple McPherson blended religious fundamentalism, faith healing, and show-biz glitz.

exuded sexuality and unlimited energy as she spread her message of "joy, joy, joy," highlighted by colored lights and Hollywood productions. Her "International Institute of Foursquare Gospel" prospered to the point of building a large Angelus Temple in Los Angeles to accommodate 5,000 and mounting a successful radio show. Sister Aimee gained her greatest fame in 1926 when she disappeared, only to emerge in the desert with an elaborate tale of kidnapping and heroic escape. The skeptical noted that her shoes were unscuffed and her dress clean. Evidence that the disappearance was a hoax grew with testimony about a fling with a married man. Her reputation was tarnished, but thousands of the faithful hysterically welcomed her survival from her "ordeal." When she died of an overdose of sleeping pills in 1944, her church had six hundred branches. She was the forerunner of a later generation of televangelists.

Prohibition

Protestant crusaders saw the passage of the Eighteenth Amendment, outlawing the manufacture, sale, and importation of alcoholic beverages, as a great victory. On the night of January 15-16, as Prohibition went into effect, there were midnight services in thousands of Protestant churches and joyous victory bells chimed. Billy Sunday confidently predicted, "The slums will soon be only a memory. We will turn our prisons into factories . . . ." Many urban middle class reformers agreed. They believed that liquor helped cause poverty, worker inefficiency, dysfunctional family life, and political corruption.

At first, it seemed as though the reformers' expectations would be realized. Saloons closed; arrests for public drunkenness fell, and alcohol consumption by the lower classes declined. Poorer Americans could not afford illegal liquor. The increasing resistance of urban Americans, however, crippled the crusade.

Enterprising "businessmen," known as bootleggers, quickly stepped into the void. They produced dreadful concoctions of hard liquor such as Jackass Brandy, which caused internal bleeding, and Soda Pop Moon, which contained poisonous alcohol. According to one story, when a suspicious customer sent a sample of his bootlegger's liquor to a chemist for analysis, the reply began, "Dear Sir, your horse has diabetes." In 1927, the death toll from ingesting these potent brews was 11,700. Adulterated Jamaican ginger extract left 20,000 people in "jake paralysis."

Only the prosperous could afford to drink regularly without jeopardizing their lives. But they greatly increased their alcohol consumption as "rum runners" regularly smuggled good quality liquor from Canada and Europe. "Speakeasies" openly operated in cities throughout America. Neither Congress nor the states provided adequate money to enforce the prohibition law. Reporters noticed Harding's bootlegger delivering cases of liquor to the back door of the White House. Prosecution, despite some colorful agents, was erratic, judges uninterested, and juries unwilling to convict. Journalist H. L. Mencken noted that, "The business of evading Prohibition and making a mock of it has ceased to wear any aspects of crime, and has become a sort of national sport."

As whiskey took on the taste of "forbidden fruit," speakeasies became the "in" places to be seen. There were, supposedly, thirty-two thousand in New York City with a mere two hundred agents assigned to close them down. "Texas" Guinan, who greeted her customers with a cheerful, "Hello suckers," presided over the most famous establishment. She was celebrated for hurling humorous insults at raiding federal agents as the band broke into "The Prisoner's Song." While earlier saloons had barred women customers, speakeasies welcomed them, in a rather odd step forward for women's rights. Alcoholism increased among the affluent for the first time.

The public willingness to evade prohibition provided unforeseen opportunities for organized crime. One observer noted, "Because bootlegging provided such resources in money and organization, an unprecedented consolidation and centralization of organized crime occurred." Big-time criminals expanded, and, like businessmen, rationalized their operations. The age of the gangster as city businessman began. In cities like Chicago, "the only completely corrupt city in America," competing gangs engaged in open combat to control liquor operations. One article estimated that 1,291 people were murdered in mob warfare in the late 1920s, 500 in Chicago alone. Few of these cases were ever solved. The bloodshed rarely endangered ordinary citizens. "It is a war in which the non-combatants are safer than they were in Belgium," remarked one observer.

Al Capone seized control of Chicago's crime network after years of relentless conflict. A lavish funeral and huge crowds of mourners followed each gangland slaying. The climax occurred on St. Valentine's Day, 1929, when Capone's men trapped seven members of a rival mob in a garage and executed them with submachine guns. Capone ruled Cicero, a Chicago suburb, once kicking the mayor down the steps of City Hall for not following orders. At his height, Capone's network of rackets was earning him over $100 million a year. He had become a hero to many, a modern Robin Hood. Organized crime became a means for immigrant inner-city young men to achieve social mobility. Capone argued that he was nothing but an ordinary businessman: "All I do is to supply a public demand. I do it in the best and least harmful way I can." Despite the untiring efforts of a ten-man Justice Department squad ("the Untouchables") to destroy his operations, it was a conviction for income tax evasion that finally brought Capone down. Although he was widely publicized and celebrated, his reign was relatively brief.

The growth of organized crime and the open flouting of the law seemed to many to prove the futility of Prohibition. The "drys," however, felt confirmed in their belief that cities had demonstrated the decline of morals. All that was required, they argued, was more zealous enforcement of the law. The issue continued to divide American politics and public discourse.

The Ku Klux Klan

Throughout the country in the 1920s, people joined organizations promising fellowship and devotion to true Americanism. These included the Rotary, Moose, Elks, Lions, and American Legion. The Ku Klux Klan was the fastest growing of these fraternities, easily surpassing the newly formed American Legion. The Klan's revival (It had been a powerful factor in the Reconstruction era.) began with the showing of D.W. Griffith's spectacular motion picture, *Birth of a Nation*, in 1915. This movie epic, which revolutionized the nature of films, depicted the heroic knights of the Klan saving the South from brutish black tyranny and lust, after the Civil War. The film helped inspire "Colonel" William Simmons to revive the Klan as a "100 percent pure American," white Protestant fraternity. The group did not take off until 1920 when Simmons hired two expert fund raisers from the Southern Publicity Association to recruit members. They hired an army of salesmen (called "kleagles") to sell memberships at ten dollars each, which Simmons, the promoters, and the salesmen would split. Sheets, horse robes, and initiation water bottles were additional costs. What had begun as an elaborate con game rapidly grew to a potent organization with four million or more members.

Its success was partly a result of its ideology, which was "at once anti-Negro, anti-Alien, anti-Red, anti-Darwin, anti-Modern, anti-Liberal, Fundamentalist, vastly Moral, militantly Protestant" in the words of a distinguished historian. It also enabled the Klansman to relieve his personal frustrations by becoming a crusader "for White supremacy, religion, morality, and all that had made up the faith of the Fathers . . . ." The revived Klan was flexible in its use of local hatreds and fears, expanding its anti-black base. In Texas it appealed to anti-Mexican feelings, in California to fear of the Japanese, in the Northeast to anti-Semitism and anti-foreign sentiments, in the South to racism and anti-Catholicism. While Klansmen rationalized that they wanted to bring about a return to a fantasy world of small-town virtues, free of pre-marital sex, marital infidelity, and disrespect for authority, their actions showed their fear and hatred of anyone who was different from them in race, religion, or ethnicity. The Klan, with its parades and burning crosses, added color and excitement to dreary small-town life. It also grew rapidly among newly urbanized people, particularly those less well educated and economically marginal.

A part of the Klan's excitement, especially in the Southwest, was its violence, a heritage of its Reconstruction days. "Night-riders" flogged or tarred and feathered accused prostitutes, bootleggers, gamblers, adulterers, and lawyers with black clients. In the summer of 1922, in Mer Rouge, Louisiana, the bodies of two outspoken opponents of the Klan were found in

Members of the Ku Klux Klan terrorized blacks and other minorities.

a lake, horribly mutilated. Despite the imposition of martial law, witnesses were afraid to testify, and the jury acquitted all eighteen men accused of the ghastly crime. In Kokomo, Indiana, in response to Klan propaganda that the "Pope was finally pulling into town . . . to take over," a mob stoned the southbound train from Chicago.

Although the Klan even gained a foothold in the industrialized Northeast, more opposition arose there. In 1923 some ten thousand New Jersey Klansmen demonstrated and burned a 62-foot cross not far from Manhattan. But when the Klan tried to organize in Perth Amboy, New Jersey in the same year, local Catholics and Jews joined forces to mob their meeting place and forcibly drive out the "Ku Kluxers." Immigrant Catholic workers in Pennsylvania coal and steel towns attacked Klan demonstrators who came in chartered trains "to give the micks something to think about." Crusading reporters won awards for exposing the activities of the Klan.

Despite this opposition (or perhaps because of it), the political power of the Klan continued to grow. The governor of Oklahoma, who sought to curb Klan lawlessness by calling out the National Guard, was impeached. The Klan was instrumental in electing governors in states as diverse as Georgia, Ohio, Colorado, Oregon, Maine, and six others, as well as fourteen senators. (At least five of the senators and four of the governors were Klan members.) Up-and-coming young politicians, like Hugo Black of Alabama (later to become a very liberal Supreme Court justice), felt they had to join the Klan to succeed. In 1925, thousands of hooded Klansmen marched twenty abreast down Pennsylvania Avenue to demonstrate their strength to an astonished national capital.

There was no state in which the Klan seemed more secure in its power than Indiana. There, the Klan had elected a governor and boasted more than 400,000 members. David Stephenson, the "Grand Dragon," bragged, "I am the law in Indiana." He had amassed a personal fortune from his Klan activities and expected to be elected to the Senate in 1926. In 1925, however, he and his bodyguards forced a reluctant secretary on a train to Chicago. There he raped and brutally bit her, leading her to poison herself with a lavatory cleanser. She survived long enough, however, to give a complete statement to doctors and police. Stephenson was sentenced to life imprisonment. When the pardon he had confidently expected from his "pal" in the governor's seat failed to develop, he gained his revenge by implicating many of

Indiana's political leaders in a web of pervasive corruption. These sensational events and revelations badly tarnished the Klan's pretensions as moral guardians of America. The remaining leaders struggled over the spoils. By 1930, the Klan's membership had fallen to 50,000. The "Imperial Wizard" of the Klan sold its Peachtree Street Palace to the Roman Catholic Church.

Nativism and Immigration Restriction

Klansmen were not the only Americans hostile to foreigners. The growing numbers of foreign-born deeply troubled many old stock Americans. They worried about the "undesirable" Catholics and Jews from southern and eastern Europe who flocked to the already problematic big cities. Two well-known psychologists declared, "The intellectual superiority of our Nordic group over the Alpine, Mediterranean and Negro groups has been demonstrated." Other "experts" agreed with the *New York Times* that our nation was in danger of becoming "mongrelized." Besides their supposed intellectual inferiority, the "new" immigrants were labeled as dangerous Bolsheviks and anarchists and more likely to be crazy or paupers.

Americanization committees tried to enforce cultural conformity. In some cases, feelings reached a fever pitch. In 1920, in West Frankfort, Illinois, mobs formed to drive every foreigner (in this case Italians) out of town. For three days they raged through the streets, burning all Italian homes and stoning and beating their inhabitants.

Eventually, the Americanization movement lost its momentum. Its followers shifted their efforts to immigration restriction. The vast majority of Americans agreed that immigration had to be curbed. The first efforts, literacy tests, succeeded only in setting higher standards, rather than in restricting the numbers of immigrants. Woodrow Wilson had vetoed efforts to impose quotas, but in 1924, Calvin Coolidge signed the National Origins Act, announcing that "America must be kept American."

The new law cut the total number of immigrants in any one year to 164,000 (compared to the million who entered in 1921). It also limited each nation to 2 percent of the number of people of that "national origin," living in the United State in 1890. Since most southern and eastern European immigrants had arrived after 1890, the not-very subtle aim was clearly to keep those "undesirables" out. Under this system, for example, 66,000 immigrants could come from Great Britain, but only 5,800 from Italy and 2,700 from Russia. To satisfy California nativists, the law completely excluded Asians. This needless slight deeply angered the Japanese. (They had earlier agreed to limit Japanese migration to America in the Gentleman's Agreement of 1907.) One protester committed harikari (suicide) in front of the American Embassy in Tokyo and relations with Japan worsened.

One, perhaps unintentional, result was the soaring rate of unrestricted immigration from the Western Hemisphere. Thousands of Mexicans poured across the border to seek a better life in the Southwestern United States. Many became migratory farm workers, earning very little and living in dreadful conditions.

The Case of Sacco and Vanzetti

The trial, conviction, and execution of Sacco and Vanzetti vividly demonstrated both the powerful currents of anti-foreign feeling and the deep divisions in American society. In 1920 a five-man band of robbers held up a shoe factory in South Braintree, Massachusetts, seizing the payroll and killing the paymaster and guard. Witnesses described the killers as Italians. A few weeks later the police arrested Nicola Sacco and Bartolomeo Vanzetti, two Italian immigrants, a shoemaker and a fish monger, well known in the area for their anarchist activities. Both were carrying loaded pistols.

The trial took place in 1921. The testimony on both sides was far from conclusive. Neither the money nor the getaway car was ever traced to the two men. Eyewitness descriptions changed to fit the defendants more closely as the date of the trial arrived. Historians have since analyzed, dissected, and redissected the evidence. Some have suggested that ballistic tests on Sacco's gun point to his involvement. Few, however, have argued that the trial was fair. Judge Thayer, who presided, was clearly hostile to Sacco and Vanzetti whom he described to friends as "those anarchist bastards." In the atmosphere of the time, it was easy for an Anglo-Saxon New England jury to feel that foreigners were suspicious types who could not be believed. Anarchists were probably also murderers. Aliens who had dodged the draft in World War I were undoubtedly guilty of something.

Judge Thayer found the men guilty of first degree murder and sentenced them to death. This was not the end of the case. It was, instead, the beginning of a worldwide outcry. Prominent liberal and radical intellectuals and Italian-Americans took up their cause. For six years they secured stays of execution and uncovered new evidence, including a confession by a convicted killer and recantations by prosecution witnesses. In 1927 the governor of Massachusetts appointed a distinguished advisory commission, headed by the president of Harvard, (a member of the Immigration Restriction League) to review the evidence. While noting "a grave breach of official decorum" by Judge Thayer, the commission upheld the conviction. Demonstrations erupted throughout the world. A famous newspaperman wryly commented, "What more can the immigrants from Italy expect? It is not every person who has a president of Harvard throw the switch for him." The words of the eloquent Vanzetti further convinced his supporters of the two men's innocence: "Never in our full life could we hope to do such a work for tolerance, for justice, for man's understanding of men as we do by accident . . . That last moment belongs to us—that agony is our triumph." They were electrocuted on August 23, 1927.

Five days later, enraged police broke up a funeral march by fifty thousand mourners. To Sacco and Vanzetti supporters, the death of "these two good men" proved that justice and change could never be achieved through the "system." Intellectuals and reformers moved sharply to the left. In *The Big Money*, John Dos Passos bitterly expressed their views. The narrator, thinking of the early settlers who hated oppression, reflects on recent events:

> America our nation has been beaten by
> strangers . . . who have taken the
> clean words our fathers spoke and made
> them slimy and foul. . .
> they have built the electric chair and hired
> the executioner to throw the switch.
> All right we are two nations . . . .

No event reflected the cultural divide between the two Americas more than the Sacco and Vanzetti case.

POLITICS AND GOVERNMENT IN THE TWENTIES

The politics of the 1920s did not reflect those deep divisions. Instead, the Republican presidents and congresses mirrored the admiration of big business that most Americans felt. After the disillusionment caused by years of reform and war, Americans yearned for stability. They wanted a leadership that would turn the clock back to an earlier time when government and business were partners. (Business would be the senior partner.) H.L. Mencken, whose cynical commentary defined the Twenties, noted, "Today no sane American believes in any official statement of national policy . . . Tired to death of intellectual charlatanry, he turns despairingly to honest imbecility." The comment of famed lawyer, Clarence Darrow reflected the mediocre (or worse) quality of leadership: "When I was a boy I was told that anybody could become president; I'm beginning to believe it."

President Harding and His Scandals

Warren G. Harding, the first president of the 1920s, was a handsome man who looked as though central casting had sent him to play the role of president. He was a kindly, good-natured moderate whose ignorance of issues and unconcerned lack of savvy horrified the White House press. "I can't hope to be the best President this country ever had," he once admitted, "but if I can, I'd like to be the best loved." In the White House, Harding remained the same small-town politician he had always been. He enjoyed playing cards with his "Poker Cabinet" and relished his cigars and illegal cocktails. He also seems to have maintained a small house for his mistress and their child. (In 1927 she wrote a best selling account of the relationship, *The President's Daughter*.)

Harding made some well-received appointments to his cabinet. These included Charles Evans Hughes, the 1916 presidential candidate as Secretary of State; Henry Wallace, a well-respected authority, as Secretary of Agriculture; and Herbert Hoover, the wartime food administrator as Secretary of Commerce. Some also cheered the appointment of "the world's second richest man," Andrew Mellon, as the Secretary of Treasury. Hoover, who in many ways dominated the cabinet, pushed for voluntary business associations to cooperate in building a prosperous economy. Mellon opposed government regulations and urged slashing taxes on the wealthy.

"Uncle Warren" could be generous and tolerant. He spoke out against mistreatment of Southern blacks to an astounded segregated audience in Birmingham, Alabama. His civil liberties record compared favorably with Wilson's repressiveness. Wilson had twice refused to free the imprisoned socialist leader Eugene Debs after the war was over, while Harding pardoned Debs on Christmas Eve, 1921. At Harding's invitation, Debs even visited the White House for a talk and declared, "Mr. Harding appears to me to be a kind gentleman." Harding also freed virtually all the two hundred federal political prisoners who remained from the war and the subsequent Red Scare.

Harding worked hard to fulfill the obligations of office. He labored at personally answering routine White House mail. He struggled to make the right decisions about intricate economic and legislative questions. But his intellectual limitations and inability really to understand the issues drove him to despair. He went for treatment of his nervous disorders to a sanitarium in Battle Creek, Michigan, run by the eccentric Dr. Kellogg, the cereal king.

The president's most tragic flaw was his tendency to persuade himself that the political cronies he enjoyed as pals must be honest and able. "Warren, it's a good thing you wasn't born a gal," his father supposedly once remarked, "You'd be in the family way all the time—you can't say no." Virtually everyone in the know warned Harding against appointing as attorney general the wheeler-dealer who had helped make him president. To Harding, loyalty was the prime virtue. "Harry Daugherty has been my best friend from the beginning of this whole thing," he informed one protester. "He tells me that he wants to be Attorney General and by God he will be Attorney General." The result: Daugherty and his friends set up a "little house on K street" to buy and sell pardons, appointments, licenses, and government surplus.

Upset by the plight of disabled war veterans, Harding was proud of his creation of the Veterans Bureau to help them. As its head, he appointed Charles Forbes, a supposed Medal of Honor winner who was also a hustling go-getter. The bureau became the major spender in the government and its head renowned for his lavish life style. Cleanliness seemed to be his fixation. He bought enough floor cleaners to last a hundred years and paid 98 cents a gallon for cleaner that usually cost a nickel. Forbes' chief assistant, informed of an impending senate investigation, committed suicide, as did a close associate of Daugherty.

As evidence of the scandals and mismanagement reached him, the despondent president confessed to a journalist, "I have no trouble with my enemies . . . . But my friends, my God-damned friends . . . they're the ones that keep me walking the floor nights." The president complained of chest pains and faintness. His doctors urged rest and approved an unhurried rail tour of Alaska. Instead, Harding brought his card-playing buddies along and played bridge compulsively for hours on end. He also insisted on making dozens of speeches along the way. By the time the train reached San Francisco, the president had collapsed. After some inept medical treatment by his doctor/crony, Harding's death (probably from a heart attack) was announced on August 2, 1923. The public was unaware of the brewing scandals. Millions waited along the tracks in silence or softly singing hymns as the casket passed by, reacting as though they had lost a latter-day Lincoln. Harding, in his death, was lavished with the love he had always wanted.

The Teapot Dome Scandal, the worst of the Harding administration disgraces, surfaced shortly after Harding's death. Secretary of Interior, Albert Fall, had been a senator from New Mexico known for his hostility to conservation. He had gained control of federal naval oil reserves. He promptly granted drilling rights to two millionaire oilmen in return for almost $400,000 in "loans." Fall became the first cabinet member in American history convicted and sentenced to prison for crimes in office. His disgrace and the publicity given to the other scandals forever blemished the image of the until-then beloved president.

Silent Cal

The public was entranced when Colonel John Coolidge administered the oath of office by the light of a lantern at the family farm to his son, Calvin Coolidge. The farm was in a part of Vermont that had remained, in the words of William Allen White, journalist and Coolidge biographer, "like the interior of some cool museum preserving colonial life." As vice president, Coolidge had been virtually unknown to the public. One of his most ambitious efforts had been an article entitled "Are the Reds Stalking our College Women?" (The answer was yes.)

The new president was a quiet, private man, a Puritan in an age of excess. White called his biography of Coolidge, *Puritan in Babylon.* The commonplace virtues of "silent Cal" reassured the public. He attempted to sit on the front porch of the White House in a rocking chair, but when crowds gathered, he gave up that small-town pleasure. He opened the doors of the oval office at 12:30 each day and, for a half hour, he shook more than 1,000 hands. He believed in as little government as possible, rarely worked more than four hours a day, and slept 12 hours or more each night. As one writer noted, "He aspired to become the least President the country had ever had; he attained his desire."

Sophisticated observers sneered at the dour little man with his obvious limitations. Alice Roosevelt Longworth said he "looked as if he was weaned on a pickle." When informed of his death, the author Dorothy Parker asked, "How could they tell?" The public, on the other hand, admired his integrity and assumed that his "curious shell of sardonic silence" was evidence of deep thought. He made them forget the earlier Republican scandals. His personal honesty and frugal life style made the people feel secure.

On a more serious level, Coolidge combined his belief in minimal government with a reverence for big business. "The business of America is business,"

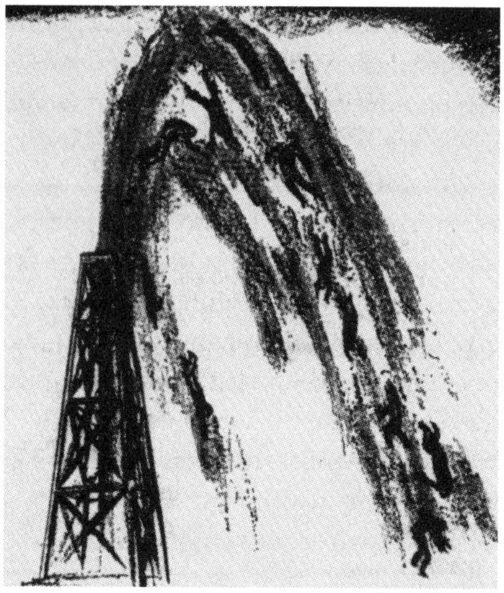

This cartoon pictures the Teapot Dome spewing out oily crooks.

he declared. "The man who builds a factory builds a temple. The man who works there, worships there." Mellon, the millionaire Treasury Secretary became his chief adviser, lowering taxes for the wealthy and increasing the widening gap between rich and poor, while balancing the budget. Tariff rates climbed to all-time heights to aid manufacturers. At the same time, Coolidge twice vetoed efforts to provide government aid to farmers noting, "Farmers have never made much money. I don't believe we can do much about that." He even turned down aid to victims of one of the worst Mississippi River floods in history (500,000 homeless and 500 dead). The government, Coolidge lectured, had no responsibility to protect people "against the hazards of the elements." He sincerely believed that government's main goal should be "not to embark on any new ventures." Earlier progressive reforms had brought high costs, complications, and thousands of deaths in the war. The public embraced the Coolidge view of limited government.

The Election of 1924

In February 1924 the ghost of a different activist America vanished with the death of Woodrow Wilson. The official Republican slogan in the 1924 election was, "Coolidge or Chaos," but most Americans preferred, "Keep Cool with Coolidge." The nation was enjoying the "Coolidge prosperity." Even farm discontent had eased, seeming to vindicate the policy of doing nothing. During the campaign Coolidge characteristically remained in Washington allowing Charles Dawes, his energetic running mate, to do all the campaigning.

A bitterly divided Democratic Party met at New York's Madison Square Garden in the midst of a devastating heat wave. Differences over Prohibition and the Klan tore the party apart. (A resolution to condemn the Klan failed 543-542.) The most dramatic event of the convention was the reappearance of Franklin Roosevelt whose promising political career had seemingly been destroyed by a devastating attack of polio some years earlier. When Roosevelt painfully pulled himself erect and, in his ringing voice, nominated Al Smith, (New York's governor) as the "Happy Warrior," the convention erupted in wild cheers. Roosevelt seemed to some observers to be "the real hero of the convention." His "adversity" had made him "the one leader commanding the respect and admiration of delegations from all sections of the land." That would prove to be the case in the future. In the meantime, the convention remained deadlocked for 102 ballots between Smith, the urban Catholic, and William McAdoo, Wilson's Treasury Secretary who represented Southern rural Protestant interests. Finally, the weary delegates compromised by nominating John W. Davis, a gentlemanly Wall Street lawyer who was almost as conservative as Coolidge.

Progressives attempted to regroup by nominating the elderly ailing "Fighting Bob" La Follette who sought to revive earlier progressive ideas of activist government reform. Barely half the public bothered to vote. Coolidge won a lopsided victory with almost 16 million votes, nearly twice that of Davis. La Follette received 17 percent of the vote, an impressive total compared to that of other third party candidates in our history. The voters had, however, basically endorsed the status quo.

Foreign Policy

The people seemed to believe that by rejecting Wilson's League, they could safely ignore the world. President Coolidge reinforced that view in 1925 when he declared, "The people have had all the war, all the taxation, and all the military service they want."

In Russia, Lenin died, and an unknown, Stalin, ruthlessly seized power. In Italy, Mussolini brutally eliminated all opposition. Magazines wrote enthusiastically about how this unusual Italian actually made the trains run on time. These events barely penetrated American consciousness.

Although American investments and exports skyrocketed in the Twenties, the nation refused any commitment outside the Western Hemisphere. America even rejected membership in the World Court. Two rare exceptions were the Washington Naval Conference of 1922 and the Kellogg-Briand Pact of 1928. In the first, the United States, Britain, Japan, France, and Italy agreed to reduce somewhat battleship tonnage to a fixed ratio. In the Kellogg-Briand Pact, sixty-one nations piously resolved to renounce aggressive wars. Everyone seemed to have gotten something for nothing. It was, as one writer has observed, "painless, toothless, and gutless."

A nation that had suffered neither defeat nor destruction decided that only European dishonesty stopped the Germans from paying reparations to the Allies and the Allies from repaying their debts to America. Few realized that these issues were intertwined and related to the economic well-being of the world. They agreed with Coolidge who concluded, "They hired the money, didn't they?" Although America eventually produced plans to lower debt demands, high tariffs made it virtually impossible for the Europeans to earn enough money to repay even the reduced amounts. Continued American insistence led to European resentment of an America described by Winston Churchill as "Uncle Shylock."

Unwillingness to fund adequately the American armed forces further illustrated the distaste for any foreign involvement. General Billy Mitchell, the foremost exponent of air power, demonstrated conclusively in 1923 that planes could sink battleships. Military and political leaders totally ignored his crucial lesson. Mitchell was eventually court-martialed and forced to resign.

The government, Americans felt, should help find foreign markets for American business and might intervene in the Western Hemisphere, but it should avoid any international commitments. The famed critic, George Jean Nathan, reflected the attitude of the Twenties when he wrote that millions of deaths overseas, "would not matter to me in the least. What concerns me alone is myself, and . . . a few close friends. For all I care, the rest of the world may go to hell at today's sunset."

Business Influence and the Decline of Progressivism

The results of the 1924 election marked the high water mark of the triumph of business influence in government. Mellon was able to win even further reductions in taxes on the wealthy, arguing that the benefits would "trickle down" to the less fortunate. A skeptical Nebraska progressive remarked, "Mr. Mellon himself gets a larger personal reduction than the aggregate of all the taxpayers in the state of Nebraska." The leaders of the very industries they were supposed to regulate ran the main regulatory agencies.

Former President William Howard Taft was appointed Chief Justice of the Supreme Court. The role of the Court, he announced, was "to prevent the Bolsheviki from getting control." Under his direction the Court held a national child labor law unconstitutional, struck down minimum wages for women, and softened anti-monopoly rulings. Encouraged by the favorable attitude of courts and government agencies, big business went on a merger binge. Organized labor, by contrast, suffered a precipitous decline. Courts routinely granted injunctions against picketing or boycotts and sanctioned mass arrests of strikers.

The decline of the Teddy Roosevelt wing of the Republicans and the disorder among the Democrats seemed to signal the final collapse of progressive reform. The voters, however, did elect a core of determined, though often frustrated, reformers. These included old style Western progressives and new urban liberals such as Senator Robert Wagner and Congressman Fiorello LaGuardia of New York. Their successes at the federal level were minimal, but they did better at the state and local level where the ideology of progressive Republicans shifted to the more urban Democratic Party. Progressive-led campaigns resulted in workmen's compensation programs and aid to women with dependent children in many states. Governor Al Smith in New York started the first public housing program.

Most Americans were uninterested in reform. One young woman exemplified the attitude of many: "We're not out to benefit society . . . or to make industry safe. We're not going to suffer over how the other half lives." Coolidge's comments in his inaugural address reflected the general satisfaction, "No one can contemplate current conditions without finding much that is satisfying and still more that is encouraging."

PROSPERITY AND THE CONSUMER SOCIETY

The booming prosperity of America in the 1920s dazzled visitors from abroad. One English observer noted, "In the world's history can there have been such a display of wealth, power and energy as is spread out across the whole continent; never such feverish activity . . . ." The visitor was troubled, however, by the cost: "the ruthlessness, the concentration, the unsleeping demand for efficiency." Americans did not seem to have any such doubts. They believed that a new age of unending affluence was at hand.

The great boom era began with a bust. The sudden cancellation of government contracts and the rapid return of veterans to the labor market made the adjustment from war to peace time very difficult. A sharp recession, characterized by steep declines in production and employment, struck from 1920-21. Recovery came by 1922, confirming the faith many economists had in the inevitability of regular business cycles. The economy then entered a "new era" of dramatic economic growth. Unemployment fell to as low as 3 percent and national income grew at an annual rate of 5.6 percent. (That growth rate has never been matched in any comparable era in American history.)

Technology and the Consumer

Technological advances were at the root of this spectacular growth. Industrial output almost doubled,

France demanded war reparations from Germany.

with remarkable increases in worker productivity. Mass production techniques, utilizing the moving-belt assembly line, made this possible.

A new age of electricity had dawned. Electricity powered 70 percent of American industry by the end of the era. Although many parts of rural America remained untouched, more than 60 percent of American homes were also wired for electric power. This made possible the production and sale of an amazing array of new electric appliances including refrigerators, washing machines, vacuum cleaners, fans, and mixers, as well as phonographs and radios, and a huge stimulus to the economy.

An extensive chemical industry also arose. Its efforts led to new alloys, synthetic materials such as rayon, and preserved foods. The quantity of gasoline that could be refined from one gallon of crude oil tripled.

Corporate structures "modernized" as well. Corporations continued the wartime consolidations that a friendly government still encouraged. A handful of big firms dominated major industries. By 1929, the two hundred largest companies owned half of the nation's corporate assets. Within the corporations, management was "rationalized" and "professionalized." Unlike the old-fashioned individualistic and autocratic style of Henry Ford, the day-to-day activities of most modern corporations were in the hands of trained professional managers. It was the beginning of the "organization man."

The old progressive fears of big business expansion and domination disappeared. The prospects of unending economic growth and prosperity, fueled by continuous technological advances, dazzled Americans.

The Automobile Age

Above all, American prosperity rested on the automobile. At the turn of the century, the automobile had been a toy of the rich. Woodrow Wilson once complained, "Nothing has spread socialistic feeling in this country more than the automobile; to the countryman it is a picture of arrogance and wealth, with all its independence and carelessness." Henry Ford had revolutionized the industry by 1914 when he had offered his workers an unprecedented wage of five dollars a day in return for a speed up in the assembly line. By 1925, the Ford plant turned out one enormously popular Model T every ten seconds. The price fell to $290, about three months wages for a typical worker.

The "Tin Lizzie," as the Model T was lovingly called, was the object of many affectionate jokes. You didn't need a speedometer, ran one, because at 15 mph the windshield rattled; at 20 the fenders shook; and at 30 your fillings fell out. But as Ford's production was merrily rolling along, a new style executive, Alfred P. Sloan, had taken control of General Motors. Unlike Ford, an eccentric self-taught "tinkerer," Sloan was an M.I.T. graduate. He reorganized GM so that each division was a self-contained entity, run by expert managers. Sloan used modern marketing methods to introduce annual model changes, "planned obsolescence," and a variety of colors. (Ford had said that you could have the Model T in any color you liked, "so long as it's black.") For $90 more, the Chevrolet offered such conveniences as a self starter (no more standing in the rain cranking and swearing) and head lights that did not depend on the speed of the engine to work. GM also encouraged installment buying, creating the General Motors Acceptance Corporation to provide credit. By 1927, two-thirds of all automobile sales were bought on time payments, and Chevrolet had overtaken Ford in sales.

Suddenly, in May 1927, Ford shut down the Model T plant. He and his son, Edsel, drove the last (15,007,003rd) Model T off the line into the pouring rain. Ford and his men had to retool completely his giant factory to create a new car. One historian has written, "The magnitude of the reorganization which had to be completed within the calendar year . . . was something new in American industry." Without planning or any research department, Ford produced the new Model A by November 1927. Buyers had already ordered half a million cars, sight unseen. Huge crowds poured into the showrooms around the country, requiring mounted police to control them. It was a great public event. The new model, with its clean lines and improved convenience, proved to be enormously popular. One song declared, "Henry's Made a Lady out of Lizzie." Automobile registrations grew from 9 million to over 26 million in the decade. The United States was manufacturing about 85 percent of the world's automobiles.

The automobile industry had a tremendous impact on the American economy and lifestyle. It stimulated the growth of such related industries as steel, rubber, glass, and petroleum. It led to America's oil dependency. It created the national highway system and its resulting spread of restaurants, motels, and service stations. America's love affair with the automobile caused the neglect and ultimate decline of the railroads. Suburban development increased, as well as real estate booms in distant Florida and California.

While one working class woman enthusiastically announced, "I'll go without food before I'll see us give up the car," critics blamed the automobile for the decline of family togetherness and private morals. The enclosed cars, they argued, were nothing more than "portable bedrooms." For most Americans, however, the rapid growth of motor-vehicle registrations created an optimistic faith in technological progress.

The Age of Advertising

The demand for automobiles and the other goods upon which the consumer economy rested was stimulated by the flourishing advertising business. By 1929, advertising earnings had jumped to $3.4 billion, more than all expenditures for formal education put together. Many advertisers followed the behaviorist theories of the psychologist John Watson. Watson believed that human beings could be easily manipulated. The authors of *What About Advertising?* argued that the advertiser "must recognize the extreme mental stupidity of the vast majority of his audience." They believed that the average American had the mental capacity of a twelve-year-old and would believe anything, presented in the right way. That way would be to aim at the emotions with a hard-sell approach.

Advertisers often played on the public's deepest anxieties. The hazards of life could destroy the unwary. "Halitosis," a new term for bad breath, was discovered to sell Listerine. "B.O." (body odor) could destroy any relationship unless the afflicted used Lifebuoy soap. The menace of pyorrhea (gum disease) seemed worst of all, hitting "four out of five" Americans. Those who failed to use Forhan's gum treatment were depicted wearing white masks to hide their hideous mouths. Even the Encyclopedia Britannica claimed that it could save the marriage of a dull young woman, "one year married and all talked out."

Other products trumpeted their benefits. Cigarettes could make you slimmer, promised Lucky Strikes with its slogan, "Reach for a Lucky instead of a sweet." The heroism of the crew of the *S.S. America* in saving thirty-two Italian sailors was a result of their smoking Luckies. Fleischmann's discovered that its yeast was a "health food," which could cure constipation, lack of energy, and even acne. Famous people willingly accepted money to give testimonials for such dubious products as useless "nerve tonics."

Advertising also worked to advance a new era of consumption. It would be a world of luxury and pleasure. A GE refrigerator could be a magnet for envious guests to admire in your kitchen. ("The owning of such a refrigerator is a form of health and happiness insurance.") Shiny new plumbing fixtures would show that you had arrived. Albert Lasker, often credited as the father of modern advertising, was able to skirt prohibitions against using words like "menstruation" or "sanitary napkin" and successfully launch the newly invented Kotex. When American orange growers produced far more fruits than Americans ate, Lasker began a campaign to get people to drink orange juice every day.

To many Americans, advertising was the new gospel. Bruce Barton, an advertising executive (founder of the giant firm B.B.D.& O.), wrote *The Man Nobody Knows*, the number-one best seller of 1925 and 1926. In it Barton discovered that "the real Jesus" was an outgoing organization man who had forged "twelve men from the bottom ranks of business" into "an organization that conquered the world." Christ, had he lived in the Twenties, would certainly have been an advertiser. Advertising, Barton explained, "as a force . . . is as old as the world. The first four words ever uttered, 'Let there be light,' constitute its charter." The success of advertisers made spending a major national pastime.

Farmers and Workers: The Limits of Prosperity

"The rich get rich and the poor get children," a 1921 song snickered. The booming economy left many behind. Spurred on by the all-time high prices during World War I, farmers had greatly expanded production. They had gone into debt to finance increased mechanization. After the war, prices and land values collapsed, leaving debt-ridden farmers with no chance to recover. As they increased productivity, prices fell even further (wheat, corn, and hay by more than 50 percent). For most American farmers, the 1920s was more a decade of depression than of prosperity. Foreclosure signs appeared on the fences of thousands of deserted farms. The owners had loaded their rickety Model Ts with their meager possessions and headed to the highways. The Department of Agriculture estimated that 19 million rural Americans had given up and gone to live in the cities.

The story for workers was mixed. Real wages for factory workers rose modestly and hours decreased. Business profits, however, increased seven times as much as wages. The wages of unionized workers rose rapidly. They generally earned twice as much as the unorganized. Nevertheless, union membership declined from over 5 million to 3.4 million by the end of the decade. The increase in mass production techniques accelerated the trend away from skilled hand labor where union labor had predominated. With the approval of a sympathetic government and courts, business- men, like Henry Ford, discouraged union organizing by using hired thugs and friendly police forces to intimidate physically union organizers.

"Welfare capitalism," based on the idea that the interests of workers and employers were identical, was even more effective in obstructing unionization. The General Electric Company pioneered in the view that workers should not be treated like machines. The cooperation of the workers, gained through better treatment, would increase production. With the growth of the industrial relations movement, companies began to hire personnel managers, trained to deal with workers. Some giant corporations introduced stock purchase plans, medical programs, group insurance, and credit unions. Companies like U. S. Steel saw no contradictions between welfare capitalism and the continued use of anti-union spies and strict controls in company-run towns.

Scientific management introduced more efficient machinery and speedups in production. Many workers complained that the new work disciplines required by these machines stripped the employees of their humanity. In nineteenth century factories, for all their evils, workers and bosses were often able to establish personal relationships. Visitors to the factories would meet the laborers. Now, as one worker complained, visitors were brought in to admire the new machinery. Charlie Chaplin's film, *Modern Times*, brilliantly satirized the plight of the modern workman.

The large number of workers who did not share in the general prosperity was even more worrisome. The wages of the unskilled barely increased at all. The textile industry was in dire straits. Textile mills had abandoned their historic homes in New England to seek nonunion labor and considerably lower wages in the South. Many New England mill towns were devastated. By the mid-1920s, the Southern textile industry was, itself, suffering serious decline as a result of foreign competition, the new "miracle" fabric, rayon, and the reduced demand due to shorter skirts.

Hours rose and wages fell below the poverty level. Even employed factory workers in more prosperous industries lived in constant fear of plant shutdowns or layoffs. Miners, particularly in coal-producing areas, also suffered from the competition of oil. Despite a series of bitter strikes, neither their wages nor their working conditions showed any signs of improvement.

Almost 42 percent of American families had annual incomes of less than $1,500, the poverty level. Of the 26 million American families in the mid-1920s, 6 million were listed as "chronically destitute." Less than half the homes in America met *Fortune* magazine's "minimum standards of health and decency," which included electricity, inside toilet and running water, and regular garbage removal. There was, indeed, poverty amidst the prosperity. Chief Justice Taft expressed the view that the country was fortunate to have a government committed to allowing "the people to work out for themselves the prosperity they deserved." Many Americans agreed with his assumption that the rich and successful merited their wealth, while the distressed farmer or poorly paid worker received precisely what each "deserved."

LIFE IN THE TWENTIES

In many ways the Twenties represented a better life for millions of Americans, particularly those in the ever-increasing middle class. Life expectancy, as a result of public health programs, rose from 55 to 60, the greatest increase ever in one decade. Tuberculosis, once called "the Great White Plague," was now an illness confined to the very poor. Other infectious diseases also declined.

Other health news was not so positive. Heart disease and cancer replaced the older diseases as the leading causes of death. Cigarette consumption had gone from 15 billion to 100 billion. Sugar use tripled. Drug addiction increased with the growth of cities. Doctors and pharmacists filled increasing demands for opium and morphine. With the support of the American Medical Association, the authorities arrested doctor-suppliers, criminalizing drug addiction.

American education was transformed. Only one-fourth of the high school-age population attended secondary school at the end of World War I. By 1930, more than half attended high school. Every state now had compulsory education laws. Even colleges and universities experienced enormous growths in enrollment.

These healthier, better educated Americans, above all, wanted to enjoy life. They did not want to be troubled by problems and issues. Ernest Hemingway's hero in *A Farewell to Arms* expressed their views when he declared, "I was always embarrassed by the words sacred, glorious and sacrifice . . . ." The attitudes of the young led the way in this "Age of Flaming Youth."

Cities and Suburbs

The 1920 census marked a great turning point in American history. For the first time, a majority of the nation's people were counted as living in cities. Although the definition of what constituted a city was somewhat questionable (2,500 or more inhabitants), the announcement had symbolic importance. It seemed to confirm the demise of the rural way of life. There were now a dozen cities with populations of more than 600,000. During the 1920s this trend continued. Steel, oil, automobile, and commercial and service centers boomed. Even greater growth took place in warm climate resort cities like Miami and San Diego.

An increase in corporate administrative and service headquarters led to an enormous boom in the construction of downtown skyscrapers. By 1929, there were 377 buildings at least 20 stories tall. City and state governments were spending large sums of money in constructing new roads, improving streets, and regulating traffic with such amazing new equipment as the traffic light.

Ironically, just as America was officially described as an urban nation, suburban development, which would ultimately undermine the cities' growth, was also increasing. By 1920, the growth rate of suburbs was greater than that of cities for the first time. Industries began to move out of the central city. Increased use of electric power made greater flexibility in location possible. The assembly line required sprawling single or two-story plants in areas where cheap land was available. Many white workers moved out of the cities to be near their work. The newly available inexpensive automobiles made it possible for workers to move out into areas lacking mass transportation. Retail establishments followed the movement to the suburbs. In 1923 Kansas City, Missouri developed the nation's first suburban shopping center. Others quickly followed.

The growing decentralization of industry and retailing led to increased building of roads. The construction of "parkways" began in the 1920s, stimulating automobile commuting and recreational trips. Decisions to pave gathering places and stress easy movement destroyed nineteenth century city neighborhoods. The new suburban expansion, coupled with continued growth of cities and rising automobile use, caused the formation of metropolitan districts (cities and their suburbs). By 1930 there were 93 such areas with populations over 100,000.

The Empire State Building had 102 stories and space for 25,000 tenants. In 1950, 222 additional feet were added.

African-American Life in the Twenties

A substantial portion of the migrants into the nation's cities was African American. Conditions in the rural South worsened as the boll weevil destroyed cotton farms and the rebirth of the Ku Klux Klan reinvigorated racial repression. "I'm tired of this Jim Crow, gonna leave this Jim Crow town," one blues song proclaimed. Black newspapers spread word of job opportunities in growing industries, encouraged by Ford's expressed willingness to hire black workers on the assembly line. This "Great Migration," in which some 1.5 million African Americans moved into America's cities, was a remarkable and unprecedented redistribution of American population

In reality, they met rising tides of prejudice. They were forced to squeeze into overcrowded slums, restricted by fearful whites from moving to better housing. In addition, despite Ford's example, few factories or construction firms were willing to hire blacks. (In Philadelphia less than 1 percent of the 43,000 factory workers were blacks, 15 percent of the population.) Most employed black women worked as domestics. The church was the central institution in the lives of African Americans who had moved from the rural South. Barbershops and beauty parlors were also significant social institutions for urban blacks. Hairdressers were part of the black elite that also included doctors, lawyers, teachers, and ministers. In fact, Madame C. J. Walker, considered the first American woman self-made millionaire, became rich by manufacturing skin creams, "whiteners," and hair-straighteners for black women. As black ghettoes spilled into adjoining neighborhoods, they often met bitter, even violent, resistance.

One response to this discrimination was an upsurge in black protest organizations. The conservative Urban League attempted, with limited success, to find jobs for blacks in the cities. The National Association for the Advancement of Colored People (NAACP) fought school segregation in the North and worked hard for a federal anti-lynching bill. After a bitter debate (one Southern congressman declared, "When these black fiends keep their hands off the throats of the women of the South the lynching will stop."), the House voted to make lynching a federal crime by a 2-1 margin. Southerners filibustered the bill to death in the Senate. The threat of possible federal action, coupled with the NAACP publicity campaign, did succeed in bringing about an enormous decline in the number of lynchings.

A. Philip Randolph was far more radical and militant than the two mainstream organizations. He decided to organize a black union, the Brotherhood of Sleeping Car Porters. Although their work was largely menial—making beds, attending to passenger comforts—porters were comparatively well paid and were among the elite of the community. College-educated black men often found that jobs as Pullman porters were all they could get. (In one deadly train wreck, his Dartmouth Phi Beta Kappa key identified the porter.) The union had its setbacks and advances, but it gave Randolph and, through him, black workers a "Harvard-accented voice" in the labor movement.

The Brotherhood of Sleeping Car Porters was one of the few unions with black members.

West Indian immigrants who lived in black communities in American cities tended to be more confident, enterprising, and ambitious than Southern migrants, as a result of their history. Marcus Garvey, who came from Jamaica, preached pride in blackness. He formed the Universal Negro Improvement Association (UNIA) to further black separatism, capitalism, and eventual migration to Africa. The UNIA newspaper refused to accept ads for skin whiteners or hair straighteners. Garvey's colorful costumes and charismatic personality appealed to working class people, many of whom bought stock in his Black Star shipping line. Eventually, undermined by crooked officers, the line went bankrupt. Garvey was convicted of mail fraud on very dubious evidence, sent to jail, and then deported. His message of "race and color consciousness," however, remained a potent one for many years to come, having a profound impact on later black nationalism.

In the 1920 census there were less than 50,000 blacks living in New York. By the end of the decade, there were 300,000, two-thirds of whom crowded together in Harlem. As Harlem became a black ghetto, it also developed into the center of African-American intellectual and cultural activity. The "Harlem Renaissance" bloomed in the 1920s, the black version of the cultural dynamism of the era. Nearly every important black writer and intellectual flocked *Home to Harlem*, the title of a Claude McKay work. Writers and poets explored the lives and often contradictory role of black people in America. "Yet do I marvel at this curious thing: To make a poet black and bid him sing," declared Countee Cullen. Langston Hughes, less ironically and more defiantly, professed pride in being "Negro," "Black as the night is black, Black like the depths of my Africa."

Nightclubs and theaters also demonstrated the variety and vitality of black culture. Bessie Smith sang her plaintive blues. Jazz had moved up the Mississippi from the whore houses of New Orleans to Memphis and Chicago. From there it came to Harlem clubs through Duke Ellington and many others. Langston Hughes recalled the Twenties as "the period when the Negro was in vogue." Whites had discovered Harlem

Marcus Garvey offered black pride to the urban blacks of the eastern cities.

as a place to escape from dull upper and middle class life. They crowded into places like the Cotton Club where white-only audiences watched black performers. The more daring went to "black and white" night spots where the races actually mixed. Broadway even featured its first all-black review, *Shuffle Along*.

Rebellious white intellectuals, youths, and bored society people were part of the fad for everything black. They felt the pull of the exotic and "primitive." White patrons supported many aspiring black writers and artists. The whites expected confirmation of their stereotypes about "African soul" from their proteges. When Langston Hughes insisted on writing about black American workers, his generous patron dropped him. Once the Depression struck, Harlem was "no longer in vogue." White supporters departed and, as Langston Hughes ruefully remarked, "The ordinary Negroes hadn't heard of the Negro Renaissance. And if they had, it hadn't raised their wages any."

The Jewish Experience

Jews from Eastern Europe were among the flood of "new" immigrants who had arrived in America from 1890-1914 and crowded into American cities. By 1920, Jews were 20 percent of the population of New York City. The restrictive immigration laws, aimed at all eastern and southern Europeans, led to a drastic decline in Jewish immigration. Only 73,000 Jewish immigrants entered the country from 1924-31. The children of the earlier immigrants wanted to become a part of American society. They aspired to the American dream as defined in the 1920s.

They met with discrimination in employment, particularly in such white collar areas as banking and commercial offices. (The New York Telephone Company announced that it could not hire Jewish women as operators since their arms were too short for the switchboards!) Better housing, resorts, and country clubs were also restricted. Despite these obstacles, Jews succeeded to a remarkable degree. Although most remained working class, a substantial number moved up to the middle class, particularly the second generation Americans. Many were small businessmen in light manufacturing or sales. Barred from the major heavy industries, the more adventurous entrepreneurs entered the riskiest new ventures, particularly the film industry. A cultural stress on education and study led others into the professions: medicine, law, and teaching.

In spite of these successes, intensified anti-Semitism appeared to threaten the hopes and security of American Jews. Major American universities, such as Harvard, and most professional schools instituted quotas to limit the number of Jews in their student bodies. Jews were startled when police in the small town of Messina, New York in 1928, rounded up the local rabbi to question him about the disappearance of a little girl. The police had heard that Jews used the blood of Christian children in a religious ritual. This was an alarming appearance of the European medieval "blood libel" on American soil. (The child was found the next day.)

What is more important, the eccentric Henry Ford had turned his attention to the promotion of anti-Semitism. In the 1920s Ford became increasingly autocratic and distrustful of others. He purchased the newspaper, the *Dearborn Independent*, and increased its circulation to 700,000 by requiring his auto dealers to distribute it. The paper launched a lengthy anti-Semitic campaign, arguing inconsistently that Jews were both radical Bolshevik revolutionaries and Wall Street capitalist conspirators. It ran such "exposes" as "The Jewish associates of Benedict Arnold." The paper also serialized a Czarist Russian forgery, *The Protocols of the Elders of Zion* to "prove" an international Jewish conspiracy and then distributed it in book form, *The International Jew*. In 1922, a *New York Times* correspondent reported from the headquarters of a young politician in Munich: "The wall beside his desk in Hitler's office is decorated with a large picture of Henry Ford . . . there is a large table covered with books, nearly all of them are a translation of *The International Jew* . . . published by Henry Ford." After losing a libel suit by one Jewish victim of the paper's rantings, Ford released a public apology. He declared that he did not know about the nasty slanders issued in his name for seven years and asked for forgiveness. By 1929, Ford was paying tribute, in a radio address, to "the great benevolence of the Jewish people . . . their eagerness to make this world better . . . stamps them a great people." Although Ford never again returned to his earlier obsession, the ugly forces of hate he had helped release remained and led to far more serious consequences in the thirties.

The New Woman—Sexuality and Consumerism

"Cigarette in hand, shimmying to the music of the masses, the New Woman and the New Morality have made their theatric debut upon the modern scene," one observer proclaimed in the middle of the decade. Increasing sexual permissiveness, as symbolized by the independent, self-indulgent flapper, was an enduring image of the 1920s. There was a new mood of sexual emancipation, particularly among young urban middle class women. The idea of the great Austrian psychoanalyst, Sigmund Freud, that sex was central to the human experience, gained widespread acceptance. Popularizers oversimplified his theories to mean an end to all sexual restraint. Popular culture reinforced this view in "hot" movies, songs with titles like, "I Need Lovin'," and cheap books such as, *One of Cleopatra's Nights*. The young flapper was a "liberated" woman who showed her assertiveness and rebelliousness by bobbing her hair, wearing cosmetics (used only by prostitutes a generation earlier), smoking cigarettes in public, raising her hemline, and dancing the Charleston uninhibitedly.

"If all the girls at the Yale prom were laid end to end, I wouldn't be surprised," Dorothy Parker wrote. Other observers were more distressed than amused. The flapper's defiance of rules, such as a willingness to "pet" in her boyfriend's car and other assertions of female sexuality, was worrisome to traditionalists. Alarmist articles with such titles as, "These Wild Young People," filled magazines.

There was some validity to the view that sexual behavior was changing. Later exhaustive studies by Dr. Alfred Kinsey showed that women of the 1920s generation were twice as likely to have premarital sex as their mothers' generation. The sexual revolution aided in the dramatic decline of prostitution. The institution of "dating," marked a substantial change from the era of adult-supervised "calls" paid at home by male suitors. Now that women were conceded to be sexual beings, they expected romantic and sexual gratification in marriage. "Companionate marriages" were promoted as the ideal. Perhaps as a result, the divorce rate tripled from 1890 to 1930, rising to 18 out of every 100 marriages.

Margaret Sanger, who had launched the birth control movement in the Progressive era as a radical form of direct action by working-class women, reshaped her program to fit the new era. She won the support of academics and physicians by stressing eugenics arguments that birth control would keep the unfit poor from reproducing. She reinvented the birth control movement as a middle class reform by emphasizing the possibilities of transforming sex from "biological necessity" to "a psychic and spiritual avenue of expression." Now women could be liberated from "loathing, disgust, or indifference to the sex relationship" and from "involuntary motherhood," to experience sexual satisfaction in marriage. Middle class women, able to obtain illegal diaphragms from physicians, became the main advocates of birth

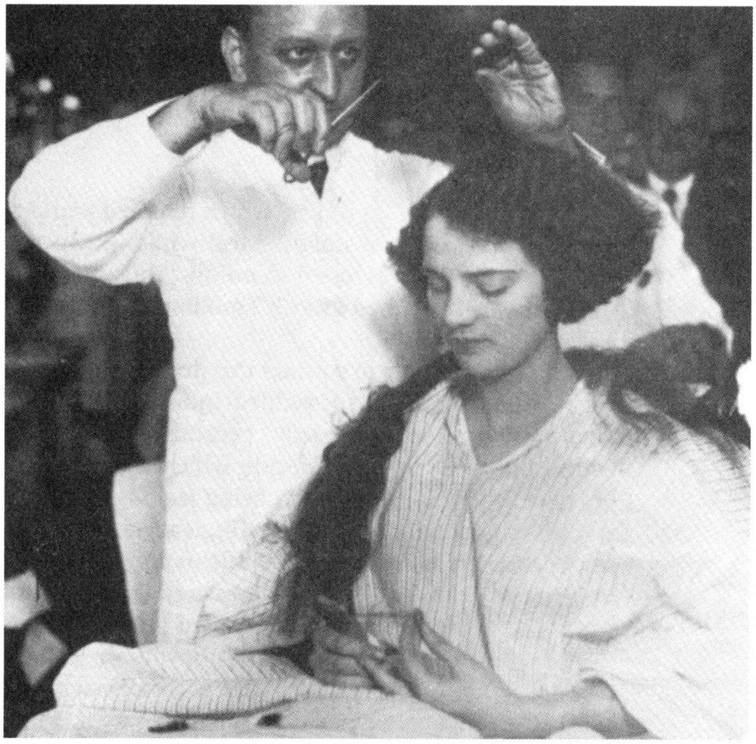

The "bob" symbolized the breezy independence of the 1920s woman.

control. Abortion rates also grew. New York City was the site of a thriving abortion clinic industry protected by payoffs to police and politicians. It has been estimated that there were almost one million criminal abortions each year, with perhaps as many as 50,000 deaths.

The apparent liberation of women in the Twenties was, in reality, severely limited. The "new woman" used her increased sexuality to find a husband, rather than to follow an emancipated life style. Far from identifying with other women, as Progressive-era feminists had, she regarded them as potential competitors and avoided the traditional female friendships. Same-sex relationships declined in the race to attract the opposite sex. Colleges increasingly began to prepare women for their appropriate roles. Business and home economics emerged as new fields for male and female specialization. New courses with titles like, "Motherhood" and "The Family as an Economic Unit" encouraged traditional roles. In contrast to the earlier era when about half of women's college graduates never married, in the 1920s college women were marrying at increasingly earlier ages, often before they completed their degrees.

Most women willingly abandoned being flappers to become wives and mothers. The responsibility of keeping "the thrill in marriage" rested with the wife. Advice manuals sternly informed women that marriage was their "vocation." Only marriage could satisfy all their needs, and any outside activities could pose a danger. Women's magazines exhorted them to reject careers and devote themselves to run-

Margaret Higgins Sanger was the founder of the American Birth Control League (1921).

A 1920 flapper poses beside her roadster, December 1927.

ning the home. Dorothy Dix, a widely syndicated columnist, informed her readers, "A man's wife is the show window where he exhibits the measure of his achievement." The first edition of Emily Post's *Etiquette* appeared in 1923 to advise the newly prosperous about proper behavior. "Infant and Child Care," the most widely read government publication, disseminated Dr. John Watson's behaviorist theories on raising children. Children were to be fed strictly by the clock and taught that crying would be rigorously ignored. Anxious wives and mothers could relieve anxieties by following the French guru, Coue, reciting twenty times a day, "Every day, in every way, I am getting better and better."

Women could also fulfill their roles by becoming avid consumers. Even flappers were defined by the products they purchased like silk stockings, cosmetics, ready-made clothing, and cigarettes. Advertisers stressed that household appliances, canned goods, and other products would "liberate" women from "constant drudgery." Toastmaster trumpeted, "The Toaster that FREED 465,000 homes." Modern studies have demonstrated that most of the new conveniences did not cut time spent in housework because of increasing demands for cleanliness.

Unmarried women did continue to work while waiting to find husbands. Some young married women attempted to combine careers and marriage for the first time. The numbers of working women increased, although their proportion in the work force remained the same. More women entered lower levels of the business world as office clerks, secretaries, switchboard operators, and saleswomen. The more than forty thousand beauty parlors, which opened in the decade, provided a new vocational option. Protective progressive measures that limited women's working hours and regulated conditions added to male/female income gaps by making women less desirable employees. Wage gaps between men and women increased. Working-class women, the majority of whom were immigrants or blacks, continued to labor at dismally low levels of pay.

While more educated women became professionals, they surged into traditionally female "service" professions, such as teacher and librarian. Social work, a new profession, began to replace upper-class settlement house volunteers. By the end of the 1920s, there were twenty-five thousand trained social workers, largely women. Male professions increasingly closed ranks against women. With strict quotas on female applicants and the refusal of most hospitals to appoint women interns, the number of female physicians fell by one-third. The proportion of women graduate students also declined as a result of tighter quotas. The press celebrated such examples of female achievement as women in aviation, like Amelia Earhart, and successful entrepreneurs, like Helena Rubenstein. These, however, were exceptions, rather than the vanguard of a new era.

Suffragists had believed that the passage of the Nineteenth Amendment, granting women the right to vote, would permanently transform American politics. After some mild efforts to win the expected "women's vote," the political parties quickly realized that no voting bloc existed for "women's issues." Women seemed to vote just as men did. (The "gender gap" would not appear until much later.) Feminist reform groups of the Progressive era languished or disappeared. Alice Paul and her National Woman's Party continued the struggle by proposing an Equal Rights Amendment to the Constitution in 1923. She attracted few supporters and quickly got into conflict with those who favored protective laws for women. Most younger women were turned off by both the equal rights and social reform branches of feminism. They associated feminism with loneliness and spinsterhood, not the "fun" of the brave new era. An article in *Harper's* in 1927 noted that young women felt contempt for those "who antagonize men with their constant clamor about maiden names, equal rights, woman's place in the world, and many another cause."

LEISURE TIME AND AMERICAN CULTURE

A popular song of the Twenties proclaimed, "'Aint We got Fun!" This reflected the image of a decade in which spending on amusement and recreation rose by 300 percent at a time when prices of other

Alice Paul and her National Woman's Party compaigned for an equal rights amendment to the Constitution.

things remained relatively stable. White collar workers, whose numbers were growing, generally had two days a week off and received annual vacations. Even industrial workers saw their workweek decline to five-and-a-half days. The availability of increased leisure time led city dwellers, in particular, on a frantic search for "fun" and escape. The United States became the entertainment leader of the world.

There seemed to be an unending appetite for fads and "ballyhoo." New games and activities attracted middle class families with increased incomes. Mah-jong, a tile game imported from China, became the rage of middle class women. The crossword puzzle craze launched Simon and Schuster, which became one of the nation's major publishing houses. Some thirty thousand miniature golf courses were built to accommodate the new enthusiasts of this activity. Camping became the most popular vacation activity, causing visits to national parks to rise from 5 million to 40 million per year. The new Miss America contest helped revive the fortunes of Atlantic City. Daring dances, like the Charleston and Black Bottom, attracted "Flaming Youth." The marathon dance mania tested the health of many. For some strange reason, people liked to stand around and watch others dance for endless days and nights until the dancers dropped from exhaustion or even heart attacks. "Shipwreck" Kelly introduced a particularly silly fad, flagpole sitting. The sitter would perch on top of a flagpole for as many as ten days, as thousands looked on.

The Movies

Mass entertainment was provided in many forms. Vaudeville shows drew family audiences with magic, animal, and juggling acts; song and dance performers; and, most of all, comedy that rested heavily on ethnic and racial stereotypes. As popular as vaudeville was, the extraordinary growth of the motion picture industry rapidly surpassed its appeal. The new industry was, in the words of one of its pioneers, a "Marvel of science, mirror of art, product of the ingenuity of man . . . . You are King in the Land of Mechanical Wonders . . . . You are great. You are the agent of the age . . . ."

Enormous crowds flocked to the movies. From 1927-29, weekly movie attendance was estimated at 110 million when the total population was 120 million and weekly church attendance was 60 million. People could find refuge from their daily lives in ornate movie "palaces." In the big cities these dream palaces had crystal chandeliers, plush carpets, velvet-covered seats, huge organs, even stuffed peacocks and stars glittering on ceilings. In smaller towns the movie theater was often the most recognizable building. Since it was expected that everyone in a community would go at least once a week, some three or four times, it was not uncommon for a town of ten thousand to have a theater that seated three thousand.

Comedy predominated in the era of the silent film, an intensely visual medium. Charlie Chaplin, the tramp-clown, was the most famous and best loved star of the age. His comedy satirized middle class pretension and materialism. There were other great slapstick comics like Buster Keaton, Harold Lloyd, and "Fatty" Arbuckle. (Fatty was the victim of the

The first Miss America was Margeret Gorman of Washington D. C. crowned in 1921.

first great Hollywood sex scandal and was driven from films despite a jury acquittal in the death of a "starlet.")

Sexuality quickly became a potent draw. Clara Bow, the "It girl," replaced Mary Pickford, the more Victorian "America's sweetheart," as the leading female star. Lurid ads promoted films with titles like, *Forbidden Fruit, Ladies of Pleasure, The Golden Bed*, and *Women Who Give*. These promised, "beautiful jazz babies, midnight revels, petting parties in the purple dawn" and "pleasure-mad daughters, sensation-craving mothers . . . ." When women's clubs complained, Cecil B. DeMille, the most influential film director, switched to Biblical spectacles like *The Ten Commandments*. There, he managed to find a Biblical setting for his sexual revelry.

In 1927 filmmaking was revolutionized. Warner Brothers, a film company whose fortunes seemed to be declining, released the first full-length feature film with sound, *The Jazz Singer*. The film was a tremendous hit, despite the warnings of critics that Hollywood was self-destructing by eliminating "the soul of the film—its eloquent and vital silence . . . ." The public formed long lines to see the "talkies" and broke into applause when they ended. The increase in Warner Brother profits from $30,000 to $17 million led other companies to follow suit. Some of the old stars were destroyed when their voices or accents were unsuitable to their images. New stars, like Greta Garbo, Gary Cooper, and Jean Harlow, were discovered. Mickey Mouse made his debut in 1928 in a short film by the young Walt Disney. Movies were more popular than ever as Hollywood offered "its great bargain sale of five and ten cent lusts and dreams," in the words of John Dos Passos.

Walt Disney left behind an enduring legacy.

Radio

Americans were willing to pay well to avoid boredom. Despite its tinny tones, the Gramophone enabled the listener to crank a handle and dance to popular music or even enjoy the soaring notes of Enrico Caruso (probably the most popular opera singer ever). The radio extended these pleasures. "Tin Pan Alley" in New York became the center of a burgeoning songwriting industry featuring such composers as Irving Berlin, the son of immigrants, and Cole Porter, the sophisticated WASP (White, Anglo-Saxon Protestant). People could now enjoy the music of the big bands on a regular basis. They could thrill to the play-by-play calls of baseball games and the blow-by-blow descriptions of boxing matches. They could learn election results and hear speeches by political leaders. (Franklin Roosevelt was the first American president to understand this potential.)

The phenomenon began in 1920 when KDKA in Pittsburgh, the first commercial station, transmitted news of Harding's election. In 1921 a Newark station broadcast the Giants' win over the Yankees in the World Series. By 1922, there were 576 licensed stations. They began hiring announcers whose rich syrupy voices were equally comfortable introducing variety programs or reporting sports spectacles or major disasters. The first network, the National Broadcasting Company (NBC), began in 1926. The Columbia Broadcasting System (CBS) followed in 1927. Each attempted to outdo the other in its appeal to the largest possible number of listeners.

Few enterprises have succeeded as rapidly. Radio sales had increased from $1 million in 1920 to $400 million in 1925. Radio's reach transcended class and regional boundaries. A 1929 presidential commission reported, "On the roof of practically every tenement house on the lower East Side numerous radio antennae are in evidence." By 1930, 40 percent of American homes owned radios. Advertisers soon realized the potential of having their messages reach millions of homes. They began to sponsor programs where their "commercials" could be repeated over and over again.

Like the movies, radio contributed to the standardization of American culture, surmounting the divisions in American society. Throughout the nation, families followed serials like "The Green Hornet." Housewives never missed "Portia Faces Life" and other daily "soaps." "Amos'n' Andy" was the most popular show of all. It ran five nights a week for 15 minutes. It followed the adventures of two black stereotypes who were proprietors of the "Fresh-Air Taxicab Company of America, Incorpulated." In the tradition of stage "burnt-cork" humor two whites wrote and acted the parts. Everybody seemed to listen and rearrange schedules to hear the show. Even President Hoover was a buff, inviting its stars to the White House. Pepsodent toothpaste, the show's sponsor, realized millions in sales.

Radio had brought the country together, but not everyone applauded the results. Lee DeForest, whose invention of the vacuum tube made the whole thing possible, was dismayed by what had happened to his "child." "You have debased this child" he complained, "you have sent him out on the streets . . . to collect money from all and sundry for hubba hubba and audio jitterbug. You have made him a laughing stock to intelligence . . . ."

In 1927, the image of Herbert Hoover's face was transmitted from Washington to New York on a tiny screen. Television had made its first tentative American appearance. Its challenge to both radio and movies remained in the future.

Mass Sports

The emergence of the modern consumer culture, a result of rising incomes, led to the growth of organized sports. Sports mania gripped almost every city in the nation. Organized sports offered cities and groups within them a feeling of community and special identity. At a time of the ascendancy of technology and the assembly line, Americans yearned for the dramatic and unpredictable.

Millions jammed parks and stadiums to view athletic events. Intercollegiate football contests brought in $21 million by the late 1920s. In the era of the revived Klan, Catholics in the cities became fervent fans of the "Fighting Irish" of Notre Dame and their renowned coach, Knute Rockne. The attendance of 130,000 at the Dempsey-Tunney heavyweight championship fight in 1926 broke all records.

Above all, baseball became "the National Pastime." The sport had been seriously shaken by the "Black Sox" scandal that broke in 1920 and pushed every other story off the nation's front pages. It was revealed that eight Chicago White Sox players had taken bribes to fix the 1919 World Series. The scandal caused the reorganization of major league baseball through the appointment of Judge Kennesaw Mountain Landis as commissioner with unlimited powers. (Despite the subsequent acquittal of the players, Landis banned all of them from organized baseball for life.) Landis gave baseball a new image of integrity. (The movies followed this successful example by appointing a "czar" to censor films.) The sport also gained a new legal foundation when the Supreme Court ruled that it was exempt from antitrust laws. Baseball's rise in popularity was even more attributable to the phenomenal rise in batting averages and home runs. In 1923, a record 300,000 fans watched the New York Yankees defeat the New York Giants in six games.

Large numbers of Americans used their added leisure time to participate in sports. Tennis was the favorite of many. Golf became an obsession for millions. By 1927, there were five thousand golf courses, most of them built in the 1920s.

Currents of Culture

The growth of universal secondary education meant that most American adults read more regularly. Many new magazines appeared in the Twenties, several with circulations over a million. *Reader's Digest* and *Time* were among the most successful. Intellectuals were more likely to read H.L. Mencken's *American Mer-*

cury and his attacks on the materialistic middle class whom he called the "booboisie." The sophisticated *New Yorker* may well have been the best-written of all. Book sales also increased enormously as the newly founded Book-of-the-Month Club and the Literary Guild competed with the quaint old-fashioned book store. The number of new book titles doubled in the decade.

The anguish felt by many in the developing intellectual class vividly demonstrated the split between the "two Americas." They rejected both the old rural fundamentalist values and the newer middle class embrace of materialism and self-satisfaction. Many felt so alienated that they fled the country for Paris where they were known as "the Lost Generation." Ironically, this was a decade of unequaled creativity.

There was probably more outstanding writing in the Twenties than in any other single decade of American history. The decade began with the 1920 publication of Sinclair Lewis' *Main Street*, "the most sensational event in twentieth-century American publishing history." The novel, an unsparing portrait of the bleakness and conformity of small-town middle America, sold an astounding 3 million copies. *Babbitt* (1922), Lewis's next novel, was an even greater success. Babbitt, the "hero" of the book, became a synonym for the small businessman who unthinkingly embraces the middle class obsession with material success. F. Scott Fitzgerald became the symbol of the lost generation in his reckless life style, as well as his novels. His works depicted "flaming youth" and their "vast carelessness" that would ultimately destroy "the greatest, gaudiest spree in history."

Ernest Hemingway was probably the most important of this group of American writers. His spare, uncluttered prose, in books like *A Farewell to Arms*, perfectly captured the disillusioned spirit of the times. He coupled a rejection of the moral values of war with a fascination with its violence. Eugene O'Neill was the towering playwright of the era. His passionate plays lifted American theater from silly melodrama to worldwide prominence. American fiction has since followed many of the themes of the Twenties—rejection of small-town mores, preference of the young to the old, preoccupation with sex and violence.

The other arts also expressed the creativity of the 1920s. Adventurous architects transformed cities with ever more daring skyscrapers. Artists, like Georgia O'Keeffe, boldly experimented with audacious colors and forms. Serious composers drew upon American folk music and the rich tradition of black jazz. (George Gershwin's *Rhapsody in Blue* was the best example of the latter.) Despite their cynicism, most American writers and artists reflected rather than rejected the dynamism of the era.

Heroes and Other Celebrities

As the Victorian value system continued to erode, individuals felt increasingly powerless in a complex and bureaucratic society. They longed for heroes who had achieved individual fame outside the "system." That explains the phenomenal popularity of Lindbergh. The media helped create other celebrities who quickly surpassed the traditional heroes of business or politics. The media in a consumer society helped create these "stars" of movies and sports.

In their films, Hollywood heroes defeated sword-wielding villains or saved innocent whites from "savage" Indian attacks. In the nineteenth century theater, heroes had been depicted as winning the rich man's daughter through good character. In silent films, Rudolph Valentino prevailed through his personal allure. The early movie stars earned enormous salaries and lived glamorous lives, promoted by the new profession of press agent and relentlessly covered by magazines and newspapers.

Rudolph Valentino, star of *The Sheik*, was the undisputed male sex symbol. Men throughout the nation attempted to emulate his appeal by growing sideburns, greasing their hair, and batting "bedroom eyes" at their girlfriends. When the "Great Lover" died suddenly at the age of 31 in 1926, his funeral caused a frenzied outbreak of mass hysteria. A famous actress arrived with four thousand roses and a song solemnly announced, "There's a New Star in Heaven Tonight."

Just two days after the great Valentino delirium in New York, enormous crowds turned out to cheer for 18-year-old Gertrude Ederle. "Trudy," as she was affectionately called, was the first woman to swim the English Channel and had done so in a time that broke the old male record by two hours. The parade in her honor was the greatest ever seen in the city, surpassing Pershing's reception at the end of the war. (Lindbergh's welcome would soon overtake Trudy's ceremony.)

Above all, sports idols dominated the public eye and heart in the 1920s. "Never before, or since, have so many transcendent performers arisen contemporaneously in every field of competitive athletics as graced the 1920s," according to two long-time sports journalists. Part of the acclaim was due to the efforts of public relations men and the exaggerated images created by sports reporters and radio broadcasters. A good deal, however, was the result of the public need for heroes who projected images of power and immediate success.

The 1920s was the "Golden Age" of American boxing. Tex Rickard, the "King of Sports Promoters," understood the public craving for heroes. He found his man in Jack, "the Giant-Killer" Dempsey. Dempsey was quickly bringing in million-dollar gates. He loved his life as a celebrity with its movie contracts, product endorsements, and vaudeville performances. The two fights pitting Dempsey, the ruthless brawler, against Gene Tunney, the "scientific" boxer, were each dubbed, "The Battle of the Century." Public excitement was so great that approximately 60 million Americans listened to the rematch on eighty-two radio stations. Seven collapsed from heart attacks during the seventh round with its legendary "long count." Tunney, the victor, an educated man who relied on defensive finesse, did not fit the public image of hero. Boxing's appeal declined.

The media found the perfect football player in Red Grange, the "Galloping Ghost." His specialty was the long run, often culminating in a touchdown. He quickly capitalized on his fame at the University of Illinois by hiring an agent and turning professional in the middle of his senior year. Professional football, up to that point, had received little respect since it was associated with immigrants and working-class people. Grange was able to attract huge crowds to the Chicago Bears' games and made enormous sums of money from various endorsements. "Kid," Babe Ruth warned him, "don't believe everything they write about you."

The great British playwright, George Bernard Shaw, supposedly once asked, "Who is this Baby Ruth? And what does she do?" There were few Americans in the 1920s who would have asked such a question. Babe Ruth was "The Sports Hero" of the era. (Only Lindbergh exceeded his popularity.) Ruth represented the ultimate fulfillment of the American dream of success; the natural, unrestrained man who revolutionized baseball with his power. He had overcome a grim and neglected childhood to rise, by the age of 19, to the big league Boston Red Sox, first as an outstanding pitcher, then a great hitter. The high-living Red Sox owner, needing money to finance a Broadway show, sold Ruth to the New York Yankees. (The Red Sox subsequent lack of post-season success became known as "the curse of the Bambino.") In his first year with the Yankees, 1920, Ruth hit 54 home runs, more than any other **team**. The public responded to his awesome power with great enthusiasm. His mammoth blasts seemed to challenge

"Red" Grange of the University of Illinois

Babe Ruth was adored by millions of baseball fans. Between 1926 and 1931, Ruth averaged 50.3 home runs a year.

the dominant world of the organization man and scientific rationality. He loved to play the game, and he also loved incredible quantities of bootleg liquor, junk food, and casual sex. The public forgave his excesses and adored his love of children and visits to their hospital beds. They marveled at his childlike delight. Yankee attendance doubled. In 1923 they were able to move into their own ball park, Yankee Stadium, "the house that Ruth built." Newspapers all over the nation ran a syndicated box, "What Ruth Did Today." Home run production and batting averages soared throughout the game and, with them, public excitement. In 1927 Ruth hit 60 home runs on what was probably the best team ever, "Murderer's Row." Not only did Ruth revive and save the game of baseball, he remains the nation's premier athletic hero to this day.

Public obsession with celebrities often extended to the far-from-heroic. Organized crime kings, like Al Capone, received celebrity status through images of forceful success. The press fueled popular fascination with the marriage of 51-year-old "Daddy" Browning and his 15-year-old bride, "Peaches." Their breakup even made the front page of the normally sober *New York Times*. Clarence Darrow got as much publicity for saving thrill killers Leopold and Loeb from execution as he later did for the Scopes trial. Jimmy Walker, the flamboyant mayor of New York, became a folk hero by spending all his time and energy living the good life, writing songs, selling favors, visiting speakeasies, and flaunting his mistress. He won reelection overwhelmingly against Fiorello LaGuardia (who would later become the city's greatest mayor). The showman, Earl Carroll, gave the most famous party of the time, which was to culminate in a champagne bath by a nude chorus girl with the guests drinking champagne from her tub. When she fainted, the party ended, but the publicity led to Carroll being sentenced to a year in jail for serving illegal liquor.

The press fed the national fixation on sensational crimes. In the Hall-Mills case, a well-respected minister was found shot to death with a married church choir singer at his side. Passionate love letters were discovered near them. Despite frenzied newspaper coverage by over three hundred reporters, the jury acquitted Mrs. Hall and her brothers. In the Snyder-Gray case, Ruth Snyder and her married lover bludgeoned her husband to death. The sleazy little murder vied with Lindbergh's flight for headlines in 1927. The public was startled that such an act could take place in a middle class home by a woman, "so like the woman across the street that many an American husband was soon haunted by the realization that she also bore an embarrassing resemblance to the woman across the breakfast table," as one observer noted. The grim picture of Ruth Snyder dead in the electric chair was a widely displayed cautionary image.

THE END OF AN ERA

The most discussed event in college sports in 1929 may well have been the emblem of the end of the "Roaring Twenties." At the annual Rose Bowl game, when Georgia fumbled the football, Roy Riegel, California's center, picked it up. Eluding his opponents, twisting away from tackles, Riegel ran for 60 breathtaking yards towards the wrong goal line! (One of his own team mates finally intercepted him at the three-yard line.) "Wrong Way" Riegel, one of the "heroes" of 1929, symbolized, perhaps, the direction in which the nation was also heading.

The Election of 1928

Coolidge had been even more gloomy than usual towards the end of his term. The strange death of his son from a foot infection devastated him. On vacation in the Black Hills of South Dakota, he summoned reporters to a press conference. There, he handed each a slip of paper on which was typed: "I do not choose to run for President in nineteen twenty-eight." He offered not a single word of explanation to the baffled reporters.

Few elections in American history have more graphically demonstrated the divisions in American society than the election of 1928: Rural America vs. Big City; "Wet" vs. "Dry"; Protestant vs. Catholic Irish. Both candidates were self-made men, but they were "as far apart as Pilsner and Coca Cola." Secretary of Commerce Herbert Hoover easily won the Republican nomination. A Quaker from a small town in Iowa, Hoover was orphaned at the age of ten. He was the embodiment of the ideals of self-reliance and rugged individualism so admired at the time. He had worked his way through Stanford University to become a millionaire mining engineer. Before entering the cabinet, he had dedicated his life to public service and humanitarian activities as wartime food administrator and leader in food relief efforts abroad. In contrast to Harding and Coolidge, he was considered somewhat progressive, a believer in the president as leader of a modern economy. He was a strong advocate of the cooperation of government and business.

The Democrats turned to Al Smith. Smith, the son of Irish immigrants, had gone all the way from a Lower East Side tenement in New York to the governor's mansion. He was the first Roman Catholic ever to run for the presidency. Although personally conservative, he had amassed a record of effective progressive reforms as governor. He was also an outspoken opponent of Prohibition. Smith launched a spirited campaign throughout the country but turned off many small town voters with his New York City accent, style, and wisecracks. ("My opponents couldn't get elected on a laundry ticket.") As a Roman Catholic and a "wet," he represented everything rural Americans believed was evil in a rapidly changing urban America.

The intensity of the anti-Catholic campaign that was launched against him stunned Smith. A flood of pamphlets and newspapers swept across the South

Herbert Hoover, the Republican candidate, stressed continued economic prosperity.

Al Smith campaigned from a train platform in his familiar brown derby.

and other areas, claiming that Smith was building a tunnel to connect to the Vatican; that the Pope would set up a White House office; that Protestant children would be forced to go to Catholic schools. Eleanor Roosevelt later wrote, "If I needed anything to show me what prejudice can do to the intelligence of human beings, that campaign was the best lesson I could have had." (Thirty-two years later, John F. Kennedy would again have to face the forces of anti-Catholic intolerance.)

The conclusive issue of the campaign was undoubtedly the "Coolidge prosperity" for which Republicans took the credit. "We in America today," Hoover announced, "are nearer to the final triumph over poverty than ever before in the history of any land. The poor-house is vanishing from among us." The Republican ad campaign promising "A chicken in every pot, a car in every garage," was topped by some enthusiasts who confidently predicted *two* chickens and *two* cars. In the resulting sweep, Hoover had 21 million votes to Smith's 15 million, cracking the solid Democratic South and even carrying Smith's own New York. Franklin D. Roosevelt, a reluctant candidate for governor of New York, was one of a small number of leading Democrats to survive the Republican landslide. There were a few other positive signs for the Democrats. So many more people voted, that Smith received twice as many votes as Davis had in 1924. What was more important, Smith carried all twelve of the nation's largest cities whose significance would increase in the future.

Calvin Coolidge left office convinced that he had achieved his goals. "The country," he informed Congress, "can regard the present with satisfaction, and anticipate the future with optimism." As he departed, many people firmly believed that he was one of the greatest presidents ever. That view did not last a year.

The Crash of an Era

Despite rising signs of problems, the Coolidge boom continued into 1929. Much of its momentum depended on spiraling speculation. As one observer noted, "Everybody speculated, everybody believed 'prosperity' was eternal . . . ." From newspapers and business journals, to Wall Street, and even to university theorists, speculation was widely defended. It was argued that Columbus and the western pioneers who built the nation had been speculators and even "Christ himself took a chance." Greed had become the defining feature of the era. Stories, largely untrue, circulated about scrubwomen now riding to work in chauffeured limousines, fueling the frenzy to get rich as quickly, and with as little effort, as possible. The 1925-6 Florida land boom was a cautionary tale ignored by most Americans. Land prices had risen to dizzying heights as lots in swamp areas sold for $20,000 or more. Miami grew so fast that it was known as "the Magic City." Then, in September 1926, a hurricane devastated the area, leaving four hundred dead and fifty thousand homeless. The land boom collapsed, leading to thousands of bankruptcies, foreclosures, and shattered dreams. By 1928, Miami was one of the most inexpensive cities in America.

Few people learned a lesson from the Florida disaster. In August 1929, a millionaire industrialist, in an interview in *Ladies Home Journal*, declared, "I am firm in my belief that anyone not only can be rich but ought to be rich." He recommended investment in the Stock Market as the means to achieve that goal. Many joined in the speculative frenzy known as the "Great Bull Market." Contrary to popular myth, the ordinary American was not involved. Most shareholders came from the wealthy or urban upper middle class. New securities, in the words of one historian, "were manufactured almost like cakes of soap" to make quick profits from their sale. Stock prices soared through the stratosphere. In four years the market value of all stocks had risen from $27 billion to $87 billion in paper value. Brokers willingly lent speculators as much as 75 percent of a stock's price, leading to increased buying on "margin." By 1929, brokers' loans had risen to $8.5 billion. Mellon's tax cuts for the rich gave them more money to speculate on the market. By the fall of 1929, the average stock was selling at more than 100 times its earnings value.

The Crash finally came on "Black Thursday," October 24, 1929. Panicky selling orders jammed the lines of the Stock Exchange, but it was difficult to find buyers. Leading bankers collected a pool to buy millions of dollars worth of stocks to instill confidence in the market. For a few days, it seemed to work. "The worst is over . . . . General conditions are good," one leading broker announced. On "Black Tuesday," October 29, the bottom fell out. A guard described the bedlam on the Stock Exchange floor: "They roared like a lot of lions and tigers . . . . It was like a bunch of crazy men. Every once in a while when Radio or Steel would take another tumble, you'd see some poor devil collapse and fall to the floor." The panic demolished $30 billion in market stock value. By mid-November, stock prices were half their October highs. Some millionaires, like Joseph Kennedy and John D. Rockefeller, began buying stocks at bargain prices. "Sure he's buying," said comedian Eddie Cantor of Rockefeller, "Who else has any money left?" Many of the "new" rich, like Cantor and Jack Dempsey, America's first millionaire athlete, lost their entire fortunes. Will Rogers, the era's most beloved humorist, complained, "You stand in line to get a window to jump out of."

Many people believed that the Crash was a necessary correction that would not change American life very much. At the end of 1929, the *New York Times* chose the expedition of Richard Byrd to the South Pole as the most memorable event of the past year. As for the economy, the paper's editorial noted with relief, "the patient" was on the road to a complete recovery. Henry Luce of *Time* magazine, picked this moment to launch his new business magazine, *Fortune*, convinced that the "business slump" would last no longer than a year. President Hoover proclaimed that there was no reason to panic: "The fundamental business of this country, that is, production and distribution of commodities is on a sound and prosperous basis." He was wrong.

The market crash would not have led to the Great Depression had there not been fundamental flaws in the economy of the 1920s. We have seen that farmers, textile workers, and miners were already in a virtual depression. Wages of workers lagged far behind profits. Tax policies favoring the rich had increased the uneven distribution of income. (By 1929, the 24,000 richest families had incomes three times as

Crowds gathered on Wall Street in response to the stock market crash of October 1929.

great as the 6 million poorest.) Much of the added income of the wealthy went to luxurious living and speculation. (The income of the wealthiest 1 percent had risen 75 percent in the decade.) Remarkable gains in productivity led to a need for increasing consumption. But demand was leveling off, and businesses refused to give workers wage increases that might have created new consumers for their products.

Spending on durable goods, like housing and automobiles, began a precipitous decline. By the end of 1928, the key construction industry had gone into a serious descent. Automobile sales seemed to have reached their "saturation" point. By August of 1929, automobile factories began laying off thousands of workers. One culprit was installment buying. Millions of American families were deeply in debt for the first time in American history. While they carried much less debt than people do today, they were far more worried about it. Noticing the slowdown in the economy and the market crash, they felt particularly vulnerable and further cut down on spending. The resulting 10 percent decline in consumer spending led to further reduction in production and layoff of workers. These, in turn, had still less to spend and the cycle continued its downward spiral. Unlike Europe, the United States had no unemployment insurance to cushion the blow.

Other factors also helped cause the Depression. The banking system was shaky at best. Rural banks, dependent on farmers, failed at alarming rates (1,000 in 1926 alone). Even stronger urban banks were caught up in the prevailing obsession with risky speculation. When stock prices disintegrated, brokers demanded that their loans be repaid, and buyers tried to remove their savings from banks. Bankers, in a bind for cash, called in loans to brokers. The banking system collapsed under the burden of impossible-to-meet obligations. European economic difficulties, which were worsened by higher American tariffs, also contributed to the depression. High tariffs destroyed foreign trade and left America with no place to sell its overprotected goods. The unwillingness of the government to regulate unchecked speculation or dubious banking practices added to the problems. Most experts firmly believed that the business cycle was an inevitable part of capitalism. They waited for the depression to "bottom out" and the cycle to rise again.

CONCLUSION

The Twenties have been labeled the "era of excess," as a result of its emphasis on consumerism, entertainment, speculation, and "fun." It was also a genuinely "new era" in American life, characterized by mass production, technological change, bureaucratization, and the rise of cities and suburbs. In grappling with the forces of change, the nation was bitterly divided. The old rural Protestant America struggled with the new urban secular society. Prejudices and intolerance surfaced amidst the strains but so did a rich cultural dynamism. Despite the huge national identity crisis, a modern society emerged. As the decade ended, however, some observers worried that the system, so carefully constructed, was nothing more than a house of cards. "May we not fear," the critic Edmund Wilson wrote at the end of 1929, "that what this year has broken down is . . . the capitalist system itself?—and that even with the best will in the world, it may be impossible for capitalism to guarantee not merely social justice, but even security and order." As the nation entered the Thirties in the grip of the most devastating depression in American history, many Americans felt similar misgivings about the nation's future.

Chronology

1915 Ku Klux Klan is revived, reaches heights in 1920s

1917-1925 Great migration of Southern blacks into Northern industrial cities

1920 Eighteenth Amendment, prohibiting alcoholic beverages, goes into effect
Nineteenth Amendment, granting women suffrage, ratified
KDKA, first commercial radio station, begins broadcasting in Pittsburgh
Sinclair Lewis publishes *Main Street*; F. Scott Fitzgerald, *This Side of Paradise*
Warren G. Harding elected president on pledge of "return to normalcy"

1921 First Miss America beauty pageant held in Atlantic City, New Jersey

1922 High tariff rates restored
Sinclair Lewis publishes *Babbitt;* T. S. Eliot, *The Wasteland*
Supreme Court declares child-labor law unconstitutional

1923 Equal Rights Amendment written by Alice Paul
Harding dies
Calvin Coolidge becomes president
Teapot Dome and other scandals revealed

1924 National Origins Act passed, imposing quotas on immigration
Calvin Coolidge re-elected president

1925 Scopes trial on teaching of evolution takes place in Tennessee
F. Scott Fitzgerald publishes *The Great Gatsby*
Ku Klux Klan scandal in Indiana destroys its power

1926 Ernest Hemingway publishes *The Sun Also Rises*; Langston Hughes, *The Weary Blues*
Further reduction in tax rates for high incomes demonstrates "trickle down" theory

1927 *The Jazz Singer*, first sound motion picture, released
Henry Ford retools and introduces Model A
After long struggle, Italian immigrant anarchists, Sacco and Vanzetti, are executed
Charles Lindbergh completes first successful solo transatlantic flight
Babe Ruth hits 60 home runs

1928 Herbert Hoover defeats Alfred E. Smith, first Catholic candidate for president
Walt Disney releases first Mickey Mouse cartoon

1929 Robert and Helen Lynd publish *Middletown*, pioneering sociological study
William Faulkner, *The Sound and the Fury*
Ernest Hemingway, *A Farewell to Arms*
Stock market crashes (October 24)

SUGGESTED READINGS

Frederick Lewis Allen, *Only Yesterday* (1931).
Lois Banner, *American Beauty* (1983).
Loren Baritz, ed., *The Culture of the Twenties* (1970).
Edith L. Blumhofer, *Aimee Semple McPherson* (1993).
Ellen Chesler, *Woman of Valor: Margaret Sanger and the Birth Control Movement in America* (1992).
Stanley Coben, *Rebellion Against Victorianism: The Impetus for Cultural Change in 1920s America* (1991).
Robert Creamer, *Babe* (1974).
Kenneth S. Davis, *The Hero: Charles A. Lindbergh* (1959).
Ann Douglas, *Terrible Honesty: Mongrel Manhattan in the 1920s* (1995).
Susan J. Douglas, *Inventing American Broadcasting* (1987).
Lynn Dumenil, *The Modern Temper: American Culture and Society in the 1920s* (1995).
Paula Fass, *The Damned and the Beautiful: American Youth in the 1920s* (1977).
James J. Flink, *The Car Culture* (1975).
Neal Gabler, *An Empire of Their Own: How the Jews Invented Hollywood* (1988).
John Kenneth Galbraith, *The Great Crash, 1929* (1955).
Ray Ginger, *Six Days or Forever?* (1958).
Allen Guttmann, *A Whole New Ball Game* (1988).
Ellis W. Hawley, *The Great War and the Search for a Modern Order* (1979).
John Higham, *Strangers in the Land: Patterns of American Nativism, 1860-1925* (1955).
Kenneth T. Jackson, *The Ku Klux Klan in the City, 1915-1930* (1967).
William Leach, *Land of Desire: Merchants, Power and the Rise of a New American Culture* (1993).
Daniel L. Lewis, *When Harlem Was in Vogue* (1981).
Fred J. Macdonald, *Don't Touch That Dial: Radio Programming in American Life 1920-1960* (1979).
Nancy MacLean, *Behind the Mask of Chivalry: The Making of the Second Ku Klux Klan* (1994).
Daniel Pope, *The Making of Modern Advertising* (1983).
Joan Shelley Rubin, *The Making of Middlebrow Culture* (1971).
Francis Russell, *Tragedy in Dedham: The Story of the Sacco-Vanzetti Case* (1971).
___, *The Shadow of Blooming Grove* (1968).
Arthur M. Schlesinger Jr., *The Crisis of the Old Order* (1957).

Chapter Nineteen

THE DEPRESSION AND THE NEW DEAL

European immigrants eventually became assimilated, and once that process was complete, they quickly proved themselves to be "worthy "citizens," whose contributions were especially noteworthy in the nation's cultural and social life. One "immigrant" who gained such acclaim during the 1930s was motion picture director Fran Capra. Today, he is probably best remembered for his last successful picture, ***It's a Wonderful Life****, shown ever year at Christmas—sometimes in its new "colorized" version—to millions of American viewers. In the movie, George Bailey, a kind and compassionate small-town savings-and-loan officer (played by Jimmy Stewart, one of Capra's "regular" stars) is almost destroyed by a wealthy, greedy, and malicious banker. So distraught by his impending ruin, George was on the verge of committing suicide when he is visited by an angel who shows him what life would have been like in Bedford Falls—his town—had he never been born. Taking a page out of the Dicken's classic,* ***Mr Scooge****, which was also made into a movie in the 1930s, Capra shows George, accompanied by his angle/guide, wandering through a coarse, corrupt, degraded town as he realizes that his life does indeed have value. He returns to the real Bedford Falls to find that his family, friends, and neighbors have rallied together to rescue him from his financial woes and affirm his value to them and theirs to him.*

When ***It's a Wonderful Life*** *premiered, Frank Capra was already one of Hollywood's most popular and successful directors. Virtually every one of his 1930s films were critical and commercial successes. They had won two academy awards for best picture (and Capra himself won best director in 1934). Capra's artistic and creative talents were undoubtedly remarkable; equally impressive was his vision. His pictures were enthusiastically embraced by Depression-era Americans because Capra's personal social and political views resonated clearly with those of his fellow citizens as they struggled through a decade of unprecedented uncertainty and anguish.*

Capra, a Sicilian immigrant, came to the United States with his family in 1903. The Capras made their way to California where young Frank grew up. After working his way through college, Capra found a job in the still-young movie industry in his home state and eventually became a director of feature films. His great breakthrough came in 1934, with the romantic comedy, ***It Happened One Night****, which has since become a classic in that particularly film genre. The picture, starring Clark Gable and Claudette Colbert, won five Academy*

Awards, including best picture and best director. Over the next seven years, Capra built on that success by making a series of poignant sociopolitical commentary pictures, which helped to establish the director as a powerful voice of an old-fashioned vision of democracy and American life. Capra's pictures expressed his romantic notion of small town America and the virtuous and noble common man who came from such an environment, while simultaneously revealing his distaste for cities, his contempt for opportunistic politicians and demagogues, and his condemnation of what he considered the amoral (often immoral) capitalist marketplace. In ***Mr. Deeds Goes to Town,*** *(1936) a simple man from a small town inherits a large fortune, moves to the city, and—not liking the greed and dishonesty he finds there—gives the money away and moves back home. In* ***Mr. Smith Goes to Washington,*** *(1939), a decent man from a western state is elected to the U.S. Senate, refuses to join in the self-interested politics of Washington, and dramatically exposes the corruption and selfishness of his colleagues. The rugged Western's actor, Gary Cooper, played Mr. Deeds, while the epitome of small town innocence and virtue, Jimmy Stewart, played Mr. Smith. In 1941, as the United States was about to enter World War II, Capra made* ***Meet John Doe,*** *once again starring Gary Cooper. In the picture, Cooper plays an ordinary man manipulated by a fascist cartel to dupe the public on their behalf. He comes to his senses just in time and by threatening suicide, rallies ordinary people to turn against the evil plans of the fascists. He then disappears into the night.*

Capra was entirely conscious of the romantic populism that he brought to his pictures. "I would sing the songs of the working stiffs, of the short-changed Joes, the born poor, the afflicted," he once wrote, in an apparent allusion to one of his creative heroes, the great American chronicler through poetry of the common folk, Walt Whitman. "I would fight for their causes on the screens of the world." He was intensely patriotic, a characteristic of many successful immigrants, and he believed passionately that the United States stood for individual opportunity and was defined by the decency of ordinary people. He was not, he said (in an effort to distance himself from the communists) a "bleeding heart with an Olympian call to 'free the masses.'" Indeed, he loathed the term "the masses" and found it "insulting, degrading." He saw the people, rather, as a "collection of free individuals. . .each an island of human dignity."

When the United States entered World War II, Capra collaborated with the government (and the Walt Disney studios) to make a series of pictures designed to explain to new soldiers what the war was about—a series known as ***Why We Fight****. Capra contrasted the individualistic democracy of the American small town with the dark collectivism of the Nazis and Fascists. He poured into them all his skills as a filmmaker and his romantic, patriotic images.* ***It's a Wonderful Life****, released a year after the war, continued his evocation of the decency of ordinary people. In the decades that followed, Capra, although he was still a relatively young man, and although he continued to work, ceased to be an important force in American cinema. The sentimental populism and comic optimism—the two central themes of his 1930s pictures—no longer appealed to post-war audiences. Post-war filmmakers and their audiences wanted harder, more realistic movies, and thus Capra faded into motion picture obscurity by the 1960s. A romantic to the end, Capra was never fully able to adjust to the vagaries of the post-war film industry. In a time of crisis, however, Capra had helped his viewers find solace in his romantic vision of the American past—in the warmth and goodness of small towns and the decency of common folk.*

THE DEPRESSION

As discussed in the last chapter, the soaring hopes of the 1920s abruptly vanished with the October 1929 stock market crash. The decade of the 1930s thus became one of the most traumatic and critically important eras in the Republic's history. Indeed, many would conclude that after the Civil War, the Great Depression marked the second most pivotal crisis in the nation's history. However, under the leadership of Franklin Delano Roosevelt and his "New Dealers," the Republic met the crisis with unprecedented activism, ultimately changing the course of domestic history down to the present. Indeed, to many Americans the New Deal represented "The Third American Revolution"—as much a pivotal turning-point in the nation's history as Independence and the Civil War.

Herbert Hoover, the personification of the 1920s business ethos, was humiliatingly rejected by a desperate and disillusioned electorate in the 1932 presidential election. Under the leadership of his successor, FDR, the national government implemented bold, innovative programs and policies, which offered material and emotional relief to millions of suffering and distraught citizens. Perhaps more important than such solicitude was FDR's determination to create a new relationship between the federal government and the Republic's citizens. Included in that new dynamic was also a reformation of the executive branch of government. In many ways, as will be illustrated in this chapter, FDR, like his beloved cousin, Theodore Roosevelt, and like Abraham Lincoln and Andrew Jackson, will significantly augment the power, prestige, and expectations of that office. In many ways, FDR was the inaugurator of the modern presidency, establishing during his four terms much of what we expect from our presidents down to the present moment. FDR will set the criteria by which we will judge all future executives, and if they fall short of those standards or hopes, then, like Herbert Hoover and many others, they will be historically relegated to that most undistinguished category of being one term presidents.

In the end, as will be seen, the New Deal did not end the Great Depression; World War II ultimately did. However, FDR's and the New Deal's importance lies in the fact that from the 1930s on, the American people could turn to their government not only as the guarantor and protector of their liberties but as a source of assistance in time of need and provider of equal opportunities for all. In short, the New Deal laid the foundation for postwar liberalism (the welfare state), which as will be seen in later chapters, will become the new American creed, replacing by the 1960s the conservative, laissez faire business ethos (rugged individualism) that had dominated the American value system since the end of the Civil War. FDR and his New Dealers will make it the federal government's responsibility to henceforth ensure that all Americans would have a minimum standard of well-being during their lives.

President Herbert Hoover's belief in limited government hurt his programs to deal with the Depression.

HERBERT HOOVER

The Technocrat as President

At his 1929 inauguration, Herbert Hoover told the American public that, "We in American today are nearer to the final triumph over poverty than ever before in the history of any land. The poorhouse is vanishing among us." The nation had not yet reached that goal, he acknowledged, "but given a chance to go forward with the policies of the last eight years, we shall soon with the help of God be in sight of the day when poverty will be banished from this nation." Those words came back to haunt Hoover, for in eight short months after making that speech, the nation's economy began its declension, ultimately collapsing into the worse financial crisis in the Republic's history. Hoover and his reputation were among the first casualties, along with the reverence for business that had been the hallmark of the New Era.

In one of the cruelest ironies in twentieth-century United States history, Herbert Hoover was inaugurated president only eight months before the nation's greatest economic calamity struck. Coming into office in March 1929, Hoover possessed all the requisite credentials for a successful and popular tenure. He embodied the rags-to-riches ideal, having risen from poor orphaned beginnings to graduating from Stanford University with an engineering degree. By the age of thirty Hoover had become one of the world's most successful mining engineers. Before the United States' entry into the Great War, Hoover directed a private American relief agency that fed millions of civilian victims of a war-ravaged Europe. For his efforts, Hoover was acclaimed the "Great Humanitarian," and such status led Woodrow Wilson to name him head of the Food Administration once the United States entered the war. Under his directorship, the Food Administration was responsible for feeding and aiding in a variety of other ways hundreds of thousands of dispossessed postwar Europeans. As a reward for his achievements, Hoover was appointed Secretary of Commerce by the 1920 Republican victor, Warren G. Harding, and remained at that post until becoming president in 1928. Indeed, in an era of lackluster presidents with equally mediocre cabinets, Herbert Hoover was a paragon of professionalism and competence.

Because he favored efficiency and growth, Hoover thought of himself as a progressive, but his reluctance to use the government as an agency of change and reform alienated him from prewar progressives, still committed to the reform ethos of early twentieth-century progressivism. Having lived most of his adult life abroad, he had never even voted in a presidential election. Aware of his political limitations, Hoover confided to a friend: "I have no dread of the ordinary work of the presidency. What I do fear is the exaggerated idea that I am sort of superman, that no problem is beyond my capacity." He added prophetically, "If some unprecedented calamity should come upon the nation I would be sacrificed to the unreasoning disappointment of a people who expected too much."

Hoover's initial responses to the depression were clear and firm. If the cooperative principles behind the modern economy were correct, as everyone seemed to embrace, Americans should then use them to stabilize the economy and then recover prosperity. "Progress is born of cooperation," the president reminded citizens. "The Government should assist and encourage these movements of collective self-help by itself cooperating with them." During the first two years of the crisis, Hoover turned to the "associational" principles he had followed as secretary of commerce, with its emphasis on "voluntary cooperation." For business, Hoover sponsored meetings and forums, hoping to convince the heads of the major corporations that his idea was the best approach to recover the economy. Hoover made it clear to these individuals that they need not worry about the possibility or specter of direct government intervention, nor was there a need for a massive overhaul or reform of the American industrial corporate system. In short, Hoover believed that the industrial chieftains were altruistic enough and savvy enough to embrace his ideas, realizing that his proposal was the only way of not only eventually restoring employment and prosperity but of saving American capitalism as well. Unfortunately, as will be seen, American businessmen disappointed Hoover, and their refusal to accept his ideas helped to plunge the economy ever deeper into depression.

For labor, Hoover won a promise from business leaders to spread the work in their firms rather than simply fire a percentage of their employees. For agriculture, the new Federal Farm Board issued large amounts of credit so that the commodity cooperatives could keep their products off the market and halt the decline in farm prices. For hard-pressed Americans everywhere, Hoover made the president's office the coordinator (but not the provider) of private, voluntary relief. Between 1929 and 1932 donations for relief increased about eightfold, a remarkable accomplishment by any previous standard. Viewing the economy as a national system, Hoover was the first president in history to attack depression systematically.

The Deepening Depression

But Hoover, like the economy, took a grim downturn in the middle of 1931. As his sense of control over affairs began to slip, he became more rigid, more isolated, more disillusioned, and frustrated by his inability to deal with the vast specter of oppressive forces. Particularly disturbing was big businesses' refusal to cooperate and enact his policies. Most only paid lip-service to the president's idea of cooperation, while others—too many—flat-out refused to acknowledge, let alone implement, any of his suggestions. As a consequence, unemployment in the industrial sector continued to rise as corporations continued to cut costs by laying off workers, something Hoover did not want to happen and believed would not if his advice had been heeded. So overwhelmed and despairing did Hoover become by 1932, that the White House became a funeral parlor. The president, never a charmer, looked, as one visitor remarked, as if a rose would wilt at his touch. In that mood, Hoover called together the villains of Wall Street who, in the president's view, had fed the Great Bull Market instead of facilitating legitimate business. When he demanded that they make massive new investments, they stalled. Finally, Hoover accepted the inevitable: the necessity of government intervention, as least as far as offering federal funds for credit. Thus, in 1932, the Reconstruction Finance Corporation was created, which, in that year, invested $1.5 billion in private enterprise, ranging from loans to ailing banks and to corporations willing to build low-cost housing, bridges, and other public works. The RFC was the biggest peacetime federal intervention in the economy to that point. The Home Loan Bank Board, set up that same year, offered funds to savings and loans, mortgage companies, and other financial institutions that lent money for home construction. Meanwhile, to ease the pressures on international finances, Hoover issued a moratorium on the payment of war debts owed to the United States by its former allies against Germany.

Unfortunately, Hoover refused to offer the same generosity to suffering Americans. Still devoted to the concept of rugged individualism, Hoover believed it an anathema to even contemplate the possibility of offering Americans in dire need direct federal relief. The idea of inaugurating the concept of the welfare state was an idea that never crossed Herbert Hoover's mind. Every citizen, he believed, must rely for survival on his or her own efforts. To give money to the poor, he insisted, would destroy their desire to work, undermine their sense of self-worth, and erode their capacity for citizenship. Critics pointed to the hypocrisy in such an attitude by reminding the president that in 1930 he refused a request of $25 million to help feed Arkansas farmers and their families but approved $45 million to feed the same farmers' livestock. And in 1932, shortly after rejecting an urgent request from Chicago for aid to help pay its teachers and municipal workers, Hoover approved a $90 million loan to rescue that city's Central Republic Bank.

By 1932 the president's policies lay in shambles. The exceptionally high Hawley-Smoot Tariff, which Hoover had signed in 1930, was intensifying worldwide depression by cutting off the flow of international trade, virtually locking out of American markets foreign manufactured goods. Employers discarded their programs for spreading the work, and unemployment shot above 12 million. Local relief funds, both public and private, evaporated. As commodity prices fell, the Federal Farm Board simply ran out of credit. Farmers burned their crops or left them unpicked as with cotton because it no longer paid them to market the crop. In some Midwestern county seats, silent men with hunting rifles closed the courts so that their mortgages could not be foreclosed. It was no wonder that by the spring of 1932, there had emerged a groundswell of protest and resentment toward the president and his uncaring policies and attitude.

The Death Knell of Herbert Hoover: The Bonus Army March

In the spring of 1932, a group of World War I army veterans mounted a particularly emotional challenge to the Hoover administration and its policies. In 1924, Congress had authorized a $1,000 bonus for Great War veterans in the form of compensation certificates that would mature in 1945. But now veterans were demanding the bonus immediately. Spearheaded by a group from Portland, Oregon, veterans decided to take action. Starting from that city and calling themselves the Bonus Expeditionary Force, they hopped onto empty boxcars of freight trains heading east, determined to stage a march on Washington. As the impoverished "army" traveled eastward, many surviving on handouts from sympathetic citizens, their ranks swelled, reaching 20,000 vets, including

Veterans of the Bonus Army camped outside Congress in Washington, D. C., demanding bonuses promised to them during World War I.

wives and children. Upon their arrival in Washington, the Bonus Army encamped in the Anacostia Flats, southeast of the Capitol, and petitioned Congress for early payment of the promised bonus. The House of Representatives agreed to allocate the funds, but the Senate rejected the bill. Hoover supported the Senate, and, more importantly, refused to meet with any of the Army's emissaries. To Hoover, the gathering represented not a plea for help but, rather, a sign that potential revolution was on the horizon. Nothing could have been further from reality. By July 1932, after two months in Washington, the Bonus Army was becoming desperate for help. Hoover, however, was intransigent; a "siege mentality" now overcame the president as he secluded himself in his fortress, the White House, with the Potomac serving as his "moat" of protection. After a group of veterans who had been staying in abandoned Washington apartments scuffled with police (who many claim were sympathetic to the veterans' plight), Hoover called on federal troops led by Army Chief of Staff Douglas MacArthur and 3rd Cavalry Commander George Patton to drive the veterans out. The troops attacked the veterans' Anacostia encampment, razed their tents and shacks, and dispersed with rather brutal force the "protestors." In the process, more than one hundred veterans were wounded, and one infant was killed.

News that impoverished veterans and their families had been attacked in the nation's capital intensified an already growing anti-Hoover sentiment. Those who suspected that Hoover never cared in the first place about the plight of the poor and dispossessed were now convinced that Hoover was a callous, paranoid man, willing to use force to suppress cries for help. His days in the White House were numbered.

During the years 1921-29 relatively little was expected of the president as an individual. The modern political economy was, after all, a complex impersonal system, not the product of a particular administration, and it appeared to operate on its own momentum. But when the thoroughly national system broke down, only the national government had the scope and authority to repair it. Because the executive branch dominated the national government, people naturally looked there for help. However, only a handful of past presidents infused the Oval Office with the energy and personality essential for its sustained vitality and preeminence within the federal structure. Consequently, throughout much of the nation's history, Congress actually dominated the national government because few presidents possessed either the willingness or the ideological inclination, or personal requisites, to assert executive authority and power. That was definitely true for both Warren G. Harding and Calvin Coolidge. Herbert Hoover certainly had the academic background to be an effective president, but he lacked both the personality and the willingness to use the full power of his office to address the crisis. The longer the depression, the more the American people turned to Hoover, not to Congress, to lead them out of the wilderness. Hoover was judged by new, demanding standards, and because he failed to deliver the people from the crisis, the popular verdict condemned him. By 1932 millions who had no other place to turn were blaming Hoover in a bitter, personal way for their troubles. A humane man with great administrative skills, Hoover lacked the flexibility, political instincts, and inspirational leadership required by the ordeal. Millions of Americans wanted desperately to believe that a brave new leader with a magic touch might still transform the toad of depression into a dazzling prince of prosperity. Thus, though knowing very little about their new "prince," the American electorate turned completely against the Republicans and their president in the 1932 election. In that year, the Republicans were voted out of office after having dominated national politics (excepting Woodrow Wilson's two terms) for 36 years. Hoover received only 39.6 percent of the popular vote and just 59 (of 531) electoral votes. FDR and the Democrats won a resounding, landslide victory. When he left the presidency in 1933, Hoover was a bewildered man, reviled by the people for what they took to be his indifference to suffering and his ineptitude in dealing with the economy's collapse. FDR's overwhelming victory, however, should not be viewed as a mandate for him or his "New Deal." Americans were desperate for hope and change and were simply willing to give the man with a "magic" name a chance, and if he proved to be as ineffective as his predecessor, then four years from now, they would turn to someone else as the hopeful "messiah."

FRANKLIN DELANO ROOSEVELT

THE LORD OF THE MANOR: FDR

It is hard to believe today that Franklin Delano Roosevelt was a man of mystery to many Americans in 1932. Though no doubt name recognition helped his credibility—he was the distant cousin of Theodore Roosevelt, a strong leader and exceptional president—few Americans, outside of his native New York, knew much about his background and experience. FDR was born in 1882 into a patrician Anglo-Dutch family whose pedigree on both sides dated back to the colonial period. By the time of his birth, the Hyde Park manor where he was raised had been in the family for over 200 years. In short,

FDR grew up among people who were convinced of their superiority in matters of ancestry, intelligence, and leadership. His education at Groton, Harvard College, and Columbia Law School was typical of the path followed by the sons of America's blue-blood elite. Though wealthy, the Roosevelt clan's holdings paled in comparison with that of some of their friends and neighbors, such as the Rockefellers, Carnegies, and Harrimans, whose fortunes ranged between $50 and $100 million or more. Interestingly, the Roosevelts disdained the nouveau riche parvenus, which many of the industrial elite were. Particularly galling to the older elite like the Roosevelts was the new elite's vulgar displays of wealth, their lack of taste and etiquette, their indifference to the natural environment, and their hostility toward those less fortunate than themselves. In short, the behavior and attitudes of the new-wealth industrial capitalists lacked that most important ingredient of quality rearing: a sense of noblesse oblige. In FDR's view, his cousin, Theodore, was the embodiment of this virtue and thus worshipped him and wanted to emulate his political career. Thus, in 1907, FDR began his ascent, following almost verbatim in the tracks of his beloved "Uncle Teddy." Like TR, FDR envisioned first a seat in the New York State Assembly, then he would be appointed assistant secretary of the navy, and then he would become governor of New York, vice-president of the United States, and then president of the Republic. Incredibly, this is almost exactly what happened (except that FDR became a state senator rather than an assemblyman, and he lost his 1920 bid for the vice presidency).

The governorship of New York and the presidency might have eluded him had he not been transformed by personal calamity. In 1921, at the age of 39, FDR was stricken by one of the most deadly afflictions of the time, polio, which luckily did not kill him but instead took away the use of his legs. Before becoming paralyzed, FDR's career, both professionally (the practice of law) and politically, was not that outstanding. He owed his political ascent more to his famous name than to actual acumen or hard work. He was charming, gregarious, and popular among associates in the New York Democratic Party. He was quite the bon vivant, a playboy in many ways, who devoted more time and energy to socializing and sailing, partying and, unfortunately, womanizing, than

First Lady Eleanor Roosevelt played an active role in her husband's administration. She became a prominent figure in high-level decision making. This was a sharp change from the roles of previous First Ladies. Eleanor had an unwavering commitment to social justice. She and Franklin had six children, however, she eventually found time for her own political career. She became the eyes and ears for her wheelchair-bound husband and traveled extensively, touring the depression-scarred nation.

he did developing a devotion to career and family. However, after his illness, FDR spent the next two years bedridden, and while confined to his bed, he seemed to experience an Ignatian revelation, a reformation of character and spirit, a desire to eschew his past life and forge a new one with a determination and seriousness of purpose conspicuously absent during his earlier years. He developed a sense of humility and compassion for those suffering misfortune that would later enable him to reach out to the millions caught in the Great Depression. FDR's physical debilitation also transformed his relationship with his wife, Eleanor, with whom he shared a testy and increasingly loveless marriage. Eleanor's dedication to nursing FDR back to health forged a new bond between them. More conscious of his dependence on others, FDR now welcomed his wife as a partner in his career. Eleanor soon displayed a talent for political organization and public speaking, a gift that surprised those who knew her only as a shy, awkward woman. She would become an active, eloquent First Lady, her husband's trusted ally and political confidant, and a key player in the formation of American liberalism. Indeed, many regard her as this nation's greatest First Lady.

Speaking from his campaign train in 1932, FDR conveyed his message of optimism to a weary nation.

Roosevelt Liberalism

During his four years as governor of New York, FDR initiated various reform programs, many of which reflected his attachment and homage to progressivism. Other programs, however, seemed to embody a new reform impulse called liberalism, which called for government intervention in economic matters while maintaining libertarian views on questions of personal behavior. As the 1932 election approached, FDR appeared to be increasingly gravitating toward this new ideology. By the time of his nomination, FDR seemed wholly committed to implementing this new ethos after his election. In a rousing call to action, the future president told his supporters in his acceptance speech at the Chicago Democratic convention, "Ours must be the party of liberal thought, of planned action, of enlightened international outlook, and of the greatest good for the greatest number of citizens." He promised "a new deal for the American people."

In his campaign, however, FDR did not always emphasize this call to activism. Always searching for a middle ground between conservatism and liberalism, FDR, at least during the hustings, appeared more of a moderate than a liberal. He was too shrewd of a politician to embrace an ideology that most Americans either did not understand or were, at best, uncertain of. Moreover, within his own party, the conservatives, especially those from the South, still wielded significant power, and the majority of them were not all disposed toward liberalism. FDR thus sometimes spoke of using the powers of the federal government to stabilize the economy but in the same breath he reassured the conservatives that he was at heart a non-interventionist who had no intention of destroying all that was "sacred" in American life: the preservation of rugged individualism, which was

Roosevelt used the radio to reassure the American people.

code for maintaining adherence to the principles of laissez faire and the conservative ethos. Though FDR started his presidency as a "moderate conservative," as will be seen later in the chapter, as the New Deal evolved and became more popular and defined, FDR moved both himself and his agenda to the left. By the time of his 1936 reelection, the New Deal no longer reflected its initial conservative restraints. By that time, the influence and ideas of the liberal coalition in his cabinet had prevailed, and thus the New Deal would become the progressive reform foundation upon which subsequent Democratic presidents, most notably Lyndon Johnson, would attempt to build the most ambitious liberal edifice: The Great Society.

In point of fact, FDR made only two outright promises during the campaign: to repeal Prohibition and to balance the budget. Thus, the nation had to wait until March 4, 1933—the day FDR was sworn in as president—to learn what the New Deal would bring.

"President Roosevelt"

The reversal in presidential character and personality between Hoover and FDR could not have been more striking. Hoover, one associate remarked, "didn't like the human element." FDR reveled in it. Not only did he mix easily with all kinds of people, but he also made them feel that intuitively he sympathized with them. Hoover, taking no one's counsel, thought he knew what the nation wanted. Unlike Hoover, FDR welcomed the challenge of selling his programs to a demoralized nation. A master of popular phrasing, simple analogies, and, most important, the media, especially the radio, FDR had a strong, warm voice that reached into millions of American homes through his famous "fireside chats," which began on the second Sunday after his inauguration, were bits of genius in the use of a mass medium. Whereas Hoover had behaved like a distant autocrat, upbraiding the American people for their lack of fortitude, FDR projected the image of a kindly grandfather, gathering his children around him to read them a soothing bedtime story called the New Deal. He always spoke in a plain, friendly, reassuring voice that went far to calm the fears and anxieties of the forlorn and discouraged. In his first chat, he explained the banking crisis in simple terms but without condescension. "I want to take a few minutes to talk with the people of the United States about banking," he began. An estimated 20 million Americans listened. To hear the president speak warmly and conversationally—as though he were actually there in the living room—was riveting. An estimated 50,000 Americans wrote letters to FDR within days of his inaugural address. Millions more, many of them barely literate, would write to him and

Harold Ickes, was a serious-minded man with a reputation for absolute incorruptibility. Reporters dubbed him "Honest Harold."

Eleanor over the next few years, thanking them for all they had done, or simply writing to them to air their troubles. Americans, regardless of party affiliation, began to hang portraits of FDR in their homes, often next to a picture of Jesus or the Madonna. Where Hoover cast somber eyes downward, the tilt of FDR's chin and the cocky angle of his cigarette holder invariable gave the sense of a man looking upward; an individual filled with confidence and optimism, which his perpetual public smile radiated.

Urging "bold experimentation" for a devastated land, FDR attracted a swarm of newcomers to Washington, a curiously mixed but effective group of advisers. For secretary of the treasury, FDR selected his close friend and Hyde Park neighbor, Henry Morgenthau, whose conscientiousness and loyalty made him indispensable to the president. For secretary of agriculture, FDR appointed Henry Wallace, the son of Harding's secretary of agriculture, whose broad liberal vision compensated for his occasional inattention to practical matters. Another liberal Republican, Harold Ickes, became secretary of the interior and watched over his domain with a fierce jealousy and a scrupulous honesty. From his New York administration, FDR brought both the first woman to hold a cabinet post, Frances Perkins, to become secretary of labor, and the tough, dedicated administrator of relief, Harry Hopkins. All of these individuals served to the end of FDR's presidency.

The administration also drew people who had never before influenced government policy: an obscure Montana professor named M.L. Wilson with a proposal for limiting agricultural production; Raymond Moley, Rexford G. Tugwell, and Adolf Berle of Columbia University, the "brains trust" of FDR's 1932 campaign, with ambitions to improve the economy's organization; social workers with plans to aid the unemployed, disabled, and the aged; and many more. Together, this polyglot of human intelligence, vision, and a zeal for change composed the "New Dealers." During FDR's long tenure this term became part of the nation's everyday language—

Harry Hopkins was the head of FERA, the Federal Emergency Relief Administration. He was a longtime Roosevelt colleague. He became so closely associated with Roosevelt and the New Deal that reporters called him the assistant president. In his first two hours in office, Harry Hopkins distributed $5 million of relief.

Secretary of Labor Frances Perkins was the first woman cabinet member. She was one of several women appointed by FDR to posts previously held only by men.

used with affection by some with hatred by others to express their strong feelings about FDR and his administration.

Behind FDR's easy public style and gracious private manner lay a keen, calculating politically savvy mind that always sought to direct—control—people and events. Indeed, FDR was never the benign father figure he made himself out to be. Behind closed doors, he was arrogant, temperamental, and often vituperative beyond description when dealing with individuals who dared question or criticize his ideas or policies. Always looking to expand the power of the presidency, as well as the Democratic Party, FDR often used the New Deal for those ends rather than for the nation's welfare. His public image was skillfully crafted. Compliant, if not intimidated, news photographers agreed not to show him in a wheelchair or struggling with the leg braces and cane he used to take even small steps. For his part, FDR often sought to hide the true purpose of much New Deal legislation behind the façade and rhetoric of "for the good of the people." Such manipulation and media control worked. Policy failures rarely seemed to adversely affect his appeal.

The din of demands around his powerful office never ruffled him. Moreover, reflecting his progressive background, FDR brought to office a firm faith in the principles of his "Uncle Teddy's" New Nationalism: He wanted business to organize, industry by industry; and agriculture, commodity by commodity. He believed that an efficient labor, with rights protected by the federal government, not forced by unions, and private financial institutions working with industry and agriculture could restore prosperity. The government had only to assist them in regaining their strength and finding their proper places in the system. FDR would experiment—but within these boundaries. Not surprisingly, the new president selected equally orthodox or conservative men for the crucial administrative posts of the early New Deal: Hugh Johnson and Donald Richberg in business affairs, George Peek and Chester Davis in

Banks closed during the depression. One of FDR's first moves as president was to close all of the banks, allowing only those that were solvent to reopen.

agriculture, and Jesse Jones for the RFC, and Lewis Douglas for the Bureau of the Budget. All of these individuals were known conservatives; indeed, some of them, like Jones from Texas, notoriously so. FDR never wanted to appear to be too far left, and thus with men like Jones in his cabinet, he was able to deflect much criticism from the right, which often accused him of trying to move the country toward socialism. FDR's conservative appointees' influence was more than checked by the imaginative, liberal appointees, among them Ben Cohen and Tom Corcoran, who set the long-term tone and direction of the New Deal.

To his credit, FDR used his popularity and executive power to strengthen American democracy at a time when democracy was crumbling around the world. However, during his thirteen years in the White House, he set in motion tendencies that would long plague American politics: a shift in overwhelming power to the executive branch, a steady expansion of the size and reach of federal bureaucracies, and a widening gap between political appearance and political reality and substance.

The "Hundred Days"

FDR's most pressing priority upon assuming office was to try to remedy the nation's banking system, which had collapsed by March 1933. The president responded with his fine sense of style and an instinctive moderation. By inauguration day several states already had closed their banks as accumulating panic spread from banks in the agrarian regions toward America's financial centers, principally in the cities of New York and Chicago. On March 4, 1933, the day FDR took his oath of office, the major banking houses in both those cities finally succumbed and closed as well. As a result of those doors closing, the entire system stopped functioning. FDR immediately declared a nationwide "Bank Holiday," dispatched expert teams to investigate and classify all banks as either strong, wavering, or hopeless, and started a transfusion of over a billion dollars from the RFC into the banking system. The president spoke soothing words; in less than two weeks 90 percent of the frozen deposits were again available to customers, and all over the country money came out of mattresses to fill the banks. It was an exemplary performance in the service of a free-enterprise system, and Wall Street joined Main Street in cheering the president. "In one week," the journalist Walter Lippmann declared, "the nation, which had lost confidence in everything and everybody, has regained confidence in the government and itself."

Only after the financial crisis eased did FDR turn to the structural reform of banking. A second

Glass-Steagall Act (1933) separated commercial banking from investment banking. It also created the Federal Deposit Insurance Corporation (FDIC), which assured depositors that the government would guarantee up to $5,000 of their savings. The Securities Act (1933) and the Securities Exchange Act (1934) imposed long overdue regulation on the New York Stock Exchange, both by reining in buying on the margin (and other speculative practices) and by establishing the Securities and Exchange Commission to oversee the stock market's daily operation and enforce the new regulations and laws, as well as authority to investigate improprieties and punish the violators with fines, loss of licenses, and imprisonment if the infraction was especially egregious. FDR wanted to ensure Americans that from this point on the market would never "crash" again because of the activities of nefarious, greedy speculators.

FDR's treatment for the banking emergency and subsequent policies to regulate the stock market revealed the broad strategy of the New Deal's first months—"The Hundred Days." Among the many popular prescriptions for halting an apparently endless economic decline, none appealed more to the president's spirit than a nationwide surge of activity that headed upward instead of downward. Mobilize confidence, synchronize energy, and prosperity would return because throughout the land people would suddenly behave as if it *were* returning. To a president who told Americans "that the only thing we have to fear is fear itself," that kind of grandiose bootstraps operation made perfect sense. As Roosevelt took office, he called Congress into special session, plied it with proposals, and during a whirlwind hundred days, guided through fifteen major laws, the greatest outburst of far-reaching legislative activity in United States history—and most of it emanating from the Oval Office, not Congress.

SAVING THE PEOPLE

Although a fiscal conservative at heart, FDR understood the need to temper financial prudence with compassion. Congress responded swiftly in 1933 to the president's request to establish the Federal Emergency Relief Administration (FERA), granting it $500 million for relief to the poor. To head it, FDR appointed a brash, young liberal reformer, Harry Hopkins, who disbursed $2 million during his first two hours on the job. True to his Roosevelt heritage, FDR was as much a conservationist as his beloved "Uncle Teddy" and was thus as interested in expanding the national park system and preserving the nation's natural beauty. The creation of the Civilian Conservation Corps (CCC) would be a logical and natural compliment to this interest. Also inspiring FDR to create the CCC was a less altruistic concern: the rise in juvenile delinquency and crime, especially in the urban areas. What better way to "nip this problem in the bud" than to transport the potential offenders hundreds if not thousands of miles (primarily to the Far West and Southwest) from temptation and put them to work in the outdoors, doing something not only constructive but aesthetically pleasing and physically and spiritually fortifying as well. Functioning like an army boot camp, the program provided full room and board, as well as a paycheck, of which they were allowed to keep only a small portion of. The lion's share of the money went into a "savings account" so when they finished their tenure (a maximum of two years) they would have something to start their new life with. A percentage of their pay was also sent home to help out there. During its existence the CCC put 2.5 million single young (primarily ages 18-25) white males (not until 1937, thanks largely to the admonishments of Eleanor Roosevelt, did FDR create a CCC for young African American men) to work planting trees, halting erosion, building national parks, putting out forest fires, and otherwise improving and protecting the environment. The CCC became one of the most successful and popular of the work programs.

In the winter of 1934, FDR launched the Civil Works Administration (CWA), an ambitious work-relief program, also under Harry Hopkins's direction, that hired 4 million unemployed at $15 a week and put them to work on 400,000 small-scale infrastructure government projects. This particular work program focused on providing jobs for working class or blue-collar Americans. For middle class Americans threatened with the loss of their homes, FDR won congressional approval for the Homeowner's Loan

Begun in 1933, The Civilian Conservation Corps (CCC) contributed to the development of the nation's natural resources.

Corporation (1933) to refinance mortgages. These direct subsidies to millions of jobless and home-owning Americans lent credibility to Roosevelt's claim that the New Deal would set the country on a new course.

The NRA and AAA

From this array of legislation, two programs formed the heart of the early New Deal. The Agricultural Adjustment Act (AAA) and the National Industrial Recovery Act (NIRA). During his first year in office, FDR was confident he could recover the economy, not from relief but through agricultural and industrial cooperation. He regarded the AAA, passed in May 1933, and the NIRA, passed in June, as the most important legislation of his Hundred Days. Both were based on the idea that curtailing production would trigger economic recovery. By creating scarcities in both agricultural and manufactured goods, FDR's economists reasoned, they could restore the balance of normal market forces. In short, FDR and his advisers believed, and to a degree, rightly so, that overproduction in both economic sectors had contributed to the depression. By artificially creating shortages, demand for goods would then exceed supply, prices would rise, and revenues from massive sales would climb. Farmers and industrialists, earning a profit once again, would increase their investment in new technology and hire more workers, and prosperity and full employment would be the final result.

The NIRA represented a continuation of Hoover-inspired government-sponsored business cooperation. Its most important provisions authorized each specialized segment of business to prepare a code of self-governance and established the National Recovery Administration to supervise the process. As director of the NRA, FDR appointed the brash, loud World War I veteran, General Hugh Johnson, an experienced public affairs man, who immediately launched a circus of a campaign to enlist all Americans behind his program. Through parades—a massive one down New York City's Fifth Avenue— public rallies—he staged an elaborate NRA celebration in

Yankee Stadium— evangelical speeches, and assorted hoopla, Johnson made the Blue Eagle, the NRA's emblem of cooperation, synonymous with the New Deal itself, and he counted on public opinion to make it correlative with Americanism. Indeed, blue eagles soon sprouted everywhere—on storefronts, at factory entrances, and on company stationary— usually accompanied by the slogan "We Do Our Part." Americans everywhere joined the campaign, and morale soared.

Johnson's first task was to persuade industrialists and businessmen, large and small, to raise employee wages to a minimum of 30 to 40 cents an hour and to limit employee hours to a maximum of 30 to 40 hours a week. The intent was to reduce the quantity of goods that any factory or business could produce. Next, Johnson brought together the largest producers in every manufacturing sector and asked them to prepare codes of fair competition. In the NRA's first four months, business groups wrote over seven hundred constitutions to govern their affairs. Where one or more large firms dominated an industry, the NRA relied on them to prepare the codes; where no company controlled an industry, the NRA turned to a trade association. Although these "blue codes" varied from industry to industry, they usually included some agreement on prices, wages, and the acceptable limits of competition. The only integration among them was a common commitment to stabilization, a common freedom from antitrust prosecution, and a common dependence on the industrial groups themselves to regulate their own members. Johnson exalted the spirit of cooperation and swore at the "slackers" but never coerced businessmen into joining "the club" nor of having to adopt the "blue codes." Johnson's policy of non-coercion was backed by his boss, FDR.

Section 7a of the NIRA authorized workers to organize and bargain in their own behalf, and some labor leaders, most notably John L. Lewis of the United Mine Workers, exulted that the government was now their sponsor. "THE PRESIDENT WANTS YOU TO JOIN THE UNION!" Although the NRA did not actually encourage an independent labor movement, it provided labor with other important benefits: it fostered a national pattern of maximum hours and minimum wages, and it eliminated child labor and the sweatshop.

In the summer and fall of 1933, the NRA codes drawn up for steel, textiles, coal mining, garment manufacture, rubber, and other industries seemed to be working. The economy picked up, and people began to hope that an end to the depression was near. However, in the winter and spring of 1934, economic indicators plunged downward once again, and manufacturers, blaming the NRA, began to evade the provisions of the codes. Also contributing to the growing anti-NRA sentiment was the fact that from the program's beginning, small businesses felt left out of the grand plan and discriminated against because of their size. Moreover, small businesses could not adopt the minimum wage guarantees nor any of the other codes because they simply could not afford to do so. Their profit margins were already slight, and to have to pay a minimum wage to workers and other benefits, while simultaneously cutting back on production, was something they could not do without going out of business. Thus, by 1934, many small businessmen cried out against the NRA, asserting that it violated free enterprise and that the New Dealers responsible for it were conspiring to eliminate the small businessman altogether. In short,

The government's purpose for creating the NRA, to benefit both factory owner and workers, is depicted in this 1933 cartoon.

small businessmen believed that the real intent of the NRA was to consolidate industrial production, ensuring that in the future only a handful of major producers would supply the nation's manufactured goods. Though such was not the planned intent of the program, there was nonetheless sentiment in the White House among some New Dealers that the industrial sector would be better off if there was less "competition."

Government committees set up to enforce the codes were powerless to punish violators. By the fall of 1934, it was clear that the NRA had failed. When the Supreme Court declared the NRA codes unconstitutional in May 1935, FDR allowed the agency to die. By then, New Dealers had given up on the idea that limiting production in the industrial sector would promote recovery.

The other cornerstone of the early New Deal was the May 1933 Agricultural Adjustment Act. The fundamental objective of this program was to increase farm income by artificially creating shortages. By decreasing supply and increasing demand, it was hoped that farm income would rise to a level of "parity," or equality, with the farmers' purchasing power just before World War I, the supposed "golden years" of farm production and income. The act was a veritable grab bag of alternatives. It included provisions from almost every farm program proposed in the twentieth century: marketing agreements, commodity loans, export subsidies, government purchases, and—reminiscent of William Jennings Bryan—even currency inflation. To these familiar devices, the government added the New Deal favorite of production restrictions, aimed at reducing agricultural surpluses at the source. During its first months the Agricultural Adjustment Administration (the AAA) used production cutbacks as a way of getting emergency cash relief to the countryside. In midseason farmers were paid to plow under their crops and slaughter livestock, a bitter expedient with so much hunger in the nation. After 1933 the AAA expected each farmer growing a particular crop to reduce production by a nationally fixed percentage.

From the moment it was promulgated, the act was guaranteed to arouse farmer opposition and thus destined to fail. Many farmers, proud of their work ethic, did not readily accept the idea that they were to be paid more money for working less land and husbanding fewer livestock. Most egregiously, the AAA made no provisions for the countless sharecroppers, tenant farmers, and farm laborers who would be thrown out of work by acreage reduction. In the South, the victims were disproportionately black. A Georgia sharecropper wrote Harry Hopkins of his misery: "I have Bin farming all my life But the man I live with Has Turned me loose taking my mule [and] all my feed. . . .I can't get a Job so Some one said Rite you."

The AAA programs also proved inadequate to the plight of Great Plains farmers whose economic problems had been compounded by Mother Nature. Just as the depression rolled in, the rain stopped falling on the plains. The land, stripped of its native grasses by decades of excessive cultivation, dried up and turned to dust. And then the dust began to blow, sometimes traveling 1,000 miles across open prairie. Dust became a fixed feature of daily life on the plains, which soon became known as the "Dust Bowl." The dust covered furniture, floors, and stoves, as well as penetrating people's hair and lungs. The worst dust storm occurred on April 14, 1935, when a great mass of dust, moving at speeds of 45 to 70 miles an hour, roared through Colorado, Kansas, and Oklahoma, blackening the sky, suffocating cattle, and dumping thousands of tons of topsoil and red clay on homes and streets. Despite government assistance via the Soil Conservation Service, which helped instruct Plains farmers with new cultivation techniques and subsidies, hundreds of thousands of dispossessed, desperate Plains farmers left the region, primarily migrating to California via the now famous Route 66. This exodus of humanity was the most significant and largest internal movement of citizens in the history of the nation. This "Okie" migration (They were called that because most, but not all, of these migrants came from Oklahoma.) made famous in John Steinbeck's *The Grapes of Wrath,* disturbed many Americans, for whom the plight of these once-sturdy yeomen became a symbol of how much had gone wrong with the American dream.

In 1936 the Supreme Court, as it did a year earlier with the NRA, declared the AAA unconstitutional because its mandated limits on farm production were considered an illegal restraint of trade. Thus, in a matter of one year's time, the two most important programs of the New Deal were shot down by the judicial branch. As will be seen later in this chapter, FDR did not take these defeats lightly. Indeed, he took them as personal affronts to both his power and agenda to uplift the nation. He was so angry at the Court—"those nine old men" as he referred to the justices—that he decided it needed to be "reformed." But he was too shrewd of a politician to challenge the Court before being reelected. Once that was accomplished, he went full-steam ahead with his plan to "reform" the judicial branch of the federal government.

The use of subsidies, begun by the AAA, did eventually bring stability and prosperity to agriculture. But the costs were high. Agriculture became the most heavily subsidized sector of the nation's economy, and the Department of Agriculture grew into one of the government's largest bureaucracies. Rural poor, black and white, never received a fair share of federal benefits. Beginning in the 1940s and 1950s, they would be forced off the land and into the cities of the North and West.

REBUILDING THE NATION

In addition to establishing the NRA, the NIRA also launched the Public Works Administration (PWA). The PWA was given a $3.3 billion budget to sponsor internal improvements that would both refurbish and expand with new construction the nation's infrastructure of roads, bridges, sewage systems, hospitals, airports, and schools. The labor needed for these projects would shrink the relief rolls and reduce unemployment, especially among the industrial working class. The projects themselves could be justified in terms that conservatives approved: economic investment rather than short-term relief.

The PWA authorized the building of three major Western dams—The Grand Coulee, Boulder, and Bonneville—that opened up large stretches of Arizona, California, and Washington to industrial and agricultural development. It funded the construction of the Triborough Bridge in New York City and the 100-mile causeway linking Florida to Key West. It also appropriated money for the construction of thousands of new schools and public libraries between 1933 and 1939.

Many black tenant farmers and sharecroppрrs were evicted from the land and pushed deeper into poverty.

The Tennessee Valley Authority

If there was one piece of legislation passed during the First New Deal that represented a strategy for economic recovery different from the one promoted by the NRA it was the Tennessee Valley Authority Act of 1933. Simply called the TVA, this particular approach called for the government—rather than private corporations—to directly foster economic development throughout the vast watershed area of the South known as the Tennessee Valley. This vast river basin winds through parts of six southern states and in the areas where these rivers flowed poverty was widespread because of the inhabitants' inability to control these rivers, especially during the rainy season. Flooding was endemic, and thus the towns and farms along the rivers were destroyed every year by the surging rivers. Thus the primary objective of the TVA was to control the flooding of the Tennessee River while simultaneously harnessing its water power to generate electricity, develop local industry (such as fertilizer production), improve river transportation, and, in the process, ease the poverty and isolation of the region's inhabitants. In some respects the TVA's mandate resembled that of the PWA, but the TVA had greater authority over economic development, which reflected the influence of New Dealers such as Rexford G. Tugwell, who were committed to statism: the creation of government-planned and government-operated enterprises. Although advisers such as Tugwell never publicly admitted so, they were drawn to certain socialist ideas such as public ownership of key industries and utilities.

The TVA's accomplishments were impressive. The program built, completed, or improved more than twenty dams, including the massive Wheeler Dam near Muscle Shoals in Alabama. Hydroelectric generators were also constructed at many of the dam sites, providing the region's population with electricity for the first time. Indeed, the TVA became the nation's largest producer of electricity, and the low rates it provided consumers forced private utility companies to reduce their rates as well. The TVA also constructed waterways to bypass unnavigable stretches of the river, reduced flooding, and taught farmers how to prevent soil erosion and use fertilizers. In short, the project, with all of its different permutations, brought the Tennessee River Valley and its inhabitants into the twentieth century with a massive, government-planned and operated rural reclamation project.

Although the TVA was one of the New Deal's most touted successes and boldest experiments in government planning (as well as coming dangerously close to socialism), it generated little enthusiasm for more ambitious programs in national planning. Only a handful of New Dealers—and most of them equivocated when pressed on the issue—wanted FDR to nationalize established industries. Though it had never been done before, the TVA made it acceptable for the government to intervene to bring prosperity to an impoverished region. However, neither FDR, the majority of Congress, or the American people favored any further extension of governmental power that such programs would necessitate. Contrary to what many conservative critics of the era asserted, and even after the depression was over, neither FDR or the New Deal embraced the idea of the federal government as a substitute for private enterprise. Nonetheless, when FDR wanted to sum up his proudest domestic achievement as president, he often cited

FDR at the Grand Coulee Dam in Washington. October 2, 1937
Photo credits:
FDR Presidential Library

the TVA. Today, delegates at a Democratic National Democratic Convention would snicker in baffled disbelief if a speaker saluted FDR for his greatest accomplishment: rural electrification. But the symbolic significance of the TVA and similar projects can hardly be exaggerated. They were thought of as not mere public utility companies but as the pilot projects of a new and "futuristic" way of life. FDR, many of his allies and supporters, believed the TVA provided a model for a new kind of technological civilization superior to that of the early industrial era. In 1937, Baker Brownell, a professor at Northwestern University, wrote that the TVA was "building more than a dam. It is building a civilization. The visitor here [at Norris Dam] is looking into the next century."

Power-generating dams were to New Deal state capitalists what steel mills were to communists and what stock exchanges were to the neoliberal free-marketeers of the late twentieth century—not just institutions but icons. Here is a song from *Power,* a 1937 pro-New Deal play: "All up and down the valley/They heard the great alarm;/The government means business/Its working like a charm/Oh, see them boys a-comin'/Their government they trust/Just hear their hammers ringin'/They'll build that dam or bust."

The region that underwent the most dramatic transformation thanks to New Deal-state-capitalist development projects was the West. There, dam construction and other infrastructure ventures brought agrarian societies, which had been bypassed by the age of steam power, directly into the second industrial era of electricity and internal combustion engines in tractors, trucks, and cars. Between 1933 and 1939, per capital payments for public works projects, welfare, and federal loans in the Rocky Mountain and Pacific Coast states outstripped those of any other region. When FDR assumed office, the United States, in many ways, was still two countries—an industrialized country, the Northeast, surrounded by a backward agrarian country, the Southern/Western periphery. As already seen, FDR's task in industrialized America was to get the factories going again by putting money into the pockets of the industrial working class, among

PWA workers began construction of Boulder Dam in 1933. The Public Works Administration's projects created new jobs for skilled workers.

other initiatives. But in the South and West, there were hardly any factories and only a small urban, industrial working class. These regions had more in common with the Northeast of the 1830s, before it industrialized, than with the Northeast of a hundred years later. FDR had to revive existing industries in the Northeast and build them from nothing in the West and the South.

Central to Western development and inspired by the success of the TVA was the program of dam building that became one of the New Deal's most enduring legacies, especially in the West. For decades Western land and agricultural capitalist developers wanted to dam the region's major rivers to provide water and electricity for urban and agricultural development. The costs, however, were prohibitive, even to the wealthiest entrepreneurs, until the New Deal offered to help with federal dollars. Via the dispensing of funds through the Bureau of Reclamation, a previously underutilized federal agency, the bureau oversaw the building of the Boulder Dam (later renamed Hoover Dam), which brought drinking water for southern California, irrigation water for California's Imperial Valley, which eventually became the fruit and vegetable "basket" of the nation, and electricity for Los Angeles and southern Arizona. The greatest construction project of all was the Grand Coulee Dam on the Columbia River in Washington, which created a 150-mile long lake. Together with the Bonneville Dam (also on the Columbia), the Grand Coulee gave the Pacific Northwest the cheapest electricity in the nation and created the potential for significant economic and population growth. The Bonneville and Grand Coulee Dams made the state of Washington the largest per capita recipient of New Deal funds. The benefits of this dam building program, in terms of economic development and population growth, did not come to fruition until the post-World War II years. Also, dam building in the West was not seen as a threat to established capitalist businesses because the government did not actually build the dams itself (as it did under the TVA) but rather hired private contractors to do the work, who became rich in the process. In short, Western dam construction was meant to aid primarily agricultural development—agribusiness as it turned out—not the poor, and it was intended to aid private enterprise, not bypass it.

It must be remembered that unlike post-World War II liberals, FDR and his contemporaries were less concerned with the redistribution of income from one group to another than with using the new technology and organizational techniques to develop the nation's productive human and natural resources. Instead of rejecting modern industry (as many agrarians did) or modern corporations (as socialists did), New Deal liberals, true to their Progressive heritage, wanted to regulate industrial capitalism to the degree that they could guide it to promote democratic social and political goals. Their main objective was geographic decentralization of both productive industry and people. Industry, concentrated in the Northeastern manufacturing belt, should be dispersed throughout the country. Population, too, should be relocated, especially from the crowded urban areas of the Northeast to the South and West. The working classes of that region, living in crowded, unsanitary conditions, should be encouraged to move to low-density suburbs and village-like "garden cities." The decentralization of industry and population would tend to promote both equality among regions and classes in the United States. The nation would no longer be a collection of resource-producing regions functioning as colonies of a single industrial area, the Northeast. Instead, the country would become a federation of balanced regions, each with a mix of manufacturing and agriculture. As the population left the crowded Northeastern industrial cities for the small, spacious, planned communities in the South and West, the wages of the urban workers who remained would rise. New Dealers believed that the key to accomplishing that vision was to implement a comprehensive infrastructure projects program, utilizing the technologies of the second industrial revolution: electricity (hydroelectric dam networks) and the internal combustion engine (highways for cars and trucks). New Deal liberals believed their "planning policies represented a "third way" between laissez faire capitalism and state socialism. While they experimented with production quotas in certain economic sectors like agriculture and to a lesser degree in industry, one could not equate their policies with Soviet-style economic planning. By planning, the New Dealers meant a flexible and eclectic combination of zoning, public works, and the providing of public credit that would attract private enterprises to develop certain regions of the country, particularly the South and the West, in a desired direction. Though this conception began with programs like the TVA, its full realization did not occur until after World War II and, more precisely, not until the 1970s and 1980s.

POPULIST OPPOSITION TO THE NEW DEAL

In their desire to rally popular support for such New Deal programs as the NRA, FDR and the New Dealers unleashed new political forces that they would have to reckon with by 1935. Though opposition to the New Deal emerged from both the Right and the Left, initially it was a group of left-leaning dissidents who defied easy ideological classification, who posed the greatest threat to FDR and the New Dealers. The great fanfare created to boost popular support for key programs, such as the NRA, raised the people's expectations that recovery was on its way. Perhaps more important, it freed them from their torpor; the people now believed that if they came together en masse (which the NRA encouraged), they could effect significant changes, or at the very least their clamors for reform would be heard, and FDR and his Brains Trust would implement the desired policies. This politicized electorate also made it clear to the New Dealers that if they could not achieve economic recovery, in the name of *all* the people, then the people would turn to others who could. Early popular criticism of the New Deal was not directed at FDR but at his advisers and at the Democratic Congress. Still, the president worried that the breadth and depth of the insurgency threatened his political survival. However, once FDR overcame his initial trepidation, his political instincts and shrewdness "kicked in," and he was able to defeat these potential usurpers by embracing or "co-opting" many of their ideas. In the end, FDR had little to fear from these individuals, for the people, though attracted to these men's programs, were not going to forsake the man who already had delivered to them so much more than anyone in history had to date.

Some critics were disturbed not only by the New Deal's failure to bring recovery but also by what they perceived as the conservative orientation of many early New Deal programs. Banking reforms, the AAA, and the NRA, they asserted, all favored large economic interests, an assessment that was not unfounded or that inaccurate. In their opinion, FDR had failed in his promise to uplift the ordinary people,

Louisiana Senator Huey Long founded the Share Our Wealth Society. The society advocated a redistribution of wealth to lessen the gap between the rich and poor in America.

the "forgotten Americans," whom they claimed was their principal concern.

The Rise of the Demagogues: Huey Long and Father Charles Coughlin

Of the above individuals, the most alarming to the Roosevelt administration was the "Kingfisher," Senator Huey P. Long of Louisiana. Long had risen to power in his home state by engaging in demagoguery: that is, by exploiting the fears, prejudices, and general feelings of alienation and hostility of middle and lower class Louisianans toward the conservative political oligarchy that controlled the state. This powerful coterie of bankers, oilmen, sugar planters, and utility company owners, primarily located in the southern part of the state, ruled Louisiana with an iron grip. Long's strident attacks on these interests won him the governorship in 1928, and from that office, he launched an all-out war on these individuals and their various enterprises. Long's purge of these men was so thorough and forceful that they were left with virtually no political power whatever. Many claimed that Huey had become a dictator, which in effect, he had. Long, however, remained popular with the Louisiana electorate, in part because of his flamboyant, charismatic personality and captivating oratory, and in part because he "delivered the goods." He built roads, schools, and hospitals; revised the tax codes, distributed free textbooks; and lowered utility rates. To pay for his progressive programs, which he boasted were for the benefit of the common people, Long taxed wealthy Louisianans into the "poor house." Barred by law from succeeding himself as governor, Long ran in 1930 for a seat in the United States Senate and won easily. Huey was now ready to take his ideas, first introduced in Louisiana, to Washington and to the American people in general.

Long supported FDR for president in 1932, but within six months of the president's inauguration, Long broke with Roosevelt, believing that FDR had broken his promise to deliver the American people from the plutocracy's continued abuse. Long lampooned the rich as "pigs swilling in the trough of luxury." In attacks on New Deal programs, he alleged that "not a single dime of concentrated, bloated, pompous wealth, massed in the hands of a few people has been raked down to relieve the masses." Long, like FDR, mastered the use of the radio, which contributed most directly to his growing national popularity.

But demagogic rhetoric would not be enough to get people to turn against FDR and the New Deal; he needed to offer them something significantly more.

As an alternative to the New Deal, he advocated something he had introduced as governor: taxing the wealthy to force a redistribution of wealth "down to the people." He named his program the Share-Our-Wealth Plan. The government, he claimed could end the depression easily by using the tax system to confiscate the surplus riches of the wealthiest men and women in the nation and distribute these surpluses to the rest of the population. That would, he claimed, allow the government to guarantee every family a minimum "homestead" of $5,000 and an annual income of $2,500. Long's mastery of the radio helped to create a membership in his Share-Our-Wealth Clubs of 10 million Americans, or so the senator claimed. Regardless of the accuracy of the number, Long's idea was popular with millions of unemployed, suffering, and disillusioned Americans, searching for a scapegoat for their woes. A majority of the clubs' rank and file came from middle-class people: independent proprietors who operated their own farms, businesses, and shops; self-employed doctors and lawyers; and plumbers, carpenters, electricians, and other contractors. Many members of these groups perceived the apparent big business favoritism of the New Deal programs as a direct threat to their future economic and social well-being. Substantial numbers of Share-Our-Wealth Club supporters also came from highly-skilled and white collar sections of the working class—railroad workers, bricklayers, postal workers, teachers, department store sales clerks, and others who aspired to a middle class income and status. By 1935 FDR considered Long as the most likely challenger to his presidential reelection bid. Indeed, in the spring of 1935, a poll by the Democratic National Committee disclosed that Long's popularity might be enough to attract more than 10 percent of the vote if he ran as a third-party candidate, enough to tip a close election to the Republicans. But before that campaign began, Long was assassinated. In an act of revenge for his wronged father-in-law by the Long machine, a young physician, Carl Weiss, shot Huey on the night of September 8, 1935 as the "Kingfisher" stood chatting with aides outside the Capitol in Baton Rouge. Though not instantly killed by Weiss' one shot, which lodged under Huey's ribs, two days later, largely as a result of poor surgery, the "Kingfisher" died.

Meanwhile in the Midwest, Father Charles Coughlin, the "radio priest," delivered a message similar to Long's. At first a warm supporter of the president and the New Deal, which he called "Christ's Deal," by 1934, Coughlin had become a harsh critic. In his weekly sermons broadcast nationally from his home parish in Royal Oak, Michigan, Coughlin proposed a series of monetary reforms—remonetization of silver, issuing of greenbacks, and nationalization of the banking system—that he insisted would restore prosperity and ensure economic justice. Coughlin's sermons were listened to by an estimated 30 to 40 million Americans. By late 1934, Coughlin had become disheartened by what he claimed was FDR's failure to deal harshly with the "money powers," which he contended were running the New Deal. The NRA was a program to resuscitate corporate profits. Coughlin called for a strong government to set national priorities and force, if necessary, business, labor, agriculture, and even white-collar professionals to do its bidding to help recover the economy and usher in a more "just" capitalist system. In 1934 Coughlin founded the National Union of Social Justice as a precursor to a political party that would challenge the Democrats in the 1936 election. By 1935, Coughlin began moving to the right, endorsing in his "sermons" fascists like Benito Mussolini and his corporative state, as well as Il Duce's ruling by decree rather than by democratic consent, which Coughlin believed FDR should be doing as well "in the name of the people." As Coughlin's disillusionment with the New Deal intensified, his admiration for the fascists dictators grew more pronounced. Most disturbing and alarming was his increasing anti-Semitism, which permeated his radio talks. Reflecting his growing approval of Hitler and Mussolini, Coughlin claimed that Jewish bankers were master-minding a world conspiracy to suppress the toiling masses. Although Coughlin was a spellbinding speaker, he failed to build the NUSJ into a viable political entity. After the 1936 election, Coughlin, embittered, moved further and further right, denouncing both Jews and democracy with incredible vituperation. His condemnations were so extreme and outright vicious that many radio stations refused to allow him airtime. Despite his fanaticism, millions of ordinary citizens continued to believe that the "radio priest" was their savior.

Another popular figure was Francis Townsend, an elderly California physician who claimed that the way to end the depression was to give every citizen over the age of sixty $200 a month, provided they retired (thus freeing jobs for younger, unemployed Americans) and spent the money in full (which would pump needed funds into the economy). By 1935, the Townsend Plan had attracted the support of more than 5 million older men and women. While the plan itself made little progress in Congress, the idea's popularity helped build support for the Social Security system, which Congress did approve in 1935.

None of these self-styled reformers showed much skill at transforming his popularity into disciplined political parties that could compete with either of the two major parties in elections. Moreover, though all three individuals—Long, Coughlin, and Townsend—were appealing orators with large public followings and masters of the new medium of radio, their speeches or sermons were more tirades or rantings against the established order than offering realistic, viable alternatives. Though Long's taxation scheme sounded good on paper and to desperate ears, in reality, there was no way the federal government would or could implement, or Americans in general support, such a blatant violation of the sanctity of private property that such a confiscatory program of taxation represented. Coughlin's initial ideas of government protection of labor's rights was sound, but his drift to the far right with his embracing of fascism and anti-Semitism negated what legitimate message he might have had. Townsend, the "mildest" of the three dissidents, whose idea of aid to the elderly was not seen as "crackpot" or "hair-brained" or even "radical" but sound and decent, for if any group of Americans were in need and deserved some sort of federal assistance it was the nation's elderly. This was why Congress eventually enacted the Social Security Act and perhaps would not have acted as swiftly had it not been for Francis Townsend.

Members of the Roosevelt administration considered dissident movements— and the broad popular discontent they represented—a genuine threat to the president. An increasing number of advisers were warning FDR that he would have to do something dramatic to counter their strength.

THE "SECOND DEAL"

The populist insurrections of 1934-35 forced a reluctant FDR to move to the left. Though personally and ideologically hesitant to move the New Deal down that path, the people had moved that way, and being the consummate politician, FDR knew that if he hoped to be reelected, he had to shift the New Deal in that direction as well. FDR's rhetoric (in which could be heard some of the tirades of Huey Long), suddenly took on an anticorporate tone. He called for the "abolition of evil holding companies." He attacked the wealthy for their profligate and unpatriotic ways. He clamored for new programs to aid the poor and the downtrodden. In short, FDR wanted to "connect" with the people and turn them away from radical solutions and, in the process, to win reelection. Thus, in the spring of 1935, Roosevelt launched the so-called Second New Deal.

The new programs represented both a new focus and direction in New Deal policy. To help him develop programs reflecting this new direction, FDR turned to reform-minded businessmen, investment bankers, lawyers, economists, and labor leaders who embraced a new theory and thus advocated a new approach to hopefully ending the depression: underconsumptionism. Supporters of this idea believed that underconsumption, or an endemic weakness in consumer demand, had caused the Great Depression. Individual consumers simply had not had enough money during the twenties to buy what the nation's industries produced. Thus, the key to recovery was not to limit production as the First Deal had implemented but rather to increase Americans' purchasing power through a variety of government policies. These policies included government support for strong labor unions to force up wages; higher social welfare expenditures to put more money in the hands of the poor; and a significant increase in public works projects to increase the number of Americans working and thus earning and spending money. The underconsumptionists did not worry about a federal deficit that increased public works programs would create. The government could always borrow funds from private sources and, in fact, considered such an approach a crucial antidepression device. Those who received government assistance would have additional income to spend on consumer goods; and producers would profit from increases in consumer spending. In short, government borrowing would increase the money supply or "inflate" a deflated economy and eventually would put an end to the depression. This "fiscal" approach to economic downturns, which the depression in effect was, represented a reversal of traditional thinking that a government should always maintain a balanced budget. In the 1940s this new theory became known as Keynesianism, named after its originator, the British economist John Maynard Keynes. From 1935, the United States' economy became essentially Keynesian; that is, the government would henceforth do whatever was deemed necessary through various fiscal and monetary policies to revitalize a sluggish or "depressed" economy. Many politicians and economists rejected this new approach, believing that deficit spending would only create a debt-ridden government. FDR himself remained a fiscal conservative but was willing to give the new idea a try.

One of FDR's first actions reflecting his change in attitude toward big business was his proposal to finally break up the great utility holding companies and spoke venomously of monopolistic control of their industry. Indeed, at the time, thirteen utility companies controlled 75 percent of the nation's electric power. The Holding Company Act of 1935 was passed, but frantic lobbying by the utilities led to revisions that sharply limited its effects. A companion measure to the Holding Company Act was the Congressionally-created Rural Electrification Administration, which oversaw the bringing of electricity at reasonable rates to hundreds of thousands of rural households. This New Deal agency was especially important to the South and West, largely rural regions where few inhabitants had electrical power. Indeed, the REA along with the Western dam projects mentioned earlier were the cornerstones of Western modernization. Finally, Congress passed the Emergency Relief Appropriation Act, a $5 billion measure that dwarfed similar legislation passed during the first New Deal. FDR gave part of this sum to the PWA and CCC so those work-relief programs could continue and used another portion to create yet another work and guidance program for primarily high school and college students, the National Youth Administration (NYA), which in Texas was directed by a future president and liberal, Lyndon Baines Johnson.

The Federal Art Project employed these artists to work in a New York City gallery. Many of the project's paintings and murals depicted scenes of American life during the Depression.

FDR, however, directed most of the new relief money to a new agency, the Works Progress Administration (WPA). This new work program was headed by the irrepressible Harry Hopkins, who was now referred to as "Minister of Relief." Though much of the WPA's money and focus continued or expanded infrastructure refurbishing and new construction, significant funds were funneled into an entirely new direction for the first time: the arts. Thanks largely to the exhortations of Eleanor Roosevelt, the WPA was largely responsible for not letting American cultural life die during the Great Depression. The WPA funded a vast program of public art, supporting the work of thousands of painters, architects, writers, playwrights, actors, and intellectuals. Beyond extending relief to struggling artists, it fostered the creation of art that reflected and spoke of and to the values, customs, and lifestyles of ordinary Americans. All across the land, WPA artists adorned public buildings with colorful, story-telling murals, usually with a theme that showed how thanks to FDR and the New Deal, people were working and happy again. Photographers also traversed the nation, capturing with their cameras the suffering of hundreds of thousands of especially rural Americans. In many ways FDR used the WPA not only as a major work-relief program but also as a means of boosting morale. FDR also used the program to ensure, by the use of various artistic mediums, that future Americans would never forget how Depression-era Americans overcame the trauma of the second most severe crisis in the Republic's history, thanks largely to FDR and his New Deal. By the time the decade of the 1930s ended, the WPA, in conjunction with an expanded RFC and the PWA, had brought about the building of 500,000 miles of road, 100,000 bridges, 100,000 public buildings, and 600 airports. The New Deal transformed the nation's urban and rural landscapes. Everywhere they turned they found concrete examples of its accomplishments.

Equally alarming to the upper classes was FDR's tax reform proposals, a program conservatives labeled as a "soak-the-rich" scheme, which, when compared to all previous taxation policies, it indeed did seem to "discriminate" against more affluent citizens. Politically, FDR's intention with his tax reform bill was to slow Huey Long's Share-Our-Wealth momentum, which it did by establishing the highest and most progressive peacetime tax rates in history. Unfortunately, as is still true today, the actual impact of these rates was limited, and many wealthy individuals found ways to escape them altogether. In retrospect, FDR's tax reform bill was put into "effect" not because he wanted to see a genuine redistribution of wealth, which he opposed, but rather for purely political reasons: he hoped to curtail the "Kingfisher's" growing popularity by stealing "his thunder." If FDR could present to the people a more realistic and viable plan than Long, then, come 1936, the president could win back those wayward voters.

Without question, the most momentous piece of legislation to come out of the Second New Deal was the 1935 Social Security Act. From the beginning of the New Deal, important cabinet members such as Secretary of Labor, Frances Perkins, had been pressuring FDR to create a system of federally sponsored social insurance for the elderly and the unemployed. FDR had consistently opposed such a measure until now. Like with his tax reform bill, FDR was responding politically rather than with any great conviction that such assistance was the right thing to do for such individuals. Regardless of FDR's motivation, the Social Security Act laid the foundation of the modern welfare state. The act established several distinct programs. For the elderly, there were two types of assistance. Those who were presently destitute could receive up to $15 a month in federal aid. More important for the future, many Americans presently working were incorporated into a pension system, to which they and their employers would contribute by paying a payroll tax; it would provide them with an income on retirement. Pension payments would not begin until 1942, and at that time, eligible persons would receive only $10 to $85 a month. Broad categories of workers (including domestic servants and agricultural laborers, occupations overwhelmingly dominated by African Americans and women) were excluded from the program. Nonetheless, the act was a crucial first step in building the nation's most important social "net" for the elderly.

Labor Resurgent

The emergence of a powerful trade union movement in the 1930s was one of the most important political and social developments of the decade. It occurred partly in response to government efforts to enhance the power of unions, but it was also a result of the increased militancy of American workers and their leaders. During the 1920s most workers rarely challenged their employers or demanded recognition of their unions. Moreover, shrewd employers such as Henry Ford, with their promotion of "welfare capitalism" in their industries, were able to greatly curtail the appeal of unionization among their workers. Also affecting unionization during the 1920s, especially among ethnic/immigrant workers, was the trend toward Americanization at school, at work, and in popular entertainment, which not only made unions appear unnecessary but also anti-American at a time when working class ethnic Americans wanted to "fit in" and be accepted. The Depression, however, rapidly changed working class sentiment toward both unions and labor militancy. The Depression heightened the sense of awareness and shared experience among workers as few working-class families escaped the distress and despair of the early 1930s. The increased politicalization of the working class first became apparent in the 1932 election when many workers voted for FDR. The NRA helped to transform their despair into hope. As already noted, it set guidelines for wages and work hours that if implemented by employers would improve working conditions. Moreover, clause 7(a) of the NIRA granted workers the right to join unions of their choosing and bound management to recognize unions and bargain with them in good faith. As a result, millions of workers, encouraged by such government promotion and protection, joined unions in 1933 and 1934.

Initially, union members' demands were quite modest. They wanted employers to observe the provisions of the NRA codes. They wanted to be treated fairly by their foremen, and they wanted management to recognize their unions. Few employers, however, were willing to give them any say in their working conditions. Most ignored the NRA's wage and hour guidelines and even used their influence over the program's code authorities to get worker requests for wage increases and union recognition rejected. Workers appealed directly to FDR and Hugh Johnson for a redress of their grievances, but their pleas went unanswered. Workers now decided to take matters into their own hands. In 1934 they staged 2,000 strikes across the country and in virtually every industry. Most of the strikes attracted little attention and were peaceful; some, however, were not, as they escalated into violent, bloody confrontations between workers and police. Such became the situation at the Electric Auto-Lite plant in Toledo, Ohio, in May 1934 when 10,000 surrounded the place and blocked all entrances and exits until the company agreed to shut down operations and negotiate a union contract. Management refused, called out the police to "remove" the striking workers, and the inevitable occurred: for seven bloody hours a pitched battle raged between strikers and the police as the latter resorted to the use of fire hoses, tear gas,

This cartoon criticizes the Social Security Act for identifying people by their assigned social security number. The program was financed by both the employers and the employees, and the money was placed in a combined account controlled by the government. A negative criticism was that this payroll tax would take money out of the economy and reduce the amount of money in circulation.

and gunfire to disperse the workers. Worker resistance, however, was more resilient than anticipated, forcing the governor to call out the National Guard, which succeeded in forcing the workers to disband but not until after more gunfire was exchanged and two workers lay dead. More violent and prolonged confrontations between police and striking workers occurred in Minneapolis and San Francisco. In the former city, from May through July 1934, National Guardsmen, police, and private security forces fought striking truck drivers and warehousemen that in the end left four dead and hundreds wounded. In the City by the Bay, striking longshoremen fought employers and police in street skirmishes throughout the month of July, in which two were killed and scores wounded. Employers there had hoped to break a two-month old strike with the use of force, but their attempt at intimidation only succeeded in gaining sympathy for the longshoremen, who were able to rally to their cause 100,000 additional workers in the transportation, construction, and service industries, who all walked off their jobs in a secondary supportive strike. As a result, for two weeks the city of San Francisco was virtually shut down. In the end, in both cities, politically astute municipal and state authorities intervened and eventually helped the workers win important concessions from employers.

The above strikes and confrontations between workers and police paled in comparison to the largest and most violent strike of 1934, which began on September 1, 1934, when 400,000 textile workers from Maine to Alabama, went on strike. Workers previously unwilling to unite because of ethnic and religious differences threw all that aside and bonded together against a common foe: textile mill owners. All of a sudden, New England Catholic Europeans joined with white Protestants from the Southeast to battle their respective employers. Both groups insisted that they were Americans first, bound together by class and national loyalties that transcended ethnic and religious identities. In the first two weeks of September striking workers brought cotton production to a virtual standstill. Mill owners tried to bring in replacement workers and hired private security forces to protect them but that only caused greater anger among the workers and the result was violent confrontations between strikers and the police. In northern communities such as Saylesville and Woonsocket, Rhode Island, full-scale riots erupted, causing several deaths, hundreds of injuries, and millions of dollars in property damage. Similar encounters took place in the South, where local vigilante groups, claiming workers to be communists, sided with the police and National Guardsmen to beat up strikers, kill union organizers, and help to incarcerate hundreds of strikers in barbed wire camps.

The often brutal suppression of strikes and other labor protests made workers more determined than ever to organize and use such unity to combat management's obvious refusal to accept the right of their workers to join unions. For that purpose, in 1935, John L. Lewis of the United Mine Workers, Sidney Hillman of the Amalgamated Clothing workers, and the leaders of six other unions that had become alienated by the AFL's lack of support seceded from that organization and formed a new consortium called the Committee for Industrial Organization, later renamed the Congress of Industrial Organizations. The new union's priority was to organize the millions of nonunion workers, regardless of skill level, gender, or race, into effective unions that would strengthen labor's political power. Hillman and Lewis made it clear that their new organization was pro-FDR and pro-New Deal and thus would vote *en masse* for the president and his party. Lewis and Hillman also pledged their union's financial support for FDR and pro-labor Democrats. Needless to say, FDR was euphoric about such support, and by his next campaign labor had become part of the New Democratic coalition. The passage of the Wagner Act and the creation of the NLRB in 1935 enhanced the labor movement's status and credibility. Because of the CIO's platform, labor union membership skyrocketed, and in short order union members began flexing their new muscles.

In late 1936 the United Auto Workers, a CIO affiliate, took on General Motors, considered by many the most powerful corporation in the world. Determined to improve wages and hours, as well as recognition of their union, workers in the Flint, Michigan plant took over the operation by employing a new tactic, the "sit-down strike," which saw workers simply, literally sit down at their job site and remain there until their grievances were redressed. For the first time in 50 years, a governor refused to call out the National Guard to end the strike. Frank Murphy, the governor of Michigan, wanted to avoid the violence and bloodshed he knew would ensue if he did and instead urged GM management to recognize the UAW and its right to collectively bargain on behalf of its workers. General Motors capitulated after a month of resistance. The CIO-UAW victory was followed up by another major triumph over a notorious anti-union corporation, United States Steel, which also announced that it too was ready to negotiate a contract with the CIO. In short order, the CIO successfully took on and won recognition and concessions from two of the most notorious anti-union corporations in the country.

As the CIO triumphed over big business, labor's stature in the nation grew along with its size. Many writers and artists, funded through the WPA, used their respective mediums to further popularize and establish the labor movement as America's first and best hope—the voice of the people and the embodiment of the nation's best and truest values—community, cooperation, and ethical individualism. Murals sprang up in post offices and other public buildings depicting blue-collar Americans at work, with faces reflecting a sense of pride and dignity as a result of their new status. Broadway's most celebrated play in 1935 was Clifford Odett's classic *Waiting For Lefty,* a raw drama about taxi drivers who confront their bosses and organize an honest union. Audiences were so inspired by the play that they often spontaneously joined in the final chorus of "Strike, Strike, Strike," the words that ended the play. *Pins and Needles*, a 1937 musical about the hopes and dreams of garment workers that was performed by actual members of the International Ladies Garment Workers Union (the play-within-the play, a new, Depression-era genre used by both Broadway and Hollywood during this time, especially in musical productions), became the longest-running play in Broadway history until *Oklahoma* broke its record of 1,108 performances in 1943.

Movies and novels also reflected the change of values brought forth by the labor movement. Both mediums celebrated the decency, honesty, and patriotism of ordinary Americans. In *Mr. Deeds goes to Town* (1936) and *Mr Smith Goes to Washington* (1939) director Frank Capra delighted audiences with stories of simple small-town heroes vanquishing the evil forces of wealth, corruption, decadence, and the abuse of power. Likewise, John Steinbeck's classic, *The Grapes of Wrath,* the best selling novel of 1939, told the story of an Oklahoma family's fortitude in surviving eviction from their land, migrating westward, and their exploitation in the "promised land" of California. In 1940, famed Hollywood westerns' director John Ford put Steinbeck's novel on the screen and made

Workers strike at an auto body plant in 1937. Labor unions gained in number and power during the 1930s.

one of that year's most acclaimed pictures. Moviegoers found special meaning in the declaration of one of the story's main characters, Ma Joad: "We're the people, we go on." In themselves and in one another, Americans seemed to discover the resolve they needed to rebuild a culture that had surrendered its identity to corporations and businesses.

THE DEPRESSION, THE NEW DEAL, AND A CHANGE IN VALUES

As reflected in labor's platform, as well as in the above mentioned movies and plays, many New Deal liberals and intellectuals were harsh critics of what conservatives believed should dictate the marketplace—amorality and its concomitant tenets of individualism, acquisitiveness, and egotistical behavior. These values informed the American political economy from the nation's founding through the 1920s. The Great Depression, however, destroyed much of the myth surrounding classical economic thought and its attendant values. As the 1930s progressed, Americans increasingly rejected those values and embraced instead the ideals of "moral economics"—the promotion of cooperation, justice, and compassion, especially a humanity inherent in a government's policies of protecting workers' rights and interests, as well as those of middle class consumers. Broadly stated, historically Americans have been torn by two opposing sets of values. Both are individualistic but one emphasizes cooperation, the other competition. Worker organizations have tended to promote cooperative individualism while businessmen have been the strongest advocates of acquisitive individualism. Middle class support of one or the other of these ideals is determined largely by historical/economic conditions. For example, during times of relative prosperity, many in the middle class have tried to emulate the upper classes and so adopted their values—the acquisitive ethic. The 1920s, 1950s, and 1980s serve as the best examples of such value acculturation in the twentieth century. During hard times, on the other hand, like the 1930s, many in the middle class identified with the working class cooperative ethos and thus, along with the working class, looked to the government—the embracing of liberalism—to ameliorate, if not rectify, the economic and social inequities caused by the amoral marketplace—unfettered capitalism.

Often American intellectuals and academics have found themselves in conflict with the popular mood. Such was the case for many of the nation's intelligentsia in the 1920s. However, during the 1930s, (and to some degree again in the 1960s), intellectuals and the common folk found enough social and economic commonality that they momentarily found themselves traveling ideologically parallel courses. Intellectuals and Depression victims alike criticized the effects of capitalism, though the latter not as explicitly or as harshly as the former. The Depression rapidly forced millions of Americans to rethink their devotion to traditional values, especially those associated with laissez faire capitalism. Even the American Dream itself was questioned by many citizens. The economic collapse of the 1930s, at the very least, called for a readjustment in values. Searching for new values, some intellectuals found hope and inspiration in the idealization of peasant societies or regional agrarianism in the United States. More turned to the legacy of Marxist socialism or other manifestations of socialist thought. What 1930s intellectuals and common folk had in common was a search for a life of community and sharing as opposed to the acquisitive individualism of modern industrial capitalism.

The Rise of the Radical Third Parties

One of the most important repercussions of labor unrest was the emergence of left-leaning third party movements. In Wisconsin, for example, Philip La Follette, son of "Battling Bob" La Follette of Progressive-era fame, was elected governor in 1934 and 1936 as the candidate of the radical Wisconsin Progressive Party, which advocated, among other things, unemployment compensation and farm loans. Perhaps more disturbing to New Dealers was his anti-liberal rhetoric. Indeed, La Follette publicly proclaimed in 1934 that "We [the Progressive party] are not liberal!" He further announced that "liberalism is nothing but a sort of milk-and-water tolerance. . . . I believe in a fundamental and basic change. I am a radical." La Follette believed there was "no alternative to conscious distribution of income," and thus in his opinion and that of his party, "this American principal of popular government, and the constitutions conceived to secure it, were not designed to sustain any particular economic system." Just what La Follette had in mind as an alternative to capitalism, he never really articulated. Yet, his rhetoric found receptive ears in his home state as former Wisconsin Democrats and even some Republicans embraced La Follette's attack on New Deal "liberalism" and voted for his party rather than for Roosevelt's Democrats.

In Minnesota, the Farmer-Labor Party, a fusion of discontented farmers and urban laborers, rose to challenge and defeat Democratic New Dealers. Led by Governor Floyd Olson, who was elected in 1930, the party completely dominated state politics from that year until the end of the decade. The party's platform echoed that of Wisconsin's Progressive Party, with Olson using the same radical rhetoric of La Follette, declaring that capitalism was "on trial for its life," and that it was "steeped in the most dismal stupidity." Olson's relief agenda for his citizens far outstripped FDR's modest early approaches, with Olson threatening conservatives in the legislature that if they did not enact his relief bills he would declare martial law. Olson stated that those who opposed his measures "because they happen to possess considerable wealth will be brought in by the provost guard. They will be obliged to give up more than they are giving up now." Olson further announced that as long as he was governor there was "not going to be any misery in the state if I can humanly prevent it." "I hope," Olson told wildly cheering crowds, that "the present system of government goes right down to Hell." Like La Follette, Olson took great pride in being a "radical," using that term constantly to describe his ideology and that of his party's. Olson announced he was a "radical," not a liberal, because he wanted "definite change in the system. I am not satisfied with tinkering, I am not satisfied with hanging a laurel wreath upon burglars and thieves and pirates and calling them code authorities or something else." Olson went even so far as to intimate that he was a closet-socialist, when again, to a rousing ovation, he declared that "When the final clash comes between Americanism and fascism, we will find a so-called 'red' as the defender of democracy." As the rise to power of both La Follette and Olson indicated, the overwhelming majority of Minnesotans and Wisconsinites wanted more drastic change than the New Deal was producing.

The same message emanated from California in 1934-36. Instead of forming a third party, discontented Californians took over the Democratic Party. In the Golden State, former Socialist Party candidate and famous author Upton Sinclair led the anti-New Deal charges. In a book titled *I, Governor of California, And How I Ended Poverty: A True Story of the Future,* Sinclair outlined his plan. The novelist described how he would be nominated and elected, and how as governor he would create a production-for-use economy in the midst of capitalist California. Sinclair predicted that he would totally eliminate poverty in the state in less than four years. The central feature of Sinclair's End Poverty in California (EPIC) was the concept of production-for-use. The profit system, the writer argued, had produced itself into a depression. Under it, increased productivity was a curse because workers were not paid enough to buy what they made. This "fact" led to unemployment, idle factories and farms, and storehouses full of goods, especially food products people desperately needed but were destroyed while millions went hungry. To remedy this, Sinclair proposed that the state take over the idle land and factories and permit the unemployed to use the land and machines to provide for their needs. Sinclair also advocated the establishment of land colonies to produce food for the hungry and state-owned and operated factories to meet other needs. Suffice it to say, Sinclair's "new socialism" terrified California conservatives because it amounted to the old concept of a "moral economy of provision" as opposed to the political economy of the free market. Despite conservative opposition, which became vicious in its falsehoods and accusations labeling Sinclair an atheist (actually he was a Christian Democrat) and a free lover—he was a devoted husband—and of course a communist—the only thing Sinclair had in common with the communists was mutual animosity—his EPIC swept the Golden State like an old-fashioned Awakening. However, come election time, the conservative coalition and its massive propaganda campaign against Sinclair, which included "newsreels" with

Hollywood actors portraying Okies and people with putative Russian accents endorsing the novelist, was too much for EPIC to overcome. Sinclair was defeated by a closer-than-anticipated margin. However, like elsewhere in the mid-thirties, Sinclair's defeat confirmed the leftward drift of American attitudes in another way. In order to win, the Republican Acting Governor, Frank Merriam, a borderline reactionary, felt constrained to speak favorably of the New Deal, calling for a thirty-hour workweek and endorsing the Townsend Revolving Pension Plan. Conservatives had to pose as progressives to have a chance of winning at this time. The American political structure as a whole had tilted definitely leftward.

Surprisingly, the American Communist Party (CP) at this time never became strong enough to pose a real political threat either in any of the states or nationally. In the early thirties, especially during Hoover's administration, the party had success in rallying to its platform homeless urban African Americans in the North, southern white and black sharecroppers, and Latino and Filipino agricultural workers in the West. Among those individuals the party mobilized them into unions and unemployment leagues. The CP also played significant roles in the Minneapolis and San Francisco strikes. The party reached its zenith of membership (80,000 by 1938) when it stopped preaching world revolution in 1935 and, instead, began calling for a "popular front" of democratic forces against fascism. Despite its new "popular front" ideology, the party remained a dictatorial organization that took its orders from Moscow. Membership turnover was high, as many left the party after learning about its authoritarian character. Interestingly, like the other movements noted above, the party's most important contribution to thirties politics was to channel popular discontent into unions and other political parties that, in turn, would force New Dealers to respond to the demands of the nation's dispossessed and forgotten.

THE 1936 ELECTION: FDR Reelected and Democratic Party Ascendancy

Despite the "thunder from the left" and the anxiety it caused FDR and the New Dealers, in the end, come election time, the president had little to fear from the populist insurgents. FDR was simply too shrewd a politician to allow an upstart, no matter how popular they or their rhetoric was, to unseat him. By moving the Second New Deal to the left, he not only silenced the populists, by "stealing their thunder" as it was, but also ensured both a victory for himself and his party. In his 1936 reelection campaign, FDR labeled the conservatives and corporate moguls and "economic royalists" who had "concentrated into their own hands an almost complete control over other people's property, other people's money, other people's labor—other people's lives." He called on citizens to strip the economic royalists of their power and "save a great and precious form of government for ourselves and the world." Voters responded by giving FDR the greatest popular mandate—for himself and his New Deal—in the history of American politics to that time. "The Messiah" received 61 percent of the popular vote; his hapless Republican challenger, Alf Landon of Kansas,—who even lost his own state—received only 36 percent. Only two states, Maine and Vermont, having between them a "whopping" 8 electoral votes went for Landon.

FDR's landslide represented not only overwhelming endorsement for the president and his New Deal but the beginning of Democratic/liberal ascendancy. From this moment forward, the Democratic Party became the party of reform and the party of the "forgotten American." Perhaps more important for the Democratic Party's future, FDR, via the New Deal, began to assemble the various interest groups or coalitions that would sustain the party and keep it the majority party for the next five decades. Not until the 1980s would the New Deal coalitions dissolve, allowing conservative Republican candidates such as Ronald Reagan to capture the presidency. But until that decade, these various groups kept the Democratic Party in power. For example, one of the party's key future "blocs" were African Americans, especially northern urban black folk, who deserted the Republican Party en masse and voted Democrat. African Americans calculated that their interests would best be served by the "Party of the Common Man." Also, ethnic, working class Americans, especially those of Italian, Irish, and Jewish heritage, voted

This is a meeting of the Communist Party in Detroit, Michigan. The Communist Party organized women and men into neighborhood organizations to fight evictions and gain relief for the unemployed.

overwhelmingly Democratic. And finally, FDR did well among the Anglo-Saxon middle class, many of whom were grateful to him for pushing through the Social Security Act.

As noted above, FDR's move to the left was politically motivated—to get himself and his party reelected. Upon closer examination of the Second New Deal's "concern for the common people" legislation, many of the most important measures fell far short of their supposed intention of uplifting the downtrodden and the oppressed. For example, the Holding Company Act did little to break-up the big trusts, and FDR's promise to deliver the nation's poor, like farm workers, were not covered by the Social Security Act or by the National Labor Relations Act. Consequently, thousands of southern black sharecroppers and Mexican-American farm workers in the Southwest were excluded from their protections and benefits. Not until the late 1960s did Southwestern and California farm workers achieve any such benefits. As will be seen, they will attain such status largely by their own initiative and by the perseverance of their leaders such as Cesar Chavez. No white southern Democrat was going to vote for a bill that would improve the economic or social condition of southern blacks. Moreover, FDR only fleetingly mentioned, and with great hesitation, the possibility of anti-lynching legislation or voting rights or any guaranteeing or protecting black folks' basic civil rights.

FDR's populist rhetoric also obscured the fact that many big business enterprises throughout the nation, but especially in the West, where corporations such as Kaiser of California and Brown and Root of Texas, enthusiastically supported the Second New Deal because it gave them such massive and lucrative infrastructure contracts to build dams and other projects. In the Midwest and East, FDR's corporate supporters included real estate developers, mass merchandisers (such as Bambergers and Sears, Roebuck), clothing manufacturers, and the like. All of these New Deal supporters were convinced that prosperity depended on high, stable levels of consumer spending and were thus willing to tolerate labor unions, welfare programs, and high levels of government spending. They had no intention, however, of surrendering either economic or political power. Though on the one hand the Democratic Party definitely became the party of the common people, on the other, it also became the party of big business. From one constituency came the votes; from the other came money to finance the campaigns. The conflicting interests of these two groups often led to great strife and disunity in the party, especially in the latter decades of the twentieth century, and ultimately helped contribute to the party's loss of majority status.

Forgotten Americans

As alluded earlier, the New Deal was designed to ameliorate conditions for white middle and working class Americans. By the 1930s, this category included (because of their sheer numbers and potential political "value"), southern and eastern European ethnic groups—Italians, Slavs, Poles, and other previously discriminated groups from those European regions. Indeed, by the 1930s, a very high percentage of individuals from these groups had been assimilated, or at least acculturated, into mainstream WASP society, and, perhaps more important, as they became politicized, they joined the Democratic Party almost en masse. By the early 1930s, their potential political power was realized, especially in the urban North and West where no Democratic politician could afford to ignore their power. FDR understood their importance well, for he was a product of New York Democratic politics where such men as Al Smith and Robert Wagner, and others had organized the "ethnic vote" even before 1920. Thus, after becoming president, FDR made sure that New Deal largesse—PWA and CWA infrastructure projects and other relief measures—found their way into the urban enclaves where these "voters" lived. As a result, Jewish Americans and Catholic Americans, especially those descended from southern and eastern European stock, voted for FDR in overwhelming numbers. Though FDR and many of his WASP New Dealers were closet anti-Semites and anti-Catholic, and did nothing to alleviate such sentiment in the nation, they at least helped to promote the belief among these ethnic Americans that they were overcoming the stigma of their heritage and would someday soon no longer be considered second-class citizens. Such would not occur, however, until after World War II.

More important to the rise in status and importance for southern and eastern Europeans was their strong working class presence. In many of the mass production industries in the Northeast, Midwest, and the West, they formed the majority of the workforce and thus made crucial contributions to the labor movement's rebirth and especially to the CIO's formation in 1935. Ever the astute and ambitious politician, FDR realized this early on in his presidency and thus accommodated their demands because he understood and feared the power they wielded through their labor organizations.

Unfortunately, the New Deal, on the whole, paid little attention to the needs of African Americans and Mexican Americans. New Dealers believed that the issues of capitalism's viability, economic recovery, and the inequality of wealth and power in white society took precedent over the social problems of racial and ethnic discrimination. Few 1930s liberals were ready or willing to address these deep-seated social issues; their priority remained saving American capitalism and if along the way the quality and quantity of life for minorities could be improved with a modicum of resistance then that was fine. Because they were disproportionately poor, most minority groups did not benefit from the populist and pro-labor New Deal reforms. In many ways, the New Deal did more to intensify racial discrimination than it did to ameliorate it. This was especially true for African Americans living in the South. Their northern counterparts, however, benefited somewhat from New Deal legislation, especially those black folk living in northern industrial centers. There, they joined unions, particularly the CIO, which welcomed them, and voted. As alluded earlier, beginning in the 1936 presidential election, large numbers of northern blacks voted Democratic instead of Republican because they had received some attention from the New Deal. Yet, even in the North, in programs like the CWA, black workers received less pay than whites for doing the same work. In the South, black folk were barred from voting, excluded from AAA programs, and denied federal protection from white reprisals when they tried to form their own farmer unions. Perhaps most unsettling was FDR's refusal to support anti-lynching legislation, a key objective of the decade's civil rights activist.

Not all New Dealers ignored the plight of African Americans. Particularly concerned for their welfare was the First Lady, who almost single-handedly did more to help black folk than any New Dealer, including her husband. Eleanor Roosevelt spoke out frequently against racial injustice. In 1939 she resigned from the Daughters of the American Revolution when the organization refused to allow black opera singer Marian Anderson to perform in its concert hall. With the support of another civil rights advocate, Secretary of the Interior, Harold Ickes, Eleanor "pressured" her husband to sponsor the idea of permitting Anderson to sing from the steps of the Lincoln Memorial. On Easter Sunday, 1939, 75,000 people gathered at the memorial to hear Anderson sing while demonstrating their support for racial equality. FDR did not attend.

Though FDR succumbed to his wife's admonishments to appoint a few African Americans to second-level posts in his administration, he was never willing to make the fight for racial justice a priority—it was just too risky politically. FDR was not about to alienate white southern senators who controlled key congressional committees for the sake of even the most modest of civil rights proposals. Like the rest of his white cabinet, FDR believed that economic issues far outweighed in importance the racial ones. As already established, FDR was the consummate politico who was always calculating potential political loss or gain. In his mind, support of civil rights legislation would be a definite political loss, not a gain, and thus only with the greatest of reservation would he expend any political capital on supporting even the most circumscribed civil rights bills. Unlike other groups, such as northern ethnics, African Americans at this time were not yet strong enough as an electoral constituency or as a reform movement to force FDR to accede to their wishes.

Perhaps more adversely affected by the Depression years than African Americans were Mexicans and Mexican Americans. The plight of Hispanic folk was especially harsh in the Southwest, where at this time the majority lived. The most devastating manifestation of racial prejudice toward Mexican and Mexican Americans was repatriation, which actually began during the Hoover administration but was continued during the early New Deal years. Repatriation meant the returning of immigrants to their land of origin. As the depression worsened, and white Americans in certain regions looked for scapegoats for their woes, the Hoover administration in 1931 announced a plan for repatriating illegal aliens and giving their jobs to American (white) citizens. This policy focused on Mexican immigrants in the Southwest, especially those in California and Texas, the two western states with the largest Hispanic population at the time. Local governments in those two states were more than willing to enforce the law for they were eager to eliminate the minority poor from their relief rolls. Between 1929 and 1935, the federal government repatriated 82,000 Mexican immigrants in "raids" that occurred on businesses and homes. Those unable to prove his or her legal status with the necessary documentation were deported. California and Colorado authorities went even further than what was intended. Threatening to remove them from the relief rolls, California officials "persuaded" 12,000 unemployed Mexicans in the Los Angeles area to leave, offering them free railroad tickets to Mexico as a further "inducement." Colorado authorities secured the departure of 20,000 Mexicans through similar techniques. Suffice it to say, such a dragnet by federal, state, and local governments created a climate of fear within the Hispanic community and consequently 500,000 more returned to Mexico voluntarily. This total equaled the number of Mexicans who had come to the United States in the 1920s. Most revealing was the fact that in the ranks of the repatriated were a significant number of legal immigrants who were unable to produce their immigration papers, the American-born children of illegals, and most egregious, thousands of Mexican Americans who had lived in the Southwest for generations.

Life grew more difficult for those immigrant Mexicans who stayed behind. Harassed by government officials, Mexicans everywhere sought to escape public attention and scrutiny. In Los Angeles, where their influence had been felt and accepted in the 1920s, they now retreated into the separate community of East Los Angeles. To many, they became the "invisible minority." Mexican Americans did receive some benefit from the New Deal, especially from the program's pro-labor legislation. Those Chicanos living in urban areas and who worked in blue collar industries, such as in the cannery and garment sectors, joined CIO-affiliated unions in large numbers and won concessions from their employers. But most Chicanos lived in rural areas and thus were agricultural workers. The National Labor Relations Act did not protect their right to organize unions, while the Social Security Act excluded them from the new federal welfare system. The New Deal, in short, offered the rural Chicano majority virtually nothing.

Interestingly and ironically, the only group of truly "forgotten Americans" whose lives were significantly improved by New Deal liberalism were Native Americans. From the 1880s to the 1930s, the federal government had pursued a policy of removing Native Americans to reservations, and once they were confined there, they were egregiously neglected in hopes they would all soon die off. As noted in a previous chapter, the 1887 Dawes Act called for the dismemberment of tribal lands and the parceling out of such domain to individual owners in the hope of transforming a nomadic, hunting people into docile and sedentary farmers. Such a policy would have been welcomed most enthusiastically by black Americans, but it was totally rejected by Native Americans. By 1933 nearly half the Indians living on reservations whose land had been allotted were landless (They had been swindled out of their land by greedy white land speculators.), while those who still had their land were living in deserts or on land so marginal that no white person would want it. The shrinking land base in combination with a growing population intensified Native American power. Compounding this growing problem was the desire of "assimilationists" in the 1920s who put pressure on the Bureau of Indian Affairs (BIA) to outlaw all Indian religious ceremonies, to take Indian children from tribal communities and place them into federal boarding schools, and impose limits on the length of men's hair. This draconian policy was finally redressed during FDR's presidency, especially by John Collier, whom the president appointed to run the BIA. Collier brought to his agency the same kind of energy and efficiency that Harry Hopkins had injected into New Deal relief programs.

Collier was one of the few New Dealers who shared Eleanor Roosevelt's genuine humanitarianism and altruism. He was determined to improve the life of one of the nation's most "forgotten" citizens. No sooner was he in office that he pursued a policy of relentless pressuring of other New Deal agencies to include Native Americans. For example, a full Native American CCC was created, and Indians also were employed in numerous other agencies on projects to improve reservation land, as well as to educate Native Americans in land conservation methods. Collier also exhorted Congress to pass the Pueblo Relief Act, which compensated the Pueblo Indians of Colorado for land taken from them in the 1920s. The 1934 Johnson-O'Malley Act was also passed, which gave federal money to states to provide for Indian health care, welfare, and education. Collier also pushed for the repeal of the once-mandatory federal boarding schools for Indian children and instead promoted their enrollment in local public schools. Perhaps one of his most important accomplishments was the allowing of Native Americans to once again practice their traditional religions. He also created the Indian Arts and Crafts Board, which promoted Indian artists and helped them to market their works.

The centerpiece of Collier's agenda was the Indian Reorganization Act of 1934 (also known as the Wheeler-Howard Act). This act revoked the allotment provisions of the Dawes Act by restoring tribal lands and granting Indians the right to establish constitutions and bylaws for self-government. It also provided support for new tribal corporations that would regulate the use of communal lands and appropriate funds for the economic development of the reservation. This was a landmark act that ended the assimilationist policy pursued by previous administrations. The act recognized that Native American tribes possessed the right of self-determination and self-government, as well as the right to control their own cultural and economic well-being. It reflected Collier's commitment to what we would call today "cultural pluralism," a doctrine which celebrates and accepts diversity in American society and seeks to protect that diversity from those who believe in "Americanism"—code for the belief that all peoples living in the United States should acculturate WASP values, mores, and norms. This was the assimilationist position. Collier hoped that his policy of cultural pluralism would invigorate traditional Indian cultures and tribal societies and sustain both for generations.

Cultural pluralism was not a popular idea in depression America, for too many white Americans believed it only caused greater division and the potential for racial or class warfare. Collier thus encountered opposition everywhere: from Protestant missionaries and cultural conservatives who wanted to continue the assimilationist policy; from white farmers and businessmen who feared that the new legislation would protect Indian lands from their acquisition; and even from some Indian groups who had embraced assimilation, while others viewed the IRA as one more attempt by the federal government to impose the "white man's will."

One such tribe that believed the IRA was another white conspiracy against Native Americans was the Navajo, the nation's largest tribe, who voted to reject its terms. For a variety of reasons, other tribes joined with the Navajo in rejecting the IRA, but a majority of the tribes—181—nearly 70 percent of the total—supported Collier's agenda and organized new tribal governments under its auspices. Thanks to Collier and the BIA many Native American tribes gained significant measures of freedom and autonomy. The New Deal, then, showed considerably more sensitivity to the needs and aspirations of Native Americans than had previous administrations. FDR's approval and support of Collier's reforms is interesting because for once there was no political gain to be had. Does that mean FDR was genuine in his concern and support for a truly neglected and oppressed people? Unlikely. Because Native Americans had been abused and oppressed for so long, and had become a truly invisible people, FDRarginalized people, despite his help, and thus still forgotten. Not until the 1970s would Native Americans demand their tribal rights and thus finally realize Collier's dream of cultural pluralism.

The New Dealers

For the academics, policymakers, advisers, counselors, and bureaucrats who designed and administered the rapidly expanding programs and agencies of the New Deal, the years 1936-1938 were heady ones. Never before had the federal government employed so many individuals to carry forth its policies and programs. Even the activism of Theodore Roosevelt and his coterie of progressives paled compared to the flurry of activity and passion that emanated from the Oval Office during these years. Fired by idealism and dedication, they were confident they could make the New Deal work. In the euphoria that set in after FDR's 1936 landslide victory, which the New Dealers interpreted as a popular mandate for their ideas, they devised countless schemes to expand the government's role especially in the nation's economic affairs. For example, the Farm Security Administration was created, an agency designed to help improve life for tenant farmers, sharecroppers, and farm laborers. In 1938, they drafted and got passed the Fair Labor Standards Act, which finally outlawed child labor, set minimum wages and maximum hours for adult workers, and put the federal government on its way to providing a home for all Americans by initiating low-cost housing projects in many urban areas.

Although the New Dealers proclaimed that all their efforts and ideas were for the "people," in reality the New Dealers were members of a new technocratic elite that had little in common with the nation's plain folk. Few were genuine humanitarians determined like a Collier to uplift and protect the truly downtrodden and oppressed. Most were motivated by the prospect of building a strong state committed to prosperity and justice but, concomitantly, to order and stability. They delighted in the intellectual challenge and technical complexity of social policy. They did not welcome interference from those they regarded as less intelligent or motivated by outworn ideologies. In short, the majority of the New Dealers were well-educated, university graduates, often animated to do the right thing for the people by an inherent sense of noblesse oblige. Many were the progeny of some of the oldest, wealthiest, most prestigious families in America upon whom it had always been incumbent to serve the public and protect the commonweal from the excesses of democracy as well as from the abuse of power by big business. They were social conservatives at heart and by temperament, but they were willing to experiment with socioeconomic reform (or social "engineering" if such efforts could guarantee a more prosperous and stable society and economy).

Not all of the New Dealers had been raised among wealth and privilege as was the case generally with earlier generations of reformers. To his credit, FDR was the first president since his cousin Teddy to welcome Jews and Catholics into his administration. Some became members of the president's inner circle of advisers, men such as Thomas "Tommy the Cork" Corcoran, Jim Farley, Ben Cohen, and Samuel Rosenman. These were men who had struggled from immigrant beginnings; they were "street smart," ambitious, politically savvy young men who brought to the Oval Office quick minds and mental toughness.

Though the New Deal offered opportunity to ethnics, a few blacks, Catholics, and Jews, such was not the case for women. The New Deal offered American females very little, especially when it came to the issues of greater economic opportunity, sexual freedom, and full equality. One reason why the issue of women's rights found few supporters was that the suffrage movement, after its 1920 triumph, had lost its momentum. Another was that prominent New Deal women, such as Frances Perkins, did not vigorously promote equal rights. They concentrated instead on "protective legislation"—laws that safeguarded female workers, who were thought to be more fragile than men. Those who insisted that women had "special" needs in the workplace could not easily argue that women were the equal of men in all respects. The most significant deterrent, however, to feminism was the general, pervasive male hostility that the depression only exacerbated. Men of all classes experienced a degree of emasculation during the Depression years because so many had lost their identity as the "bread winner" and provider of economic security for their families. For such men, being unemployed and then having to accept relief—the dole—unleashed feelings of inadequacy. The unemployment rates of men, especially among the ranks of blue-collar workers, tended to be higher than those of women, many of whom worked in white collar occupations, which were less vulnerable to job cutbacks. This fact only made unemployed men feel even more emasculated and useless. Resentment toward women, particularly those with jobs, intensified. The American male was not ready to accept the possibility that his wife or daughter could be a breadwinner.

This male anxiety had political and social consequences. Several states passed laws forbidding the hiring of married women. New Deal relief agencies were reluctant to authorize aid for unemployed women. The labor movement, even the more egalitarian CIO, made the protection of the male wage earner one of its principal goals. The Social Security pension system did not cover waitresses, domestic servants, and a host of other female-dominated occupations. Male fears of being emasculated and the venting of such anxiety became so intense during the 1930s that many artists, especially those involved in cartoon/comic strip production, started to project a strident "masculinism" in their work. Mighty Superman, the new comic-strip hero of 1938, reflected this male fretfulness. Superman was depicted as a working-class hero who, on several occasions, saved workers from mine explosions and other disasters caused by the greed and negligence of villainous capitalists. Superman's greatest vulnerability, besides kryptonite, was his "fatal" attraction to the sexy and aggressive working woman, Lois Lane. He was never able to resolve his dilemma by marrying Lois and then making her a kept woman because the continuation of the comic strip demanded that Superman repeatedly be exposed to kryptonite and female danger. However, in other media, such as the movies, producers faced no such technical obstacles. Anxious men could go to the local motion picture theater and find comfort from the conclusions of such pictures as *Woman of the Year*, in which Spencer Tracy (in many ways the epitome of masculinity) persuades the ambitious Katherine Hepburn to exchange her successful newspaper career for the bliss of motherhood and domesticity. From a thousand different points, 1930s politics and culture made it clear that woman's proper place was in the home. Faced with such intense, sometimes virulent opposition to breaking the confines of domesticity, it is not surprising that female activists failed to make feminism a part of New Deal reform.

Stalemate, 1937-1940

By 1937-38, the New Deal began to lose momentum and popularity, especially among increasing numbers of middle class Americans. Though initially supportive of the working class and its cooperative ethos, labor's increasing militancy, exemplified by the CIO's rise to prominence, began alienating the middle class. After the UAW's victory over General Motors in 1937, other workers began imitating the successful tactics pioneered by the Flint, Michigan auto workers. The sit-down strike became ubiquitous across the nation. Many middle class Americans were becoming disturbed by labor's growing power and apparent radicalism. To many members of the middle class, FDR had taken the New Deal too far to the left and thus wanted him and the party to "calm things" done. This was the moment the right had been waiting for since 1936 to regain power. Prior to this time, the conservatives had been unable to stop the Rooseveltian juggernaut. Now, with the middle class support waning for the New Deal, the right resurrected itself and began to aggressively assault both the president and his program as having gone too far to the left and endangering democratic republican government. Though the conservatives' criticisms found receptive ears, ultimately forcing FDR to move back to the center and curtail the more ambitious, left-leaning social reform programs of the New Deal, at really no time was the president ever in jeopardy of losing favor with the American people nor of being denied a third term.

"The Arrogance of Power": The Court Packing Debacle

Unfortunately for the fate of New Deal liberalism, its allegedly greatest proponent, FDR, helped to cause its final demise. One year after receiving the greatest electoral landslide in American political history and an apparent mandate for his New Deal, FDR committed what proved to be one of the greatest political blunders of his career: his attempt to "pack" the Supreme Court by adding a new justice for each sitting justice who, having served at least ten years, did not resign or retire within six months after reaching the age of 70 (with a proviso that no more than six additional justices would be appointed). FDR's stated reason for his plan was that the current justices were too old and feeble to handle the large volume of cases coming before them. It became rapidly apparent to many Americans that it was not the justices who were "feeble" but that FDR's excuse to expand the Court was "feeble" at best. What prompted one of the savviest political presidents in history to commit such a mistake? Simply put, in FDR's mind, for the New Deal to move forward, that is to further the advance of the welfare state, he had to find a way of "removing" the last obstacle to that end. He believed the most effective way of doing that without arousing too much opposition was to propose the idea of simply adding more justices to the bench. Naturally they would be liberals and thus no further New Deal legislation would go the way of the NIRA, the AAA, and Guffy Coal Act—all shot down by the Court in 1935-1936 largely because they reflected an improper delegation of power to the executive branch. In that assessment, the Court was "strictly" correct; however, FDR had believed he did have such power and that the Court was wrong in denying him the exercise of that prerogative, which he insisted came under the "necessary and proper" clause of the Constitution.

Much to FDR's amazement, few Americans bought his "plan." It was perceived by many to be a high-handed attempt to concentrate even greater power in the executive branch, removing the last check on his already immense control of the government. Congress, in the eyes of many Americans, had become nothing more than a rubber stamp for the president's agenda. Southerners were especially aroused by the plan for they read into it a "conspiracy" by FDR and his Yankee New Deal liberals, led by "That Woman," Eleanor Roosevelt, to secretly appoint liberal justices who would upset their region's racial order.

Throughout the nation, the Court packing crisis proved to be the beginning of the end of New Deal liberalism and the conservatives' ascendancy. Conservatives had made little headway a year earlier by denouncing the welfare state but now found Americans more receptive to attacks on Court reform. The president's plan, they maintained, proved that he was dangerously power-hungry and that he aspired to be a dictator. The charges, though wildly exaggerated, resonated well with many Americans who were troubled by the advance of the European dictatorships. *The Dallas Morning News* expressed these fears when it editorialized: "Perhaps it is a little difficult for Mr. Roosevelt, who is entirely self-convinced as to the

In the 1930s, most factory jobs were divided into women's work and men's work. Women's work, such as sewing clothes, usually paid less than the jobs done by men.

integrity of his motives, to see that the objection is not giving the particular present executive unlimited power but to giving it to any President. The objection is to a practical dictatorship which Mr. Roosevelt seeks in his conviction that the purity of his motives will overcome the drawbacks of a nation in political servitude. Unfortunately, the obsession in the case of all dictatorships is the same."

Very few Americans supported the packing plan because they did not associate it with immediate, tangible, or direct benefits, as they did earlier New Deal measures such as relief programs, agricultural price supports, old-age pensions, and unemployment insurance. As conservative attacks on the bill mounted, FDR's motives assumed a darker hue. As the editor of the conservative *Texas Weekly* declared, "His [FDR's] proposal to subjugate the judiciary strikes at the roots of the American constitutional form of government, and the people have the right to know precisely why he proposes so drastic a step. If there is to be a Newest Deal, some further incursion into the political unknown, we should like to know what he has in mind."

Needless to say, FDR was stunned by the widespread opposition to his plan. Once he realized the blunder he had made, FDR decided to back down and allowed the plan to go down to defeat in the Senate in July 1937. From this point on, FDR's earlier zeal to push the New Deal further to the left by expanding the welfare state seemed to dissipate with each passing month. To be sure, there were a few more social welfare programs left in the New Deal, but they were not as enthusiastically, nor as adamantly, pushed as they were earlier. FDR's hesitant behavior contrasted sharply with the impression of energy and purpose he had conveyed in 1933. The administration became less committed to restructuring the economy and more interested in stabilizing it and producing growth. Historian Alan Brinkley maintained that by 1938 New Dealers "were no longer much concerned about controlling or punishing 'plutocrats' and 'economic royalists,' an impulse central to New Deal rhetoric in the mid-1930s. Instead, they spoke of their commitment to providing a healthy environment in which the corporate world could flourish and in which the economy could sustain 'full employment.'"

That FDR's once supposed passionate devotion to social welfare programs should decline so precipitously after 1937 was not surprising when one remembers that he was never as committed to social reform or to championing organized labor as he publicly let on. FDR was not a left-wing social democrat. Pressured by leftists in his party and by populist demagogues like Huey Long, FDR reluctantly supported the 1935 Social Security Act on the condition that it be solvent and designed according to "insurance principles." Nor was he as pro-union as his rhetoric led many to believe. He despised the "dole" for able-bodied citizens, preferring work programs like the CCC to welfare checks for non-workers. FDR was also a late convert to Keynesian economic theory, which only became the foundation of liberal political economy after his death. Most interesting, he resisted to the end leftist pressure to sponsor anti-lynching and civil rights laws, partly because he did not want to alienate southern white Democrats, but also because, unlike Eleanor, he shared the racial prejudices of most white Americans of his time—a fact illustrated by his support of Japanese-American internment during World War II.

THE RECESSION OF 1937-1938

Whatever hope FDR may have had for a quick recovery from the court-packing fiasco was dashed by a sharp recession that hit the country in late 1937 and 1938. FDR had mostly himself to blame for the downturn. The expanded work program of the Second New Deal helped stimulate the economy to the degree that in 1937 production surpassed the highest level of 1929, and unemployment dropped to 14 percent. Confident the depression was easing, FDR made the mistake of cutting back on the federally sponsored work relief programs that sustained the supposed "recovery." The Federal Reserve tightened credit, and new payroll taxes took $2 billion from wage earners' income to subsidize the Social Security pension fund. That withdrawal would not have hurt the economy had the money been returned to circulation as pensions for retirees. Instead, the money was held with no pensions scheduled to be paid until 1941. Once again, the economy lacked a sufficient money supply, and, once again, the stock market crashed. By October 1937, the market fell by almost 40 percent from its August high. By March 1938, the unemployment rate soared back to 20 percent.

The widespread distress resulting from the 1938 recession badly hurt Democrats in the 1938 midterm elections. Republicans won a smashing victory, gaining 81 House seats and 8 seats in the Senate. The Congress that assembled in January 1939 was the

This cartoon depicts the Democrat's mascot, the donkey, abandoning Roosevelt after his proposal to change the number of justices. Congress had changed the number of justices several times in the previous century. However, the "Court packing" would load the Court in Roosevelt's favor.

most conservative of the New Deal years. Since all the Democratic losses had taken place in the North and West, particularly in such key states as Ohio and Pennsylvania, Southerners were now once again in a strong position, and they were in no mood to see any further extension of the welfare state, in any capacity. The House contained 169 non-southern Democrats, 93 southern Democrats, 169 Republicans, and 4 third-party Representatives. For the first time, FDR could not form a majority without the help of Southerners and Republicans. Most observers agreed that the president could, at best, hope to consolidate but certainly not extend the New Deal. FDR admitted as much when he delivered his annual message in January: "We have now passed the period of internal conflict in the launching of our program of social reform. Our full energies may now be released to invigorate the processes of recovery in order to preserve our reforms."

By the end of 1938 it had become clear that any new ambitious goals faced an uncertain future: the New Deal had essentially come to an end as congressional opposition now made it difficult, if not impossible, for FDR to enact any major new programs. More important, perhaps, in ending the New Deal was the threat of world crisis, which hung heavy in the political atmosphere. FDR was gradually growing more concerned with persuading a reluctant nation to prepare for war than with pursuing new avenues of reform. With such retrenchment at the national level, the way was now open for conservatives to mount an all-out attack on New Deal liberalism. FDR would continue through the war years to say that the New Deal was not dead but on the "back-burner." But everyone knew the New Deal had run its course.

CONCLUSION

Elected in 1932, Franklin Roosevelt dominated the nation's history for the next thirteen years. He had few qualms about using the powers of the federal government to combat the Depression and reform society. Dire economic problems gave him unprecedented opportunities to redefine the federal government's relationship with the American people.

Americans' expectations created opportunities for FDR, but he faced serious constraints as well. Crisis or not, there were political and ideological limits on how much the president could change and how much he wanted to change. Many on the political left saw FDR's election as a chance to reform society, to achieve social justice for all, and to restructure American capitalism to make it more human and responsive to the needs of the common people. But FDR had no intention of abandoning corporate capitalism or restructuring American society. Roosevelt's choices were thus shaped by public and political expectations and constraints as they intersected with the economic and social needs caused by the Depression. The result was the New Deal, a three-part barrage of legislation designed to bring about economic recovery, relief for Depression victims, and reforms to better regulate the economic sector. In the end, the New Deal did not end the Depression nor did it even provide adequate relief for the most destitute. However, the New Deal's legacy saw the emergence of the federal government, especially the executive branch, as the most powerful and important level of government in the nation. Before the 1930s, people had looked to local, county, and state governments for help. After the New Deal, people looked to Washington for assistance, and government and politics were forever changed.

Thanks to the New Deal's extension of public relief to millions of Americans, we have come to accept the legitimacy of the welfare state. We recognize that many individuals in our society need such assistance to survive. In sharp contrast to progressivism, the reforms of the New Deal endured. Voters returned FDR to office for an unprecedented third and fourth terms. And these same voters remained wedded for the next forty years to FDR's central idea: that a powerful state could enhance the pursuit of liberty and equality.

Chronology

1929 Herbert Hoover assumes the presidency
Stock Market crashes on "Black Tuesday," October 29

1930. Congresses passes Hawley-Smoot tariff, raising duties to all-time high on many foreign goods

1931 2,000 U.S. banks fail
Austrian bank failure triggers European depression.

1932 Unemployment rate reaches 25 percent
Reconstruction Finance corporation established
Bonus Army marches on Washington
FDR defeats Hoover for presidency

1933 FDR assumes presidency
Hundred Days legislation defines First New Deal
Roosevelt administration recognizes the Soviet Union "Good Neighbor" policy toward Latin America launched
Reciprocal Trade Agreement lowers tariff

1934 Father Charles Coughlin and Huey Long attack conservatism of First New Deal
2,000 strikes staged across the nation
Democrats overwhelm Republicans in off-year election Radical political movements emerge in Wisconsin, Minnesota, California, and Washington
Indian Reorganization Act restores tribal land, provided funds, and grants limited right of self-government to Native Americans.

1935 Committee for Industrial Organization (CIO) formed Supreme Court declares NRA unconstitutional
FDR unveils his Second New Deal
Congress passes Social Security Act
National Labor Relations Act (Wagner Act) guarantees workers' right to join unions
Holding Company Act breaks up utilities' near monopoly
Congress passes Wealth Tax Act
Emergency Relief Administration Act passed, funds WPA and other projects
Rural Electrification Administration established
Number of Mexican immigrants returning to Mexico reaches 500,000

1936 FDR defeats Alf Landon for second term
Supreme Court declares AAA unconstitutional
Congress passes Soil Conservation and Domestic Allotment Act to replace AAA
Farm Security Administration established

1937 United Auto Workers defeat General Motors in sit-down strike
FDR attempts to "pack" the Supreme Court
Supreme Court upholds constitutionality of Social Security and National Labor Relations acts
Severe recession hits.

1938 Conservative opposition to New Deal does well in off-year election
Superman comic debuts
Fair Labor Standards Act passed

1939 75,000 gather to hear black opera singer Marian Anderson perform at Lincoln Memorial.

1940 FDR reelected for unprecedented third term
New Deal is over as nation engages in military preparedness and begins aid to Great Britain, only nation still standing against Hitler's attempt to conquer Europe

SUGGESTED READINGS

Anthony Badger, *The New Deal: The Depression Years* (1989).
Barton J. Bernstein, ed. *Toward a New Past; Dissenting Essays in American History* (1968).
Michael Bernstein, *The Great Depression: Delayed Recovery and Economic Change in America, 1929-1939,* (1987).
Alan Brinkley, *The End of Reform: New Deal Liberalism in Recession and War* (1995).
David Burner, *Herbert Hoover: A Public Life* (1979).
Lizabeth Cohen, *Making a New Deal: Industrial Workers in Chicago, 1919-1939* (1990).
Paul K. Conklin, *The New Deal* (1975).
Cletus E. Daniel, *Bitter Harvest: A History of California Farmworkers, 1870-1941* (1981).
Roger Daniels, *The Bonus March* (1971).
Michael Denning, *The Cultural Front: The Laboring of American Culture in the Twentieth Century* (1997).
Melvyn Dubofsky and Warren Van Tine, *John L. Lewis: A Biography* (1977).
Sidney Fine, *Sitdown: The General Motor's Strike of 1937-1937* (1967).

Steve Fraser and Gary Gerstle, eds. *The Rise and Fall of the New Deal Order, 1930-1980* (1989).

Frank Friedel, *Franklin D. Roosevelt: A Rendezvous With Destiny* (1990).

Colin Gordon, *New Deals: Business, Labor and Politics in America, 1920-1935* (1940).

Linda Gordon, *Pitted But Not Entitled: Single Mothers and the History of Welfare* (1994).

Ellis Hawley, *The New Deal and the Problem of Monopoly* (1967).

Dorothy Ray Healey and Maurice Isserman, *California Red: A Life in the American Communist Party* (1990).

Abraham Hoffman, *Unwanted Mexican Americans in the Great Depression: Repatriation Pressures, 1929-1939* (1974).

Herbert Hoover, *Memoirs: The Great Depression* (1952).

Irving Howe and Lewis Coser, *The American Communist Party, 1919-1957* (1957).

Barry D. Karl, *The Uneasy State, the United States from 1915-1945* (1983).

Lawrence C. Kelley, *The Assault on Assimilation: John Collier and the Origins of Indian Policy Reform* (1983).

Robin D.G. Kelley, *Hammer and Hoe: Alabama Communists During the Great Depression* 1990).

David Kennedy, *Freedom From Fear: The American People in Depression and War, 1929-1945*(1999).

Harvey Klehr, *The Heyday of American Communism: The Depression Decade* (1984).

Joseph P. Lash, *Eleanor and Franklin* (1981).

Nelson Lichtenstein, *The Most Dangerous Man in Detroit: Walter Reuther and the Fate of American Labor* (1995).

Richard Lovitt, *The New Deal and the West* (1984).

William F. McDonald, *Federal Relief Administration and the Arts* (1968).

Robert S. McElvaine, *The Great Depression* (1984).

Barbara Melosh, *Engendering Culture: Manhood and Womanhood in New Deal Public Art and Theater* (1991).

Greg Mitchell, *The Campaign of the Century: Upton Sinclair's EPIC Race for Governor of California and the Birth of Media Politics* (1992).

Mark Naison, *Communists in Harlem During the Great Depression* (1990).

James T. Patterson, *The Struggle Against Poverty, 1900-1980* (1981).

Richard Pells, *Radical Visions and American Dreams: Culture and Social Thought in the Depression Years* (1973).

Albert V. Romasco, *The Poverty of Abundance: Hoover, the Nation, the Depression* (1965).

Vicki Ruiz, *Cannery Women/Cannery Lives: Mexican Women, Unionization, and the California Food Processing Industry, 1919-1950* (1987).

George J. Sanchez, *Becoming Mexican American: Ethnicity, Culture, and Identity in Chicano Los Angeles, 1900-1945* (1993).

Lois Scharf, *Eleanor Roosevelt: First Lady of American Liberalism* (1987).

Arthur M. Schlesinger Jr. *The Age of Roosevelt: The Crisis of the Old Order* (1957).

____, *The Coming of the New Deal* (1958).

____, *The Politics of Upheaval* (1960).

Jordan Schwarz, *The New Dealers: Power Politics in the Age of Roosevelt*, (1993).

Harvard Sitkoff, *A New Deal for Blacks* (1978).

Graham D. Taylor, *The New Deal and American Indian Tribalism: The Administration of the Indian Reorganization Act, 1934-1935* (1980).

Studs Terkel, *Hard Times.*

Richard M. Vallely, *Radicalism in the States: The Minnesota Farmer Labor Party and the American Political Economy* (1989).

Geoffrey Ward, *Before the Trumpet: Young Franklin Roosevelt, 1882-1905* (1985).

Susan Ware, *Holding Their Own: American Women in the 1930s* (1982).

Harris G. Warren, *Herbert Hoover and the Great Depression* (1959).

T. H. Watkins, *The Great Depression: America in the 1930s* (1993).

____, *Righteous Pilgrim: The Life and Times of Harold Ickes, 1874-1952* (1990).

Nancy J. Weiss, *Farewell to the Party of Lincoln: Black Politics in the Age of FDR* (1983).

Blanche Wiesen, *Eleanor Roosevelt*, vol. 1 (1992).

Joan Hoff Wilson, *Herbert Hoover: Forgotten Progressive* (1975).

Chapter Twenty

THE "GOOD" WAR: World War II

It was a Sunday morning, December 7, 1941. Americans were home relaxing, listening to the radio and reading the Sunday papers. The children were absorbed in the comics: Popeye was being bashed in the head for trying to make Olive jealous; Flash Gordon was in trouble for stealing an "enemy" plane suspiciously resembling a Japanese model. The newspapers reported conflicts overseas and exchanges of threats and ultimatums. Few were concerned. We were having problems adequately caring for our own people. Under no circumstances should we be involved in disputes between "Chinks and Japs" or in trying to solve the problems of Europe. "We had already solved Europe's problems in World War I, and what good had that done?" It was inconceivable that anyone would dare to attack us. Hadn't Admiral Clark Woodward, in a syndicated newspaper column, assured us that the Japanese armed forces were inferior fighters and our economic restriction would deter any possible military ambitions?

So when the distinctive voice of H.V. Kaltenborn, the radio commentator, interrupted regular programs to inform Americans that the Japanese had attacked the American fleet in Pearl Harbor, most Americans were astounded. "This shouldn't have happened to us. We were Americans, they were Japanese . . . Jesus Christ, how the hell'd this happen," one man wondered. To a seventeen-year-old girl, the seriousness did not sink in. The thing that really bothered her about Pearl Harbor Sunday was that they weren't playing dance music on the radio. To most Americans, however, the attack created a new atmosphere—a tremendous surge of excitement and patriotism. In Seattle, a band of young people roamed the city smashing windows and lights to insure total blackout that evening. A Princeton junior rushed to the recruiting office and found a line so long that he had to wait until the next morning to enlist. Americans rushed off to fight the war, "a good war, a war we could understand." No wonder those who survived it call it "the last of the good wars."

THE WORLD DRIFTS TO WAR

It might seem odd to us today that Americans had so resolutely refused to acknowledge the ominous events taking place in other parts of the world. While Americans turned inward, struggling with the effects

THIS WORLD TODAY

FINAL MORNING EXTRA

San Francisco Chronicle

U.S. AT WAR!

PARATROOPS LAND IN PHILIPPINES!

America at War!

Japs Bomb Hawaii, Invade Thailand

350 Slain—Then Tokyo Declares War on U. S., Britain; President Roosevelt Will Go Before Congress Today!

Pacific Coast Springs to Wartime Alert; Leaves Are Canceled, Guns Manned

FDR on Air

Raiders Fly From Hidden Aircraft Carrier; Guam Is 'Surrounded'; Wake Falls

Raids Took a Heavy Toll, Hawaii Says

INSIDE

U. S. Faces War; Losses May Be Heavy, Nation Warned

The *San Francisco Chronicle* for December 8, 1941.

of the Depression, totalitarian Italy, Germany, and Japan were becoming increasingly aggressive and dangerous. Mussolini had gained control of Italy back in 1922 by taking advantage of economic and social discontent. He continued to suppress all opposition and create a one party fascist state, proclaiming, "We have buried the putrid corpse of liberty."

Fanatic militarists seized power in Japan and launched a systematic policy of expansion in Asia. In 1931, using a flimsy cover story of assault by Chinese railroad workers, the Japanese occupied the vast Chinese province of Manchuria and installed a puppet government. A lengthy investigation by the League of Nations came to the not-very-surprising conclusion that Japan had indeed committed aggression, and the League voted to "condemn" Japanese actions. Japan demonstrated its contempt for the toothless international organization by simply withdrawing from the League. Although Japan's actions were a clear threat to the Open Door policy, President Herbert Hoover refused to consider economic sanctions. Instead, he embraced the Wilsonian notion of "nonrecognition." The American and international powerlessness emboldened the dictators to further aggression. Within a month of the U. S. warning, Japanese cruisers were shelling Shanghai and preparing to invade China.

Adolf Hitler, who took power in Germany in 1933 at virtually the same time as Franklin Roosevelt in the United States, posed an even greater menace. (The lives of these two men were ironically and inextricably intertwined for the following twelve years until they died in April 1945, within two weeks of each other.) Hitler swiftly established a brutal dictatorship, boasting that the German master race would rule the inferior "mongrel" races of Europe in a thousand-year empire. First, however, the nation must be purged of the "subhuman" Jews whom he blamed for Germany's defeat in World War I. A series of racist laws severely limited the civil and economic rights of German Jews. The world stood by silently, allowing the 1936 Olympics to take place in Nazi Germany. The American Olympic Committee, to avoid antagonizing the Nazis, even removed the American Jewish track star, Marty Glickman, from his running events.

"Today Germany, tomorrow the world," the Nazis had proclaimed. They rapidly moved to make their boast a reality. They rearmed in open violation of the Treaty of Versailles. In 1936 Nazi troops reoccupied the "demilitarized" German-speaking Rhineland. Earlier, Mussolini had attacked the North African country of Ethiopia where his tanks and planes barely prevailed against the spears and flintlock rifles of the native troops. In alliance with Mussolini, Hitler intervened to aid Francisco Franco in his rebellion against the elected government of Spain. The dictators used the vulnerable civilian population of Spain to test new weapons and techniques of air warfare. The three aggressor nations, Germany, Italy and Japan, signed treaties of alliance and defense in 1936. This ultimately led to the creation of the Rome-Berlin-Tokyo Axis, binding them together in destruction and war.

In 1938 German storm troopers marched into Vienna, annexing Austria, in yet another violation of the Treaty of Versailles. Not to be outdone, the Japanese had begun a full-scale invasion of China in 1937. The democratic nations of Europe were reduced to hand wringing at these various acts of aggression and the League of Nations to unenforceable declarations of sanctions. The United States remained aloof from the troubles of others.

Bolstered by his easy successes, Hitler turned his attention to democratic Czechoslovakia and demanded that he be ceded a strategic region, the

Sudetenland, the home of many ethnic Germans. A conference was held in Munich in September 1938. The Czechs and their potential Russian allies were excluded. The British and French agreed to all of Hitler's demands in return for his promise not to ask for anything else. A triumphant British Prime Minister, Neville Chamberlain, returned to cheering throngs of his countrymen to announce that he had achieved, "Peace in our time." Within six months, however, his words became a mocking symbol of the futility of appeasement (giving in to dictators) as Nazi troops marched into the rest of a greatly weakened Czechoslovakia. The United States had played no role at Munich. "It is always safest and best to count on nothing from the Americans but words," Chamberlain noted. Finally, the British and French resolved that they could not allow Hitler to continue his unopposed conquest of Europe and warned him that the consequences of any further aggression would be war.

Not surprisingly, Hitler was unimpressed with the new found Western backbone. In August 1939 he dropped a bombshell by signing a nonaggression pact with his arch-foe Joseph Stalin of the Soviet Union, ensuring that he would not have to fight on two fronts. On September 1, 1939, a hot Saturday, the German armed forces surged into Poland. When he was informed, Roosevelt understood the significance immediately, "It's come at last. God help us all," he sighed.

The British and French honored their commitments by declaring war. They were not, however, able to save Poland. The Poles fought gallantly, using cavalry and antiquated weapons against twentieth century military technology. The German *blitzkrieg* or "lightning war" coordinated tank, plane, and troop movements with ruthless efficiency. The Russians attacked Poland from the East, and the doomed country fell to superior forces in three weeks.

After a few months of nervous quiet in the dark winter that followed the fall of Poland, Germany suddenly struck at Denmark and Norway and easily subdued them in April 1940. The *blitzkrieg* knifed through Belgium and Holland in twenty-three days and launched an attack on France. Only an heroic effort by the Royal Navy and an unlikely flotilla of English pleasure and fishing vessels were able to save over 300,000 British soldiers from total annihilation at the beaches of Dunkirk. Their equipment and the field were left to the Germans.

A few weeks later, on June 22, 1940, the Nazis piled humiliation on top of defeat. They forced the demoralized French to sign a document of surrender in the same railroad car where the Germans had signed the armistice in 1918 ending World War I. Only Britain stood against Hitler's total triumph. Thousands of Nazi planes dropped bombs on British cities. Sympathetic radio and news reports chronicled the heroic British resistance. Winston Churchill, the new British Prime Minister, asked for American assistance, "Give us the tools, and we will finish the job." How would the American public respond to the stunning events of 1939-1940?

Employing *blitzkrieg* tactics, a motorized division of German troops drives through a ravaged town.

WINSTON CHURCHILL

NEUTRAL IN WORD AND DEED

For many Americans, during those years of anxiety and conflict, as the world crashed toward the abyss, events in Europe and Asia might as well have been taking place on Mars. Americans were uninterested in the early years of the rise of fascism. As more Americans began to understand the significance of events unfolding in Europe and Asia, most passionately believed that we should avoid involvement in another war at almost any cost.

Novelists and poets of the 1920s had expressed the increased American revulsion against war. A series of popular "exposes" in the 1930s, with titles like *Merchants of Death*, had argued that America had been dragged into World War I through the evil machinations of arms dealers and bankers. A series of Senate committee hearings from 1934 to 1936, led by Gerald Nye of North Dakota, "revealed" the obvious—that munitions' makers had made a great deal of money in World War I. Although the committee failed to discover any sinister conspiracy, an angry public was only too ready to believe the worst. The same rich manufacturers who had brought the Depression must have reaped enormous profits over the bodies of innocent young men.

Led by the American Student Union, a peace movement spread through the nation's college campuses. In the spring of 1936 half a million students joined a "peace strike" in which they stayed out of classes to attend antiwar activities. A 1937 Gallup poll showed that 70 percent of Americans now believed that the U. S. should not have entered World War I, and an astounding 95 percent believed we should stay out of any future world war.

From 1935-37, applying the supposed "lessons" of 1917, Congress passed a series of Neutrality Acts. These were designed to prevent the kind of circumstances that had "dragged" us into World War I. They outlawed arms sales and loans to nations at war and declared that Americans traveling on ships of such nations would do so at their own risk. By failing to distinguish between victims and aggressors, these laws benefited the fascist powers who had already armed themselves. A provision, added in 1937, allowed nations at war to buy "nonmilitary" supplies, if they paid in advance and carried them on their own ships. This had the potential to favor the British with their naval superiority. Congress hoped that this would enable American manufacturers to sell their goods overseas without involving us in any conflict.

President Roosevelt was unwilling to get ahead of American public opinion. In 1936 he declared, "I hate war. I have passed unnumbered hours . . . thinking and planning how war may be kept from this nation." While he sincerely desired peace, he never worked to educate the public about the growing fascist menace.

When the Japanese overran North China in 1937, Roosevelt appeared to move cautiously toward a more activist policy. In a speech in Chicago he suggested that the peace-loving nations should act collectively to "quarantine" aggressors because "we cannot have complete protection in a world of disorder in which confidence and security have broken down." Although he gave no concrete suggestions of what measures should be taken, the public reaction was decidedly mixed. Roosevelt remarked, "It's a terrible thing to look over your shoulder when you are trying to lead—and to find no one there." He quickly retreated into silence. When Japanese planes bombed Standard Oil tankers and a U. S. gunboat, *Panay*, killing three, the U. S. government accepted a Japanese apology for the "accident." Most Americans supported this meek response. Over 70 percent believed that we should withdraw from the Far East completely.

One group of Americans, American Jews, watched world events with increasing trepidation. The intensifying brutality of Hitler's anti-Semitic policies was a matter of grave concern. Like most Americans, Jews were more concerned with the domestic economic issues of the depression than with events abroad. They were against the neutrality laws and believed that the appeasement at Munich was a serious mistake. They were fearful, however, of causing an increase in American anti-Semitism if they overplayed "the Jewish hand in America as it was overplayed in Germany before the present suppression." Fully two-thirds of the American public already believed that Jews had "too much power" in the country. The very visible presence of such Jews as Treasury Secretary Henry Morgenthau among Roosevelt's circle of close advisers led to snide remarks about the "Jew Deal."

Hitler's remorseless war against the Jews reached its culmination of violence on November 9, 1938, with *Kristallnacht*, the "Night of the Broken Glass." Using the pretext of the assassination of a minor German embassy official in Paris by a grief-stricken young Jewish man, the Nazis unleashed a rampage of destruction. Thousands of Jewish-owned shops were looted and destroyed, homes were vandalized, and two hundred synagogues were burned. In addition, thousands were thrown into camps, and Jews were barred from virtually all occupations. This was a foreshadowing of the "final solution," Hitler's extermination policy, carried out during World War II.

American Jews reacted by organizing protests, picking up support and sympathy from the general public who believed it was unsporting to bully a defenseless minority and burn down its "churches." The American government responded with a mild protest and the recall of its ambassador to Germany "for consultation." Josef Goebbels, the German Minister of Propaganda, sardonically replied to the protests, "If there is any country that believes it has not enough Jews, I shall gladly turn over to it all our Jews." Roosevelt expressed his shock that "such things could occur in the twentieth century," but he evaded the issue of allowing any more German Jewish refugees.

Jews fled Germany by the thousands, seeking haven from the rising brutality. Hundreds of famous and distinguished Jewish scholars, writers, and scientists were welcomed in America, including the cadre of physicists who were instrumental in creating and building the atomic bomb. The masses of ordinary refugees, however, were not so lucky. Immigration quotas were not liberalized to admit them. Led by a bitterly anti-Semitic Assistant Secretary of State, Breckinridge Long, consular officials blocked the desperate petitioners from even filling the German quota.

American Jews feared that requests for government intervention on behalf of German Jews would be seen as special pleading. Although most Americans claimed to deplore the German persecution, 75 percent opposed allowing any more "Jewish exiles from Germany." Congress in 1939, reflecting overwhelming public sentiment, refused even to relax the quota to admit 20,000 Jewish refugee children. The wife of the Commissioner of Immigration commented, "20,000 children would all too soon grow up to be 20,000 ugly adults." The result of such a policy, of course, was that the children would never be able to grow up at all.

A graphic demonstration of these attitudes occurred in June 1939. The ship *St. Louis*, carrying nine hundred desperate Jewish refugees who were refused expected landing permits in Havana, was denied permission to unload its passengers in Florida. A Coast Guard cutter even stood by to foil any attempt to jump off the vessel and swim ashore. Although it had come within sight of the lights of America, the *St. Louis* was forced to sail back across the Atlantic to deliver most of its hapless passengers to certain death.

FROM NEUTRALITY TO WAR

The outbreak of war in Europe led to a gradual retreat from isolationism in America. With the backing of most of the American public, Roosevelt called a special session of Congress to revise the neutrality laws. Munitions could now be sold to the Allies on a "cash and carry" basis. Arms began to flow across the Atlantic to Britain and France. The public had come around to favoring aiding the Allies short of war, but less than 30 percent agreed that we should enter the war if the Allies seemed on the verge of defeat.

The fall of France was particularly sobering to many Americans. The United States had many sentimental ties to a romantic Paris, now blighted by the image of Nazi storm troopers marching in triumph down the *Champs Elysees*. Jerome Kern expressed this anguish in his popular song, "The Last Time I Saw Paris." Some active interventionists joined the "Committee to Defend America by Aiding the Allies," chaired by William Allen White, a famed Kansas editor and a Republican. White warned that it was "impossible for a free country and a free people to live beside Hitler's world enslaved."

As German bombs rained down on England, Congress considered a proposal for the first peacetime draft in American history. Outside a thousand protesters sang, "Ain't Gonna Study War No More." The regular army numbered only 137,000 in 1939, but ultimately Selective Service processed some twenty million men and funneled eleven million into the armed services. Service in the peacetime army was limited to one year and confined to men aged 21 to 35. A Gallup poll showed that most young men were willing to accept a year of compulsory military service. The first mass registration went through with few hitches. Only a small number of Indian tribes (Seminole and Hopi) boycotted registration claiming they were still at war with the United States or not obliged to obey any American law. (During the war, most Native Americans fought bravely in the armed forces.)

At the same time that he pledged to keep our country out of the war, Roosevelt abandoned any pretense of impartiality to strengthen defenses and aid the beleaguered British. Radio reporters, such as Edward R. Murrow, broadcast vivid descriptions of the bombing of London and the heroism of the Royal Air Force to the public. Their reports helped convince most Americans that we should assist British war efforts. In September of 1940, Roosevelt dared to issue an executive order transferring fifty "old" destroyers to the British in exchange for leases on British bases in the Western Hemisphere. He was also able to obtain an increase in appropriations for airplanes and other defense needs.

This "tilt towards the British" angered anti-interventionists and led to the formation of America First. Although they represented a minority of Americans after the fall of France, isolationists remained strong in the Midwest, particularly among Republicans and old-time progressives such as Senator Robert LaFollette Jr. of Wisconsin. They also appealed to German-Americans and Irish-Americans. Charles Lindbergh, the famed flying hero, was their most renowned spokesman. Reflecting the persistent anti-Semitism of the era, Lindbergh concluded that the three main groups pressing for war are "the British, the Jewish, and the Roosevelt administration." He warned the Jews not to push too hard because "they would be among the first to feel its consequences." His wife added that while fascism might well be evil, it was the "wave of the future" that could not be defeated. Others, like Joseph Kennedy, American Ambassador to Great Britain, simply believed the European war did not concern us. "This is not our war," he declared. Roosevelt privately complained that Kennedy was an appeaser and "a pain in the neck to me."

During these months of crisis in 1940, Roosevelt decided to break with tradition and run for a third term. The Republicans passed over their front runners, all of whom were isolationists. Instead, they nominated a dark horse liberal Republican, Wendell Willkie, a utilities executive. Although Willkie was an internationalist who favored aid to Britain, he proclaimed, "I will never send an American boy to fight in a European war." Roosevelt, in turn, assured American parents, "Your boys are not going to be sent into any foreign wars." Both men, thus, underplayed the possible military consequences of the crisis in Europe. Americans seemed to agree with Mayor Fiorello LaGuardia of New York that they preferred "Roosevelt with his known faults to Willkie with his unknown virtues." Roosevelt won with a reduced, but still substantial, majority, 27 to 22 million.

Women from various mothers' groups conducted a pray-in to protest the passage of the Lend-Lease Act.

Once the election was safely over, Churchill notified FDR that Britain could no longer afford to pay for necessary equipment. America, Roosevelt informed the people, must become "the great arsenal of democracy." A bill, introduced in January 1941, allowed the president to "lend, lease, or otherwise dispose of" war supplies to nations whose defense was vital to the United States. Roosevelt argued that the policy was similar to offering a garden hose to a neighbor whose house was on fire. You don't ask your distressed neighbor to pay you in advance (cash and carry). You just expect the hose to be returned once the fire is out. Others agreed with the view of Senator Robert Taft of Ohio that a better analogy would be to "chewing gum. You don't want it back." Senator Burton Wheeler, in a more vicious comparison, described lend-lease as similar to the AAA crop destruction of the 1930s: "It will plow under every fourth American boy."

Despite the intense debate that included a Capitol prayer meeting by the "Mother's Crusade" against lend-lease, Congress passed the measure in March 1941 with considerable public support. American aid proved to be of vital assistance to the British war effort and in bolstering British morale.

In June of 1941 Hitler astounded the world by breaking his alliance with the Soviet Union and launching a surprise invasion, hoping to gain control of vast Soviet resources. Most experts expected a rapid Soviet collapse. But, like Hitler, they greatly underestimated the Soviet ability to fight back. When the Soviets mounted an effective resistance, Roosevelt extended lend-lease to the Soviet Union. Anti-Communists were angered, but Churchill supported the decision, concluding, "If Hitler invaded Hell, I would make at least a favorable reference to the Devil . . . ."

In August Roosevelt met with Churchill off the coast of Newfoundland to discuss strategy. Although Eleanor Roosevelt fretted over Churchill's night owl proclivities that denied her husband adequate sleep, the two world leaders hit it off famously. They established the closest relationship ever held between an American president and foreign leader. They also drew up the Atlantic Charter, an unofficial statement of war aims. These included a peaceful, disarmed world that embraced the "Four Freedoms"—freedom of speech, freedom of worship, freedom from want, and freedom from fear. The United States and Great Britain had clearly become allies.

By this time, in the fall of 1941, American destroyers were escorting convoys as far as Iceland and stalking German submarines thereafter to report their whereabouts to British commanders. Incidents at sea were inevitable. The president deliberately deceived the public when the Germans attacked the tracking destroyer, *Greer*. Stating that the *Greer* was an innocent vessel carrying only passengers and mail, and that the Nazis were "the rattlesnakes of the Atlantic," Roosevelt ordered the navy to "shoot on sight" any hostile ships.

At the end of October a German submarine sank the destroyer *Reuben James*, causing the death of 115 American sailors. At Roosevelt's urging, Congress authorized the arming of American merchant ships and the transport of lend-lease supplies directly into war zones. Nothing remained of the 1930s neutrality legislation that had been designed to keep us out of war. The United States was already involved in a limited war. Roosevelt declared to a concerned public in a fireside chat, "Never before since Jamestown and Plymouth Rock has our American civilization been in such danger."

Isolationists at the time, as well as later historians, have argued about Roosevelt's European policies. They insisted, with some validity, that he gradually increased American involvement and did not tell the whole truth to the American public. Recent sources confirm, however, that he really did hope to stay out of the conflict until the last possible minute. In 1941 America obtained German codes and used the German naval messages to avoid, rather than provoke, incidents. Roosevelt had been proven right in his belief that first Britain, then the Soviet Union, would successfully hold on against the Nazis. He hoped to aid the Allies, but keep America from the fighting, remarking, "The time may be coming when the Germans and the Japs will do some fool thing that would put us in. That's the only danger of our getting in."

TOWARD PEARL HARBOR

Roosevelt was preoccupied by events in Europe. Since Hitler seemed by far the more dangerous enemy, the president hoped to avert any showdown with Japan. He particularly sought to avoid provoking Tokyo into any conflict before the completion of the "two-ocean navy" Congress had authorized. "I simply do not have enough navy to go around," he remarked to an aide in mid-1941. Earlier in 1941, a large portion of the fleet was fortuitously transferred from the Pacific to the Atlantic to protect shipping.

Hitler had always given as an excuse for his aggression the need for **lebensraum**—"living space" to expand. Encouraged by his success, the Japanese also insisted on the need for a "Greater Asia Co-Prosperity Sphere" where they could obtain raw materials and food for their rapidly growing population and modernized economy. Their determination was matched by American insistence on the Open Door Policy. At the same time, Japanese pillaging of Chinese cities, including the slaughter of 300,000 in Nanking, alienated the American public. The United States pursued a gradual policy of economic pressure, hoping to give the Japanese time to reconsider their actions and to encourage moderate leaders. America eventually instituted embargoes on scrap iron, steel, industrial chemicals, and oil and ultimately froze Japanese assets in America. However, Hitler's conquest of Europe led Japanese leaders to believe that the raw materials of French Indochina and the Dutch East Indies could replace embargoed goods.

By the fall of 1941, the Japanese had decided on war. They would seize Southeast Asia and talk with the United States but proceed with war if Americans did not concede all demands. They expected to win great victories in the early stages of the war, to be followed by a stalemate and a peace reaffirming Japanese conquests. Grim militant expansionists, led by General Hideki Tojo, toppled the more "moderate" Japanese government. The government kept its decision for war from its own diplomats, so they could seem to be negotiating in good faith. The one thing they did not want was any settlement that would interfere with the rush to war. On the night of December 6, American experts deciphered an unyielding message from Tokyo to the Japanese ambassador to Washington. "This means war," Roosevelt concluded upon reading it.

Military experts had expected the Japanese to attack British and Dutch possessions in Southeast Asia and were debating how to respond. Instead, the Japanese gambled that a surprise air raid on the U.S. naval base at Pearl Harbor, Hawaii, would destroy the American Pacific fleet. That would enable them to solidify their Asian conquests by neutralizing the United States.

The Japanese attack came at dawn, Hawaii time, on December 7, 1941. Waves of Japanese dive-bombers and torpedo planes soared across the harbor to bomb the anchored ships and strafe the planes parked wing tip to wing tip. Luckily, the two American aircraft carriers, still with the Pacific fleet, were out at sea. But the damage was devastating. In less than three hours most of the aircraft and many of the unprotected naval vessels were destroyed or damaged. More than 2400 Americans were dead, and 1100 were injured.

The next day, the Japanese attacked General Douglas MacArthur and his troops in the Philippines and pounded Malaya and Thailand. Roosevelt appeared before a stunned joint session of Congress where he called on the American people to avenge "a date that will live in infamy." Congress passed a Declaration of War against the Empire of Japan with only one dissenting vote (Jeannette Rankin who had also voted against entry into World War I).

These events have led "revisionist" writers to claim that the government knew of, or even invited, the attack beforehand to push America into the war. Why, these writers asked, were the battleships and planes so close together and open to attack? Why had Roosevelt sent the Pacific fleet from the West Coast to the more vulnerable base in Hawaii? Why didn't junior officers report last minute warnings of blips on their radar screens?

There were serious errors. These were, however, human, rather than conspiratorial. The planes and ships were so close together to guard against possible sabotage. The fleet was sent to Hawaii as a warn-

Japan launched a surprise attack on the United States at Pearl Harbor on December 7, 1941. Hitler declared war on America four days after the Pearl Harbor attack.

Franklin D. Roosevelt signed a war declaration against Japan after the attack on Pearl Harbor.

ing to Japan. In addition, all the so-called experts allowed racist presuppositions to color their evaluations of Japanese abilities. Admiral Gene LaRoque remembered, "We were so proud, so vain, and so ignorant of Japanese capability. It never entered our consciousness that they'd have the temerity to attack us." Americans believed that "nearsighted" Japanese couldn't see well enough to bomb targets accurately. They also "knew" that the makers of "junky equipment" could never build good weapons. "We thought," concluded Admiral LaRoque, that "they were of a lesser species."

As for Roosevelt's supposed maneuvers to get America into war, it is hardly likely that he would deliberately destroy elements of the very navy he was working so hard to rebuild. The president was trying to avoid a war in Asia that would have likely led to a war on two fronts. He clearly believed that the Germans were the greater danger. The Japanese, however, had been determined to follow a course of inevitable conflict.

As it turned out, the great Japanese "success" at Pearl Harbor ultimately proved to be a strategic and tactical disaster. The navy repaired and returned to service all the supposedly "sunk" battleships, except the *Arizona* and the *Oklahoma*. Several played key roles in subsequent American naval victories. What is more important, as anyone familiar with the history of the *Maine* or the *Luisitania* could have predicted, an unprovoked attack could only unite the American people behind the war effort. Even Senator Burton D. Wheeler, a leading isolationist, proclaimed, "The only thing to do now is to kick hell out of them." Thus, the Japanese surprise attack destroyed its basic strategy of neutralizing the United States and, ultimately, guaranteed defeat.

Roosevelt briefly worried that he would not be able to fight the greater menace of Nazi Germany. Hitler solved this dilemma, even though the Tripartite Pact required him to help only if Japan was attacked. Despite the pleas of his advisers, on December 11, he declared war against "half Judaized and the other half Negrified" America. Mussolini quickly followed suit. Americans now united behind the massive effort needed to defeat the Axis powers. Isolationism and appeasement were discredited for a long time to come.

In 1942 the military situation seemed hopeless. In the Battle of the Atlantic German submarines destroyed Allied ships at a faster pace than workers could produce new ones. The Japanese conquered Hong Kong, Singapore, the Dutch East Indies, and the Philippines and seemed well on their way to realizing their imperial ambitions in Asia. Could a society as determinedly nonmilitary as the United States was at the time meet the challenge of totalitarian militarism?

THE CITIZEN-SOLDIER

Increased draft calls and enlistments enormously enlarged the armed forces. By the end of the war 15 million men and 350,000 women had served. Local draft boards, which determined who was to go to war, often took the heat from people who suspected them of favoritism, especially as casualties rose. Deferments were granted to married men, particularly "Pre-Pearl Harbor Fathers." Many boards were suspicious of marriages entered into, and children conceived, after that pivotal date.

Boards also received letters from "patriotic Americans," pointing out people they might have overlooked. One woman urged consideration of her "shiftless" son-in-law who would benefit from military discipline. Another begged, "Please locate Enoch Calhoun and put him in the service. He has deserted his family and took another woman with him."

After 1943 deferments were based mainly on the importance of one's occupation to the community or to the war effort. Physicians, dentists, defense plant workers, and, most particularly, farmers and farm workers could gain exemptions. Actors and professional athletes had the highest proportion of draftees, largely for symbolic reasons. The public tended to be suspicious when seemingly healthy celebrities gained deferments, so the army began to waive defects that might have disqualified others "to satisfy public opinion." Jimmy Stewart, the actor, won great public approval when he went on a weight-gaining diet to meet army requirements.

The GI, so-called because everything he was given was government issue, received four to six months of physical training and indoctrination. The citizen-soldier tended to hold a firmly negative attitude about army life, despite efforts to improve morale. He cynically joked about "SNAFU—situation normal, all fouled up." A report to the army warned that the 1940 man was "a different breed of cat" from his 1917 counterpart. "The present breed (mark well) is questioning everything from God Almighty to themselves." Perplexing authorities, he would ignore a new post recreation hall for a scroungy town pool hall to "get away from the Goddamn Army." The typical soldier was an infantryman, as represented by Willie and Joe—craggy, unshaven, and disheveled. These were the characters of a syndicated cartoon first drawn by Bill Mauldin when he was an 18-year-old GI. These remain forever symbols of the World War II soldiers.

The army spent a great deal of effort to improve morale, especially for overseas troops. Entertainers, like Bob Hope, were encouraged to tour overseas. The American military even filled cargo space on flights to North Africa with hundreds of crates of Coca-Cola, to the dismay of the British. Soldiers received cigarettes at almost every turn, leading, perhaps, to increased addiction. Five million pictures of actress Betty Grable, the most popular "pin-up," were distributed to fighting men. Interestingly, she represented the wholesome, supportive girlfriend or wife many men dreamed of meeting when they returned from war, rather than an overtly erotic sex goddess. When she became a mother in 1943, it only seemed to add to her appeal.

The American armed forces were given constant reassurance of their superiority, leading to self-confidence, even in adversity. One striking photograph shows grim German guards leading American prisoners-of-war through Rome. The captured Americans are waving, smiling, and making V-for-victory signs. The novelist, Robert Kotlowitz, recalled how he, like most soldiers, truly believed that the war was a struggle between "good and evil . . . Right and wrong. Us and them." He saw the world "in simple adolescent terms, for I was still an adolescent. And that is why it was easy for me to hate the enemy."

The men came from small towns or farms or city neighborhoods. Most had never been anywhere else. Now they found themselves in strange places, running into exotic people, "as well as into one another, whom they found equally exotic." They learned to depend on one another and that became the most important thing. "The reason you storm the beaches," one remarked, "is not patriotism or bravery. It's that sense of not wanting to fail your buddies. There's sort of a special sense of kinship."

The experiences of the fighting men in the European theater were very different from that of the Pacific. The number of killed and wounded in combat was higher in Europe, due to the larger quantity and superior quality of German artillery. Psychological casualties were greater in the tropical jungles of the Pacific. There malaria often claimed more victims than the Japanese. The climate and terrain of Europe generally compared to that of the United States. In 1944 many soldiers in Europe would go AWOL (absent without leave) for short periods as self-prescribed treatment for combat exhaustion. (When the American army first crossed the Seine near Paris, ten thousand GIs took off to see the city.) By contrast, the Pacific islands were strange and forbidding. There were few AWOLs, since there was no place to go. Venereal disease rates were only a tiny fraction of those in Europe. The heat, mosquitoes, and rain led one soldier to cry, "It's hell living here in the Pacific."

Despite denunciations of Nazi "barbarism," letters home show a lack of deep hatred towards German soldiers. Unlike the Japanese, Germans surrendered when the situation was hopeless. They were "exactly our age. They were boys like us." There was little real dislike of German soldiers who fought an "honest fight and lost." On stationary fronts firing often stopped when ambulances appeared or when food was brought. Both sides followed "Tacit rules of conduct."

The mood was very different on the other front. *Yank* magazine ran an article about tossing grenades into caves where Japanese troops hid, shooting anyone who came out, whether armed or not. One soldier-reader expressed the view that it was an inhumane practice. His comment drew hundreds of responses. "We are fighting back-stabbers," said one. Our motto, another suggested, should be, "Kill the bastards." Interestingly, this attitude did not come only from experiences fighting the Japanese. Men serving in Europe or still at home exhibited the same feelings about the Japanese. The roots of these attitudes came from a sense of racial and cultural superiority, reaffirmed by the attack on Pearl Harbor. It was reinforced by the belief that the Japanese themselves violated rules of warfare, as shown by the Bataan Death March in which thousands of American and Filipino prisoners died. It was true that the Japanese military took a dim view of surrender, which they regarded as dishonorable. In retaliation, many American outfits took no prisoners. This made intelligence officers, who had hoped to obtain information from prisoners, very unhappy.

There was a widely held belief that Japanese soldiers, who lacked Western "feelings," were better suited to jungle warfare and night fighting. But American intelligence officers who read the letters of Japanese troops knew that, like American GIs, the Japanese soldier wrote of the jungle as a sinister place, complained about American snipers and tricks, and had similar gripes about food, officer privileges, and men with soft jobs at home.

The heaviest fighting took place in the last fourteen months of the war. In the last six months of 1944, 12,000-18,000 Americans were killed each month, and 40,000-60,000 were wounded. Death by friendly fire, called "amicide," was rarely discussed. Attacks by U. S. aircraft were common enough that soldiers dubbed the U. S. 9th Air Force, "the American Luftwaffe." One investigation in the Pacific estimated that 12-16 percent of the deaths had been caused by American weapons.

If a man was wounded, his odds for survival were excellent. Only 3.5 percent of the wounded who survived to reach medical facilities subsequently died. The use of transfusions and the development of penicillin helped to bring about this substantial improvement over earlier wars.

Prisoners of War

Some ninety-five thousand Americans became prisoners of war in Europe, and twenty-five thousand in the Pacific. Both Axis powers routinely violated the Geneva Convention in their treatment of enemy prisoners, particularly in forcing them to aid in the manufacture of war supplies. Despite Hitler's stated preference for executing prisoners, the German record was generally better than the Japanese. The Germans, however, did use prisoners as miners under terrible conditions. In December 1944 an SS unit murdered many American prisoners in the Malmedy Massacre. Prisoners of the Germans, nevertheless, did receive letters from home and packages from the Red Cross. Prisoners in the Pacific were not given any letters or parcels, even those with medical supplies. The Japanese regarded those who allowed themselves to be captured as contemptible. The prison guards tended to be misfits who deliberately mistreated and humiliated their charges. The Japanese displayed airmen, shot down over Tokyo, in a cage in the zoo. More than 90 percent of the Pacific POWs had been beaten, one in three died, and half of the survivors qualified for veteran's disability after the war.

In contrast, there were nearly 500,000 German POWs held in more than 500 camps in the United

States, including old CCC camps, gyms, and even the Santa Anita race track. Farmers and businessmen used some of them to fill labor shortages. They were employed in lumber production, road and farm work, and, ironically, at a kosher meat packing firm in New Jersey. One proposal, seriously considered, then rejected, was to recruit a POW "German Volunteer Corps" to fight the Japanese. The POWs at Fort Lewis held a huge party for Hitler's birthday, complete with a Nazi banner. Several others escaped and joined American society. The last one surrendered in 1985.

African-American G.I.s

In Salina, Kansas, a black soldier, refused service at a local restaurant, watched in disbelief as six German POWs were accommodated at the lunch counter. This was typical of the contradiction inherent in fighting a war against racism with a segregated army. Black American servicemen had to fight dual enemies—Hitler and Jim Crow. In many training camps blacks were not allowed to use white servicemen's clubs or recreational facilities and were not given their own. German POWs rode in the front of streetcars in the South, black soldiers in the back. Even the blood supply was segregated—plasma from blacks and whites stored separately. Ironically, the process for storing plasma had been invented by Dr. Charles Drew, an African-American physician.

The newsreels spoke lyrically about "Legions of colored troops, dramatic evidence of American solidarity and the fight for freedom." In reality, numerous clashes resulted from the use of MPs to make sure blacks stayed "in their place," enforcing Jim Crow laws in the South and establishing a color line in England. At least fifty black soldiers were killed in these racial conflicts.

Some 1.2 million African Americans served in the armed forces in World War II. As in 1917, blacks were, originally, almost exclusively in labor battalions—loading, cleaning up, digging, working as "domestics abroad as well as at home." Despite earlier American history (the Civil War, the Indian wars, San Juan Hill), most military experts believed the myth that blacks could not be trusted in combat. Secretary of War Stimson stated, "Leadership is not embedded in the Negro race yet and to try to make commissioned officers to lead men into battle—colored men—is only to work a disaster to both."

One of the tasks of some black naval units was to load ammunition on ships under conditions that violated all safety standards. In July 1944, in the worst home front disaster of the war, two ships, a pier, 202 black men, and some whites were blown up at a California naval depot. Ten days later, the remaining men were ordered back to the same work, and fifty were court martialed for refusing to do so. The white officers, responsible for the fiasco, went unharmed and unpunished.

In 1944, as war casualties rose, a few black units were permitted to go into combat. This was partially a result of a "Fight for the Right to Fight" campaign, launched by the NAACP and the black press, and supported by Eleanor Roosevelt. These units proved themselves in battle. General Patton exhorted the 761st Tank Battalion to "establish a record for yourself and . . . for your race" and to "make a liar out of me." (He once said that blacks were incapable of the technical abilities needed in tank warfare.) They were awarded 293 Purple Hearts, 60 Bronze, and 11 Silver Stars in a unit of 750 men.

General Arnold, of the Army Air Corps, said that blacks could never be fighter pilots, since they could not withstand "high g forces," because of "the simpler configuration of their brains." The 332nd Fighter Group, better known as the Tuskegee Airmen, proved him wrong. They were carefully screened and trained, creating an elite group of the brightest and most fit. Generally, they flew escorts for bombers. After more than 15,000 sorties and 1500 missions, they were able to brag that they never lost a bomber, while destroying or damaging 409 enemy aircraft. The group won 95 Distinguished Flying Crosses. Included were men who later became a Mayor of Detroit, a Manhattan Borough president, a congressman, a Secretary of Transportation, and a college president. The last, one of the first Americans to shoot down a German jet, later concluded, "Our success ended segregation."

While civilian America continued to maintain segregation, the military began to change. Although somewhat halfheartedly, an effort began in 1944 to integrate training camps. As early as mid-1942, black officers were graduating from integrated Officer Candidate Schools at a rate of two hundred a month. Three years after the war, under the order of President Truman, the armed forces became the first American institution to integrate.

The war also gave black veterans greater self-esteem and increased expectations, as they understood the irony of "fighting fascism and letting racism run rampant." This change was exemplified by the experience of a young black lieutenant who boarded a military bus at Fort Hood, Texas, and was ordered to "get to the back of the bus where the colored people belong." Since the army had already officially desegregated its bases, he refused to move. The Officer of the Day called him "uppity," and he was tried for insubordination. The military tribunal took only a few minutes to find him not guilty. His name was Jackie Robinson and, a few years later, he became the first black major league baseball player, integrating American professional sports.

Women in the Military

In World War II, for the first time, the military ceased to be an exclusive male club, in which the women worked only as nurses. Female leaders like Eleanor Roosevelt had pressed for a military role for women. In May 1942 the military formed the Women's Auxiliary Army Corps (WAACs) to perform four traditional jobs at reduced pay—secretarial, telephone, driving, and cooking. By the following year, "Auxiliary" was dropped from the title. WACs gained equal ranks and pay and were allowed to perform 406 jobs, almost all traditionally female. The navy began its own corps, the WAVEs. One woman, who rose to Master Sergeant, recalls that she had to overcome a threat by her father to "kill himself" if she was so unfeminine as to enlist. Harassment by resentful men and the restrictiveness of an olive drab girdle were part of her daily routine. But, despite these and other limitations, she remembers, "You felt enthused, just like the men who signed up."

From 1942 to 1944, 1800 WASPs (Women Air Force Service Pilots) were trained. They flew every type of plane, including the B29 Super Fortress, which they were allowed to fly to demonstrate to balky men that "even women could fly" it. The women constantly worried about sabotage. In one case sugar was found in a gas tank. When a utility plane crashed, the army sent the male pilot's body home with honors, but the WASPs themselves had to take up a collection to send home the unacknowledged body of his female copilot. A great deal of hostility was directed against the nontraditional activities of "Jackie Cochran's glamour girls." One magazine article sarcastically suggested that "these 35 hour female wonders" trade flying outfits for nurse's uniforms. "But that would be downright rub and scrub work—no glamour there." On December 22, 1944, the army disbanded the WASPs without any public commendation. Their efforts were not officially acknowledged until 1977.

Gays in the Military

The war also had a great impact on another minority group in the military—gay men and women. Before the war, the armed forces neither excluded nor discharged homosexuals, unless they were convicted of performing homosexual acts. As the war began, psychiatrists "reformed" military policy so people diagnosed as homosexuals would be given undesirable discharges, rather than going to prison. They developed screening procedures to discover "medical problems" of suspect "unfit" personality types. Recruits were asked if they "liked girls" or were curious about masturbation. Examiners evaluated whether each man seemed effeminate or "too sensitive" or was interested in being a dancer or interior decorator. While the psychiatrists saw these policies as being more humane, the new emphasis on homosexuality led some officers to conduct witch hunts and imprison suspected homosexuals in "queer stockades." Gays awaiting discharge filled the psychiatric wards of some military hospitals.

Thousands of patriotic homosexuals faced the dilemma of weighing the sacrifices inherent in military service against those of remaining civilian at a time of national crisis. Most took the chance

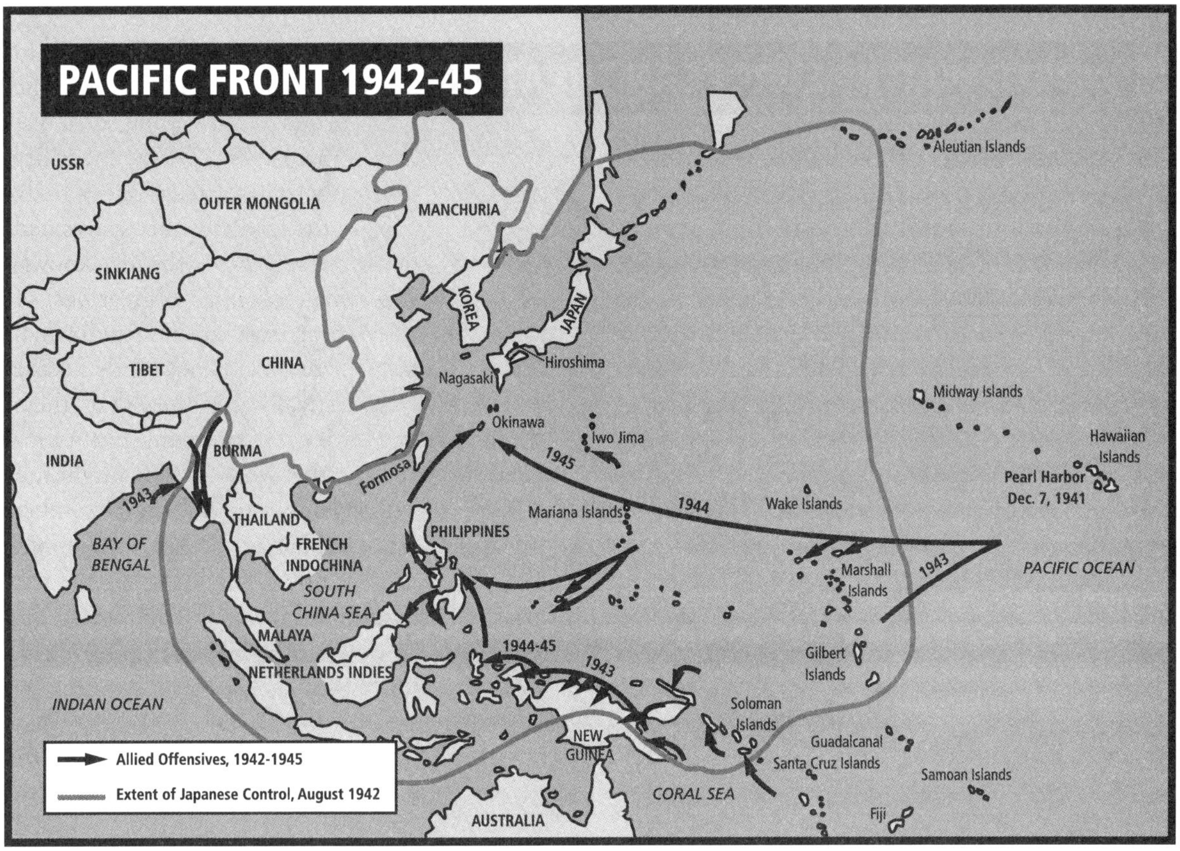

of being eventually discovered and stigmatized in the service. "Everyone in my age group went into the service that year—and you would have been ashamed if you didn't go in," said one. Those who made it in realized that "you had to form relationships very discreetly and privately."

Ironically, the war mobilization helped loosen restraints that had once isolated gays and lesbians. The draft placed thousands of homosexuals in gender-segregated barracks where, for the first time, they could find each other and discover the gay life in the cities. Like other GIs, they fought and died in all theaters of the war. The Veterans Benevolent Association, founded in 1945, was the first significant gay membership organization in America. The homosexuals who served in World War II fought one war for their country and another to protect themselves against their own government. Fifty years later, the issue of the role of gays in the military still causes controversy.

THE WAR FRONTS

While Winston Churchill was shocked by the news of Pearl Harbor, he was also excited. "We have won the war," he thought and then slept "the sleep of the saved and thankful." Within two weeks, he was in America to discuss strategy with Roosevelt. To most Americans Japan was the number one enemy because of its sneak attack. Outside the big cities, in America's heartland, many people neither knew nor cared about the European conflict. A March 1942 opinion poll showed that 70 percent wanted to crush Japan first. The two Allied leaders, however, reaffirmed their earlier plan to assign the highest priority to the European theater, since Germany was seen as the more dangerous enemy.

Although the Allied military situation appeared grim in 1942, there were glaring weaknesses in the Axis alliance. Both Germany and Japan were fighting two front wars without any strategic coordination.

They had to commit huge armies to Russia and China at great costs of supplies and manpower. Both were so brutal in their occupation of conquered countries that they made implacable enemies of local populations. Valuable resources had to be used to maintain control.

The Allies, also, had important strengths, particularly Soviet manpower and American productive capacities. In 1940, FDR astounded the country by calling for the unheard-of production of 50,000 planes per year. By the end of the war, American factories had turned out more than 300,000 planes.

The big Three Allied leaders—Stalin, Roosevelt, and Churchill, despite differences,—were able to focus their efforts on the common goal of defeating Hitler. Stalin, whose people were suffering catastrophic losses, demanded that the Allies relieve the pressure by opening a second front in Western Europe. (It was said that the Soviet Foreign Minister knew four English words—“yes, no, and second

The Allied forces faced the German General Rommel in North Africa.

front.") Churchill persuaded Roosevelt that there were not enough men and equipment to mount such an attack. Despite the objections of some American generals, FDR agreed to Churchill's idea of starting the offensive in North Africa. The postponement of the second front to 1943, and later until mid-1944, helped to increase Stalin's paranoia about the motives of his capitalist partners.

In spite of the early concentration on defeating Germany, the first successes came in the Pacific. In mid-1942, the American navy won a surprisingly decisive victory at the Battle of Midway, breaking Japanese Pacific naval superiority, sinking aircraft carriers, and destroying hundreds of enemy planes. By August 1942, American forces began to mount an offensive against Japanese-held islands. The grim and costly six-month struggle by the marines at Guadalcanal was the precursor of the bloody "island hopping" campaign to come.

In November 1942, American and British troops, commanded by General Dwight D. Eisenhower, landed in North Africa in "Operation Torch." They swept eastward, defeating the "Desert Fox," the famed German commander, General Erwin Rommel, by May 1943. Despite orders to fight to the death, more than 300,000 Axis troops surrendered. By drawing substantial German forces into a new theater of war, the African campaign provided significant relief to the beleaguered Soviet army.

At the same time, German and Soviet armies, each with more than a million men, faced each other at Stalingrad in the Soviet Union. In the four months of this battle, the Soviets lost more men than the Americans did in the entire war. However, at the end of the battle, the Germans had lost an entire army, and the Red Army was able to go on the offensive along a thousand mile front.

By the end of 1942, the Allies were also beginning to turn the tide in the Battle of the Atlantic. They sank two-thirds of the German submarines by incorporating modern radar into an increasingly sophisticated antisubmarine warfare campaign. In early 1943, the American and British air forces began round-the-clock bombing of Germany. The hundreds of tons of bombs dropped on Hamburg destroyed a good part of the city, killing some sixty thousand people.

In a meeting at Casablanca in January 1943, Roosevelt and Churchill agreed to invade the Axis' "soft underbelly," Sicily and Italy, after victory in North Africa. They also declared that they would accept only the "unconditional surrender" of the Axis powers. Despite later criticism that this demand was a tragic mistake that steeled the enemy resolve and prolonged the conflict, at the time most

American soldiers land on the coast of France.

Americans believed that Germany and Japan had to be totally defeated. No other option would have been politically or emotionally acceptable. In any case, no policy, no matter how generous, could have swayed the leaders of Germany and Japan from their self-destructive course. Within two months of the landing on Sicily, Italy surrendered. But Mussolini fled to German troops who had poured into the country. It took the Allies eight more months of painful, bloody fighting to drive the 150 miles to Rome. They were still fighting in Northern Italy when the war ended.

The Big Three met again in Teheran, Iran, late in 1943. There the Allies agreed to launch the often delayed "second front," Operation Overlord, the invasion of Normandy, France in mid-1944. Stalin also again agreed to enter the war against Japan, once Germany was defeated.

Under the command of the new Supreme Allied Commander, General Eisenhower, D-Day, the greatest amphibious (land and water) landing in the history of warfare, began on June 6, 1944. Hitler realized that the Allies were coming, but encouraged by deliberate Allied misdirection, he had decided they would land at Calais, the port closest to Britain. Dummy parachutists were dropped on several locations to confuse the Germans further, causing Hitler to delay sending two available reserve divisions. On June 6, the first assault troops established beachheads along the coast of Normandy. Over the next few days, 1.5 million soldiers landed. Hedgerows on the Norman farms, which served as effective barriers for

MacArthur lived up to his pledge to return to the Philippines.

the German defenders, slowed the Allied offensive. However, Allied tanks were able to break through German lines. The retreat turned into a rout. On August 25, a Free French division, accompanied by the American Fourth Infantry, liberated a Paris "mad with joy." By mid-September, the Germans had been driven out of France and Belgium.

In December 1944, in the deluded hope that a military setback would lead the British and Americans to realize that their true enemy was the Soviet Union, Hitler ordered a final desperate winter offensive in southern Belgium. The Germans succeeded in pushing the Allied lines back 50 miles, trapping the 101st Airborne. (Its commanding officer gave the famed reply, "Nuts," to a German demand for surrender.) American troops, initially surprised, fought tenaciously and stood fast in the "biggest, most stunning and confusing battle of the Western Front." The Battle of the Bulge delayed the invasion of Germany by about a month and cost 77,000 American casualties, but Hitler lost 200,000 irreplaceable men and hundreds of tanks. Both in the West and the East, little stood in the way of Allied conquest of Germany.

The battles for the control of the Pacific and its island groups were fought preeminently by Americans. Here, there was no battle front or clear line between opposing forces. Both sides relied on carrier-based aircraft.

As late as 1943, only about 15 percent of Allied resources were allotted to the Pacific war, which, thus, proceeded more slowly. After the fall of Guadalcanal in early 1943, a series of naval engagements and amphibious operations succeeded in destroying Japan's carrier air power and the offensive capabilities of its fleet. American forces seized airfields within bombing range of Japan. By January 1945, the flamboyant General MacArthur had kept his earlier dramatic promise to return to the Philippines. He became, with the help of a public relations campaign, America's most recognizable military hero.

Although Japanese leaders realized that the war was lost, they refused to consider surrender, with disastrous consequences. Beginning in March 1945, B29s launched bombing attacks on major Japanese cities. The firebombing of Tokyo swept destruction through its wooden structures and killed 100,000 people. But the Japanese fought on.

THE HOME FRONT

The massive war effort required a total mobilization of American society by the government. A week after Pearl Harbor, Congress granted the president extraordinary authority in the War Powers Act. Soon, hundreds of wartime agencies were regulating most aspects of American life. These included the War Production Board, the War Labor Board and the

FDR, General MacArthur and Admiral Nimitz in Pearl Harbor, Hawaii. July 26, 1944

Office of Price Administration. At the end of 1942, the OPA imposed strict price controls to prevent the runaway inflation experienced in World War I.

Roosevelt explained that "Dr. New Deal" had given way to "Dr. Win the War." After Republicans won additional seats in Congress in 1942, a conservative coalition was able to kill WPA, CCC, and new bills designed to aid education and introduce national health insurance. However, basic New Deal reforms, such as Social Security, remained in place. The war actually led to a tremendous growth in the size of government and in the power of the presidency, which had already been significantly increased during the Depression. Federal spending and the deficit both increased ten fold. To win the war, the federal government had almost doubled the total that the government had spent since its founding in 1788!

The government had to increase taxes to meet those expenses. The number of Americans required to file returns and pay taxes quadrupled. Total tax revenues increased more than twenty times. In 1943 the payroll deduction system was introduced to make tax collection more efficient. It became a permanent feature of the tax structure. In a widely seen cartoon short, the OWI enlisted Donald Duck to explain the new system and convince the public that it was their patriotic duty to comply. The Treasury Department commissioned the great American composer, Irving Berlin, to write, "I Paid My Income Tax Today" to reinforce a willingness to share the burden of fair taxation:

> I never felt so proud before
> To be right there with the millions more
> Who paid their income tax today.
>
> You see those bombers in the sky,
> Rockefeller built them,
> So did I!
> I paid my income tax today!

Bugs Bunny, as well as human celebrities, helped sell war bonds to the public with the slogan, "Buy a share of freedom today." Their efforts and the limitations on consumer spending made it the most popular way to save. Bonds paid almost half the costs of the war.

The miracle of production may well have been America's most significant victory. Within two years, American factories were producing twice as much as the combined output of the three Axis nations.

It was, as one observer noted, "a case of Scripture turned upside down, plowshares were beaten into swords (or their twentieth century equivalents: tanks, mortars, planes, bombs)." Two-thirds of all industrial production was war production. Much of the astonishing increase was the result of connections between big business and the military. Large corporations had more experience producing the huge volume needed. They were given generous contracts, loans, tax write-offs, and suspension of antitrust rules. Henry J. Kaiser, for example, used government loans and prefabrication techniques in his giant West Coast ship yard. He lured workers with superior wages and benefits, including child-care facilities. He managed to reduce the production time of a Liberty cargo ship from six months to twelve days. Corporate profits rose 70 percent, and large corporations increased their dominance over the economy. Some people worried about the rise of what was later called, "the military-industrial complex."

To an extent unimaginable under the New Deal, the war created prosperity for ordinary Americans as well. The hard times of the Depression "as though by some twentieth century alchemy were transmuted into Good Times." It even caused the only major improvement in income distribution in modern times. The rich certainly did not grow poorer, but, because of more regular employment and overtime pay, real wages of industrial workers rose almost 50 percent. As a result, the income share of the richest 5 percent declined from 24 to 17 percent. The war aided in the development of an expanding middle class.

Organized labor grew more rapidly than at any other time in its history. Except for a dramatic and unpopular coal miners' strike, labor unrest was limited and had little impact. As the worst of the war ended, more strikes occurred, particularly of the "wildcat" variety. Many people condemned the strikers with the slogan, "There are no strikes in fox holes." They replied, "There are no profits either."

At the beginning of the war, one Iowa farmer told another, "What we needed was a damn good war and we'd solve our agricultural problems." The other, who had a son about to enter the service, later killed in combat, replied, "Yes, but I'd hate to pay with the price of my son. It's too much of a price to pay." Because of the war, farmers finally did overcome the hard times they had experienced in the 1920s and 1930s. Farm production rose dramatically, even though farm population had fallen. Output per worker and farm income both doubled. On the radio, listeners could hear the words of a nursery rhyme parody, "The farmer's in the dough." The use of scientific advances and consolidations created "agribusinesses" and changed the face of American farming.

Science and the Atomic Bomb

The government created the Office of Scientific Research and Development to use the talents of scientists, particularly refugees from Axis countries. They produced improved radar, sonar, anti-aircraft guns, and other military devices. They also saved lives with the development of insecticides, pesticides, drugs to stop the spread of malaria and syphilis, and mass production of miracle drugs like penicillin. One result was a three-year increase in the average life expectancy.

The atomic bomb was the most sensational and lethal development. German scientists had discovered fission, releasing energy by splitting a uranium atom. Late in 1939, the great physicist, Albert Einstein, convinced FDR of the importance of atomic science and the danger to humanity if the Nazis developed atomic weapons. Within a few years, the largest research and development effort in history was underway, code named the Manhattan Project. General Leslie Groves, a tough, wily administrator, was placed in charge. The original purpose was to beat the Nazis in the race for atomic weapons, a grim goal clearly understood by the refugees from fascism, who were the leading scientists on the project. As far as they knew at the time, Japan was never in this race. The government committed more than $2 billion in federal funds and 160,000 people in 37 facilities to the top-secret effort. Despite major technical breakthroughs, scientists were still working feverishly to produce a usable weapon as 1945 and the war's conclusion approached.

Consumers, Advertisers, and Entertainment

The wartime stimulation of the economy was marvelous for the American consumer. Despite taxes, rationing, and wage and price controls, people found themselves able to buy amenities long denied to them. Wartime shortages created frustrations, but the average family income climbed well above 1938 levels. People moved about to find better jobs in defense industries or to follow servicemen to their camps. Buses were filled with passengers. Railroads made money on passenger travel for the first time in 15 years. The "sunbelt" cities of the South, Southwest, and Pacific Coast boomed. Women, with $8 billion more in their purses, spent freely. The sales of women's clothing doubled despite shortages. With restrictions in many areas, Americans spent their extra money on entertainment and recreation, particularly motion pictures and night clubs. During the war, New York was known as "fun city." Even scarce and rationed goods could be bought for the right price on the black market. Jewelry sales mounted because as one jeweler noted, "People are crazy with money. They purchase things . . . just for the fun of spending." On December 7, 1944, the third anniversary of Pearl Harbor, Macy's had the biggest selling day in its history.

Advertisers tried to encourage the urge to spend and to prepare the public for a postwar of plenty. Formfit urged the purchase of its bras "for the *support* you need in these hectic days of added responsibility." Western Electric predicted, "Some day Johnny . . . will climb out of his foxhole into a world freed from the fear of dictators. When that day comes, the telephone . . . will help to place all peoples . . . on friendly speaking terms." In a Nash Kelvinator refrigerator advertisement, a woman with her chin held high addressed her heroic soldier-husband, "I know you'll come back to me . . . and when you do . . . you'll find . . . everything your letters tell me you hold dear. I will be wearing the same blue dress I wore the day you went away . . . . Everything will be here, just as you left it," except, of course, for the shiny new refrigerator in the kitchen. Another ad asked, "Is This Worth Fighting For?" It showed a typical American living room with a fireplace and the western pine walls of the advertiser. That, in fact, did symbolize what many Americans felt the war was about. The *Saturday Evening Post*, addressing Admiral Yamamoto, the planner of the Pearl Harbor attack, declared, "Your people are giving their lives in useless sacrifice. Ours are fighting for a glorious future of mass employment, mass production, and mass distribution and ownership."

Now that Americans had more money than ever, there were restrictions on spending it. People could afford steak every night, but they could not buy it. It was frustrating enough, joked a shipyard worker, "To make you want to save money." The slogan was, "Do with Less so They'll Have Enough." Americans practiced consumer patriotism. "Save newspapers, save scraps, save America." They improvised. Cigarettes went to servicemen, so civilians rolled their own. Twenty million families planted "victory gardens," which eventually produced 40 percent of the food grown. As nylon supplies dropped, nylon stockings were unavailable (except on the black market for $5 a pair). Women made do with liquid leg make-up. When the government ordered a 10 percent reduction in the cloth in women's bathing suits, the desired result was achieved by replacing the full 1930s style suit with a skimpier two-piece model. "The difficulties and damages of the situation are obvious. But the saving has been effected—in the region of the midriff," noted the *Wall Street Journal.*

For all the mistakes and bureaucratic bumbling, the system of controls worked. The OPA's 5600 boards registered every American family for rationing and generated five billion forms a year. It was remarkable that everything worked as smoothly as it did. Few people were badly inconvenienced, and, certainly, nobody starved. Americans accepted cuffless trousers and "imitation chocolate that tasted like soap and imitation soap that did not lather." Having survived the Depression, meatless Tuesdays and other aspects of rationing did not seem so difficult to the average American.

The Office of War Information was designed to help shape public opinion and to protect the American myth, so Americans could "tell the good guys from the bad guys." The mass media cooperated. *Time* magazine entitled an article about Iwo Jima,

"Rodent Extermination." The author concluded, "The ordinary Jap is ignorant. Perhaps he is human. Nothing . . . indicates it."

Hollywood churned out scores of films showing the brave struggle against Japanese barbarism and German viciousness, movies like *Bataan, Wake Island, Thirty Seconds Over Tokyo, Purple Heart, Sahara*, and *Lost Patrol*. All of these featured a clean-cut valiant young middle-American fighting man or a grizzled, no-nonsense "sarge" surrounded by his ethnic buddies—the Irish cop, the Jew and/or Italian from Brooklyn, the Southern farm boy, a cross section of America (except for blacks). Their unity enabled them to withstand enemy soldiers or even torture. (A similar view was expressed in the song about "The Little Yellow Bellies who Meet the Cohens and the Kellys.") Other films presented the lesson that even your German or Japanese friend could not be trusted. In *Lifeboat*, a "serious" film, only the tough American workingman is able to deal with the immoral Nazi sneak.

Propagandists ordered socurity posters because of worries about spies.

Billboards warned Americans that "Loose Lips Sink Ships" and "Carelessness is the Enemy Fifth Column." Some movies reflected the same concerns. Fifth columnists, spies, and saboteurs could be everywhere, disguised as ordinary Americans. In the Hitchcock film, *Saboteur*, the enemies are spoiled idle rich folk who refer to the masses as the "moron millions." The hero, an innocent American worker, declares that the issue is "love and hate," and "the world's choosing up sides." Some longed for the simpler past depicted in escapist, nostalgic films like *Meet Me in St. Louis*. The big hit on Broadway was *Oklahoma*, where the singer belts out, "The land we belong to is grand."

Captain Midnight, Jack Armstrong: All American Boy, and Hop Harrigan, all radio heroes, fought the enemy and spies. Superman and other comic strip heroes also went to war. Radio and juke boxes played numbers like, "We Did it Before and We Can Do it Again," "Let's Put the Axe to the Axis," "Praise the Lord and Pass the Ammunition," and "Good-bye Momma, I'm Off to Yokohama," the first hit of 1942. As the war went on, songs reflected the longings and feelings of lonely women and of love interrupted. These included, "They're Either Too Young or Too Old," "Don't Sit Under the Apple Tree With Anyone Else But Me," and the melancholy, "Saturday Night is the Loneliest Night of the Week."

The hunger for wartime news increased the circulation of popular magazines. Radio audiences reached record levels, as people sought the latest information. The voices of Edward R. Murrow and Eric Severeid, reporting from the battle fields, became as familiar as old favorites Jack Benny and Fred Allen.

The war had a major impact on the national pastime, baseball. One paper declared, "Baseball is more than a National Game. It is America's anchor . . . American boys play ball. 'Play ball' is their battle cry, not 'Heil Hitler.'" Baseball Commissioner Kennesaw Mountain Landis asked Roosevelt if he wanted the game to shut down for the duration of the war. FDR, who was a huge baseball fan, replied, "I honestly believe it would be best for the country to keep baseball going." He warned, however, that individual players would have to go into the service, even if it hurt the quality of the game. Eventually, 340 major leaguers and 3000 minor leaguers served in the war. Hank Greenberg, the first major leaguer called in the peacetime draft, re-enlisted when Pearl

Harbor was attacked. The great pitcher, Warren Spahn, survived the Battle of the Bulge. Bob Feller, chief of a gun crew, kept in shape by jogging around the deck between Japanese air attacks. Most stars played baseball for the army or navy to boost morale and raise funds. The public continued to come to games, even though most of the remaining players were well past their prime. The St. Louis Browns even employed Pete Gray, a one-armed outfielder. The 1945 World Series was so bad that one observer said it reminded him of "the fat men against the tall men at the company picnic." In 1943 an "All-American Girls' Professional League" was formed to appeal to baseball-deprived fans. Even though the players were coached on femininity and wore skirts, the league drew one million fans in one year.

People who were children during the war remember it as an exciting era. They watched movies in which the Allies always won. Favorite candy bars disappeared; weird-tasting gum replaced Wrigley's; ice cream gave way to orange and vanilla sherbet; and Spam sandwiches replaced rationed meat. The Green Hornet's Japanese pal became Filipino. The Dragon Lady in "Terry and the Pirates," after a long criminal career, was now urging her band to "Follow me against the invader who threatens to engulf China." Comic heroes fought in the war against "Japs who looked like monkeys with their thick glasses." Children ducked under desks in air raid warning drills. They participated in the war effort by buying ten cent savings' stamps, as classes competed against each other. They became "Uncle Sam's Scrappers" and "Tin-Can Colonels." They collected "old tires, old rubber raincoats, old garden hoses, rubber shoes, bathing caps, gloves," as the president had requested. They saved "tin foil" from packages and rolled it into balls. One 13-year-old collected more than 100 tons of paper in three years. One girl recalled that they were encouraged "to pray that a lot of Germans and Japs got killed." In her Catholic girls' school, "We were taught, in no uncertain terms, that God was on our side." Children believed that every contribution they made was important in defeating the Axis.

The nation's schools felt the impact of the war. Thousands of teachers quit to join the armed forces or find a better paying defense job. Schools in rural areas and new boom towns were particularly short-handed. High school enrollments plummeted as teenagers were now able to find work. Colleges admitted more women to fill empty seats. The military sent almost a million servicemen to college to acquire needed skills. At one point, Harvard granted four military certificates for every bachelor's degree it awarded. Higher education became increasingly dependent on federal government grants, subsidies, and contracts.

Ordinary civilians were involved in the war in other ways. There were constant fears of invasions by enemies who were "spotted" everywhere. (German submarines, along the Atlantic coast, did manage to put some spies ashore on Long Island and Maine. All were captured in New York City.) Twelve million Americans were involved in Civil Defense. Many took part in crash courses in firearms. Some manned positions on top of light houses, church steeples, and hill tops to spot enemy aircraft. Families whose sons were serving in the war put a blue star in the window. If the serviceman was killed, the star became gold.

The war often forced young couples to make immediate decisions whether to marry or wait and see if their love could survive the war. Everything was sped up. It was not surprising that the divorce rate jumped. Marriage and birth rates also soared. More surprising was the number of quickie marriages that lasted. Wives of servicemen often waited weeks or months without getting letters. Some men were gone two years and were never able to get home. Young wives volunteered, donated blood, prayed, and worried. Mostly, they waited. A poignant popular song, "I'll Be Seeing You," captured their emotions.

Women on the Home Front

No event had a more revolutionary effect on the lives of women than World War II, although views about gender roles hardly changed. Reversing the Depression-era efforts to keep women out of the labor force, the federal government suddenly discovered "the vast resources of womanpower." With so many men in uniform, the government tried to persuade women to go into defense jobs to "help save lives" and "release able-bodied men for fighting." Songs like "We're the Janes Who Make the Planes," and

"Rosie the Riveter . . . She's making history, working for victory," appealed to women's patriotism. Women were assured that these jobs were no more difficult than housework and, therefore, no challenge to traditional female roles. "If you've sewed button holes . . . on a machine, you can learn to do spot welding on airplane parts. If you've used an electric mixer in your kitchen, you can learn to use a drill press," a government publication declared.

More than 6.5 million women did enter the workforce during the war. Many performed highly skilled jobs that had been always considered "male." Most of the new workers were married and middle-aged, unlike earlier female workers. Gains were particularly striking for black women. Some 300,000 of them were able to leave domestic and farm labor for better paid factory jobs. Women found great satisfaction in their work and in its importance to their country. "We were happy to be doing it . . . . Workers from other ships would look at us and see that we were welders and it was a terrifically wonderful thing," one recalled. She felt great joy at the "beautiful, beautiful ships" she helped build. They were also thrilled by their new income that gave them, for the first time, a chance at a middle class life style. It was truly a miracle!

Most Americans believed this change was a temporary war time situation. A War Department brochure maintained, "A woman is a substitute, like plastic instead of metal." Companies found ways of getting around regulations requiring equal pay for equal work. One way was to classify jobs as "heavy" and "light." Women were placed in the latter category and earned about 65 percent of what men did for the same work. The reluctance to supply day-care centers for the children of war workers was evidence of the persistence of traditional expectations. Most agreed with Mayor LaGuardia of New York that even the worst mother was better than the best facility. There were fears of worsening juvenile delinquency as women worked, and the term "latch-key child" was coined at this time.

One woman remembered, "They were hammering away that the woman who went to work did it to help her man, and when he came back, she'd cheerfully leap back to the home." Although women did lose their defense industry jobs when the war ended, they enjoyed the money and the feeling of self-worth it gave them. As the same woman observed, they got a taste for independence. "Like that of Wrigley's chewing gum found in the pack of every GI, its flavor was longer lasting." Despite expectations, women

"Rosie the Riveter," a song extolling women workers, was popular during the war. This photograph is by Margaret Bourke-White.

During World War II many African Americans used nonviolent direct action against prejudice.

remained in the work force after the war, although in more traditional female jobs at lower pay levels. The war had expanded their world. "I feel," said one "Rosie," "that was the beginning of women's liberation—we showed we could do it."

African Americans at Home

African Americans experienced a similar revolution of rising expectations, as their lives were substantially altered by the war. In 1940 three-quarters of the black population still lived in the rigidly Jim Crow South. The pull of jobs in the cities of the North and West caused more than a million to leave the South. It was the beginning of one of the greatest mass migrations in American history. The portrayal of the war as a fight against Nazi racism led to greater black self-awareness and militancy. Black leaders advocated the "Double V—victory over our enemies at home and victory over our enemies in the battlefields abroad." Most black Americans fought loyally for their country, agreeing with the great heavyweight champion, Joe Louis, "America's got lots of problems, but Hitler won't fix them."

A. Philip Randolph, head of the Brotherhood of Sleeping Car Porters, the most powerful black labor union, wanted blacks to be able to share equally in the new prosperity. In 1941, he threatened to bring 100,000 blacks to a March on Washington right to "the White House lawn" if the president did not eliminate bias in federally subsidized employment. After procrastinating to avoid offending Southern Democrats, Roosevelt compromised by issuing an executive order to prohibit racial discrimination in defense industries. The Fair Employment Practices Commission (FEPC) was established to enforce the policy. Although the understaffed FEPC was not able to do much about complaints, labor shortages caused more than two million blacks to obtain jobs in industry. The average wage of black workers quadrupled during the war, rising to 65 percent of white wages.

The membership of the largest civil rights organization, the NAACP, grew from 50,000 to 500,000, as it pushed for voting rights. A new organization, the Congress of Racial Equality (CORE), was founded in 1942 to use nonviolent direct action against prejudice. One of their demonstrations was a sit-in at a Chicago restaurant that had refused to serve blacks. Pickets at Yankee Stadium carried signs saying, "If we are able to stop bullets, why not balls?"

The shortage of labor may have opened factory doors, but intolerance and racism remained. The federal government accepted "local standards" in housing and education, including segregation. A government documentary, *War Town*, unwittingly illustrated this. It showed defense plant workers as they left the gates separating into two groups—whites to go to their houses and blacks to theirs in a different direction.

Thousands of blacks came into Detroit, the capital of the defense industry. Most lived in a crowded, filthy rundown ghetto known, ironically, as Paradise Alley. Interracial tensions grew when blacks tried to move into a new housing project built for them at the edge of a Polish neighborhood. A strike of 25,000 Packard workers, to stop the promotion of

Some Hispanics were nicknamed "Zooters" because of their suits. Police arrested the Zooters, who were often the targets not the causes of violence with white sailors.

three blacks, made the situation worse. The strikers shouted, "We'd rather see Hitler and Hirohito win than work beside a nigger." *Life* magazine characterized wartime Detroit as "a keg of powder with a short fuse." Finally, on a steamy hot Sunday in June 1943, racial war erupted. White mobs dragged African Americans out of trolleys and movie theaters to assault them, and blacks smashed and looted white stores. Federal troops arrived to bring peace, after twenty-five blacks and nine whites were killed, and seven hundred people were injured. When the federal government told the city of Philadelphia to solve its shortage of streetcar drivers by hiring blacks, the union rebelled, arguing, "The next thing they will be marrying our sisters." Other race riots broke out in Los Angeles, Mobile, and New York.

Nevertheless, as the war went on, even in Detroit, jobs and living conditions improved for African Americans. The new baseball commissioner, a Kentucky politician named "Happy" Chandler, reflected the beginning of changing attitudes, "If a black boy can make it on Okinawa and Guadalcanal, hell, he can make it in baseball." The new opportunities in the North created hope. In 1944, for the first time, black votes played a significant role in the re-election of Roosevelt. Gunnar Myrdal, the Swedish author of the 1944, *An American Dilemma*, a pioneer study of race relations, believed that "not since Reconstruction had there been more reason to anticipate fundamental changes in American race relations."

Other Minorities

In the West, Mexican Americans also experienced new opportunities and serious difficulties. Wartime shortages led American growers to import **braceros** (temporary workers) from Mexico, under contract. There were also thousands of illegal Mexican immigrants working under substandard conditions on large farms. Thousands of other Mexican Americans left agriculture to improve their living standards in defense industries.

In Los Angeles, young Mexican Americans asserted their own culture by wearing "zoot suits"—long, large-lapelled, broad shouldered jackets and baggy, tapered pants in vivid colors. Servicemen were angry at the young "draft dodgers" who roamed the streets. When the rumor spread, in June 1943, that a sailor had been stabbed by a **pachuco** (Mexican American), thousands of sailors and soldiers rioted through the streets of Los Angeles. They grabbed residents wearing zoot suits, ripped off their clothes, and beat them up. Mexican Americans, with their clothes in shreds, filled the jails. Los Angeles officials praised the rioting servicemen, and the city council made it a misdemeanor to wear a zoot suit. However, a disproportionate number of Mexican Americans served bravely in the armed forces and, like blacks, anticipated a better life after the war.

American Jews also discovered that fighting a war against Nazism did not automatically doom prejudices. A poll showed that 47 percent of Americans thought that Hitler had picked on the Jews because they were too powerful in Germany. Forty-six percent believed that Jews "have too much power in America." When a few Jewish refugees were rescued and put up at a fort in Oswego, New York, locals, angry at "Eleanor's folly," called them "refujews." (Eleanor Roosevelt had led the rescue effort.) One Jewish soldier was taken aback when a fellow GI read a poem over the post loudspeaker: "When we finish with the Germans and the Japs, we'll come back and kill the Jews and the blacks." When he confronted the bigot with "I'm the Jew you're gonna kill," he was assaulted. He later noted wryly, "The experience gave me another interpretation of World War II."

Franklin Roosevelt had been appalled by the violations of civil liberties he had witnessed during World War I, when he was Assistant Secretary of the Navy. He wanted to avoid the mob attacks on foreigners, the spying on neighbors, and the suppression of dissent that had characterized the earlier conflict. In World War II, conscientious objectors were scorned by the public as "damn yellow bellies." Some were sent to Civilian Public Service camps, where they received no pay. The Mennonites became the nation's first smoke jumpers. Jehovah's Witnesses, who refused to serve in any capacity and, worst of all to the public, refused to salute the flag, were sent to prison. (They were executed in Nazi Germany.) In general, however, the government treated dissenters more fairly than they had in World War I.

"Enemy aliens" also had fewer problems than in the earlier war. At first, German and Italian immigrants, who were not citizens, were somewhat restricted in traveling and urged not to "speak enemy languages." However, German and Italian Americans looked like everyone else. The public may have seen Italians as a little darker skinned, but they did produce great ball players like DiMaggio. Roosevelt was eager to retain the support of Italian voters, so he lifted the restrictions on Italian aliens on Columbus Day, 1942. Many Americans sympathized with the plight of these German and Italian Americans and "treated the war led by their native countries as a source of embarrassment, something like an uncle who had become a petty crook." The Japanese, on the other hand, could not blend in so readily, "Our relations had not married their children."

Japanese Americans During the War

A woman recalls the image of Japanese in films. "They sure as heck didn't look like us. They were yellow little creatures that smiled when they bombed

A Nisei toddler waits to be taken to a detention camp.

The 442d Regimental Combat Team fought some of the bloodiest battles of the war.

our boys . . . . The Japanese were all evil." Years of warning about the "Yellow Peril" combined with super-patriotism when the war began. In the hysteria that followed the attack on Pearl Harbor, people believed that the Japanese had attacked the Golden Gate Bridge. The *San Francisco Examiner's* headline screamed JAPANESE INVADE WEST COAST. Almost immediately, people turned on Japanese Americans living on the West Coast. Rumors spread that they were setting forest fires as arrows pointing to military installations. Milkmen refused to deliver milk to them. A funeral parlor proclaimed, "I'd rather do business with a Jap than with an American."

These popular feelings, and some evidence that onshore shortwave operators may have assisted Japanese submarine shellings on the coast, helped persuade Roosevelt to agree to an executive order allowing the roundup and relocation of Japanese Americans on the West Coast. Two-thirds of the 120,000 living on the coast were **Nisei**, born in the United States. "A Jap's a Jap," declared the Commander of West Coast Defenses. "It makes no difference whether he's an American citizen or not . . . . The Japanese race is an enemy race." The lack of evidence of any Japanese acts of disloyalty, merely confirmed his suspicions, "The fact that no sabotage has taken place to date is just a disturbing . . . indication that such action will be taken."

Japanese Americans were told to report to assembly centers and given 48 hours to pack their things and dispose of their property. "We are going into exile as our duty to our country," one Japanese-American leader announced. Most lost everything, as whites made the rounds, looking for "fire sale prices." A newspaper columnist wrote, "I am for immediate removal of every Japanese . . . to a point deep in the interior . . . . Herd 'em up, pack 'em off. . . . Let 'em be pinched and hungry . . . . Personally, I hate the Japanese. And that goes for all of them." The detainees were sent hundred of miles to desolate Western areas. The conditions in the detention camps were primitive. Detainees lived in crude black

Prime Minister Winston Churchill of Great Britain, President Franklin D. Roosevelt of the United States, and Premier Joseph Stalin of the Soviet Union (seated left to right) during the Yalta Conference in February 1945.

tar paper barracks, lacking any privacy. They were surrounded by barbed wire and guard towers with machine guns and searchlights. Internees were asked to sign a humiliating loyalty questionnaire in which they agreed to "forswear any form of allegiance to the Japanese Emperor." Eventually, many showed their resilience by forming bloc organizations, constructing swimming pools, planting gardens, and building educational institutions.

When given a chance, thousands of Nisei enlisted in the armed forces. "We wanted to show the rest of America that we meant business," said one. The all-Japanese 442nd Regimental Combat Team, which served in Italy and France, became the most decorated military unit in World War II: the 4500 men amassed 18,000 individual decorations. Their slogan, "Go for Broke," was well demonstrated by their breaking through German lines to rescue a besieged Texas unit, the "Lost Battalion." Parents, still in prison camps, were awarded combat medals for their sons who had died for their country.

In *Korematsu v. United States* (1944), the Supreme Court upheld the constitutionality of the relocation as a wartime necessity. Justice Murphy, who dissented, characterized the removal as "one of the most sweeping and complete deprivations of constitutional rights in the history of the nation." By this time, the hysteria had lessened, and those who could find jobs were allowed to leave the camps. As a result, the Japanese-American population scattered throughout the country to areas where anti-Japanese prejudice was less pervasive. When one family returned to California after the war, their shed was dynamited, and shots were fired into their house. The older people were devastated by their experience. "They not only lost their homes, they lost the sense that they belonged," a grandson wrote. They became dependent on their children who were able to prosper in postwar America. Only a tiny trickle elected to go to Japan after the war. In 1982 the government condemned the relocation as "race prejudice" and "war hysteria" and apologized for a "grave injustice." A few years later, Congress voted to compensate each interned Japanese American with $20,000.

POLITICS AND DIPLOMACY

The war did not cause a suspension of domestic politics. Franklin Roosevelt appeared to be noticeably weakened by his years of fighting the depression and war. Although only 62, he seemed years older, and many wondered whether he would seek a fourth term in 1944. One week before the Democratic Convention, Roosevelt announced, "As a good soldier . . . I will accept and serve." Conservative Democrats forced him to drop his liberal vice president, Henry Wallace, in favor of a little-known Missouri Senator, Harry S. Truman. The Republicans nominated the moderate young New York Governor, Thomas E. Dewey. Dewey, who had few disagreements of substance with FDR, emphasized the president's failing health. But the improvement on the military front, and the feeling of many that, if Roosevelt was worn out, it was in service to his country, resulted in a fourth term for the president. It was the closest of his victories—he gained 53 percent of the popular vote. The New Deal coalition may have been showing cracks, but the weary president had to turn his attention to international diplomacy.

In February 1945 Roosevelt met with Churchill and Stalin for the last time at Yalta on the Black Sea. He was tired and ill. Roosevelt's aims were to set up a viable international organization, redeeming the promise of Woodrow Wilson and, above all, to make sure that the Soviets would enter the war against Japan. American military leaders felt that Soviet participation was essential to avoid a blood bath in the invasion of Japan. Stalin did reaffirm his commitment to enter the Pacific war "two or three months" after the defeat of Germany. In return, he would regain territory lost to Japan 40 years earlier and concessions in Manchuria. Stalin also agreed to a United Nations Conference to be held April 1945 in San Francisco. He insisted, however, on Soviet preeminence in Eastern Europe, particularly Poland, the pathway in both world wars for German invasions of Russia. Roosevelt and Churchill reluctantly accepted a vague Soviet promise to hold "free elections" in Poland "as soon as possible."

Later, critics charged that a sick, dying Roosevelt was duped by Stalin or, perhaps, even "soft on communism." The faultfinders, however, forgot that military realities favored the Soviets, whose armies had already overrun Eastern Europe. They stood 50 miles from Berlin at the time. There was no way, short of war, to dislodge them. Roosevelt was realistic in this regard. When an aide complained of the vagueness of Stalin's promises for Poland, FDR replied, "I know. But it's the best I can do for Poland at this time." It also may well be that Roosevelt was more correct than his critics in his assumption that Stalin was more interested in protecting Soviet security than in stirring up world revolution.

A weary president appeared before Congress to declare that the new world organization would "provide the greatest opportunity in all history to achieve real peace." His increasing frailty was apparent to a shocked public. For the only time in his political career, he delivered the speech seated and commented on the weight of the steel braces on his legs. In March, American troops crossed the Rhine, capturing Cologne and surrounding the Ruhr industrial heartland of Germany. The end was near. Roosevelt went to his vacation home in Warm Springs, Georgia, to rest for the upcoming United Nations Conference. On April 12, 1945, while sitting for a portrait, he complained of a "terrific headache." He died within two hours of a cerebral hemorrhage. Most Americans, old enough to remember, can recall exactly where they were when they learned of the president's death. Although some die-hard Roosevelt-haters expressed delight, the nation, as a whole, had not been so grief-stricken since the assassination of Lincoln. Roosevelt represented a wise leader and father figure, the only president many Americans had ever known. "We're finally winning this war, and now he'll never know," one GI remarked sadly. Eleanor Roosevelt said that people told her, "They missed the way the president used to talk to them."

Harry Truman now faced the overwhelming task of replacing Roosevelt. In the short time he had been vice president, Truman had rarely met with Roosevelt and knew virtually nothing about FDR's plans. No one had bothered to tell him about the top-secret

This serviceman, as well as the entire nation, mourned the death of FDR, a man who had tried to meet the challenges of the Depression and a global war.

work on the atomic bomb. "Boys," Truman told reporters, "if you ever pray, pray for me now . . . I feel like the moon, the stars, and all the planets have fallen on me." Truman did display remarkable decisiveness in office, some believed to cover his inadequacies. He quickly got into disagreements with Stalin whom he profoundly distrusted. Some historians feel that his decision to reduce economic assistance to a devastated Soviet Union was the opening salvo of the cold war. Averill Harriman, a diplomat and public official, believed, "If FDR had lived, the cold war wouldn't have developed the way it did, because Stalin would have tried to get along with Roosevelt. FDR had a facility of keeping negotiations open . . . ."

THE FINAL DAYS OF TRIUMPH AND TRAGEDY

Although Hitler had danced when he learned of Roosevelt's death, believing it might change the tide of the war, by the last week of April American and Soviet troops met in Germany and embraced at the Elbe River. One Jewish American captain had the pleasure of accepting the surrender of a German general to whom he insisted on speaking in Yiddish. The Soviets had overrun Vienna and were arriving in the suburbs of Berlin. On April 30, Hitler committed suicide in his bunker far beneath the streets of Berlin—he wanted to avoid the fate of Mussolini whose body had been mutilated by angry partisans. His last order, which was ignored, was to flood the Berlin subways filled with Germans seeking shelter from the bombardment. On May 2, Berlin fell to the Soviets. Germany surrendered on May 7.

V-E Day brought great jubilation. "V-E Day, oh such a joyous thing . . . . I was ecstatic . . . when the GIs and Russian soldiers met, they were all knights in shining armor saving humanity," one woman fondly recalled. "To see fascism defeated, nothing any better could have happened to a human being," said a Jewish soldier. "I always felt very lucky to have been a part of it." But the joy was short-lived as Americans had to turn to the Pacific war, and word began seeping out of the horrors Allied troops were encountering in their liberation of Europe.

The Holocaust

The advancing armies were dumbfounded at the indescribable barbarism of the concentration camps. The Nazis had implemented the "final solution," an attempt to exterminate all of Europe's Jews, as well as Gypsies, homosexuals, and other "inferior" peoples. Extermination centers were constructed to kill people in gas chambers and burn them in ovens. The Nazis murdered six million Jews (including 1.5 million children) and five million other people. Western officials had known of the slaughter since 1942. The State Department attempted to keep information about the "final solution" from reaching the public. By 1943 word had leaked out, and hundreds of church sermons and newspaper articles informed Americans of the terrible butchery. A mass protest rally was held in Madison Square Garden in New York. Concerned Jewish leaders desperately sought intercession from the American government. The president and his

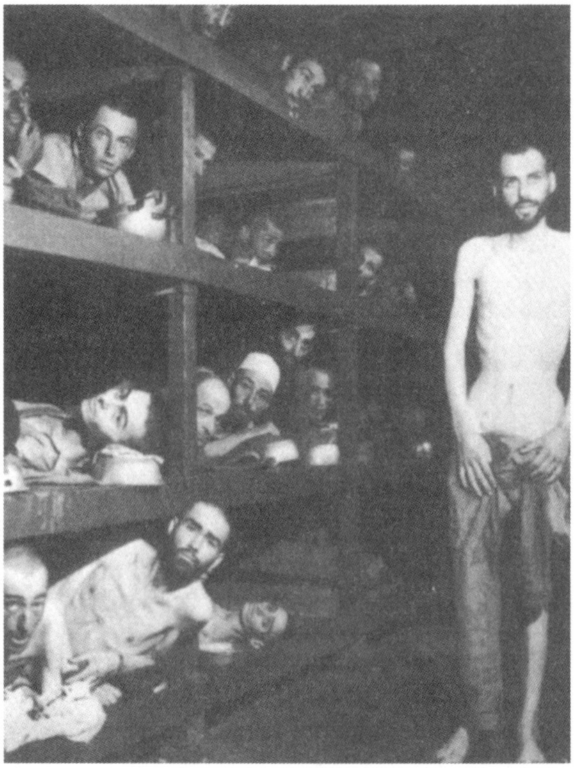

Prisoners look from their bunks at the Buchenwald concentration camp. Many died from disease, maltreatment, and starvation. The camp was opened in July 1937 and liberated by American troops on April 11, 1945.

A row of ovens reveals the cremated remains of the bodies of Jews sent to their deaths in gas chambers.

advisers responded that the best way to save the Jews was to win the war as rapidly as possible. While European Jewry was being destroyed by the Holocaust, American Jews were divided over whether to press for a homeland in Palestine. By 1944, Henry Morgenthau, secretary of the treasury and the only Jew in the cabinet, had grown increasingly alarmed by the actions of the State Department. He sent Roosevelt a report, "The Acquiescence of this Government in the Murder of the Jews." This led to the creation of the War Refugee Board and to the erection of refugee centers in Europe, saving thousands, but coming too late to save millions. Although the United States had aerial photographs of Auschwitz and other camps by 1944, the Allies refused to bomb either the rail lines to the camps or the gas chambers to interrupt the murders.

American troops, who liberated the camps, had seen a great deal of combat, but they "couldn't believe human beings could treat other humans this way." They saw skeletal corpses, stacked like cordwood, shorn of recyclable clothing, hair, glasses, and gold teeth. At Dachau, they came upon a garage filled with human bone dust from the crematorium, which was to be used as fertilizer for nearby farms. "You heard these things, but you never believed 'em. It's typical of American people I guess. You don't believe it until you see it," one soldier commented. Those who saw never forgot. A doctor in command of an Armored Division Medical Company remembered Buchenwald fifty years later. He saw ovens with human bones in them and lampshades made from tattooed human skin. The commanding general ordered local city officials and their wives to clean the camp so they could see the results of Nazism. At the time, the doctor noted, "I was dulled. I can't recall any particular effect . . . . but over the years, I am driven to relive what I saw. Every time there are films about the camps, I have to see them and then I cry."

Only about 110,000 of Europe's Jewish population had been able to find refuge in America, a number so meager that it haunted American Jews. Graphic photographs and films, and the testimony of survivors who arrived in America, seared the Holocaust into the consciousness of American Jews. Although they lacked any real power to change government policy, they felt enormous guilt at not having done enough. As a result, they began to organize to become more effective advocates and to make sure that such horror could never happen again.

The Dropping of the Bomb and the End of the Conflict

Meanwhile, the bloody conflict in the Pacific ground on. Marines had received a foretaste of the struggle

Unimaginable atrocities of the death camps shocked Americans

to come in 1944 on Saipan. There, both Japanese soldiers and civilians hid in caves. Told that the marines had achieved status by killing their own parents and would torture and murder them, the Japanese committed suicide by leaping to their deaths from cliffs. (Some who balked were beheaded by Japanese troops.) Of forty thousand on the islands, only one hundred survived. Japanese extolled the "glorious acts," while Americans saw only fanaticism.

Early in 1945, a marine assault force invaded the tiny island of Iwo Jima, a place that "looked like nothing that belonged on earth. It looked like another planet." It took six weeks and thousands of casualties to dislodge the Japanese soldiers from tunnels and concrete bunkers in "eight square miles of unadulterated hell." The famous photograph of the marines planting the American flag on Mt. Suribachi became a symbol to all Americans of the valor of American fighting men.

Between April and June 1945 on Okinawa, 370 miles from Japan, determined defenders, including 3500 **kamikaze** (suicide pilots), inflicted 50,000 American casualties. (The kamikaze brought terror to the American psyche, convincing many that the Japanese would always fight to the bitter end.) The battle degenerated into a yard-by-yard, cave-by-cave flushing out of soldiers and civilians with artillery and flame throwers. It was "a netherworld of horror" in which "life had no meaning." Over 100,000 Japanese soldiers died, including their commander who disemboweled himself in his command post cave rather than surrender. Fire, suffocation, and sword also took the lives of 100,000 civilians. An invasion of Kyushu, the southernmost of Japan's home islands, was scheduled for November 1, 1945, with the main island of Honshu targeted for March 1946. If the resistance on these small islands had been so fierce and costly, what would an assault on Japan itself have entailed?

Just before sunrise on July 16, 1945, a fireball arose from the desert in Alamagordo, New Mexico with "the brightness of several suns at midday." Scientists of the Manhattan Project had finally detonated their first atomic explosive device with the force of 20,000 tons of TNT. The mind-boggling sight inspired J. Robert Oppenheimer, the scientific director of the project, to quote Hindu texts about Shiva, god of destruction, "Now I am become death, the destroyer of worlds."

Truman learned of the successful bomb test on his way to his first meeting with Stalin and Churchill. The Allied leaders met from July 17 to August 2 in a palace in the elegant city of Potsdam, just 15 miles from the heart of shattered Berlin, and down the road from Wannsee, where the "final solution" had been planned. (Churchill, whose party lost an election, was replaced in the middle of the conference.) The world leaders agreed to a plan for occupying Germany. Stalin was not impressed with Truman, "that noisy little shopkeeper," but he did agree to enter the Pacific war within a month. "Fini Jap when that happens," Truman noted in his diary. However, Truman also had his "ace in the hole," the bomb, which was to be dropped if Japan did not surrender by August 3. Truman casually informed Stalin that he possessed a weapon of "awesome destruction." Stalin appeared uninterested, probably because he already knew about the bomb from his spy network and was working on one of his own. On July 26, a rather vague ultimatum was issued to Japan, threatening "inevitable and complete destruction," using the "full application of our military power" if Japan did not surrender unconditionally. Tokyo ignored the Potsdam Declaration, perhaps unaware of its true meaning.

In the darkness at 2:45 A.M. on August 6, 1945, a B29 bomber, called the *Enola Gay*, left Tinian Island in the Pacific. At 8:15 A.M., it arrived over the city of Hiroshima and dropped its cargo, an 8900-pound uranium bomb nicknamed "Little Boy." When the bomb exploded, it filled the plane's cabin with an intensity that one crew member likened to a "photographer's bulb going off." When the plane turned to look, the city seemed "like a pot of black boiling tar." On the ground human beings were vaporized where they stood or suffered agonizing burns. One 12-year-old saw charred bodies "laid down like in a fish market, all burned black. They could hardly be recognized as male or female." Her father could not identify her in the hospital because, "My skin had hardened like stone, my lip was pulled up, my chin was adhered to my neck." A huge firestorm erupted in the center of the business district. Nearly 100,000 were killed instantly, and 50,000 were dead by the end of 1945. The scientists had not known about radiation poisoning.

The Japanese government did not send any messages to the Allies acknowledging the catastrophe. Two days later, as scheduled, the Soviet Union entered the war and quickly steam-rolled over Japanese forces in Manchuria.

On a humid sunny August 9, early in the afternoon, in the city of Nagasaki, an "all clear" had been sounded after earlier false alarms. People were emerging from bomb shelters. One 13-year-old looked up and saw two parachutes floating down. This was followed by "a blinding flash, the sky filled with fire." He was thrown across the road. When he regained consciousness, he looked down and realized that his "skin had peeled away in sheets." A second atomic bomb (a more powerful plutonium bomb called "Fat Man") had been dropped from the belly of another B29, the *Bock's Car*. In the blink of an eye, the center of the port city was obliterated. Two-thirds of the 240,000 residents were killed or horribly injured.

The Tokyo regime was badly split over what kind of peace offer, if any, to accept. An American pilot, shot down over Japan on August 8, had lied to his Japanese interrogators, telling them that the United States had 100 more bombs and Tokyo would be the next target. At the same time, the Soviet entry into the war was an enormous blow to the Japanese who had hoped that Stalin would remain neutral. The Minister of War and top military leaders wanted to continue the struggle. However, for the first time, the Emperor intervened, warning his ministers that a continuation of the fight "means nothing but the destruction of the whole nation." Despite an attempted coup and a mutiny by die-hard militarists, the Emperor prevailed. He spoke directly to his people on the radio on August 15, urging acceptance of the peace terms. Truman, who had confided that he did not want to kill any more women and children, approved terms that implicitly accepted the retention of the Emperor. These terms might have been politically impossible for the president to accept before the bomb had repaid the "treachery" of Pearl Harbor. The famous surrender ceremony took place on September 2 on the battleship *Missouri*.

The servicemen, preparing to be shipped over to the conflict, felt, as Churchill put it, that the bomb was "a miracle of deliverance." Said one, "We're sitting on the pier in Seattle sharpening our bayonets when Harry dropped that beautiful bomb. The greatest thing ever happened. Anybody sitting at the pier . . . would have to agree." Some cried with relief, "We were going to grow up to adulthood after all." One unit went so wild with joy at the news of the surrender that every soldier took a gun and started shooting. With all the bullets flying, "32 men out of our outfit were killed that night by stray celebrating bullets." To civilians as well, V-J day was "the biggest party in the history of the nation." There was an orgy of drinking, kissing, screaming, and having fun without feeling guilty. It took San Francisco "about a week to recover from the hangover." Americans felt good about the war. Evil had been defeated. The forces of light had prevailed.

In 1945, 85 percent of the public supported what seemed to be Truman's unassailable decision to drop the bomb. Fifty years later, a Gallup Poll showed that only 44 percent of the public supported that decision. Critics later noted that, even at the time, other options had been suggested. Some of the atomic scientists signed a petition urging that the United States demonstrate the bomb on a desert or uninhabited island first, giving the Japanese a chance to surrender before the bomb was used on civilians. Military leaders like Generals George Marshall and Dwight D. Eisenhower and Admiral Leahy questioned or opposed the use of the bomb without warning.

Revisionist historians have argued that American officials knew at the time that, even without the bomb, the Japanese government was prepared to surrender soon. The Japanese were waiting for Truman's reassurance that they could keep the Emperor. These revisionists have argued that there is little historical basis for the often-cited assertion that up to a million Americans would have died invading Japan. They suggest that a racist tendency to see the Japanese as subhuman "monkeys" or "rats" made it easier to drop such a destructive weapon on them. These critics also contend that the real purpose of using the bomb was to demonstrate American power to intimidate the Soviet Union and crowd it out of potential gains in the Pacific war.

While it is undoubtedly true that some of the president's advisers saw the bomb as an implied threat to the Soviet Union, many people feel that the speedy end to the war and the saving of American lives were foremost in Truman's mind. He believed the Japanese would ignore any warning and might concentrate on shooting down the plane carrying the bomb. Military experts worried that a demonstration might not work. America and its president would look ridiculous, particularly since there were only two bombs ready for use at the beginning of August.

Japanese revisionist historians have pointed out that it is not so clear that Japan was prepared to surrender, even if concessions were granted on the Emperor's role. In August 1945, a senior Japanese naval officer proposed a huge suicide attack on the Allies that might "sacrifice 20 million Japanese lives." The Emperor's top adviser later said that the peace faction in the government had been "assisted by the atomic bomb in our endeavor to end the war."

Once the moral threshold of deliberately killing civilians had been crossed in the firebombings of Dresden and Tokyo, the A-bomb seemed nothing more than an easier, less risky way of conducting strategic bombing. (Of course, the Germans and Japanese had obliterated those lines long before.) Certainly, after years of research and billions of dollars spent, once the bomb was successfully tested, it is hard to imagine any American president refusing to use it or opting to invade Japan. "For what sane power, with atomic weapons in its arsenal," sociologist Kai Erikson has asked, "would hurl a million more of its sturdiest young men on a heavily fortified mainland?"

A half century later, the issues posed by the bombing had not been resolved. One psychiatrist has argued that the bomb plunged America into fifty years of troubled denial of the nation's capacity to "inflict and . . . ignore mass death." Philip Morrison, an A-bomb physicist, believed, sadly, that Hitler had created the legacy of war, "When we beat the Nazis, we emulated them . . . I became callous to death." Perhaps, the ultimate legacy was that all the world did as well.

CONCLUSION

World War II left death and destruction in its wake. Civilian casualties greatly exceeded the number of soldiers who died. The death toll probably reached 60 million, of which 25 million were in the Soviet Union. As the war memorial in Dresden declared, "How many died? Who knows the number?" Approximately 300,000 American fighting men and women died. Protected by two oceans, alone among the combatants, few American civilians were killed, and American cities were not destroyed. The costs in lives, suffering, destruction, and dislocation in the rest of the world, however, were on a scale never seen before. Some have asked whether such a price could ever be worth paying. The alternative of a fascist victory in which, as one historian has noted, "a new dark age was to descend on the earth . . . a world dominated by evil," would have been even more appalling.

"World War II changed everything," a retired admiral declared. The structure of the American economy was affected as trends towards bigness and centralization accelerated in business and agriculture. The size of the national debt guaranteed that the role of the federal government in the economy would continue to grow. The power of the presidency, as well, was greatly enhanced. The placement of training facilities and defense industries in the South and West played an important role in rearranging the American economy and population. The development of science and technology during the war showed their potential for creating a better world in the future, as well as the possibilities of mass annihilation.

Many Americans worried about how returning veterans would adjust to a peacetime world. "They Won't All be Psycho-Neurotics," was the dubious reassurance of an article in the *Saturday Evening Post* in April 1945. Although there may have been some small shocks, the reabsorption turned out to be relatively easy. The average GI had never been attracted to the military way of life. He came home to a genuine welcome, "the sort any home town accords to members of a winning team after a well-played game." He was aided by continued economic expansion and prosperity. He benefited from the bounty of government programs, such as education benefits and low-cost home loans. Statistics showed that veterans did very well economically, moving up rapidly. Despite the horrors many had faced, most had fond memories of their service. One rifleman observed, "In a short period of time, I had the most tremendous experience of all, of life, of fear, of jubilance, of misery, of hope, and of endless excitement. I honestly feel grateful for having been a witness to an event as monumental as anything in history."

Black GIs were the exceptions. They had come from being welcomed warmly as liberators abroad and expected more dignity and respect at home. One black soldier, stopping in Georgia on his way home by bus, made the mistake of reaching inside a white waiting room to fill a cup with water. Although he was in uniform, local whites beat him unconscious for his effrontery. This experience turned the GI, Hosea Williams, into a civil rights leader. The conditions to which the black servicemen returned led not only to bitterness but also to a revived struggle for human rights.

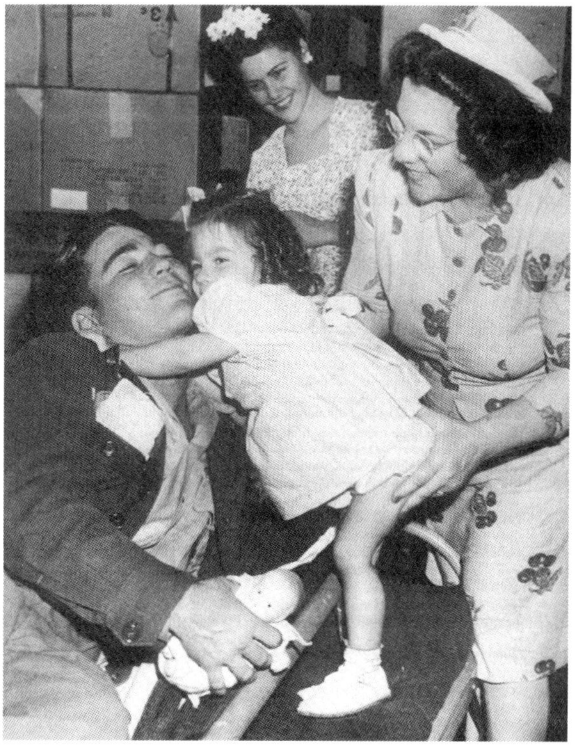

This man returns to his family in 1945. He was wounded in the invasion of Normandy.

Many believed that the experience of Rosie the Riveter was nothing more than a "cultural hiccup." It wasn't. The nature of women's roles had been altered forever even though obstacles remained. Japanese Americans regained, and even improved, their place in American society. The stark images of the face of evil as revealed in the Holocaust made anti-Semitism far less acceptable, and both political parties pledged to support the establishment of a Jewish homeland in Palestine. Americans had become a more mobile people. The necessities of rebuilding a war-torn world helped maintain growing American productivity and prosperity.

On the world scene, the United States assumed a role that would have been unimaginable only five years earlier. An article in *Harper's* in the 1970s explained:

> In 1945 . . .the United States inherited the earth . . . what was left of Western civilization passed into the American account. The war had also prompted the country to invent a miraculous economic machine that seemed to grant as many wishes as were asked of it. The continental United States had escaped the plague of war, and so it was easy enough for the heirs to believe that they had been anointed by God.

But, there was also another new superpower. The Soviet Union was as intent as the United States on reshaping the postwar world in its image. The European colonial empires in Africa and Asia rapidly dissolved and became centers of contention. People worried that the fragile new peace could disintegrate, just as it had after Versailles. Above everything loomed the shadow of the atomic bomb, bringing fear as well as caution. It was all too clear that another world war would be the last. The "good war" that "had to be fought" was over. Americans declared, "We'll never have to do it again." Perhaps the new United Nations would see to that. But, as one observer noted, "Liberty, like truth, is a piece of unfinished business."

Chronology

1922 Mussolini grabs power in Italy

1928 Kellogg-Briand pact renounces war

1931 Japan invades Manchuria

1933 Hitler seizes power in Germany
United States recognizes Soviet Union
Franklin Roosevelt declares Good Neighbor policy in Latin America

1935 Neutrality Act seeks to shield America from world conflicts
Italy invades Ethiopia

1936 Germany reoccupies Rhineland
Spanish Civil War begins
Second Neutrality Act passed

1937 Japan invades China
Roosevelt urges "quarantine of aggressors"
Third Neutrality Act passed

1938 Germany annexes Austria
Munich Conference gives Hitler Sudetenland in Czechoslovakia

1939 Nazi-Soviet non-aggression pact signed
Germany's invasion of Poland starts World War II (September 1)
Cash-and-carry agreement concludes between U. S. and Britain

1940 German *blitzkrieg* conquers most of Western Europe, including France
Isolationists, like Charles Lindbergh, form America First
Roosevelt re-elected to unprecedented third term
U. S. agrees to destroyers-for bases deal with Britain
America institutes first peacetime draft

1941 Lend-lease plan enables Britain to obtain needed war materials on credit
Germany invades Soviet Union
Roosevelt establishes Fair Employment Practices Commission (FEPC)
American ships skirmish with German submarines in North Atlantic
Atlantic Charter, signed by Roosevelt and Churchill, states war aims
Japan attacks Pearl Harbor (December 7) and U. S. enters World War II

1942 Japan captures the Philippines
Japanese-Americans interned in camps
U. S. navy wins first victories in battles of Coral Sea and Midway
Top secret Manhattan Project started to develop atomic bomb
War Production Board and Office of Price Administration created
Allies invade North Africa
First news of the Holocaust reaches United States

1943	Soviets win victory at Stalingrad Allies invade Italy—Mussolini overthrown and Italy surrenders to Allies Race riot breaks out in Detroit "Zoot suit" riots erupt in Los Angeles
1944	Allies launch D-Day invasion of Normandy (June 6) GI Bill of Rights passed Roosevelt wins fourth term as president U. S. recaptures Philippines
1945	Big Three meet at Yalta Roosevelt dies (April 12); Harry Truman becomes president Germany surrenders (May 7) V-E Day U. S. drops atomic bombs on Hiroshima (August 6) and Nagasaki (August 8) Japan surrenders (August 14); V-J Day ends World War II

SUGGESTED READINGS

Michael C.C. Adams, *The Best War Ever* (1994).

Stephen E. Ambrose, *The Supreme Commander: The War Years of General Dwight D.Eisenhower* (1970).

Allan Berube, *Coming Out Under Fire: The History of Gay Men and Women in World War II* (1990).

Michael Beschloss, *The Conquerors: Roosevelt, Truman and the Destruction of Hitler's Germany, 1941-1945* (2002).

John Morton Blum, *V Was for Victory* (1976).

David Brinkley, *Washington Goes to War* (1988).

Tom Brokaw, *The Greatest Generation* (1999).

A. Russell Buchanan, *Black Americans in World War II* (1977).

James McGregor Burns, *Roosevelt: The Soldier of Freedom* (1970).

Peter N. Carroll, *Odyssey of the Abraham Lincoln Brigade: Americans in the Spanish Civil War* (1994).

John Costello, *Virtue Under Fire: How World War II Changed Our Social and Sexual Attitudes* (1985).

Robert Dallek, *Franklin D. Roosevelt and American Foreign Policy, 1932-1945* (1979).

Roger Daniels, *Prisoners Without Trial: Japanese Americans in World War II* (1993).

Lewis A. Erenberg and Susan E. Hirsch, *The War in American Culture: Society and Consciousness During World War II* (1996).

Carlo D'Este, *Eisenhower: A Soldier's Life* (2002).

Bill Gilbert, *They Also Served: Baseball and the Homefront* (1992).

Sherna B. Gluck, *Rosie the Riveter Revisited* (1987).

Doris Kearns Goodwin, *No Ordinary Time: Franklin and Eleanor Roosevelt: The Home Front in World War II* (1994).

John Hershey, *Hiroshima* (1946).

Lee Kennett, *G.I.: The American Soldier in World War II* (1987).

Richard Lingeman, *Don't You Know There's A War On?* (1970).

Deborah E. Lipstadt, *Beyond Belief: The American Press and the Coming of the Holocaust* (1993).

Mauricio Mazon, *The Zoot Suit Riots* (1984).

William O'Neill, *A Democracy At War: America's Fight At Home and Abroad in World War II* (1993).

Geoffrey Perrett, *There's a War to Be Won* (1991).

___ ,*Days of Sadness, Years of Triumph: The American People, 1939-1945* (1974).

Richard Polenberg, *War and Society* (1972).

Gordon W. Prange, *At Dawn We Slept: The Untold Story of Pearl Harbor* (1981).

Leila Rupp, *Mobilizing Women for War* (1978).

Leon Sigal, *Fighting to a Finish* (1988).

William Tuttle Jr., *"Daddy's Gone to War": The Second World War in the Lives of America's Children* (1993).

Gerhard Weinberg, *A World At Arms: A Global History of World War II* (1994).

Allen M. Winkler, *Home Front U.S.A.* (1986).

David S. Wyman, *The Abandonment of the Jews: America and the Holocaust, 1941-1945* (1984).

Chapter Twenty-one

THE COLD WAR: The Truman-Eisenhower Years

"But I don't want to lose my job as a machinist. This is the best money that I have ever made. I don't want to go back to clerking in a department store." Many Rosie the Riveters echoed this sentiment as industry quickly forced women out of their jobs when the men returned home from World War II. The women's experience of knowing that they could do "difficult" but well-paid work just as well as men was but one of many war experiences that helped to shape the cold war era. Black men, who had served in the segregated armed forces and were made officers of all black units, expressed similar sentiments. Having experienced leadership in the army, many were determined not to go back to segregated menial life again. Finally, there were the changes made possible by the GI Bill. As young men from Turtle Creek, Pennsylvania, neither Bill Norris n or his best friend, Layman Allen, expected to be anything but laborers. World War II and the GI Bill changed all that for them and a generation of Americans. Looking back on a career as a U.S. Circuit Judge, Bill Norris said about himself and University of Michigan law professor Layman Allen, "Princeton opened all those doors for us. But the GI Bill opened the doors to Princeton." If only those were the only memories of this period. But there was that other war. "Kiddies, send a stamped self-addressed envelope to WCVI radio Connellsville, Pennsylvania and get your free map of Korea. Use your crayons to trace the daily advance of American forces as we beat back the Godless Communists!" Leading the nation at the beginning of this period of intense changes was the man who had succeeded to the presidency: Harry S Truman.

TRUMAN PRESIDENCY

After twelve years of the leadership of Franklin Roosevelt, Americans wondered what their new president was like and if he would be equal to the tasks of post-war America. Some said he looked and talked like what he was: a failed haberdasher. Without question, he was a contrast to the beloved FDR.

FDR came from a comfortable background with inherited wealth. Truman had grown up on a small farm outside Independence, Missouri in relative poverty. FDR was a Harvard graduate who had been educated at private schools; Truman could not afford a college education. FDR had never served in the military even though he was Assistant Secretary of the Navy in World War I. In contrast, what changed Truman's life was his service in World War I as a captain. There he found that he had leadership skills.

When Truman returned from the war, he and a partner began a haberdashery business. They were soon bankrupt. Although it took him many years, Truman eventually paid back every debt incurred in the bankruptcy. With business closed to him, Truman became a professional politician beginning his career as a county judge.

He was next elected to the United States Senate where he chaired a committee to investigate war mobilization. His relentless search for evidence of price gouging brought him national attention. Truman was decisive, feisty, and loyal. He was also profane and had a temper. The most famous example of these last traits was the letter he wrote during his presidency to a music critic, Paul Hume, who had panned the singing of his daughter Margaret. Hume had written a critical review for the *Washington Post* of Margaret Truman's first Washington concert as a coloratura soprano. In his letter Truman wrote, "Some day I hope to meet you. When that happens you'll need a new nose, a lot of beef steak for black eyes, and perhaps a supporter below!"

Truman's presidency began with a myriad of problems in both domestic and foreign affairs. The most pressing was foreign affairs. Our old war time ally, the Soviet Union, now opposed the United States. While our support of the Soviets in World War II was a partnership of convenience, Roosevelt had thought the United States could work with the Soviet leader, Joseph Stalin, to prevent future wars. It soon was obvious that this was not possible. The factors that influenced the development of this new form of conflict, the cold war, can only be understood if the nature of Soviet Communism is clear.

Karl Marx, the father of Communism, based his theories on class conflict that he thought was inevitable. He believed that capitalism was the last stage in the evolution to a utopia where the proletariat, the workers of all countries, would control the government. Marx fully expected that the proletarian revolution would begin in one of the most heavily industrialized nations; instead, it began in one of the more backward, Czarist Russia. Under Lenin, the leader of the revolution, and his successor, Stalin, the Soviet Union followed a foreign policy that was a mixture of world revolution and the old czarist policy of expansionism. The United States was prepared for neither.

UNITED NATIONS

Roosevelt had obtained a consensus among the war-time allies to establish a new international organization to replace the defunct League of Nations. Accordingly, on April 25, 1945, delegates from fifty nations met in San Francisco to draw up the charter of the UN. The UN could admit additional members by a two-thirds vote of the General Assembly, which included delegates from all member nations.

The other permanent agency was the Security Council, which had five permanent members (United States, Union of Soviet Socialist Republics, Great Britain, France, and China) and six elected members. Each permanent member had veto power over any action. The Security Council might investigate any dispute, recommend settlement or refer the dispute to the International Court, and take measures including a resort to military force. The UN was lodged at Lake Success, New York with a permanent home planned in New York City.

There was also a consensus that those responsible for the atrocities of World War II should face trial and punishment. The Potsdam Conference gave final approval to the principle of war-crime trials. Both German and Japanese officials went on trial for crimes against peace, against humanity, and against the established rules of war. Out of twenty-two Nazis tried at Nuremberg, twelve were sentenced to death, three to life imprisonment, and four to shorter terms. In Tokyo, twenty-five Japanese were tried with seven sentenced to death, sixteen to life imprisonment, and two for short term imprisonment. Thousands of others were tried in national courts. The accused offered the excuse that "they were just following orders." It was not accepted. Fifty years later it was revealed that many Japanese who had conducted biological experiments on allied prisoners had escaped punishment even though the United States knew of the experiments. There were also many Nazi scientists whom the U. S. protected because they could be helpful in the new cold war against the Soviets.

POSTWAR PROBLEMS: EUROPE AND THE MIDDLE EAST

Americans hoped that the Yalta and Potsdam agreements with the Soviet Union would stand. The Yalta agreement had divided Germany and Berlin into occupation zones with a divided Berlin within the Soviet Zone. At Potsdam, Truman accepted the reality of the border that the Soviets had established between themselves and their satellite Polish state. When the Americans, British, and French successfully blocked any Soviet claims to reparations from their western zones, the Soviets stripped $3 billion a year from East Germany. It soon became clear that the Soviets were not going to keep the agreements but instead were intent on keeping what they had. To the Soviets, this was just providing a buffer zone between them and the Germans who had invaded them twice in less than twenty-five years. They also thought that it paralleled American control in Japan and Western control in most of Germany and Italy.

As early as 1946, Stalin had pronounced international peace as impossible "under the present capitalist development of the world economy." His statement impelled George Kennan, a foreign service officer, to spell out the roots of Soviet policy and to warn that the Soviet Union was "committed fanatically to the belief that with the United States there can be no permanent *modus vivendi*, that it is desirable and necessary that the internal harmony of U.S. society be disrupted, the traditional way of U.S. life be destroyed, the international authority of the U.S. be broken, if Soviet power is to be secure."

The turning point in the relationship came with the Moscow Conference of 1947. The foreign ministers met to discuss the question of German political and economic unification. The Soviet Union would agree to economic unification on two conditions: that they share in the control of industry of the Ruhr Valley and the recognition of their claims for ten billion dollars in reparation. The West rejected this. Nor was there any agreement on political unification. This conference ended any hope of friendly cooperation between the Communist and non-Communist worlds. It also marked the beginning of the policy of containment.

By 1947 Kennan was back at the State Department and presented his ideas for a proper response to the Soviets in *Foreign Affairs* under the pseudonym "X." ". . . it is clear that the main element of any United States policy toward the Soviet Union must be that of a long-term, patient but firm and vigilant containment of Russian expansive tendencies." Kennan thought that there was a strong possibility "that Soviet power, like the capitalist world of its conception, bears within it the seeds of its own decay, and that the sprouting of those seeds is well advanced." This became America's basic foreign policy stance during the cold war. While Kennan later wrote that his recommendation applied only to Europe, future administrations applied it world-wide.

The first action under the policy of containment was the Truman Doctrine: the policy of the United States to support free peoples who were resisting attempted subjugation by armed minorities within or by outside pressure. The first application of this doctrine was in Greece and Turkey.

For centuries the Russian Empire had sought a warm water port to give them access to the Mediterranean. The Soviet Union continued this policy by pressuring Turkey to yield control of the Dardanelles, as well as areas on the Black Sea. The pressure on Greece was less direct, but it had been fighting Communist forces within Greece, who were receiving aid from Communists in three neighboring states since 1945. Great Britain had been aiding both Greece and Turkey, but in 1947 informed Truman that it could no longer continue this aid. Truman asked Congress for $400,000,000 in military and economic aid to Greece and Turkey. After two months of debate, Congress authorized all that the president requested, as well as sending military and civilian experts. By 1949, U. S. aid had saved Greece and Turkey. It was the first success for containment.

While the problems in Greece and Turkey required military and monetary aid, the problems in the rest of Europe were economic. By 1947, a severe drought and a harsh winter made Europe a "rubble heap and a charnel house, a breeding ground of pestilence and hate" in Winston Churchill's words. Amid the chaos, the Communists were flourishing. While aid from the United Nations had prevented starvation, it did nothing to aid economic recovery.

The American answer was the Marshall Plan. George C. Marshall, the former general who had coordinated U.S. wartime planning, was now secretary of state. In May 1947 Marshall unveiled the plan in a commencement address at Harvard University. American aid was offered to any European nation who would coordinate its efforts for recovery and present the United States with a program and specification of its needs. Marshall stated: "Our policy is directed not against country or doctrine, but against hunger, poverty, desperation and chaos."

This promise of economic assistance included the Soviet Union and the eastern European nations that comprised the Soviet bloc. Some members of the Soviet bloc did turn up at the planning meeting but were ordered home "from the imperialist" scheme. In December Congress passed the European Recovery Program and in June 1948 funded it with an initial $4 billion. The total cost of the program that saved Europe was $10.25 billion. We also poured money into rebuilding Japan. Since the U. S. was the only major economic power after World War II, the Marshall Plan also benefited the United States.

With the failure of the Moscow Conference, the United States, Great Britain, and France decided to unify their three zones to create West Germany and West Berlin. Unification proceeded with the creation of a representative government that would control its domestic affairs and have limited control over foreign affairs. The ban on rearmament remained, and the military occupation would continue. The U. S. then invited the West Germans to participate in the Marshall Plan.

Berlin Airlift

The Soviets tried to shut off ground access to Berlin in June 1948. The plan was to force the Allies from West Berlin, which was in Soviet-controlled East Germany. Truman responded with a massive airlift that delivered 4,500 tons of food and coal a day! It operated for eleven months. The strain of the blockade was not without its humorous encounters. The Soviet commander's gas main ran through West Berlin so the Americans shut it off. When the Soviets attempted to move his furniture through the American zone to another home, the Americans seized the furniture. There was also the spectacle of

The Marshall Plan helped to rebuild wartorn Europe.

the Berlin children who waited outside the fence at the airport for the candy bars thrown to them by American pilots as they waited for their planes to be unloaded. Eventually the Soviets lifted the blockade. The first major encounter of the cold war showed that neither side wanted to turn it into a "hot" war.

As the change in the world order became clearer in 1948, Congress authorized the president to develop collective defense pacts under the UN charter. This was the beginning of the **North Atlantic Treaty Organization** (NATO), a defensive alliance of Britain, France, United States, Belgium, Netherlands, Luxembourg, Canada, Denmark, Iceland, Italy, Norway, and Portugal. It later included Greece, Turkey, Germany, and Spain. It marked the first treaty of alliance the United States had had since the Franco-American Alliance of 1778 during the American Revolution.

The last big foreign policy decision with long term consequences came in the Middle East. In 1947 the United Nations proposed to partition Palestine into Jewish and Arab states. The Arab states fiercely resisted to no avail. May 14, 1948, Jewish leaders proclaimed the independence of Israel. The United States, disregarding its oil interests in the Arab states, recognized it in minutes. The Arab states immediately went to war. A temporary truce and peace were worked out in May 1949, and Israel was admitted to the United Nations.

A domestic policy decision that was destined to have long-range effects on foreign policy was the National Security Act of 1947. Passed in response to the Pearl Harbor intelligence debacle, the National Security Act of 1947 created a National Military Establishment headed by the secretary of defense. It also created a Joint Chiefs of Staff and, most importantly, the Central Intelligence Agency (CIA). The CIA, which was the replacement for the wartime Office of Strategic Services (OSS), was designated to coordinate intelligence gathering. It was permitted neither covert actions nor any domestic activities. But the act contained a big loophole that would in time allow the CIA to engage in both: authority to perform "such other functions and

The Berlin airlift provided food and fuel for West Berliners. Children waited for candy that American pilots dropped in tiny parachutes.

duties related to intelligence" as the National Security Council might direct. While the activities under the Truman administrations were limited, the CIA would enter a new era of activity under succeeding administrations.

THE COLD WAR: JAPAN, CHINA, AND VIETNAM

Japan

A Far Eastern Commission, speaking for the eleven powers that had fought against Japan, existed to make policy. In reality, however, it was the Supreme Commander for the Allied Powers, General Douglas MacArthur, who controlled Japan. Under MacArthur's administration the Japanese docilely accepted the changes that revolutionized their nation. These included the shrinking of Japan to four islands; the renunciation of war; the punishment of war criminals; and the institution of a constitutional monarchy with woman suffrage. There was also an attempt to institute a more democratic economy. These last changes ended when the occupation ended.

China

U. S. policy was not so successful with other major Asian powers. During World War II, both the Nationalist Chinese (Kuomintang) and the Communist Chinese had worked together to defeat the Japanese. American foreign policy was based on the erroneous belief that this situation would continue and that the two could join together in a post-war democratic China. What the United States did not know was that during the final months of the war when the Communists were retaking the interior in the Northwest and North, the Soviets were sending them assistance. It was soon clear that only action by the United States could save China from a civil war.

In November 1945 Truman sent newly retired General George C. Marshall to China with two instructions: seek a truce in the fighting; and obtain political unification through a conference of the Nationalists, Communists, and other groups. The underlying assumption was that the only legal government in China was the Nationalist government. After spending a year in China, Marshall returned home and reported to Truman that there was no hope of compromise because of extremist elements on both sides. It was a situation that the United States would find often: dedicated Marxists on one side and the criminal element of corrupt elite on the other.

While the United States continued to recognize the government of Chiang Kai-shek, it had lost faith in Chiang's ability to solve China's problems and, therefore, did not supply the massive military aid that Chiang would have needed to win. The United States undertook a progressive disengagement from the Chinese situation as the Truman administration concentrated on the problems in Western Europe. The expectation was that eventually the nationalist interests of the Chinese would overcome their Communist ideology so that they would, like Marshall Tito in Yugoslavia, go their own way and not be dominated by the Soviet Union. At that point, the administration thought, China, like Yugoslavia, would want to establish good relations with the United States. In the midst of this, the United States ascertained that the Soviet Union had exploded an atomic bomb. A week after this news, the People's Republic of China was inaugurated; Chiang was in Formosa and Mao Zedong and his Chinese Communists were in control of mainland China. In future years, Republicans would charge the Democrats with losing China. Historians still disagree on the issue of whether China could have been saved.

Soon after the Communist take over in China, Truman decided to build the "Super" hydrogen bomb that would have ten times the destructive force of the bombs dropped on Hiroshima and Nagasaki. In fact, its "trigger" was a nuclear explosion!

Vietnam

At the settlements at the end of World War II, Churchill had prevailed on Roosevelt to return Indochina to France, its former colonial master. In 1945 Ho Chi Minh, the leader of the Communist

Vietnamese, declared Vietnamese independence using the stirring phrases of Jefferson's Declaration of Independence. Nevertheless, the Allies gave France their approval to reassert dominance in the area. By 1946, the French were fighting Ho Chi Minh and his Independence League, the Viet Minh. Few natives of either Vietnam, Laos, or Cambodia supported the French who had been too slow in fulfilling their promises of independence. The French choice for a ruler of Vietnam, the Emperor Bao Dai, did not gain an enthusiastic response like that given to Ho Chi Minh. While the United States did not send troops, American money supported the French effort.

DOMESTIC POLICY

As soon as the war ended, Americans began to demand the return of their men. Accordingly one of Truman's first acts was the demobilization of 9 million men and a few women from the army and navy. This reduced the military to 1.5 million, with Congress asking for more reductions. By 1950 there were 600,000 men in the military. In his memoirs Truman termed this "the most remarkable demobilization in the history of the world, or disintegration if you want to call it that."

The return of the men from war presaged social and economic changes whose repercussions have not yet ended. The first result came in 1946 with a baby boom that continued until the early 1960s. The second result took a bit longer since it was tied to the GI Bill of Rights passed in 1944 by a margin of one vote. This act provided veterans with money for education, vocational training, and medical treatment, as well as loans for homes or business.

Despite predictions by opponents of the bill that the educational benefits would be ignored, American colleges and universities were flooded with 2.2 million veterans taking advantage of the higher education provisions. This group included 60,000 women and 70,000 African Americans. Many veterans were married, so the colleges had to establish married housing or vetvilles. At a cost of $5.5 billion this first GI Bill produced 450,000 engineers, 240,000 accountants, 238,000 teachers, 91,000 scientists, 67,000 doctors, 22,000 dentists, 17,000 writers, and thousands of other professionals of all types. Estimates of the return on this investment range from $3-$4 for every dollar spent. Along the way, it enabled new millions to enter the middle class and led to the most equitable distribution of wealth in American history. In 1949 the richest 5 percent owned only 19.3 percent of the wealth. By comparison in 1998, 97 percent of the wealth was controlled by 5 percent of the people. The GI Bill also fueled the economy, helped to prevent a post-war depression, and led to inflation.

Unions, which had not gotten much of an increase in wages during the war, now began to strike. When the mine owners refused to accept the United Mine Workers' demands, Truman, using war powers, took over the mines. In the railroad strikes, it was the workers who refused the agreement, so Truman took over the railroads until the strike was settled.

Such decisive actions made it obvious that Truman was not going to be just a caretaker president. He next sent a program to Congress that called for an enlarged New Deal. It included expansion of unemployment insurance, extension of the Employment Service, a higher minimum wage, a permanent Fair Employment Practices Commission, slum clearance and low rent housing, regional development of the nation's river valleys, and a public works program.

Although there were the usual fights with the Congress, the Employment Act of 1946 was passed that set up a Council of Economic Advisors to advise the president on employment needs. There was also the Atomic Energy Act, which gave civilians power over the new force and authorized only the president to use it in war.

In the off-year election of 1946, people voted for a Republican controlled Congress, which was anti-labor, and passed the Taft-Hartley Act of 1947. This banned the closed shop, which required that only union workers be hired, but permitted a union shop, which required that workers must join a union within a short period of time after they are hired. While it included provisions against unfair union practices, it also required union leaders to take oaths that they were not Communists. Truman's veto restored his credit with labor, but the bill was passed over his

This is a post World War II housing project established on the edge of a metropolitan area.

veto. Its biggest effect was that Southern states passed right-to-work laws that banned union shops.

The Republican Congress also passed a tax cut that Truman vetoed on the grounds that while production and employment were high, the federal deficit should be reduced. Congress overrode his veto.

Truman recommended and Congress passed a law changing the order of presidential succession so that the Speaker of the House and the President Pro-tempore of the Senate, both elected officials, came before the secretary of state and other cabinet officials. In a swipe at FDR, Congress passed and the states ratified the Twenty-second Amendment, limiting presidents to two terms or not more than a total of ten years should they serve out part of a previous president's term. It did not apply, however, to Truman.

Civil Rights

On February 2, 1948, Truman sent a civil rights message to Congress, the first in American history. He called for anti-lynching laws, anti-poll tax laws, the establishment of a Fair Employment Practices Commission to prevent discrimination by employers and unions alike, an end to discrimination in interstate travel, and a request that the claims of Japanese Americans who had lost their property and had been confined because of their racial origin be acted upon. (The latter was not approved until the Reagan administration.) Truman also announced that he had ordered the secretary of defense to end segregation in the armed forces. When asked to soften his civil rights views, Truman, whose ancestors were Confederates, replied, "...my stomach turned over when I learned that Negro soldiers, just back from overseas, were being dumped out of army trucks in Mississippi and beaten....as President I know this is bad. I shall fight to end evils like this."

ELECTION OF 1948

Republican successes in the 1946 election seemed to indicate that the Republicans could take the presidency, especially since the Democratic Party was divided. Henry Wallace, who had served as one of FDR's vice-presidents and who wished for closer relations with the Soviet Union, ran on the Progressive Party ticket. Truman ran for the Democrats, and Thomas E. Dewey ran for the Republicans. The Republican platform was conservative and international; the Democrats included a civil rights plank and the enactment of federal anti-lynching and anti-poll tax laws. When the Democrats met in convention, the Southern Democrats, or Dixiecrats, bolted and nominated Strom Thurmond, later a Republican Senator from South Carolina, for president. The Dixiecrats wanted to split the electoral vote so that no one would have a majority. This would result in the presidential race being thrown into the House of Representatives, which the Republicans controlled. Under this scenario a deal could be struck to prevent any attempt at civil rights.

With the Southern Democrats alienated from the national party, Truman's strategy was to appeal to the black vote in the North. With a strong civil rights platform and his executive order to desegregate the military, Truman was well positioned to gain the black vote. The four party race also benefited Truman since it put him right in the middle of the political spectrum. With the Progressives putting forth a leftist campaign and the Republicans and Dixiecrats a rightist one, Truman became the moderate in the ideological middle.

Thomas Dewey, the GOP candidate, had run for president against Roosevelt in the 1944 election. He had an admirable record as an anti-Mafia prosecutor and a competent governor of New York. However, he seemed to think that he was automatically going to win the election. He followed the conventional belief that Truman was a bumbler and a sure loser. Not all Republicans were enamored of Dewey. Teddy Roosevelt's daughter, Alice, derided him as, "The little man on the wedding cake."

As Truman traveled around the country on a whistle-stop train tour, criticizing the "do-nothing" Republican 80th Congress, a man yelled out, "Give 'em hell, Harry." Truman replied that he just told the truth, and they considered that hell. Whatever the case, it reaffirmed Truman's image as a fighter.

On November 1, 1948, the Gallup organization published the results of their last poll taken between October 15 and 25. It gave Dewey the winning edge of 49.5 to Truman's 44.5. To the surprise of everyone but Truman, Truman won the election, the greatest upset in American political history. We now know that in close elections, voters make their decision the weekend immediately before Election Day. Thomas E. Dewey and his supporters were so confident of winning that the *Chicago Tribune* even published a headline issue announcing "Dewey Defeats Truman." It was an issue of the *Tribune* that Truman delighted in holding up for photographers. One congratulatory telegram to Truman was from General Dwight Eisenhower. In it he stated: At no point in the political history of the United States was there a "Record of greater accomplishments than yours, that can be traced so clearly to the stark courage and fighting heart of a single man." Along with the presidency, the Democrats also carried both houses of Congress.

Truman worked with Congress to increase the minimum wage to $.75 an hour and to increase coverage under the Social Security Act. A National Housing Act, extension of rent control, farm price supports, slum clearance, and support for the Tennessee Valley Authority also passed. The Dixiecrats, however, gave the cold shoulder to civil rights, national health insurance, federal aid to education, and subsidies for farm incomes rather than farm prices.

Truman's next four years in the White House were ones of declining popularity and increasing problems. Shortly after the election, the Trumans moved from the White House to Blair House while the White House was totally gutted and rebuilt with the exterior walls still standing. This was necessitated when a leg of daughter Margaret's piano came through the ceiling of the room beneath it! While they lived in Blair House in 1950, two Puerto Rican nationalists attempted to assassinate Truman. In the ensuing gunfire, a White House policeman was killed along with one of the Puerto Ricans. Had the assassins waited a few hours, they might have had a better chance of killing Truman at an outdoor speech.

SECOND TERM

Foreign policy issues became paramount during Truman's second administration, and the worst problems were in Asia. Here the issue of China had been bubbling away for all the years that Truman had been president. The problems with U. S. policy were two-fold. Chiang had retired to Formosa, an island 100 miles off the coast of China, where he set himself up as a government in exile. The second problem was that Mao was more of a Communist than a pragmatist and was vociferously anti-American. The Chinese knew that it was more important for them to have a good relationship with the Soviets with whom they shared a border than with the distant United States. On February 14, 1950, Red China and the Soviet Union announced the signing of a mutual-defense treaty. Soon the administration would face the Republican charge of "losing China."

In the midst of these foreign policy concerns were highly interrelated domestic concerns. One was the trial of Alger Hiss with the accompanying rise of a young Republican representative from California, Richard Milhous Nixon, a member of the House Committee on Un-American Activities (HUAC). The other was the beginning of a phenomenon called McCarthyism. Both were concerned with the subversive activities of Communists or Communist sympathizers called fellow travelers. One danger was that any one who disagreed with the ideology of their accusers could be called a Communist, fellow traveler, or comsymp (Communist sympathizer).

Alger Hiss was a former mid-level State Department official who had become president of the Carnegie Endowment for International Peace. Whittaker Chambers, an editor from *Time* and admitted former Communist, accused Hiss of Communist sympathies. Nixon was a HUAC supporter of Chambers. When Chambers testified before the HUAC where he was backed by Nixon, he enlarged his charges and accused Hiss of espionage. At a crucial point in the investigation Chambers produced microfilm documents that he claimed Hiss had passed to him in 1937 and 1938. The

Harry Truman displays the headline on the front page of the *Chicago Tribune*, which had declared Dewey the winner.

documents that had been hidden in a pumpkin on Chambers' farm were known as the Pumpkin Papers. In December 1948 Hiss was charged with perjury for denying these allegations under oath. He could not be charged with espionage because the statute of limitations had expired. After two trials, a federal jury convicted Hiss in January 1950, and the judge sentenced him to five to ten years in a federal prison. To his defenders, Hiss was the victim of a conservative conspiracy led by Richard Nixon. To his accusers, he was a symbol of a naive government policy that was leaving the United States vulnerable to its worst enemy. Although Hiss is now dead, as are Chambers and Nixon, the case is still discussed and, while Hiss denied it to his dying day, all available evidence points to his guilt. The case did help propel Nixon to the United States Senate and from there to the vice-presidency.

HUAC also conducted a series of investigations on Communist infiltration of the film industry. This resulted in the imprisonment of a group of writers, directors, and producers known as the Hollywood Ten. One of the people who testified before the committee was Ronald Reagan, a six-time president of the Screen Actors Guild, the union for film actors. As union president, Reagan tried to remove suspected Communists from the movie industry and made strong anti-Communist statements to HUAC.

HUAC also investigated one of the most popular stars of the 1950s, Lucille Ball. Ball had once registered to vote as a Communist to please her elderly grandfather. When her husband defended her before their popular TV show, *I Love Lucy*, he said the only thing red about Lucy was her hair and even that was dyed.

The other politician who rode the issue of communism to fame was Joseph McCarthy, the junior senator from Wisconsin. Friendless and generally considered a failure, he was looking for an issue that might raise him out of obscurity. Communist subversion was that issue. In February 1950 in a speech to Republican women in West Virginia, McCarthy waved a piece of paper on which he said were the names of 205 known Communists in the State Department. Later he made essentially the same speech but said it was fifty-seven "card carrying" Communists. This speech made the headlines and soon gave birth to a new term in American political history, "McCarthyism." In a follow-up speech to the Senate, which went on for five hours, he claimed eighty-one names.

Alger Hiss, who had been a prominent State Department official, was convicted in January 1950.

Although McCarthy had no evidence that there was even one Communist, he soon was no longer obscure. Despite his hard-drinking recklessness, moderate and liberal Republicans did not reject him. Many conservative Republicans gave him unconditional support including Senator Robert Taft from Ohio, son of President William Howard Taft, who was planning a run for the presidency in 1952. The only Republican to challenge McCarthy was Senator Margaret Chase Smith, the only woman in the Senate. She declared that she did not want to see the Republican Party ride to a midterm victory in 1950 on the "four horses of calumny—fear, ignorance, bigotry, and smear."

As early as 1947, Truman had been concerned about the political issue of Communists in the government. Partly as a reaction to HUAC, Truman issued an executive order establishing an elaborate Federal Employees Loyalty and Security Program. It did serve to pull the rug out from under his Republican detractors in Congress. However, years later in private conversations with friends, Truman conceded that it had been a mistake. The Truman administration also indicted and convicted eleven leading Communist Party officials under the Smith Alien Registration Act of 1940. The Supreme Court upheld the constitutionality of the act, and they were sent to prison.

However, these programs did not provide any cover against the charges that McCarthy made. Truman showed his ethical standards when he refused to leak a huge file on McCarthy's bedmates to the press. As author John Hersey has reported, Truman said, "You must not ask the President of the United States to get down in the gutter with a guttersnipe. Nobody, not even the President of the United States, can approach too close to a skunk, in skunk territory, and expect to get anything out of it except a bad smell." His only defense against McCarthy's charges would be the truth.

KOREAN WAR

Korea was Truman's biggest foreign relation problem in his second administration. To facilitate the surrender of Japanese troops in Korea, it had been divided at the 38th parallel into a Soviet zone and an American zone. Just as the Soviets would not agree to political or economic reunification in Germany, they would not agree to it in Korea. Although the United Nations set up a Temporary Commission to hold elections, they were excluded from North Korea. In South Korea a constitution was written for the Republic of Korea with Syngman Rhee, a ruthless man, elected as the first president in 1948. In the North the Soviets organized a Democratic People's Republic with Kim Il Sung as president. Each government aspired to control the entire peninsula, but North Korea was better equipped with tanks and heavy artillery. The United States had equipped the South with defensive weapons only. When the Soviet and American armies left, military might belonged to the North. Saturday, June 24, 1950, Truman received the news that North Korea had invaded South Korea. It was a complete surprise.

Within a few hours Truman asked for a meeting of the United Nation's Security Council, which declared the North Korean aggressors by a vote of 9-0 and called for the cessation of hostilities and the withdrawal of North Korean forces. It was 9-0 because the Soviet ambassador was boycotting UN meetings to protest the non-recognition of Communist China. While fifteen nations responded to the call for troops, the military was heavily composed of South Korean and American troops. The response of the American public was that, of course, we could easily defeat a third rate power such as North Korea. Radio stations even offered free maps of Korea so that American children could follow the advance of American forces.

Because of their superior fire power and training, the North Koreans pushed the South Korean forces to the extreme southeast corner of Korea at Pusan. MacArthur notified Truman that a complete collapse of South Korea was imminent and that combat forces must be used, Truman discussed the matter with congressional leaders who advised against a war resolution. Accepting their advice, Truman used his presidential authority to send troops. He also called for the support of the UN. Since the Soviets were still absent and therefore unable to veto it, the resolution to use armed force to stop the invasion in a "police action" passed. One caution came from the Secretary of Defense Olin Johnson: to give MacArthur detailed instructions "so as not to give him too much discretion." The immediate response was positive: Truman was praised by Democrats and Republicans alike for his bold action.

MacArthur showed his military brilliance when he unveiled a plan to stage an amphibious invasion at Inchon on the western coast of Korea and within easy distance of the southern capital at Seoul. Although military odds makers gave the chances of success as 5,000 to 1, Truman backed MacArthur. The invasion took place on September 15, and the North Koreans were soon routed. Truman now gave MacArthur permission to liberate the North. Containment seemed to be giving way to liberation. On October

The Korean War was a war of containment.

2 Chinese Prime Minister Zhou En-lai sent a warning to Washington via the Indian Ambassador to China: Peking did not object to South Korean troops entering North Korea. However, if American troops crossed the border, China would enter the war. In the flush of the Inchon invasion success, the momentum of events could not be stopped. The State Department, Pentagon, and White House all considered the warning to be a bluff. However, Truman made clear that MacArthur was only authorized to cross the 38th parallel if there was no sign of major intervention in North Korea by the Chinese or the Soviets.

October 7 the first American troops crossed the 38th parallel. A week later Truman flew to Wake Island to meet with MacArthur about the final phases of the war. MacArthur indicated that the formal resistance would end by Thanksgiving and that by Christmas the Eighth Army would be back in Japan. He expected that the United Nations would hold elections in January 1951 and that a military occupation would end shortly after that. When Truman asked about the possibility of Chinese or Soviet intervention, MacArthur reported very little chance of either. While Truman and MacArthur talked, the first Chinese troops had crossed the Yalu River, the Korean-China border.

By the end of October, MacArthur, in direct violation of his orders that only South Korean forces were to be allowed near the Chinese and Russian frontiers, ordered all his forces to drive northward at full force. UN forces first encountered the Chinese on October 26. By November 6 MacArthur was calling the Chinese response wanton aggression. On November 24 MacArthur announced an "end the war offensive." Rather than formal resistance ending on Thanksgiving, the day after Thanksgiving 250,000 Chinese Communists swarmed across the Yalu River. Within two days, MacArthur's forces were fleeing south in what became the longest retreat in American military history. The UN forces retreat involved some of the worst and most tragic fighting of the war in sub-zero temperatures for which they were totally unprepared. So disastrous was the retreat that it has been compared to Napoleon's withdrawal from Moscow, which destroyed the French army in the winter of 1812-1813.

MacArthur now wanted to fight a total war even if it meant taking on China directly. Since China had a defensive treaty with the Soviet Union, this would have meant the start of World War III. Omar Bradley, the Chairman of the Joint Chiefs, said it was the wrong war at the wrong place with the wrong enemy. Newly appointed Secretary of Defense General George Marshall favored getting out of Korea with honor. There must be no all out war with China.

The press, which had long glorified MacArthur, now went on the attack. *Time* charged him with being responsible for the worst military disaster in history; the New York *Herald Tribune* said that MacArthur could no longer be accepted as the final authority on military matters. MacArthur soon began to rewrite history by saying that it was not his fault. He denied that his strategy had been the cause of the Chinese intervention. He blamed his lack of success in combating the Chinese forces on Washington-imposed restrictions.

While MacArthur was waging war in the media, a new commander, Matthew Ridgway, took command of the Eighth Army in the field and, after some consolidation, began to push forward. Soon the Americans were again at the 38th parallel. Meanwhile in Tokyo, MacArthur's utterances became increasingly bizarre: he proposed massive air attacks on Manchuria. This was followed by a new twist: depositing radio-active wastes from atomic manufacture along the Yalu River. When MacArthur learned that Truman planned a statement about negotiations to end the war, MacArthur released his own declaration in which he threatened to expand the war into China and offered to meet with the Chinese commander-in-chief to reach a settlement that sounded very much like Chinese unconditional surrender. When MacArthur wrote to Republican House Minority Leader Joseph Martin that there was no substitute for victory and that the Nationalist Chinese of Chiang Kai-shek should join the battle, it was the last in a series of acts of insubordination. Despite the fears of Truman's advisers that there would be vicious attacks on Marshall, Bradley, and Truman himself, April 11, 1951, Truman fired MacArthur and replaced him with General Matthew Ridgway.

There was an immediate political and public outcry over MacArthur's firing. The Republican congressional leaders called for Truman's impeachment. One Republican Senator declared that the U. S. was in the hands of Russian spies who were directing "a secret coterie." Opposition ranged from longshoremen who walked off their jobs in protest to a Baltimore women's group who wanted to march on Washington. Truman was even burned in effigy in Massachusetts and California. Probably the most extreme reaction was that of a Protestant minister from Houston. He became so upset dictating a telegram that he died of a heart attack. Despite this, most newspapers, including some staunch Republican papers, praised Truman for asserting civilian control of the military. Nevertheless, when MacArthur returned home for the first time in fourteen years, he received a hero's welcome including parades and a chance to address a joint session of Congress. We know today that Truman had received information from American spies that made it all too clear that MacArthur's rhetoric on the Nationalist Chinese and war with China was actually more than that. He was determined to start World War III, a nuclear war in Asia, with himself as the American commander.

By June 1951, negotiations began on an armistice that the Eisenhower administration would finalize in June 1953. One problem that turned up during this conflict was the brainwashing of American prisoners who then turned against their own government. This was accomplished by sleep deprivation. Americans at home could not understand how in the few short years between World War II and the Korean War, American soldiers had so changed that they would cooperate with the enemy. Questions were raised to determine the responsibility for such moral failures. One answer was to blame it on the soldiers' mothers.

Another problem that remained hidden for fifty years was, at least, one atrocity Americans committed that seemed like a precursor of events at My Lai in Vietnam. American infantry and pilots massacred Korean civilians hiding under a bridge at No Gun Ri. For years the Army rejected claims by Korean survivors that American troops were involved. In the fall of 1999, however, three hundred witnesses including former G.I.'s came forward to support the victims' accounts.

During his last year and a half in office, Truman was beset by revelations that some in his administration were involved in influence peddling and other scandals. He seemed incapable of realizing that any of his people would dishonor the offices they held by illegal acts.

ELECTION OF 1952

Although the Twenty-second Amendment did not bar Truman from running for re-election, a 23 percent approval rating marked the end of any thoughts of such a run and, in truth, Truman was ready to return to Independence.

The man Truman wanted to succeed him was Adlai Stevenson, the governor of Illinois, who, to Truman's distress, was playing the role of reluctant candidate. In July Stevenson finally decided to run against Estes Kefauver, a senator from Tennessee who held the lead in committed votes. After the second ballot, Truman intervened to see that support would go to Stevenson. Senator John Sparkman of Alabama ran with Stevenson. Problems quickly arose between Stevenson and Truman when it seemed that Stevenson agreed with the Republicans that there was a "mess" in Washington.

The Republicans were expecting a landslide victory on the issues of Communists, corruption, and Korea, no matter who their candidate was. As the year progressed, the GOP nomination turned into a battle between Dwight Eisenhower, who represented the Eastern moderate wing of the party, and Robert Taft, who was the darling of the conservative wing. Despite many scurrilous rumors about Ike and his wife, Mamie, he won the Republican nomination on the first ballot. To balance the ticket, ideologically, geographically, and demographically, Ike chose as his vice-president Senator Richard M. Nixon from California.

In September the press revealed that wealthy southern California businessmen had established a secret trust fund for Nixon. Many of Ike's advisers counseled him to dump Nixon from the ticket. Instead, Nixon went on TV to explain the fund. He then asked people to wire their verdict to the Republican National Committee. When Ike refused to say when he would make his decision about Nixon's future, Nixon used an unfortunate choice of words to push Ike. "There comes a time in matters like this when you've either got to shit or get off the pot." Ike never forgot the phrase. No one had ever presumed to speak to him like that. Later Ike told Nixon, "You're my boy!"

One of the low points in the campaign was Eisenhower's October speech in Wisconsin with Joe McCarthy sitting behind him on the stage. Ike's aides had been telling the press all that day that Ike planned to give a tribute to George Marshall, whom McCarthy had labeled a traitor over the fall of China. When he made the speech, Ike omitted the tribute to Marshall. Instead, Ike charged that the Reds in Washington had caused the fall of China, as well as the surrender of the nations in Europe. Many criticized Eisenhower who seemed to be so intimidated by McCarthy that he directly criticized the man who had recommended him for the post of Supreme Allied Commander in World War II.

The high point of Ike's campaign was also in October when he promised that, immediately after his election, he would go to Korea. Those who favored winning the war thought Ike meant he would go to see how this could be accomplished. Those who favored an armistice thought Ike meant that he would go to Korea to end the war. In either case, Americans were certain that Ike would take charge and end the war. Ike's lead at the polls increased in response to this. Two weeks later the election results followed predictions with the Republicans sweeping both the presidency and the Congress, although by slim majorities. When Ike was inaugurated, the frosty relationship between the president-elect and Truman was clear to all.

EVALUATION OF TRUMAN

The total renovation of the White House was one of the things that Truman was most pleased with completing during his second term. In April 1952 the White House was again open to the public. Truman took the American public on a television tour that all three networks covered. They were the only television broadcasters in 1952. Truman's love of the history of the White House was obvious to all, and it helped to raise his standing with the American people.

When Truman retired from the presidency and wanted to make arrangements to move his personal family belongings to Independence, a Washington, D.C. bank refused to give him a loan without a co-signer. His former Secretary of State Dean Acheson, who was a wealthy man, agreed to co-sign the loan. Truman's wife's family even owned the house in Independence that Truman lived in. In 1953 there was no pension for former presidents or congressmen; Truman's only source of income was his pension from his service as a captain in WW I. A man of honor who had no intention of selling his fame as president by serving on corporate boards or giving speeches, Truman faced some hard financial times. Five years later in 1958 Congress agreed to provide all former presidents with a pension of $25,000 a year, which was one fourth the annual presidential salary, money for staff, office space, and free mailing privileges.

Truman stepped into the presidency with almost no briefings from FDR. Despite this, he successfully ended World War II, resisted Soviet expansionism, extended the ideals of the New Deal, and confronted the issue of segregation. In the years since his presidency, Truman's stature has increased. Historians have consistently rated him one of the near-great presidents.

EISENHOWER YEARS

The Eisenhower years are often seen today as a golden time of peace and prosperity, family values, and traditions—a time when everything was right in America. Such is not the case. For example, teenage pregnancy was at an all time high with many out of wedlock births. While the economy was good and many Americans were prosperous, it was a prosperity that left many Americans in poverty. Twenty-five percent of the population was poor, and there were no food stamps, Medicare, and few federal housing programs. One third of American children lived in poverty, as well as 60 percent of the elderly. The prosperity that existed was directly related to federal policies such as the GI Bill with its easy access and low down payments for homes. Before World War II banks required 50 percent down and financed homes for only 5-10 years. By the 1950s you could buy a home with 10 percent down under the Federal Housing Administration and pay for it over 30 years at an interest rate of 2-3 percent. If you were a veteran, it was possible to get a mortgage for one dollar down!

Although most families were still intact in the 1950s, there were problems below the surface. For example, the problem of battered wives was blamed on the wives, not the husbands. Psychoanalysts like Helen Deutsch said such a wife was a "masochist who provoked her husband into beating her." She also proclaimed that a "feminine" woman left the initiative to the man and renounced her own needs to experience herself through her identification with her man. Another family problem hiding beneath the surface was incest. When Marilyn Van Derbur became Miss America in 1958, most thought she came from a typical American middle class family. No one suspected her respectable successful father of sexually molesting her from ages 5-18. Years later, she discovered that he had done the same to her sisters. Her mother, like many wives of the times, denied that the incest had occurred.

The roots of such passivity on the part of women can be traced back to society's view of women in the post-war period. A 1947 best seller was *The Modern Woman: The Lost Sex* by Marynia Farnham, a psychiatrist, and Ferdinand Lundberg, an historian. They declared that feminism was an illness and that an independent woman was a contradiction in terms. The authors also claimed that war and depression were a result of women leaving homes and families. In their view the women's rights movement had caused women to reject their natural, sex-based instincts in a futile attempt to become imitation men.

Most of the problems of society were blamed on women. Dr. Benjamin Spock in his best selling *Baby and Child Care* cautioned that mothers who wanted to work and leave their children should seek counseling. The good mother was the one who was always there for her children while at the same time never being overprotective. This last was to guard against the condition called "Momism." After World War II, author Philip Wylie castigated women as evil mothers who smothered and devoured their children by keeping them dependent and immature because there was nothing else in their lives. Such mothers created men who could not function in wartime as soldiers. Adding fuel to this debate about the role of women were such cold war icons as J. Edgar Hoover, head of the Federal Bureau of Investigation

Dwight D. Eisenhower

(FBI), who saw mothers as the first line of defense against the "twin enemies of freedom—crime and communism."

WOMEN'S ROLES

For a while it did seem that women were returning to the life of domesticity with enthusiasm. Early marriages and a rising birth rate characterized the 1940s and 1950s. Suburbs bloomed, and woman as consumer became an increasingly popular concept.

Post-war fashions also showed a new feminine image as the Dior silhouette took hold: long full skirts, defined bustlines, and tiny waists. In the 1950s the "baby doll" style was introduced with greater emphasis on the feminine image: belted waists, padded brassieres, and full skirts over layers of crinoline petticoats. Shoes had three inch heels that had to be reinforced with steel to avoid breakage. The idea was to emphasize slim beautiful legs. In reality the shoes worked to make women more passive and contributed to many sprained ankles, as well as foot and back problems.

While the emphasis was on the typical American suburban housewife, the truth was that this applied to only a minority of American women. Millions lived either in cities or farms. Many suffered from poor health, unemployment, and poverty. Poor women could not remain at home; they had to work. This was especially true of African-American women. Despite 40 percent of African-American women having small children at home, they had to work outside their own homes for survival. The only good news was that, with the labor shortage, department stores began to hire black saleswomen and office managers began to hire black clerical workers. Most black women, however, remained in the domestic sphere.

While it was possible to get jobs in the traditional female occupations, other jobs were closed to women, a fact made evident by the gender separated listings in the want ads. An agent for a large insurance company reported that his company did not recruit female college graduates for jobs since they did not expect to have a career and the few that did changed their plans in a few years. Because the only jobs left open were more tedious and allowed no room for ambition, college women often quit them in a few months. It was a double bind because they were not hired for "women's work" since they would become bored and leave, and they were not hired for "men's work" since they might marry and leave.

The technology that dominated the 1950s was not an unmixed blessing for women either. Since they had all of these machines to save time, society thought women should be able to do more. By the end of the 1950s although labor saving devices proliferated, the women's housework time actually increased from slightly less than fifty-two hours per week to fifty-four.

Life magazine in 1956 had a special issue on the ideal American woman: mother of four, wife, hostess, volunteer, and home manager but, above all, a conscientious mother who spent hours with her children helping them with their homework and listening to their problems. In essence, she was a sweet and innocent homebody. Television had a different view and showed the American housewife in "I Love Lucy" where Lucille Ball played a lovably comic but ditzy Lucy Riccardo. The irony is that Lucille Ball was the brains behind the success of "I Love Lucy" and its production company, Desilu. Even the sex sirens of the day such as Marilyn Monroe and Elizabeth Taylor combined aggressive sexuality with a certain artlessness and naivete that made them less threatening and

Living the ideal suburban life was difficult for most African-American women. They found employment in menial, low-paying jobs, such as this woman cleaning a Greyhound bus.

more of a sex object. Monroe's wide-eyed charm, physical voluptuousness, and natural sex appeal made her the most famous international sex symbol of the twentieth century.

SUBURBAN LIFE AND THE AUTOMOBILE

With the end of World War II, Americans were able to renew their love affair with the automobile. While Congress had passed the Interstate and Defense Highway Act in 1944, which provided $1.5 billion for road building and improvements in the first three post-war years, it soon proved inadequate. Very little of it was spent for limited access highways like the Pennsylvania Turnpike, which had proved its worth during the war in carrying shipments of Pittsburgh steel east to the Atlantic ports. While California began building the much admired freeways, tollways continued to be the answer in the East. By the end of the 1950s it was possible to drive from New York to Chicago via tollways, which included links to Philadelphia, Pittsburgh, Cleveland, and Toledo. Few people thought of what these limited access highways would do to the Mom and Pop businesses that were soon consigned to oblivion.

The growth of highways at the same time spelled the end of the other major mode of transportation: rail. The first to go was the Pacific Electric Railway (PER) that served the Los Angeles area. Although it was probably always doomed by Angelenos' love of their cars, a General Motors led consortium including Firestone, Standard Oil of California, and Philips Petroleum hastened its demise. The consortium bought up rail systems and replaced them with bus service. In all, over one hundred transportation systems were involved in the West and Midwest with the PER being the largest. In 1949, in federal court, the members of the consortium were found guilty of anti-trust violations because GM produced buses in their Yellow Coach Division. Some suggested that the purpose of the consortium was more sinister. Since profits on the bus lines were minimal, the real purpose may have been to get local governments to improve highways to the benefit of all members of the consortium. It seems clear that, with or without the aid of GM and its associates, the interurbans, rail lines connecting urban areas, would have declined if for no other reason than their lack of flexibility.

The demise of the interurbans isolated those who lived in the poverty areas of large cities such as the Watts neighborhood of Los Angeles. It also made possible the exurbs, as the distant communities surrounding core communities were named. While the suburbs sprang up because of the rail system, the exurbs were dependent on the car. That changed the nature of the life of the commuter who could easily spend fifteen to twenty hours a week just traveling to and from work. Nor were exurb women excluded from this since most shopping, schools, and other services also required a car. With people spending so much more time in their cars, automotive manufacturers began to put greater emphasis on comforts to keep the driver happy: radios to make the traffic congestion more bearable; improved heating and air-conditioning to even out the extremes in the American climate; and automatic transmissions and power steering to reduce the strain of stop and go driving.

To lure buyers into the showrooms and to break the back of the minor car manufacturers, the Big Three (General Motors, Ford, and Chrysler) put an emphasis on styling. The first of their products to show this was the Chevrolet Corvette, unveiled in 1953. Described as one of the sexiest looking vehicles to come off an assembly line, the 'Vette was sold primarily on styling rather than engineering and went on to become the most successful sports car made in America. The accent was on aviation type styling, which often included aviation type names. For example, the 1950 Oldsmobile 88 had a "Rocket" engine; the Mercury had a "jet-scoop hood." The minor car companies never caught up, although Studebaker-Packer did come out with some designs that were on par with the Big Three. Their lack of chrome and fins, however, defined their lack of success with the public.

The automobile also included sexual images in a way to make them a fetish. The body of the car was curvaceous, with a symmetry that was like the female human form. It was designed to create an erotic whole. No one did it better than Cadillac. A 50s sex symbol, Jayne Mansfield, not only owned and died in a Cadillac, she was one. Other companies followed suit, and the ads showed this. The car was desirable, something to be possessed, and then transformed into a slave to man's desires. Some historians report that this was all unconscious to the consumer and to most of society, but teenage boys in the 50s often described their girlfriends as a car model. Just as Jayne Mansfield was a Cadillac and Doris Day a Lincoln Continental Mark IV, so were their girlfriends.

As the car population increased, the need for improved national highways became more evident. In 1954 Eisenhower established a committee to look into the issue of creating a network of limited access highways. Ike had been in charge of an army convoy that had crossed the country in 1918. He knew well the military value of such a network of roads. In addition, the construction of such a network would stimulate the economy. In 1956 Congress passed the Interstate Highway Act, which provided for the construction of 41,000 miles of toll-free highways. The federal government would provide 90 percent of the funds and establish standards for their construction, while leaving administration and maintenance to the individual states. Levies on trucks, tires, gasoline, and related products would raise money and channel it through a Highway Trust Fund. These limited access highways were part of a system called the National System of Interstate and Defense Highways. The expectation was that vehicles on these limited access highways would move at 70 miles per hour, although many went much faster.

While the interstate highway system was a boon to the tourists and the truck industry, there were some humorous stories involving the first motorists who encountered the cloverleaf pattern that provided the access and egress from the highway. There were jokes about commuters who never reached the main lanes of the interstate but spent hours trapped in the cloverleaf going on and off, on and off, on and off.

The construction of the interstate system had unforeseen effects in both cities and rural areas. In cities, the webs of urban expressways often destroyed long-established neighborhoods. While this problem existed throughout the nation, the work of Robert Moses in New York City produced some of the worst examples of such destruction. In the rural areas, the interstate spelled the end of the Mom and Pop businesses that were on the side roads. In both areas, urban and rural, there was the growth of the strip mall often located near the new motels like Holiday Inn and Howard Johnson's, a cross between the urban hotel and the auto-court. They also propelled the growth of franchises such as Harland Sander's Kentucky Fried Chicken and Ray Kroc's McDonald's. Travelers appreciated the efficiency, cleanliness, and guarantee of a product that was the same across the entire nation. The strip mall evolved into the enclosed shopping mall that encouraged year round shopping. The first was opened in 1956 in Edina, Minnesota, a suburb of Minneapolis. And that, in its turn, marked the demise of the shopping center in the central city.

EISENHOWER ADMINISTRATIONS

During the Eisenhower years, technology became an important element in the lives of American citizens. It was seen in the new cars they drove down the interstate highway system, the television that showed them the civil rights struggle and Elvis, the airplanes that transported them across the country in record time and protected them from attack as part of the Strategic Air Command, the computers that made missiles possible, and the atom and hydrogen bombs that added to the anxiety of modern life.

It was also during the supposed placid years of the 40s and 50s that sexual activities became a focus of academic study at Indiana University. Here, in 1942, Alfred Kinsey, a world authority on gall wasps, founded the Institute for Sex Research to investigate human sexual behavior. Kinsey and his associates collected data by interviewing some 18,000 men and women. Kinsey published his results in *Sexual Behavior of the Human Male* in 1948 and in *Sexual Behavior of the Human Female* in 1953. Both books caused considerable controversy over the subject matter and the methodology. Nevertheless, Kinsey made the study of human sexual behavior a respectable field of study. In recent years sociologists have criticized his methods of data collection, which they believe gave inaccurate and misleading data.

To fight all of these changes as well as "Godless Communism," there was a new emphasis on so-called traditional religion and traditional values. Congress responded by inserting the phrase "under God" in the Pledge of Allegiance. June 14, 1954, Flag Day, CBS carried the ceremony of the first use of the "under God" phrase on its morning show. Religious programming was on the television not only on Sunday but also in prime time with the Baptist Reverend Billy Graham and his evangelical crusades and Roman Catholic Bishop Fulton J. Sheen whose show rated higher than the popular comedian Milton Berle who was in the same time slot. Although religion seemed to many to be a prop for the status quo, there was still that kernel of the social gospel that would re-emerge in the 1960s in the civil rights movement.

Americans generally thought that they knew the new president well. Dwight Eisenhower was the third of six sons born to a religious farm family in Abilene, Kansas. Ike was a star athlete but an average student. Despite this, both Ike and his older brother, Milton, wanted to attend college. However, the family could not afford it. The brothers agreed to alternate helping each other through school. For a few years Ike worked at a dairy with his father so that he could provide money for Milton's college expenses. Then Ike learned that he could attend West Point for free if he scored high enough on the entrance exam. Before this point, Ike had shown no interest in a military career.

Ike gained the appointment to the United States Military Academy. At West Point Ike continued his athletic career until he injured his knee. From the beginnings of his military career, his superiors recognized his superior ability as an organizer. This served him well and eventually led General Marshall to promote him over many others to lieutenant general and eventually to recommend to FDR that Ike be the Supreme Allied Commander in World War II.

After the war ended, Ike served as president of Columbia University in New York City and later as the first Supreme Commander of NATO. During all these years, Ike had stayed so far away from politics

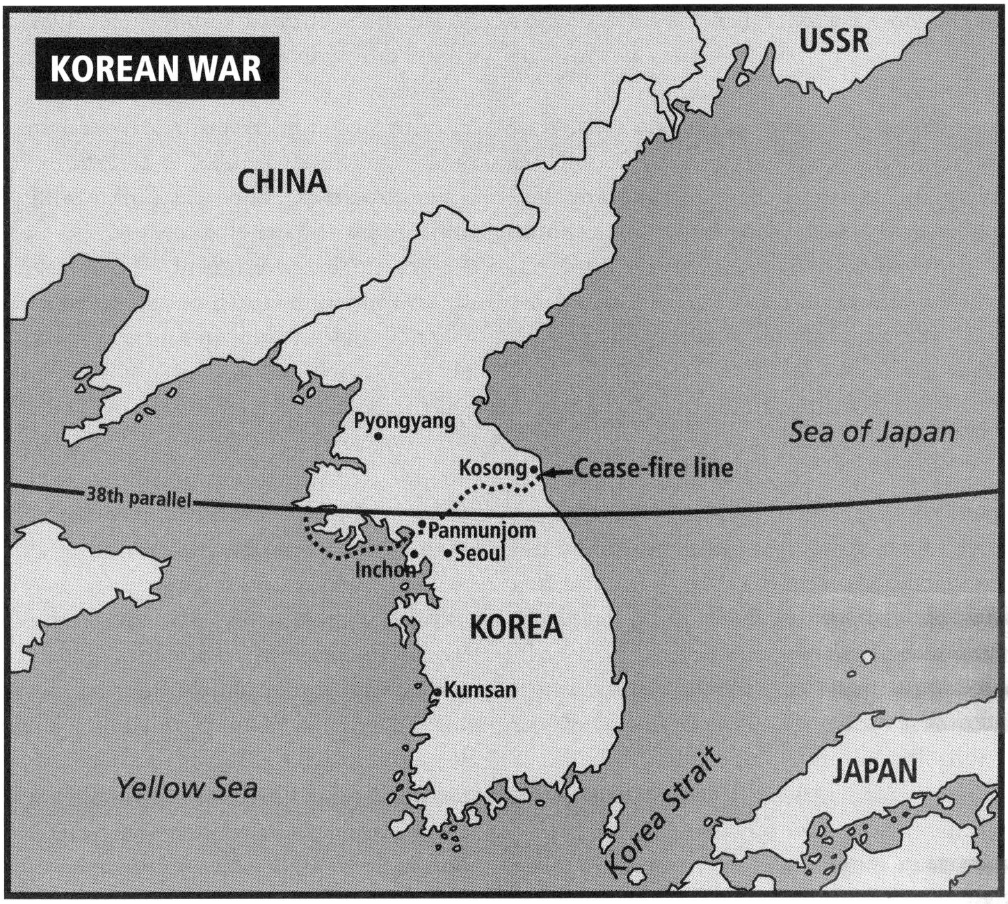

that no one knew whether he was a Democrat or a Republican. Both parties had tried to draft him to run on their ticket in 1948.

While Ike had a wonderful disarming grin, he was also a man who had a temper. In that regard, he had a lot in common with his predecessor. Still, Americans had no problem in saying "I Like Ike" and voting that preference.

The End of the Korean War

The first item that Eisenhower had to deal with was a resolution of the Korean War. During the 1952 campaign, Ike's Secretary of State John Foster Dulles had condemned the Truman policy of containment and said that it would be replaced with one of liberation. In reality, the policy of liberation was nothing but domestic campaign rhetoric. Rather, the new policy could be summed up in these watchwords: domino theory and brinkmanship. The domino theory was just a spin on containment. Defense of a nation might be required because if that nation fell, all the other nations in that area of the world would fall just like a line of dominos. Brinkmanship involved using the threat of nuclear attack or bringing the United States to the brink of war.

In Korea Ike faced two problems: dealing with the Red Chinese and dealing with Syngman Rhee and the South Koreans. The Chinese had to be convinced that it was in their interests to settle the issue of repatriation of prisoners of war and agree to an armistice. That was accomplished by brinkmanship. John Foster Dulles told the Indian Prime Minister Jawaharlal Nehru, who was a conduit to the Communist Chinese, that the United States might feel compelled to use atomic weapons if a truce could not be arranged. Even without this, the Chinese certainly knew that the United States could deliver bombs to the Chinese mainland from the island of Okinawa. This "threat" is particularly interesting in view of a letter that Ike wrote after the bombing of Hiroshima and Nagasaki in which he criticized Truman's use of the bomb.

The issue with Rhee was to get him to keep an armistice. Ike sent an emissary to Rhee to tell him that if he did not cooperate, all American troops and aid would be withdrawn. Rhee finally realized that it was futile to try to go it alone. On July 26, 1953, the truce was signed, and the war in Korea came to an end. Ike regarded this as one of his greatest achievements.

CIA and Foreign Policy

Ike appointed John Foster Dulles' brother, Allen, head of the CIA, which now became very active in covert operations around the world. The first overthrow of a government took place in Iran in 1953 under the leadership of Kermit Roosevelt, Teddy Roosevelt's grandson. The plan was to depose Iranian Prime Minister Mohammed Mossadegh and replace him with the former leader Shah Mohammed Reza Pahlavi. Mossadegh had seized the British owned Anglo-Persian Oil Company. The British and American oilmen told Ike that Mossadegh was a Communist. Here was the perfect place to use the CIA to implement American policy. As Ike's biographer Stephen Ambrose has written, "Eisenhower's fundamental belief [was] that nuclear war was unimaginable, limited conventional war was unreasonable, and stalemate was unacceptable." That left only covert activities.

In Iran the CIA used what became its traditional methods: bribery of army officers, use of paid rabble rousers to manipulate public opinion, and the installation of someone who would agree with Western economic policy even if having no interest in the establishment of a democratic government. It was very successful; Mossadegh was removed, the previously deposed Shah was reinstalled, and American oil companies were given 40 percent of Iranian oil. During the time that Roosevelt was planning the overthrow, Brigadier General H. Norman Schwarzkopf, who had reorganized the Shah's police force in 1940, arrived in Iran and became part of the operation. The police force was the Shah's agency of suppression. Despite over a billion dollars in American aid, there were no social or economic reforms, which were greatly needed.

The successful events in Iran set a precedent for presidents to use the CIA as a quick fix for foreign policy problems. Soon the CIA would perform a similar task in Guatemala where the Communists dominated the government. The worst crime was the expropriation of 225,000 acres of the best land of United Fruit Company, an American owned company and the major economic power in Guatemala. United Fruit had powerful connections in the United States, including the Dulles' brothers. John Foster Dulles' old law firm, Sullivan and Cromwell, had long represented United Fruit, and Allen Dulles had served on the United Fruit board.

The CIA chose a leader for the *coup d'etat* and provided an air force and American pilots. It took less than two weeks for the overthrow. The first thing the new leaders did was to disenfranchise illiterates who were 70 percent of the population. When a "free" election was held, it was to vote yes or no on the question of Castillo-Armas continuing as president. It was no surprise when he won. The government soon took 800,000 acres of land from the peasants, returned to United Fruit Company the land it had lost, and repealed laws guaranteeing worker rights and the rights of labor unions. This was just the first of many military dictators.

The rationale for the CIA's activities in Latin America goes back to recommendations made by George Kennan in 1950. From Kennan's viewpoint it was better to have a strong regime in power than a liberal government that might be penetrated by the Communists because of the freedoms that it permitted its people. Kennan wanted U.S. policy in Latin America to protect the United States' source of raw materials; to prevent military exploitation by the Communists; and to prevent the Latin Americans from being turned against the U.S. through psychological mobilization. By 1954, thirteen of the twenty countries in Latin America were under military dictatorships. To protect United States interests in Latin American nations, the U.S. Army operated the School of the Americas, first in Panama and later at Fort Benning, Georgia. Here, army officers and police were trained in repression, torture, and murder that they then went home and carried out. The United States Army has consistently denied that the School of the Americas taught torture, but the activities were confirmed in the 1990s.

FOREIGN POLICY CRISES

In October 1956, just in time for the fall presidential election, which was a rematch of Eisenhower versus Stevenson, two foreign policy problems moved to the fore: a revolution in Hungary and the Anglo-French-Israeli attack on Egypt. During the 1952 campaign John Foster Dulles had preached liberation, and over the almost four year administration the United States had encouraged people in the satellite nations to push for their freedom. The Hungarians took the U. S. at its word, but there would be no liberation. Instead, Soviets moved in to crush the revolt leaving poignant pictures of unarmed men throwing stones at Soviet tanks. The U. S. did permit thousands of the Hungarian refugees to enter the country.

The situation in Egypt was more complicated. Gamal Abdel Nasser had overthrown the Egyptian king and taken control of the country. In December 1955 the United States and Great Britain offered to help Nasser build the Aswan Dam, which was his pet project. In April 1956 Egypt joined with other Arab nations to form an anti-Israel alliance and then recognized Red China and withdrew its recognition of Nationalist China. As a result of congressional pressure, John Foster Dulles had to withdraw the Aswan offer. The Soviets moved in quickly to replace the United States. Now the British, French, and Israelis decided to secretly coordinate attacks on Egypt with Israel attacking the Sinai and France and Britain moving in to "protect" the Suez Canal. At the UN both the U.S. and U.S.S.R. condemned the Anglo-French action, and it was abandoned December 22, 1956.

U-2 Spy Plane

During the second Eisenhower administration, the CIA hit the top of its technical expertise with the building of the U-2 reconnaissance plane. Built in 1956 in seventeen months at $19 million ($3 million under budget), it was designed for the latest cameras, which used high resolution film. U-2s would fly over the Soviet Union filming whatever areas interested the CIA.

Secretary of State John Foster Dulles frequently took a hard line stand in foreign affairs.

These were not the first flights over the Soviet Union. Strategic Air Command (SAC) under General Curtis Le May had sent SAC bombers, which were loaded with nuclear and thermonuclear weapons, in unauthorized flights over the Soviet Union. In May 1956 alone, SAC had flown twenty-seven flights over Soviet airspace in an attempt to intimidate the Soviets. In part because Ike did not completely trust the military, he gave control of the U-2 to the CIA. Before each flight, Eisenhower had to give permission for the use of a ten-day period. From the first, the Soviets had tracked the U-2 and had complained through diplomatic channels about the flyovers. It was clear that eventually the Soviets would develop the capabilities to bring a U-2 to earth. Sooner came in 1960 when Eisenhower was preparing for a Big

Four (the Americans, British, French, and Soviets) meeting in Paris. Ike hoped that he could get Soviet Premier Nikita Khrushchev's agreement on a nuclear test ban treaty as a first step toward arms control and an agreement on Berlin.

There had only been two overflights in 1960, and those were primarily because the Soviets had fired their first intercontinental ballistic missile. Eisenhower approved the final flight as long as it was completed by May 1. The CIA thought that even if the Soviets shot down a U-2, they would never admit it because they would have to admit that the flights had been going on for a while and that they had been unable to stop them. In any event, the CIA was sure that neither a plane nor its pilot would survive a downing. A contract pilot, Francis Gary Powers, left the U-2 base in Turkey for his flight. The Soviets shot down his U-2 and arrested him. The CIA knew something was wrong and reported the plane as "lost." The Soviets kept quiet about the capture of Powers and the plane until May 5 when Khrushchev made a speech denouncing the U. S. for its aggressive provocation. Eisenhower had the National Aeronautical and Space Administration (NASA) issue a release that it was a weather plane that was lost. On May 6 Khrushchev released a photo of a wrecked plane that was not the U-2. The U.S. stuck to its weather story, and Khrushchev sprung his trap by showing part of the U-2 and its still alive pilot, Powers. Next, Eisenhower authorized the story that Powers had not been authorized to fly over the Soviet Union. When the summit finally took place, Khrushchev lambasted Eisenhower for the overflights and demanded that he apologize. Then the Soviets walked out of the meeting. Any hope Eisenhower had for détente or peace had been ruined by his decision to authorize the U-2 flights. The Soviet Union tried Powers and sentenced him to prison. The U. S. later traded a Soviet spy for Powers.

Cuba

The CIA also played a role in Cuban affairs after Fidel Castro gained power. The United States had supported the rightist dictator, Fulgencio Batista. On January 1, 1959, he fled Cuba as Fidel Castro entered Havana. Castro was soon executing Batista's officials after public trials that were more like Roman circuses. It became clear that Castro planned a socialist revolution and opposed foreign control of the Cuban economy. When he began land reform and nationalization of foreign owned property, relations with the U.S. worsened. Some believe that by rejecting Castro's requests for loans and other aid, the United States lost its chance to influence the revolution and pushed Castro further to the left.

The United States did not like Castro's seizure of British-American refineries, which would not process Soviet oil. Although Eisenhower was never able to determine to his satisfaction whether Castro was a Communist, he did determine that he wanted to get rid of him. In July Ike ordered economic sanctions against Cuba by reducing the sugar quota for 1960 and eliminating it for 1961. Sugar was the main Cuban crop.

In August 1960 Eisenhower met with the CIA to see what progress had been accomplished on a four-point program that he had approved in March. On point one, no leader for a government-in-exile could be found because the Cubans who were anti-Castro could not work together. Point two, which was a propaganda offensive, was underway. Point three, a resistance movement within Cuba, was a total failure. Progress was being made on point four, which was the creation of a para-military force in Guatemala from Cuban exiles. These four points formed the basis of the later Bay of Pigs invasion.

The other anti-Castro activity that the CIA directed was the assassination attempts that involved the American Mafia. Castro had shut down the American Mafia's gambling, dope, and vice dens in Havana. Some of the assassination plans can only be described as bizarre. They included using Mafia hit men, poisoning his cigar or coffee, and giving him something to make his facial hair fall out. None of the plots succeeded, but they kept on trying. It is unclear whether Eisenhower directly ordered such attempts. Since he was the author of the "plausible denial concept," either case could be true. Certainly, the CIA thought they had approval.

Eisenhower had appointed General Jimmy Doolittle chair of a committee to investigate the

CIA. The 1954 report concluded: "It is clear that we are facing an implacable enemy whose avowed objective is world domination by whatever means and at whatever cost. There are no rules in such a game. Hitherto acceptable norms of conduct do not apply." Whether this was the way it should have been, this was definitely the reality as far as the CIA was concerned. Shortly after Allen Dulles took the realm, the Agency began a program of covert use of biological and chemical weapons. The purpose was to turn humans into robots that could be programmed to kill on command. The guinea pigs would be Americans. Some like the addicts at a drug treatment center in Lexington, Kentucky were informed and asked to consent to the use of experimental drugs. Most were not. The agency was mainly interested in d-lysergic acid diethylamide, more popularly known as LSD. When the tests showed that the addicts did not respond to control for long periods of time or at long range, LSD was tested on "normal" people rather than drug addicts. Some died from these experiments. Others had long term mental problems. These activities did not come to public notice until the 1970s.

A young Fidel Castro lead his followers in the early stages of the Cuban Revolution.

One man who died was Frank Olson, an Army scientist from Fort Detrick, Maryland, the Army's biological research center. Unknown to his family Olson worked for the CIA and had done research on LSD and the spreading of anthrax and other toxins. He was found dead 10 stories below his hotel room in New York City. The death was ruled a suicide, but the story is much more complicated than it appeared.

In 1975 Olson's family discovered part of the story when a commission headed by Vice President Nelson Rockefeller revealed that the CIA had given an Army scientist LSD with the result that he jumped from a hotel window. A later congressional investigation identified that Army scientist as Frank Olson. The family decided to sue the federal government for damages and to find out the truth. To prevent the suit, the Ford administration proposed that Congress pass a Private Bill of $750,000 to settle the claim. This was done to keep other information from becoming public, such as the CIA's assassination manuals. One of the preferred assassination methods described in the manual was to drug or stun victims and then throw them from 75 feet or more to a hard surface.

Over the years Frank Olson's son, Eric, discovered bits and pieces of the story, and in 1993 he had a forensic pathologist perform an autopsy on his father's exhumed body. The autopsy concluded that Frank Olson had been struck on the head and then thrown from his hotel window to his death.

The last tantalizing piece of the story was the discovery in late 2002 of a memo in the Gerald Ford Presidential Library from Vice President Dick Cheney, then a White House Aide, to Secretary of Defense Donald Rumsfeld, then serving as Ford's chief of staff. This memo warned that a lawsuit might require revealing highly classified national-security information and the illegal activities of the CIA. A second memo from the White House counsel that was routed through Cheney and Rumsfeld suggested the need to settle the case to prevent any court settlement appearing as money to cover up CIA activities.

Numerous Cubans emigrated to the United States after World War II.

The agency was also interested in biological warfare, and, in 1960, Dr. Sidney Gottlieb, who was head of the Agency's Technical Services Staff, was on his way to Africa to assassinate Patrice Lumumba, the Congolese national leader, with bacteria that would cause a fatal disease. Before Gottlieb could succeed, Lumumba was captured and killed by a rival.

One of Eisenhower's strengths as president was his knowledge of the military and the politics and ploys it used to increase its budget. It was much harder to contest an Eisenhower military budget cut than it was other president's. It was, however, not impossible, as Curtis Le May proved, when he created the notion of a "bomber gap" and went to Congress to lobby for more bombers for SAC. It also did not protect Ike from charges that there was a missile gap after the Soviets had beaten the United States into space with the launching of their satellite, Sputnik, in the fall of 1957.

Nuclear War Threats

Eisenhower used the threat of nuclear war more often than any president before or since. Whether he was bluffing, no one knows for sure. Ike reportedly told Lyndon Johnson, when Johnson became president, that he had let the Chinese know that he would not hesitate to bomb China. He also threatened atomic warfare over Quemoy and Matsu, two islands off Formosa. Eisenhower saw no difference between atomic warfare and conventional warfare. For this reason he ordered the deployment of nuclear weapons as close to the Soviet Union as possible. This included loading SAC bombers, which were on standby twenty-four hours a day, with both nuclear and thermonuclear weapons.

By 1954, both the United States and U.S.S.R. had exploded hydrogen bombs and achieved a "balance of terror," as Churchill called it. The United States had tested the first hydrogen bomb, "Big Mike," on Bikini Atoll in the Pacific Ocean. It was much larger than expected. The cloud formed a canopy that was over one hundred miles wide on a stem that was thirty miles high. The fireball had vaporized the entire island and lifted into the air over 80 million tons of solid material. It left a circular crater two hundred feet deep and more than a mile across. It was, indeed, a balance of terror.

Another problem of the nuclear age was the Pentagon's loss of thermonuclear weapons, Hydrogen

Bombs. In 1958 the Air Force had four major accidents involving H-bombs. Two of them have never been recovered.

In February 1958, two Air Force jets crashed off the Georgia coast, and the bomber pilot was told to jettison his H-bomb. He dropped it near the mouth of the Savannah River where he thought it could be easily recovered. This was a primitive version of the H-bomb that weighed four tons and had 100 times the explosive force of the A-bomb dropped on Hiroshima. It was equipped with a plutonium trigger and armed with 400 pounds of TNT. The big danger was not that there might be a thermonuclear explosion but rather that the TNT might explode on contact and send radioactive debris across the area where it fell. The H-bomb jettisoned near the Savannah River did not explode and rescue efforts ceased on April 16, 1958 as the Pentagon reported to the Atomic Energy Commission in a request for a replacement. That bomb is still buried off Warsaw Sound, and there are no plans to recover it.

A second H-bomb was accidentally dropped in March 1958 in Florence, South Carolina, and the TNT in this one exploded causing extensive damage on the ground and several injuries, as well as spewing radioactive debris across the area. The remainder of the H-bomb was recovered.

Vietnam

In 1954 the United States also began the long trek to Vietnam. That year, the French lost the battle at Dien Bien Phu and were preparing to leave. Ike did consider American intervention via a single air strike using three atomic bombs, which we would then deny ever using. It was also at this time that the domino theory was enunciated. On April 7, 1954, Ike said at a news conference: "You have a row of dominos set up, you knock over the first one, and what will happen to the last one is the certainty that it will go over very quickly." In July, the Geneva agreements were signed calling for nation-wide elections in Vietnam in two years. The United States did not sign the Geneva agreements and instead worked to get the South East Asian Treaty Organization (SEATO) organized to establish a defensive line in Asia. By September, SEATO included France, Britain, Australia, New Zealand, Thailand, the Philippines, Pakistan, and the

After the Soviets launched Sputnik in 1957, Americans feared possible attacks and focused on civilian defense. Drills were routinely held in the schools.

United States. A special protocol was added to the treaty extending coverage to Indo-China

Soon the CIA was running the policy in Vietnam. When Ho Chi Minh took over in North Vietnam, the United States helped those who wished to get to South Vietnam and pushed Ngo Dinh Diem, who had been in exile at a Catholic seminary in New Jersey, as the next premier. Because the Communist leader of North Vietnam, Ho Chi Minh, would be the winner in any free elections in 1956, Eisenhower effectively blocked them. He next agreed to assist Diem "in developing and maintaining a strong, viable state, capable of resisting attempted subversion or aggression through military means." In return for United States aid, Diem was to institute needed reforms. When the French left, Diem ousted the emperor and had himself installed as president. By 1957, when the North Vietnamese guerrilla forces, the Vietcong, began attacking South Vietnam, the United States was stuck with Diem. Later, as a past-president, Eisenhower advised both Presidents Kennedy and Johnson to declare all out war in Vietnam and seek victory, not negotiations, threatening nuclear war if necessary.

DOMESTIC POLICY

Although Eisenhower saw McCarthy as a problem, it was one that he did not address until McCarthy began attacking Eisenhower's own appointees rather than Truman's. The battle ground was the United States Army. McCarthy was investigating it for the promotion of supposed Communists. Ike remained behind the scenes having his press secretary leak negative information on McCarthy and sending Richard Nixon to challenge McCarthy for television coverage. The Army-McCarthy televised hearing served only to humiliate McCarthy. Eisenhower hastened the destruction by encouraging Republican senators to push for a formal censure vote against McCarthy that spelled the end of his career.

Economic Policy

Eisenhower's economic policies were focused on limiting the federal government's role in the economy, lessening governmental regulation, fighting inflation, and balancing the budget. To achieve these, Ike fought for lower taxes for industry and capital and turned over the tideland oil reserves to the states. While he tried to hold down the increase in individual social security benefits, he also expanded the number of workers covered so that, at the end of his administrations, five-sixths of the paid work force were under Social Security.

Eisenhower promoted new and stronger forms of government-business cooperation, which harkened back to the approach of Herbert Hoover in the 1920s. Businessmen were also the most frequent invitees to the stag dinners that Ike held. Antitrust prosecutions declined and were replaced by more cooperative arrangements, such as pre-filing conferences, consent decrees, and pre-merger clearances. Even these did not completely please his business colleagues. In addressing the national housing shortage, Ike set up a national advisory committee that was composed of realtors, builders, bankers, and pro-administration politicians hostile to the competition of the federal public housing. The result was the Housing Act of 1954, which did little for the poorest segments of the population. New federal policies did clear slums, but they provided no alternative housing for the poor who were now permanently displaced from their former urban homes. In his second administration Ike pushed for the passage of the Landrum-Griffin Act of 1959, which had anti-union provisions that pleased his corporate backers. A small but important favor to some of his backers was the repeal of the penny tax for each label placed on the top of a whiskey bottle. This saved Seagrams and other distillers millions of dollars.

Health Issues

In his first term Ike had two serious health problems. In September 1955 he suffered a heart attack while on vacation in Colorado. Unlike the ailments of his predecessors, Ike's heart attack was revealed to the American public. By Christmas Ike was fully recovered and back in Washington. In early June 1956 Ike had an attack of ileitis, a severe inflammation of the lower intestine, which was described in detail.

Televisions became popular in American homes by the late 1940s. It became the center of family life in prosperous households.

These health problems did nothing to shake the faith of the American people in Ike's ability to serve as president.

Television

One of the technological advances of great importance was the growth of television. Its importance in the post-war year cannot be over emphasized. TV changed how Americans received their news, helped to homogenize the nation, and affected the cost of presidential campaigns.

The number of households with television grew from several thousand in 1946 to over fifteen million in 1952. By 1955 more than two-thirds of all American homes had television. Advertising dollars were tremendously increased in the 1950s rising from a mere $170 million in 1950 to passing $1 billion by 1955. While the first television shows included the documentary series, Edward R. Murrow's "See It Now," it soon degenerated into a bland menu of situation comedies that pictured women as zany madcaps or saccharine sweet housewives. Fathers did not do much better. They were often pictured as stumbling incompetents. Much of the media was saturated with violence, either in the Old West or in police dramas and even children's shows.

In no case did television deal with the Other America of the poor, the homeless, and the dispossessed. Blacks, Native Americans, and Hispanic-Americans were invisible on TV. The media did, however, depict teenagers but in the worst possible light as zip gun toting hoodlums with hair slicked back into ducktails. And TV gave American adults the first look at rock and roll. White performers such as Buddy Holly, Bill Haley, and others had adapted the rhythm-and-blues of the black community into the new rock and roll. The first major hit was Haley's "Rock Around the Clock." No performer, however, had the magic of Elvis Presley, an ex-truck driver from Tupelo,

Mississippi. Between January 1956 and his induction into the armed forces in 1958, Presley recorded fourteen consecutive million-selling records. His popularity was so great that he was asked to appear on the "Ed Sullivan Show," which was the mecca for entertainers. However, to maintain respectability, his gyrating pelvis, which was his trade mark, could not be shown. Millions of American teenagers tuned in only to be disappointed to see Elvis from the waist up.

Television did, however, show Americans how black Americans were being treated when they peacefully protested for their civil rights whether it was attending school or boycotting buses. For the first time many white Americans outside of the South saw how blacks were treated.

CIVIL RIGHTS

Ike was not committed to civil rights although he did believe in law enforcement. He confessed to aides that, while he believed in legal and economic equality of opportunity, he opposed social mingling. After the Little Rock crisis Eisenhower backed completely away from the civil rights struggle in the South. He thought the *Brown* decision was a mistake and would require thirty to forty years to implement in the more moderate Upper South and border states. He was quite disgusted with the decisions of the Supreme Court under Chief Justice Earl Warren and referred to Warren's appointment as "the biggest damn fool mistake I ever made." Under Chief Justice Earl Warren the Supreme Court entered an activist phase where the Court began to make decisions with social implications. Such decisions were against Ike's idea of a limited government.

Brown Decision

Pauli Murray had an unpublicized effect on the *Brown* decision. Murray, who found sexual discrimination at Howard Law School and labeled it "Jane Crow," began work at Howard on a paper later completed at Berkeley, which would be important in the *Brown v. Board of Education of Topeka* decision of 1954. In 1946 Murray urged NAACP lawyers to work to overturn *Plessy v. Ferguson* (separate but equal) on the basis that segregation was a violation of the Fourteenth Amendment's equal protection clause. She argued that separate but equal put blacks into both a social and legal position that was inferior and that did violence to the personality of the individual who was affected. To support her position, she used social science data. This was the tactic that Thurgood Marshall employed in developing the strategy in the *Brown* case. By using black and white baby dolls, Dr. Kenneth Clark and his wife Mamie Phipps Clark were able to show that black children would always choose the white baby dolls because segregation had made them feel inferior. The *Brown* decision declared in words similar to Murray's that to separate Negro children from others of their age and qualifications created "a feeling of inferiority as to their status in the community that affect their hearts and minds in a way unlikely to ever be undone" and thus violated the equal-protection clause of the Fourteenth Amendment. Separate but equal was inherently unequal. A year later the Court ordered the states to desegregate with "all deliberate speed."

Emmett Till Case

In 1955 white men were still killing blacks in Mississippi with impunity, but now a case came to the attention of the whole nation. Emmett Till was a fourteen-year old Chicago boy visiting his grandfather, Mose Wright, outside Money, Mississippi. On a dare, he entered Byrant's Grocery and Meat Market and told Carolyn Bryant, "Bye Baby" after he had purchased some candy.

Three days later, Roy Bryant, a truck driver, and his brother-in-law, J.W. Milam, came to Wright's cabin and took Till away. When his body was found in the Mississippi River, it had been weighted down with a cotton-gin fan. He had a bullet in his skull, one eye gouged out, and his forehead was crushed on one side. The mutilation was so bad that the body could only be identified from a ring. *Jet* magazine published pictures of Till to ensure that all of black America saw what happened. Further publicity came when the national media covered the trial of Bryant and Milam. Some compared the expected acquittal to the Holocaust in Nazi Germany. The publicity increased again two months after the trial when Bryant and Milam sold their story for $4,000. In the story they admitted the murder and tried to justify it because Till had not begged for mercy or seemed repentant.

Montgomery Bus Boycott

One of the papers that had given a prominent display to the Till case was the *Montgomery Advertiser*. Three months later three women, two black and one white, pushed the civil rights movement forward in Montgomery, Alabama. They were Rosa Parks, Jo Ann Robinson, and Virginia Foster Durr. Parks and Robinson were granddaughters of slaves while Durr was the granddaughter of a slave owner.

Virginia Foster Durr had grown up in Birmingham, Alabama, the outspoken daughter of a racist preacher. She was educated at Wellesley College where she first associated with blacks on the basis of equality. After she married Clifford Durr they moved to Washington, D.C. where they had become active in the National Association for the Advancement of Colored People (NAACP), an involvement that they continued when they moved to Montgomery, Alabama.

Two of the Durrs' friends in Montgomery were Mr. E. D. Nixon, the head of the local NAACP, and Rosa Parks, secretary of the NAACP. Parks was a woman who had the bearing and demeanor of a middle-class woman even though she was from a working class background and earned her living as a seamstress. In 1955 Virginia Durr arranged for Parks to attend the Highlander Folk School in Tennessee on a scholarship. It was one of the few places in the South where blacks and whites mixed freely, and for that reason bigots called it communistic. Parks returned from the school more committed than ever to the civil rights movement.

The third woman, Jo Ann Robinson, was the youngest of twelve children and the first member of her family to graduate from college. After getting an MA in English, she moved to Montgomery where she taught at the black Alabama State College and became active in the Dexter Avenue Baptist Church. Because Robinson owned a car, she did not experience the segregation on busses in Montgomery and elsewhere in the South until she took a bus to Cleveland to visit relatives. Her experience in being forced to the back of the bus helped lay the foundation for the decision to overturn Montgomery's law governing segregation on buses.

The opportunity to do so came December 1, 1955, when Rosa Parks refused to give up her seat in the black section to a white person. She was arrested and jailed. When Nixon could not bail her out, he called upon the Durrs to aid him. After Rosa was out on bail, Parks and the others discussed whether they should have the charge dismissed on a technically. The other alternative was to test the constitutionality of segregation. Parks' husband was very afraid and chanted in the background, "Rosa, the white folks will kill you. Rosa, the white folks will kill you." But Rosa Parks was determined to test Montgomery's Jim Crow laws.

Jo Ann Robinson had also been at work. As soon as she heard of Park's arrest, she called some of her trusted students, and they ran off tens of thousands of flyers, which were distributed by the Women's Political Caucus. The flyers asked Montgomery blacks to stay off the city busses. That Monday no blacks rode the busses, and Parks was tried and convicted but decided to appeal. It was at this point that Martin Luther King, Jr. entered the scene. There was a mass meeting at Holt Church where King gave an impassioned speech that spoke of the power of non-violent resistance. The boycott continued, and King became the leader of the movement that eventually gave birth to the Southern Christian Leadership Conference (SCLC). The foot soldiers, however, were the women who walked for months rather than ride the segregated busses. The boycott led the Supreme Court of the United States to rule in 1956 in favor of a lower court decision striking down the city's segregated seating practices.

In 1999, Parks was honored for her contributions to the civil rights movement with the prestigious Congressional Gold Medal of Honor, the highest civilian award bestowed by the United States government.

Little Rock

The next major civil rights crisis was in Little Rock, Arkansas, where in 1957 nine black teenagers were chosen to integrate Central High School. Governor Orville Faubus called out the Arkansas National Guard to bar them from entering the school. After attempting to reason with Faubus, Eisenhower was forced to send in the 101st Airborne Division and the federalized Arkansas National Guard to protect the nine teenagers. Each student was assigned a soldier to protect him or her, but the soldiers could not blunt the forces of terrorism that were loosed upon these nine teens. There were organized campaigns of terrorism: telephone threats, insults and assaults, groups of attacking mothers, restroom fireball attacks, rogue policemen, acid-throwers, stalkers, economic blackmail, and even a price upon the head of one student, Melba Pattillo Beals. An uncle, who was a deputy sheriff passing for white and a member of the Ku Klux Klan, warned Beals that the KKK planned to skin Beals alive. This was meant literally. Beals' family got her out of town and out of Arkansas to save her life.

Not all whites were opposed to integration. One friend of Beals was a white student, whose true identity is still hidden by the pseudonym Link. Link came from a prominent family and was part of a gang who came to attack Beals. Instead, he saved her by throwing her his car keys which enabled her to escape. He also became her spy. Another was the white soldier assigned to protect her. Finally there was the Quaker family in California who took her in so that she could finish her high school education in safety.

Sit-Ins

The last civil rights action in the Eisenhower years took place in Greensboro, North Carolina and was led by four freshman college students from North Carolina Agricultural and Technical College. All four were members of the NAACP Youth Council and had discussed what they could do about segregation. They decided to go to the local F.W. Woolworth Company and ask to be served at the all white lunch counter. Before approaching the lunch counter, the four had made purchases. When the white waitress refused service, they pointed out that another counter in the same store had served them. The students sat there until the store closed. Unsure of what to do next, they sought assistance from the Congress of Racial Equality (CORE), which sent a representative to organize more sit-ins. The SCLC also lent its support. Soon there were sit-ins all across the country organized and led by both black and white college students. Eventually the students founded their own organization, the Student Nonviolent Coordinating Committee or SNCC.

While African Americans made progress in the 1950s through the *Brown* decision and the Montgomery boycott, other minority groups did not fare as well. Only Asian Americans began to move into the middle class primarily due to the heavy use of the educational benefits guaranteed under the GI Bill. Both Hispanic Americans and Native Americans made little headway in ending discrimination against them. One third of Hispanic Americans lived below the poverty line. The Native Americans were the poorest of any minority group. The Seminole Indian Tribe sent a petition to Eisenhower in which they stressed that they were neither inferior nor superior to white men; they were Indians who had a different outlook from white men and wished to retain that. The plea was unanswered.

ASSESSING THE COLD WAR AND EISENHOWER

American and Soviet misunderstandings of each other were virtually unavoidable. American principles, such as self-determination and democracy, conflicted with the Soviet ideals of spheres of influence. Soviet leaders wanted buffers to protect them from another invasion by Germany. The only other principle that the Communists held to was world revolution. The United States wanted them kept out of the Western Hemisphere so the Monroe Doctrine was now made multinational. All states in the Western Hemisphere eventually agreed that an attack on one was an attack on all, whether the attack was from outside or inside the hemisphere. There was some misinterpretation of

Whites protested the integration of their junior high school in Little Rock, Arkansas. They did not want change and charged that many of the civil rights workers were really communist infiltrators who stirred up the local black communities. Resistance was especially strong in states in the Deep South where a majority of whites still clung to a belief in white supremacy and staunchly favored states' rights over those of the federal government.

Kennan's containment. He later said that he listed five regions of the world: United States, United Kingdom, Rhine Valley with adjacent industrial areas, Union of Soviet Socialist Republics, and Japan, where military strength could be produced in quality and only one of those was Communist. Containment was to see that none of the four others fell into communism.

The cold war was a huge change for the United States. It became a nation committed to a major and permanent National Military Establishment with a National Security Council, CIA, and later National Security Agency for monitoring media and communications for foreign intelligence. The United States had entered into peacetime alliances for the first time. It was a far cry from 1796 when George Washington warned against "those over-grown military establishments which...are inauspicious to liberty" and advised that the United States "steer clear of permanent alliances with any portions of the foreign world."

Eisenhower had wanted his legacy to be one of peace. This was clear from a 1953 speech, "The Chance for Peace," given before the American Society of Newspaper Editors. In it he welcomed the Soviets post-Stalin offer to limit the arms race.

> Every gun that is fired, every warship launched, every rocket fired signifies... a *theft* from those who hunger and are not fed, those who are cold and not clothed. This world in arms is

> not spending money alone. It is spending the sweat of its laborers, the genius of its scientists, the hopes of its children....We pay for a single fighter plane with a half million bushels of wheat. We pay more for a single destroyer with new homes that could have housed more than eight thousand people. This is not a way of life at all, in any true sense. Under the cloud of threatening war,...it is humanity hanging from a cross of iron.

His farewell address carried out this theme when Eisenhower warned about the dangers of the military-industrial complex. "This conjunction of an immense military establishment and a large arms industry is new in the American experience....In the councils of government, we must guard against the acquisition of unwarranted influence, whether sought or unsought, by the military-industrial complex. The potential for the disastrous rise of misplaced power exists and will persist." With the new importance of technology, Ike warned of the dangers of a "government contract becom[ing] virtually a substitute for intellectual curiosity" in directing university research. The new circumstance created the dual danger "of domination of the nation's scholars by Federal employment" and the shaping of policy by a scientific/technological elite.

Rated by historians as a high average president, his two greatest legacies are the building of the inter-state highway system, the largest pubic works project in American history, and his work for peace. Although not a boaster, Eisenhower once summed up his presidency: "The United States never lost a soldier or a foot of ground in my administration. We kept the peace. People asked how it happened—by God, it didn't just happen, I'll tell you that."

ELECTION OF 1960

The Democrats had met in Los Angeles and had nominated Senator John F. Kennedy from Massachusetts who in a surprise move chose Senator Lyndon Johnson from Texas as his running mate. The first surprise was that Kennedy wanted him and the second was that Johnson accepted, trading in his power as Majority Leader in the Senate for the vice-presidency. In recent years Kennedy's long time secretary, Evelyn Lincoln, has revealed that she was present when Kennedy discussed the issue with his brother, Robert. Johnson wanted the nomination and had some of J. Edgar Hoover's secret FBI files on Kennedy's extensive womanizing. According to Lincoln, Johnson used this as leverage to secure the vice-presidential nomination despite the opposition of both Kennedy brothers.

The Republicans nominated Nixon who had no serious opponents. For his vice-president Nixon chose Henry Cabot Lodge, Jr., the man Kennedy had defeated in his first senatorial campaign. A problem arose between Nixon and Eisenhower because Nixon was stressing his eight years of experience as vice-president and wished to show himself as having a leading role in the decision making process of the administration. This, however, was precisely the area in which Ike was the most sensitive because of Democratic charges that he reigned rather than ruled. Ike also saw the election as a referendum on his eight years as president, while Nixon saw it as Nixon vs. Kennedy. While Nixon wanted Ike to campaign for Nixon as indispensable and a leader, Ike campaigned in defense of his own actions. Another problem arose when Nixon separated himself from the administration on the issue of defense spending. Ike could not help but interpret that as a rejection of all that he had stood for.

Neither candidate seemed an embodiment of the national purpose. Nixon had served as vice president under Eisenhower for eight years and was famous for a kitchen debate with Nikita Khrushchev. Here Khrushchev said "we will bury you" and Nixon replied that the U. S. makes more color TVs. Nixon had also developed a reputation for duplicity and was popularly known as "Tricky Dick," who concealed his true self under a series of masks. Kennedy seemed equally calculating. His record in the Senate was undistinguished although he was an author of a Pulitzer Prize winning book, *Profiles in Courage*, which caused some pundits to say that his career showed more profile than courage.

Three events helped to shape the election: religion, the debates, and civil rights. As the first

Catholic to run since Al Smith lost to Herbert Hoover in 1928, Kennedy sought immediately to dispel the religious issue by giving a speech before the Houston Ministerial Association in which he said that "the separation between church and state is absolute." This helped to neutralize the religious issue.

Nixon made a key mistake when he agreed to a series of TV debates with Kennedy, the lesser known of the two candidates. Nixon's strong suit had been his experience. The first debate turned out to be the most important. Nixon had just come out of the hospital where he had been treated for an infected knee. He looked wan while Kennedy was tanned and seemed the epitome of vigor. The results of the first debate showed that Kennedy could hold his own. His poise made him seem the equal if not the superior of Nixon to the TV audience but not the people who had listened to the debate on radio. He was a candidate made for the television media; it brought out his charisma. In the words of one bemused southern senator, Kennedy combined the "best qualities of Elvis Presley and Franklin D. Roosevelt!"

During the campaign Martin Luther King, Jr. was sent to jail during a sit-in in Atlanta. Both Nixon and Kennedy were working behind the scenes to help King, but it was only Kennedy who called Mrs. King to express his sympathy. His brother, Robert, also called a judge in Atlanta and the mayor to see if they could expedite King's release. The day after John Kennedy's phone call, King was released on bail. His father, Martin Luther King, Sr., said, "It's time for all of us to take off our Nixon button." According to the Gallup poll, Kennedy received 68 percent of the black vote, more than a 7 percent increase over what Stevenson had gotten.

Ike was no help to Nixon either. In answer to a press conference question as to what idea of Nixon's Ike had adopted, Ike responded that if given a week, he might think of one. Although he called Nixon to apologize and express his regrets, it was too late. The damage had been done. Even though Ike campaigned for Nixon in October, his focus was still on his own administration rather than what Nixon might do in leading the U.S. in the 1960s. November 8, 1960, one of the closest elections in American history was decided by less than 120,000 popular votes: John Kennedy would be the 35th President of the United States.

CONCLUSION

Post World War II Americans felt good about their many accomplishments. In foreign affairs they had held the line against the Communist menace in Europe and Asia, rebuilt Europe and sustained military dominance. Domestically the middle class had grown as a result of the G.I. Bill and the economy was good. Beneath the accomplishments, however, were signs of upheaval. There was now a communist nation in the Western Hemisphere: Cuba; twenty percent of Americans were not benefiting from the good economy; minorities and women had begun demanding their rights; teenagers were listening to Elvis. Nevertheless, the average American little suspected that an era was ending and that what would follow would change the nation and their lives forever.

Chronology

1945 Franklin Roosevelt dies; Harry Truman becomes president
United Nations established
Indochina returned to French control

1946 Iron Curtain speech—Winston Churchill
Coal miners' strike
1,000,000 GIs to college
GOP wins Congress
Spock's *Baby and Child Care Book* published
Vietnam declares its independence
Baby Boom begins

1947 Truman doctrine
Taft-Hartley Act
Marshall Plan
Levittown development started
Containment policy developed by George Kennan
Central Intelligence Agency (CIA) established
Marynia Farnham and Ferdinand Lundburg, *The Modern Woman: The Lost Sex*

1948 Israel founded
Berlin blockade and Airlift
Truman orders end to segregation in the armed forces and sends the first civil rights message to Congress
Truman-Dewey election with Truman victor in greatest upset in American history

1949 NATO established
Communist victory in China
Soviets detonate atomic bomb

1950 Truman authorized hydrogen bomb
Joseph McCarthy announces that there are Communists in the government
Korean War begins
China enters Korean War and U. S. begins the longest retreat in U. S. military history

1951 MacArthur fired for insubordination
Rosenbergs convicted of espionage
Armistice talks begin
Twenty-second Amendment—limits on presidential term of office

1952 First hydrogen bomb exploded
Eisenhower elected
White House renovation completed

1953 Korean Truce signed
CIA supported coup in Iran
Earl Warren appointed Chief Justice

1954 Army-McCarthy hearings
Brown v. Board of Education of Topeka
CIA intervention in Guatemala
"Under God" inserted in Pledge of Allegiance
U.S.S.R. explodes hydrogen bomb
South East Asian Treaty Organization (SEATO) established

1955 Emmett Till murder
Montgomery Bus Boycott

1956 Interstate Highway Act
Suez Crisis
Eisenhower re-elected
Hungarian Revolution
U-2 spy plane built
Eisenhower agrees to support Diem in Vietnam

1957 Eisenhower Doctrine
Civil Rights Act (first since Reconstruction)
Little Rock desegregation of schools crisis
Sputnik launched

1958	Halt of atomic tests by U. S. and U.S.S.R. National Aeronautical and Space Administration (NASA) founded
1959	Castro comes to power in Cuba Landrum-Griffin Act passed
1960	U-2 incident Second Civil Rights Act Sit-ins begin Election of John Fitzgerald Kennedy
1961	Eisenhower's farewell address—military industrial complex

SUGGESTED READINGS

Stephen E. Ambrose, *Eisenhower: Soldier and President* (1990).

Melba Pattillo Beals, *Warriors Don't Cry: A Searing Memoir of the Battle to Integrate Little Rock's Central High School* (1994).

Christopher Finch, *Highways to Heaven: The Auto Biography of America* (1992).

Alonzo Hamby, *Man of the People: A Life of Harry Truman* (1995).

George F. Kennan, *American Diplomacy, 1900-1950* (1951).

_____, *Memoirs 1925-1950* (1967).

David McCullough, *Truman* (1992).

John Ranleagh, *The Agency: The Rise and Decline of the CIA from Wild Bill Donovan to William Casey* (1986).

Richard Rhodes, *Dark Sun: The Making of the Hydrogen Bomb* (1995).

Lisle A. Rose, *The Cold War Comes to Main Street: America in 1950* (1998).

Stanley Sandler, *The Korean War: No Victors, No Vanquished* (2000).

Sam Tannehaus, *Whittaker Chambers, A Biography* (1997).

Warren A. Trest, *Air Commando One: Heinie Aderholt and America's Secret Air Wars* (2000).

Stanley Weintraub, *MacArthur's War: Korea and the Undoing of an American Hero* (2000).

David Wise and Thomas B. Ross, *The Invisible Government* (1962).

Chapter Twenty-two

HOPE TO DESPAIR: Kennedy-Johnson Years

Inauguration day in 1961 was crisp and cold with snow piled everywhere in Washington. Matching the untypical weather was the address that John F. Kennedy gave that day. It was at once a call to patriotism and selfless dedication to the good of the nation. As Kennedy called the nation to ask "what you can do for your country," he set the youth of all races afire with the notion that they could change the nation and even the world. The drama of this beginning was matched three years later with the drama of its end. The shock of the assassination was such that over thirty years later, 300,000 Americans wrote to advice columnist, "Dear Abby," to answer the question, "Where were you when President Kennedy was shot?"

"I was in the Peace Corps and had been teaching English in a small town in Thailand for just two months. The shy young Thai student who lived with me came and told me in Thai that President Kennedy had died. I couldn't imagine why he would die suddenly, and said, 'Oh, you must mean that his father has died.' No, no, she said, and kept explaining in Thai what had happened. I didn't know the Thai word for 'assassinate' so I couldn't understand her. Finally she got her English lesson book and pointed to a drawing of a fellow shooting a gun, next to the sentence, 'He fired a shot.' Then I knew."

M.J.B. Van Nuys, CA.

"I still feel the loss as if a member of my family had been killed. I was twenty years old that year and just about idolized John Kennedy. I don't think I will ever forget."

M.B. Gadsden, AL.

"My husband and I were working in the yard as it was a beautiful November day. I could hear the telephone ringing and ringing. I finally went in to answer it, and it was Mrs. L., a woman who liked to be first with any news. She told me that John Kennedy had been killed. I yelled for my husband to come in as I turned on the TV. We spent the next four days in front of the TV crying and wondering what would happen next."

MGK, Ruffs Dale, PA.

THE KENNEDY ADMINISTRATION

The thousand days of the Kennedy administration that began the 60s with the "High Hopes" of Kennedy's campaign song turned to a decade of hopelessness, distrust of the federal government, and despair over the war in Vietnam. Not even the passage of civil rights legislation in the fallen president's honor could assuage these feelings that grew as the decade passed into history.

The two men whose presidencies comprised these years were as different in background, personality, and goals as any two presidents could be. John Fitzgerald Kennedy came from a privileged Boston background. The Roman Catholic Kennedy was also a Harvard graduate, a hero in World War II, and a U. S. Senator. In contrast, Lyndon Baines Johnson was a Texan from a family that had lost the money it once had. He had worked his way through a state college and trained to be a schoolteacher. Johnson had served as Majority Leader in the U. S. Senate for nearly a decade where he had displayed the greatest gift for compromise since Henry Clay. It was a shock to political observers and his friends when he accepted the Democratic nomination for vice president. Where Kennedy was seen as cool and intellectual, Johnson was viewed as earthy and volatile with an in-your-face style of confrontation. Kennedy's goals were limited while Johnson sought to outdo his hero, Franklin D. Roosevelt. Kennedy, one journalist wrote, was the first of all the presidents to be a Prince Charming. Johnson was described as Machiavelli in a Stetson. While Kennedy described his administration as the New Frontier and put an emphasis on sending a man to the moon and returning him safely to earth, Johnson named his programs the Great Society, which

President Kennedy, Director F.B.I. Hoover, and Attorney General Kennedy, White House, Oval Office. Feb 23, 1961. Photo credit: Abbie Rowe, National Park Service/JFK Library

would eliminate poverty. Kennedy had an intellectual interest in the problem of poverty, while Johnson's political career displayed a long-standing concern for humble people and the cause of civil rights. As one of his biographers has described Johnson, he was a man of both light and dark impulses. The Great Society programs showed his light side while the involvement in Vietnam showed his dark.

Domestic Affairs

When Kennedy was choosing his cabinet, he put the accent on youth and Eastern Establishment. His most controversial appointment was his younger brother, Robert, for attorney general, who many people believed did not have the qualifications for the position. Robert immediately began to pursue the Mafia and those members of American unions who were involved with the Mafia. Years later, Kennedy's cabinet and advisers were described as "the best and the brightest."

Kennedy's appointment of Adlai Stevenson to the post of U. S. Ambassador to the United Nations gave J. Edgar Hoover, head of the FBI, one more chance to denigrate Stevenson and mischaracterize his record. Although Republicans and Democrats alike lauded him, the FBI chose to conclude its report by calling him "a controversial figure."

Although the Congress was overwhelmingly Democratic, it was firmly in the grip of the Southern conservatives who blocked Kennedy's efforts to increase federal aid to education, provide health insur-

The United States competed with the Soviet Union in the space race.

ance for the aged, and create a Department of Urban Affairs, as well as initiatives for unemployed youth, migrant workers, and mass transit. It also blocked a tax cut.

There were some successes with Congress: defense appropriations increased even more than requested; a Developmental Loan Fund to help Latin America called the Alliance for Progress; a new housing act; raising of the minimum wage from $1 to $1.25 an hour; an increase in Social Security benefits; and the Peace Corps. The biggest success was the Trade Expansion Act, which led to the Kennedy Round of Negotiations and a 35 percent reduction in tariffs between the United States and the European Common Market.

Space Program

When Kennedy took office, the United States was still sensitive to its failures in the Space Program and the success of the Soviets, first into space with the launching of Sputnik in 1957. To counteract this, Kennedy sought to make the United States first on the moon. By 1962, criticisms of the goal began to surface about the lack of military value of the Apollo program. Ike wrote an article for the *Saturday Evening Post* in August 1962 in which he endorsed space research but not a crash program to the moon. If prestige was sought, why not through industrial and agricultural productivity. ". . . [W]hy let the Communists dictate the terms of all contests?" he asked. Despite the criticism, the program continued until its successful conclusion under the presidency of Richard Nixon. One positive impact of the space program was that it helped to stimulate the economy. At the time, the economy sustained a growth rate of 6 percent while inflation was under 1.3 percent. This was a remarkable accomplishment.

THE GREAT SOCIETY

After the Kennedy assassination, Johnson used his legislative skills to push a torrent of legislation through Congress. Johnson was aware that "every day I'm in office, I'm going to lose votes. I'm going to alienate somebody." Using his honeymoon period, Johnson pushed through the Great Society legislation, working the Congress at a pace unseen since the First 100 Days of the New Deal. Virtually the entire agenda of liberalism was enacted from poverty programs to Medicare and Medicaid. The interest in poverty was a combination of Johnson's own interest and a legacy of the Kennedy administration.

Michael Harrington in his book, *The Other America*, detailed the problem: "40-50 million people were mired in a culture of poverty hidden from sight and passed on from one generation to another." Television made the problem vivid to the public by accentuating the relative deprivation of the poor. The poor saw how different they were from middle-class Americans, and this revelation left many fatalistic about their condition. Harrington described the poor as hopeless and passive, yet prone to bursts of violence; lonely and isolated, yet often rigid and hostile. Kennedy read the book and asked his advisers to investigate the problem and suggest a plan of action. When Johnson became president, he was determined to act in a big and bold way. In January of 1964 the Council of Economic Advisors reported that 9.3 million American families, about 20 percent of the population, were below the poverty line of $3,000 a year for a family of four.

Passed partly as a memorial to the slain Kennedy, the anti-poverty programs included the Economic Opportunity Bill, Job Corps, Head Start, work-study, and Volunteers in Service to America (VISTA). The Job Corps trained young people in marketable skills. Head Start was a program for pre-schoolers from poor families. Work study was a program for poor people who were either in high school or college. VISTA was a domestic version of the Peace Corps, encouraging community action. These programs were the basis of the Great Society. The revenues generated by the 1964 tax reduction of over $10 billion would pay for these programs. This tax cut generated one of the longest sustained economic booms in American history. In theory it was liberalism triumphant but Johnson, unlike his hero, Franklin Roosevelt, had no Harry Hopkins to monitor activities, and many programs were plagued with administrative snafus.

One example is the Economic Opportunity Act, which sought to train and place the hard-core poor in jobs. This was a new clientele for the State Employ-

Watching the lift-off of the first American in space. (L-R) Vice President Johnson, Arthur Schlesinger, Adm. Arleigh Burke, Mrs. Kennedy. White House, Office of the President's Secretary. May 5, 1961. Photo credit: Cecil Stoughton, White House/ JFK Library

ment Services. When new incentives were given, the State Employment Services often grabbed anyone off the street, even criminals or drug addicts, so that they could meet their quotas. There were cases where criminals and addicts were given advances once they entered the training programs, which they then used to support their habits. Meanwhile, the Civil Service employees could report another successful placement. Such activities almost guaranteed that the programs would not last.

Two priorities of the Great Society were health insurance and aid to education. The American Medical Association had long been opposed to health insurance, but now that Johnson had the votes, they got on the bandwagon. Johnson signed the final bill, which was broad and included both Medicare, a federal program for those over 65, and Medicaid, a state-federal program for the poor.

Johnson's proposed $1.5 billion in federal aid to elementary and secondary education was directed at poverty-impacted school districts regardless of whether they were public or parochial. With his first-grade teacher looking on, Johnson signed it in the dilapidated one-room schoolhouse he had attended.

Because many of the pockets of poverty were found in the southern Appalachian Mountains, the Appalachian Regional Development Act was passed to provide $1.1 billion for programs in remote mountain coves. The Housing and Urban Development's low cost 240,000 units and $2.9 billion for urban renewal were to remedy urban poverty. There were also funds for rent supplement for low-income families added in 1966.

The biggest domestic concern of both administrations, however, was the Civil Rights movement, which could not be controlled from Washington.

CIVIL RIGHTS

Under the first Reconstruction in the 1860s, it was the Radical Republicans in Congress who had ensured the passage of the three great civil rights amendments: Thirteenth, Fourteenth, and Fifteenth. The Second Reconstruction was quite different. The presidents and the Congresses were in the position of reacting to rather than leading the Second Reconstruction.

This Second Reconstruction was the work of ordinary Americans who sought to change the conditions under which all minorities in America were forced to live. Obtaining rights guaranteed in the Constitution was difficult if you were black, Chicano, Indian, or female. The new movement began with Rosa Parks in 1955 and built up with the sit-ins in Greensboro, North Carolina, in February of 1960.

While black leaders had some hopes that the Kennedy administration would be willing to move on civil rights legislation, activists did not wait. In May of 1961 freedom riders from the Congress of Racial Equality (CORE) began to test a 1946 U. S. Court decision that prohibited discrimination against interstate travelers. While national groups, such as CORE, organized parts of the movement, much progress was made due to acts of individual Americans demanding freedom.

One of these was black veteran James Meredith who asserted his right to attend the University of Mississippi in 1962. Governor Ross Barnett refused to allow Meredith to enroll. Kennedy had to send federal marshals to enforce the law. Angry white mobs attacked the federal marshals, and two people were killed in the melee. Kennedy then had to send in federal troops to restore order. Although the president was willing to send federal forces to maintain order, he was not yet ready to call for additional federal legislation to protect the rights of black Americans.

By 1963 Martin Luther King, Jr. had decided to force Kennedy to act and called for federal legislation by launching non-violent demonstrations in Birmingham, Alabama. To combat the peaceful demonstrations, the Police Chief Eugene "Bull" Connor used attack dogs, tear gas, and electric cattle prods that millions saw on TV. In June Governor George Wallace stood in the doorway of the University of Alabama to prevent two blacks from enrolling. The National Guard was called, and Wallace was forced to obey a Court desegregation order. That evening Kennedy spoke to the nation: "If an American, because his skin is black, cannot enjoy the full and free life which all of us want, then who among us would be content to have the color of his skin changed and

The work of the Congress of Racial Equality (CORE) drew on the talents of whites as well as blacks. Members participated in voter registration drives and the Freedom Rides on interstate buses. The sign at the left refers to the 1964 murders of three civil rights workers, including two whites, Andrew Goodman and Michael Schwerner.

stand in his place? Who among us would be content with the counsels of patience and delay?" That night Medgar Evers, head of the Mississippi branch of the National Association for the Advancement of Colored People (NAACP), was murdered. After four hung juries, his accused murderer, Byron De La Beckwith, was finally convicted of the crime in 1995.

The culmination of the 1963 drive was the August March on Washington by over 200,000 peaceful marchers singing "We Shall Overcome." In the afternoon Martin Luther King, Jr. gave his "I Have a Dream Speech" from the Lincoln Memorial. In the cadence of the Baptist minister that he was, King chanted over and over again, "I have a dream," and then listed his vision for the future of a land where "all of God's children, black men and white men, Jews and Gentiles, Protestants and Catholics, will be able to join hands and sing in the words of that old Negro spiritual 'Free at last! Free at last! Thank God almighty, we are free at last!'" One result of the march was that Kennedy endorsed a pending omnibus civil rights bill.

After Kennedy's death, Johnson called for the passage of the Civil Rights Act as a memorial to Kennedy. July 2, 1964, Johnson signed the most far-reaching civil rights measure ever enacted by Congress. It outlawed discrimination in hotels, restaurants, and other public accommodations. It required that literacy tests for voting be administered in writing and defined anyone who finished the 6th grade as literate. The attorney general could bring suits for school desegregation. An Economic Opportunity Commission was established that administered a ban on job discrimination by race, religion, national origin, or sex. That same year the Twenty-fourth Amendment was ratified outlawing the use of the poll tax to deny people the right to vote in federal elections. A 1966 Court decision applied the ruling to state elections.

Birmingham, Alabama firefighters used high intensity fire hoses to knock down civil rights demonstrators. The hoses were powerful enough to tear bark off trees. These pictures aroused sympathy for the civil rights movement.

College students became active in the movement in 1964 in the Mississippi Freedom Summer Project where one thousand students helped blacks to register to vote in Mississippi and to become members of the Mississippi Freedom Democratic Party (MFDP). For many African Americans it was the first time they realized that they could vote. This work was dangerous both for the students and for those registering to vote. One student recorded that July 18: "...Four of us went to distribute flyers announcing the meeting. I talked to a woman who had been down to register a week before. She was afraid. Her husband had lost his job. Even before we got there a couple of her sons had been man-handled by the police." Fanny Lou Hamer was one of the women who lost her job and saw her husband also lose his because they had the temerity to register to vote. Undeterred, Hamer joined the MFDP and sought representation at the 1964 Democratic Convention. Although she was not seated at the 1964 convention, she was the chair of the Mississippi delegation in 1968.

Mississippi in 1964 was not much different from the Mississippi of the 1950s when Emmett Till was killed and dumped into the Mississippi River. A college student recorded in Tchula, July 16: "Yesterday while the Mississippi River was being dragged looking for three missing civil rights workers, two bodies of Negroes were found—one cut in half and another without a head. Mississippi is the only state where you can drag a river any time and find bodies you were not expecting. Things are really much better for rabbits—there's a closed season on rabbits." Despite the threats of violence and actual violence, the civil rights workers remained undeterred in their quest for justice.

In 1965, King and the Southern Christian Leadership Conference (SCLC) announced a drive to register 3 million blacks in the South. The center of the activity was in Alabama. Here the state police, rather than protecting the peaceful marchers, violently sought to disperse them. They even used high intensity fire hoses to knock down the demonstrators. Johnson had to send in the National Guard and army military police to protect them. Several days after the march concluded in Montgomery, Johnson went before Congress to ask for a Voting Rights Act that suspended state literacy tests and authorized federal examiners to register voters. Where states or coun-

An African American being attacked by a police dog during the protest demonstrations in Birmingham in 1963

ties had fewer than half the adults voting, literacy tests were suspended and the attorney general was authorized to dispatch federal examiners to register voters. He climaxed his speech with "And we shall overcome." The Voting Rights Act became law.

Black Power

In 1964 only 34 percent of Americans thought that blacks were trying to move too fast but by 1966 the percentage was 85. One of the things that caused this change was the Watts Riot in Los Angeles in August 1965, which came at the end of the week in which Johnson had signed the Voting Rights Act. The Watts riot was the first of more than one hundred riots that took place over the next three summers. These riots broke the coalition of organized labor, intellectuals, minorities, and the poor that had united in the Democratic Party. Johnson's appointment of Thurgood Marshall, a former NAACP attorney who had argued the *Brown* case, as the first black justice on the U. S. Supreme Court did nothing to ease the situation. By 1967 Americans saw tanks in Detroit rolling through the streets and soldiers from the 101st Airborne using machine guns to deal with snipers. Blacks now used violence and destruction on themselves and the areas in which they lived.

Black Power became the new rallying cry. King was now seen as an "Uncle Tom," someone who worked too closely with the white power structure to be trusted. Stokeley Carmichael became head of the Student Non-Violent Coordinating Committee (SNCC) in 1966 and ousted whites from the organization. H. Rap Brown, who succeeded Carmichael, urged blacks to "Get you some guns" and "Kill some honkies."

The most articulate spokesman was Malcolm X. Malcolm was born in Omaha, Nebraska as Malcolm Little. His father was a Baptist minister who was a follower of Marcus Garvey, a black nationalist of the 1920s. When Malcolm was six, his father was murdered by the Ku Klux Klan in Lansing, Michigan. When his mother suffered a nervous breakdown, the state welfare department took eight Little children. Malcolm soon was sent to a reform school and began a life of crime that lasted until he was imprisoned for burglary in 1946. While in prison, he became interested in the teachings of Elijah Muhammad, the leader of the Black Muslims, who taught that Christianity was the "religion of white devils." One result was that Malcolm spent the rest of his time in prison educating himself.

Malcolm left prison in 1952, joined a black Muslim temple, and took the name of Malcolm X. In 1964 he made a pilgrimage to the Islamic holy city of Mecca in Saudi Arabia. He then renounced his previous teaching that whites were evil and began to advocate racial solidarity. He adopted an Arabic name and became El-Haji Malik El-Shabazz. When Malcolm broke with Elijah and founded his own organization, Black Muslim assassins gunned him down.

A positive outcome of the Black Power movement was a pride in culture and color. An Afro became the hair style, and the chant was "black is beautiful." This last was doubly important since there was color prejudice within the black community itself. Those

The Watts riot of 1965 was one of more than 100 urban riots in the 1960s.

who were lighter in skin tone were given more prestige than their darker hued brothers and sisters. This was also the time when black studies programs were established with African-American history as their centerpiece.

WOMEN AND THE CIVIL RIGHTS MOVEMENT

Much of the civil rights movement believed that racism's effect was more pervasive on the black male who was emasculated by his lack of economic power and thereby lost "control" of his wife and children. This resulted in black men losing their self-respect. Many civil rights leaders saw strong black women as a detriment to the black community and socially destructive. Civil rights leaders often called black women traitors to the greater cause of civil rights.

At first, black women saw their lives shaped more by racism than sexism and often distrusted the feminist movement, which seemed more for white women. This situation changed as, increasingly, black women pursued higher education and entered the professions. Now, besides racial discrimination, they also faced sexual discrimination.

Malcolm X , a militant black nationalist, urged African Americans to get their freedom "by any means necessary."

"Jane Crow"

During the 1960s there was a rebirth of the feminist movement that had stagnated since the 1920s. As was true in other periods of our history, women who were involved in the Civil Rights movement soon came to realize that there was a link between racism and sexism. Before this awakening, women had responded to the same arguments used after the Civil War that black rights were more important than the rights of women. One battlefield for the new movement was equal rights.

Alice Paul's Equal Rights Amendment from the 1920s had not received political support from groups except conservative Republicans and southern Democrats, who opposed the protective legislation for women that it would outlaw. Across the country married women faced restrictions in their ability to sign contracts, sell property, have access to credit, and to serve on juries. In many states women who became pregnant had to quit their jobs. That all began to change with the election of John Kennedy and his appointment of Esther Peterson as head of the Women's Bureau in the Department of Labor.

Peterson had discovered the labor movement at college in the 1920s and soon became a labor advocate. Through her lobbying work, she met Kennedy when he was a freshman congressman from a blue-collar district in Boston. She supported Kennedy's career and was rewarded with the directorship of the Women's Bureau. From here she played a key role in the women's movement.

Because the Kennedy margin of victory was so narrow, Peterson suggested that he and the Democratic Party needed to expand their base by winning over women. Kennedy appointed her executive vice-chair of his Presidential Commission on the Status of Women (PCSW), which was chaired by former first lady and former ambassador to the U.N., Eleanor Roosevelt.

The PCSW wanted the federal government to serve as a model by leading the assault against dis-

The women's liberation movement of the 1960s

Feminists demonstrated at the Miss America pageant in Atlantic City, New Jersey, in 1968. They protested the conditioning of women to "beauty" standards to get male approval. Bras, girdles, and hair curlers were thrown into a "freedom trash can."

crimination based on sex. Before the commission filed its report, Kennedy ordered an end to separate civil service listings for men and women. The PCSW decided that the answer to the question of protective legislation for women was to extend the same protection to men.

The final report was a mixture of liberation and tradition. It stuck with the idea that it was the responsibility of men to support their wives, and it refused to change social security legislation to allow a widowed man to stay home to care for his children as women did. But it did recommend paid maternity leave, an increase in widow's benefits, and extensive child-care services for all income levels.

Women's median income dropped from 63.9 percent of that earned by men in 1955 to 60 percent in 1960. In 1963, Congress passed the Equal Pay Act, which applied only to businesses actually engaged in interstate commerce rather than the broader definition of "affecting" interstate commerce. It mandated equal pay for equal work rather than the broader equal pay for comparable work. Despite the narrowness of its application, in ten years 171,000 employees won $84 million in back pay under the act.

Rather than supporting the ERA, Peterson agreed with Pauli Murray that women could win equality by pursuing cases under the "equal protection" clause of the Fourteenth Amendment. Murray wanted to demonstrate that "Jane Crow" sexual discrimination was just as abhorrent to the Constitution as the racial discrimination of Jim Crow.

The first Jane Crow case was filed by the American Civil Liberties Union (ACLU) in 1965 in Lowndes County, Alabama. Lowndes was known as "blood Lowndes" because a clique of white men terrorized black men and kept all women, black or white, in their place by killing anyone who challenged the status quo. The ACLU lawyers, including Murray, challenged the jury selection system that barred all black men through discrimination and all women by statute. In 1966 the federal court in Montgomery ruled in *White v. Crook* that the Fourteenth Amendment applied to women as well as blacks.

New Feminists

The middle class became conscious of the women's movement in 1963 when Betty Friedan, a college-educated housewife, published *The Feminine Mystique*. One of her questions was: "What kind of a woman was she if she did not feel this mysterious fulfillment waxing the kitchen floor?" Friedan examined the role of the media in propagating the idea that the only happy woman was the housewife and that women who worked outside the home always came to a bad end. She noted that training women to be appropriate mates for ambitious men seemed to be the real goal of women's education. *The Feminine Mystique* also indicted Freudian psychology because it equated the impulse to achieve with masculine striving, bad mothering, and sexual maladjustment. It was a best seller with all the major women's magazines publishing excerpts. At times the media distorted Friedan's message into an attack on housewives, which was untrue.

Women's Rights in the Johnson Years

Alice Paul saw her chance to push for equal rights when civil rights legislation was being discussed in 1964 as one of the results of the Kennedy assassination. At Paul's urging, the word "sex" was inserted into the civil rights bill that prohibited discrimination in employment.

Many liberals opposed the bill because it would remove protective legislation. Women legislators like Martha Griffiths of Michigan rallied support for it, and it won 168-133 with most of the support coming from Southerners and Republicans. Pauli Murray got the Johnson administration to drop its opposition by pointing out that the omission of "sex" would weaken the civil rights bill by neglecting black women. They also persuaded Johnson to include "sex" as one of the grounds for prohibiting discrimination. He did this in Executive Order 11375, which governed policies for businesses with government contracts. Such contracts affected one-third of the labor force.

The Civil Rights Act of 1964 set up an agency to enforce the provisions of the act, the Equal Employment Opportunity Commission (EEOC). The first head publicly declared that he would not enforce the sex provision. To force the issue, a civil rights group for women was needed, and the informal Washington network prevailed on Friedan to start it. Thus, the National Organization for Women (NOW) was born in October 1966.

NOW called for a fully equal partnership of the sexes as part of the human rights revolution. It demanded a national system of health care and an end to all practices that denied women opportunities even if they were under the guise of protective legislation.

The passage of the Civil Rights Act of 1964 did not mean that the battle was over. An EEOC commissioner told Friedan that he was interviewing "girls" for the position of Assistant General Counsel. Friedan informed him that since the lawyers applying for the job would surely be over twenty-five, calling them girls was like calling a forty-five year old black man a "boy." The days of the "girls" were over, and the days of women were beginning.

As expected, NOW's first target was to force the EEOC to follow the law. NOW supported a sex discrimination suit brought by stewardesses against the airlines' policy of forcing them to retire when they married or reached age thirty or thirty-five. NOW also fought an EEOC ruling that sex-segregated newspaper ads did not constitute discrimination. Television networks were invited to cover a small demonstration that forced EEOC to hold hearings. The result was new rulings favoring the NOW position.

At the 1967 NOW convention, the abortion rights issue was added to its agenda. Some women split from NOW over this and in 1968 formed the Women's Equity Action League (WEAL), which considered abortion too divisive an issue for a woman's group to take a stand on. Instead, WEAL concentrated on educational and economic issues. NOW and WEAL were soon joined by the National Women's Political Caucus (NWPC), which was a bipartisan organization of women who would work on women's issues on the state level.

MEXICAN AMERICANS

Mexican Americans and others of Latin American heritage constituted another group that began to push for more rights. Many Mexican Americans had been brought into the U. S. during World War II in the bracero (hired hand) program and made up about 10 percent of the agricultural workers. As the war ended, both the U. S. and Mexico considered the program successful. During the Korean War, a new law was enacted to bring workers in again. It was in effect from 1951 to 1964. When it was brought up for renewal in 1960, there was a seven-month debate over its extension. Finally, in December 1964, the bracero program was over. This ending had important consequences for the organizing of Mexican-American field workers since it would no longer be easy to import strike breakers.

The first Chicano (Mexican Americans) to receive national recognition was César Chávez who headed the National Farm Workers' Association (NFWA). In May 1965 the NFWA joined in the Delano Grape Strike in the San Joaquin Valley of California.

Chávez grew up as a typical Mexican-American migrant. He attended about thirty different schools before he eventually completed the seventh grade. After service in the U. S. Navy, Chávez became involved in the organizing of farm workers. Two years after the founding of the NFWA, that was more a cooperative than a union, there were 1,000 members in the southern San Joaquin Valley.

Chávez believed the Delano strike had a chance of success because it would now be more difficult for the companies to bring in strikebreaking workers from Mexico. By presenting the strike as a broad movement for social justice, rather than just a wage-and-working-conditions issue, Chávez was able to build broad public support. He also made full use of a wide range of civil rights and religious groups, including the California bishops of the Catholic Church. This was brilliant since it effectively deprived the union's opponents of the chance to charge the union with being communist.

Chávez was also able to get the Democratic governor of California, Edmund "Pat" Brown, and the Democratic senator from New York, Robert Kennedy, to support the grape strike. After a five-year struggle, 50 percent of the table-grape growers had signed agreements with the union. In acknowledgment of his contributions, California in 2001 made César Chávez Day a state holiday.

Latina women were also being liberated. In Los Angeles and New York, they began to raise civil rights issues. One California Chicana informed her friends that times have changed. "We can stand up! We can talk back! It's not like when I was a little kid and my grandmother used to say, 'You have to especially respect the Anglos.'"

NATIVE AMERICANS

As the civil rights movement gained strength, Indian organizations became active participants. Indians wanted their rights not only as American citizens but also to maintain distinct political and cultural communities. They met success in both goals.

Indians were routinely made beneficiaries of civil rights legislation, such as the Fair Housing Act, the Equal Opportunity Act, and the Voting Rights Act, which created special protections for them as persons whose primary language was not English. The status of their tribes as distinct political communities was also recognized in civil rights legislation of the New Frontier and Great Society, which included Indian tribes as governments eligible for participation. The result was a renewal of Indian confidence and pride as they learned that they could assert their rights without worry about termination, the dismantling of tribal government, the redistribution of tribal assets to tribal members, and the end of federal services to individual Indians.

The most interesting piece of legislation was the Indian Civil Rights Act of 1968, which required tribal governments to afford to persons under their jurisdic-

César Chávez organized Mexican-American farm workers to boycott against grape and lettuce growers who practiced discriminatory practices.

tion the civil rights guaranteed in the Constitution. The freedom of religion provision, however, did not prohibit a state religion. This protected the rights of a number of theocratic tribes. It also protected the tribes against states that sought to exercise jurisdiction over the tribal lands.

Once their rights as American citizens were firmly established, they sought to assert their rights as tribal citizens. Treaty rights and the right of tribal self-government would become the new focus. Against all odds, Indians prevailed in federal court in protecting rights that were recognized over a century earlier in various treaties. Although the final resolution of some of the cases took until the 1980s, the Indians did succeed in curtailing state power in the areas of taxation, civil court jurisdiction, and Indian child welfare proceedings.

FOREIGN POLICY

When Kennedy took office after winning the closest presidential election since 1888, he was immediately faced with a foreign policy problem: Cuba.

Though a small island, Cuba consumed more of Kennedy's time than any other area of the world. The first concern was a covert Central Intelligence Agency (CIA) operation conceived under the Eisenhower administration to overthrow Castro. The plan involved the use of the American Mafia. In September of 1960, Robert Maheu, an ex-FBI agent and free lance CIA agent, approached Johnny Roselli, Santos Trafficante, and Sam Giancana with a deal to kill Fidel Castro for $150,000. All three were high-powered men in the Mafia and could see economic benefits to eliminating Castro and regaining control of the drugs, gambling, and prostitution in Cuba that they had previously run under Castro's predecessor. There were a number of unsuccessful high tech assassination attempts. Planning for the invasion of Cuba began at the same time and soon developed into a full-bodied World War II model underground-movement plan with an amphibious invasion.

Before leaving office, Eisenhower severed American-Cuban relations and briefed Kennedy on the CIA plan for 1,500 anti-Castro Cubans to invade their homeland. The Joint Chiefs of Staff assured

Kennedy that the plan was feasible. Diplomatic advisers assured him that the invasion would inspire indigenous uprisings against Castro. Few expressed doubts about the plan before it was executed. Later a book, *Group Think*, was written about the phenomena of individuals fearing to speak against what they perceive to be the group norm. The planning for the Bay of Pigs invasion was the most infamous example of group think in our history.

The scheme was poorly planned and poorly executed. Failures in intelligence, operations, decision-making, and judgment doomed the invasion. The CIA overestimated the effectiveness of the opposition to Castro, while at the same time underestimating the effectiveness of the Cuban military. CIA planners, such as agency head Allen Dulles, were less than candid with Kennedy out of fear that he would cancel the operation. While Kennedy did not cancel the operation, he refused to support it with U. S. air cover once its failure was apparent. When the invasion force landed, Castro subdued it in three days and captured 1,200 men. A *New York Times* columnist said the United States "looked like fools to our friends, rascals to our enemies and incompetents to the rest."

Later that year, Castro began negotiations for the release of the Cuban exile brigade members in exchange for food and medicine. At the same time Castro's chief lieutenant, Ernesto "Che" Guervara, initiated contact with a Kennedy aide, Richard Goodwin, to see if a *modus vivendi* (temporary agreement) could be achieved with talks on trade, compensation for nationalized property, and the question of the Guantanamo Naval Base. The Kennedy administration rejected the overture.

The fiasco at the Bay of Pigs led, in turn, to problems with the Soviet Union and, ultimately, the Cuban Missile Crisis of 1962. Instead of driving the Soviets and the Communists from Cuba, the botched invasion drove the Cubans and the Soviets closer. Fearing another invasion, Castro sought military aid from the Soviets. The U. S. response was CIA sabotage: contaminating goods leaving European ports for Cuba and bribing foreign manufactures to supply faulty equipment and parts. All of these simply pushed Cuba more toward the Soviets. The CIA next renewed its efforts to kill Castro. They tried poisonous cigars, pills, and needles. Nothing worked.

At the Pentagon some people were calling for a first strike nuclear policy regarding Cuba. By September 1962, the CIA reported that the Cuban military buildup with Soviet aid was in response to a belief that the United States would attempt to overthrow Castro by one means or another. The CIA saw the buildup not as a Soviet initiative but as a response to Castro's request for help. The Soviets began to install missiles in Cuba. On October 14, 1962, CIA U-2 spy plane photographs showed the missiles. Kennedy was determined that they had to go. The choices eventually narrowed down to a so-called surgical air strike and a blockade of Cuba. The blockade was renamed "quarantine" since a blockade is an act of war. Monday, October 22 the president announced to members of Congress and then the public the discovery of the missiles and the quarantine.

Nikita Khrushchev, the Soviet Premier, blustered that Kennedy was pushing mankind to the abyss of a nuclear war. There were some tense days as five Soviet ships steamed to Cuba with supplies. At the last minute, they stopped short of the quarantine line, and World War III was avoided. October 28 Khrushchev agreed to remove the missiles and added, "We should like to continue the exchange of views on the prohibition of atomic and thermonuclear weapons, general disarmament, and other problems relating to the relaxation of international tension." The entire world breathed a sigh of relief. What was unknown to the general public in 1962 was how close we were to nuclear war because of actions of U.S. military personnel. The Commander of the Strategic Air Command (SAC) issued an alert on an open radio so that he could impress the Soviets that planes were in the air loaded with nuclear and thermonuclear bombs. During the alert an American airplane strayed into Soviet airspace over Siberia. In another instance a navy commander dropped a depth charge on a Soviet submarine. Unknown to the U.S. Navy was that the Soviet submarines were carrying nuclear-tipped torpedoes. One that patrolled in the area around Pearl Harbor had orders to attack the U.S. base if war broke out.

The positive results of the crisis were: the establishment of a "hot line" between Washington and Moscow to prevent the accidental beginning of war and the negotiation of a treaty to stop nuclear testing in the atmosphere. As Kennedy put it, "A journey of a thousand miles begins with one step."

Other peace initiatives followed. On June 10, 1963, Kennedy gave a speech at American University in which he renounced the *Pax Americana*, a peace enforced by weapons of war. Some historians judge this the most important speech of the post-1945 era. He asked Americans to re-examine their attitudes toward the Soviet Union and its citizens. Kennedy concluded the speech with the announcement that both the British and Soviets had agreed to talks to limit nuclear testing and that the U. S. would unilaterally halt atmospheric testing. Both the British and the Soviets hailed the speech, which was published in total in both Soviet papers *Izvestia* and *Pravda*. Kennedy seemed willing to end the cold war. The sale of surplus American wheat to the Soviets and Kennedy's September speech to the U.N. proposing that the U. S. and U.S.S.R. do the big things together, such as the trip to the moon, were two additional indications of this change. Khrushchev turned down the offer. Nor was the offer well received in the Senate, which kept funding for the space program while putting a rider on the bill forbidding a joint lunar landing without the consent of Congress.

The ending of the Cuban Missile Crisis, however, was not the end of problems related to Cuba. By March of 1963, Kennedy realized that Cuban exiles had developed links with right-wing political groups in the U. S. as well as criminals who were professional gun runners stealing armaments from the U. S. military. Kennedy ordered restrictions on unauthorized exile activities including training camps in the United States. At the same time, Castro tried to seek some accommodation with the U. S. In the fall of 1963 Kennedy authorized a member of the U.N. staff to work up an agenda with the Cubans. There is evidence that Kennedy was also pursuing non-formal contacts through a French journalist who was going to Cuba to interview Castro. During this interview both men received word of the Kennedy assassination. There have been no attempts at a détente with Cuba since then.

Europe

Two months after the Bay of Pigs, Kennedy met Soviet Premier Khrushchev in Vienna where the So-

President Kennedy and his brother, Attorney General Robert F. Kennedy, confer during the Cuban missile crisis. The entire world was frightened over the possibility of a nuclear conflagration that could be so devastating.

viet leader sought to intimidate the young American president. When Kennedy returned home, he called up the Reserve and National Guard units and asked Congress for $3.2 billion more in defense funds.

Shortly after this meeting, Khrushchev built the Berlin Wall thus making the Iron Curtain in East Germany a concrete reality to prevent East Germans from fleeing communism. On his last trip to Europe in 1963, Kennedy gave a speech in front of the Berlin Wall pointing out that the West did not have to build a wall to keep its own people in; only the Communists had to do that. In what became a memorable phrase Kennedy stated that the proudest boast a free man could make was that he was a Berliner. He then repeated it in German to mass cheers, applause, and some confusion since the phrase in German meant that he was a German pastry.

Peace Corps

One of Kennedy's foreign policy initiatives that still remains today was the Peace Corps, whereby young and old Americans went to various second and third world countries to provide assistance to the people. Although many of the members were recent college graduates, some were like Lillian Carter, the mother of future president Jimmy Carter, who, at age 65, went to India to use her nursing skills.

One of the requirements of the Corps was that the volunteers had to learn the language of the country to which they were being sent and to live like the natives of the area. Although the Peace Corps was not overtly political, there was often an ideological battle for the peoples of the third world. When volunteer Tim Scanlon asked a Peruvian Indian chief how Scanlon could be of help to his people, the chief replied, "Will you be willing to come here when it snows and you have to leave your jeep and walk twenty miles in five foot snows? The Communists will."

Vietnam

Vietnam was the foreign policy area that had the most military and domestic repercussions. The whole of Southeast Asia was a simmering caldron of conflict during the 1960s. Laos and neighboring Cambodia had been declared neutral in the Geneva Accord of 1954, but both were involved in their own struggles while at the same time serving as a conduit for troops and supplies going from North Vietnam to South Vietnam.

The focus was on Vietnam, which represented both a political and economic prize to whatever interests dominated it. As the decade opened, the two major forces were the Communists under Ho Chi Minh in North Vietnam and the South Vietnamese under American-backed Premier Ngo Dinh Diem.

A religious conflict added to the usual conflict between competing ideologies. The population of North Vietnam was originally heavily Catholic. However, after the Communists gained power, many Catholics fled to the primarily Buddhist South. Premier Diem was a Catholic with one brother a prominent Catholic Bishop and another the head of the secret police, a position that included CIA involvement and drug running.

Kennedy demanded that Diem begin to resolve some of the economic and social problems of South Vietnam in return for American support. Diem did not deliver on his promised reforms, and Kennedy refused to increase the American military presence, although he sent more and more advisers. Between 1961 and 1963, the advisers increased from 2,000 to 16,000.

By 1963 things were coming to a head over the Diem regime. Buddhist monks began committing suicide by setting their gasoline-soaked bodies afire. American TV news showed films of this immolation. When dissident generals proposed a *coup d'etat*, Henry Cabot Lodge, the American ambassador, assured them that Washington would not stand in the way. The U. S. offered to fly Diem into exile, but he chose to stay and was killed in the *coup*. The new government was not an improvement, as the generals were no more interested in reform than Diem.

In September 1963 Kennedy declared, "In the final analysis it's their war. They're the ones who have to win it or lose it. We can help them as advisors but they have to win it." Documents declassified in December 1997 prove that shortly before Kennedy's death, military leaders were proceeding with plans to withdraw American advisors from Vietnam. An

President Kennedy greets Peace Corps volunteers on the South Lawn of the White House. August 8, 1962. Photo credit: Abbie Rowe, National Park Service/JFK Library

October 4, 1963 memo from Maxwell Taylor, then chairman of the Joint Chiefs of Staff, declared that, "all planning will be directed toward preparing Republic of Vietnam forces for the withdrawal of all United States special assistance units and personnel by the end of the calendar year 1965." It continued that the plan was to withdraw 1000 military personnel by the end of 1963. The Joint Chiefs, unhappy with the plans, were pushing for war against North Vietnam. The first one hundred advisors had returned to the U. S. when Kennedy was assassinated on November 22, 1963. The following day, Johnson, the new president, reversed Kennedy's policy of withdrawal.

After JFK's death, Johnson sank the United States into the most disastrous war in our history. How this happened is partly explained by LBJ's obsession with failure. His personal history permitted him no retreat, and he saw Vietnam as a test. He also believed in the domino theory first stated by Eisenhower: "You have a row of dominos set up, you knock over the first one, and what will happen to the last one is the certainty that it will go over very quickly." If the Communists overran South Vietnam, Ike had reasoned, communism would then take over in other countries of Southeast Asia. Johnson thought the answer in Vietnam was to get in and out quickly. Led by some of the so-called "best and brightest" of the Kennedy administration, Johnson soon committed American combat forces.

The road to making the civil war in Vietnam into an American war began in 1964 with the authorization of the bombing of North Vietnam in

Ho Chi Minh (left) meets China's Chairman Mao during his travels in Asia.

retaliation for the death of nine American advisers. Johnson thought the bombing would boost South Vietnamese morale and get them to enact reforms. For the North it was an attempt to drive them to the bargaining table. Johnson was trying strategies that had worked for him as majority leader in the U. S. Senate: the carrot and stick of compromise. Neither Johnson nor his advisers seemed able to grasp that the Vietnamese were playing by rules that admitted no compromise or bargaining.

Gulf of Tonkin

The decision to send combat troops came out of one of the most unusual encounters of the period. The U. S. had military ships in the Gulf of Tonkin off the coast of North Vietnam. In August 1964 a novice sonar man on the *U.S.S. Maddox* reported to his captain that he had seen torpedo runs and that the ship was under attack. The *Maddox* fired its own torpedoes, although they could not see any ships, and began evasive action. The sonar man continued to report torpedo runs. Navy flyers, including Commander James Stockdale, later an admiral and 1992 vice presidential candidate with Ross Perot, flew over the area searching for North Vietnamese ships. He reported: "Not a ship, not the outline of a ship, not a wake, not a reflection, not the light of a single tracer bullet. Nothing." The first reports were immediately sent on to Washington. Later reports advising that caution be exercised since the whole report may have been in error were ignored. The truth is that there were no ships and no attack.

Nevertheless, Johnson told the American people on national TV that the North Vietnamese had attacked two American destroyers, the *U.S.S. Maddox* and *U.S.S. C. Turner Joy* on August 2 and 4 in the Gulf of Tonkin. Congress passed the Gulf of Tonkin Resolution, which authorized the president "to take all necessary measures to repel any armed attack against the forces of the United States and to prevent further aggression." Only two senators voted against it. Years later, when the full story was known, many senators, who supported the resolution

because they believed the president, said they would have voted against it had they known the full story. In 1995 former Defense Secretary Robert McNamara visited Vietnam and asked General Vo Nguyen Giap of North Vietnam if there had been an attack. He confirmed that there had not.

Years later, Johnson told one of his biographers that if he hadn't gotten Congress to back him on the Gulf of Tonkin Resolution, the "commies" would have seen it as a sign of weakness, and his Republican opponents would have cut his heart out in the 1964 presidential election. The recent release of Johnson tapes reveal that he wondered "how we get the hell out of there."

Under Johnson, the war took on all the aspects of total slaughter. The line between military targets and civilians ceased to exist. When General William Westmoreland was challenged about bombing civilian targets, his response was that "it does deprive the enemy of a population." An American commander justified the shelling of the village of Ben Tre by saying that it "had to be destroyed to be saved."

The emphasis on the numbers game, where the military was constantly inflating casualty figures, was one of the problems. In previous wars, success or failure was determined by the capturing of military objectives. In Vietnam it was measured by body counts. The following conversation between Major General William E. Dupoy, Joint Chiefs of Staff, and Arthur Goldberg, Johnson adviser, illustrates the problem:

Dupoy: "There were 230,000 enemy in the order of battle. We have killed approximately 80,000 of them."

Goldberg: "...how many seriously wounded, would

you say there were for every one killed?...what's the ratio of seriously wounded to killed?

Dupoy: "About ten to one, sir."

Goldberg: "...can we agree three to one as a conservative figure for those rendered ineffective by wounds? Is that all right, General?"

Dupoy: "Yes, sir, that's all right."

Goldberg: "...by my count if you have 240,000 seriously wounded plus 80,000 killed, for a total of 320,000 out of an order of battle of 230,000, General, who the hell are we fighting out there?"

American support for the war eroded faster than the will of the North Vietnamese to tolerate casualties. Opposition began on college campuses in 1965. The rise of a New Left movement was one reason for the opposition. This included the Students for a Democratic Society (SDS) founded at the University of Michigan by Al Haber and Tom Hayden. At a 1962 meeting in a United Auto Workers' Hall in Port Huron, the SDS issued its Port Huron Manifesto, touching on most of the themes of the 1960s except for the Vietnam War that was added later. They stressed opposition to human degradation, as symbolized by racism in the South, and the threat of the cold war.

The University of California at Berkeley was another center for student activity, where the main issue became free speech. In the early 1960s Berkeley residents cared about two issues: peace and race. By 1960 the town of Berkeley was one fifth black, but blacks were almost invisible on campus or in town. In 1964 the Berkeley student chapter of CORE attacked job discrimination in the area. Recruitment for their activities took place at card tables set on city property along the edge of the campus. The students passed out leaflets, solicited funds, and gathered names.

Some of the students had worked in 1964 for civil rights in Mississippi where their eyes had been further opened to injustice. When they returned to campus, they expected to recruit more students to this cause. The president of the University of California system banned the recruitment tables. The students demanded an end to the regulation forbidding political activity on campus. They demanded the rights of free speech guaranteed by the First Amendment.

The regulations shifted many times so that no one really knew what was banned and what was legitimate. When the students moved their recruitment tables into the heart of the campus, the Berkeley administration called the police. The students then staged a sit-down and got police permission to use the roof of the police car as a podium to address the crowd. One speaker called the administrators a "bunch of bastards" who were exercising illegitimate authority.

To emphasize the "fascist" aspects of the university administration, the students planned a sit-in in one of the major halls on campus. They occupied all four floors. The college president became desperate and after getting a false report that a student had broken into an office, Governor Pat Brown ordered that the students be arrested. Seven hundred and seventy-three students were arrested, the largest number of arrests in one day in California history.

As sit-ins took place at other prestigious universities across the nation, they helped to cause a break between parents of the World War II generation and their children. Parents, who had made sacrifices in World War II and who had scrimped and saved so that their children could be educated, could not understand their ingratitude and their rebellious ways. The draft resistance movement further enlarged this break. Fathers who had fought in World War II or the Korean War could not understand why their sons had become draft dodgers.

Draft Resistance

In 1965, individuals began joining together to resist the Vietnam draft. For some it meant a break with their families as they contemplated going to Canada. Others asked their fathers to "save" them from the draft by getting them a safe post in the National Guard. Some were more confrontational and joined with their friends to burn their draft cards while chanting: "Hell no! We won't go." Momentum gathered slowly, and in July 1966 anger at the Vietnam buildup resulted in a New Haven group returning their draft cards to the local board.

While individuals and groups were protesting the war, some governmental officials were having second thoughts, too. In 1966 William Fulbright, chairman of the Senate Foreign Relations Committee, began a congressional investigation. George Kennan, the author of the containment policy, said containment was not the proper policy for Asia. General James Gavin said General Westmoreland's military strategy had no chance of achieving victory. By May 1967 even Secretary of Defense Robert McNamara seemed to be losing his faith in the war when he said, "The picture of the world's greatest superpower killing or injuring 1,000 noncombatants a week, while trying to pound a tiny backward nation into submission on an issue whose merits are hotly disputed, is not a pretty one."

As was true of the Civil War, the Vietnam War was turning into a rich man's war and a poor man's fight. Black Muslims felt the full force of the law when they refused on the ground of religion to fight in any war not declared by Allah. In 1966 Muhammad Ali, who had become heavyweight champion of the world under the name Cassius Clay, asked his draft board in Louisville, Kentucky for Conscientious Objector (CO) status. They said his beliefs were insincere. Ali replied that if he was not sincere, why would he give up millions of dollars and lose his public image? If Ali had accepted the draft, he would have been sent into armed services boxing exhibitions in Vietnam. Instead, he was convicted in 1967 for refusing induction, sentenced to five years in prison, and stripped of his heavyweight championship. Four years later, while he was free on bond, the Supreme Court reversed the conviction on technical grounds.

While the government could prosecute a few individuals, it could not deal with masses. That was the goal of the draft resisters: 100,000 acts of defiance. This resistance was organized in the fall of 1967 with scores of educators and religious leaders supporting it. These included the famous pediatrician Dr. Benjamin Spock and the head of campus ministry at Yale, Rev. William Sloane Coffin. Attorney General Ramsay Clark chose to prosecute both Spock and Coffin. Their convictions were reversed, but the Justice Department did convey a public image of vigorous enforcement of the draft law.

Congress reacted by making the burning of draft cards a crime with punishments ranging up to five years. Resisters defied the law and were promptly jailed. Once the movement gained momentum, the Justice Department became more selective in its prosecution. During the height of the resistance in 1967-1968, fewer than fifty were indicted, and forty were convicted.

Some draft boards were over zealous in their prosecutions. Robert Craig received mail at home while he was away at college. His father had recently died, and his mother did not want her only son to go to Vietnam so she returned all letters to the draft board without telling her son. He was prosecuted and convicted of draft evasion.

In the South the induction notices were often sent to "trouble makers" who were active in the civil rights movement. Mrs. Jeanette Crawford of New Orleans was a civil rights activist with three draft-age sons. When she refused to testify before the Louisiana House Committee on Un-American Activities, her three sons were ordered to report for induction. The oldest, James, who had already served thirteen years in the army, was accused of not registering for the draft. The FBI staked out the Crawford home in hopes of capturing him. This was impossible since he was serving with the U. S. Army in West Germany. His brother Warren refused induction and received the highest penalty in the Vietnam Era—six concurrent five-year sentences.

Not all draft resisters remained anonymous. Many of the leaders of the Baby Boom generation that came to power in the 1980s never served in Vietnam. These men were from both political parties. They include former Republican Vice President Dan Quayle and President George W. Bush, who obtained much sought after slots in the National Guard; Republican Newt Gingrich, former Speaker of the House, who got a family man deferment; former Republican Senator Phil Gramm from Texas, who had an educational deferment; and former Democratic President William Jefferson Clinton, who used a number of maneuvers to escape the Vietnam War. Some of those who served include Republican Senator John McCain of Arizona, who was a prisoner of war caged like an animal; former Democratic Senator Robert Kerrey of Nebraska, who lost a leg in the war; Democratic Senator John Kerry of Massachusetts, who founded

Vietnam Vets Against the War; and former Democratic Vice President Albert Gore, Jr., who served as an Army journalist.

Tet Offensive

On November 24, 1967, the CIA warned that an enormous flood of Vietcong infantry was coming down the Ho Chi Minh Trail. The military ignored the warning and, thus, the January 1968 Tet Offensive came as a total surprise. The shock of the Tet Offensive, the sight of an enemy swarming all over the American Embassy in Saigon and indeed all over Vietnam, forced a public reckoning. Soon college campuses exploded with more than two hundred major demonstrations in the first six months, involving forty thousand students. Walter Cronkite of CBS News, deemed the most trusted man in America, announced that the U. S. was involved in a stalemate with no hopes of victory. Although the result was a major military defeat for the Vietcong, the American people had already turned. Johnson's popularity fell to 35 percent. Each day Johnson could hear the protesters outside the White House chanting, "Hey, hey, LBJ. How many kids did you kill today?" Other protesters shouted obscenities. In February 1968 the CIA, Clark Clifford the new Secretary of Defense, and Johnson's advisers all concluded that the war could not be won. The best that could be achieved was a stalemate. They advised disengagement and withdrawal.

Johnson's worst nightmares were beginning to come true: loss in Vietnam, Richard Nixon emerging as his GOP opponent, and Robert Kennedy thinking of challenging him for the Democratic nomination. In March of 1968 the voters in New Hampshire gave Eugene McCarthy, a little known Democratic Senator from Minnesota, 42 percent of the vote in the presidential primary. Four days later Robert Kennedy entered the race. On March 31, three days after the final meeting with his advisers, Johnson announced at the end of a televised speech: "Accordingly, I shall not seek and I will not accept, the nomination of my party for another term...." Instead, Johnson pledged to devote the rest of his term to finding a way to end the war.

At the same time the draft resistance movement became more violent. The Catonsville Nine led by the Berrigan brothers, one a priest and the other a former priest, used the same napalm the army was using in Vietnam to destroy 378 draft files. Government reaction was swift and severe. The Berrigans were caught, tried, convicted, and sentenced to prison.

What really crippled the draft process was not the resisters but the lawyers who were working within the system. The case of Daniel Seeger of New York began the unraveling of the system. Seeger had asked for an exemption as a conscientious objector. His draft board refused, since Seeger did not belong to a pacifist sect. The case went to the Supreme Court, which ruled that he qualified because of his personal religious beliefs. That did not mean that draft boards would begin to abide by this change in law; they didn't. Increasingly lawyers told their clients that they should challenge the legality of the draft board decisions, and the resisters began to win. In 1968 a small group of Washington lawyers established the *Selective Service Law Reporter,* which published decisions, regulations, and legal analysis.

The demands of the Vietnam War did not increase the safety record of the Pentagon, which continued to lose H-bombs in the 1960s. In 1966 a bomber carrying four H-bombs crashed off the Spanish coast. Three of the bombs landed near the coastal village of Palomares. The TNT charges in two of them exploded and showered the area with uranium and plutonium. The fourth bomb landed eight miles off shore and is still there in 2,850 feet of water. In 1968 a B-52 caught fire on a flight above Greenland and crashed into North Star Bay near Thule Air Base. The impact detonated the TNT in all four H-bombs and scattered uranium, tritium and plutonium over a 2,000 foot radius. The thermonuclear assembly was encapsulated in the ice and the rescue crew had to work in -70 degrees to recover it. Showing their sense of humor, the recovery work crew called it "Dr. Freezelove."

Another effect of the Vietnam War was the Johnson administration's use of the U.S. Army to spy on civilians. The Army employed more than 1,500 plainclothes agents to watch any anti-war demonstration of twenty people or more. They infiltrated civil rights protests, set up phony news organizations, and misdirected busloads of anti-war demonstrators. They were seeking to prove that communists were responsible for opposition to racial segregation and the war in Vietnam. When it was over, the Army had collected information on more than a million law-abiding American citizens. Its nefarious activities were revealed when Christopher H. Pyle, former Army Captain in Army intelligence, testified before the Senate Subcommittee on Constitutional Rights in 1971.

POPULAR CULTURE

Popular culture changed dramatically in the 1960s as the first wave of the baby boom generation entered college. Many rejected what they saw as the materialistic life style of their parents. Some became hippies and lived in communes. Others experimented with drugs and sex. Many did all three. The center for the hippie movement was the Haight Ashbury district of San Francisco, although groups were found throughout the nation.

Surveys indicated that half of the college students had tried marijuana. A minority followed the lead of Harvard Professor Timothy Leary who urged students to experiment with hallucinogenic drugs like LSD or "acid," telling them to "turn on, tune in, drop out."

Some of the rock groups like the Grateful Dead and the Jefferson Airplane popularized a new style called "Acid Rock," which had a heavy beat and lyrics that promoted the youth agenda of radical politics, sexual promiscuity, and drugs.

In 1964 a change came into popular music with the British invasion of the Beatles who appeared on the popular television program, the Ed Sullivan Show. At first, the Beatles seemed like angelic choirboys whose hair was a bit too long and who sang lovely romantic songs. That soon changed, and their music, too, took on all the aspects of the youth culture. There seemed to be drug messages in their songs whether it was "I want to turn you on" or a hidden message about LSD in "Lucy in the Sky with Diamonds." It was, however, their 1967 album, *Sergeant Pepper's Lonely Hearts Club Band,* that ignited a summer of emotional release and youth unity. In contradistinction there was the hard rock of Mick Jagger and the Rolling Stones, another British group.

The 60s also saw soul music moving into the popular mainstream with the Motown sound of the Supremes from Detroit. Music now became part of the resistance movement as the young listened to Bob Dylan, Arlo Guthrie, Pete Seeger, and Joan Baez sing songs about draft resistance and peace.

Sexual experimentation was made easier with the marketing of oral contraceptives in 1960. The Pill freed women from the dangers of unwanted pregnancies but not the dangers of sexual diseases.

The festival held at Woodstock, New York in August 1969 was the symbol of the counter culture. Hippies, Vietnam War protestors, civil rights supporters, and those who experimented with sex and drugs attended. Surprisingly the festival was planned by four young executives who were interested in venture capitalism. The partners expected somewhere between 50,000 and 100,000 people so they rented a field from a local dairy farmer as the site. It soon became clear that the event was going to draw a much larger crowd. On August 15, when the festival began, an estimated 400,000 people were in attendance. The band scheduled to open the festival could not get to the site because of the traffic jams. Some of the greatest performers of the 1960s performed there, including Janis Joplin, Ravi Shankar, Arlo Guthrie, and Joan Baez, as well as bands including The Who; Crosby, Stills, Nash and Young; the Jefferson Airplane; The Grateful Dead; Sly and the Family Stone; and Creedence Clearwater. Jimi Hendrix ended the three-day event with a free-form solo guitar performance of "The Star Spangled Banner." In spite of the large numbers, the event was peaceful. It was later documented in the motion picture, *Woodstock.*

There was also a theological component of pop culture: the new consciousness movement of the "Death of God." This was an anti-theology that said the evils of Auschwitz and Hiroshima meant there was no God. Hopeful theologians like Harvey Cox expounded not that "God Is" but that rather "He Is Not Yet." There was also a reborn interest in Eastern religions, fueled by the Beatles who made their own trip to India.

Of course, people who were hippies, sexually promiscuous, or tried drugs were a minority of the baby boomers. Many saw all of this as a sign of moral decay, a beginning of the end. Questions of social and moral behavior soon entered the political arena where they remain today.

A DECADE OF ASSASSINATIONS

The three political assassinations were perhaps the most troubling aspect of the 1960s. The first was the assassination of John F. Kennedy, followed in 1968 by the killing of Martin Luther King, Jr., and then Kennedy's brother, Robert.

In November 1963 John Kennedy with his wife Jackie and Vice President Lyndon Johnson made a trip to Texas. In preparation for the 1964 election, JFK wanted to settle an internal dispute in the Texas Democratic Party. While riding through the streets of Dallas in an open car, Kennedy was hit in the throat and brain by rifle bullets that caused his death. Very quickly, the Dallas police arrested a suspect, Lee Harvey Oswald, who worked in the Texas Book Depository Building on the square where the president was murdered. No one knew the immediate implications of the plot, nor who else might have been targeted. Matters became more unsettled when Jack Ruby killed Oswald on live TV while Oswald was being moved from one jail to another.

To ease the fears of the American people, newly sworn-in President Lyndon Johnson set up a commission headed by the Chief Justice of the United States Supreme Court, Earl Warren. Members of the commission also included former CIA Director Allen Dulles and future president Gerald Ford. The commission did not have an investigative arm but instead only reviewed the information that was presented to it by the FBI and other agencies. Despite requests from Jack Ruby that he be brought to Washington, D. C. to testify, no attempt was made to secure his story. The commission accepted that Lee Harvey Oswald was the lone assassin who was killed by Jack Ruby, another lone assassin. The most persuasive presentation of the Warren Commission theory can be found in Gerald Posner's *Case Closed*, which some members of the media and some historians have endorsed.

Both the FBI and the CIA had their own secrets that they wished to protect. FBI head J. Edgar Hoover's confidential sources linked Oswald to organized crime and Cuban exiles and indicated that he should have been placed on the Security Index. Hoover did not want to reveal that this had not been done. The CIA did not want the news out that it had been working with the Mafia to assassinate Castro. At the first meeting ex-head of the CIA, Allen Dulles, provided the commission with copies of an article claiming that most political assassinations resulted from lone madmen.

Within a short time the reaction to the Warren Commission Report went from praise to condemnation and generated a flood of critical books, which has not yet ended. One result was the 1978 House Select Committee on Assassinations, which surmised that the most likely conspiracy involved Cubans associated with anti-Castro organizations in the United States and that it might have included the criminal element. The committee documented the ties Mafia Boss of New Orleans Carlos Marcello's had with Jimmy Hoffa, ex-head of the Teamster Union whom Attorney General Robert Kennedy had sent to prison; Santos Trafficante, Mafia Head of Miami whom Castro had jailed in Havana for a time; and Oswald, Ruby and members of the New Orleans Cuban community. While the committee was meeting, and before he could testify, Sam Giancana was killed in what had all the earmarks of a gangland hit. Johnny Roselli, a lower level Mafioso who testified to the committee, was killed and his body stuffed into a drum. He was later found off the Florida coast. In the 2001 *Science & Justice*, the journal of Britain's Forensic Science Society, D. B. Jones detailed a new analysis of recorded police radio transmissions that provided new confirmation that there were shots fired from the grassy knoll, an indication of more than one shooter, which put Kennedy in crossfire. With such revelations coming on a regular basis, it is no surprise that thirty-five years after the assassination, 80 percent of the American public believed that Kennedy's and Oswald's deaths were part of a huge conspiracy.

The Conspiracy Case

Some people maintain that there is evidence of interconnections between the Cuban exile community, Jack Ruby as gun runner, organized crime bosses, the CIA, the FBI, drug traffickers, leaders of the military-industrial complex, and the Dallas Police Department.

The Cuban exile community was very anti-Kennedy since the unsuccessful invasion of Cuba at the Bay of Pigs and the agreement not to invade Cuba made with Khrushchev during the Cuban Missile Crisis. The CIA's rejection of the Cuban exiles' military plan in the Caribbean, intended ultimately to goad the U.S. into war with Cuba, had leaked between November 8, 1963, and its official announcement on November 19. In the same interval the FBI received reports of a plot to assassinate the president in Dallas. It was verified in 1964 that Oswald had many associations with the militant CIA-funded Cuban exiles.

The predecessor to the CIA, organized crime, and the United States military had a history of working together since World War II. The military obtained Lucky Luciano's release from prison to work with the navy in the invasion of Sicily. This had continued with the CIA's plans to use the Mafia to assassinate Castro.

FBI head J. Edgar Hoover also had questionable ties to Meyer Lansky, the Mafia boss who organized the syndicate that controlled a large proportion of the crime in the United States and turned Las Vegas into a gambling mecca.

Some believe that Oswald's three years in Russia and activities on behalf of Castro prove that the Communists killed Kennedy. Others maintain that the original Warren Report was basically correct and the conspiracy theory is unproven. That is the argument of Gerald Posner in *Case Closed*.

And actions of the Kennedy family helped to fuel conspiracy theorists. There was contention about the casket in which Kennedy's body had been placed in Dallas and the casket it was in when it arrived at Bethesda for the autopsy. The Dallas mortician swore that he had placed the body in a bronze casket. The Navy corpsman present at the autopsy said that it had arrived in a different one. When Kennedy's body lay in state it was in a casket of mahogany.

In 1999 the National Archives released information that the casket had been damaged in transport and had been loaded aboard a military plane and dropped into 9,000 feet of water off the Maryland-Delaware Coast. This was done because the family feared that it might become an object of morbid curiosity and because the Mayor of Dallas did not want it to become a public focus.

Upon Kennedy's assassination there was a dramatic change in U. S. Vietnam policy. From a slow withdrawal of advisers to active participation with ground troops, the change in presidents marked a dramatic reversal of policy.

Since 1961, Johnson had been an ally of Air Force General Curtis LeMay, and both had been unrelenting in their efforts to get Kennedy to introduce combat troops in Vietnam. Members of the defense industry joined them in this lobbying effort. Hoover's sexual dirt on the Kennedys began to surface in late June 1963 after the president's peace speech at American University. Such tidbits as "What high American official was involved with Marilyn Monroe?" appeared in the Drew Pearson-Jack Anderson column of June 29, 1963. On the same day the Hearst paper in New York linked "one of the biggest names in American politics" to the Ward sex-ring in Great Britain, which had brought down a member of the British cabinet. It was John Kennedy.

For decades the national press had ignored the private sexual affairs of national politicians. However, not many were as active as John Kennedy. His most serious indiscretions were with women who had ties to organized crime. Judith Campbell was involved with Mafia Don Sam Giancana at the same time that she was having an affair in the White House with Kennedy. And Hoover was aware of every move that Kennedy made.

There were also some questions about Oswald, whom Johnson described as a "curious fellow." Oswald had served in the U.S. Marines and had been stationed for a time at Atsuge Air Base in Japan where the U-2 spy planes were based. He eventually defected to the Soviet Union and then reclaimed his citizenship after living in the U.S.S.R. for a few years. At the time of his arrest, Oswald was carrying a Department of Defense ID, which was only issued to those injured on active duty who needed medical privileges or those who were civilian employees overseas. This last tidbit of information was uncovered as a result of the demand for the release of more assassination information after the Oliver Stone movie, *JFK*. It had been buried for years in the files of the Dallas Police Department. In preparation for the 40th anniversary the Muchmore film, which shows the fatal head shot much better than the more famous Zapruder footage, is being remastered and restored with digital technology. Although it has been forty years since the assassination, the issues it raised have not been put to rest nor has the distrust in the federal government to which it gave rise. When the Clinton-appointed Assassinations Committee announced the release of the Kennedy Assassination files in the fall of 1998, they stated that one result of the government secrecy was an increased distrust of the federal government.

Election of 1964

When Johnson came to the presidency, it was as a man committed to the space program as a model of the role government should play in society and the role technology should play in government. To LBJ the space program was the beginning of the revolution of the 60s. It showed what could be done with proper organization and dedication, which could then be applied to other problems such as education and Medicare. This became clear in the 1964 campaign when Johnson promised a technocracy that would free U. S. from poverty and create the Great Society. His opponent, Barry Goldwater, a conservative Republican Senator from Arizona, was firmly behind individual initiative and a balanced budget, as well as behind the government's involvement in the military-industrial complex that Ike had warned against in his farewell address. While the priorities were debated, the basic premise of a technocracy where the state would direct change was not. While Johnson supported the Apollo program, Goldwater wanted the space program under the military with the race to the moon abandoned in favor of the development of antiballistic missiles and laser weapons.

Johnson was elected in his own right in 1964 against Goldwater, who scared Americans with his proposals to abolish the income tax, sell the Tennessee Valley Authority, and overhaul Social Security. He also seemed trigger-happy with his plans to bomb North Vietnam. Goldwater had voted against both the nuclear test ban and the Civil Rights Act. He claimed there was a silent majority who would vote Republican if only they quit having "me-too" candidates. He had one convert, Strom Thurmond, a former Dixiecrat who had run against Harry Truman in 1948, who became a Goldwater Republican. During the campaign, Johnson promised that "We are not about to send American boys nine or ten thousand miles from home to do what Asian boys ought to be doing for themselves." Johnson won with 61 percent of the total vote, the largest landslide given any preceding modern president. The Democrats also controlled the House and the Senate.

Evaluation of JFK

John Kennedy remains one of the most powerful, complex, and controversial actors in American history. In a long series of Gallup Polls a majority of Americans still regarded Kennedy as the greatest of all American presidents.

With Kennedy's murder, all peace initiatives ended. The ascension of Lyndon Johnson led to one of the most crucial reversals in American foreign policy. All the unanswered questions about the murder from who had actually killed him and why resulted in a cynicism in the American worldview that has yet to end.

Much of Kennedy's appeal can be attributed to his good manners, vitality, wit, self-deprecating humor, and disarming casualness, which made him the most attractive man of his generation. He articulated a sense of hope and connected the young people to the government in a way not seen since the death of his brother Robert. He conveyed a lofty standard of excellence and yet his own tastes were mundane. He could be vindictive and petty and

Vice President Lyndon Johnson took the oath after the murder of John Kennedy.

seemed to have an enormous ego and vanity. Those traits, however, were not evident to the public.

Just like Kennedy's womanizing was unknown to the general public so was the state of his health. He looked like a strong vigorous man, and his only known ailment was back trouble. In truth he suffered from adrenal insufficiency, colitis, and osteoporosis. All of this was uncovered by historian Robert Dallak who was given access to Kennedy's medical records as he researched a new Kennedy biography to be published in 2003, *An Unfinished Life: John F. Kennedy, 1917-1963.*

Dallak described the medical records as revealing the "quiet stoicism of a man struggling to endure extraordinary pain and distress." The records revealed he had so much pain from three fractured vertebrae from the osteoporosis that he could not put a sock or shoe on his left foot unaided. Despite the constant pain, presidential tapes of Kennedy during the Cuban missile crisis and at other times show him lucid and in complete command.

The final analysis of Kennedy must be based on whether the country was in better shape as a result of his presidency and to what extent he achieved his stated goals. In the area of foreign policy he accomplished several significant goals including the strengthening of the military and the atmospheric test ban treaty. Of the major foreign policy crises facing Kennedy in 1961, only Vietnam remained at his death. Furthermore, he did much to improve the image of the United States in the newly emerging nations of Africa and Asia. Kennedy also emerged as the father of the space program.

In the domestic sphere, he promoted economic growth, provided on-the job training, updated Social Security and the minimum wage, and reduced job discrimination against women. He eased farm problems, responded to the problem of juvenile delinquency and the needs of mental retardation, implemented the first significant housing program since 1949, and began urban renewal. Under his administration the Twenty-third Amendment was

Mrs. Kennedy and her children leave the Capitol building. (L-R) Peter Lawford, Attorney General Kennedy, Patrica Kennedy Lawford, Caroline Kennedy, Mrs. Kennedy, John F. Kennedy Jr. November 24, 1963
Photo credit: Abbie Rowe, National Park Service/JFK Library

passed, giving residents of the District of Columbia the right to vote in presidential elections. The fight against organized crime, which he and his brother Robert had begun, ceased upon his death.

The Kennedy administration had few scandals, and the men he appointed were an exceptional group of public servants. To the end Kennedy remained a positive role model: charming, optimistic, and positive. Historians have consistently ranked him as an above average president.

Evaluation of Johnson's Presidency

Johnson saw himself as the executor of John Kennedy's legacy, a legacy that Johnson saw himself creating. Kennedy had defined a key core of goals for his presidency: tax cuts, a civil rights bill, federal aid to education, improving life in the cities, medical care for the aged, and a poverty program. Johnson worked to have legislation in these areas passed, and it was here that he was at his best.

With the Civil Rights Act of 1964, the Voting Rights Act of 1965, and the Supreme Court's decision in 1964 in *Reynolds v. Sims* (one man, one vote), the administration completed the crucial work of the abolitionists, which had been left undone after the Civil War. This was one of Johnson's greatest accomplishments.

Johnson's strength was his knowledge of how to get legislation through Congress. A good example of this is how he got his federal aid to education bill passed. He saw to it that both the National Educa-

Signing of Civil Rights Act of 1964. July 2, 1964, by Cecil Stoughton. Photo credits: LBJ Library Photo

tion Association and the National Catholic Welfare Conference were on board for the program, which gave assistance to the impoverished child and not to the school attended. It was passed four months after it went to the Congress.

Despite his strengths, Johnson also had a turbulent and infantile nature. He was prone to bullying his staff and advisers with verbal tirades, fits of temper, and even physical abuse. He kicked Vice President Hubert Humphrey in the shins so often that Humphrey once showed the scars to a newsman.

In 1965 Johnson took the U. S. into a war that turned out to be the longest in our history. He became personally involved in the war even to the extent of choosing bombing sites. He also took the involvement on a personal level. ". . . if I got out of Vietnam and let Ho Chi Minh run through the streets of Saigon, then I'd be doing exactly what Chamberlain did in World War II. . ." [And then] "there would be Robert Kennedy . . . telling everyone that I had betrayed John Kennedy's commitment to South Vietnam. . . . That I was a coward. An unmanly man. A man without a spine." Once LBJ took a thing personally, his pride and vanity knew no bounds. Despite sending more than half a million troops into Vietnam and dropping more explosives than were used by all sides in all theaters of World War II, the military was unable to win.

His undoing was the cost of the Vietnam War, hidden from both the American people and Congress. He finally was forced in September of 1967 to ask Congress for an increase in taxes in the form of a 6 percent surcharge. To get this, he had to agree to a decrease in domestic spending, ending expansion of the Great Society programs.

Johnson has not received the rating from historians that he so much wanted. He has consistently been rated as an average president. Johnson was a larger than life figure with great gifts and tragic flaws.

Martin Luther King, Jr. talks with President Lyndon B. Johnson in the Oval Office, White House. December 3, 1963. By Yoichi R. Okamoto. Photo credits: LBJ Library Photo

Assassinations of Martin Luther King, Jr. and Robert Kennedy

During the presidential election year, 1968, two more assassinations took place. The first occurred in April when Martin Luther King, Jr. was assassinated in Memphis, Tennessee. He had gone there to support sanitation workers striking for union recognition. Although James Earl Ray was soon arrested and confessed to the murder, he later recanted in prison. The King family had questions about his guilt and was seeking a trial for Ray when he died in prison in 1998. However, they were successful in getting Attorney General Janet Reno to take another look at the assassination.

Some believe that it was King's speech in 1967 against the Vietnam War that brought his end. After the speech in which he said the greatest purveyor of violence in the world is "my own government," J. Edgar Hoover wrote to Johnson that it was clear King "was an instrument in the hands of subversive forces seeking to undermine our nation." Hoover had been tapping King's phones and keeping him under surveillance since the Kennedy administration.

King announced a new campaign in April 1968 that would use civil disobedience to force Congress to help the poor. The Poor People's Campaign wanted Congress to pass a comprehensive anti-poverty act with full-employment, guaranteed annual incomes, and a half million units of low cost housing a year. The intelligence community knew from their listening devices that King had broadened his campaign to include a peace movement to shut down the Pentagon.

When King was assassinated, Robert Kennedy was campaigning for the Democratic Party presidential nomination in Indianapolis. Thanks to his efforts, there was no riot in Indianapolis. Other cities were not so lucky. The King assassination set off riots in over sixty American cities with the worst in Chicago and Washington, D. C.

On June 6, Robert Kennedy, who had just won the California Democratic presidential primary, was assassinated as he went through a Los Angeles hotel kitchen after celebrating his victory. The assassin was a Palestinian immigrant, Sirhan Sirhan, who was captured at the scene. Robert Kennedy was the sole candidate who appealed to whites and blacks, the less privileged, and the middle class. With Kennedy gone, the idealism of the early 60s was dead, and the presidential nomination was open for Johnson's vice president, Hubert H. Humphrey.

ELECTION OF 1968

August 1968 the Democratic convention was held in Chicago to nominate Hubert Humphrey. Richard Daley, the Mayor of Chicago, remembering the riots after the King assassination, determined that nothing like that would happen at the convention. Daley had called for twenty-four thousand police and National Guardsmen to keep order. It was a disaster. The New Left was there to protest the Vietnam War. The additional police soon added to the chaos as they arrested people indiscriminately and behaved in a savage and ruthless manner. Millions watched on TV as the police bashed the heads of the protesters and others. One of those arrested was a conservative Republican county coroner from Indiana who was in Chicago on business. Like many others, he was in the wrong place at the wrong time.

Richard Nixon who had reinvented himself since his disastrous loss of the governorship of California in 1962 was running hard for the nomination. Ike, who had been ill, finally endorsed Nixon right before the convention. By that time, Nixon did not need his endorsement since he was on a roll toward the nomination.

For his vice president Nixon chose Spiro Agnew, the governor of Maryland, in part because of his harangue of black leaders over the riots in Baltimore. In essence, Agnew blamed them for not being out on the streets stopping the riots.

Nixon said that he was listening to the great silent majority of Americans who did not protest and break the laws but instead paid their taxes and went to work—those who loved their country. The main issue of the election, however, was the Vietnam War. Nixon claimed that he had a secret plan to stop the war in Vietnam. It was so secret that it was never revealed, even after the election.

The election was full of tricks from both sides. In October Johnson was moving toward a bombing halt and peace. Nixon used Anna Chan Chennault to get President Thieu of South Vietnam to refuse to cooperate. It was truly overkill, as Thieu had no intention of committing political suicide for either Johnson or Humphrey. The Johnson-Humphrey administration found out about the Nixon plan because they were using an illegal wiretap on his phones.

When it was falsely reported that an agreement had been reached, Nixon moved to undercut Johnson. He did this by mounting a campaign to convince the American people that Johnson had sold out the people of Vietnam, and he kept this up right to Election Day.

On October 31, five days before the election, Johnson announced that Hanoi had agreed to expanded peace talks and he had therefore ordered a bombing halt. The expanded talks would resume November 6, the day after the election. On a nationwide television broadcast the Monday before Election Day, Nixon said that he had heard a report that in the last two days "the North Vietnamese are moving thousands of tons of supplies down the Ho Chi Minh Trail, and our bombers are not able to stop them." He made the whole thing up keeping to the political tactics that he had used in his very first election campaign. On November 2 the Government of Vietnam announced that it would not sit down with the Vietcong.

On the other side, Johnson and Humphrey were not being honest that serious peace talks were to be held on Wednesday. The politicians were all playing their own games and lying to the American people while American men and money were spent with abandon.

George Wallace, the governor of Alabama, became a third party candidate who appealed to people on the issues of welfare, growth of the federal government, and race. His running mate, retired General

Curtis LeMay, however, scared many Americans when he said that the U. S. should just "nuke" Vietnam. Despite this, Wallace got 13.5 percent of the popular vote.

Nixon and Agnew won by a narrow margin of 800,000 votes. Nixon won in 1968 with less votes than he had gotten in 1960 when he lost! He was the first president since Zachary Taylor in 1848 to win the presidency while his party failed to carry either the House or the Senate.

CONCLUSION

The election of 1968 marked the end of the liberal consensus in American politics, which had supported government activism at home and abroad. The American people wanted calm after the chaos of their last eight years; they wanted the end of the Vietnam War. Government was now seen as an enemy that could not be trusted and that needed to be restrained. It was the beginning of the conservative resurgence.

Chronology

1960 Sit-ins at lunch counters
John Kennedy elected president

1961 Peace Corps
Alliance for Progress
Bay of Pigs
Berlin Wall erected

1962 Cuban Missile Crisis
James Meredith enrolls at Old Miss

1963 Civil Rights demonstrations in Birmingham
March on Washington
Test Ban Treaty
Diem Assassination
Kennedy Assassination
Betty Friedan, *The Feminine Mystique*

1964 Job Corps
Head Start
Mississippi Freedom Summer
Civil Rights Act
Economic Opportunity Act
Gulf of Tonkin Incident
War on Poverty
Johnson-Goldwater Election

1965 Americanization of Vietnam War
Assassination of Malcolm X
Medical Care Act
Civil Rights March: Selma to Montgomery
Voting Rights Act
Watts Riot
Grape strike in California
Opposition to draft

1966 Black Power
National Organization of Women (NOW)

1967 Anti-War Demonstrations
Race riots in Newark, Detroit
March on Pentagon
Thurgood Marshall, first African-American appointed to the U. S. Supreme Court

1968 Tet Offensive
Indian Civil Rights Act
Johnson not to seek re-election
Martin Luther King, Jr. assassinated
Robert F. Kennedy assassinated
Violence at Democratic Convention
Vietnam Peace talks
Nixon elected president

SUGGESTED READINGS

Stephen Ambrose, *Nixon: The Triumph of a Politician 1962-1972* (1989).

James N. Giglio, *The Presidency of John F. Kennedy* (1991).

Doris Kearns Goodwin, *Lyndon Johnson and the American Dream* (1991).

Paul R. Henger, *In His Steps: Lyndon Johnson and the Kennedy Mystique* (1991).

Frederick E. Hoxie, *Indians in American History* (1988).

Ray LaFontaine and Mary LaFontaine, *Oswald Talked: The New Evidence in the JFK Assassination* (1996).

Alfred McCoy, *Politics of Heroin: CIA Complicity in the Global Drug Trade* (1972).

Myra MacPherson, *Long Time Passing: Vietnam & the Haunted Generation* (1984).

Matt S. Meier and Feliciano Rivera, *The Chicanos: A History of Mexican Americans* (1972).

John Newman, *JFK and Vietnam* (1992).

Thomas G. Paterson, *Kennedy's Quest for Victory: American Foreign Policy, 1961-1963* (1989).

Glenda Riley, *Inventing the American Woman: A Perspective on Women's History 1865 to the Present* (1986).

W. J. Rorabaugh, *True Stories from the American Past* (1993).

Peter Dale Scott, *Deep Politics and the Death of JFK* (1993).

Harvey Wasserman, *America Born and Reborn* (1983).

Where were you when President Kennedy was shot? Memories and Tributes to a Slain President as told to DEAR ABBY (1993).

Chapter Twenty-three

THE SEVENTIES: The Crisis of Confidence

Early in the morning of June 17, 1972, five men broke into the Democratic Party headquarters at the Watergate apartment and office complex only a mile from the White House. They wore surgical gloves and carried lock-picking tools, camera, mace, and wire-tapping devices to replace faulty bugs installed in an earlier break-in. The techniques used by the burglars were so primitive and the equipment so shoddy that they would have "appalled the CIA, the Mafia, the New York Police Department or the KGB," in the words of one observer. The incompetent criminals carefully placed tape across the latches of the spring locks on the door to the Democratic headquarters. A guard on a routine inspection noticed the tape and removed it. The burglars, noting that the tape was no longer in place, re-installed it in the same conspicuous way. The guard, returning an hour later, alertly observed the reappearing tape and summoned the police.

The Nixon administration had targeted Washington to demonstrate its commitment to law and order. The newly effective Washington patrol system rushed a car to the scene at 2:00 A. M. On the sixth floor of the Watergate building, the police burst in to discover the culprits who pleaded, "Don't shoot, we give up." The inept criminal band included four Cuban-Americans who thought they were striking a blow against Castro, and James McCord, the "wire man." McCord was a former CIA agent and current security chief for the Committee to Re-elect the President (CREEP). The cash they carried in $100 bills could be easily traced through serial numbers to CREEP. Papers found on the perpetrators linked them to two CREEP officials: E. Howard Hunt, a former CIA agent, and G. Gordon Liddy, a former FBI employee.

The logic behind the break-in was difficult to discern. Apart from the size of its considerable debts, it is hard to figure out what possible secrets of any significance could have been discovered by tapping the phone of the Democratic National Committee. The burglars, undoubtedly, were comfortable in the belief that their superiors in CREEP (who now included John Mitchell, the former attorney general) could easily cover up the episode and arrange for their release.

Despite these expectations, a grand jury indicted the five burglars, as well as Hunt and Liddy. The administration quickly developed a cover story to ensure that any links to criminal activities stopped at Hunt and Liddy. The break-in, according to this tale, had been "deplorable, an excess of zeal, unauthorized, illegal, regrettable." Neither the media nor the public picked up Democratic cries of a cover-up in the 1972 election campaign. There was nothing to link the White House to this "third-rate burglary." President Nixon won a landslide re-election victory. After thanking White House Counsel John Dean, for his role in containing the damage, the president darkly threatened all of those he believed "have tried to do us in." All his enemies were "asking for it and they are going to get it." A lawyer for the Washington Post was "a guy we've got to ruin... We are going to fix that son-of-a-bitch." How had such an intoxicating victory turned into such a dark moment? Would the beleaguered White House staff be able to contain what Dean described as a "cancer on the Presidency?"

NIXON THE MAN

Historian Garry Wills recalled his feelings at a 1968 George Wallace rally:

> We have now a vast middle range of the comfortable discontented. They are not as Nixon knows, the kind who march or riot. They just lock their doors. And they vote. They do not, most of them, go to Wallace rallies, but those who do go speak for them in growing measure. This is the vague unlocalized resentment that had such effect in the 1968 campaign, tainting all the air around talk of law and order. America itself, like her major cities, has blight at the core, not in the limbs and extremities. As I stood bewildered like most reporters, in the insane din of that Wallace rally, saw a crowd of eight thousand tormented by a few hundred, I realized at last what had not sunk in at Miami's riot, or Chicago's. I realized this is a nation that might do anything. Even elect Nixon.

Indeed Nixon's life-long ambition was finally achieved. Did this victory symbolize the death of liberalism? Many "silent Americans" believed liberalism had scarred the nation's cities and college campuses and propelled the seemingly unending bloody carnage in the jungles of Southeast Asia.

Few politicians in American history have been so well prepared but so ill-suited to occupy the Oval Office as Richard Milhous Nixon. Born in 1913 to Quaker parents, he grew up in the small southern California town of Yorba Linda. World War II interrupted his plans to start a law practice in Whittier, California. After serving as a naval supply officer in the Pacific, Nixon returned to his native state, where he enjoyed a meteoric rise in the national political arena. Elected first to the House of Representatives and then to the Senate, he went on to serve eight years as Dwight Eisenhower's vice president.

From the outset his was a political life of enormous contrasts. It was a career marked by great promise but undermined by equally great character flaws. Richard Nixon was the quintessential outsider, who somehow always needed to define himself in this manner, even when he became the ultimate insider. At his second inauguration in 1972, despite his overwhelming victory, Henry Kissinger wrote, "Nixon moved as if he were himself a spectator, not the principal....There was about him this day a quality of remoteness, as if he could never quite bring himself to leave the inhospitable and hostile world that he inhabited...." John Ehrlichman, an aide who loved the president, recalled, "There was another side to him, like the flat, dark side of the moon."

Even in his first campaign for Congress in 1946, Nixon did not hesitate in capitalizing on the strongly anti-Communist post-war sentiment by questioning the loyalty of his Democratic opponent. His innuendoes about the incumbent's supposed associations with subversive elements led to a surprise Nixon victory. He achieved considerable national prominence as a member of the House Un-American Activities Committee. His greatest public visibility came from his role in the investigation of accused spy Alger Hiss. When he ran for the Senate four years later against Helen Gahagan Douglas, he continued to rely on insinuations about loyalty by labeling Douglas "the Pink Lady."

Nixon survived revelations of a "slush fund," established by California businessmen to keep him in "financial comfort." He remained Eisenhower's vice president, despite Eisenhower's evident distaste for him. During the 1952 campaign, Nixon had continued his "redbaiting" by charging that a Democratic victory would bring "more Alger Hisses, more atomic spies." After a close defeat by the Kennedy machine in the 1960 presidential election, Nixon

Richard M. Nixon in a campaign motorcade standing on the back of car gives the "V" sign. January 28, 1970 Photo credit: Nixon Presidential Library

went on to lose his bid for the governorship of California in 1962. His political career seemed over. He even announced to the press, "You won't have Dick Nixon to kick around any more." But working hard behind the scenes, occupying the center of his party, and declaring himself to be a "New Nixon," he succeeded in resurrecting himself from political death. He campaigned vigorously for Republican candidates, accumulating political IOUs. He went on to win the presidential nomination and election in 1968. Despite his triumph, Nixon remained insecure, angry, and paranoid in his conviction that enemies, particularly the "eastern liberal establishment," were conspiring to get him.

Nixon surrounded himself with hard-working, clean-cut looking, ambitious, tough, and unswervingly loyal aides. They reflected his identification with the "silent majority" who had grown weary with the lawlessness and "moral permissiveness" of the Sixties. In his first inauguration, Nixon promised to work on behalf of national unity, promote fiscal conservatism, support minority rights, fight crime, and bring peace to Southeast Asia. In many ways this very solemn and lonely man was attempting to steer a moderate Eisenhower-like course. It was a course he would never find. As one historian who has studied both those men wrote, "Eisenhower was a man full of love for life and for people, while Nixon, sadly, was a man who all too often gave in to an impulse to hate."

At first, however, the celebration of the first man on the moon symbolized the unity promised by the new president. On July 21, 1969, only seven years after President Kennedy had announced a gigantic program to counter the Soviet space challenge, astronaut Neil Armstrong stepped out of Apollo 11's lunar module to walk on the surface of the moon. Armstrong declared to the enthralled millions who were watching on television, "That's one small step for man, one giant leap for mankind." Americans were thrilled and proud when Armstrong and fellow astronaut Buzz Aldrin planted an American flag on the moon. A plaque declared, "Here men from planet earth first set foot on the moon, July 1969 A. D. We came in peace for all mankind." Many hoped that the peace announced in space might also come to earth, particularly in the continuing morass of Vietnam.

AMERICA'S LONGEST WAR

Nixon, who viewed himself as the consummate expert in foreign affairs, recognized that the war in Vietnam was his most immediate international problem. Vietnam was, in fact, the driving force behind virtually every other issue. He chose his old friend William P. Rogers, Eisenhower's second term attorney general, to be Secretary of State. Rogers remained in that position until 1973, when Henry Kissinger, the national security advisor from 1968 to 1973, replaced him. Kissinger, almost from the beginning, was Nixon's real ally in implementing his grand design in foreign policy. Kissinger, a refugee from Nazi Germany, had a distinguished academic career and was widely viewed as a highly respected expert on military and foreign policy.

Kissinger came to recognize that he and Nixon were pragmatic realists who wished to reshape cold war policies. Vietnam was their chief obstacle. It prevented détente with the People's Republic of China and, most importantly, the Soviet Union. Furthermore, the war fueled inflation, stimulated domestic disorder, and drained U. S. military might. Ending American involvement in Vietnam without loss of international credibility was the central issue Nixon and Kissinger had to address.

Vietnamization and the Nixon Doctrine

In the spring of 1969, Nixon and Kissinger began implementing a strategy of "Vietnamization." This de-escalation of American involvement was intended to achieve a number of objectives, including continued protection of the South Vietnamese government by intensifying U. S. bombings. In addition, South Vietnam was to become more militarily self sufficient by assuming a larger role in the fighting. The president understood that both the public and the troops had grown increasingly weary with the seemingly unending conflict. "I'm not going to end up like LBJ," Nixon swore, "holed up in the White House afraid to show his face on the street. I'm going to stop that war." By 1972, only 50,000 American troops remained in that war-ravaged part of the world.

In July 1969, the president announced the Nixon Doctrine. The Nixon Doctrine, reflecting the president's characteristic pragmatism, acknowledged that the United States could no longer maintain its current level of overseas commitments. America had to rely much more heavily on regional allies to prevent the further spread of communism. Nixon declared, "this approach required our commitment to helping our partners develop their own strength. In doing so, we must strike a careful balance. If we do too little to help them—and erode their belief in our commitments—they may lose the necessary will to conduct their own self-defense or become disheartened about the prospects of development. Yet, if we do too much and American forces do what local forces can and should be doing, we promote dependence rather than independence."

Escalation

The peace talks, which Henry Kissinger continued in great secrecy between 1969-71, reached a stalemate. This led the administration to exert more military, economic, and diplomatic pressure on the North Vietnamese. Nixon hoped this intensified pressure would end the conflict and win the acceptance of the Saigon government. He achieved this by undertaking bombing excursions into the neutral nations of Laos and Cambodia, where the enemy supposedly maintained supply bases. Nixon concealed these operations from the public from March 1969 until he announced the invasion of Cambodia in April 1970.

The strategy did not succeed. The Paris Peace Talks soured further as the North Vietnamese government remained implacable. The seemingly inactive United States anti-war movement came alive, when in October of 1969 the Vietnam Moratorium Committee brought over 250,000 protesters to a Washington, D. C. demonstration. As they marched past the White House, they demanded an end to the hostilities. The Cambodian invasion, which seemed to many to be reescalating the conflict, ignited the most extensive college protests in American history. Tragedy struck on May 4, 1970, when National Guardsmen shot and killed four Kent State University students. Ten more were wounded. Although Nixon regretted the deaths, he told Americans that "when disaster turns to violence, it invites tragedy." Only ten days later police on the Jackson State College campus in Mississippi killed two African-American students and wounded another twelve.

The country's mood did not improve after the 1970 revelations about American atrocities at My Lai. This episode brought to question not only the morality of the war itself but that of United States ground forces. How was it possible that an American platoon could have obliterated a small Vietnamese village of several hundred men, women, and children? Led by the inexperienced lieutenant William Calley, the unit had lined up women and old men in front of ditches and mowed them down, gang-raped young girls, and blown babies apart with hand grenades. Could the war have disintegrated to the kind of blood bath the United States had supposedly intervened to prevent in the first place? At Calley's trial, his commander declared, "Every unit of brigade size had its My Lai hidden some place."

The Cambodian invasion also brought out strong responses on Capitol Hill. What had happened to the congressional power to declare war? Was the checks and balances system no longer working? Congress, determined to recapture its lost powers, repealed the Gulf of Tonkin Resolution. Congress also tried to design proposals to restrict the commitment of additional U.S. troops.

When the United States withdrew its forces from Cambodia at the end of June 1970, none of the invasion's objectives had been achieved. In fact, the situation considerably worsened. The invasion ended Cambodia's doggedly preserved neutrality. This provoked a civil war in which hundreds of thousands died and led to the rise to power of the horrifying Khmer Rouge rebels who massacred at least a million more. When the failure of the South Vietnamese Army denied him further expansion of the war into Laos in February 1971, Nixon determined to protect the survival of South Vietnam with air power. But hopes to cut the Ho Chi Minh trails through repeated bombing proved no more successful for Nixon than it had for Lyndon Johnson.

Problems continued to mount for the administration when, in June of 1971, the *New York Times* published the so-called *Pentagon Papers*. This was a top-secret official investigation of U. S. policies in Vietnam prepared in the Johnson administration. Leaked by a former Defense Department official, Daniel Ellsberg, the *Papers* were politically damning. Although they contained nothing about the Nixon years, Nixon feared they would undermine public trust in the government and tried to prevent their further publication by securing an injunction. The Supreme Court overturned the order. The *Pentagon Papers* revealed extensive government duplicity, including covert U. S. activity in Southeast Asia as well as the depth of deception and intrigue of three previous administrations. Clearly, as 1971 ended, Nixon and Kissinger were deeply frustrated.

The End at Last

Vietnamization was not working as expected. Television broadcast the routing of South Vietnamese forces in the Laos venture of February 1971. Its failure was clear for all to see, as desperate South Vietnamese soldiers tried to grab on to retreating American helicopters. Encouraged by this success, the North Vietnamese government mounted an Easter Offensive in 1972. It was their largest military campaign since 1968. Not willing to abandon Vietnamization, Nixon responded with increased military action. The American military mined North Vietnam's major harbors and B-52s pummeled its cities. Although this revived the antiwar protest movement, the White House reported a public

Dr. Daniel Ellsberg holds an impromptu news conference outside federal building in Boston while his wife, Patricia, waits behind him after he was released on bond. Mrs. Ellsberg accompanied her husband in court for the arraignment.

outpouring of more than five to one in favor of the president's actions. Later insiders revealed that the Committee to Re-elect the President had paid for thousands of phony telegrams of support. A public opinion poll in 1971 revealed that 71 percent of Americans thought it had been a mistake to send American troops to Vietnam, and 58 percent believed the war was immoral. The Communist offensive, however, stalled by mid-June 1972. This led the North Vietnamese to reassess their position at the negotiating table. By October, both sides were willing to be more conciliatory.

In fact, on October 26, 1972, Henry Kissinger announced, "Peace is at hand." The presidential election was only days ahead. Secretly Kissinger and Le Duc Tho, the North Vietnamese foreign minister, had agreed to a cease-fire. All remaining United States troops were to be withdrawn. All U. S. prisoners of war were to be released. And, most importantly, from the North Vietnamese perspective, their troops were allowed to remain in the South.

Henry Kissinger's October announcement was unfortunately premature; except for the effect it may have had on the outcome of Nixon's 1972 landslide. No one seemed to have anticipated the reaction of South Vietnamese President Thieu, who obdurately rejected the offer. Nixon decided to back him and ordered the Christmas bombing of Hanoi and the North. After eleven days, the bombing stopped. Large sections of Hanoi lay in ruins, a hospital had been leveled, and over two thousand civilians were dead. Thieu was now informed he would have to accept the next proposal offered or go it alone. The talks resumed for another week, at which time President Thieu did agree to a settlement little different from that proposed in October. Ironically, the United States of America ended its active involvement in the war on the very day that Lyndon Baines Johnson died of a heart attack—January 23, 1973.

But neither peace nor democracy came to Southeast Asia. The cease fire, itself, collapsed. In November of 1973 the United States Congress passed the War Powers Act, over Nixon's angry veto. The act established a sixty-day limit on any presidential commitment of American troops to foreign campaigns, unless the Congress voted to continue the action. Meanwhile, the fighting resumed in Vietnam. At last, in the spring of 1975, the South collapsed. President Thieu fled his faltering nation on April 21 and on April 30, the South officially surrendered. After thirty years of turmoil many wondered what, if anything, had been accomplished.

Despite being elected largely on the wave of disillusionment with the Vietnam War, it had taken Nixon four years, massive destruction in Vietnam, Laos and Cambodia, and 20,000 additional American lives to end the conflict. Overall, the war cost over $150 billion and 58,000 American lives. More than a million Vietnamese had also lost their lives. Despite the warnings of a "domino effect," other Asian nations, outside of Vietnam, Laos and Cambodia, did not fall to a resurgent Communism. Vietnam and China, supposed allies, soon returned to their historic animosity.

One result of America's defeat, the deeply held opposition to the war and the brutality of guerrilla combat, was that returning veterans did not receive public recognition for their sacrifices. At best, a public, that wished to forget the painfulness of Vietnam, ignored them. At worst, Americans thought of them as brutalized, dangerous, or drug-crazed. One veteran bitterly recalled the "feelings of rejection and scorn that a bunch of depressed and confused young men experienced when they returned home from doing what their country told them to do." Eventually, most were able to readjust to civilian life (although one-sixth of the three million who served suffered from posttraumatic stress disorder). One worried years later, "We have adjusted too well. Too many of us have lost touch with the horror of war...we lose the intensity...I wish we were more troubled."

A New Direction in World Affairs

If the president and his chief foreign policy expert and ally, Henry Kissinger, could not rightly proclaim a "Peace with honor" in the Vietnamese war, they could correctly claim to have dramatically changed international affairs in other arenas. They charted a course all succeeding administrations have followed.

As the war in Southeast Asia ground on, Nixon and Kissinger worked behind the scenes to reshape foreign policy worldwide. Henry Kissinger continued the well-established Kennedy and Johnson administrations' trend of moving the control of foreign policy into the White House, rather than relying on international organizations like the United Nations. The policy was a reflection of Kissinger's and Nixon's shared world view that the post World War II world, ruled over by the United States and the Soviet Union, was gone. Growing nationalism, coming from the Third World, was directed at the United States in its sphere of influence in the world and at the Soviets in theirs. As a result, both superpowers found the freedom to flex their muscles increasingly restrained.

Both Richard Nixon and Henry Kissinger understood the growing split between China and the Soviet Union. Several bloody border clashes demonstrated the rapidly worsening relations between these two communist nations. The split provided the U.S. with a diplomatic window of opportunity, as each of the communist powers felt compelled to draw nearer to the United States. In his first inaugural speech Nixon had spoken of a new "era of negotiation" rather than another "era of confrontation." What could be more surprising to all than a reversal of two decades as the world's chief anti-Communist by being the president "to open China," and cause "an arms-control agreement with Russia?" The timing was ideal. Unlike Presidents Truman, Kennedy, and Johnson, Nixon had no Nixon to accuse him of selling out to the communists.

Proceeding cautiously, Nixon began to refer to China as the People's Republic rather than Red

President and Mrs. Nixon at the Great Wall of China.
February 24, 1972 Photo credit: Nixon Presidential Library

China. Following the suggestion of the President of the International Table Tennis Federation, Premier Zhou En-Lai invited American players to visit China. In April 1971 an American table tennis team arrived. In receiving the players at the Great Hall of the People in Beijing, Mr. Zhou declared, "We have opened a new page in the relations between the Chinese and American people." So-called "Ping-Pong diplomacy" underlay serious diplomatic negotiations between the two nations. Within two months, Henry Kissinger secretly visited China and set up Nixon's extraordinary trip to China in February-March of 1972. (At the same time a delegation of Chinese table tennis players toured the United States.)

The president's plane landed in the People's Republic on February 22, 1972. He remained there for nearly a week—the longest state visit ever made by a president to a foreign country. No other modern American president had visited China. American television cameras showed a smiling Nixon and his entourage on escorted trips to the Great Wall and the Imperial Palace. Images of official rice-liquor toasts and Nixon learning to eat with chopsticks signaled a true historic milestone. Over twenty years of hostility had ended. Although full diplomatic relations between these countries would have to wait for the Carter administration, Nixon's visit was undoubtedly the single key event in relations between the United States and the People's Republic of China.

This also proved to be true for relations between the Soviet Union and the United States. Russia, apprehensive about rapprochement between China and the U.S., maneuvered closer to America as well, just as Nixon and Kissinger had hoped. As he had with the Chinese, Kissinger made a secret visit to Moscow. Soviet President Leonid Brezhnev and Kissinger discussed improving relations between their respective countries. Late in May of 1972 Nixon himself traveled to Moscow and signed an arms control treaty with Brezhnev. The Strategic Arms Limitation

Treaty (SALT I) froze International Ballistic Missile (ICBMs) deployment. The two powers were limited to two hundred antiballistic missiles (ABMs), and two ABM systems each. The treaty limited the number of strategic missile launchers each nation could have for a five-year period. It did nothing, however, to slow down the buildup of the far more dangerous Multiple Independent Re-entry, or MIRVs. Clearly SALT I could not have prevented a future nuclear war. It was, however, a very real beginning to a thaw in the cold war. It also enhanced Richard Nixon's standing as a man of peace.

Détente progressed on other fronts as Nixon and Brezhnev concluded agreements on trade and technological cooperation. The Soviet government even agreed to purchase $750 million worth of grain from American farmers over three-years. Numerous athletic and cultural exchanges followed. The world appeared to have become a safer place. Nixon and Kissinger's diplomatic revolution was complete, albeit limited.

Other Foreign Initiatives

The Nixon-Kissinger diplomatic revolution did not apply to all other American overseas commitments. By 1971 while both Nixon and Kissinger viewed much of the rest of the world as a kind of footnote to Sino-Soviet-U.S. relations, they were certainly aware of the economic significance and potential in resources and markets elsewhere. Politically, they recognized a potential Third World challenge to American influence in organizations such as the United Nations. Therefore, they determined not to let affairs in Latin America, Africa, and the Middle East disrupt détente.

Foreign policy in Latin America was, consequently, very much a continuation of quite traditional cold war practices. Like Lyndon Johnson before him, Nixon continued to isolate Castro's Cuba and ensure that there were no additional communist regimes in the Western Hemisphere. Using tactics he had learned in his Eisenhower years, the president approved covert operations designed to topple the Marxist, but democratically elected, government of Salvador Allende in Chile. The CIA worked to disrupt the economy and, at the same time, fund opposition groups. The strategy worked. In three years the Chilean economy was in a shambles. In 1973 the military overthrew and killed Allende, replacing him with the oppressive military administration of General Augusto Pinochet. The United States quickly denied any role in the coup but just as quickly recognized the new government.

Nixon had also indicated that United States policy would retaliate against governments that nationalized U. S. owned companies, unless they were adequately compensated. The United States government might withhold aid or influence multilateral institutions, for example the World Bank, to veto aid. Policies such as these did little to enhance the image of America in the rest of the Western Hemisphere.

Policy in Africa also deviated little from the past. Like its predecessors, the Nixon administration sought to strengthen and broaden its relationships with white governments, including Rhodesia, South Africa, and the Portuguese-run Mozambique and Angola. In troubled Angola, for example, the CIA financially supported both the Portuguese and those fighting to gain their independence from Portugal. This sowed the seeds for the civil war that erupted in 1975, following Angolan independence. The United States, along with South Africa, covertly supported one faction in the conflict. The Soviet Union supported the other. Congress, maintaining that the United States should not be actively cooperating with racially oppressive governments like that of South Africa, cut all funding. Eventually, a leftist leaning administration assumed power in Angola causing the Nixon administration to rethink its policies. Thereafter the administration distanced itself from South Africa and Zimbabwe (the former Rhodesia). America established stronger economic ties and supplied arms to other black African nations.

Perhaps no place outside the Sino-Soviet-U.S. orbit was more volatile, and thus more likely to upset détente, than the oil rich Middle East. President Nixon, himself, had referred to this area as a "powder keg." The situation had worsened after the 1967 Six-Day War. Victorious Israel had agreed to cede most of the territory they occupied in return for peace and direct negotiations, but the Arab states

Arrival ceremony welcoming King Faisal of Saudi Arabia. May 27, 1971
Photo credit: Nixon Presidential Library

refused. The Palestine Liberation Organization, or PLO, organized in 1964, had pledged to destroy Israel and regain all the land lost by Arab Palestinians in successive conflicts. Their so-called "war of attrition," using terrorist tactics, exacerbated an already tense situation. Their terrorism included hit-and-run raids on Jewish settlements, hijacking jets, and even murdering Israeli athletes at the 1972 Olympics in Munich, Germany.

In this atmosphere of continued tension, war erupted again in October 1973. Syria and Egypt launched a surprise attack on the Jewish holy day of Yom Kippur. Moscow backed the Arab states and the United States, Israel. Israel was able, with some American assistance, to hold on and begin a counterattack. The Nixon administration forced its ally into accepting a cease-fire, rather than pursuing its advantage. The oil-rich Arab states sought to avenge Arab defeats by imposing an embargo of crude oil on the United States and her allies through the Arab influence within the Organization of Petroleum Exporting Countries (OPEC). The embargo, which lasted from October 1973 to March of 1974, resulted in a major energy crisis.

Henry Kissinger, concerned about the Soviet influence in militant Arab nations and the impact of ongoing oil shortages, spent the two years following October 1973 in so-called "shuttle diplomacy." He succeeded in negotiating two Israeli-Egyptian disengagement agreements and one between Israel and Syria. The Arabs also agreed to end the oil embargo. Of course, the larger objective of Kissinger's diplomacy was to firmly establish the United States as a major Middle East peace broker, while diminishing the Soviet Union's role. This policy proved successful for the most part. In general, the Nixon administration had helped to create a new, more pragmatic era in American foreign policy.

DOMESTIC POLICY

The president-elect was never truly interested in domestic policy. In 1968 Nixon reportedly said he "always thought this country could run itself domestically without a President." To his political intimates, he confessed domestic issues bored him. Yet, like all presidents before him and since him, Nixon wished to be portrayed favorably in history as a reformer. How tragic, then, that this paradoxical politician would eventually be destroyed on his least favorite of battle fields.

Perhaps this is not as surprising as it first appears. Despite his many years in national public life, the new president mistrusted government and was profoundly suspicious of all those he considered political insiders. Nixon despised the so-called liberal eastern establishment so intensely that he needed not just to discredit them but rather to obliterate them. Adlai Stevenson once characterized "Nixonland" as "the land of smash and grab and anything to win."

The ever embattled Nixon preferred not to work with either the Congress or his cabinet. Instead, he surrounded himself in an almost fortress-like way with a small cadre of personal aides accountable only to Richard Nixon. None held cabinet titles. Thus Henry Kissinger, national security advisor, not secretary of state William Rogers, had the major voice in key foreign policy decisions. In domestic affairs, the president consulted almost exclusively with H. R. "Bob" Haldeman and John Ehrlichman labeled by the White House press corps as the "Germans."

"Nixon's Nixon," Vice President Spiro Agnew, a former governor of Maryland, became the administration's hatchet man. His role was to be the president's mouthpiece on domestic issues. Perhaps the most divisive voice in the administration, Agnew took on all those segments of American society that the administration held responsible for national domestic woes. These included educators, so-called defeatists, the news media, student protesters, and liberal Supreme Court justices. Like a ferocious warrior with clever speech writers, he attacked with allitera-

Nixon with John Ehrlichman. February 12, 1973
Photo credit: Nixon Presidential Library

tive verbal assaults. To the great delight of political conservatives, he depicted the power structure as "sniveling," "hand-wringing," and "deserv[ing] the violent rebellion it encourages." Intellectuals were "an effete corps of impudent snobs." He characterized the media as "nattering nabobs of negativism" and television newscasters as "a tiny and closed fraternity of privileged men."

The new president faced a formidable obstacle in the Democratic control of Congress. Nixon was the first president since 1849 to face both Houses of Congress dominated by the opposition in his first two years in office. Despite this, Nixon began his first term as the thirty-sixth president of the United States on a positive note, promising to "bring us together." In his first inaugural address, the president stated, "We cannot learn from one another until we stop shouting at one another. . . ."

The New Federalism

This tone of moderation was as Eisenhower-like as it was politically pragmatic. Nixon called for a new kind of conservatism, that he described as a new federalism. The new federalism acknowledged and accepted the basic outlines of a welfare state. It did not propose a massive undoing of Lyndon Johnson's Great Society social programs but hoped to make federal programs much more accountable to state and local governments. In the Revenue Sharing Act federal tax funds would be released to states, counties, and cities to better meet local priorities. Federal controls and restrictions were reduced. Conservative Republicans objected to the plan because it did not significantly decrease federal spending. Nevertheless, in October of 1972, Congress passed the act. In its twelve-year existence the program dispersed some $83 billion to state and local governments. This represented the first major shift in political power, responsibility, and accountability from the national to the local level since the New Deal.

The administration also sought to confront the complex dilemma of the nation's welfare system by calling upon Daniel Patrick Moynihan, a Democrat who had helped Lyndon Johnson shape many of the Great Society programs. The Nixon administration proposed the Family Assistance Plan that Nixon hoped would revolutionize the welfare system and assure his place in history. Under this program, a family living in poverty would receive an annual guaranteed income of $1,600 plus $860 in food stamps. At the time, the payments to many welfare recipients were actually below this amount, as was the income of many of the working poor.

Democrats criticized the proposal, considering the benefits excessively low. Other liberals objected to its provision that required mothers of young children to accept substandard employment. Overwhelmingly, conservatives opposed the plan because of its costs and the potential of increasing the numbers receiving welfare. One Southerner worried that poor African Americans would be unwilling to work low paid jobs: "There's not going to be anybody left to roll those wheelbarrows and press these shirts." Interestingly Michael Harrington, whose book *The Other America* had virtually begun the 1960s war on poverty, referred to the plan as perhaps "the most radical idea since the New Deal."

Philosophically, Richard Nixon did not entirely oppose the basic concept of welfare. Yet he and Moynihan shared the view that the existing system destroyed personal initiative and esteem. Many others also held the system responsible for the destruction of families. Concerns about the welfare system grew out of a very real increase in the number of those on some kind of government assistance, primarily in Aid to Families with Dependent Children (AFDC). In 1970 the AFDC caseload was about 2.2 million families, a 30 per cent increase in that year alone. Overall, by 1972, about 6 per cent of all Americans were receiving welfare.

The proposal to revolutionize the welfare system went down to defeat on Congress in both 1969 and 1971. Nixon's commitment to the plan seemed to fluctuate, especially as the election approached. Of it he said, "I did not want to be in a losing fight with conservatives...in an election year." However, in the 1972 State-of-the-Union address, the president offered the nation "a New American Revolution." Components of the package included revenue sharing, health care and anti-pollution programs, a major reorganization of the executive branch of government, and, again, welfare reform. Administrative interest waned once more as the plan bogged down in the Democratic Congress. The revolution was aborted.

Despite the failure of welfare reform, the Nixon administration enhanced governmental regulatory powers in many areas. Much of what was done dismayed staunch conservatives, especially in the president's own Republican Party. Nixon expanded the Job Corps, supported federal subsidies in housing for low and middle income families, made food stamps more accessible, allowed for direct federal assistance to the handicapped and elderly, and increased Medicaid and Medicare benefits. In his first term, the Twenty-sixth Amendment was ratified, granting eighteen-year-olds the right to vote.

The Environment

Nixon's actions in vital environmental issues were, perhaps, most controversial. After the Cuyahoga River in Cleveland, Ohio caught fire in 1969 and a major oil spill occurred off the coast of Santa Barbara, California, Americans became increasingly alarmed about the despoliation of the environment and the wanton plundering of natural resources. Major cities like Los Angeles choked with smog. Lake Erie and other major bodies of water were declared dead. Many believed that action was essential.

Nixon sided with the nation's corporate leaders. They maintained that establishing environmental standards would increase the prices of American products and thereby decrease their world-wide competitiveness. But the Democratic-controlled Congress moved ahead and enacted numerous laws to protect the environment against the further abuses. These restricted the use of pesticides, protected endangered species, safeguarded coastal lands, and controlled strip-mining activities. Other legislation assured consumers of product safety. Regulations established maximum levels for the amount of pollutants released into the air and water.

Americans celebrated their first Earth Day on April 1, 1969. Demonstrations advocating strong government action led the ever pragmatic Nixon to understand that his administration needed to respond. He supported the National Environmental Act (1969), requiring federal agencies to prepare an analysis of the environmental impact of proposed projects, and the establishment of the Environmental Protection Agency (EPA) in 1970. Its task was to enforce all environmental regulations. In 1970, Congress also created the Occupational Safety and Health Administration (OSHA) to safeguard workers against work-related accidents and disease. Although he never really sympathized with the environmental movement, Nixon nevertheless signed the Clean Air Act in 1970, establishing strict national standards for air quality. He also agreed to the Clean Water Act and the Pesticide Control Act in 1972.

Civil Rights, the Supreme Court, and Other Americans

Richard Nixon's presidential victories in 1968 and then again in 1972 rested, in part, on his appeal to the so-called Silent Majority. These Americans, considered the heart of the Nixon-Agnew constituency, were fed up with policies they believed catered to minorities and societal malcontents through social experimentation. They complained about rising crime rates, domestic unrest, increasing drug use, oppressive taxation, pornography, and minority protests. By supporting them, Nixon and the Republican Party attempted to establish a strong political foundation with the middle class and its supposed values. These were the Americans who would prove to be the essence of a revitalized Republican Party for many decades to come.

The president appointed his friend, former law partner, and campaign manager, John Mitchell, as attorney general. An avowed conservative and outspoken proponent of law-and-order, Mitchell helped the administration pass a very tough new criminal justice law for the District of Columbia. He worked to isolate radical and student groups through infiltration and prosecution under a newly passed anti-riot law. Holding African Americans and other civil rights advocates responsible for much domestic disorder, Mitchell testified against the extension of the Voting Rights Act, due to expire in the summer of 1970.

The administration also moved against another favorite conservative target—the Supreme Court, as part of a larger plan, called the Southern Strategy. It was a bold attempt to establish a new Republican stronghold in the once solidly Democratic South. Nixon and Mitchell succeeded in many of their political objectives. The Johnson administration and the Democratic Congress had made sure massive racial desegregation of southern schools would finally occur when Richard Nixon took office. But Mitchell and Nixon decided to shift responsibility for forced integration to the federal courts. In the summer of 1969, the United States Justice Department asked for a federal judge to delay desegregation of some thirty-three school districts in Mississippi. When the Supreme Court responded by ruling against the Justice Department, white Southerners could not hold the president responsible. Instead, they focused their vitriol on the already despised Court. At the same time, Nixon would not appear responsible for thwarting the course of civil rights.

The president also had opportunities to reshape the Court into a much more conservative body. The first such occasion occurred when Nixon's old California Republican rival, Earl Warren, retired as Chief Justice. Perhaps no single individual was held more responsible for the perceived loosening of social restraints during the preceding decades than Earl Warren. In replacing him, Nixon could strike back on behalf of the Silent Majority and perhaps begin to undo the civil rights and civil liberties activism Warren had so ably defended.

Nixon's choice, who met with little opposition, was Warren Burger. He was a man of moderately conservative views and considerable federal court experience. Real opposition mounted when the next Court vacancy occurred. The Senate rejected both of Nixon's nominees, one for obstruction of civil rights and conflict of interest and another for being clearly unfit to serve on the Court. (One senator actually defended the latter by declaring that "there are lots of mediocre judges" and that mediocre people also deserved representation on the Court.) Despite the failures of these appointments, Nixon had enhanced himself and his party in the South.

Eventually, Harry Blackmun, a respected conservative from Minnesota (who ultimately proved to be not so conservative at all) filled the vacancy. Two more appointments followed: a distinguished jurist from Virginia, Lewis Powell, and the uncompromisingly conservative William Rehnquist of Arizona. Despite these changes, the Court upheld forced busing to advance integration, allowed the death penalty only under very circumscribed situations, and restricted the government's right to wiretap suspected subversives. In 1973, this supposedly more conservative Burger Court affirmed a woman's right to abortion in the landmark case of *Roe v. Wade*. The failure of Nixon's Court to do his bidding was a demonstration that the tides of history could not be turned back. It also showed that the decisions of justices, appointed for life, cannot be predicted or controlled.

Nixon vowed in his 1968 campaign to eliminate many of the programs of the Great Society as wasteful and symptomatic of an excessively strong centralized federal government. His administration eliminated the Office of Economic Opportunity and the Model Cities Program. A Nixon spokesperson proposed that the time had come "when the issue of race could benefit from a period of benign neglect," rather than governmental activism. To this end, the administration considerably reduced the number of federal investigations intended to determine how well communities in the nation were complying with school desegregation rulings. When the Court ruled in favor of busing students to integrate schools, Nixon used television to demand, unsuccessfully, that Congress enact legislation to prevent forced busing. And yet, in his characteristically contradictory way, in 1970 Nixon orchestrated the desegregation of school systems in seven defiant states (Alabama, Arkansas, Georgia, Louisiana, Mississippi, North Carolina and South Carolina). One not particularly sympathetic observer noted that the Nixon administration had "accomplished more to desegregate Southern school systems than had been done in the 16 previous years." He characterized Nixon's actions in this matter as "the outstanding domestic achievement of his administration."

The Economic Crisis

From his predecessor, Lyndon Johnson, the new president inherited not only the messy protracted

Vietnam war but an ever spiraling rate of inflation. Johnson's economic policy of "guns and butter" (the war and an ambitious program of social reform) had created a serious economic situation. Nixon faced an inflation rate of 5 percent and a budget deficit of $25 billion. As prices rose at an alarming rate, workers demanded higher wages. The result was an economic vicious cycle.

Because of his faith in the private sector's power to turn around the economy and the Republicans' distrust of government intervention, Nixon initially seemed unable to take direct action to stop the spiral. Instead, he focused on balancing the budget by reducing government expenditures. Simultaneously he strongly encouraged the Federal Reserve Board to maintain a tight money and high interest rate policy. His hoped this would lessen inflation.

The immediate consequence of what the president called his "game plan," was a deepening economic crisis, the first recession since 1958. The Dow-Jones average dropped about three hundred points; the sharpest drop in over thirty years. As businesses failed, the Democratic Party coined a new term—"Nixonomics." Unemployment reached 5.8 percent by 1970. This was a 2.5 percent increase in less than two years. The Gross National Product (GNP) also declined. But, even worse, inflation did not subside. Internationally, this translated into overpriced American goods coupled with a weaker dollar. For the first time in almost one hundred years, the United States had a deficit in the balance of trade of nearly three billion dollars.

Besieged by critics and facing a worsening economic downturn, the president at first held fast to his "game plan." But, by the summer of 1971, Nixon realized his hand was forced. "Stagflation" (economic stagnation and inflation), as it came to be known, did not let up. Nixon announced Phase I of a new economic policy. This included devaluing the dollar, ending the old international monetary system based on gold-dollar convertibility. A 10 percent surtax on all imported goods accompanied this action. Finally, Nixon imposed a ninety day freeze on all wages and prices.

Conservative Republican voices like those of Senator Barry Goldwater from Arizona and California governor Ronald Reagan decried this new direction of their party. Nonetheless, Phase I seemed to be somewhat successful. During the first part of 1972, industrial production rose, as did the stock market. On the eve of the 1972 election campaign, the economy was the healthiest it had been since Nixon assumed office, and it contributed to his landslide re-election.

Phase II began in the summer of 1973 with a new sixty day price freeze, but prices soared again as soon as the freeze was removed. This resumption of inflation was not necessarily the result of a failed Nixon economic policy. Higher prices had much more to do with major increases in the cost of imported oil. The United States purchased about 36 percent of its crude oil supply from OPEC nations who raised oil prices by almost 400 percent from 1970 to 1973. Beginning with the winter of 1973-74, OPEC nations imposed an oil embargo on the United States and the other Western nations who had allied themselves with Israel in the Yom Kippur War of 1973. Uncontrollable inflation was only one consequence of OPEC's action. The other was unprecedented-long lines of angry Americans waiting at their neighborhood filling stations in the following administrations.

THE FINAL CRISIS

Never forgetting his losses or even his narrow victories, like the 1968 election, Richard Nixon quickly moved against his perceived political enemies. This was part of his strategy to appeal to the Silent Majority and emphasize law and order. Indeed, to liberals, law and order became code words for Nixon's antipathy toward social progress and his innate distrust of the intellectual elite. It came, as well, to play a large role in his re-election campaign in 1972.

The president was more than willing to use all the powers at his disposal to oppose all those elements he either feared or distrusted. These included civil rights activists, minorities, anti-war protesters, the government bureaucracy, and various radical groups. To achieve his ends, Nixon ordered the all-powerful Internal Revenue Service to audit tax returns and the Small Business Administration to deny loans. The president directed the Central Intelligence Agency to investigate and compile dossiers on dissidents in direct violation of the law limiting its activities to the international area. He enlisted the Federal Bureau of Investigation in illegal wire tapping and bogus arrests, based on highly questionable charges. Playing on the nation's fears, Nixon cajoled the Justice Department to prosecute political dissenters in media enhanced trials.

But his profound distrust did not stop there. Beginning in the spring of 1969, shortly after the bombing of Cambodia, Nixon ordered the wiretapping of phones following press leaks concerning the new direction of the war. The taps included not only telephones of members of the press but also those of members of his National Security Council. The following year, Nixon convened a meeting in the White House of top officials to propose methods of dealing with "the leak problem." Suggestions included increased electronic surveillance, additional legal "mail coverage," and a relaxing of restrictions on illegal mail coverage; increased number of informants on college and university campuses across the country; removal of all restrictions on "surreptitious entries" (meaning break-ins and burglaries); and the creation of an International Group on Domestic Intelligence and Internal Security. FBI director, J. Edgar Hoover, blocked the plan, largely because he believed it would undercut his power.

In June of 1971, the *New York Times* began to publish the *Pentagon Papers*. Nixon determined that there would be no further leaks of secret government information. To that end, he established a special "plumbers" unit within the White House, headed by E. Howard Hunt, a long-time veteran of the CIA, and G. Gordon Liddy, a former FBI agent. They were specifically directed to discredit anyone who leaked information to the media. Their initial target was the man responsible for releasing the *Pentagon Papers*—Daniel Ellsberg. Failing to find the expected discrediting information, they pursued their search by breaking into the office of Ellsberg's psychiatrist and searching his files, to no avail.

White House aides prepared an "enemies list." It came to include several hundred Americans who were prominent in various social and political arenas. The list ranged from liberal movie stars like Paul Newman to university presidents. The type of mentality involved in creating the list was well characterized by a White House aide, who said, "Anyone who opposes us, we'll destroy. As a matter of fact, anyone who doesn't support us, we'll destroy."

Although he failed to secure a Republican majority in Congress in the 1970 election, Nixon acted aggressively to assure his re-election in 1972. He didn't want to simply win, he wanted to humble his opposition. To assure this outcome, the attorney general, John Mitchell, formed the Committee to Re-elect the President, ominously, or appropriately, best known as CREEP. Staffed with people who were experts in political "dirty tricks," CREEP both harassed potential Democratic contenders and spied on them. White House "plumber" Liddy eventually generated the elaborate scheme to spy on the Democrats. His plans included the bugging of their national headquarters in the Watergate complex that led to the arrest of all five men who had broken in.

The Election of 1972

As amazing as it is in retrospect, the break-in and subsequent arrests did not figure significantly in the 1972 election. Too many layers removed Nixon from the bungled burglary at this juncture of history. Nonetheless, he immediately took action to cover-up the evidence. Nixon soon learned many of his top aides had been involved in some way in the crime. Publicly he adamantly proclaimed that no one in his administration "was involved in this bizarre incident." Although the public believed him, Nixon took the initial steps down the path of self-destruction. He ordered staff members to pay off those arrested with CREEP hush money. He warned the CIA to keep the FBI out of the investigation on the bogus grounds that national security issues were at stake. Finally, Nixon told those around him to lie under oath should it prove necessary. The president privately insisted, "I don't give a [expletive deleted] what happens. I want you all to stonewall it, let them plead the Fifth Amendment, cover-up, or anything else...."

One of the most remarkable things regarding the Watergate break-in is that it was so totally unnecessary. Nixon's re-election in 1972 was assured.

Candidates that might have posed the most serious opposition to Nixon either destroyed themselves or were wrecked by "dirty tricks." An assassin shot the most serious spoiler of all, former Alabama governor George Wallace. As a result of his wounds, the paralyzed Wallace had to abandon the race. This removed an opponent who might have taken some right-wing support from Nixon.

The result was as expected. Nixon received almost 61 percent of the popular vote and captured the electoral college 520 to 17. His well-meaning opponent, Senator George McGovern of South Dakota, was soundly defeated. The "prairie populist," as some called McGovern, was a long-time and strong opponent of the war in Vietnam. Although he captured the peace movement advocates, many Americans regarded McGovern's promise to end U.S. involvement and reduce the defense budget by $30 billion with suspicion. Although they wanted the war to end, they did not want to abandon the nation's role in international affairs.

McGovern's other issue of his own personal integrity as compared to Richard Nixon's was weakened by public perceptions that he was a politically inept radical. The Democratic National Convention of 1972 reinforced this image. After the 1968 Chicago convention debacle, a new more liberal and activist element captured control of the party, a change McGovern had aided. In 1972, the old New Deal coalition of big city bosses, organized labor and its leaders, and southern politicians was gone. The youthful and non-traditional, particularly women and minority groups, replaced it. Images of McGovern as a supporter of busing and legalized marijuana helped doom his candidacy. One traditional labor leader who normally supported Democrats denounced McGovern as "the candidate of amnesty, acid, and appeasement."

The dove on George McGovern's campaign button symbolized his opposition to the war in Vietnam. He also became a symbol of other liberal causes, including women's rights.

Yet the 1972 Nixon landslide bears closer examination. Voters may well have been rejecting McGovern, rather than embracing Nixon. Outside of the presidency, the Republicans gained little elsewhere in the election: twelve seats in the House—while the Democrats gained two Senate seats. In addition, voters demonstrated a pronounced tendency toward ticket splitting. Only 55.7 percent of all those eligible to vote did so, a tendency toward public disinterest that has continued to the present time. This rather sad commentary on the electoral process was all the more serious as the most critical political crisis since the days of the Civil War was about to unravel.

Watergate and the Undoing of the Nixon Presidency

Despite the public's tendency to ignore the Watergate break-in and the initial success of the cover-up, *Washington Post* reporters, Bob Woodward and Carl Bernstein, kept the case on the front pages. They exposed the direct connection between CREEP, "dirty tricks," and the break-in.

In a 1973 trial, Hunt, Liddy, and the five burglars were convicted. The hard-nosed federal trial judge, John Sirica, refused to believe that the burglars had acted on their own and threatened them with long prison sentences. As a result, one of the conspirators admitted that he and the others had committed perjury during the trial and testified about the role of well-placed White House aides in the break-in.

A grand jury was convened to examine the charges. At the same time, the Senate created its own special investigating committee, chaired by the crafty Sam Ervin of North Carolina. White House counsel John Dean, who feared that he was the designated administration scapegoat, admitted there had been a cover-up and that Nixon had ordered it. In a vain attempt to distance himself from the growing scandal,

Nixon announced the firing of Dean and the resignations H.R. Haldeman and John Ehrlichman, both of whom were involved in the cover-up. Next, the president appeared on television and promised the American public there would be no "white wash." Nixon seemed to be true to his promise when he made Elliot Richardson his new attorney general. Richardson, in turn, named Archibald Cox of Harvard Law School as the special Watergate prosecutor. Both men were well known for their unquestioned integrity.

At the televised Senate hearings, John Dean in a demonstration of an almost photographic memory, revealed sensational details about "enemies" and cover-ups. His assertions seemed impossible to prove until another presidential aide almost casually revealed, "Well...yes, there's a recording system in the President's office." It seemed that there was an extensive cache of Oval Office tapes, recorded regularly since 1970. Both Ervin and Cox asked for any tapes discussing Watergate. Nixon refused to comply, citing Executive Privilege. When Cox attempted to secure the tapes through a court order in October 1973, the president ordered Richardson to fire Cox. Richardson resigned rather than comply. The deputy attorney general, who also rebuffed the president, met the same fate. Only the solicitor general, Robert Bork, would comply in what became known as the "Saturday Night Massacre." These actions outraged the public and the president's popularity rating fell to an unprecedented 27 percent.

Nixon's situation was dire. In the middle of the tape struggles, he had to confront reports that he spent $10 million of federal money on his own homes and paid federal income taxes of less than $1,000 in 1970 and 1971. (Later, it was revealed that Nixon owed a half million dollars in back taxes.) It certainly did not help that, at the same time, Vice President Spiro Agnew had to resign from his office. Agnew pleaded no contest to charges of income tax evasion and the acceptance of bribes while governor of Maryland. The president nominated the popular House minority leader, Gerald R. Ford of Michigan, to replace the dishonored and disgraced Agnew. Ford became the vice president under the provisions of the Twenty-fifth Amendment to the Constitution, ratified in the wake of the Kennedy assassination of 1963.

Cox was gone, but Nixon had an equally formidable opponent in his new special prosecutor, Leon Jaworski, a prominent Texas attorney. Jaworski eventually took Nixon to court to force surrender of the tapes. In the interval, the president released a laundered version of transcripts. While still not directly linking him with the cover-up, even these highly censored documents revealed Nixon at his worst. They contained large gaps of information and frequent references to "expletive deleted." The president exposed himself as narrow-minded and vengeful. Even the Republican newspaper, the *Chicago Tribune,* wrote of Nixon, "We have seen the private man and we are appalled."

In June 1974, the Supreme Court unanimously ruled the tapes had to be turned over to Judge Sirica. The decision stated that although there were "constitutional underpinnings" for executive privilege, such privilege "cannot prevail over the fundamental demands of due process of law in the fair administration of justice." The Court went on to declare that neither "the doctrine of the separation of powers nor the need for confidentiality of high-level communications...can sustain an absolute, unqualified presidential privilege of immunity from judicial process under all circumstances."

Shortly after the Court ordered Nixon to surrender the tapes, the House Judiciary Committee adopted its first article for the impeachment of Richard Nixon. After several painful days of testimony, the majority voted to impeach the president for obstruction of justice and presidential abuse of power. Hoping against hope that he might still be able to remain in office, Nixon went on television on August 5, 1974, to admit he had made "mistakes" by withholding relevant evidence. He surrendered three tapes that confirmed Dean's testimony and vividly demonstrated Nixon's role in the cover-up. This was, indeed, the "smoking gun." Even diehard Nixon supporters reluctantly favored impeachment. They did so because, as one expert wrote, here was abundant evidence of a "systematic obstruction of justice for more than two years....a weapon so redolent

On Aug. 8, 1974, facing expected impeachment over the Watergate cover-up scandal, President Richard Nixon went on nationwide television and announced his resignation, the first American president to do so. The next day he left office after an emotional farewell to members of his staff and cabinet. With him are wife Pat and daughter Tricia.

of powder, so smeared with prints that no defendant could hope for acquittal."

Watergate involved more than a break-in and its subsequent cover-up. It was the most serious abuse of presidential power in American history. In the twentieth century the presidency had become the central institution in the federal government, establishing the legislative agenda, creating the national budget, and even circumventing congressional power to declare war. Nixon had carried the "Imperial Presidency" to its most extreme. He refused to spend moneys appropriated by Congress, constantly invoked executive privilege to avoid questions about his decisions, and even attempted to create a colorfully uniformed "palace guard." But the fall-out from Watergate brought his bid for unbridled executive power to a crashing end. The American system of checks and balances did work, as the creators of our Constitution had envisioned.

Key Republican congressional leaders, led by respected conservative Senator Barry Goldwater, told Nixon that impeachment and conviction were inevitable. Finally, on August 8, 1974, Richard Nixon announced his resignation. The following morning, he bade a tearful and revealing farewell to his cabinet and staff. "Never get petty," he advised them, "always remember, others may hate you, but those who hate you don't win unless you hate them, and then you destroy yourself." This complex man, who had so abused presidential powers, fell because of his inability to practice his own advice.

THE INTERREGNUM YEARS: 1974-76 GERALD FORD

The surprising elevation of Gerald Ford to the vice presidency following the resignation of Spiro Agnew

Members of the White House staff watch from the balcony as Gerald Ford and his wife, Betty, escort resigning President Richard Nixon and his wife to a helicopter on the White House lawn.

in October of 1973 was surpassed by his ascendance to the White House only eleven months later. It was an unprecedented time and place for a man who had never been elected to national office. A major economic recession, energy shortages, and the final collapse of the South Vietnamese government all compounded the crisis of leadership that confronted him.

A long-time Congressman from western Michigan, Ford was a very different character than Richard Nixon. He was an amiable and well-liked man, personally conservative, and regarded as honest, trustworthy, and humble. Lyndon Johnson had once noted, cynically and unkindly, that Ford's problems resulted from having played football at the University of Michigan without a helmet! Well aware of his unique role under unique circumstances, as well as of his own personal limitations, he informed the American people they had "a Ford, not a Lincoln" as their president. "Our long national nightmare is over," the new president declared. For many Americans his more open temperament seemed a refreshing change from Nixon's arrogance, cynicism, and paranoia.

Ford's honeymoon with the nation, however, was short-lived. On September 8, 1974, he granted a full pardon to Nixon saying, "My conscience tells me that only I, as president, have the constitutional power to firmly shut and seal this book." Instead, angry Americans believed that Ford and Nixon had struck some kind of a political deal, despite the lack of evidence to support this charge. By pardoning Nixon, the new president unintentionally linked himself to the Watergate scandals. Ford did replace most of what was left of Nixon's White House staff but retained Henry Kissinger. In fact, Kissinger held two positions in the Ford years—National Security Advisor and Secretary of State. The public clearly demonstrated its discontent by overwhelming Democratic victories in the congressional elections of 1974.

If the pardoning of Nixon had been intended to heal the nation's wounds, so too was the September 16, 1974 proclamation offering clemency to approximately 28,000 Vietnam War era draft evaders and military deserters. A form of limited amnesty would be granted in return for a sworn oath of allegiance and performance of twenty-four months of alternative public service. As for those already convicted for draft evasion or desertion, the president created a nine member clemency board to review their cases. Although Ford's proclamation never used the controversial term "amnesty," it was a step toward what the president called the "reconciliation...and restoration of essential unity of Americans within which honest differences of opinion do not descend to angry discord and mutual problems are not polarized by excessive passion."

Domestic Policy

Although Ford prided himself on his good relations with both Houses of Congress, he had difficulties in working with a Congress controlled by Democrats. As a congressman, Ford had voted against virtually every Great Society initiative. In the White House, he vetoed a variety of social welfare, environmental, and public-interest bills—fifty-three vetoes in just over two years. He called bills to provide federal aid to education and federal laws to regulate strip-mining too expensive or inflationary. He also vetoed the 1974 "freedom of information" proposal, which would have granted American citizens greater access to government documents. To the great dismay of civil-rights supporters, Ford was an outspoken opponent of Court mandated school busing. Congress overrode many Ford vetoes.

President Ford announcing his pardon of Richard Nixon from the Oval Office. September 8, 1974. Photo credit: Gerald R. Ford Library

The satire of comedian Chevy Chase on the popular television program, *Saturday Night Live*, bolstered the public perception of President Ford as an inept bungler. The president's propensity to bump his head when disembarking from Air Force One and to hit spectators with golf balls reinforced this image. His handling of the economic situation did not inspire greater confidence. When Ford came to the White House, the inflation rate was already more than 10 percent and the unemployment rate was 7 percent, largely as the result of rising oil costs. Consumer prices rose 12 percent in 1974 and 11 percent more in 1975.

Ford, far less flexible than Nixon, responded to rising inflation in a much more traditional Republican fashion by tightening the money supply, reducing government spending, and raising interest rates. Ford also launched his voluntary "Whip Inflation Now" (WIN). American refusal to buy overly expensive goods and willingness to stop demanding higher wages would supposedly defeat inflation. The president announced the program at a national press conference with WIN buttons for the press corps to wear in their lapels. WIN proved to be totally inadequate in dealing with the economic crisis. The nation plunged into the most severe economic recession since the Second World War as unemployment rates reached 11 percent.

Although congressional insistence on tax cuts, greater benefits, and public works projects somewhat alleviated the problem, economic woes continued for the duration of the Ford presidency and then lingered into the Carter years. These weaknesses were part of a larger American crisis that manifested itself most dramatically as urban decay. For a "people of plenty," as historian David Potter had once characterized Americans, this was a difficult reality to comprehend. The hallmarks of the 1950s and early 1960s—steady growth rates of over 3 percent per year, relatively stable prices reflected in low inflation rate, and unemployment rates of only 4.5 percent a year—were long gone.

As early as the late 1950s, the postwar economic boom enjoyed by most Americans was winding down. The United States had helped rebuild the industrial infrastructure in Europe and Japan with the latest technology. Meanwhile, in the "Rust Belt" of Ohio, Michigan, and Pennsylvania, obsolete plants and outmoded production systems meant American industries were no longer competitive. Corporations failed to invest in outmoded plants, preferring short-term profits. Highly paid unionized workers, expecting lifetime employment, suddenly found that their jobs had permanently disappeared. The consequence of the combination of these factors was that the United States was outproduced at exactly the same time American markets were opening up to foreign imports. During the 1970s, Japanese production increased by some 7 percent, while U.S. productivity was on the decline. Fundamental shifts in the structure of the economy and manufacturing system further eroded American manufacturing capability. America's economic productivity had once been based on the manufacturing sector, particularly heavy industry such as railroads, steel, and, later, automobiles. By the 1950s, the economy was beginning to shift from the manufacturing to the service sector, based on high technology, especially computers and information.

Energy shortages added to these alterations. Americans were energy gluttons who consumed about one-third of the world's fuel supply, although only 6 percent of its population. The United States came to rely all too heavily on foreign oil that, by 1973, was one-third of all oil consumed. That is why the OPEC price increase and embargo, driving the price of a barrel of oil from $5 to $12 in about three months, had such a severe impact

The Johnson administration's escalation of the Vietnam conflict in 1965 made this situation worse. Combined with domestic spending for the Great Society programs and no tax increases, the war led to a growing national debt. Especially during the late 1970s, the American penchant for living beyond one's means greatly accelerated. Household and business borrowing increased more than three-fold. The great credit expansion helped drive up prices on everything. Although most Americans suffered as a result, the crisis was most visible in the nation's cities. One factor in the decline of American cities was the deterioration of their economic essence, manufacturing.

In the cities, working class people experienced increasing difficulties in finding jobs. At the very bottom were those minorities, African Americans and Hispanics, who lived in blighted inner cities. Their unemployment rate was often three times as high as that of the rest of the work force. These people formed a virtually permanent underclass.

In Youngstown, Ohio and Pittsburgh, Pennsylvania steel mills stood idle. In Detroit, Michigan the largest automobile manufacturer in the world, General Motors, laid off 6 percent of its domestic work force. Thousands of others were put on temporary leave. Chicago lost 326,000 manufacturing jobs between 1967 and 1987. New York City lost more than half a million. By late 1975, New York was near financial collapse. It was unable to meet its payroll and pay its bonds. President Ford let it be known that it would veto any federal bailout bill passed by Congress. A headline in a New York newspaper ruefully summarized his attitude: "Ford to City: Drop Dead." After Congress agreed to grant the city a loan, however, he backed off, and the city survived. Cleveland, Ohio was less fortunate as it became the first major American metropolis to default since the days of the Great Depression.

Foreign Policy Under Ford

A long-time supporter of the war in Vietnam, Gerald Ford had the misfortune of occupying the White House during the debacle of the final days of that conflict. In April 1975, as the network television cameras recorded the scene, the public watched the pathetic evacuees scramble for helicopters attempting to flee Saigon. Ford blamed Congress for the sorry spectacle.

Two weeks later he achieved a small victory of sorts. The communist regime in Cambodia captured an American cargo ship, the Mayagüez. Ford authorized a military rescue. Americans reacted favorably to this macho response, ignoring that 41 men died to free the ships' 39 crew members. One proud senator gloated, "It shows we've still got balls in this country."

The retention of Henry Kissinger signaled Ford's initial support of Nixon's détente policy with the Soviet Union and China. The new president met with Soviet leader, Leonid Brezhnev, in 1974 and made some advances towards further arms-limitations. This led to the Helsinki Accords the following year where the two superpowers and other European leaders accepted the existing post-World War II boundaries of Europe, including Soviet-dominated Eastern Europe. Both also agreed to a rather lengthy list of human rights and freedom to travel.

Election 1976

As the bicentennial year of American independence grew nearer, Ford decided he wanted to govern in his own right. Even though he had the advantage of incumbency, his record did not inspire enthusiasm. Furthermore, the Republican Party was badly divided. Opposition came from the well-organized right-wing, which supported the former California governor, Ronald Reagan. In primaries across the nation, Reagan attacked détente with the Soviet Union, lamenting the "collapse of the American will and the retreat of American power." But, in the end, the president weathered the assault and barely prevailed.

The Democrats were also divided in 1976. Massachusetts Senator Edward Kennedy, the brother of the late president, might well have been the strongest candidate, but the terrible 1969 incident on Chappaquiddock Island hovered over him. Kennedy was driving a car involved in an accident in which a young woman drowned and was never able to provide a satisfactory explanation of his actions. Since the Democrats seemed unable to find a suitable candidate with nationwide support, a most unlikely individual emerged, James Earl (Jimmy) Carter, Jr. This "born-again" Christian was a graduate of the U. S. Naval Academy who served in the nuclear submarine fleet. When he returned to Plains, Georgia, Carter entered his father's peanut business that he successfully rebuilt. His entire political career consisted of a one term stint in the Georgia Senate and one successful term as the Governor of Georgia. This total lack of national political experience, however, was exactly what the American public seemed to want after the imperial presidencies of Lyndon Johnson and Richard Nixon and the perceived ineptness of Gerald Ford.

Secretary of State Henry Kissinger, General Secretary Leonid Brezhnev, President Ford, and Foreign Minister Andrei Gromydo during the Helsinki Summit. August 2, 1975 Photo credit: Gerald R. Ford Library

Sensing that Americans wanted something very different, this intelligent and ambitious Georgian swept the Democratic primaries by offering himself as a political outsider. He argued that, "the vast majority of Americans are outsiders. We are not going to get changes by simply sifting around the same groups of insiders,...the same unkept promises." He emphasized the very things that post-Watergate weary Americans wanted to hear—honesty in government and traditional values. Appearing in campaign ads dressed in blue jeans, he introduced himself to the voters as Jimmy and promised them in his soft spoken southern accent that he would "never tell a lie to the American people."

Jimmy Carter was an excellent representative of the "new" South. This was a South that accepted racial integration. Carter once told a member of the powerful racist White Citizen's Council that rather than pay them the $5 membership fee, he would flush the money down the toilet. But he was equally well rooted in the old South of evangelical faith. Carter considered himself a man of principle, honesty, human decency, and family values.

Carter began the campaign against Ford with a whopping 33 point lead. Neither candidate, however, generated much enthusiasm from the electorate. Less than 54 percent of them turned out at the polls. Carter's early lead dwindled, but he held on to win a very narrow victory (49.98 percent of the popular vote and 297 electoral votes to 240 for Ford).

The 1976 election revealed significant trends in race and class. Remarkably, almost 90 percent of African Americans voted for Carter, the native Georgian. They represented his margin of victory in seven southern states and pivotal northern states like Ohio and Pennsylvania. Carter also carried the overwhelming majority of Mexican-American votes. In general, the new president appealed most strongly to the alienated and disaffected segments of society. On the other hand, Ford received most of his support from more affluent, white, better educated Americans, particularly suburbanites. Although native son, Carter, carried the South, the solid South was a phenomenon of the past. This once political monolith had become increasingly industrialized, urbanized, more heavily populated, diverse, and Republican. As the 1980 federal census would subsequently reveal, the new population center of the nation was now in the Sunbelt. The long time power base of the Democratic Party, in big labor, was gone as well. As the economic infrastructure of the country underwent massive changes, so too had the membership and power of America's unions. These changes were to have profound meaning collectively, not only for the Democratic Party, but for the nation as a whole.

THE "OUTSIDER" AS PRESIDENT

Avoiding the bullet-proof limousine used since the Kennedy assassination, Jimmy Carter, his wife Rosalynn, and their daughter, Amy, walked the 1.2 miles hand-in-hand from the Capitol to the White House. On that bitterly cold day of his inauguration, the new president wore an ordinary blue suit. Symbolically, he was rejecting so many of the trappings of the not too distant past. Even the politically savvy editor of the *Washington Post* felt moved, encouraged, and hopeful about the future. But good intentions and appearances were not enough. The complexity of the problems confronting the nation, combined with Carter's inexperience, and lack of direction or clear political philosophy, soon put his administration in trouble.

Although hard-working, decent, and very intelligent, Carter could also seem inflexible and suspicious of federal "insiders." His administration was a reflection of the man. The president selected well established and experienced Democrats for his cabinet. Those closest to him, however, were personal friends, known as the "Georgia Mafia," who had no more national experience than Carter did. At lower administrative levels, Carter appointed many liberal activists, Kennedy and McGovern supporters. Many of them were women and African Americans. The problem was activists, party insiders, and close friends were not likely to work well with one another. And they did not. Carter largely ignored the Democratic Congress, which was furious when it saw the first Carter budget. Carter eliminated projects dear to many congressmen without consultation. The ensuing budget battle established the pattern of the relationship between Carter and Congress. By the middle of 1977, most of the president's proposals were buried in the legislature.

Domestic Programs—Energy

The economy and energy costs were the most immediate problems confronting the new president on the domestic front. Of the two, energy took top priority with Jimmy Carter. He believed that excessively high energy costs caused the nation's economic woes, due to the simple fact that Americans were consuming far more energy than the nation was producing.

Calling the energy crisis the "moral equivalent of war," Carter appealed to the American public by urging them to lead more simple lives. Small individual reductions in energy consumption would yield large savings. To that end, the president proposed that more people use public transportation, wear sweaters, and lower their thermostats. He also introduced major energy legislation in the Congress, advocating increased domestic production along with conservation. The program included requiring energy savings in auto engineering, the creation of the cabinet Department of Energy, funding for the research and development of alternative fuels, and regulation and taxation to curtail excessive profit making in the energy industry.

The Department of Energy was operating by October 1977, but the other proposals were bogged down as lobbyists for oil, natural gas, and automobile industries besieged Congress. Eventually, Congress did pass legislation to allow for increases in the price of natural gas, encourage home energy conservation, and provide for increased automobile fuel efficiency. New increases in oil prices beginning in 1978, a result of serious oil shortages, finally led to funding for the development of alternative energy sources. Again, Americans waited in long lines at their nearby gas station.

Use of alternative energy sources was very controversial. Nuclear energy use fell under serious

President Jimmy Carter and Rosalynn Carter at the Inaugural Ball. January 20, 1977. Photo credit: Jimmy Carter Library

scrutiny after an almost catastrophic nuclear power plant accident at Three Mile Island in Pennsylvania. Nuclear power advocates had long argued that it was the energy source of the future. They maintained it was safe, cheap, clean, and abundant. The serious energy problems of the 1970s increased the emphasis on this alternative. Opponents argued that nuclear power was very likely dangerous to the environment and humans.

Their dire predictions seemed to be coming true when, on March 28, 1979, the power plant on Three Mile Island had a serious accident. A thousand citizens had to be evacuated from the area after the plant released a radioactive gas cloud. Although the experts prevented a meltdown, it took them more than two weeks to shut the plant down. President Carter continued to speak favorably about continuing the commitment to nuclear energy, but the disaster clearly complicated his energy problems. The incident seriously damaged the credibility of nuclear energy as an alternative energy source.

Domestic Programs—The Economy

Carter first tried to deal with the "stagflation" he inherited from the Ford and Nixon years by reducing unemployment. In his first year in office, he cut federal tax rates and initiated a public works program. National unemployment rates did fall to about 5 percent by the end of 1978. He met with no success in reducing inflation, however. Some of this failure was the result of the president's lack of leadership skills, especially his inability to work with Congress even though it was controlled by Democrats. For the most part, however, the problem of inflation was structural and beyond his control.

The United States was not yet prepared to compete in the emerging global economy. West Germany, Taiwan, Japan, and Korea all cut into American markets. The near bankruptcy of one of the big three automobile manufacturers, the Chrysler Corporation, reflected this most dramatically. In 1980, Congress agreed to save the company by granting it a $1.5 billion loan that the company eventually repaid.

The continuing rapid increases in energy prices set by OPEC helped cause rising inflation rates. During Carter's last two years as president, prices continued to rise at rates well in excess of 10 percent. Nothing seemed to work. Neither the appointment of conservatives to head the Federal Reserve Board and institute high interest rates nor the call for voluntary citizen restraint proved effective. By 1980, an election year, inflation rose more than 13 percent while interest rates climbed to an unprecedented 20 percent.

As the situation worsened in the summer of 1979, the president went on a retreat to Camp David, Maryland. For ten long days he reflected on the situation and returned to address the nation. In his bleak sermon he seemed to be blaming the American people for the nation's "crisis of confidence." Following what the press derisively called the "national malaise" speech, Carter asked for the resignations of some of his cabinet members. Neither of these actions solved the nation's problems—problems which more and more Americans were coming to believe were beyond the capabilities of the president. Carter's approval rating fell to 26 percent, lower than Richard Nixon's during the depths of the Watergate scandal. Overseas events at the same time undermined the public's confidence in Carter even further.

Foreign Policy

Foreign policy provided some of the greatest triumphs of the Carter administration, but it also helped cause his ultimate defeat. Just as the United States was struggling to find its place in the new global economy, there was a similar struggle to redefine its role in international affairs. The end of the war in Vietnam seriously diminished American prestige and position. Public opinion surveys revealed an increasing lack of support for foreign intervention. One expression of this disengagement was the passage of the War Powers Act of 1973. Revolutionary nationalist movements in other parts of the world, especially in Latin America and the Middle East, seemed to limit American ability to take charge of events.

Carter's expressed foreign policy objectives included: continued détente with both the Soviet Union and China; the elimination of nuclear weapons; the eradication of poverty in the Third World through social and economic development; and fostering human rights worldwide. Unfortunately, he was not always clear about how he planned to implement these goals. Furthermore, because Jimmy Carter lacked experience in foreign affairs, he relied very heavily on others. The problem was he chose two experienced foreign policy experts whose basic outlooks were considerably at odds with each other. His secretary of state, Cyrus Vance, and his national security advisor, Zbigniew Brzezinski, were often in conflict. Vance was an establishment man and Washington insider, who wanted to pursue social, economic, and human rights objectives. Brzezinski, a Polish refugee, from Communist dominated Eastern Europe, was an uncompromising Cold Warrior. He cared little about social and economic goals outside of Europe and the Soviet Union and possessed virtually no knowledge about or interest in the Third World. Jimmy Carter recognized the differences that these two men brought to the foreign policy of his administration but felt he could build the necessary bridges to bring them together. The consequence was a foreign policy that often seemed inconsistent.

At the outset, these problems were not apparent. Building on foundations established in preceding administrations, Carter achieved a number of foreign policy successes. The death of long-time dictator Mao Zedong in 1976 opened the door for further improvements in relations with China. Carter reestablished full formal diplomatic relations with China as of January 1, 1979, opening the door for further commercial and cultural exchanges. This completed U.S./China détente begun by Richard Nixon in 1972. A few months later, Carter also met with the clearly ill Soviet leader, Leonid Brezhnev, to complete the drafting of a SALT II arms limitation agreement to restrict missiles, bombers, and nuclear warheads.

His deeply-held moral principles were the foundation of Carter's approach to foreign affairs. He believed that the United States must foster human rights throughout the world. He spoke out against repression of dissidents and Jews in the Soviet Union and against apartheid in South Africa. The administration used economic sanctions, with some success, to pressure a number of countries, such as Argentina and Chile, to stop oppressing their citizens. Sometimes, however, pragmatic security considerations took precedence over the cause of human rights as in China and Iran.

Carter and Vance worked hard to negotiate two treaties to relinquish control of the Panama Canal to the government of Panama by 1999. Both men believed the United States would be acting in the best spirit of a good neighbor, fostering human rights, and improving America's strained relations with Latin America. Carter stood firm despite the 80 percent public disapproval and criticism from Ronald Reagan and other conservatives that this was another example of U. S. loss of nerve. After a bitter debate, the Senate approved the treaty with only one vote to spare.

Carter's greatest foreign policy victory occurred when he applied his moral authority to the troubled Middle East. Despite the shuttle diplomacy efforts of Henry Kissinger in the Nixon/Ford years, the state of war between Egypt and Israel had not ended. Kissinger, however, established the foundations for the United States to be the major power broker in the area. Surprising everyone, the President of Egypt, Anwar Sadat, announced in 1977 that he was traveling to Israel to negotiate directly with the Prime Minister of Israel, Menachem Begin. This was an amazingly courageous act. It raised the very real possibility that Egypt would become alienated from all the other Arab states. Not only did this happen, but in 1981 Islamic extremists would assassinate Sadat for his pragmatic and far-sighted vision.

Sensing a real opportunity in the wake of Sadat's visit to Israel, Carter invited both Begin and Sadat to join him at Camp David, Maryland in September 1978. After a thirteen day retreat, the three men emerged with a framework for future negotiations. Begin and Sadat agreed to a future peace treaty in which Israel would return the Sinai Peninsula, seized in the 1967 war, to Egypt. In return, Egypt would recognize Israel's right to exist. When talks broke down again, Carter flew to Cairo and Jerusalem to nail down the agreement. On March 26, 1979, Carter presided over a special White House ceremony for the signing of the first peace treaty between Israel and an Arab state. Later both Begin and Sadat received Nobel Peace prizes for their efforts. The peace settlement was far from perfect. It left many major issues unresolved, particularly those concerning Palestine refugees and the claims of Palestinians for nationhood. In addition, many Arabs, led by Syria, and the Palestinians condemned the treaty. Despite these limitations, hopes for a final peaceful settlement in one of the most volatile places in the world now appeared possible. This was Jimmy Carter's finest hour in office.

Shortly after this greatest success, however, the foreign policy of the Carter administration began to unravel. Carter's insistence on human rights already jeopardized détente. On this issue the Russians reacted with considerable outrage. It was at this time that Soviet repression against dissidents like nuclear physicist, human-rights advocate Andrei Sakharov was intensifying. There was also the issue of restricting the emigration of Soviet Jews.

Nowhere was the conflicted nature of the Vance vs. Brzezinski and Carter foreign policy more evident than in relation to the Soviet Union. Working quietly behind the scenes to reverse détente, Brzezinski persuaded Carter to undertake the construction of new high tech weapons—MX missiles to replace the Minutemen ICBMs and Trident submarines. Thus, whatever the fate of SALT II, a new arms race would be a certainty. The new SALT II agreement reached with the Soviets and signed by President Carter pleased very few people in the United States. Liberals thought the armament cuts were not deep enough, while conservatives thought too much had been given away. Conservative groups, many of whom were supporting presidential hopeful Ronald Reagan, demanded a massive arms buildup. Reagan claimed a "window of vulnerability" existed in the United States.

The president withdrew SALT II as it came up for a vote in the Senate in December 1979. The Soviets had invaded Afghanistan, a mountainous country on the southern border of the USSR, where a pro-Soviet government was in danger of collapsing in the face of Muslim opposition. Carter proclaimed that the invasion was "the gravest threat to peace since 1945." Apparently he interpreted it as a Soviet move toward the Indian Ocean and the Persian Gulf.

Jimmy Carter and Omar Torrijos signing the Panama Canal Treaty. June 16, 1978. Photo credit: Jimmy Carter Library

The president followed words with tough action by reinstituting the draft, banning the sale of high tech materials to the Soviets, and embargoing the export of grain to the Soviets. He followed this with a boycott of the 1980 Moscow Olympic Games.

These measures did not bring an end to the Russian invasion of Afghanistan, an invasion that resulted in a protracted guerrilla war. In time, that war proved as disastrous for the Soviet Union as Vietnam had been for the United States. They too learned a lesson on the limits of military power. For President Carter, Afghanistan meant the renewal of the cold war, the death of détente, and the ruin of much of his foreign policy.

If Jimmy Carter's finest hour had been his role in the settlement of the Middle Eastern conflict between Israel and Egypt, he was to suffer his greatest humiliation in the Middle East. It took place in Iran, an oil rich state that had once provided a barrier against Soviet influence in the area. That nation was ruled by the Shah of Iran, a loyal American ally who had been restored to power through CIA intervention in 1953 to thwart Marxist nationalists. The Shah repaid his allies by allowing the United States to install electronic listening equipment along the border his country shared with the Soviet Union. He bought huge stashes of the most sophisticated weapons available from the United States. The Shah's enormous purchases helped America deal with the balance-of-payments' crisis. Unlike other countries in the region, he continued to sell the United States oil during the 1973-74 embargo (although at inflated prices). But the Shah also ruled autocratically, using SAVAK, the brutal secret police, to suppress any dissent. Many Iranians blamed the United States for training the torturers.

Like other presidents before him, Carter mistakenly believed that the Shah was a popular leader. Beginning in the 1960s, the Shah had undertaken a massive modernization program intended to improve both social and economic conditions in his nation. Its consequence was widespread political and social unrest. The Shah had alienated every sector of his country, apart from his military and westernized middle and upper class citizens. The continuing oppression angered leftist intellectuals. At the other end of the social spectrum, reactionary Shiite Muslim ayatollahs (religious leaders) and mullahs (priests) indoctrinated the devout Iranian peasantry. They taught that the Shah was a blasphemous ruler who had contaminated Iran with Western values and sold out to the "Great Satan," the United States.

By the late 1970s the Shah's government teetered on the edge of disaster. The once mighty ruler vacillated between intensified terror and liberalization. In Washington, Carter waffled between standing fast with the Shah and preparing for a new Iranian government. Carter tried to do both.

After months of turmoil and uncertainty, the Shah left the country in January of 1979 for a "vacation." He never returned. Ayatollah Ruhollah Khomeini, the central figure of the Shiite Muslim resistance, returned from Paris where he was living in exile and established a repressive Islamic republic. Hundreds of the Shah's supporters were executed. Westernization in Iran not only ended, it was undone. More than anything, this new fundamentalist Islamic state asserted that the United States was the major source of evil in the world. Khomeini's hatred of the West was so intense that normal diplomatic relations were impossible.

The situation was so bad, few believed it could get worse. But matters deteriorated even more when the desperately ill Shah requested to come to the United States for cancer treatment. Distinguished Americans, like David Rockefeller, pressured the beleaguered president to grant the request. Well-placed Iranian officials warned Carter that to do so would result in reprisals against Americans. He decided that it would be morally wrong to deny the request to a long-time loyal friend who was dying. On November 4, 1979, an angry Iranian mob stormed the American embassy in Tehran and held the Americans inside captive.

Menachem Begin, Jimmy Carter, and Anwar Sadat during one of the Camp David Summit meetings. September 7, 1978. Photo credit: Jimmy Carter Library

Iran demanded the return of the Shah to stand trial, in exchange for the hostages. Fifty-three Americans remained in captivity for 444 days. Feeling personally responsible, Carter agonized over what he could do. As Carter obsessed over his powerlessness, so did the nation. Newspapers and television reported each day of the captivity, each one a further international humiliation. The television program, *Nightline*, began as a daily report on the continued plight of the hostages.

The crisis intensified the divisions between Vance and Brzezinski. Vance advocated negotiation. Brzezinski pushed for force, maintaining that international respect for the United States was far more important than a few lives. In April 1980, Carter agreed to a desperate hostage rescue attempt. It ended in failure. Eight crewmen lost their lives when their helicopters crashed and burned in the Iranian desert. Vance, who had always opposed the mission, resigned as Secretary of State. This embarrassing defeat, perhaps unfairly, reinforced the image of presidential incompetence.

An agreement to free the hostages could be reached only after the Shah's death in 1980 through the efforts of both the Algerians and Canadians. They were finally released on January 20, 1981, the day Carter left office. The entire episode revealed the real limitations of traditional foreign policy in dealing with terrorism and terrorist governments. This revelation of American impotence also crippled Jimmy Carter's chances for re-election in 1980.

THE CHANGING FACE OF AMERICA IN THE 70S

The failures in the administrations of Richard Nixon, Gerald Ford, and Jimmy Carter may have been affected by much larger issues confronting the United States. These included economic competition in a new global economy, establishing a place in the post Vietnam world, and coming to terms with significant internal changes. How would Americans adjust to these domestic transformations?

Demographic transitions produced a striking new reality. The 1980 federal census revealed more than half of all Americans now lived in either the South or the West. Population rates in the East and Midwest, in contrast, were stagnant. Northern cities were the greatest losers. The Sunbelt states of California, Florida, and Texas gained the most. Because corporate America re-located in these states, young professionals and skilled workers were compelled to follow. Thus, in the decade when New York City almost went bankrupt and lost close to a million residents, the hub of the nation's oil industry, Houston, Texas, grew by 26 percent. By 1980, Houston's population reached 1.5 million, making it the fifth largest city in the nation.

Another significant demographic change was that for the first time since 1940, the birth rate began its steady decline. In 1970, there were 18.4 births for every 1,000 people, but by 1975, the rate dipped below 15. (It had been 25.3 at the height of the baby boom in 1957.) While the birth rate decreased, life expectancy increased. Importantly, the poverty rate among the elderly decreased throughout the decade. As Americans lived longer, political priorities changed. Politicians had to pay more attention to this increasingly important interest group and its concerns about Medicare, Medicaid, and, Social Security. Unquestionably, it was a group destined to be more visible and even more important on into the twenty-first century.

As it had almost a century earlier, the character of immigration to the United States underwent very important changes in both character and volume. The once European flow of humanity changed to Asian and Latin American. More legal immigrants entered the land in the 1970s, some four million, than had since the era of immigration restriction. This figure says nothing about the many thousands of others who entered illegally. By the decade's end, the annual flow of humanity into the "land of opportunity" was over 700,000. Of these, only 10 percent were European in origin. It should be noted, however, that immigration, once 10 percent of the total population each decade, declined to less than 2 percent in the 1970s.

Life Styles of the 1970s

The traditional American family, the one that most school children of the 1950s read about in the el-

After 444 days the Iranian hostage crisis ended, but it destroyed Carter's chances for re-election.

ementary grades, became increasingly hard to find as the 1970s wore on. The family found in *Fun With Dick and Jane* was no longer the sole American norm. Many couples opted not to have children. Widespread use of the reliable and easy-to-use birth control pill made this choice possible. Although marriage remained the predominant choice, there were other socially accepted options. The fastest growing of these was "living together." By the mid 1980s, unmarried partners living together, and other non-traditional households, constituted 30 percent of all households in the United States. Not all the unwed couples were heterosexual. In urban areas particularly, greater acceptance of gay life-styles led to a substantial increase in homosexual households in the 1970s and 1980s. Even among traditional couples, there were substantial changes. The divorce rate doubled between 1960 and 1980. By the mid-1980s nearly one out of two first marriages ended in divorce. Popular television sitcoms such as *Kate and Allie* replaced *Father Knows Best* in reflecting this new reality.

A 1970s social stereotype, the young urban professional or "yuppie," embraced the new life styles most enthusiastically. Yuppies were the first generation of the baby boom to turn thirty. Many were affluent Americans who, as they became well established professionally, focused on the accumulation of wealth and possessions. Although they did not totally dismiss social issues—feminism and environmentalism, for example—they were primarily concerned with self.

One of their expressions of self concern was the quest for physical fitness. Whether it was skiing, playing tennis, working out at home or in clubs, or jogging, yuppies exercised with great determination. This concern about physical well-being and the environment led to the appeal of health foods, free of chemical additives and pesticide residues. Once they discovered that cigarette smoking was directly related to a host of respiratory problems, heart disease, and cancer, many gave up smoking.

The Yuppie generation also sought to find psychological fulfillment To that end, they became involved in consciousness-raising groups and transcendental meditation. Most often these searches were harmless, but sometimes they became cults like those of the Maharishi Mahesh Yogi or Sun Myung Moon. Sometimes self-improvement turned into selfishness, a type of "therapeutic sensibility." In his thought provoking book, *The Culture of Narcissism: American Life in An Age of Diminishing Expectations*, historian Christopher Lasch maintained, "People [of the 1970s] hunger not for personal salvation, let alone for the restoration of an earlier golden age, but for the feeling, the momentary illusion, of personal well-being, health, and psychic security." Another author simply characterized his contemporaries in the 1970s as the "Me Generation."

Women

Because women in the 1970s had fewer children (less than two by the middle of the decade), they also enjoyed fewer constraints in their life styles. Smaller families, for example, meant that more women were able to enter the job market. In 1950, only 21 percent of wives worked, but by 1980, the figure was over 50 percent. This female labor force included many women with school-age children, some of whom took on part-time, seasonal, or temporary work.

Many of the new working women were middle class. The growing service economy required sales, clerical, and office workers. Elementary schools, rapidly expanding to accommodate the baby boom, required more teachers. Others entered the professions, as many more women had been able to obtain college and university education. By 1979, more women were enrolled in college than men. Between 1971 and 1981, the percentage of lawyers and judges who were women grew from 4 percent to 14 percent; the proportion of doctors from 9 percent to 22 percent. In the first half of the 1970s, the proportion of female PhDs awarded just about doubled from 11 to 21 percent. Still, most working women were subjected to economic and job discrimination. At the close of the decade, a working woman made only 60 percent of a working man's wage. Many of these women had to work due to the ever increasing pressures brought on by stagflation and the decline of wages in terms of purchasing power. They tended to view paid labor as a family necessity, rather than fulfilling any personal inclination or individual goal.

Society sent mixed signals to these "new women." In 1972, President Nixon vetoed a bill to provide a nationwide network of day-care centers to assist working mothers. He attacked the "communal approach to child-rearing" and the "family weakening implications" of the legislation. One psychologist in 1972 discussed the "fear of success" demonstrated by 80 percent of the college women in her survey. They had internalized society's continuing view "that competition, success, competence, and intellectual achievement are basically inconsistent with femininity." The resulting "fear of looking aggressive" was a limiting factor in the work world.

The push for "sexual liberation" and the new emphasis on female sexuality also had diverse consequences. By 1970, surveys among college students showed a substantial rise in premarital sex, especially among women. Magazines, like *Cosmopolitan*, trumpeted the arrival of the independent "Single Girl" who was, above all, "available." Feminists noted that women's role as a "sexual object" seemed to have increased, rather than declined. Sexual competition for marriageable men became a lifelong obsession for many. One article in *Ms* magazine on the sexual revolution commented ruefully, "Women [have] been liberated only from the right to say 'no.'"

By the beginning of the 1970s, the movement for full equality for women had developed a wide-ranging agenda and ideology. Just like the civil rights movement, the women's movement divided into two distinct camps. The moderate faction advocated working to achieve equality through the passage of specific laws. The radical faction wanted to eliminate restrictive gender roles. Both factions, despite their differences, adamantly opposed "sexism." NOW, for example, advocated passage of the Equal Rights Amendment, the establishment of a nation-wide child-care system, enactment of equal opportunity legislation, and repeal of anti-abortion laws. One historian has noted that the more "revolutionary" radicals "were indeed a vital part of the feminist campaign, if only because they made more moderate demands seem reasonable and legitimate by comparison."

One key issue for the women's movement involved the Equal Rights Amendment. First proposed in 1923, it read, "Equality of rights under the law shall not be denied or abridged by the United States or by any state on account of sex." After years of neglect, NOW resuscitated the amendment. Finally, in 1972, Congress overwhelmingly passed the amendment, and twenty-eight states promptly ratified it. Thereafter, support waned. In 1979, Congress granted its supporters three more years for ratification to take place. The amendment process for the ERA ended in 1982, only three states short of the needed three-fourths. The long and turbulent struggle for passage had pitted women in the professions against those who feared the amendment would endanger protective legislation for non-professional women workers. Other, more conservative women, worried that the amendment would threaten traditional family roles, mandate unisex bathrooms, and require drafting women into the armed forces.

Another broader cause of dissension involved sensitive and private concerns: abortion, marriage, male/female relationships, and homosexuality. "Consciousness-raising" groups sought to make women aware of sexual oppression, including rape and abuse. Some argued that they encouraged "man-hating." "Radicalesbians" argued that "Heterosexual relations locked women into second-class status." But by far the most divisive of all issues emerged following the 7-to-2, 1973 Supreme Court decision of *Roe v. Wade*, protecting a woman's constitutional right to abortion. The majority opinion asserted that "the right to privacy" guaranteed women's freedom of choice, based on the due process clause of the Fourteenth Amendment. Because of the ruling, the number of women having legal abortions greatly increased. Anti-abortion sentiment also increased.

Various religious denominations joined with conservatives and established a "Right to Life" opposition designed to oppose abortion on both legal and moral grounds. The Right to Lifers prevailed on Congress to pass the Hyde Amendment in 1976, forbidding the use of federal Medicaid funds to pay for abortions. This was most damaging to indigent women across the country. Pro-choice factions tried to respond by helping to establish privately funded abortion clinics and agencies to protect all women's right to choose.

With the advent of "sexual liberation" organizations such as Planned Parenthood found an increasing need for their services, such as birth control. By the 1970s, sexual behavior patterns of women became more similar to those of men.

Despite setbacks, feminists had made progress. Many joined forces for a massive Strike for Equality on August 26, 1970. Significantly, the Strike marked the fiftieth anniversary of the ratification of the Nineteenth Amendment to the Constitution. Women's groups all across the country established abortion counseling clinics, shelters for battered women, rape crisis centers, and feminist book stores. In 1971, Gloria Steinem and other feminists began to publish *Ms*, the first national feminist magazine. Feminists succeeded in getting sexist stereotypes eliminated from many textbooks. Such all-male strongholds as the U. S. Military Academy and the great Ivy League institutions opened their doors to women. Colleges offered thousands of women's studies courses. The armed forces integrated women in 1979 (though in non-combat roles), just as they had integrated African Americans in the 1950s.

The Supreme Court issued a number of other important opinions related to sex discrimination.

In one, the Court determined that "job-related classifications, based on gender or race, were inherently suspect." In 1976, the Supreme Court decided that, to be constitutional, a policy that engaged in discrimination based on gender had to be "substantially related to an important government objective." Finally, Congress itself took action by passing the Equal Credit Opportunity Act in 1974. Recognizing the significant increase in the number of women in the work force, it allowed women the opportunity to secure bank loans and obtain credit cards on the same terms as men.

Despite these advances, gender discrimination remained, particularly in the workplace. Changing sexual mores led to a substantial increase in single, usually female headed, households. Often these households were African American or Hispanic and, just as often, they were very poor. Although feminists had achieved many successes, they realized that there was much that still needed to be done. By the late 1970s, however, opponents of feminism were uniting under a "pro-family" emblem, and the nation was shifting to a more conservative suspicion of social activism.

African Americans

Lyndon Johnson's vision of a Great Society had included an America in which "every human being had dignity and every worker has a job . . . education is blind to color and unemployment is unaware of race." Although his programs did not succeed in creating that ideal state, there was a great deal of progress by the end of the 1960s. During the 1960s the median income of black families rose 53 percent, and the proportion of those below the poverty line fell from 55 to 27 percent.

President Nixon denounced many of the Great Society programs as wasteful and eliminated some of them. Despite the position of the president, however, changes stemming from African-American protest as well as major federal programs and efforts of the last several decades could not be entirely undone. Significant social, as well as economic, gains had already been achieved and had become institutionalized within American society. Numerous barriers impeding economic opportunity and advancement were destroyed or seriously weakened. By 1980 there were over 2 million African Americans enrolled in institutions of higher education. Affirmative-action programs and more equitable educational opportunities meant that, by 1976, twice as many African Americans held white-collar occupations than in 1960.

There were a few different African-American worlds in America by the late 1970s. The upper class of business people and professionals enjoyed their affluence and resented the lack of acceptance they met with from upper-class white society. The middle class, key supporters of civil rights and integration, lived in "gilded ghettos" and struggled to differentiate themselves from the poor in the slums.

The African-American lower classes lived in ghettos from Harlem in New York to Watts in Los Angeles. These neighborhoods included an energetic culture of churches, lodges, lively music, and soul food. But they also were centers of overwhelming problems that America had not yet addressed. By 1986, 45 percent of all African-American children in the United States were born into impoverished female-headed households. Early in 1981, the median income for a lower-class African-American family was $12,674, a little over half of its white counterpart. Even in traditionally structured lower-class families, African-American males increasingly disappeared from the work force of the nation. Profound changes in the economic infrastructure of the United States led to their elimination. The new middle-class and working-class African Americans fled and established new communities or integrated formerly all-white suburbs. A number of the more affluent professionals even returned to the South to the bustling new cities of the Sunbelt.

As great as the advances were for those who departed, the tragedy for those they left behind was equally great. The reasonably steady and well-paid jobs were gone. The best that could be found for those who remained were low paying service occupations, such as a fast-food worker, hospital orderly, or janitor. A once diverse community had become a more uniform community—one populated by "single mothers on welfare, out-of-work men hustling on the streets, drugs, gangs." In one Chicago section, where churches, banks, and stores once flourished "a population of around sixty-six thousand...had exactly one bank, one super market, but . . . forty-eight state-lottery agents, fifty currency exchanges, and ninety-nine licensed liquor stores and bars."

An insidious problem began to invade the United States in the 1970s in the growing popularity of cocaine. Although it could be found in all places and all levels of society, its use was especially pervasive in the nation's urban ghettos. The passage of strict antidrug laws like the Comprehensive Abuse Drug Act of 1970 did little to ameliorate its deadly consequences in the country's inner cities.

Despite these problems and class divisions, African Americans were still united emotionally by race. The popularity of folk hero Muhammed Ali demonstrates these feelings. Like Jack Johnson, a black boxing champion of an earlier era, Ali flouted the rules of white society. After the Supreme Court reversed his conviction for draft evasion, he regained his title and continued his colorful taunts of his opponents. As an imposing, defiant, triumphant, and charitable black man, Ali represented the aspirations of many African Americans of all classes in the 1970s. As the years went on, he became an icon in the larger society as well.

Native Americans

Perhaps no people in America were more disadvantaged than Native Americans. In 1970, the life expectancy for Native Americans was nearly ten years lower than the national average and the infant mortality rate was twice as great. At least a half million American Indians lived in conditions of abject poverty, comparable to those in the poorest nations of the world. Their homes were often unsanitary, dilapidated, and, all too frequently, abandoned automobiles. Forty percent of all American Indians lived below the poverty level, and their unemployment rate was ten times the nation's average. Disease and alcoholism were rampant on the reservations and among Indians in American cities. Angered by policies of termination and assimilation and inspired by the social activism of other groups in the 1960s, the American Indian began to organize and strike back.

Many tribes began to take legal action against the U. S. government and numerous state governments to regain land, water, hunting, and fishing privileges guaranteed to them by treaty. In one such instance, the Passamaquoddies and the Penobscots of Maine sued in 1972 to recover 12.5 million acres of land they maintained had been seized illegally by the state. In 1980, the Indians settled for 300,000 acres of land and a $27 million tribal trust fund. Earlier, in 1971, various native peoples of Alaska prevailed when they were awarded forty million acres of land and a one billion dollar financial settlement for numerous long-standing claims.

Since they were a relatively small group compared to other minorities, Native Americans could not depend on political clout based on ability to mobilize votes. They had to gain the assistance of repentant whites to achieve any real social or political change. The civil rights movement had sensitized whites to Native American culture. Native Americans were portrayed in more sympathetic ways in films such as *Little Big Man*, on television programs, and even in antipollution commercials that portrayed an Indian's grief at the exploitation of the land. Best selling books such as Dee Brown's *Bury My Hear At Wounded Knee* (1970), criticized historic white mistreatment of Native Americans. *God is Red* (1973) by Vine Deloria, a Sioux, and many other works, celebrated Native American values. Many Native Americans opposed liberal suggestions for job training programs that would have assimilated them into the white economy. They preferred efforts to make reservations more self-sufficient.

The American Indian Movement (AIM), the best known of the Native American protest organizations, staged some of the most dramatic protests. In 1969, they seized Alcatraz Island in San Francisco Bay where they remained until mid-1971. In 1972, they led a demonstration called the "Trail of Broken Treaties," echoing the "Trail of Tears" their ancestors had been forced on over a century earlier. Marching to the nation's capital, the demonstrators captured the offices of the Bureau of Indian Affairs. Their most publicized demonstration occurred in 1973, when two hundred armed Indians took over Wounded Knee, South Dakota. For seventy-one days they occupied the town that had once been the site of the 1890 massacre of the Sioux by the U. S. army cavalry. Shots were fired, and an FBI agent was killed. Some older Native Americans opposed AIM radicalism.

Native Americans stepped up their efforts to re-establish control over their tribal resources and their culture. Richard Nixon demonstrated his sympathy by appointing Indians to important positions in the Bureau of Indian Affairs. He also expanded federal programs in support of Native Americans to encourage greater self-determination. In 1975, the Indian Self-Determination and Cultural Assistance Act took effect. This important legislation gave tribes authority over the various federal programs on their reservations. It also increased their control of reservation schools.

Renewed tribal life, more public awareness of the social and economic status of Native Americans, government willingness to honor treaties, and a new attitude by federal officials were all positive indications of a more promising life and future for the American Indian. These positives did not eliminate the very real problems, such as the high incidence of alcoholism, disease, and high unemployment rates among Native Americans that persisted as the decade ended.

Hispanics

The fastest growing minority group in the 1970s was a mixture of peoples lumped together as Hispanics. Their numbers increased from 9 million in 1970 to 26 million in 1995. This significant increase was due to two factors: immigration and high birth rates. Approximately 45 percent of immigrants to America after 1960 came from the Western Hemisphere. There were also millions of illegal immigrants. This was especially true of Mexicans who, since the middle of the 1960s, crossed over the border hoping to find better lives for themselves and their families. Despite the efforts of the United States to control and curtail this great influx, it continued. Best estimates are that, by the end of the 1970s, the population of Mexican Americans had increased by around 60 percent.

Even though there are many differences in history and customs among Hispanic people, they share some similarities in religion, language, and a fusion of Spanish and Native-American values. These newest of arrivals concentrated in specific places in the country. Thus, in the Southwestern states of Arizona, California, Colorado, New Mexico, and Texas one could travel for hours at a time and see and hear only indications of Mexican-American life and culture. Puerto Ricans and Cubans settled mainly in New York, New Jersey, and Florida.

Just like the other immigrants who had come before them, Hispanics hoped to improve their lot. What they found waiting for them was poverty and discrimination. Many endeavored to retain their native language and traditions, but the language barrier was also an obstacle to educational success. The lack of a good education limited employment to unskilled and semi-skilled occupations, especially in agriculture. Mexican Americans, the largest group, demonstrate this point. Their average educational attainment was under nine years in 1970. As a result, their average income was about 60 percent of that of the rest of the population.

Puerto Ricans, who are American citizens, moved back and forth to mainland America more easily. They tended to settle in urban ghettoes in the Northeast. They entered the cities just as job opportunities were moving to suburban areas. In addition, their inability to speak English, love of large families, and suspicion of bureaucracies hampered their attempts at economic improvement. Almost half had poverty-level incomes, and nearly 40 percent received some form of welfare assistance. By contrast, most of the earlier Cuban refugees from Castro's communist regime were middle class people with a strong entrepreneurial spirit. They tended to be more successful than other Hispanic groups. In 1980, however, the Mariel boatlift brought in 100,000 more Cubans, largely of working class origin. This group encountered more problems than the earlier immigrants.

Whatever its origins, a new social activism energized Hispanic Americans. Younger Mexican Americans adopted a new name for themselves—Chicano. "Chicano" implied a rejection of Anglo society and the more moderate accommodationist Mexican American. One Texas group formed a political party, *La Raza Unida*, in 1970, committed to community control of Mexican-American counties. Some Puerto Ricans turned to militant nationalism, demanding Puerto Rican independence. One group even "occupied" the Statue of Liberty in 1977 to publicize their demands.

There were also some political gains. In 1981, two major American cities elected Mexican-American mayors: Henry Cisneros in San Antonio and Federico Pena in Denver. Earlier, in 1971, two Mexican Americans were elected state governors: Raul Castro in Arizona and Jerry Apodaca in New Mexico.

Despite these accomplishments, in reality, Hispanics exercised only a small amount of political, economic, or social power. Meanwhile, more Hispanics were entering the United States from Central and South America and the Dominican Republic. Aside from sharing a language and religion, the greatest similarity among these people was poverty. For the nation's second largest minority group, the long struggle to make a place for themselves in the United States was still a formidable task that lay ahead.

Other Americans

Immigration from Asia also increased in the 1970s. Large numbers of people arrived from Korea, the Philippines, and China, as a result of more liberal immigration laws. The Vietnam War and its subsidiary conflicts throughout Indochina led to a wave of refugees, particularly after the fall of South Vietnam in 1975. In the 1970s most Asian Americans continued to respect traditional values of family loyalty and high achievement. Some Asian Americans, influenced by other militant groups, attempted to create a pan-Asian spirit and a yellow-power movement. The basic cultural differences among the various Asian groups proved too great to surmount and the movement generated little support. Nevertheless, Asian Americans seemed more concerned about equality and less willing to accept conformity than they ever had been before.

In the summer of 1969, New York City police raided a gay Greenwich village bar, the Stonewall Inn. Although such raids had long been commonplace in the United States, this time the bar patrons fought the police. This incident and the civil disobedience that followed led to an era of "gay pride." Gays and lesbians began to "come out of the closet" and join activist organizations demanding an end to discriminatory laws and customs. They achieved some success in decriminalizing sexual acts between consenting adults. Several states repealed anti-sodomy laws. In 1973, the American Psychiatric Association removed homosexuality from its list of mental illnesses. This was only the beginning of a long and continuous struggle.

Traditional white ethnic groups found all this new militancy very unsettling. Continued swings in the business cycle and decline in blue collar jobs increased their unease. Black power movements caused white ethnic expressions of community pride. Bumper stickers began to appear announcing, "Polish power" or "Slovak power," or "Irish power." The enormous popularity of the 1977 television serialization of Alex Haley's *Roots* and the 1978 presentation, *Holocaust*, led many whites as well as African Americans to search for their own origins. Ethnic studies programs spread.

These white ethnics, however, felt threatened when the federal government in the 1970s tried to enforce open housing laws, bus children to integrate schools, and impose racial quotas in business hiring and college admissions. White ethnic groups supported Allan Bakke when he sued the University of California for denying him admission to medical school as a result of reserving places for disadvantaged minorities. In a landmark 1978 decision, the Supreme Court ruled against rigid racial quotas. Demands for "law and order," which African Americans saw as code words for prejudice, appealed to traditional white ethnic groups. As a result of these growing social tensions, many of these white ethnics began to abandon their traditional attachment to the Democratic Party.

TURN TO THE RIGHT

Ethnic groups and yuppies were not the only Americans in the 1970s to attempt a search for a more meaningful existence. Whether it was in the Reverend Sun Myung Moon's Unification Church or the International Society for Krishna Consciousness, the decade was one of religious resurgence. The growth in evangelical Protestant sects like the Southern Baptists and Assemblies of God was particularly impressive. Despite a host of differences between them, these Protestant groups, led by such men as Jerry Falwell and his Moral Majority, shared a core of common beliefs. Among these was a belief that an individual could be "born-again" as a convert to faith; a commitment to a strict moral life ruled by individual piety; and a literal interpretation of the Bible as absolute truth.

Greatly troubled by more liberal attitudes toward divorce, abortion, homosexuality, pornography, the absence of prayer in public schools, and the lack of values in popular culture, they began to engage in political activities. Jerry Falwell, a highly successful radio and television evangelist, sought to use his Moral Majority to create a political base dedicated to "family values" and the American way of life.

But Evangelical Christians were not the only Americans who had moved to the right as the decade came to its end. The old liberal New Deal coalition was in disarray. Taking advantage of society's new mood, the Republicans began cutting into Democratic bulwarks like labor unions, the South, and white ethnic Americans. Furthermore, they had mastered newly developed organizational techniques like political action committees, vehicles for effective fund raising. They also created direct-mail lists and telephone banks. Through these devices, they raised millions of dollars and got voters to turn out for their candidates.

Evangelical Christians politically represented "the human disposition to preserve what we love and to oppose changes which threatened to disrupt accustomed life-patterns." Republican Party conservatives also incorporated "possessive conservatism," which included, in the words of one political scientist, "those who have the most to lose should society undergo rapid social and economic change." Historically, this basic "defense of property rights" has been the essence of what Americans have understood to mean conservative. Added to these in the 1970s was a new respectability for a "philosophical" conservatism that expressed a great reverence for the past.

"Neo-conservative" intellectuals totally disavowed social engineering programs like racial and gender quotas in hiring and school admissions, school busing to achieve racial integration, affirmative action, and the welfare state. They represented a significant defection from New Deal and Great Society activism. They established "think tanks" that reaffirmed their faith in capitalism and individual social mobility and claimed that they believed in equality of opportunity as opposed to government guarantees of equality of outcome. They maintained it was time Americans looked to see what was right rather than wrong about their country. One man more than any capitalized on and popularized the emotional appeal of conservatism. He was the former Governor of California, Ronald Reagan.

The Election of 1980

The problems of the Carter administration intensified as the election of 1980 drew closer. The energy crisis with its staggering increases in costs of oil led to ever rising prices. The continuing Iranian hostage crisis sapped the energies of the president and the nation. The discontent of white ethnics led to their disaffection with the Democrats. Americans, who had begun to turn inward in the decade of the 1970s, as the decade ended, turned increasingly to the right. They turned to tinseltown, to Hollywood, to Ronald Reagan, a candidate who seemed to offer different solutions.

Reagan brought together the various streams of conservative thought. To a nation traumatized by the Vietnam War and the hostage crisis, he promised to restore American "strength and pride." He criticized the supposed excesses of federal government activism and promised major tax cuts in accordance with tax revolts that were spreading across the nation. His personal attributes, magnified by television, included self-confidence, cheerfulness, and, despite his 69 years, the appearance of youthful vigor. He also possessed a unique ability to reduce complex issues to the most simple explanations. In television debates Reagan constantly reminded voters of the "misery index,"—a combination of the unemployment and inflation rate that hovered at 20 percent—and asked, "Are you better off now than you were four years ago?"

The American electorate answered Reagan's question by giving him 51 percent of the vote to Carter's 41 percent. (Seven percent voted for the independent candidacy of a moderate Republican congressman, John Anderson.) The election was hardly a ringing affirmation of support for Reagan. Only 52 percent of those eligible bothered to vote. One eighteen-year-old declared, "I didn't want to be responsible for electing either one." Many merely believed it was "time for a change." Carter left office forlorn and rejected by the American people. He later reestablished his reputation by launching the most notable career of any ex-president as a leader in promoting international peace and in humanitarian activities. In 2002 Carter was awarded the Nobel Peace Prize for his lifetime achievements in these areas. But, in 1981, few regretted his departure. America seemed ready to embrace a new vision of the future.

CONCLUSION

In the decade of the 1970s public faith and confidence in government continued to decline. The revelations in the *Pentagon Papers* about deceptions in the Vietnam War and the corruption and abuses of power shown by the Watergate scandal shook public trust to the core. Although Presidents Ford and Carter demonstrated personal morality, they both lacked the political skills to restore national confidence in government. Internationally, despite a better outlook in the Middle East and restoration of relations with China, the hostage crisis demonstrated to many Americans the decline of American power in the world. Changes in American society based on the ongoing struggle for equal rights continued. The government, however, appeared helpless in coping with major economic problems of lack of growth, unemployment combined with inflation, and a seeming inability to compete in the world economic markets. In the "Me Decade," many Americans also worried that the day of American political and economic power was ending.

Chronology

1968 Richard Nixon elected president

1969 Apollo 11 lands Americans on moon
Nixon begins withdrawal of U. S. troops from Vietnam; orders secret bombing of Cambodia
"Stonewall Riot" sets in motion gay liberation movement

1970 Pentagon Pagers published
Nixon implements wage-and-price freeze
"All in the Family" premieres on television, introducing sharp social commentary

1972 Nixon visits China and the Soviet Union
Congress approves Equal Rights Amendment
Salt I Treaty signed
Break-in discovered at Democratic National Committee headquarters in Watergate
Eleven Israeli athletes killed in terrorist attacks at Munich Summer Olympics
Nixon wins landslide re-election
Nixon orders "Christmas bombing" of North Vietnam

1973 Watergate burglars tried and convicted
Native Americans demonstrate at Wounded Knee
Senate special committee investigates Watergate; scandal widens
Roe v. Wade decision issued by Supreme Court
Vietnam ceasefire agreement signed;
America withdraws its troops
Yom Kippur War between Arabs and Israel leads to Arab oil embargo and energy crisis
Vice President Spiro Agnew resigns; Gerald Ford appointed vice president

1974 House institutes impeachment proceedings against Nixon
Nixon resigns; Ford becomes president
Ford pardons Nixon for any crimes committed in his presidency

1975 Government of South Vietnam falls to communists
Khmer Rouge seize power in Cambodia and begin systematic genocide

1976 Jimmy Carter elected president

1977 Carter pardons Vietnam draft resisters
Panama Canal treaty ratified

1978 Beginning of "stagflation"—high inflation and interest rates and slow growth
Supreme Court issues *Bakke* decision against "reverse" discrimination

1979 Egyptian-Israeli peace settlement, mediated by Carter, signed at White House
Serious nuclear power accident occurs at Three Mile Island plant in Pennsylvania
Carter restores full diplomatic relations with Communist China
Oil prices double
Soviets invade Afghanistan
Iranian militants seize American hostages at embassy in Teheran

1980 Hostage crisis troubles nation; attempt to rescue hostages fails
Ronald Reagan elected president

SUGGESTED READINGS

Stephen Ambrose, *Nixon: The Triumph of a Politician, 1962-1972* (1989).
William C. Berman, *America's Right Turn from Nixon to Bush* (1994).
James A. Bill, *The Eagle and the Lion: The Tragedy of American-Iranian Relations* (1988).
Peter G. Bourne, *Jimmy Carter: A Comprehensive Biography* (1997).
Fawn Brodie, *Richard Nixon: The Shaping of His Character* (1981).
Peter N. Carroll, *It Seemed Like Nothing Happened: The Tragedy and Promise of the 1970s* (1990).
William H. Chafe, *Women and Equality: Changing Patterns in American Culture* (1977).
Ronald Dewing, *Wounded Knee: The Meaning and Significance of the Second Incident* (1985).
P.J. Dolan and E. Quinn (eds.), *The Sense of the 70s* (1978).
Martin Duberman, *Stonewall* (1993).
John Dumbrell, *The Carter Presidency: A Reevaluation* (1995).
Marian Faux, *Roe v. Wade* (1988).
L.H. Gann and Peter J.Duignan, *The Hispanics in the United States: A History* (1987).
David Garrow, *Liberty and Sexuality: The Right to Privacy and the Making of Roe v. Wade* (1994).
Paul Gottfried, *The Conservative Movement* (1993).
John R. Greene, *The Limits of Power: The Nixon and Ford Administrations* (1992).
___, *The Presidency of Gerald R. Ford* (1995).
Susan M. Hartmann, *From Margin to Mainstream: Women and Politics Since 1960* (1989).
Joan Hoff, *Nixon Reconsidered* (1994).
Burton I. Kaufmann, *The Presidency of James Earl Carter, Jr.* (1993).
Stanley J. Kutler, *The Wars of Watergate* (1990).
Nicholas Lemann, *The Promised Land: The Great Black Migration and How it Changed America* (1991).
Stanley Lieberson and Mary Water, *From Many Strands: Ethnic and Racial Groups in Contemporary America* (1988).
Matt S. Meier and Feliciano Rivera, eds., *Mexican Americans/American Mexicans* (1993).
Herbert Parmet, *Richard Nixon and His America* (1989).
William B. Quandt, *Camp David* (1987).
David Reimers, *Still the Golden Door: The Third World Comes to America* (1985).
Rosalind Rosenberg, *Divided Lives: American Women in the 20th Century* (1992).
Barry Rubin, *Paved with Good Intentions: The American Experience and Iran* (1983).
Leigh W. Rutledge, *The Gay Decade: From Stonewall to the Present* (1992).
Robert Schulzinger, *Henry Kissinger: Doctor of Diplomacy* (1989).
Ronald Takaki, *Strangers from a Distant Shore: A History of Asian Americans* (1989).
___, *A Different Mirror: A History of Multicultural America* (1993).
Reed Ueda, *Postwar Immigrant America* (1994).
Winifred Wandersee, *On the Move: American Women in the 1970s* (1988).
Theodore H. White, *Breach of Faith* (1975).
Tom Wicker, *One of Us: Richard Nixon and the American Dream* (1991).
Garry Wills, *Nixon Agnostics* (1970).
___, *Under God: Religion and American Politics* (1990).
Bob Woodward and Carl Bernstein, *All the President's Men* (1974).
___, *The Final Days* (1976).

WALK

Chapter Twenty-four

THE RISE OF CONSERVATISM: Ronald Reagan to George H. W. Bush

Although credited with ideas and policies that ended several years of stagflation, in reality the Reagan presidency marked the beginning of one of the most protracted periods of income inequality in American history. The concentration of wealth in the hands of 1 percent of the American population (who by the end of the 1980s accounted for 37 percent of the nation's private wealth—up from 31 percent in 1983, an increase of almost 20 percent) and the general acquisitiveness among the nouveau riche of the 1980s was at times as shameless and as callous as the parvenu behavior of the Gilded Age. Indeed, the Reagan years witnessed the final demise of the cooperative, ethical individualism that had transformed and informed the American economy since the New Deal—the values that came to define the nation's capitalist culture through the 1960s. By the 1980s that liberal value system had been replaced completely by a resurrected conservative, egoistical, amoral, and grasping individualism that the Reagan administration embraced and propagated in words and enacted in policies. In more pedestrian terms, the theme of money, status, and power came to dominate popular culture in the 1980s. Reagan himself set the tone when he responded to a reporter's question asking him what was best about America. "What I want to see above all," Reagan replied, "is that this remains a country where someone can always get rich." Many thousands of Americans realized the Reagan credo, making fortunes in the expansive and lucrative sectors of the economy: stock trading, real estate, business services, defense contracting, and high-tech industries. A step below those who made millions in these various enterprises were the equally covetous, aspiring, college-educated, middle-management professionals among the baby-boomers, the "yuppies" of the upper middle class, who redefined bourgeois life in America with their conspicuous consumption of gourmet foods, designer clothes, expensive automobiles, and the purchasing of homes in "gentrified" neighborhoods. The emergence of this more conservative, competitive, and materialistic sector within the baby-boom generation reflected the values revolution noted above, which the Reagan years promoted as the essence of the American Dream.

As will be seen later in this chapter, the nation's economy expanded significantly during the 1980s; wealth was created and money was made but this wealth, as believed by Reagan and his supporters, did not "trickle down" into the pockets of ordinary working Americans. Indeed, real income for the majority of the American working class declined during the Reagan years. By the close of the Reagan-Bush era (1992), the number of poor people in America had reached 36.9 million, or 14.5 percent of the population. At the time of Reagan's inauguration in 1981, the government had classified about 26.1 million people as poor, 11.7 percent of the population. While the United States during the 1980s and early 1990s became home to more billionaires than ever before, ordinary working Americans were coupon clipping and heading to Wal-Mart looking for the cheapest possible necessities with which to feed, clothe, and clean their families. All across the nation's landscape dollar stores proliferated on land that once sustained factories. While millions of Americans struggled to barely make ends meet on minimum wage incomes, executive, managerial, and CEO salaries accelerated at rates that would have shocked even the original Robber Barons of the late nineteenth century.

In the following excerpt taken from David Shipler's in-depth study of income inequality, ***The Working Poor: Invisible in America****, the problem of crushing income inequality that exploded during the Reagan-Bush years and its debilitating physical and psychological impact on the lives of millions of ordinary American citizens is revealed. Equally significant, the passage also relates the increased feminization of poverty that began during the Reagan-Bush era. Despite a growing rate of labor force participation in the 1980s, the majority of women gainfully employed earned less than a living wage. Even if employed, women usually lost ground following a divorce, especially with the end of alimony payments in most instances. Moreover, the decade witnessed a dramatic increase in "dead-beat fathers"—men who defaulted on child-support payments within one year after separation and then disappearing for years and paying nothing until they were found and ordered by the courts to make restitution or spend time in jail. However, the financial damage caused by their abandonment to wives or girlfriends and their children had long taken its toll. Whereas divorced men enjoyed a sizable increase in their standard of living, divorced women suffered a significant decline in their quality of life. During the 1980s, the number of poor families headed by women increased nearly 70 percent.*

A sharp rise in teenage pregnancy reinforced this pattern. An increasingly high percentage of these mothers were too young to have gained sufficient education or skills to secure jobs that would pay them enough to support themselves and their children. Even with income supplements from AFDC and food stamps, it was (and is) impossible for these single mothers to keep their families above the poverty line. By 1992, female-headed households, comprising 13.7 million people, accounted for 37 percent of the poor. African American and Latino women and their children made up the overwhelming majority of those living in poverty and despair.

"Christie did a job that this labor-hungry economy could not do without. Every morning she drove her battered 1986 Volkswagen from her apartment in public housing to the YWCA child-care center in Akron, Ohio, where she spent the day watching over little children so their parents could go to work. For her services, she received a check for about $330 every two weeks. She could not afford to put her own children in the day-care center where she worked. Christie is a single mom with two young children."

"Like a great many Americans, Christie suffered from stress and high blood pressure. She had no bank account because she could not keep enough money long enough. Try as she might to shop carefully, she always fell behind on her bills and was peppered with late fees. Her low income entitled her to food stamps and rental subsidy, but whenever she got a pay raise, the government reduced the benefits and she felt punished for working. She was trapped on the treadmill of welfare reform, running her life according to the ever-changing rules of welfare retrenchment. Initially the new laws combined with the good economy to send welfare caseloads plummeting. As states were granted flexibility in administering time limits and work requirements, some created innovative consortiums of government, industry and charity to guide people into effective job training and employment. In the 1990s this approached was dubbed 'workfare' and represented a total rejection of the paternalistic liberal 'welfare state' idea of the 1960s. The problem with workfare was that most available jobs had three unhappy traits: they paid low wages, offered no benefits (especially health insurance) and led nowhere." "Many who do find jobs," concluded the Urban Institute "lose other supports designed to help them such as food stamps and health insurance, leaving them no better off—and sometimes worse off—than when they were not working."

"Christie considered herself such a case. In her wallet was a computerized credit card look-alike issued by the state of Ohio. On the second working day of every month she slipped the card into a special machine at Walgreens and entered her ID number. A credit of $135 was loaded onto her chip. This was the form in which her food stamps was now issued. This was her first portion of income each month. The money was to be used for food only and not for cooked food or pet food. Christie spent this $136 immediately at the grocery but only a few days later she had to find more money for food. In order to justify receipt of this assistance to the state, every three months Christie had to take a half-day off from work (losing money) and take all her pay stubs, utility bills, and rent receipts to a caseworker who applied a state-mandated formula to figure the food stamp allotment and her children's eligibility for health insurance. When Christie completed a training course and earned a raise of 10 cent per hour, her food stamps dropped by $10 per month."

"The arithmetic of Christie's life added up to tension and you had to look hard through her list of expenditures to find fun or luxury. On the fifth she received her weekly support check from Kevin (her boyfriend and father of her son). Christie received nothing from her daughter's father who was serving a long prison sentence for assault. The same day she put $5 worth of gas in her car and the next day spent $6 of her own money to take the daycare kids to the zoo. The eighth was payday and her entire $330 paycheck disappeared in a flash. First was a $3 charge to have the check cashed (a poor person's tax like many of the associated fees with money orders, very low bank accounts, etc.). Immediately, $172 went for rent, including a $10 late fee because she never had enough to pay by the first of the month. Then, because it was October and she had started a plan for Christmas, she paid $31.47 at a store for presents that she had put on layaway, another $10 for gas, $40 to buy shoes for her two kids, $5 for a pair of corduroy pants at a second hand shop, another $5 for a shirt, $10 for bell bottom pants, and $47 bi-weekly for car insurance. The $330 was gone. She had no insurance on her TV, clothes, furniture, or other household goods. Utilities and other bills got paid out of her second check toward the end of the month. Her phone usually cost about $43 per month, gas for the apartment $3, electricity $46 and prescriptions between $8 and $15. Her monthly car payment ran $150, medical insurance $72 and cable TV $43."

As Shipler wryly observed, "Recreation for Christie and Kevin centered on food and drink. Occasionally she budgeted $15 for a bottle of Paul Masson brandy."

A PERSPECTIVE ON RONALD REAGAN'S 1980 ELECTION VICTORY

To fully comprehend the Reagan presidency's impact on the nation, it is essential to first examine the political, sociocultural, and economic forces that had been gaining momentum since 1968 that helped Reagan and other conservatives to defeat liberal Democrats, and in the process establish the Republican Party as the majority party by the early 21st century. These various impulses eventually coalesced in the formation of a "New Right" movement, propelling Reagan and other conservatives to power in the 1980s. In many ways, Reagan can thank Richard Nixon for having first exploited for political advantage the various social and cultural issues around which Republicans of both Nixon's and Reagan's era rallied to gain power. For Nixon, Reagan, and even for George W. Bush and the "neoconservatives," the general conservative backlash and resurgence began in the watershed year 1968.

Historians must be careful when using such a loaded word as "watershed" to describe a given historical moment, for they run the risk of oversimplifying the complexity of the historical process. However, if the word is used to convey the idea of a "turning point" that marks the ideological end of one epoch and the constellation of forces that sustained it, and the beginning of a new ideological era and its attendant impulses, then the historian is on less hazardous ground when defining 1968 as a "watershed" year. Just as the reign of terror of Joseph McCarthy and his henchmen ruthlessly cozened Americans' fear of communism, bringing to a standstill the collective movements for social change that had evolved out of the New Deal/World War II experience, the political agonies of 1968 represented the climax of various reform initiatives that had been gaining strength since the late 1950s. However, by 1968 many activist groups, despite the Great Society's many progressive policies, had lost faith in the liberal ethos, believing the only way to bring about genuine change was to outright attack the established order, forcing through often violent intimidation, the traditional liberal elites who controlled the reform process to deliver the promised goods. As extremism increasingly took hold of the left, such action in turn engendered an equally passionate conservative reaction, which called seriously into question the possibility of successfully resolving social tensions through civilized discourse and established political processes.

Indeed, by 1968, many Americans believed the nation was on the verge of another civil war, only this time it would be a class conflict between the politicized and "liberalized" have-nots of the lower classes and the "vital-center" haves of the middle class. It was believed that the liberal agenda embodied in the programs of the Great Society, and of course the Vietnam War, were responsible for polarizing the two antagonistic, hostile groups—one in opposition to the "Establishment" for its betrayal of the liberal ethos and the other a reaction to liberalism's wanton empowerment of the previously disadvantaged. Trade unionists and big-city ethnic bosses felt completely alienated from the party, and for the first time, white working-class voters, the heart of Democratic Party strength, began to associate the Democrats with "special interests" like minorities and feminists. Getting Polish-Catholic workers in Gary, Indiana to sit at the same Democratic table with feminists opposed to the Catholic position on birth control and with black civil rights groups demanding union membership proved impossible. To blue-collar voters, "fairness" became code for quotas for dissident groups instead of equal access for all. Thus beginning in 1968, and climaxing with Reagan's victory in 1980, the Democrats' greatest losses were among white "middle Americans"—blue-collar workers, members of labor union families, Catholics, and high school graduates—people who, from the New Deal through the Kennedy-Johnson era, formed the core of Democratic Party strength and had sustained the party in power by voting "the straight" Democratic ticket.

However, by 1968, Americans of all classes, creeds, and colors had become disappointed, alienated, and embittered by the failure of liberalism, which since the New Deal had promised to all Americans unity, stability, and social progress. As a result of liberalism's failure, an aggressive, strident, and antagonistic conservatism eagerly awaited the opportunity to reestablish its hegemony by engaging in the politics of fear and polarization, which, with only a brief respite in the 1990s, has lasted to the writing of this chapter in 2007.

Ironically, the individual most responsible for creating the blueprint strategy for the conservative (and Republican) resurgence was Kevin Phillips, who since 1968, has transformed himself into one of the Bush administration's and the New Right's most vituperative critics. However, in 1968, one would have been hard pressed to find a more zealous, venal, and shrewd reactionary than Phillips. In his manifesto, *The Emergence of a Republican Majority,* Phillips deftly outlined what would become for the next 30 years the fundamental Republican strategy for winning elections at both the national and state levels. Phillips correctly contended that the majority of white middle-class Americans had grown weary of New Deal liberalism. Indeed, in many parts of the country, but particularly in the working class, ethnic, Catholic neighborhoods of northern industrial cities (i.e., Pittsburg, Chicago, Detroit, and Cleveland to name but a few), the white South, and in the growing suburbs of the Sun Belt states, residents of those communities had come to despise liberalism, for they believed the ethos responsible for unleashing upon the land a brand of radicalism bent on the destruction of the traditional middle-class values and mores they cherished. These "silent" or "forgotten" Americans, as Richard Nixon called them, shared a common revulsion against militant minority groups, student activists, and arrogant intellectuals, all of whom along with a Northeastern liberal media elite had come to dominate the Democratic Party.

Phillips believed (as did Nixon and other aspiring Republicans of the era) that if the Republican Party focused its message of patriotism, law and order, and rugged individualism on these particular groups living in the Sun Belt—the states of the old South or former Confederacy, including Texas, California, New Mexico, Oklahoma, Arizona, and Colorado—they would not only win in 1968 but for years to come, for they would have successfully and dramatically changed the nation's political demographics, shattering in the process the Democratic Party's close to 100 years of Southern hegemony. The "Solid South" would become Republican and with such a base help carry the party to successive electoral victories, especially at the national level. Phillips' assertion proved prescient; today, all but California are Republican "red,' with the South firmly under Republican control.

Why such concerted effort on the Sun Belt states? The answer was (and is) relatively simple: the region since 1945 has become a magnet for both the American people and modern industry. It has become the natural home for political and cultural conservatism as well as the center of a revitalized, aggressive, and doctrinaire evangelical Protestantism. By the time of Reagan's election, it was clear that the majority of "Sun Belters" had remained traditional in racial attitudes and still suspicious of Northeast elitism. In the thirty years after the war, these states' populations more than doubled. Cities like Phoenix, Arizona, sky-rocketed in population from 65,000 to 755,000, and Houston from 385,000 to 1.4 million. The Sun Belt also became a haven for the new high-tech industries of aerospace, plastics, chemicals, electronics, and ultimately computers. Scientists, engineers, and other tech specialists flocked to the new industrial research "parks" in North Carolina, Florida, Texas, and especially to California, which by the end of the 1970s became synonymous with the computer industry. Indeed, the Santa Clara valley of the central coast region of northern California, an area once encompassed by fruit orchards and farms, was renamed "Silicon Valley," for as *Fortune Magazine* noted the 25-mile stretch from Santa Clara to south San Jose boasted "the densest concentration of innovative industry that exists anywhere in the world."

Moreover, these states provided Nixon and future Republicans with the ideal constituency for their strident calls for "law and order." Their attacks on the Supreme Court for its excessive liberalism resonated well with Sun Belters, as did their extolling and applauding Westerners and Southerners for their devotion to the traditional values of hard work, patriotism, and family. By zeroing in on cultural values and the emerging power of the religious right, Republicans began shifting the axis of American politics away from one that focused on horizontal issues such as income, class, and economic need toward one that centered on vertical issues such as religiosity, anti-elitism, and law and order. In short, the New Right mobilized voters around volatile social issues and middle American outrage at the excesses of the 1960s, which such individuals perceived as a concentrated assault on the most basic values and institutions of society—the family, the church, patriotism, and sexual morality.

Although the New Right had its origin in traditional conservatism, notably anticommunism, the movement accelerated in popularity by exploiting the anger among increasing numbers of white middle-class Americans against policies recently introduced to the national agenda: busing, affirmative action, feminism, abortion (the 1973 *Roe v. Wade* decision), school prayer, and new attitudes of "permissiveness" toward pornography and sexual freedom. By the late 1970s, the Republicans grasped the anger and hostility among traditional Democrats toward these issues and seized the opportunity to exploit such outrage for political gain. In effect, by 1980, the Republican Party, through its New Right supporters, claimed to be speaking for the "average American" while accusing and labeling the Democrats as the voice of special interests.

For New Righters the 1970s represented the beginning of the culture wars, with conservatives rushing to defend the ramparts against the liberal assault on the private domain of the family and other cherished values and traditional morality. The New Righters devoted countless hours and money opposing the Equal Rights Amendment, defending the "right to life" of fetuses, and seeking to ban homosexuals from teaching in the public schools. Phyllis Schlafly's 50,000-member reactionary Eagle Forum inundated legislators with mail insisting that the ERA sanctioned homosexual marriages, unisex toilets, the drafting of women in military service, and the destruction of the traditional family (patriarchal authority). Many New Right conservatives were convinced that a conspiracy existed, spearheaded by liberal Democrats and their special interest allies, such as gays and lesbians, to destroy, as one New Righter declared, "everything that is good and moral here in America." This excerpt from a leader from a New Right group to all its members best illustrates the confluence of these issues and the fear mongering engaged by the New Right in order to rally support for their various causes.

> I am rushing you this letter because the children in your neighborhood are in danger. How would you feel if tomorrow your child was taught by a practicing homosexual? Was bused twenty to thirty miles away to school every morning? Was forced to attend classes in a school where all religion is banned? If you think this could never happen, you are in for a shock!

Interestingly, the millions of Americans supporting these "anti" campaigns remained "liberal" when it came to economic issues. New Righters thus redefined the term "liberal" to encompass any group or individual who challenged their notions relative to what was right and moral when it came to parenting, sex, prayer, family discipline, and authority. They were ready to engage in righteous battle the supposed liberal conspiracy to subvert and destroy the values taught in the home and the "new morality" of individual excess and license.

Ronald Reagan and the "Moral Majority"

Bolstering the New Right revolt was the remarkable growth of a revitalized, strident, and doctrinaire evangelical Christianity, which by the end of the 1970s declared the support of more than 50 million Americans that cut across all Protestant denominations. Exploiting this resurgence of "born again" Christians for their own personal agendas were fundamentalist "tele-evangelicals" such as Jerry Falwell and Pat Robertson, and a host of others, who through weekly talk shows, either on television or the radio, like the "700 Club" or the PTL (Praise the Lord), reached millions of Americans. Falwell's "Old Time Gospel Hour" was broadcast on 225 television stations and 300 radio stations. From his base of operations in Lynchburg, Virginia, Falwell galvanized his followers into the Moral Majority movement to "fight the pornography, obscenity, vulgarity and profanity that under the guise of sex education and 'values clarification' literally pervades the literature of the public schools." Robertson urged his listeners to condemn the "humanistic/atheistic/hedonistic influence on American government. We have enough votes to run the country," Robertson, declared, "and when the people say 'we've had enough,' we're going to take over."

Most disturbing, leaders like Falwell and Robertson made it clear that politics had become religion and religion had become politics. In other words, the sanctity of the separation of church and state had no relevancy in these individuals' frame of reference. In their view, America had become a Sodom, rife with all manner of vice, corruption, and licentiousness. It was the Evangelical Right's duty to God and country to cleanse the nation of such sin, and thus in sermons and literature, they declared a holy war against abortion, the ERA, homosexuality, and for the restoration of school prayer. Falwell, who became the most dominant, visible, outspoken, and richest spokesmen for the Evangelical Right, declared that "We're going to single out those people in government who are against what we consider to be the Bible, moralist position." Leaders like Falwell expected the faithful come election time to vote according to prescribed fundamentalist criteria, which meant for candidates who were "pro-family" (code for pro-life, for the restoration of school prayer, and for a homophobic proscription of gays) and who were strong "anticommunists," which became the euphemism for hardcore conservatives who opposed the welfare state and who supported an aggressive policy against the "Godless" Soviet Union.

The New Right also perfected the concept of direct mail, which became their most important vehicle for translating diffuse concern over social issues into direct political action. This approach was the brainchild of the Texas conservative Richard Viguerie, who idolized such reactionary figures as Joseph McCarthy and Douglas MacArthur. Prompting Viguerie to develop this medium was the 1974 finance reform law that limited the amount of money any individual could contribute to a political campaign. Instead of seeing this restriction as a handicap to the conservative impulse, Viguerie and his supporters saw the situation as a massive opportunity to mobilize grass-roots support for right-wing causes. Naturally Viguerie also

Nancy Reagan looks at her husband, Ronald Reagan, as he takes the oath of office as 40th President of the U. S. January 20, 1981. Photo credit: Reagan Presidential Library

saw direct mail as a means to personal wealth, which occurred by 1980, when his firm RAVCO reported an annual income in the millions of dollars. Serving virtually all the single issue causes of the New Right, direct mail threatened to revolutionize 1970s politics.

Perhaps what made this approach so effective in garnering support was the personal nature of each letter sent. Not only were recipients' individual names on the letterhead but the requests for money or support were also intimate as well. One letter from right-wing congressman Philip Crane, for example, asked more than 80,000 citizens to join his *personal advisory* committee, as well as to make a financial donation. Direct mail, Viguerie announced boldly, "Allows a lot of conservatives to by-pass the liberal media and go directly into the homes of the conservatives in this country. . . There really is a silent majority in this country, and the New Right now has learned how to identify them and communicate with them."

Motivating most direct mail opportunists was of course voter mobilization for conservative causes. "Our purpose," one New Righter declared, is "to organize discontent." Most direct mail letters were purposely strident, seeking to anger or scare voters by exploiting their fears and prejudices on certain issues. "The shriller you are," another fundraiser declared, the easier it was to recruit supporters. "That's the nature of our beast." Thus, one anti-abortion mailing called on voters to "stop the baby killers. These anti-life baby killers are already organizing, working and raising money to re-elect pro-abortionists like

George McGovern. Abortion means killing a living baby, a tiny human being with a beating heart and little fingers . . . killing a baby boy or girl with burning deadly chemicals or a powerful machine that sucks and tears the little infant from its mother's womb." Frequently accompanied by graphic pictures, such literature almost inevitably evoked a response of some sort, and usually it came in the form of a donation for the cause.

While critics decried the New Right's approach of direct mail for fund raising as a "rape of the public," and an effort by "quasi-political entrepreneurs to discover commercial opportunities by mechanizing discontent," the recruitment efforts paid off. By sharing mailing lists and repeatedly bombarding people with their pleas for support and money, New Right direct mail operations reached approximately 10 percent of the total population at the end of the 1970s, striking fear in the hearts of liberals, whether politicians or lay leaders, who found themselves on a New Right "enemies list."

The final component of the conservative revival was the proliferation and legitimization of reactionary intellectuals through the establishing of right-wing think tanks on an academic par with their liberal counterparts. Since World War II, liberals had dominated public policy and thus the national agenda and debate on critical issues through studies from the Brookings Institution, the Ford Foundation, and the Rockefeller Foundation. Although the founders of the latter two institutes were hardly liberals, overtime, especially during the 1930s, both think tanks became liberal bastions. However, by the late 1970s, conservative think tanks had emerged, such as The Heritage Foundation, funded by millions of dollars from archconservative Joseph Coors (of Coors Brewery) that threatened liberal ascendancy in this particular, vital arena of national discourse. For the first time in American history conservatism generated an "intellectual" class and a place for them to gather to "issue papers" and treatises that would steer public policy away from the liberal ethos thus breaking liberalism's monopoly on such academic enterprises. Indeed, the Heritage Foundation promulgated most of the task force ideas of the Reagan administration.

Another of such brain trusts was the American Enterprise Institute, committed to conservative positions on both domestic and foreign policy. Such groups seized the cultural initiative, mobilizing a powerful arsenal in defense of the family, traditional white middle-class values, and a shrill, often bellicose, anticommunist foreign policy. They were aided by yet another, yet still nascent conservative manifestation, "neo-conservatism," expressed in such media instruments as *Commentary* magazine and *The Public Interest.* Interestingly, most of the early "neo-cons" were former liberals, and many were respected academics, politicians, and career foreign service diplomats and bureaucrats. For a variety of reasons, but mainly over foreign policy issues, these former liberals abandoned the Democratic Party in the years after 1968 and sought a new ideological conservative "middle" ground between the far right and far left. Their years of experience and intellectual/academic credentials proved to be a great boon to the New Right, for their presence gave the conservative cause an intellectual credibility and panache that American conservatism had always lacked. Although as alienated by and thus hostile to the liberal excesses of affirmative action and busing, the early neo-cons were not nearly as strident on these issues as the New Right had hoped. However, the New Right welcomed the neo-cons' militant anticommunism. The neo-cons authority and reputation ensured that conservative ideas would receive respect and attention and that the New Right would not be dismissed as a lunatic fringe, nor would its presence be ephemeral as was the case for the majority of earlier conservative movements.

With all these ingredients in place, by the late 1970s, the New Right had become one of the most visible and powerful political forces in American history. Through the Conservative Caucus, a sort of national directory headed by Richard Viguerie and Howard Phillips, the New Right sought to coordinate the activities, agenda, and direction of the conservative movement. The interlocking directorate of the Conservative Caucus wove together in one monolithic reactionary enterprise virtually every conservative organization from the National Right to Work Committee to the National Right to Life

Committee, to the Committee for the Survival of a Free Congress, and, most recently in 2004, the Swift Boat Veterans for the Truth, which helped defeat John Kerry in that year's presidential election. With the full-fledged endorsement of the Conservative Caucus, the Swift Vote Veterans for the Truth unleashed a vicious propaganda barrage, asserting that Kerry's Vietnam War record and service was a farce while painting Kerry with the brush of cowardice and betrayal. If there was a supposed conspiracy to change the nation's socio-cultural and political orientation, it was not emanating from the left as the New Right proclaimed, but rather from the New Right as reflected in their agenda and propaganda with their shrill, unrelenting, and vicious attacks on liberalism and its proponents.

By 1980 the New Right had embraced the candidacy of Ronald Reagan for president. They also claimed direct responsibility since 1976 (via their use of such tactics outlined above) for the defeat of such liberal giants as Gaylord Nelson in Wisconsin, Birch Bayh in Indiana, John Culver in Iowa, Frank Church in Idaho, and George McGovern in South Dakota. "We aim to take control of the culture," one New Right leader declared, and the election results—Reagan's victory and the defeat of such liberal lions as those noted above—seemed to suggest that the aim had been accomplished. Indeed, many pundits as well as Democrats, such as Massachusetts moderate Senator Paul Tsongas, interpreted Reagan's victory and the defeat of men like Bayh, Church, and McGovern as a right-wing sweep, and that according to Tsongas, "Basically the New Deal died yesterday [November 4, 1980]." If Reagan could exploit popular impressions of a conservative mandate, there was at least a possibility that he could transform appearance into reality. Perhaps most important, would Reagan and his New Right and neo-con supporters be able to resolve the cultural and social conflicts that besieged the nation? By 1980, in varying degrees, Americans of all creeds, colors, and classes had become a disassociated, frustrated, jaded, and suspicious people. Problems were huge, demanding a response as creative and imaginative as any that had been called for in the past. Despite Reagan's resounding victory, there was little evidence that America's political leaders were ready to provide solutions, or even, perhaps, to ask the right questions.

THE REAGAN YEARS

Since his days as a Hollywood movie actor, Ronald Reagan gained as much acclaim as a raconteur as his presence on the silver screen. Indeed, Reagan's story-telling abilities prolonged an entertainment career that should have ended long before it did. By the 1950s and the advent of television, Reagan's engaging and homey personality made him into one of television's most popular prime-time hosts. Thanks to his television career, Reagan also became one of the most sought after public and promotional speakers, telling huge audiences why they should buy a particular product or support a certain cause. One of Reagan's favorite yarns and one that reveals the essence of Reagan's personality and perception of life in America was the one about two young brothers, one of whom was an inveterate pessimist, the other an incurable optimist. Their parents tried to remedy their respective outlooks by giving them very different presents on gift-giving holidays such as Christmas and their birthdays. Despite such largesse, the pessimist cried in the corner, certain all the toys he had been given would break. The optimist, carefully examining a pile of horse manure, plunged happily into the dung, digging furiously and exclaiming confidently that, "I just know there's a pony in here somewhere."

The optimist's comment reflected the buoyancy, confidence, and frequent naiveté, simplicity, and imperviousness that came to define the Reagan presidency. Throughout his tenure Reagan was like the optimist. As he had during his campaign, he repeatedly rejected the notion that the country was at the abyss, about to enter an era of limits and declension. Reagan refused to accept such notions, endlessly telling Americans that they possessed all the right stuff to not only resurrect the nation from its alleged malaise but to take the United States to unimaginable new heights of domestic prosperity and international respect and presence. In the Reagan frame of reference, the United States was still John Winthrop's "city upon a hill," an exceptional, liberty-loving nation whose democratic principles and institutions still destined the country to world leadership. Reagan believed unequivocally that Americans were God's chosen people, and thus if they did not rise to their calling, if they did not fulfill their righteous, God-ordained endowment to spread democracy and American ideals about the world, they would not only disappoint God but humankind as well. In his inaugural address, he exhorted Americans to "believe in ourselves and to believe in our capacity to perform great deeds, to believe we can still resolve the problems which now confront us. Why shouldn't we believe that? We are Americans."

That Reagan sincerely embraced such tenets was obvious to everyone who knew him or heard him speak. Reagan possessed a simple, pure, impregnable vision that dissenting voices or contradictory facts could not penetrate, let alone alter. The country was in trouble, but contrary to the naysayers and other pessimists, the problems were not insurmountable. Indeed, as Reagan told Americans, all that was required was for "a new sheriff to ride into town" to clean up the mess—to rescue America, restore confidence, and sweep away all the doubters and skeptics who insisted on talking about problems rather than solutions.

Reagan's faith in the capacity of Americans to transcend all problems and emerge triumphant in every encounter, whether at home or abroad, knew no bounds. Reagan's media-savvy aides and advisors ensured such a message came across loud and clear to the American people. As one of Reagan's top "spin-doctors," Michael Deaver, later proclaimed, "We kept apple-pie and the flag going the whole time." In 1984, Deaver and others made "Its Morning Again in America" the central theme of Reagan's feel-good campaign for reelection. Then, as always, they carefully managed his public appearances, providing television reporters with a "line-of-the-day" sound bite, a trite yet catchy and encapsulating, always optimistic phrase for use in the evening news. Presented this way, Reagan struck opponents as little more than a pitchman for the conservative agenda—a national master of ceremonies or appealing mouthpiece for the New Right yet personally disconnected from reality and the events around him. As will be seen, such criticism proved to be more accurate than not, especially during his second term.

Nonetheless, some of the goals Reagan advanced, such as winning the Cold War, bolstering traditional values, and propagating the American dream of upward social mobility, resonated well with millions of voters. As noted in the introduction of this chapter, Reagan represented the triumph of New Right conservatism, and thus when he blamed liberals for being soft on communism or "permissive" about developments at home, such superficial and inflammatory rhetoric found a receptive audience among millions of citizens. As will be seen, Reagan's domestic agenda focused on using the commanding power of the presidency to dismantle the New Deal/Great Society legacy, obliterating what was left of the welfare state. Interestingly, Reagan's obsession with destroying the liberal ethos contradicted his supposed worship and desire to emulate FDR, his only real political hero. Thus, while paying lip service to his mentor, Reagan lambasted the Great Society, denounced environmentalists, condemned welfare recipients as too "lazy" to get a job, and labeled the Soviet Union an "evil empire." Reagan not only made acting on these pronouncements his *raison d'etre*, but to a degree that astonished both opponents and supporters succeeded in getting his way on many issues as well.

As will be seen, despite Reagan's refusal to often accept reality or even to entertain the possibility that his vision for curing the nation's ills was seriously shortsighted, if not flawed, Reagan left one of the most enduring personal legacies of any twentieth-century president. Indeed, as FDR and his New Deal informed the 1930s, the Reagan credo characterized the 1980s. Two qualities imbued the essence of the Reagan canon: the overwhelming tendency, if not blindness, with which he believed in a few fundamental ideas and the extraordinary skill to communicate those beliefs to the American people. In the Reagan frame of reference, liberalism—big government and the welfare state—were responsible for most of the nation's problems. Thus, such an onus needed to be lifted from the American people's backs. However, the military was good, the sole exception to the evil of government, and thus warranted unlimited support. Relative to foreign policy and reflecting a 1950s Cold War mentality reminiscent of John Foster Dulles, the Reagan creed advocated a dangerous "heating up" of tensions and rivalries with the Soviet Union because the purpose of American foreign policy was to fight and defeat communism wherever and whenever it appeared (hence the need for a strong military). Such notions as "détente" or "peaceful co-existence" with the Soviet Union were ideas or policies Ronald Reagan could not embrace. To Reagan, the Soviet Union personified evil, the United States naturally good. Thus, it was incumbent upon the United States in the service of all humanity to extirpate from the world such a menace. On the domestic scene, slashing taxes would accomplish the dual goals of making America rich and abolishing deficits. These ideas became a religious catechism, articles of faith upon which Reagan grounded his presidency. Reagan's devotion to such simple axioms was so immutable that he became impervious to all argument, evidence, experience, or reality to the contrary of what he so fervently believed. Precisely because such ideas were matters of faith, Reagan's advocacy of them was powerful, persuasive, and inspiring.

Despite his passionate devotion and articulation of his "truths," Reagan, we know now, was one of the nation's most detached executives, relying on a handful of loyal supporters to implement his vision. From the very beginning of the Reagan presidency, his closest advisors knew he would be disengaged from the daily development of policies and programs. They knew their man was a "delegator." Reagan simply had no interest and little intellectual capacity for the details of the decision-making process. Thus, few insiders were surprised when he made such statements that ICBM's could be called back after launching or that U.S. submarines did not carry nuclear missiles. Although columnists such as David Broder commented sarcastically that "when someone approaches Reagan bearing information, he flees as if from a leper's touch," Reagan apologists dismissed such criticism, declaring that unlike past presidents such as Jimmy Carter who became mired in the supposed "minutiae" of his office, Reagan did not, allowing him more time to develop his "vision."

As a result of not getting "bogged down" by details, Reagan looked perpetually fresh, buoyant, and ebullient, and in this aspect of his presidency, he indeed reflected his hero, FDR, who too seemed remarkably spry and positive. Regimenting Reagan's daily routine was his wife, Nancy, and his closest aides. Their objective was not only to ensure Reagan's "freshness" but to conserve as well his energies for the limited tasks he *had* to carry out. His wife and aides so circumscribed his day that what few responsibilities he had to perform could be completed as efficiently as possible. Their goal was to keep Reagan "sharp" enough to present the "big" decisions and policies of his administration to Congress and the public in a sufficiently clear manner. Such a controlled system required as little detailed involvement by Reagan as possible. The key to such an approach was the quality of people the president called on to implement his vision. In addition to his wife, three other individuals were responsible for running the Reagan White House and implementing the Reagan agenda, such as it was: Edwin Meese, Michael Deaver, and James Baker. These men formed a powerful insider troika; in effect they ran the government. Not even Sherman Adams and John Foster Dulles of the Eisenhower administration had such White House preeminence and control of the executive schedule and initiatives. They sat at the Cabinet table with the president, a fact that bothered many Cabinet members sense of hierarchical protocol; Meese, not the president, defined the Cabinet's agenda and moderated its discussions; and no one, not even the National Security Advisor, had direct access to the president without their approval. In theory good advisors can make such a system work, but whatever success can be accomplished depends on an executive willing and able to ask the searching questions essential to prevent the inherent dangers in the process from bringing down the administration. As will be seen, it was only a matter of time before the flaws of such an insulated and detached approach to governing would adversely affect the Reagan presidency. As Martin Anderson, the Reagan White House economic advisor, noted, "if any of his personal staff chooses to abuse his or her position, and deliberately withholds key information or misleads him, Reagan is helpless and disaster can strike."

Anderson described perfectly the fundamental cause of the Iran-Contra debacle, which resulted largely from Reagan's detached and dependent approach to governing the country.

For the moment, however, such dangers seemed only real to embittered Democrats still reeling from Reagan's landslide victory. What mattered was not the new president's executive style, his personal policies, or his excoriation of big government; rather it was Reagan's passionate call for Americans to support the simple verities of his credo. If they did, he promised he would resurrect the nation from whatever doldrums it may have fallen; that America would once more stand tall, and no one, anywhere, would ever again think about challenging the strongest power on earth.

Domestic Policy Agendas

No sooner did Reagan enter the Oval Office than he began to make good his campaign promise to dismantle the remnants of the Great Society, cut taxes, and stimulate the expansion of the military-industrial complex. With a rapidity of legislative success not seen since the halcyon days of LBJ or FDR, Reagan proceeded to perform radical surgery on the nation's economy and welfare system. In 1981, Congress agreed to cut more than $25 billion from welfare programs (with hundreds of billions more planned for future years), while slashing taxes over five years by $750 billion. Perhaps more important and ominous for the future was Reagan's securing of congressional approval to increase over a five-year period defense spending to the staggering amount of $1.2 trillion. With such a mandate, Reagan appeared to be fulfilling his pledge that during his watch the United States would not only reestablish itself as the greatest superpower but that never again would the United States be subject to humiliation at the hands of the Soviet Union.

It was in the eradication of liberal social philosophy, programs, and regulations that one sees Reagan as the embodiment of the New Right agenda, for Reagan relished this particular role more than any other, embracing his charge with the greatest vigor and enthusiasm. Not even winning congressional approval for a massive build-up of the nation's military satisfied him more. Why such elation in ending liberalism? The answer was simple: to Reagan, all of the country's socioeconomic ills since the late 1960s resulted from the continued expansion of the federal government and the welfare state. Thus, if the federal government's presence in the daily life of the nation was minimized and if all but the most essential social welfare programs or "entitlements" (i.e., social security) could be eliminated, then all would be right again in America, for the private sector would once again be responsible for the nation's well-being, as it was in the halcyon days of supposed economic growth and prosperity, the 1920s, which in Reagan's mind was the way things should be during the 1980s. No doubt Reagan embraced wholeheartedly Calvin Coolidge's adage that "the business of America is business."

However, as the economist Lester Thurow observed at the time, "The American problem is not returning to some golden age of economic growth (there was no such golden age), but recognizing that we have an economic structure that has never in its entire history performed as well as Japan and Germany have performed since World War II. We are now the ones who must copy and adapt policies and innovations that have been successful elsewhere. To retreat into our mythical past is to guarantee our days of economic glory are over." Naturally, Reagan would never countenance such an assertion, for in his view, Thurow's contention reflected the pessimism and naysaying of liberals and other "doubting Thomas'" and "Debbie downers" who talked only about nagging dilemmas, limits rather than possibilities, problems rather than solutions.

In his assault on the welfare state, Reagan made the end of affirmative action his priority. He ordered his Attorney General, William French Smith, to fight such programs in the federal courts and packed the Civil Rights Commission and EEOC with known anti-rights individuals dedicated to reversing the racial and gender policies of previous administrations. Reagan slashed food stamp benefits, eliminated 300,000 CETA jobs, cut AFDC funds—leading to a reduction of more than 10 percent in the welfare rolls—and lowered the benefits of an additional 300,000 families receiving welfare assistance.

Deregulation

Reagan proved equally passionate about deregulation, especially when it came to the environment, which he believed must be delivered to the private sector to promote economic growth. In short, Reagan saw all the environmental protection laws passed since the presidency of Theodore Roosevelt as one of the greatest handicaps to domestic economic expansion, for such laws prevented businesses access to vital resources and land essential for such development. Reagan thus ordered EPA administrator Anne Burford to delay imposing penalties on chemical companies responsible for toxic waste dumps. No one perhaps better reflected the Reagan credo relative to the environment than Secretary of the Interior James Watt, who within months of assuming his job became one of the most arrogant, venal true believers of the Reagan administration's pandering of the New Right agenda. Watt, from Wyoming, worked tirelessly to open federal wilderness areas, forestlands, and coastal waters to oil and gas companies and developers. He also undermined endangered species programs and cut initiatives to protect environmentally threatened regions. Before coming to Washington, Watt had headed the Mountain States Legal Foundation, a right-wing organization, which spearheaded the so-called Sagebrush Rebellion of western conservatives seeking to open public lands to private development.

On a positive note, Watt's aggressiveness, arrogance, and temperamental and petulant displays of public disdain for conservationists did more to galvanize the environmental movement than any previous administration or person. In response to Watt's extreme positions, membership in the Sierra Club, the Wilderness Society, and other environmental organizations skyrocketed. More than a million conservationists signed petitions demanding Watt's removal. After a series of public relations gaffes and comments offensive to various groups, Watt resigned in 1983.

Only on implementing New Right social issues did the Reagan administration fall short, but even in this capacity—on questions such as abortion, school prayer, and busing—the president enthusiastically endorsed New Right positions, frequently using executive power to back up his words. New federal rules banned the circulation of birth control information or abortion advice without parental consent, and wherever possible, Justice Department lawyers argued the New Right position on social issues that came before federal courts. As a result of such actions, by the end of Reagan's second term, the Supreme Court had substantially eviscerated previous rulings on "set aside" programs for minority and women contractors, while threatening to overturn *Roe v. Wade*. In all such activity, the administration's agenda reflected two fundamental convictions of Reagan's credo: that the least government was the best government, and that allowing the private sector to once again reign supreme offered the surest guarantee of sustained prosperity and growth.

Reaganomics

Without question, to the New Right, Reagan, and the Republicans the key to their "revolution's" success was to redeem the economy from the Keynesian ideas liberals had implemented since the late 1930s. Such adherence, they believed, had caused the economic downturns of the 1970s and early 1980s. Reagan and his supporters believed the first step in their redemption crusade was to sharply reduce personal and corporate income taxes, especially the former, which he proposed to reduce by 30 percent over the next three years. Reagan's zeal for lower taxes was both ideological and personal. He embraced, as best as his mind could, the fundamentals of supply-side economics, an anti-Keynesian approach first introduced by a University of Southern California economics professor, Arthur Laffer. Although Reagan understood the contours of the "Laffer curve," his desire to lower taxes was primarily visceral—a result in large part of his own experience with the IRS. As Treasury Secretary Donald Regan later explained, "When he [Reagan] was in Hollywood he would make about three or four hundred thousand dollars per picture. Reagan would work for three months, and loaf for three months, so he was making between six and seven hundred thousand dollars per year. Between Uncle Sam and the state of California, over 91 percent of that was

Secret service agents rush an assailant who fired six shots at President Reagan as he was leaving the Washington Hilton on March 30. This photo released by the White House shows the door on the presidential limousine being closed (right) after Reagan was pushed in, and Press Secretary James Brady and patrolman Thomas Delahanty on the ground after being hit by gunfire.

going in taxes. His question, asked rhetorically, was this: 'Why should I have done a third picture, even if it was *Gone With the Wind?* What good would it have done me?' So he loafed for a part of the year. And he said the same thing was happening throughout America. People would reach a certain peak, and they weren't willing to do the extra effort that was needed to keep us a first-class nation."

Interestingly, Reagan did not charge Donald Regan with implementing the administration's fiscal and economic policy, but rather the president entrusted such a Herculean task to a conservative ideologue, David Stockman, whom Reagan appointed to head the Office of Management and Budget. Stockman, a devoted disciple of the supply-side theory, developed a capitalist version of a Soviet-style Five Year Plan, which a Lenin or Stalin would have approved for its doctrinaire simplicity and dialectics. According to Stockman, sharp reductions in personal income taxes would encourage savings and investments, especially among employers and investors, who Stockman believed would want to make even more money by using their tax savings to expand their businesses by increasing production, which in turn would create more jobs. Such greater entrepreneurial activity would spur rapid economic growth, which would hike personal income, bringing in greater tax revenues, even at the lower rates. Deregulation of industry, in turn, would free businesses to compete more efficiently in the marketplace. Repealing environmental protection measures would release energy and resources for private development; and cutting back social welfare payments to the elderly and poor would bolster self-reliance and initiative. The overall goal, Stockman later said, was "a minimalist government, a spare and stingy creature which offered evenhanded public justice, but no more." Millions of citizens might suffer in the short run, but in the long run, the country would be strengthened "by abruptly severing the umbilical cords of dependency that ran from Washington to every nook and cranny of the nation." Reagan boasted that within three years, an unshackled economy would produce a balanced budget based on sustained growth. The cherished American "virtues" of rugged individualism, competition, and personal pride would be restored, and with the chains of government bureaucracy removed, individual Americans would once again be liberated to realize their abilities and aspirations.

Despite the defection of some Democratic stalwarts such as Senator Lloyd Bentsen of Texas, who supported Reaganomics, which gave Reagan hope that he could count on bipartisan support for his initiative, the majority of Democrats opposed the concept, rightly claiming that the tax cuts would benefit the rich more than the poor, exacerbating economic inequality. The opposition also correctly asserted that the program would expand budget deficits, the more so because the president was calling for huge increases in defense spending. As a result, Reaganomics became an exercise in self-contradiction. One could not massively expand military spending, cut taxes sharply, and still have a balanced budget. The insanity of such policies became apparent by 1982 when in that year budget deficits soared to over $100 billion, which was more than three times the largest deficit incurred during the Carters years. By 1983 the deficit reached $300 billion. "No one imagined how bad the outcome would be," Stockman later observed. "It got away from us."

Reagan must be held responsible for what James Baker called "voodoo economics." When Stockman realized that politicians, especially the Democrats who made the sustaining of the welfare state their political lifeblood, weren't going to turn against their handiwork, cutting social security and Medicare benefits to the elderly, he tried to curtail defense spending and persuade Reagan to raise revenues. The president, however, turned a deaf ear to such a plea, despite bipartisan support for such measures. "Everyone was ready," said Stockman, "But Reagan said no. He wouldn't allow it. He didn't believe there was a problem. That was his selectivity on the facts of life. The whole thing got turned into a cynical, politicized, surreal substitute for sane fiscal government." As Reagan and his aides lobbied hard for the bill in March 1981, it became clear that the measure would not pass as easily as Reagan blithely had hoped.

As the impasse intensified, fate dealt Reagan a cruel but politically auspicious hand. On March 30, 1981, deeply troubled twenty-five-year-old John Hinckley tried to assassinate Reagan as he left a speaking engagement at a Washington hotel. Firing six times with a .22 caliber pistol, Hinckley hit James Brady, Reagan's press secretary, in the head. The shot permanently disabled Brady. Other gunfire bloodied a Washington policeman and a Secret Service agent. One of Hinckley's bullets ricocheted off the presidential limousine, hitting Reagan under his left arm. The bullet eventually lodged in his lung close to his heart. An ambulance rushed him to the nearest hospital where doctors found him bleeding profusely. Surgeons operated on him for two hours to remove the bullet and save his life. Reagan's brush with death, which the public did not realize until much later, kept him in the hospital until April 11.

While Reagan recuperated, news releases informed a frightened public not only how close they came to losing their president, but perhaps more important politically, how calm and good-humored he had been. As he was being taken into the operating room, Reagan quipped to his wife, Nancy, "Honey, I forgot to duck." As doctors were about to put him under, he remarked, "Please tell me you are all Republicans." Polls recorded that his courage and joviality had caused his popularity to soar, with more than 70 percent of the people giving him favorable ratings. Upon his return to the White House, Reagan kept a low profile until April 28, 1981, when he emerged to give an eagerly awaited television speech to a joint session of Congress. Still recovering, he seized this emotionally charged occasion to call upon the legislators to enact his economic program. How could Congress defy such a popular and courageous man? Indeed, he appeared to be reprising one of his more immortal Hollywood roles, that of the great Notre Dame football legend, George Gipp, only this time "the Gipper" lives, returning to the playing field with even greater vigor and intensity than before. For the next four months Reagan and his aides unleashed upon Congress one of the most ferocious lobbying campaigns witnessed in years, with Reagan personally meeting 69 times with 467 members of Congress. The president's persistence paid off. In July Congress passed slightly modified tax and budget bills, thanks largely to the defection of "boll weevil" (conservative) Southern Democrats, whom Reagan had won over during the preceding months. In securing the measures, Reagan greatly advanced the salience of conservative economic ideas, thereby driving liberals—then and thereafter—onto the defensive. His triumph impressed many seasoned observers. Reporters declared a "Reagan Revolution" in fiscal policy. Hedley Donovan of *Fortune* wrote that the tax and budget acts represented the "most formidable domestic initiative since the Hundred Days of Franklin Roosevelt." At last, it seemed, the United States had a president who could oil the gears of government and make them turn.

Soon after the passage of the tax and budget bills, Reagan endeared himself further among the New Righters by refusing the right of the federal employees who were members of the Professional Air Traffic Controller's Organization to strike for better pay and benefits. When union members voted to strike, Reagan rejected their demands and threatened to fire them if they did not return to work in 48 hours. Reagan believed such a strike to be illegal, even though he was the first American president to have served as the head of a union—the Screen Actor's Guild of Hollywood—and who had received PATCO's endorsement in 1980. Nonetheless, Reagan held firm in his belief that if the workers went out on strike they would be endangering the nation's well being. Many Americans agreed and supported Reagan's tough stance. When his 48-hour decree passed, Reagan announced that 38 percent of the strikers had returned to work and that military controllers would replace those who were still on strike. After firing more than 11,000 air traffic controllers Reagan reassured the nation that air travel was safe and that flight schedules had returned to 80 percent normal. Reagan's action destroyed the union and sent a unmistakable anti-union message to the rest of the nation's labor organizations, making it clear that the heyday of union power and the striking worker was coming to an end.

Naturally liberals and labor leaders considered Reagan's behavior an anathema. A vengeful imperial presidency was once again looming with long-range consequences, for Reagan's actions not only broke the strike, they further demoralized organized labor. Moreover, his actions signaled to the American public that Reagan could be, and often was, a stubborn man of conviction. Conservatives naturally were euphoric, more confident than ever that they, at last, had in Reagan truly one of their own. His image as a consistent defender of a core of ideas helped him repeatedly to deflect all criticism, causing opponents to lament that he was a "Teflon President"—nothing stuck to him.

Equally appalling to liberals was Reagan's open hostility to large-scale spending for social welfare, especially when this parsimony was contrasted to the lavishness of Nancy Reagan's lifestyle and the glitter of the celebrations that surrounded the inaugural ceremonies—"a bacchanalia of the haves," as one wag commented. Nancy Reagan's wardrobe for these events was said to have cost $25,000. It seems the Reagans simply brought Hollywood excess and self-indulgence to the nation's capital and expected the American people to hold them in awe as many once did when both husband and wife were on the silver screen. Firing the air traffic controllers, liberals added, was blatant union busting. Cutting taxes for the wealthy while curtailing benefits for the poor seemed immoral. As Speaker of the House Tip O'Neill exclaimed, "When it comes to giving tax breaks to the wealthy of this country, the president has a heart of gold." A joke circulated Washington that Reagan's right hand didn't know what his far right hand was up to. Liberals, however, did not laugh. Many believed Reagan was deliberately running up deficits via tax cuts and military spending in order to starve social programs. This, they charged, was "Reagan's Revenge," a diabolical plot to destroy the welfare state, or what was left of the programs after years of chipping away at the overall system. It was up to Reagan to bring the definitive end to the New Deal-Great Society legacy, a prospect that delighted Reagan's New Right supporters. Although liberals could not prove that such was Reagan's intent, there was no doubt that the president and his conservative allies sought to cut social spending and that large deficits stymied efforts for new liberal initiatives.

While implementing Reaganomics, Stockman and his cohorts at the OMB also faced the immediate problem of inflation, which reached 13 percent by the last year of the Carter presidency. The Federal Reserve Board, under the leadership of Paul Volcker as chairman, led the charge, pushing interest rates ever higher in hopes of forcing Americans to save and invest rather than spend, which if they continued to do, would only push prices higher. This harsh medicine, coupled with a drop in oil prices, did its job. Inflation fell to around 4 percent in 1983 and held steady thereafter. However, the high interest rates necessary to curb inflation soon brought on the worst recession to hit the country since the 1930s, making prophets out of Reaganomics critics, at least temporarily. Unemployment shot up to 10 percent by 1982, and because of earlier cuts in funding for social welfare programs, the plight of the poor worsened. Moreover, as interest rates remained high, America's European allies screamed in pain as money flowed out of their countries and into the coffers of U.S. banks where their money earned unprecedented interest. As the dollar rose in value relative to foreign currency, the situation made U.S. goods more expensive abroad but allowed Americans to consume in great quantities the much cheaper foreign products. Such a scenario led to a dramatic decline in American exports and the simultaneous staggering increase in Americans buying TV's, stereos, automobiles, and a host of other products made in Japan and other countries. The result: a mind-numbing trade imbalance or U.S. deficit (the gap between exports and imports) that reached a whopping $111 billion by 1984. By that year, the United States was well on its way to becoming for the first time in decades a "debtor nation."

The industrial heartland was especially hit hard, reeling under the triple blows of slumping exports, particularly of capital goods, foreign competition, and technological obsolescence. The hard-hit auto plants, aging steel mills, and other heavy industries of the Midwest, Mideast, and Northeast laid off hordes of workers with many plants closing their doors forever. In the years 1979-1983, 11.5 million U.S. workers lost their jobs as a result of plant closings and general decline in heavy manufacturing. As a result, thousands left the "Rust Belt" and headed to the booming high-tech, oil, and petrochemical dominated economies of the Sun Belt states, particularly California and Texas, where cities like San Jose and Houston respectively became the permanent home of these new "Okie" migrants. The influx of the "rust belters" and others fleeing destitution in the Northeast or Midwest caused the populations of Sun Belt cities like Houston to explode; by 1983, Houston had become the fourth largest city in the country, with over 4 million residents; only New York, Los Angeles, and Chicago had more human beings. Not since the Dust Bowl days of the Great Depression had the country witnessed such a massive exodus of people from one part of the nation to another. To be sure, farmers suffered as well. Wheat exports fell 38 percent from 1980 to 1985, and corn exports by 49 percent. In foreclosure sales reminiscent of the 1930s, the family farm was about to disappear from the American landscape.

Soaring federal deficits added to the economic muddle. Reagan's tax cuts reduced federal revenues without immediately producing the predicted business boom, while soaring military expenditures far exceeded domestic spending cuts. With the economy sputtering, budget deficits escalating, and liberals denouncing his callousness toward the poor, Reagan in 1982-1983 grudgingly accepted a reduction in military appropriations, a slowing of cuts in social programs, new emergency job programs, and various tax increases his administration disguised as "revenue-enhancement measures." Such a reversal, however, came too late to save the Republicans from defeat in the 1982 congressional elections. In that year, the Democrats gained 26 House seats, signifying what appeared to be a clear rejection of supply-side economics. Reagan appeared headed for failure.

Such hope among liberals, however, proved illusory; by 1983, the "Gipper" was back on top as the economy rebounded. Encouraged by tax cuts, falling interest rates, and evidence that inflation had been tamed at last, consumers went on a buying binge; unemployment dropped; and Reagan's popularity revived, for sufficient numbers of Americans believed Reagan's economic policies had indeed finally worked their magic. The recovery was by no means universal, and African Americans especially continued to suffer, with their income declining relative to whites, and the percentage of those living in poverty increased. But the welfare of black Americans and many other ethnicities had never been a priority for Reagan, and for much of the rest of the nation (white America) the economic indicators were positive. By 1984 unemployment declined to 7.5 percent, and the automobile industry recovered its vitality, as did the housing market, which witnessed a boom in starts. It was the most vibrant economy since the early 1960s, and despite continued high interest rates and deficits that threatened to vault into the stratosphere, people felt good. Continued growth seemed likely, and the nation acquired once more a sense of confidence and buoyancy. Less sanguine individuals such as David Stockman and others, however, knew it would only be a matter of time before the massive deficit spending would bring economic catastrophe. As will be seen later in this chapter, the "Teflon President" would escape the fallout of his own making; his successor, George H.W. Bush, would not.

In fact, the overall economic picture of the mid-1980s, though improved, was uneven. While many of the wealthy prospered as never before, the real wages of full-time male production workers continued to stagnate. As in the 1970s, job-seekers frequently complained that the fastest growing occupations were in the low-paying jobs of the service sector; waiters and waitresses, nurses, janitors, cashiers, and truck drivers. As American manufacturing declined because of less expensive imported goods, or as increasing numbers of businesses sent their production overseas in search of cheap labor markets, blue-collar American workers lost what for many were good-paying jobs. At the very least, they had earned enough money to support an acceptable middle class existence. As a result of supply-side policies, such individuals not only lost decent paying jobs, but if they wanted to continue to work, they had to either completely retrain for another industry or take low-paying service sectors jobs in the meantime in order to put food on the table.

With better times came a wave of stock-market speculation reminiscent of the 1920s. The bull market began in August 1982 and lasted for five years. Entrepreneurs like Donald Trump, a Manhattan real estate mogul, and Ivan Boesky, a supposed genius at stock transactions, became millionaire celebrities by playing the market and engaging in a variety of other speculative (and what later proved to be questionable if not outright illegal) ventures. Indeed, not since the 1920s had the nation witnessed such a presumptive craze. The same mania to get rich quick that affected Americans in the 1920s engulfed many of their 1980s counterparts, and in many instances producing a "new breed" of the affluent, derisively referred to as "yuppies"—young urban professionals, many of whom had entered the ranks of the upper middle class by either investing in the stock market or by working in one of the many "boiler room" brokerage firms that proliferated across the nation during the 1980s. Interestingly many "yuppies" were former anti-Establishment student insurgents such as Rennie Davis, one of the founders of the revolutionary yippie movement of the late 1960s. By the Reagan years, Davis (as well as many other former 60s radicals) had transformed himself into one of the most successful brokers on Wall Street, earning hundreds of thousands of dollars annually by finding ways for other ex-1960s rebels and "drop-outs" to become part of the "new" Establishment of the 1980s.

"Yuppiedom" also connoted a certain lifestyle of consumerism on an unprecedented scale, not only in quantity but in frippery as well. As former hippies and radicals entered the ranks of middle class respectability and responsibility, they wanted and purchased the American dream writ large and in the process bought the very best their money could buy—VCR's, personal computers, telephone answering machines, cable TV, and remote controls—the latest, most expensive electronic gadgets that did not exist in 1970. The German-made BMW became a yuppie's personal car of choice, as did expensive, exotic vacations, and of course a new home, outfitted with the latest in house-ware accoutrements, in the best suburban neighborhoods. Perhaps the most disappointing aspect of this "sell out" was the fact that many former activists not only became yuppies by occupation and material identity but conservative Republicans in the process. Indeed, demographically, "thirty-something" middle class suburban whites became one of Reagan's staunchest support groups.

Reagan set the tone for the crass consumerism of the 1980s in a 1983 speech in which he declared that, "What I want to see above all is that this remains a country where someone can always get rich." Critics who deplored this message asserted that while 1970s culture, the Me Decade, had been greedy and self-absorbed, their cupidity paled in comparison to their 1980s counterparts' grasping. Thanks to Reagan's message, yuppies were becoming icons, inspiring others to want to plunge their hands into the cornucopia of goods that had seduced the United States into becoming a nation of uninhibited consumers. In short, this single-minded pursuit of wealth and possessions was commercializing virtually all of American culture and creating a new Gilded Age. "Hanoi Jane" Fonda, who in 1972 had traveled to North Vietnam to protest the war, was now making millions selling exercise videos and promoting physical fitness. Fonda rather disingenuously claimed that she gave most of her proceeds to the worker's rights causes that her then husband, Tom Hayden, former founder of the SDS and refreshingly still left-wing, was promoting. It appeared Fonda and other celebrities still wanted to associate and identify with the Left, for it was still somewhat chic, but in reality their commitment to true leftist initiatives was half-hearted at best. Especially dispiriting were reports announcing that one-third of the Yale class of 1985 were interviewing for jobs as financial analysts at First Boston Corporation. What a dramatic change from the socially conscious 1960s!

Not only did stock market speculation (and peculation) flourish in the 1980s, but so did corporate mergers and the further consolidation of various businesses into the hands of fewer and fewer owners, making a further mockery of the cherished American notions of competition and free enterprise. Chevron bought Gulf Oil in 1984 for $13 billion; GE acquired RCA (and its subsidiary NBC) for $6.3 billion in 1986. Conservatives naturally embraced and touted conglomeration, asserting that mergers helped the United States weed out its inefficient companies, invest in recent technology, and outperform foreign competition. Critics charged that such compression caused the "downsizing" and "outsourcing" of employment, wiped out well-managed small businesses, enriched already fat CEOs, smashed labor unions, and inflated prices. In the meantime, the stock market roared on. Banks and savings and loan companies, newly deregulated and flush with deposits of eager investors, ladled out billions to developers planning shopping malls, luxury apartments, condominiums, retirement communities, and office buildings.

Perhaps nowhere was this particular brand of frenzied, self-indulgent, and ostentatious speculation more manifest and abundant than in Houston, Texas, the city that came to symbolize the limitless opportunities of unfettered corporate capitalism. Houston's downtown skyline, proliferation of malls, high-rise office buildings and apartment complexes reflected the freebooting capitalism unloosed by the Reagan administration's laissez faire policies. Houston became in many ways the most flamboyant, spectacular reflection of the supposed Reagan economic "miracle." However, by the mid 1980s, as oil prices plummeted and savings and loan scandals rocked the nation, Houston in particular, "Boom Town USA," experienced one of the worst recessions in its history, mirroring in foreclosures, unemployment, and general economic declension, the financial devastation that rocked the Midwest and Mideast years earlier. It appeared by the late 1980s that no region or city, regardless of how prosperous or allegedly recession-proof, could escape the long-range repercussions and inherent flaws of Reaganomics.

The excesses noted above sparked considerable cultural criticism, especially toward the middle of the decade when a team of UC Berkeley social scientists, led by Robert Bellah, published the results of their well-regarded surveys of American values in the late 1970s and early 1980s. Reflecting a growing consensus among liberals and Reagan critics, the data concluded that during these years "American individualism may have grown cancerous" and "may be threatening the survival of freedom itself." Calling on Americans to develop more community spirit, the authors lamented that, "The citizen has been swallowed up in economic man." Yale University economist James Tobin echoed the warnings of the Bellah Report, believing the end result of Reaganomics would be the redistribution of "income, wealth, and power—from the government to private enterprise, from workers to capitalists, from poor to rich." Sadly, few Americans read, let alone heeded, Bellah and Tobin's forebodings. Ronald Reagan certainly did not, and if by some miracle he had, he no doubt would have dismissed their findings as one more cynical, liberal manifesto, put forth by disgruntled and alienated intellectuals, who simply refused to accept that he had brought "Morning in America." For the moment, Reagan could indeed bask in the sunshine of success and thus turn his attention to defeating the "Evil Empire," the Soviet Union and its communist minions throughout the world.

REAGAN CONFRONTS THE WORLD

The Soviet Union, and Crises in the Middle East and Central America

In foreign policy as well, many Americans felt a new sense of pride and confidence that Reagan not only would restore U.S. honor, respect, and might around the globe, but, in the process, win the Cold War and usher in an "American Century," a "Pax Americana," in which all the nations of the world would benefit. In short, the New Right, and in particular the movement's Protestant evangelicals, saw in Reagan (as they would later see in George W. Bush), the Final Conflict, the triumph of fundamentalist, millennial (American) Christianity over not only the satanic forces of communism but the vanquishing, as well of other anti-Christ, religions such as Islam. Indeed, it was before a convention of evangelicals that Reagan demonized the Soviet Union as "the focus of evil in the modern world." To the Soviet Union he declared a new policy of moral superiority. The arms race, he declared, was a struggle of "good versus evil, right against wrong." In one of his early press conferences, Reagan intimated that the Russians were genetically disabled, hence their propensity to lie and cheat; they simply could not help such behavior because they were inherently "defective." Not even in the heyday of John Foster Dulles and his often-deprecating jingoism did an American leader so outright insult the Soviet Union and its people. To back up his antagonistic rhetoric, Reagan lobbied and eventually won congressional approval for a 41 percent increase in defense spending. With such funding he pledged to build 17,000 new nuclear weapons.

Unlike any of his Cold War predecessors, Reagan flatly refused to engage in any arms control negotiations with the Soviets. Even the most hardline Soviet leaders, such as Leonid Brezhnev, could not believe the belligerence emanating from Washington and thus put his country's armed forces on alert status, certain that this "cowboy" of a president could at any time become "trigger happy" and start pushing buttons, unleashing a nuclear war. Possible Armageddon almost occurred when Soviet MiG fighter jets shot down a civilian Korean airliner in the fall of 1983. The act was one of incompetence and confusion on behalf of the Soviets but not one of wanton aggression. Soviet military officials genuinely believed the plane to be a spy intruder. Reagan, however, ignored all evidence that confirmed the attack as one of miscalculation and, instead, seized on the event to lead a worldwide condemnation of the Soviet Union. Reagan, of course, led the name-calling, labeling the Soviets as "inhumane," "barbarous," and "uncivilized," and accusing them of a "massacre," implying that the Soviet strike reflected the premeditated murder of innocent civilians. Although certainly taken aback by Reagan's bellicose response and diatribe, luckily for the world the Soviets did not respond in a similar fashion. Most importantly they did not over-react and threaten to militarily retaliate if Reagan wasn't muzzled. They wisely turned a deaf ear to Reagan's rantings, certain that the world would grow weary of his belligerence and world opinion would soon force him into silence, for no one would want to see World War III. Reagan did indeed "stifle himself" as events elsewhere in the world got his attention.

Perhaps nowhere in the world was Reagan's obsession with communism more intense than in the Western Hemisphere, especially in desperately poor Central America, where two nations, caught up in revolutionary turmoil, El Salvador and Nicaragua became fixations for the Reagan administration. Indeed, as he told a joint session of Congress in May 1983, "The national security of all the Americas is at stake. If we cannot defend ourselves there, we cannot expect to prevail elsewhere. . . and the safety of our homeland would be put at jeopardy." In El

Lt. Col. Oliver North takes the oath before the House Foreign Affairs Committee. North invoked the Fifth Amendment and refused to answer any questions in the Iran arms-contra aid hearing.

Salvador, the Reagan White House backed the right-wing military junta in its brutal suppression of all opposition. Certain the regime was fighting to preserve "democracy" in El Salvador, Reagan allowed the CIA and other U.S. covert agencies to send "advisors" to help the Salvadoran army put down the supposed communist insurgents. With such approval from Washington, the Salvadoran government unleashed a vicious reign of terror on its own citizens, with U.S.-trained paramilitary "death squads" roaming the Salvadoran countryside slaughtering thousands of innocent people over the course of several months. By 1984, El Salvador had been "saved" from communism. A U.S.-favored moderate, Jose Napoleon Duarte, won the 1984 presidential election, ending the rule of the military junta. However, under Duarte the "purging" (killing) of opponents continued. The Reagan administration naturally saw nothing wrong with the "removal" of "communists" from El Salvador and thus supported the Duarte dictatorship.

In Nicaragua, the Carter administration, in an attempt to atone for decades of United States-backing of the brutal Anastasio Somoza regime, had initially granted aid to the Sandinista revolutionaries, who overthrew Somoza in 1979. No sooner did Reagan enter the White House than he reversed this policy, claiming the leftist Sandinistas were turning Nicaragua into another Marxist state like Castro's Cuba. Although certainly no great fans of U.S. policy toward Central America and without question socialists in their economic vision for their country, the Sandinistas had no intention of becoming a Soviet lackey state. However, Reagan's attitude and policies, which cut off all aid to Nicaragua because they had gone "red," left the Sandinistas no choice if their country and regime was to survive but to turn to Cuba and the Soviet Union for assistance. As the Sandinistas drifted deeper into the Cuban-Soviet camp, the more determined Reagan became to overthrow the regime. In 1982, with Reagan's blessing, the CIA organized and financed a 10,000 man anti-Sandinista guerrilla army called the *contras*, based in neighboring Costa Rica and Honduras, with the avowed purpose of bringing down the "Marxist dictatorship" of Nicaragua.

Reagan and other New Right zealots referred to the *contras* as "freedom fighters" but as recently de-classified documents have shown, the majority of the individuals comprising the force were ex-Somoza thugs, mercenaries, and most revealing, many were heavily involved and profiting from drug smuggling (cocaine) for Manuel Noriega of Panama and for the Colombian cartels. Such new disclosure contradicts the stellar image of "patriots" the Reagan administration projected to the American people and the world at the time. With such full-fledged U.S. support, the *contras* conducted raids, planted mines, and carried out sabotage in Nicaragua. Their terrorist activities naturally caused the death of several thousand innocent civilians over the course of several years of covert operation.

Fearing another Vietnam quagmire, only this time in their own backyard, many Americans grew alarmed as details of this "secret" war against the Sandinistas leaked out. Thus, in 1982, led by Democratic congressman Edward Boland from Massachusetts, the House passed an amendment (the Boland Amendment) prohibiting the CIA and Defense Department from using funds to overthrow the Sandinistas. The Boland initiative revealed the continuing presence of a powerful source of political division in late twentieth-century American politics: antagonism between Congress and the executive over presidential war-making authority, a tension that had existed

The Reagans honor the victims of the bombing of the U.S. Embassy in Beirut, Lebanon, at Andrews Air Force Base, Maryland. April 23, 1983. Photo credit: Reagan Presidential Library

since the days of LBJ and his 1964 Tonkin Gulf Resolution. The amendment passed the House 411 to 0 and was signed by Reagan. The administration, however, ignored the resolution and continued to funnel money contributed by foreign governments and right-wing groups in the United States to the *contras.* Such clandestine operations increasingly came under the auspices of the National Security Council, which became the conduit for deliveries of covert aid. The two men most responsible for the venture, as well as for what would become known as the Iran-Contra scandal, were NSC director, Robert MacFarlane, and his gung-ho staff assistant, Marine Lt. Colonel Oliver North.

The continuing turmoil and conflict in the Middle East that had so frustrated the Carter presidency also affected the Reagan administration. Determined to stop the spread of militant Islamic fundamentalism, with its call for jihad against Western corruption and imperialism, the United States, trying to play the hoary balance of power game, and still smarting from the Iranian hostage crisis humiliation, sided with Saddam Hussein's Iraq in its eight-year war (1980-88) with Iran. The conflict resulted in an estimated 1.5 million Iraqi and Iranian deaths, devastated both nations' economies, and created millions of refugees. Interestingly, U.S. support of Iraq only served to embolden Saddam Hussein, who, as will be seen, believed he could dominate the Middle East for he was certain the United States would sanction his pretensions because he would be a countervailing force against the more radical Iranians and equally ambitious vainglory of Hafez Asad of Syria. In the end, America's attempt to stabilize this most volatile region of the world by attempting to play one country off against another resulted in only further antagonizing and alienating the nations involved.

Meanwhile, the conflict between Israel and the Palestinians and their Arab allies dragged on. Because of America's growing dependence on foreign oil, particularly from the Middle East (most notably Saudi Arabia), as well as its deep emotional bond with Israel, which resulted in billions of dollars of military aid and other assistance, the Reagan administration was no different than any of its predecessors in failing to achieve peace in the region. No matter how much impartiality the United States tried to demonstrate to the region's Arab/Muslim countries, such as giving substantial aid to Egypt, they knew that in the end, when push came to shove, America would always side with Israel. Such has been proven true repeatedly since Israel's existence as a nation. America's growing dependence on Middle Eastern oil has only exacerbated this problem, for many of the Arab countries that provide the United States with oil were and are violently anti-Israel and will remain so until the United States rethinks its policies relative to Israel and the Arab world. A step in the right direction would be for the United States to curtail its dependence on Arab oil. Until that happens, United States' policy in the Middle East will continue to wallow in a self-inflicted cognitive dissonance, contradiction, and potential humiliation. However, during the Reagan years such a reality never crossed the president's mind, thus the Beirut disaster of October 1983.

In 1981, Israel and the Palestinian Liberation Organization (PLO) concluded a cease-fire. However, the PLO continued building up forces at its base in southern Lebanon. In June 1982, when an extremist faction within the PLO shot and critically wounded Israel's ambassador to Great Britain, Israel naturally retaliated. Israeli troops under General Ariel Sharon, Israel's defense minister, invaded Lebanon, defeated the PLO, forcing its leaders, including Yasser Arafat, to flee Lebanon. However, the Israeli invasion only served to intensify the already bloody civil war in Lebanon between Christian and Muslim factions for control of the nation's government. Both the United States and Israel favored the Christian forces, for a Christian-dominated Lebanon not only would secure Israel's southern border with a friendly power but also hopefully give the United States, as well, a non-Muslim ally in the region. With Sharon's approval, a Lebanese Christian militia force entered two

U. S. Marines walk down a street of Greenville, Grenada after landing near the town.

Palestinian refugee camps near Beirut to search out armed gunmen. However, the raid's purpose changed dramatically into one of bloody revenge for the assassination a few days earlier of Lebanon's Christian president. The Christian partisans massacred as many as 700-800 camp residents, including women and children. An Israeli commission of inquiry found Sharon negligent for allowing the militiamen to enter the camp and recommended his dismissal but found no evidence that Sharon knew of the planned slaughter in advance. Sharon resigned as defense minister but remained in the government.

After the Beirut massacre, Reagan, for reasons still unfathomable today, ordered two thousand marines to Lebanon as part of a multinational peacekeeping force. Perhaps Reagan believed that by sending American troops to this troubled country, he would be demonstrating to the world that the United States no longer suffered from its "Vietnam syndrome," which had forced the Carter administration into a foreign policy of retrenchment. The result of such a retreat in Reagan's, the New Right's, and in many Americans' view was the resurgence of a whole host of anti-democratic, anti-American, communist movements, all of which in Reagan's mind were manipulated from Moscow. Thus to display to the world that the United States was "back," that America's vaunted strength had been rebuilt and that the nation was ready to assume its rightful place as the most dominant force in the world, Reagan sent the marines to Lebanon. Reagan, oblivious to how Lebanon's Muslim militias would see his initiative, was courting disaster, for the Muslims naturally saw the Americans as favoring Israel and the Christian side. Thus in October 1983, a Shiite Muslim on a suicide mission crashed an explosive-laden truck into the poorly guarded U.S. barracks, killing 239 marines. Other than customary public pap about the need for peace in the region and how it was the United States' responsibility to promote such an endeavor, Reagan never clearly explained how the deployment served U.S. interests, and the disaster further discredited his Middle East policy. Indeed, a bipartisan blue-ribbon investigation later blamed the tragedy on politicians in Washington who overrode Pentagon recommendations that such a move could prove disastrous. In early 1984 Reagan withdrew the surviving marines.

The Reagan administration, however, typically quickly rebounded from the Beirut disaster by invading the tiny West Indian island of Grenada, allegedly to protect the lives of American medical students threatened by a supposed Castro-manipulated Marxist dictatorship. In reality nothing could have been further from the truth, but the Reagan administration, known for its adroit timing and showmanship, and needing desperately and quickly to atone for the Beirut fiasco, invaded the island with 10,000 troops to demonstrate its resolve to contain the spread of communism in the hemisphere. After a day of skirmishing with 750 Cuban laborers constructing a new airport (only 110 of them were soldiers), Reagan declared a great American victory and the public's display of enthusiasm for Reagan and for such a trivial affair was surreally absurd. The troops "coming home" were greeted with such fanfare and adulation that one would think that they had just won one of the greatest military victories in the history of the Republic. Of course the Reagan public relations experts exploited such a *cause celebre* to its fullest political potential for the president and the Republican Party, which now assumed the mantle of having restored America's military "might" and presence in the world by vanquishing a "threat" to American security, a petty, left-leaning dictatorship on a microscopic Caribbean island. As the political commentator Elizabeth Drew noted soon after the Grenada hoopla died down, "Reagan is a political phenomenon—a man who by force of personality and marvelous stage management superimposes himself over his own mistakes."

By any objective criteria, Reagan should have been severely chastised for his arrogant and precipitous actions in both Beirut and Grenada. However, such was not to be the case in either event, for the "Teflon President" typically deflected such potential disaster by rallying the country in a tour de force television appearance in which he associated the week's two events with his own policies of American patriotism and bravery. So convincingly did Reagan articulate his foreign policy credo, and by extolling the importance of the "great victory" in Grenada, that

Geraldine Ferraro became the first woman nominated for the office of vice president when she was picked as a running mate by the 1984 Democratic presidential candidate Walter Mondale. Here she is seen campaigning with Senator Paul Simon of Illinois.

in the end, he successfully erased in the American public's mind the Beirut debacle. Reagan's peroration focused on a wounded marine in Lebanon, unable to speak, who scrawled the marine motto, "Semperfi," on a pad and handed it to a visiting general. In trying to convey this touching scene to the public, Reagan could not choke back the tears; he attempted twelve times to relate the exchange but it appeared to be too emotionally overwhelming for him at the moment. Finally, he used it to end his exhortation, in the process fusing his own leadership with the courage of the troops he commanded, celebrating their shared honor, pride, and patriotism. Within days of his speech, all other emotions or criticisms dissipated, as if trivial and selfish. Reagan's approval rating shot up 15 points, sending a clear message to the Democrats that they had a battle on their hands in the forthcoming election.

THE ELECTION OF 1984

As the 1984 election neared, liberal Democrats and many independents criticized Reagan for excessive military spending, Cold War belligerence, massive budget deficits, cuts in social programs, and assaults on the government's regulatory powers. To his detractors, jingoism abroad and selfishness at home defined Reaganism. However, the majority of Americans dismissed such accusations, believing Reagan had redeemed America from its supposed "malaise" both at home and abroad. They touted his delivering of a booming economy with an end to the inflation that had wracked the country for several years prior. They applauded his tough stance with the Soviets and the rebuilding of America's military might. Even feminists welcomed his 1981 nomination of Sandra Day O'Connor as the first woman justice on the Supreme Court. The 1984 Republican convention, brilliantly staged for TV by the powerbrokers of the RNC, became a Ronald Reagan "love-fest," hammering home both subliminally and overtly the themes of patriotism, prosperity, and, above all, the personality of Ronald Reagan, the individual most responsible for the nation's resurrection.

The Democratic hopefuls included former Colorado Senator Gary Hart, and the Reverend Jesse Jackson of Chicago who proposed a "rainbow coalition" of African Americans, Hispanics, displaced white-ethnic blue-collar workers, and all other citizens negatively affected by the Reagan Revolution. Hart emerged the early leader in most Democratic polls, but a sex scandal exploited by the tabloids and other mediums forced him to bow out of the race. Former Vice President Walter Mondale quickly filled the void, easily winning the Democratic primaries and thus the nomination. In another age and time, Mondale might have been a sure bet to win the presidency. Descending from Norwegian stock, the son of a minister and piano teacher, Mondale epitomized the nation's heartland virtues of hard work, compassion, and public service. He was also the anointed heir of Hubert Humphrey, one of the Democratic Party's and liberal America's most beloved and genuine progressives. A student leader at Macalester College, Mondale became Humphrey's protégé as Minnesota's attorney general then moved on to the U.S. senate to carry forward the New Deal/Great Society agenda. Mondale was bright, worked hard, and his colleagues respected him. After Jimmy Carter chose him as his running mate in 1976, Mondale became a full partner in the Carter administration, participating on a daily basis in governing the country and in making major decisions. He knew the tensions, ambiguities, and challenges of the Oval Office better than any person except the president himself. Mondale was ready.

Most revealing in retrospect, Mondale believed he could win—not easily—to be sure, but he was confident that if he could pull together the old New Deal coalitions, add a few allies, and appeal to Americans' sense of "fairness," maybe he could pull off a victory. In short, Mondale believed that when shown the truth and the reality of Reaganomics, that it had promoted a class struggle on behalf of the rich, they would reject both Reagan and the New Right agenda, returning to the liberal ethos that had so equitably guided the nation since the days of FDR.

With equal conviction, Mondale believed voters had become alarmed by Reagan's militarism and Cold War belligerence. Indeed, polls revealed that more than 70 percent of Americans supported a nuclear freeze with the Soviet Union. Three-quarters of a million people had demonstrated in New York City on behalf of such disarmament. Reagan's increased production of weapons of mass destruction not only fueled out-of-control deficits but also created the possibility of confrontation with the Soviets. Even an old Cold Warrior such as George Kennan, who had come to regret his own responsibility for escalating tensions between the U.S. and the Soviet Union in the aftermath of World War II, feared for America's future, believing Reagan's antagonistic hyperbole had created a "dreadful and dangerous condition" between the United States and the Soviet Union. The progenitor of containment further asserted that Reagan's rhetoric was "childish, inexcusably childish, unworthy of a people charged with responsibility for conducting the affairs of a great power in an endangered world." Whether most Americans agreed with Kennan's harsh assessment of Reagan's policies was moot. There was, however, ample evidence from polls that most citizens were deeply troubled by the possibility of Central America turning into a new Vietnam and wished as well for a shift in Soviet-American relations from confrontation to cooperation.

With these concerns as a base, Mondale was confident that he could put together a coalition of Democratic loyalists and challenge the president. Pundits blamed previous Democratic failures on the party's inability to retain traditional Democratic constituencies. Mondale thus put his efforts toward reclaiming these lost Democrats, going, for example, to the AFL-CIO, the National Education Association, the NAACP and other civil rights groups, and women's organizations for support. According to public opinion polls, the most significant new political phenomenon was the "gender gap." Women differed from men by 10 to 15 points on issues such as war and peace or social justice at home. Thus Mondale cultivated the support of groups like NOW. He also solicited the trade unions, all the while selling his case on fairness at home and relaxation of tensions abroad, especially with the Soviet Union. Such a strategy seemed to be working as Mondale swept the Democratic primaries; he appeared to be successfully lining up the troops and beginning his march to victory. When Mondale gave Jesse Jackson center-stage at the Democratic convention and then boldly chose Congresswoman Geraldine Ferraro of New York as the first female vice-presidential candidate in history, he may have solidified his ties to his party's liberal base, but in the process he only further alienated and drove into the Reagan camp the already disaffected white, working-class Democrats who had been the party's heart and soul supporters since the New Deal.

Despite Mondale's well-laid plans for victory, in retrospect that anyone could have defeated Reagan in 1984 seems absurd. The economy was booming, inflation was done, and America was strong again. Before Reagan's 1980 election, Americans had been held hostage in Iran for over a year, United States athletes had boycotted the Moscow summer Olympics, the economy was stagnant, and American morale had sunk to its lowest level since the Great Depression. By the time of the 1984 election, all that had changed. American athletes, led by Carl Lewis in track and field, swept the gold at the Los Angeles Olympics (helped in no small amount by the non-participation of Soviet and Eastern European athletes, who although would arrive undoubtedly "juiced" by performance enhancing hormones, nonetheless they would have prevented such American dominance of the games), a new patriotism (chauvinism) permeated the body politic, and the United States had demonstrated its reinvigorated military prowess in Grenada as well as in the construction and significant increase in nuclear weapons, cutting-edge aircraft (the stealth bomber), and nuclear-powered, multi-war-headed, missile-laden submarines. Nothing seemed impossible any longer. "Just about every place you look," one Reagan ad declared, showing a man painting a white picket fence, "things are looking up. Life is better—America is back—and people have a sense of pride they never thought they'd feel again." As one Reagan advisor observed, "I almost feel sorry for Mondale having to go up against this . . . it's almost like running against *America.*"

Indeed, that had been the Republican campaign strategy from the moment the 1984 election began. As a Republican staff memo instructed: "Paint Reagan as the personification of all that is right with, or heroized by America. Leave Mondale in a position where an attack on Reagan is tantamount to an attack on America's idealized image of itself—where a vote against Reagan is, in some subliminal sense, a vote against a mythic AMERICA." Reagan's aides carefully monitored his impromptu appearances, wanting to ensure Reagan said nothing embarrassing. They could not watch him, however, 24-7 and thus there were bound to be some mishaps along the way. During a warm-up for a radio address and not realizing the microphone was on, Reagan joked, "My fellow Americans, I am pleased to tell you that I just signed legislation outlawing Russia forever. The bombings begin in five minutes." While many Americans were amused (and applauded) the president's sense of humor, the Soviets were appalled. Despite such gaffes, Reagan's popularity remained intact and thus his reelection a certainty. As one of Mondale's leading advisors observed, "you couldn't touch Reagan without hurting yourself."

In the face of such odds, all Mondale could do was to hammer way at the fact that for many Americans the Reagan years had not brought "Morning again in America" but rather endless dark nights and days of poverty, despair, and discrimination. As Mondale told a Cleveland audience, in Reagan's America "it's all picket fences and puppy dogs. No one's hurting, no one's alone. No one's hungry. No one's unemployed. No one gets old. Everybody is happy." However, there was another America, Mondale declared, where the poor, the disabled, the unemployed, and the victims of bigotry were treated as part of the family (the Democratic Party) and were helped. That America, Mondale asserted, believed in community and compassion. Such Americans surely would not cast a vote for selfishness dressed up as patriotism.

Although faltering rather badly in his first of two televised debates with Mondale, which raised questions about Reagan's age—73—and whether he could still meet the demands of leadership, by the time of the second debate, his wife and aides had worked assiduously in the two week interval to recast their man. Early on in the second debate, Reagan addressed the age controversy with a characteristic quip. "I will not make age an issue in this campaign. I am not going to exploit for political purposes my opponent's youth and inexperience." As the audience roared with laughter and applause, the campaign effectively ended. As Lou Cannon later explained, "For Reagan the burden of proof was exceptionally light and he more than met it with his inspired one liner." On election day, Reagan won in a devastating landslide, rolling to victory with 59 percent of the popular vote and taking 49 out of 50 states in the electoral college for a total of 525 electoral votes to Mondale's 13. It was a day of reckoning for the Republican Party as Reagan helped to sweep away their own embarrassing showings in 1936 and 1964. Not since Nixon's slaughter of poor George McGovern in 1972 had the party and its candidate been so validated by the American people. Although the Democrats retained control of Congress and remained strong at the state and local levels, the Republicans' post-1968 dominance of the White House—interrupted only by what now seemed a momentary aberration, Jimmy Carter's single term—continued. It seemed the American people refused to recognize the intrinsic shortcomings of the Reagan credo, for to do so would be to deny their renewed faith in themselves and in their country. Even if based on an illusion, this new era of good feelings was one that people wanted to celebrate and savor for as long as possible. The question at the beginning of the second term was how long it could continue given the flawed foundation on which it rested.

Falling Apart

One of the more interesting phenomena of twentieth-century presidential history has been an administration's descent into self-destruction precisely at the moment when it is at the pinnacle of its popularity and control. Such was the fate of FDR, Lyndon Johnson, and Richard Nixon, all of whose presidencies witnessed the dramatic decline of both their stature and programs soon after winning resounding electoral victories. In all three instances the individuals themselves were largely responsible for their loss of prestige and credibility. For FDR, it was his "court packing" scheme that led to the disintegration of congressional support for his New Deal, for the initiative precipitated a powerful rebellion by conservative Democrats and Republicans who had been chomping at the bit to curtail executive power. FDR's high-handedness relative to the Supreme Court simply gave them the entrée they had been waiting for. They could now rightly accuse FDR of attempting to manipulate the nation's constitutional structure to strengthen the executive branch. LBJ's consensus began to dissipate soon after his landslide victory over Barry Goldwater in 1964, which was a mandate for his Great Society. Despite passing landmark legislation in civil rights and social welfare initiatives, it was Johnson's simultaneous escalation of the Vietnam War and his lying about his intentions relative to that nightmare that brought his presidency to its knees. Finally, Richard Nixon, who obliterated poor George McGovern in 1972 on behalf of a new Republican majority, saw his administration unravel, becoming in less than two year's time one of the most humiliated and despised regimes in American history as the Watergate scandal and the congressional hearings held to find out the extent of executive usurpation and corruption became public. The common thread running through all these presidencies was the seduction of power, a willingness to engage in deceit or illegal actions to accomplish an ulterior motive; a hubris that engulfed not just the president but the individuals around the executive who believed that what they were doing was right for the country, regardless of the legality (and wisdom) of their actions.

After 1985 it was Ronald Reagan's turn to experience many of these same pitfalls. Although the scandals and illegalities that ensnarled the Reagan administration did not bring down his presidency, they certainly tarnished Reagan's image, causing many Americans to feel duped and betrayed by an individual in whom they once felt nothing but confidence and pride. Two symbiotic "realities" or revelations were responsible for Reagan's demise in his second term. It was only a matter of time before Reagan's detached, dependent, and uninformed style of governance would catch up with him. During his first term Reagan escaped accountability for the flaws of his disengagement largely because of extraordinary good luck and because his immediate staff brilliantly buffeted him from too much public exposure. One of the biggest mistakes Reagan made during his second administration was to reshuffle his White House staff, sending to new positions the very men who had so remarkably insulated him during his first four years. James Baker became Secretary of the Treasury while the former head of that department, Donald Regan, became Reagan's new chief of staff. Tragically, we know today that Regan, unlike James Baker, could not relate to Nancy Reagan, and thus during the second term,

Nancy, not the chief of staff, exerted overwhelming influence on the president. She always had her husband's ear, but during the second term her presence and control of the president knew no bounds.

Ultimately more devastating to Reagan than listening to the advice of his imperious wife was his increasing detachment from foreign policy decisions and the delegating of such crucial matters to a group of self-righteous, arrogant individuals who came to believe they had the authority and the right to take such matters and the law into their own hands. In short, in this particular policy arena, Reagan's uninvolvement in the details of setting initiatives resulted in him becoming an accomplice in his administration's descent into hubris. Consequently, by the fall of 1987, the Reagan presidency, like so many before it, seemed poised to self-destruct, a victim of its own excesses.

Even before the Iran-Contra affair emerged, the flaws of Reaganomics began to adversely affect the economy. Sky-high federal deficits grew worse, surging to over $200 billion in 1985 and 1986, and hovered at about $150 billion for the next two years. This, coupled with the yawning trade gap, which soared to $170 billion by 1987, made the United States the world's largest debtor nation. The interest on the national debt alone took as much money as it cost to run nine government departments, including Labor, Commerce, Education, and Agriculture. It required the output of 1.5 million American workers simply to pay the interest on the debt it owed to the rest of the world. In the face of such realities, one economist concluded, "the potential for disaster is great." Such conditions became Reagan's principal economic legacies to his successor, George H.W. Bush, who, as will be seen later in this chapter, proved incapable of remedying these two most important issues, causing his reelection defeat in 1992.

Despite such pitfalls, Reagan's second term was not a complete domestic lost cause; there were some important legislative achievements. Most notable among them was the 1986 Immigration Reform and Control Act, which for the moment outlawed the hiring of illegal aliens, strengthened border controls, and offered legal status to aliens who had lived in the United States for five years. Interestingly, all such mandates have not stopped the influx of people from the southern hemisphere, and as will be seen in the next chapter, "the immigrant problem" is still alive and well, often engendering acrimonious debate among the nation's political leadership and in the public forums. The other important domestic initiative of Reagan's second term was the 1986 tax reform. This particular bill made the system fairer by eliminating many deductions—"loopholes"—which had favored the rich and establishing uniform rates for taxpayers at comparable levels. The law removed some 6 million low-income Americans from the income-tax rolls as well. With his appointment of Sandra Day O'Connor, an Arizona conservative and protégé of Barry Goldwater, Reagan also began the reshaping of the Supreme Court and the federal judiciary, in general, into increasingly more conservative institutions. Such a "right turn" relative to the judicial system, and especially in Supreme Court appointments, continued during the presidencies of George H.W. Bush and his son. Even the alleged liberal Clinton White House appointed individuals to the Supreme bench who were at best ideological "moderates."

The Iran Contra Affair and Other Scandals

Without question the most devastating blow to Reagan's credibility and popularity arose from his administration's effort to control events in Latin America, a perennial temptation for U.S. presidents. Late in 1986 a Beirut newspaper reported the disturbing news that a year earlier the United States had shipped, via Israel, 508 antitank missiles to the anti-American Iranian government. Admitting the sale, Reagan claimed his goal with the armaments sale had been to encourage "moderate elements" in Tehran to rise up against the militant fundamentalist regime and to gain the release of U.S. hostages held in Lebanon by the Iranian terrorist organization Hezbollah. The Beirut release was just the tip of the iceberg of a subterfuge, arrogance, and contempt for the law that would reach deep into the bowels of the Reagan White House. Prompting such intrigue was the intractability of the hostage problem, especially the desire to secure the release of an American CIA officer. Although Reagan himself had always insisted that the United States would never negotiate with terrorists, or ransom the hostages, he evidently failed to understand that this was exactly the nature of the bargain proposed by his aides, especially by members of what was becoming a renegade National Security Council led by Robert McFarlane and then by Admiral John Poindexter who, along with his sidekick, Marine Lt. Colonel Oliver North, took the initiative to a whole new level of deceit and abuse of power. Much to their credit, neither Secretary of Defense Caspar Weinberger nor Secretary of State George Schultz supported any phase or aspect of the scheme. Quite the contrary, from the beginning both men vehemently opposed the operation. Sadly, their wisdom fell on deaf ears. As the transactions became murkier and more complicated, even McFarlane advised calling a halt to the entire affair.

Most explosive was the revelation that North, with Poindexter's and others' approval on the NSC, had secretly diverted profits from the Iran arms sales to the Nicaraguan *contras* at the very time the Boland Amendment had been passed and, in effect, forbidding precisely such clandestine support in the overthrow of governments. However, to Oliver North and other true believers, the law was not only irrelevant but a severe retardant in America's fight against communism in the Western Hemisphere. Desperate to circumvent the congressional restraint, North and other NSC staffers solicited third-country and private contributions for the "freedom-fighting" *contras.* Over an 18-month period North and his minions received $32 million for their cause from Saudi Arabia. As the intrigue deepened and more and more players of dubious repute became involved, it became inevitable that word of the chicanery would leak, and it did, spilling across the front pages of not just every American newspaper but all the major publications throughout the world. The Reagan administration naturally tried to skirt the issues but as it became apparent that a cover-up was impossible, Reagan declared that the venture had the best of intentions—to begin to cultivate the anti-Khoumeni forces in Iran, which hopefully would result in the mullah's overthrow—a specious justification at best. Eventually all the "cover" stories were discounted, the plan to divert money to the contras revealed, and an administration that had railed against its allies for talking to terrorists was exposed as having both betrayed its own exhortations and violated its own laws.

In May 1987, a joint House-Senate investigative committee (the Tower Commission) opened televised hearings on the scandal. Perhaps most startling were the revelations made by Poindexter, North, and others that they believed they had the power to create a secret government beyond the control of laws and institutions, free to pursue a hidden agenda that they alone would have the right to define. During the hearings Poindexter declared that he had the right to lie to Congress and the press, on his own authority, without going to Reagan, since he knew what the president wanted, and after all, the people had chosen the president. Poindexter believed it was more important to refuse to inform the president of details in order to guarantee Reagan "plausible deniability" than to bring important issues for decision to him. Suffice it to say, commission officials were shocked by Poindexter's presumption.

Even more terrifying was North's testimony. Not only did North "confess" that he, Poindexter, and CIA Director William Casey (who died of a cerebral hemorrhage the day before he was to testify) had planned from the beginning of the arms sales for the funds to go to the *contras* but to finance as well "an overseas entity capable of conducting activities similar to the ones we conducted here." Even more unsettling, if not reprehensible, was North's arrogance, condescension, and obvious disdain for the commission for having the "audacity" to impugn his "patriotism," which he believed his every action in the operation reflected. After watching the North spectacle one columnist wrote that, "What we see here is a combination of right wing fervor, militaristic nationalism, and religiosity reminiscent of the stirrings of authoritarianism in Europe." Most distressing, the American public initially embraced North as a national hero, more impressed by his protestations of patriotism than by his reckless disregard for the law.

Ironically, even though the scandal seemed a sickening replay of the 1974 Watergate crisis, it was the very prospect of having yet another president, in little over a decade, having to resign in disgrace for the abuse of power that in the end saved Reagan from

President Reagan and Prime Minister Margaret Thatcher on the south lawn during her Arrival Ceremony, February 26, 1981. Photo credit: Reagan Presidential Library

humiliation and kept his popularity in tact. In short, the American people simply did not want to have to endure the embarrassing spectacle of having the world watch yet another one of their leaders either resign or be removed from office for their turpitude. To avoid such a disgrace, the American people decided that for the good of the country, which meant their own redemption, it would be better to exonerate even the worst of the culprits like North, and certainly the president, than to have to endure another Watergate debacle. Thus, the Tower Commission found no positive proof of Reagan's knowledge of illegalities but roundly criticized the lax management style and contempt for the law that had pervaded the Reagan White House. In 1989, after his indictment by a special prosecutor, North was convicted of obstructing a congressional inquiry and destroying and falsifying official documents. However, the conviction was later reversed on the technicality that some testimony used against North had been given under a promise of immunity. Although less damaging than Watergate, the Iran-Contra scandal dogged the Reagan administration's final years as a gross abuse of executive power in a zealous campaign to overthrow a Latin American government the White House found objectionable. Indeed, for a jubilant moment is seemed the "Teflon" had finally worn off. As James Reston of *The New York Times* declared, "You shouldn't be surprised. This administration has been living a life of pretense, cheating, and borrowing for over six years." Even Republican stalwarts such as Dick Cheney of Wyoming, Gerald Ford's former chief of staff noted "You have to say it's a pretty fundamental flaw that would allow a lieutenant colonel on the White House staff to operate in defiance of the law."

With a little more than a year to go in the Reagan presidency, the administration seemed completely adrift in a sea of misfortunes of its own making, paralyzed by the president's detachment and indifference and void of the energy necessary to turn things around. As *The New Yorker's* Elizabeth Drew commented, "It is hard to see how things could change sufficiently to give us a presidency that is not—and does not put the country in—danger." Despite the magnitude of the Iran-Contra crisis and the revelations about the Reagan White House the scandal brought to the fore, Reagan's personal popularity seemed unaffected. Drawing on his training as an actor, he possessed the uncanny ability to communicate warmth and sincerity and to shrug off damaging implications with a disarming joke. Within months of the hearings' ending, Reagan acted as if nothing seriously had happened; that he was still the "Gipper" whom the American people believed in and loved, and despite that little mishap called Iran-Contra, it was still "Morning in America." Benefiting Reagan most was the turn of events abroad, which if handled with alacrity and acumen, would allow his presidency to end on a triumphant note.

Reaching New Heights

Ironically, rescuing the Reagan administration from lassitude and despair was the leader of the president's

President Reagan and Vice President Bush meet with Soviet General Secretary Gorbachev on Governor's Island, New York. December 7, 1988 Photo credit: Reagan Presidential Library

arch-nemesis, the Soviet Union, Mikhail Gorbachev, who not only challenged all of Reagan's preconceptions, but even more important for world peace, accepted Reagan's rather harsh and unilateral ground rules for ending the Cold War. What made such an historic event possible was the complete about-face both men took—Reagan, one of this nation's most fervid and evangelical anticommunists since the late 1940s, became the defender of détente, while the leader of totalitarian communism transformed into a champion of democracy. For the citizens of both countries, if not the world, it was a miracle too extraordinary to contemplate.

Many Americans (especially Republicans) still boast that it was Reagan's shrewd, if not brilliant diplomacy and adroit, "handling" of Gorbachev that made the Soviets accept a "zero option" agreement relative to their nuclear missiles in Europe (in effect Reagan demanded that the Soviets dismantle the Warsaw Pact and remove all their missiles from their Eastern European bases). In reality, the Soviet system, in virtually every capacity, was collapsing by the mid-1980s, leaving Gorbachev and his followers in the politburo no choice but to seek a rapprochement with the United States so Russia could survive without enduring another upheaval like that of 1917, which brought the Bolsheviks to power. In short, by the time Gorbachev became Soviet Premier, the years of Cold War competition with the United States had finally taken their toll; the Soviets simply could not keep pace with the more dynamic and abundant United States economy, an economy that could provide its citizens with the most enviable standard of living in the world while simultaneously producing the most advanced weapons of mass destruction and conventional armaments, from planes, to ships, to infantry rifles. Moreover, by the beginning of Reagan's second term, the old hardliners within the politburo

President Reagan holds a National Security Council meeting on the Persian Gulf with National Security Advisor Colin Powell in the Oval Office. April 18, 1988. Photo credit: Reagan Presidential Library

had all either died (Yuri Andropov and Konstantin Chernenko, Gorbachev's two older predecessors) or had been cast aside by a younger generation of leaders like Gorbachev, anxious to reform Russia before it was too late.

Also affecting the Soviet Union by the time of Gorbachev's ascendancy were the repercussions of the 1979 Soviet invasion of Afghanistan, which had become for the Soviet Union a "Vietnam quagmire." Just as American military might could not, in the end, subdue the Vietcong, neither could Soviet "superiority" defeat the Afghani insurgents fighting a similar guerrilla war with arms supplied by the United States and other countries. The Soviets not only were losing a very costly war, but the Russian people had had enough of Soviet adventurism, which was causing a multitude of deprivations at home. Soviet consumers waited in lines for hours for basic necessities such as meat, bread, and toilet paper, while the government spent billions of rubles on new rockets, tanks, and trying to hold on to a country, Afghanistan, which the majority of Soviet citizens believed was a horrible waste of Russian lives and resources. Gorbachev agreed; within a year of becoming premier he pulled all Soviet troops out of Afghanistan and gave the country back to its people, which sadly became under the Taliban, an Islamic fundamentalist faction that took over Afghanistan in the early 1990s, one of the most oppressive regimes in the world; ironically a far more repressive government than the one that had invaded the country in 1979.

The final motivating factor for Gorbachev to seek détente with the United States was Reagan's startling news that the United States had developed the ultimate weapon, which would render any future retaliatory missile attacks or first-strikes by the Soviets futile—the Strategic Defense Initiative, or SDI ("star wars"). Such a device, Reagan told Gorbachev, would use laser-beam technology to build an umbrella of protection that would destroy any incoming missile. Suffice it to say, Reagan's revelation stunned Gorbachev, who probably initially believed Reagan suffered from fantastical delusions or at best was bluffing. Regardless of first reactions, Gorbachev knew that whether the United States had such a weapon was moot; he knew he could not justify to his people the building of a similar device without them exploding in revolution. The Soviet people, economically burdened for decades with sustaining military parity with the United States had had enough. It was time to end this ridiculous no-win war of nerves and saber rattling with the United States and build a new Russia. Gorbachev agreed and thus announced his commitment to *glasnost* and *perestroika* (openness, freedom, and decentralization) at home while simultaneously announcing massive cuts in Soviet arms production and a new policy of close cooperation with the United States and its western allies. No doubt such pronouncements startled the world, especially the Reagan administration, which only a few years earlier had denounced the Soviet Union as the personification of evil in the world, thus certain such a turn of events impossible. Perhaps most important, Gorbachev's overtures not only gave Reagan the opportunity to salvage his administration in the midst of the Iran-Contra controversy but the unprecedented chance of a lifetime to help end over forty years of potential Armageddon.

The question now became was the Reagan administration up to the task. Fortunately for world peace, Ronald Reagan rose to the occasion, having four summits with Gorbachev in two and a half years, breaking even Richard Nixon's record with Leonid Brezhnev in the early 1970s. In 1987 the two leaders signed the Intermediate Nuclear Forces Treaty (INF), providing for the removal of 2500 U.S. and Soviet missiles from Europe. This treaty, for the first time, eliminated an entire class of existing nuclear weapons rather than merely limiting the number of future weapons as SALT I had done. It in turn led to Reagan's historic visit to Moscow in May 1988, where the two leaders strolled and chatted in Red Square in front of the Kremlin. Historic in themselves, the INF treaty and Reagan's trip to Moscow proved a mere prelude to more dramatic events. They marked, in fact, nothing less than the beginning of the end of the Cold War. That one of America's most dedicated Cold Warriors should be the president to preside over its final phase remains one of the great ironies of recent United States history. Nonetheless, the president's luck had returned, and Ronald Reagan could leave the White House as the man who took one of the greatest steps toward world peace since World War II instead of as a leader, like Johnson and Nixon before him, embarrassed and humiliated by his own errors in judgment. But whatever Reagan's part (and it should not be ignored or downplayed), the triumph was above all a gift of Mikhail Gorbachev, who for his own reasons had entered onto the world stage with his own commitment to radical change for his country, which would most assuredly impact the United States. Indeed, as one Soviet leader humorously but poignantly announced, "We are going to do something terrible to you Americans; we are going to deprive you of an enemy."

When Ronald Reagan likened his presidency to a sheriff who had come to town to clean out all the "bad guys," he projected an image of himself that baffled many foreign observers: how could an ex-B-rated actor who played cowboys ever become president of the most powerful, richest, and advanced nation in the world? The answer was simple: it was Reagan the actor who held the key to the political history of the 1980s. He himself wondered out loud how any president who had *not* been an actor could survive the Oval Office. In his daily routine he carried out the role assigned to him. At moments of the highest drama, he aspired to Academy Award levels of performance; in his worst parts, he played a role so unrelated to reality that he ran the risk of endangering the country; and in the parts he cared about most, he conveyed the identification, vision, and intensity that could alter the course of history. It was in Moscow, before a group of intellectuals and artists that Reagan articulated his view of the presidency, declaring that acting had helped him greatly "in the work I do now." Cleverly acknowledging the work of the famous Russian director Serge Eisenstein, he went on to tell his audience that, "The most important thing is to have the vision. The next is to grasp and hold it. To grasp and hold a vision, to fix it in your senses, that is the very essence, I believe of successful leadership." In many ways, Reagan had grasped and held onto his vision. He had gotten "inside a character, a place, and a moment." Because he was so successful at playing the part, regardless of what his critics said or continue to say, Reagan left an indelible mark on history. As Reagan supporter George Will noted, the president had produced an era of good feelings. Rhetoric had been an essential component in generating such an atmosphere because Reagan "intended his statecraft to be soulcraft." Will also admitted that Reagan's always-buoyant façade had numbed "the nation's senses about hazards just over the horizon." By ignoring economic realities, disguising portents of disaster, and glossing over the increase in poverty, homelessness, and alienation, Reagan had bought time, for the moment, from the harsh consequences that flowed from implementing his credo.

THE REAGAN LEGACY: GEORGE H. W. BUSH

The person who would politically bridge the decades of the 1980s and 1990s was George H.W. Bush, Ronald Reagan's loyal (and malleable) vice-president. Although somewhat tarnished by Iran-Contra and other scandals, Reagan, thanks in large measure to Mikhail Gorbachev, left the White House with his reputation and popularity in tact. Leaving on such a positive note boded well for George Bush, who could claim that his unflinching support for the president made him Reagan's logical successor. The Republican Party agreed, and with virtually no opposition from within the party's ranks, George Bush easily captured the Republican nomination. Accepting his party's endorsement to carry forward the "Reagan revolution," Bush called for a "kinder, gentler America" and pledged "Read my lips: no new taxes." As his running mate, he selected a relative unknown lightweight, the affable but rather bland and less than perspicacious Indiana Senator Dan Quayle. It was to be Bush's good fortune to preside over the final dissolution of the Cold War and the unchallenged rise of the United States to military supremacy in the world; it was to be Bush's misfortune to inherit an economy wasting away under bloated deficits (the national debt had tripled from $1 trillion in 1981 to $3 trillion by 1988) and industrial inertia. As will be seen, it will be Bush's inability to effectively address such pressing economic issues that destined him to be a one-term president even though he had the seal of approval of one of the more popular executives in twentieth-century U.S. history. Although not to blame for these problems, Bush nonetheless, like his predecessor in many ways, blithely believed they would all go away in due time without much effort from him. Perhaps had Bush possessed Reagan's theatrical wit and charm, the same "Teflon" so-to-speak, he too

Is honesty the best policy? In the 1988 presidential election, Michael Dukakis informed Americans he would raise taxes to cut the deficit. George Bush then delivered his famous "No New Taxes" pledge and won the election. Shortly after assuming office, President Bush recanted his pledge. The tactic hurt his bid for reelection in 1992.

might have escaped unscathed and been reelected. Such was not to be George Bush's good fortune.

Although possessing no core political identity other than being attached to Reagan and elected to office in his own right only once (to the House), Bush's identification with Reagan proved to be enough to get him elected. The Democrats, on the other hand, had far more serious problems to overcome if they hoped to recapture the White House. First, and probably most devastating, was the loss of their party's core, blue collar, industrial, ethnic, Catholic workers, who had gravitated to the Republican Party in 1984, "the Reagan Democrats." Also by 1988, the transformation of the white South into a Republican stronghold was almost complete. Also hurting the party was the loss to a sex scandal of its leading contender Senator Gary Hart of Colorado. The Reverend Jesse Jackson, like Phoenix rising, once again sought the nomination, winning states like Michigan in the primaries and for a while boasting the most delegates. However, to many pundits' surprise, a relative dark horse, the dry, serious, high-tech governor of Massachusetts, Michael Dukakis, ended up the winner. To help "balance" his ticket and in hopes of winning back at least some of the less than "solid" Southern states such as Texas, Dukakis chose as his running mate, the venerable moderate from the Lone Star State, Senator Lloyd Bentsen. Dukakis owed his victory to a superior campaign organization; certainly not to his charisma or to his vision for the country, which many people in his own party had difficulty discerning.

In the electoral race that followed both candidates paid, at best, lip service to the profound issues facing the country. Rather, they favored TV-oriented "photo opportunities" and "sound bites." Bush visited flag factories and military plants. In one of the more ridiculous-looking "bites," Dukakis proved his toughness on defense by posing in a tank, with only his head popping out of one of the vehicle's portals like a jack-in-the-box. Editorial writers grumbled about the "junk-food" campaign, but fleeting visual images, catch phrases, and twenty-second spots on the evening news had seemingly become the essence of presidential politics. Little to any attention was devoted to issues like the greenhouse effect, the globalization of the economy, the proliferation of homelessness, or even the implication's of Gorbachev's revolution in the Soviet Union.

President and Mrs. Bush walk with Millie at Camp David. September 19, 1992.
Photo credit: George Bush Presidential Library

During the hustings, Bush stressed and identified himself with Reagan's achievements, while keeping his distance from the Iran-Contra scandal, which he repeatedly told the public, he was completely "out of the loop." Later evidence revealed that Bush knew more of the intrigue than he told the public in 1988. Emphasizing peace and prosperity, Bush pointed to better Soviet relations, which of course his party took full credit for, low inflation, and the 14 million new jobs created during the 1980s—an achievement unmatched by any other industrial nation. What Bush failed to note was the sector that experienced the most prodigious job growth was the military-industrial complex, thanks in large part to Reagan's belief that the Soviets could no longer engage in an intense arms race with the United

States. He fortunately was right because Gorbachev refused to play that particularly costly and dangerous game. Since the arms race component of the Cold War was now over, there soon would begin the layoffs in those defense industries stimulated by Reagan's expenditures. It would only be a matter of time before unemployment would rise, ultimately affecting the Bush administration.

In response, Dukakis emphasized his accomplishments as governor. "This election is not about ideology, it's about competence," he insisted. Dukakis hammered at the failures of the "Swiss-chesse" Reagan economy and urged "Reagan Democrats" to return to the fold. But throughout the campaign Dukakis appeared edgy, dispassionate, defensive, and simply lackluster. His dismissal of ideology made it difficult for him to define his vision for the country. Indeed, liberals in particular chafed at Dukakis' centrist position on many issues and were especially upset by his less than enthusiastic support for social welfare legislation. They wearied of his stock phrases and his repeated boasts of his managerial skills.

Most disconcerting, the campaign reflected the extraordinary hold appeals to law and order, "negative images," fear, and patriotism still exerted on the American public. The Bush team realized such a reality early on while the Dukakis team, although taking the high road on such matters, which was laudable, allowed the Republicans to paint Dukakis as weak on every issue that appeared to be important to voters, regardless of how shallow and inflammatory those topics might have been. Ironically, initially Bush's "negatives"—the "suspect" qualities people associate with a candidate—were nearly three times greater than Dukakis'. The Bush team quickly remedied that situation, and in some of the most blatantly racist and scurrilous campaign ads ever seen on television, portrayed Dukakis as a cold, effete, unpatriotic, anti-religious, soft on crime, opposed to the death penalty, liberal/intellectual. The most infamous ad depicting Dukakis in such light was the one focusing on Willie Horton, a black inmate who had been convicted of rape and assault and who, on a weekend furlough, had terrorized a Maryland (white) couple, raping the woman. The Willie Horton piece showed a revolving door letting people out of prison (black folk) and accused Dukakis of pampering criminals and endangering law-abiding citizens. "Never had the appeal to racism been so blatant and raw," the *New Yorker's* Elizabeth Drew wrote. However, as Bush campaign strategist Lee Atwater boasted, "If I can make Willie Horton a household name, we'll win the election." He was right. On November 8, 1988, Bush carried forty states, giving him 426 electoral votes, while garnering 54 percent of the popular vote. Dukakis prevailed in only ten states plus the District of Columbia for 112 electoral votes. Although losing the White House yet again, the Democrats retained control of both houses of Congress and most state legislatures.

THE GEORGE H.W. BUSH PRESIDENCY

In exhorting Americans to become a "kinder, gentler" people, and evoking the image of citizens helping one another through volunteer work, creating "a thousand points of light," Bush seemed to be attempting to break from the harsh social policies of the Reagan years. Indeed, Bush was no right-wing ideologue; a conservative on some issues yes, but in reality and temperament, Bush's politics, attitudes, and beliefs reflected more the moderate internationalism of the traditional Eastern Establishment wing of the Republican Party. Such a mentality came "natural" to Bush because he was, despite his claims to the contrary (of being a "Texan"), the scion of a quintessentially WASP Eastern patrician family. Thus, much to the dismay of his party's more doctrinaire conservatives, Bush, to his credit, did not pander to their interests or succumb to their evangelical rantings for enactment of their New Right agenda. Still the question remained: could he, or would he, deliver on both a foreign and domestic initiative for change. Not surprisingly, Bush deftly and purposefully handled most of the foreign policy crises that came his way. Although criticized by the more hawkish hard-right members of his party's supporters for not being more aggressive or assertive on specific issues, the majority of the American people, including Democrats, agreed that Bush was sure-handed and effective in pursuing his goals.

President Bush meets with the Emir of Kuwait, Jabir Al-Ahmad Al Jabir Al-Sabah in the Office of the White House to discuss the situation in the Gulf. September 28, 1990.
Photo credit: George Bush Presidential Library

The Cold War Ends

The collapse of Soviet power, symbolized by the toppling of the Berlin Wall in November 1989, proceeded with breathtaking rapidity during Bush's presidency. Germany reunited for the first time since 1945. Estonia, Latvia, and Lithuania, the Baltic republics forcibly annexed by the Soviet Union prior to World War II, declared independence; Solidarity won free elections in Poland; even in Romania, where the harshest hard-line Stalinist dictator, Nicolae Ceausescu, had brutally oppressed his people for years, was overthrown and publicly executed in a display of democratic fervor that swept through the "satellite states" of the Soviet bloc. Although some criticized Bush for not responding more boldly to these democratic uprisings, his cautious approach made eminent sense. To have reacted with the Cold War mentality and bombast a-la-John Foster Dulles might well have caused a violent counter-revolutionary reaction, especially from the Soviet armed forces already smarting from Gorbachev's demilitarization policies. Indeed, by the time of Bush's inauguration, Gorbachev was already feeling pressure from both the right and left within his country to either move Russia toward greater democracy and privatization or to suppress dissent and maintain the status quo. Were he to lose power to the hardliners, such a coup would reverse many of the positive changes that had already occurred, particularly in Eastern Europe. Thus Bush wisely but judiciously bolstered Gorbachev, publicly applauding his every effort to change Russia and doing what he could to tangibly support his initiatives. Bush correctly believed that the best way to sustain Gorbachev in power was to continue détente by disarmament initiatives. Bush thus responded to Gorbachev's overtures on arms control by cancelling the nuclear-alert status of U.S. bombers and agreed to terminate plans to build mobile long-range missiles. Through a series of summits, the two super-power leaders arrived at stunning breakthroughs on new arms control treaties that promised to reduce dramatically the nuclear weapons arsenals of the world.

Bush's diplomatic aplomb was further tested in August 1990 when the more hardliners in the Soviet military, in a last-ditch effort to reassert control, attempted a coup, which to the surprise of the world was thwarted by an outpouring of citizens rallying behind their nationalist leader Boris Yeltsin, who had become Gorbachev's most serious rival. The coup greatly damaged Gorbachev's credibility while bolstering popular support for Yeltsin and the further democratization of Russian society. Within weeks of the coup's defeat, the USSR disappeared, dissolving into 15 different nation states. By now more a bystander than a player, Bush had committed his only major error—recognizing too late Yeltsin's ascendancy and Gorbachev's decline. Bush recovered quickly, however, and made Yeltsin into an ally, beginning a new coalition wherein both world powers would act in concert to enforce peace around the globe.

One issue of vital concern was the future of the Soviet arsenal of 27,000 nuclear weapons, based not only in Russia but in newly independent Ukraine, Belarus, and Kazakhstan as well. Secretary of State James Baker worked to ensure the security of these weapons and, more importantly, to win the cooperation and promise from these republics' regimes in preventing further nuclear proliferation, especially the selling of these weapons and nuclear technology to other nations or terrorist groups. As strategic talks with Yeltsin and other leaders went forward on these issues, Bush promoted further good will by announcing major reductions in the U.S. nuclear arsenal.

For decades the superpowers had backed their client states and rebel insurgencies throughout the Third World, where competition had always been keen to either pick up new allies or in preventing a favorable regime from being toppled. As the Cold War faded, the prospect for solving some local disputes brightened. In Nicaragua, Bush proved himself to be much less of an evangelical anticommunist than his predecessor, abandoning Reagan's failed policy of financing the contras war against the Sandinistas. Moreover, by the time Bush entered the White House, the Sandinista government was self-destructing, having recently lost its most important patron, the Soviet Union, leaving only Castro's Cuba to sustain the Marxist regime, which Fidel could not do alone. Bush also distanced himself from the *contras* upon learning of their ties to the Colombian drug cartels and other questionable support groups. Bush and Congress worked out a program aimed at reintegrating the more reputable *contra* factions into Nicaraguan life and politics. Bush's willingness to reach an accord with the Sandinistas paid off in that country's 1990 elections, which saw a multiparty coalition of anti-Sandinistas emerge victorious.

Poverty, ignorance, and economic exploitation still plagued Latin America. Open guerrilla warfare continued in Peru, Bolivia, and Colombia, largely the result of conflict between government forces trying to smash the powerful drug lords and their well-armed militias. The flow of cocaine and heroin from those countries to U.S. cities reached epidemic proportions, and the Bush administration determined to stop the trade by getting rid of the individuals who served as the conduits. In December 1989, concern over the drug traffic led to a U.S. invasion of Panama to capture its dictator, General Manuel Noriega, who for years had been on the CIA's payroll. Noriega was found to have been accepting bribes and kickbacks from the cartels to permit drugs to pass through Panama and then on to the United States. Convicted of drug trafficking, Noriega received a life prison term. However, there might have been a more compelling reason for Bush to want to remove Noriega. According to documents, as well as to individuals within the Reagan administration, most notably Caspar Weinberger and George Shultz, and despite his repeated protestations to the contrary, Bush's involvement in the Iran-Contra scandal was extensive. Indeed, according to Weinberger and Shultz, not only was Bush "*in* the loop," he had also strongly advocated for the arms sales and the using of the proceeds to fund the contras. Most startling were the revelations relative to Noriega, who claimed that Bush knew of his drug trafficking but looked the other way as long as Noriega funneled some of his take to the *contras,* which he agreed to do through the CIA. Thus, there was possibly a great deal more involved in Bush's Panama invasion that just the supposed "war on drugs." Incidentally, Noriega mysteriously died in his prison cell a few years later. For the moment these revelations did no dramatic harm to Bush—he continued to stick by his "out of the loop story." What they did do was raise questions about his candor and integrity. Further investigation into Bush's involvement in Iran-Contra was about to proceed when on August 2, 1990, Iraq shocked the world by invading the neighboring nation of Kuwait. Suffice it to say, Americans now had a more important crisis to worry about than whether George H.W. Bush had lied about his role in the Iran-Contra affair; indeed to most Americans that was an episode that was over and done with, and the majority of citizens were glad it was.

Operation Desert Storm

Iraq's dictator, Saddam Hussein, had long dismissed Kuwait's ruling sheiks as puppets of Western imperialists and asserted Iraq's claims to Kuwait's vast oil fields. To a degree, Hussein's accusations and proclamations of sovereignty were historically legitimate, but none of the great powers in the past, nor at the moment, were about to acknowledge their validity, especially since Kuwait had become one of the Western industrial powers most important suppliers of oil. Moreover, under Saddam, Iraq had become a general menace throughout the Middle East, causing the other Arab nations, as well as Israel, to fear his megalomaniacal pretensions. Iraq's military program, including both chemical and nuclear weapons projects, worried many governments. During the Iran-Iraq war, however, the United States had favored Iraq over Iran and even assisted Iraq's military buildup. We now know that such aid to Iraq, which included not just arms but providing Hussein with satellite photos of Iranian positions, continued through the Reagan and Bush administrations. Indeed, Bush, even more than Carter or Reagan, had the closest ties with the dictator, opposing as president a congressional attempt to impose sanctions on Iraq for its use of chemical weapons against the Kurds and arranging for $2 billion in agricultural credits. Only 10 months before the attack on Kuwait, Bush issued a National Security directive ordering all government agencies to strengthen their ties with Iraq. Just a few days before the invasion, the U.S. ambassador to Iraq reassured Saddam that the U.S. wanted to maintain good relations with him and that the Bush administration had "no opinion" regarding Iraq's "territorial dispute" with Kuwait. Thus Saddam was justifiably shocked when Bush turned on him after he invaded Kuwait, for all along he had believed the United States would not only look the other way but even support his annexation of Kuwait as legitimate. As one reporter noted, "During a decade of extensive contacts with Washington, nothing whatever had occurred that could have led him [Saddam Hussein] to expect it"—Bush's complete about-face and determination to drive the Iraqis out of Kuwait.

Why such an abrupt change in policy? The answers were relatively simple: oil, Bush's "wimp factor" image, and Israel. The first does not need much elaboration other than Kuwait was and still is one of Europe's main oil suppliers and, thus for the sake of solidarity with the Europeans, Bush had to respond with force. Ever since he began his run to the White House, many pundits, such as the cover of *Newsweek,* had labeled Bush a "wimp" for never taking a stand on issues or committing himself wholeheartedly, passionately to a cause and articulating a resolve to problems. He appeared a man of mystery and nothing more than a loyal yes-man to Reagan. This dogged him through the early months of the campaign, but he addressed this supposed liability by delivering mean-spirited ads on television. The ads were supposed to have shown the public that George Bush could be "tough" on the issues that mattered and that his opponent was the true "wimp." Saddam's invasion of Kuwait simply provided Bush with the perfect opportunity to reaffirm in the eyes of his own citizens, as well as in those of the world, that George H.W. Bush would stand up to bullying and aggression. Lastly, Saddam Hussein's rantings about destroying Israel could never be tolerated by any U.S. president, and thus in defense of the U.S.'s long-time ally and friend, Bush had to help protect Israel from such possible attacks.

Avoiding Lyndon Johnson's mistakes during the Vietnam conflict, Bush wisely built a consensus for a clear military objective—Iraq's withdrawal from Kuwait, and once that had been accomplished, the use of force ended then and there. There would be no invasion of Iraq proper to oust Saddam Hussein. Bush had also learned from Harry Truman's experience during the Korean War that once an objective has been established and announced, any modification or deviation from that plan could have disastrous political fallout. Truman's reneging on his declaration that the United States' goal in Korea had been to drive the North Korean invaders out of the south, and once that had been accomplished the fighting was to stop, cost Truman dearly. Truman got politically greedy, hoping to erase the stigma of being "soft on communism" for supposedly allowing China to fall to the communists. Wanting to atone, Truman gave General Douglas MacArthur the green light to not only cross the 38th parallel and invade North Korea but to advance to the Chinese border, ready to "liberate" China as soon as Truman gave him the go ahead. As predicted, the Chinese, feeling their security threatened, entered the conflict, causing the war's protraction for another three years; the conflict became a travesty that should have been over with the stated results achieved in six months! China never would have entered the fray had Truman stuck to his pledge and ended the conflict after South Korea had been liberated. Bush learned from both of these past presidents' mistakes.

In his call to arms Bush eventually got the full support of Congress, the United Nations, and, most important, the American people. If United Nations' imposed economic sanctions failed to remove the Iraqi's from Kuwait, Bush was ready to deploy more than four hundred thousand U.S. troops to Saudi Arabia from where the offensive to drive the Iraqis out of Kuwait would be launched. The United Nations mandated that Saddam withdraw from Iraq by January 15, 1991. On January 12, 1991, on divided votes, the Senate and the House endorsed military action against Iraq to commence on January 16, 1991. Most Democrats voted against war, favoring continued economic sanctions instead. The air war began on January 16, 1991. For six weeks B-52 and F-16 bombers pounded Iraqi troops, supply depots, and command targets in Baghdad, Iraq's capital. The air forces of other nations participated as well because after all, this was not just a U.S. war but a United Nation's collective security response to an act of aggression. To the surprise of the coalition forces, even Syria, which was no friend of the United States, joined the "cause," largely because its equally ambitious dictator Hafez Asad saw his country's involvement in the conflict as his chance to weaken a rival; Asad had long wanted Syria to become the dominant Arab power in the Middle East but such pretense could not be accomplished as long as the United States bolstered Saddam Hussein.

In retaliation, Saddam fired Soviet-made Scud missiles against Tel Aviv and other Israeli cities, as well as against the Saudi capital, Riyadh. Americans watched transfixed as CNN showed U.S. Patriot missiles streaking off to intercept incoming Scuds. As portrayed on television, the war seemed a glorified video game. The reality of many thousands of Iraqi deaths, military and civilian, hardly affected the national consciousness. Here again Bush learned from a past president's mistake: Lyndon Johnson did not censor the Vietnam conflict; instead he allowed Americans to watch in "living color" on the nightly news American soldiers in actual combat, and frequently they watched the young men die before their very eyes. Bush was not about to let such a reality undermine his war effort, and thus, thanks to CNN reporters broadcasting live from a Baghdad hotel room, the only "fighting" the American public saw on their television sets were the bombs exploding in Baghdad after being dropped by U.S. bombers on their targets. Thus far Bush had handled the conflict with the greatest of diplomatic and political aplomb and dexterity.

On February 23, 1991, two hundred thousand U.S. troops under General H. Norman Schwarzkopf moved across the desert toward Kuwait. Although rain turned the roadless sands to soup, the army pushed on. Knowing they could not defeat the overwhelming military might of the United States, especially on land, and no doubt at this juncture despising Saddam Hussein for having placed them before such a juggernaut, Iraqi soldiers either fled or surrendered en masse. U.S. forces destroyed 3,700 Iraqi tanks while losing only three. More than 300 Iraqi soldiers died for every allied casualty. With Iraqi resistance crushed, Bush declared a cease-fire, and Kuwait's ruling family returned from various save havens where they had sat out the war. U.S. casualties numbered 148 dead—including 35 killed by "friendly fire" and 467 wounded. Perhaps the most important lesson Bush learned from the past was that once the announced objective had been attained—in this instance, Iraq driven out of Kuwait—the military operation was over. Despite pressure from Schwarzkopf and other generals to push on into Iraq and remove Saddam Hussein, Bush refrained from such action, knowing full well that such a move could adversely affect his presidency. Although Bush was tempted to "unleash Stormin' Norman" on Iraq, he wisely listened to the more judicious advice of his Chairman of the Joint Chiefs, Colin Powell, who reminded Bush of Truman's fiasco in Korea because he momentarily got politically greedy, disavowed his objective, and allowed MacArthur to cross into North Korea with dire consequences. Bush certainly did not want to suffer the same fate so he ordered his potential "MacArthur," Schwarzkopf, not to enter Iraq. Fortunately for Bush, Schwarzkopf obeyed his commander in chief.

Despite some sporadic, half-hearted campus protests, the war enjoyed broad public support. Indeed, to many Americans it was as though the shame of Vietnam had finally been exorcized. After the victory celebrations, however, the outcome seemed less than decisive. Saddam still held power. His army brutally suppressed uprisings by Shiite Muslims in the south and ethnic Kurds in the north. Saddam agreed to grant U.N. inspection teams access to his weapons-production facilities but reneged on his agreement within a few years. Despite the stunning military victory of 1991, Iraq remained a thorn in the flesh for the United States and its U.N. allies.

The Politics of Frustration

In the afterglow of Operation Desert Storm, George Bush's popularity reached an all-time high of 91 percent; not even FDR in the heyday of his presidency had attained such numbers. The lightning victory seemed to vindicate Bush, with many suggesting that anyone who had opposed the war faced political extinction. Indeed, Bush's monumental (but momentary) public acclaim in the early summer of 1991 made many prospective Democratic candidates reluctant to seek their party's nomination, for they did not want to become another Alfred Landon or Walter Mondale, suffering a humiliating electoral defeat and then historical oblivion. Thus many decided to give 1992 a pass, assuming no one could even remotely challenge Bush. Such Democratic trepidation was based on a short-term perspective. The popularity of a triumphant commander-in-chief could fade in the face of other discontents, whether in foreign policy matters or at home. In Bush's case it was the latter, a recession caused by the final fallout of Reaganomics, which inevitably was going to negatively affect Reagan's successor, which just happened to be George Bush. By the late fall of 1991, Bush's lassitude and ineffectuality in domestic matters had caused his ratings to drop below 50 percent. The *New York Times* described Bush as "shrewd and energetic in foreign policy, but clumsy and irresolute at home. The domestic Bush flops like a fish, leaving the impression that he doesn't know what he thinks or doesn't much care, apart from the political gains to be extracted from an issue." As the *Times* accurately observed, Bush cared little if anything about domestic policies, had no ideas on how to proceed, and appeared content to mouth platitudes about things not being *that* bad. "Where was the guiding concept," a Bush administration official asked. "There was none. It's been a problem for the whole Bush presidency." By January 1992, unemployment was over 7 percent; new jobs were concentrated in service industries; and even huge firms like IBM and Xerox were beginning to flounder. Yet, instead of alarm, Bush responded with indifference, even complacency. "I don't think it's the end of the world even if we have a recession," Treasury Secretary Nicholas Brady said. "We'll pull out of it again. No big deal." Rather than devise a new approach, Bush advisors recommended standing pat. "Frankly," Bush's chief of staff John Sununu said in November 1991, "this president doesn't need another single piece of legislation."

The Bush administration thus ignored the realities of a major sea of change in people's attitudes toward politics, even as all around it the tide was rushing out. Eight months after the Gulf War, fewer than 40 percent of the American people felt comfortable with the way the country was moving. A deep-seated malaise seemed to be sweeping the land: there were problems no one was addressing, issues that for too long had been swept under the rug, first with Reagan and now with Bush. Perhaps no other event better encapsulated this frustration, anger, despair, and disillusionment than the race riots that exploded in south-central Los Angeles in April 1992 after the verdict acquitting the police who had been shown beating black motorist Rodney King on videotape. For several days the release of anger and pent-up frustration raged, leaving some forty persons dead and millions in property damage, and again, reminding the nation of the desperate conditions in its inner cities. The Bush administration did little to remedy these issues. In 1990, when Congress passed a bill broadening federal protection against job discrimination, Bush vetoed the measure, claiming that such legislation encouraged racial quotas in hiring. When Bush came to Atlanta in 1992 to observe Martin Luther King Day, King's daughter, a minister, ask bitterly, "How dare we celebrate in the midst of a recession, when nobody is sure whether their jobs are secure?"

Government officials and corporate executives were going to jail for betraying their obligation to the people. Suddenly an election that had looked like a ritual coronation of the incumbent became a wide-open contest, evoking images and passions not seen in the political arena for three decades—not since the 1960s.

CONCLUSION

United States culture in the late 1970s and 1980s revealed contradictory tendencies. On the one hand, in reaction to the upheaval of the 1960s, movies, TV, and popular music provided escapism, and many middle-class citizens immersed themselves in a frivolous, acquisitive, materialism and a careerist pursuit of wealth and status not seen since the 1920s. Perhaps most important and alarming was the emergence of a conservative backlash coupled with a resurgence of evangelical religion around which conservatives organized politically to achieve their vision of a "better" America. At the same time, activist energies rooted in the 1960s found expression in a revived women's movement, a gay-rights campaign, and support for environmental causes. On the economic front, the 1980s and early 1990s saw equally divergent tendencies. The 1980s, although bracketed by recessions, brought a boom that suffused part of Reagan's America with a glow of prosperity. Millions of Americans, however, mostly in the inner cities and mostly darker skinned minorities, seemed permanently frozen out of a high-tech economy that increasingly demanded education and specialized skills. Many African Americans entered the ranks of the middle class, but the majority remained mired in inner city poverty and hopelessness, seething with a rage that the slightest provocation or insult could unleash. Throughout the era growing immigration from Latin America and Asia reshaped the nation's ethnic and demographic profile.

Internationally, U.S.-Soviet relations worsened in the late 1970s and early 1980s but improved dramatically in Reagan's second term. Endemic socioeconomic problems in the Soviet Union—perhaps hastened by Reagan's heavy defense spending, "star wars," and forcing the Soviets into yet another arms race, only this time they refused to engage—signaled nothing less than the end of the Cold War, an amazing and largely unanticipated development that would fully unfold during the presidency of Reagan's successor, George H.W. Bush. Brightening prospects on one front were matched by heightened menace elsewhere. The Middle East, in particular, wracked by ancient conflicts, brought moments of illusory hope interspersed with frustration and tragedy. As the 1980s ended, a rising tempo of terrorist attacks suggested that the nation was entering a period no less dangerous than that which Americans had faced during the darkest days of the Cold War.

Chronology

1981 Ronald Reagan takes office as president
Hostages released from Iran
Severe recession begins (to 1983)
Reagan wins major cuts in taxes and domestic spending and increases in military spending
Researchers identify cause of AIDS
Sandra Day O'Connor appointed first female Supreme Court justice
Reagan survives wounds from assassination attempt

1982 U. S. supports contra war against Sandinista government in Nicaragua
Equal Rights Amendment dies

1983 U. S. invades Grenada
Terrorist attack in Beirut kills American Marines
U. S. pulls out of Lebanon
Reagan proposes Strategic Defense Initiative

1984 Democrats choose Geraldine Ferraro, first woman vice presidential candidate
Reagan defeats Walter Mondale in land-slide for re-election as president

1985 Mikhail Gorbachev becomes leader of Soviet Union
Increase of terrorist acts like airline hijackings

1986 Iran-contra scandal begins to leak out
U. S. bombs Libyan targets
Insider trading scandals rock Wall Street
Challenger space shuttle blows up after takeoff

1987 Congressional hearings held on Iran-contra
Stock market suffers record decline
Gorbachev comes to Washington

1988 George Bush elected president

1989 Berlin Wall is torn down; Communism collapses in Eastern Europe
U. S. invades Panama
Chinese government crushes prodemocracy students in Tiananmen Square
Alaska hit by massive oil spill from *Exxon Valdez*

1990 Bush and Congress agree on tax increases to reduce budget deficit
Federal Clean Air Act is passed
Iraq invades Kuwait; United Nations imposes sanctions
Recession begins
Gorbachev wins Nobel Peace Prize as Soviet troops withdraw from Eastern Europe

1991 Soviet Union disintegrates as Soviet republics declare independence
U. S. ousts Iraqi army from Kuwait in Gulf war (Operation Desert Storm)

SUGGESTED READINGS

Mary Francis Berry, *Why ERA Failed* (1986).
Michael Beschloss and Strobe Talbott, *At the Highest Levels: The Inside Story of the End of the Cold War* (1993).
Bryan Burroughs and John Helyar, *Barbarians at the Gate: The Fall of RJR Nabisco* (1990).
Lou Cannon, *President Reagan: The Role of a Lifetime* (1990).
Theodore Draper, *A Very Thin Line: the Iran-Contra Affair* (1991).
Martin Duberman, *Stonewall* (1993).
Lawrence Freedman and Efraim Karsh, *The Gulf Conflict, 1990-1991* (1993).
Andrew Hacker, *Two Nations: Black and White, Separate, Hostile, Unequal* (1992).
Haynes Johnson, *Divided We Fall: Gambling with History in the Nineties* (1994).
— ,*Sleepwalking Through History: America in the Reagan Years* (1991).
Michael Katz, *The Undeserving Poor: From the War on Poverty to the War on Welfare* (1989).
Jonathan Kozol, *Rachel and Her Children: Homeless Families in America* (1988).
Alex Kotlowitz, *There Are No Children Here: The Story of Two Boys Growing Up in the Other America* (1991).
Nicholas Lemann, *The Promised Land: The Great Black Migration and How it Changed America* (1989).
Martin Lowy, *High Rollers: Inside the Savings and Loan Debacle* (1994).
Kevin Phillips, *The Politics of Rich and Poor: Wealth and the American Electorate in the Aftermath of the Reagan Presidency* (1990).
Arthur M. Schlesinger Jr., *The Disuniting of America* (1991).
Randy Shilts, *And the Band Played On: Politics, People and the AIDS Epidemic* (1987).
James B. Stewart, *Den of Thieves* (1991).
Gary Wills, *Reagan's America: Innocents At Home* (1987).
—, *Under God: Religion and American Politics* (1990).
William Julius Wilson, *The Truly Disadvantaged* (1987).

Chapter Twenty-five

A DIVIDED AMERICA: Bill Clinton to George W. Bush to Barack Obama

It was clear and pleasant on that September 11 morning. United Airlines Flight 93, scheduled to depart Newark at 8:01 for San Francisco, took off 40 minutes late. There were only 40 aboard the plane; 15 of them had decided to take that flight at the last minute. There was the usual combination of business and pleasure travelers. One passenger, with a heavy heart, was recovering the remains of a stepson killed in an auto accident on his honeymoon.

At 9:28 four (or three, according to the passengers) Middle Eastern men wearing bandanas hijacked the plane. One claimed to have a bomb strapped to his body. An air-traffic control tape revealed that the pilot yelled, "Get out of here!" This was followed by a breathless terrorist announcing, with bizarre decorum, "Ladies and gentlemen, here, it's the captain. Please sit down. Keep remaining sitting. We have a bomb on board." But the passengers did not passively remain seated. Through more than two dozen in-flight phone calls they learned that three planes had crashed into the World Trade towers and the Pentagon with horrendous consequences. Jeremy Gluck, a former college judo champion, told his wife that there were three other passengers as big as he. Mark Bingham had played on a championship college rugby team. Tom Burnett, a former high school quarterback, informed his wife that "a group of us" were planning to get control of the plane. Todd Beamer, a baseball and basketball player in college, prayed with a telephone operator he had reached. She heard him say, "Let's roll," at the end of their conversation. A flight attendant told her husband, "They're forcing their way into the cockpit." The passengers seemed to have broken into the cockpit using a food cart as a battering ram. In those final desperate minutes a ferocious struggle took place. At 10:03 the Boeing 757 crashed into thousands of pieces in an old strip mine outside of Shanksville, Pennsylvania. All aboard died, but they had prevented the plane from reaching its destination, the Capitol building or the White House, with further disastrous consequences.

The passengers on Flight 93 were not the only heroes of the 9/11 atrocity. Thousands of fire fighters, police officers, emergency medical technicians, and ordinary people rushed to the twin towers to help. Partially as a result of deadly flaws and failures of communication in their rescue efforts, 343 fire fighters died. One woman, after descending 80 floors, along with dozens of others, found the stairway blocked. A fire fighter broke through an office wall with his ax, locating a way out. "Come this way – move quickly," he shouted, illuminating the path with his flashlight. She and the others made it to the street at 10:24, four minutes before the north tower collapsed. The survivors did not include the firefighter. "He stayed there because there were more people behind us," she recalled.

Mohammed Salman Hamdani, a Muslim Pakistani, was a research technician at Rockefeller University. He had experience as an emergency worker, so he dashed into the towers to assist in the rescue efforts. He was never heard from again. There were insulting rumors about his disappearance and loyalty to America that were dispelled by the recovery of his remains.

The events of 9/11 penetrated the consciousness of Americans who had a sense of invulnerability. Although, "we all know that we are going to die," one observer noted, "Americans see suffering and death as aberrations." The 9/11 catastrophe, "presented us with this massive reminder of death, and how unpredictable, uncontrollable and arbitrary death can be," a social psychologist commented. The public saw the ghastly details on television: the towers collapsing, the people jumping, the billows of smoke, and felt it personally. "Everybody felt that it had happened to them." So the stories of heroism were a balm to wounded souls. The people on Flight 93 quickly acted after they learned about "the unthinkable." The son of one of the passengers said, "I think it is a message to the world that the American spirit is alive and kicking."

THE 1992 ELECTION: Bill Clinton and the Triumph of Neo-Liberalism

The recession that followed in the wake of the Gulf War, to which the Bush administration responded with passivity and a condescending, nonchalant attitude, opened the door for a Democratic victory in 1992. As is always true, the party out of power not only has to have a distinct, clear message of change to present to the people but the right person to articulate that vision and energize the party faithful. In 1988 the lackluster Democratic nominee Michael Dukakis proved not to be the right bearer of the Democratic platform, which, in the minds of many Americans, had become stale, dated, and, most important, out of touch with the post-1968 middle-class. Indeed, Dukakis' route by Bush in 1988 plunged the Democratic Party into ideological disarray, creating the perfect opportunity for a fresh face, an outsider to emerge (as Jimmy Carter had done in 1976), to not only unite the party but breathe new philosophical life into what obviously had become to many party loyalists and voters an unappealing vision. That "messiah" surfaced in the summer of 1991 in the person of William Jefferson Clinton, the 45-year-old, six-term governor of Arkansas.

Although paying respectful homage to the liberal agenda of his predecessors, Clinton, along with a host of other post-Great Society Democrats, claimed to represent a "New Democracy" in ideology and vision. They were neo-liberals who believed the party had to "center" itself and cultivate a new relationship and appeal among the middle-class, especially with its more upwardly mobile, affluent members, who since the 1980s, had moved to the right along with many traditional working class Democrats whose disaffection began in 1968. In effect, to Clinton and his neo-liberal cohorts, if the Democrats hoped to win the presidency as well as maintain the Democratic Party as the majority party, it was time for the Democracy to shed its New Deal/Great Society heritage and shibboleths and embrace instead a "new look" that reflected the interests and concerns of blue-collar and white collar middle-class voters. As noted in the previous chapter, beginning in 1968 and over the course of the next two decades, white middle-class Americans, regardless of their "collars'" color, had come to resent traditional liberalism, especially as it had manifested in the Great Society, which many middle-class white people believed had overwhelmingly catered to the underprivileged and disenfranchised literally at their class's expense. Such "favoritism" (whether real or perceived) caused wide-spread white middle-class alienation and defection, resulting in the emergence of the "Reagan Democrats" and Republican presidential landslide victories beginning in 1980.

To promote his party's new ethos and agenda, Clinton, along with other neo-liberals, created the Democratic Leadership Council in the late 1980s. In 1990 Clinton became the DLC's chairman and from that position he began putting together a new coalition of middle-class Democrats, whom he

Bill Clinton shaking hands with John F. Kennedy.
Photo credit: Consolidated News, Arnie Sachs

was confident would become the driving force in the party's transformation. In the summer of 1991 Clinton believed the time was right for him to test whether the middle-class was ready to embrace neo-liberalism and thus rejoin a redefined and refocused Democratic Party by announcing that he was running for the party's nomination. To the surprise of many, including the stalwarts of his own party, there emerged a groundswell of support throughout the country for Clinton's new "message."

Although confident he could bring back to the party the wayward middle-class Reagan Democrats, Clinton, more than the incumbent Bush, had to contend with the unsuspected and potentially damaging third-party candidacy of Texas billionaire Ross Perot, who many Clinton Democrats feared could hurt their candidate's presidential prospects. Perot, like Clinton, had great populist appeal with his pithy, "straight-talking," outspoken views on everything and a remarkable capacity (like Clinton) to be in the right place and the right time. Similar to Clinton, but more direct, Perot claimed to speak for "the forgotten Americans," who were sick of big government, especially the bureaucratic functionaries and self-serving party hacks who seemed to be "running the show" in Washington and who were tired of both major parties' political manipulation, falsehoods, and broken promises. Perot appealed to those who were ready for a take-charge kind of guy, who could look under the hood, tell them what was wrong and proceed to fix the damage without fanfare, political jargon, and something in return.

Perot's party (he liked the term "citizens group" better), "United We Stand, America," called for cutting the deficit and balancing the budget. Although allegedly "a-ideological," Perot articulated a political philosophy that was essentially conservative/libertarian, which called for less government involvement in people's lives. However, his inherent conservatism was tempered by a populist reality that many Americans still wanted a government responsive to the common people's needs and solicitous of those at the bottom. But it was Perot's folksy "straight-talk" more than anything else that appealed to so many disaffected voters, cutting across partisan lines and causing both major parties to reevaluate their traditional third-party perceptions and calculations.

Helping Perot and others disseminate their respective messages to larger audiences was the emergence of talk-show "journalism," hosted by such celebrities as Oprah Winfrey, Geraldo Rivera, and Phil Donohue. All provided politicians with an outlet to reach the American heartland via television. Although many Americans dismissed Oprah and Geraldo as jokes and thus their respective attempts at "serious journalism" to be a farce, they nonetheless accepted Larry King and his one-hour nightly CNN-sponsored interview program as legitimate. Indeed, King's show by the early 1990s became the prize media site for any aspiring candidate. Perot used his friendship with King to persuade King to let him on his program to "offer his services" to the American people as a presidential candidate. King allowed Perot the airtime, and their one hour "discussion" sans tough adversarial questions, engaged debate, or informed rebuttal, helped to catapult Perot overnight into one of the most popular third-party alternatives in several decades. (George Wallace's presence in the 1968 election represented the last of such "threats" to Democratic-Republican Party hegemony). Media control—or control of the media—suddenly took on new meaning.

Unfortunately for Clinton, as the Democratic donnybrook for president unfolded, it would only be a matter of time before Clinton's notorious philandering past would come to the fore. However, Clinton and his equally politically savvy and ambitious wife, Hillary, knew the question would arise and they and Clinton's staff prepared early on to address the inevitable. Clinton did a masterful job of convincing the press that such "indiscretions" were behind him when his 12-year affair with Gennifer Flowers hit the tabloids and then the legitimate press. Although most of the revelations about their relationship had either been exaggerated or were outright false, Clinton's campaign nonetheless entered a "free fall" in the polls. Indeed, it looked as if his gambit for the Democratic nomination was over. However, Clinton was not about to bow out of the race. Instead he chose to publicly address the issue head on, with his wife by his side. Thus on Super Bowl Sunday (January 1992), the Clintons appeared on one of television's most respected, legitimate news programs, CBS' *60 Minutes*. They did what no political couple had ever done before: confess to having past marital "problems"—Bill Clinton's infidelity—but they had now "worked" them out. As Clinton declared, "I think the American people—at least people who have been married a long time—know what [extramarital affairs] that means. Listen to what I've said; I have acknowledged causing pain [womanizing] in my marriage. I have said things to you tonight that no American politician ever has. I think most Americans will know what we're saying; they'll get it, and they'll feel that we have been more than candid." Then, to the surprise of many viewers, who got a glimpse of Hillary Clinton's often insouciant, irreverent, and brusque personality, the future First Lady, senator, and presidential candidate, added: "You know, I'm not sitting here—some little woman standing by my man, like Tammy Wynette. I'm sitting here because I love him and I respect him, and I honor what he's been through and what we've been through together. And you know, if that's not enough for people, then heck, don't vote for him."

It was an amazing commentary, both on what had happened to the political media and what it now took to survive such potentially destructive onslaughts. The Clintons took one of the greatest political gambles in modern American politics by publicly "intimating" that one spouse had not been faithful and then asking for "understanding" (mercy or forgiveness) for such a "momentary indiscretion." To the Clintons and their campaign's great relief, their ploy worked: sufficient numbers of Americans (voters!) understood the Clintons' problem and forgave Clinton for his "wandering." The free fall stopped. Indeed, after losing the New Hampshire primary to Massachusetts Senator Paul Tsongas, the Clinton campaign became a juggernaut of one primary victory after another. By the end of Super Tuesday in March 1992, Clinton had wrapped up the Democratic nomination. However, was it a nomination worth having? The attacks on his personal behavior (such as his alleged Vietnam War "draft-dodging," involvement in anti-war protests while at Oxford University, and his pot-smoking) still dogged him. He had defeated a lackluster group of Democratic challengers and now wondered if he would simply be, like his predecessors, another Democratic sacrificial lamb to a popular Republican incumbent. Indeed, Clinton was even behind in the June polls to Ross Perot. If Clinton hoped to even have a chance to compete, he had to find a way to define himself and his program in such a way that the American people would have a positive reason to support him.

Clinton concluded that he had to focus on the issue or issues that affected the majority of Americans. It quickly became apparent to the Arkansan what that issue was. As the sign in Clinton's Little Rock campaign headquarters blared, "IT'S THE ECONOMY, STUPID." That simple message had to be delivered, however, in such a way as to attract back to the party those Democrats who had defected in the 1980s to the Republican Party but who now felt betrayed by that party's disastrous economic policies, or lack thereof. Thus Clinton began to hammer away at the Bush administration, tying it to the Reagan revolution, which he rightly claimed had victimized and ignored the middle-class and lower income Americans while giving a 100 percent increase in income to the top 1 percent of the country. Clinton realized that the middle-class was the "vital center," whose votes the Democratic Party had to win if it hoped to recapture the White House. It was the nation's largest voting bloc whose values and attitudes had to be embraced and reflected in party ideology and rhetoric and whose well being had to be championed above all other interest groups. Thus in Clinton's neo-liberal litany, "fairness" meant respecting hard work and ideals of middle-class America, getting able-bodied people off welfare, and assuring that everyone, but especially the well-off, paid their fair share of taxes. In verbiage reflecting that of his idol John Kennedy, Clinton's entire economic frame of reference was premised on investment, accountability, and shared responsibility. Indeed, rarely, if ever, in speeches before middle-class audiences did Clinton call for welfare state expansion or greater government intervention in the private sector. To demonstrate that the Democratic Party no longer catered to special interests and particularly to those groups who continued to denigrate white middle-class America, Clinton went to a Jesse Jackson conference and openly criticized the black rap singer Sister Souljah, who had used lyrics that attacked white people. Clinton hoped that such a move would further highlight to white middle-class America that he represented and articulated the ideology of a new Democratic Party.

Despite public chastisements of African Americans for "white-baiting" and bashing, black voters rallied to the Clinton campaign, not only because of their traditional loyalty to the Democratic Party but because Clinton's message resonated well within the African-American community, particularly among its burgeoning middle-class, which despite setbacks during the Reagan-Bush years, still found ways to expand, albeit incrementally. Even as governor of Arkansas, Clinton had connected with African Americans. Indeed, his ability to relate to the African-American community, especially in the South, earned him the honor and recognition among many black Americans of being the nation's first "black president." Clinton also exalted what many 1960s observers predicted at the beginning of that decade: that the United States was on its way to becoming the most diverse society in the world. By the 1990s such a forecast had become true. Clinton publicly celebrated multiculturalism, asserting it to be a positive development, one that was enriching and strengthening the American character by endowing our national personality with a more global perspective and tolerance. By contrast, Clinton lambasted those Republicans who continued to see the existence of ethnic pluralism as negative and un-American. Interestingly, by embracing diversity, Clinton was helping to maintain the Democracy as coalition party by welcoming into its ranks new ethnic groups and continuing to respect the membership of the old ones. Like FDR and LBJ, Clinton believed he could hold all these groups together by devotion to a common set of rules and economic priorities.

Of course helping Clinton was the rapid unraveling of the Bush administration, which by the beginning of 1992 was in a credibility free-fall as the last zip of the Reagan boom completely dissipated. Not only was real income declining for the lower middle-class and working class but much to Bush's chagrin, Republicans around the country began expressing dissatisfaction with the administration's inertia. Tax breaks for the wealthy, deregulation initiatives, high interest rates for investors, permissiveness toward mergers, and an enormous growth in business executives' salaries all contributed to the glaring disparity between those Americans who had so much more than the majority of citizens. Indeed, not since the Great Depression had less fortunate Americans suffered more. Financial expert Felix Rohatyn decried the "huge transfer of wealth from lower-skilled, middle-class American workers to owners of capital assets and a new technological aristocracy." Millions of people, ranging from foreclosed farmers to laid-off industrial workers, were struggling to make ends meet.

Compounding Bush's economic woes was the reemergence of a revitalized Republican "hard Right" led by such reactionaries as Patrick Buchanan who waged war against the man they never believed to be a true conservative anyway. Bush tried to make peace with the far right of his party by unwisely turning over the opening night of the Republican national convention in Houston, Texas to Buchanan and his sidekick, the equally shrill and retrogressive fundamentalist Pat Robertson. The two engaged in some of the most vitriolic rhetorical overkill of the opposition ever witnessed in American political history. For several hours, to throngs of surprising numbers of enthusiastic supporters, the two railed with unseemly invective against every manifestation of the supposed "evils" unleashed by the liberal ethos since the days of FDR and the New Deal.

Both men called for a cultural and religious war to "cleanse" the nation of feminists, homosexuals, pro-choice advocates, and other alleged "deviants," all of whom they claimed were undermining daily the country's traditional moral underpinnings. It was time for 100 percent "Americanism," which to Robertson and Buchanan meant the restoration to preeminence of WASP America and its attendant values. To both men diversity and multiculturalism were code for "mongrelization," which they asserted if not checked soon, would cause the end of WASP America, the "true" Americans. Buchanan also articulated a foreign policy that was both xenophobic and isolationist. There was no gentleness, no tolerance, and no humor. By contrast to the Democratic emphasis on community, inclusiveness, and warmth, the Republicans conveyed a message of prejudice, mean-spiritedness, and anger. Bush unwisely allowed the true believers to run roughshod over the voices of Republican reason and moderation. Even Ronald Reagan could not rescue the evening. Only an acceptance "speech of a lifetime" by Bush could have salvaged his candidacy. Instead, the president arrived at the convention with two contradictory drafts that he tried unsuccessfully to combine into one, ending with a text that offered neither vision nor hope for the party.

Despite the debacle at the Republican convention, Bush continued to believe he could win by running on his laurels, acting as though he deserved reelection simply on the basis of having been president. He believed all he had to do was invoke the pride of "Desert Storm," and he would be returned to office by acclamation. Reality, however, set in by mid-summer as Bush trailed Clinton in some polls by 15 points. At that juncture, Bush asked long-time friend and adviser, Secretary of State James Baker, to leave his cabinet position and take over his campaign. But even an experienced operator like Baker could not do much without the president having a message he wanted to deliver, and that remained a mystery. As one highly placed staffer observed, "I still can't tell you what he stands for and I've worked for him for ten years."

While Bush flailed about, Clinton further amplified his image as a new Democrat by choosing as his running mate a generational peer, Tennessee senator Al Gore, Jr. Clinton's selection of Gore surprised many primarily because he was a fellow Southerner, which flew in the face of conventional wisdom that for decades had dictated that a party's candidate never choose a running mate from his own region of the country. Clinton, however, believed that by selecting Gore he could win more Southern states, essential to a Democratic victory. Since the Nixon years, the South had been increasingly gravitating toward the Republican Party; by the end of the Reagan era, the "Solid South" now meant Republican. Thus, with a fellow Southerner on the ticket, Clinton was confident he would at least win a few key Southern states, at least enough to turn the tide in his favor in the electoral college. Clinton's gambit paid off. In the election he took Arkansas, Louisiana, Georgia, Tennessee, and Kentucky, all states that four years earlier went to George H.W. Bush.

At its elemental level, the 1960s was what the 1992 election was all about. For Bill Clinton, the 1960s represented a moment of hope, a surge of moral commitment to try to make not only the United States a more equitable and just society but to bring such enlightenment to the world at large. Clinton also saw himself (albeit in a somewhat abridged capacity), as the heir apparent of liberalism, binding him as a "child' of that era to resurrect the reform impulse and fulfill the legacy bequeathed to him by his liberal forebears. Clinton believed, and thus his message was, that it was time for Americans to renew their faith in the efficacy of positive government and embrace once again the ideology that had in the past ameliorated so many of society's inequities. To Clinton, as it had been to his liberal predecessors, liberalism not only could improve the lives of those at the bottom but in the process instill in Americans a greater sense of unity and national purpose as well.

By contrast, Bush reflected the attitudes and spirit of the largely reactionary 1980s, when the conservative, self-righteous backlash, of which he was part, attempted to obliterate the last vestiges of the Great Society. To Bush and other conservatives, the 1960s was a time of excess, rancor, and counter-culture alienation that attacked the values and institutions that had made America great. It was also a decade of unwarranted government intervention and favoritism, especially toward the "undeserving elements" among the poor and "ungrateful" minorities, who used the government's largesse to line their own pockets and turn people against the very entity that was trying to help them. Liberalism did not unite Americans; quite the contrary in George Bush's view, it polarized them into warring factions, which came close to plunging the nation into a second civil war. Thus, the 1992 election's overarching theme was not the impending recession but which version of the 1960s—Bill Clinton's or George Bush's—the American people wished to honor and remember.

In the end Bill Clinton won because he possessed a strategy, a vision, and a campaign apparatus prepared to implement a winning plan. By contrast, *Time* observed that Bush was "feckless, confused, whining, and rudderless." By redefining the Democratic Party along neo-liberal lines, Clinton successfully brought back to the Democrats a good number of Reagan defectors. Clinton called his triumph "a victory for the people [the middle-class] who work hard and play by the rules. . . a victory for the people who are ready to compete and win in the global economy but who need a government that offers a hand, not a hand-out." Bush seemed oblivious to the common folk Reagan had so skillfully cultivated. Bush seemed unable to shed his blue-blood persona and image and connect with the average person. As a result, Bush won a lower percentage of popular votes (37 percent) than Barry Goldwater in 1964, Herbert Hoover in 1932, or George McGovern in 1972, three presidential candidates slaughtered by their opponents. Indeed, no incumbent since William Howard Taft (in 1912 against Woodrow Wilson and TR) had fared so poorly. Bush won a majority only among white Protestant Southerners. In the electoral college Clinton won handily, 370-168, carrying 32 states and the District of Columbia. In contrast to Bush winning only a majority among Southern white Protestants, Clinton carried the Jewish, African American, and Latino vote by large margins and even gained a plurality among people who had served in Vietnam, despite the controversy that had surrounded his alleged "shirking" and "draft-dodging" during the war years. Perot's candidacy hurt Bush more than Clinton. The Texas billionaire gained no electoral votes but did attract 19 million popular votes. Perhaps most surprising, about 55 percent of eligible voters went to the polls, a turnout that reversed 32 years of increasing voter apathy.

Most interesting were the poll revelations that women (both black and white), especially those in the workplace, had favored the Clinton-Gore ticket because they believed they would benefit from the kind

Bill, Hillary, and Chelsea walking down Pennsylvania Avenue. January 20, 1997.
Photo credits: Clinton Presidential Materials Project

of social programs that Clinton and most Democrats promoted. Compared to their male counterparts, fewer working women had employer-funded health insurance; conversely, children and their single-parent working mothers were the overwhelming recipients of food stamps and Medicare/Medicaid. Given such status of many working women, it was no surprise that they would vote for a ticket that promised programs that would ameliorate their plight. Conservatives naturally lambasted such "favoritism," derisively calling such initiatives "the Nanny State." Liberals and feminists exulted, proclaiming 1992 "The Year of the Woman." Indeed, the election saw female representation in the House of Representatives nearly double, from 28 to 47, while the number of women in the Senate tripled, from 2 to 6. Not only did the Democratic victory bode well for women politically but African Americans as well, who saw their presence in the House climb to 41 members, an all-time high.

Perhaps such an improved turnout can be attributed to Clinton's appeal among baby-boomers, for they were electing one of their own and thus took great pride in the fact that their day in the political sun had finally arrived. At the same time, as will be seen, such high expectations, especially among Clinton's own generation, made his job all the more difficult. Like his idol John Kennedy, Clinton was greeted with much the same fanfare and hope. The pressure was on him to rise to such heights and deliver the promised goods. Clinton projected the image of a youthful, exuberant, thoughtful, and brilliant leader with an equally accomplished wife (although one not nearly as glamorous or gracious as Jacqueline Kennedy), who promised to be a full partner in the White House, perhaps potentially more powerful in the public arena than any First Lady since Eleanor Roosevelt. It was almost as though the best impulses of the 1960s had come together to make a reappearance—feminism, a commitment to fairness, a modern marital relationship but one framed by devotion to family, an energetic vision about the ability to use government to make people's lives better. "What excites most people about Clinton," one magazine said, "is precisely the degree to which he speaks to their hunger for meaning and purpose, their half-conscious and often inchoate desire to transcend the selfishness and meaningless of materialistic and narcissistic society." *Time* was equally elegiac: "For years," it said in its Man of the Year issue, "Americans have been in a kind of vague mourning for something that they sensed they had lost somewhere—what was best for the country, a distinctive American endowment of youth and energy amid ideals and luck; the sacred American stuff." To the magazine, Clinton appeared to be the "messiah," providing his fellow citizens with the answer, for his victory "places him in a position to preside over one of the periodic reinventions of the country—those moments when Americans dig themselves out of their deepest problems by reimagining themselves." As one writer noted, to many baby-boomers Clinton was "our generation's second chance."

Whether any president could live up to such high hopes represented both the challenge and the Achilles heel of the new administration. Would it be possible for Bill Clinton to resurrect his version of the 1960s without alienating the very consensus that brought him election victory, who he had assured that his brand of liberalism would keep in check the excesses of the 1960s? At the same time, if he kept his promise to the middle-class that he would not allow liberalism to "run amok," then would it be possible for him to move toward fulfilling the legacy of his liberal forebears—FDR, Truman, Kennedy, and Johnson? Or would he flounder, overwhelmed by the immensity of the problems facing the Republic and victim to his own capacity for self-destructive behavior.

THE CLINTON YEARS

The Clinton presidency can be divided into two phases. From late 1992 to the fall of 1994, the Clinton administration pursued an ambitious agenda of socio-economic reform, resurrecting with a neo-liberal reinterpretation programs and policies last discussed during the liberal heyday of the 1960s. However, whatever progress Clinton had made toward change, he undermined by political miscalculation and shortsightedness and personal dissemblance and dissipation. As a result, the Republicans swept to victory in the 1994 congressional elections, after which his administration reflected little more than survival in office based on accommodations with congressional conservatives. Yet, despite an innate penchant for self-destructive behavior, which did not reach full "potential" until his second term, Clinton implemented many successful initiatives both at home and abroad during his tenure.

Clinton made embracing diversity a reality by appointing to his cabinet three African Americans—Mike Espy as Secretary of Agriculture; Ron Brown as Secretary of Commerce, and Jesse Brown as Secretary of Veteran Affairs—and two Latinos—Henry Cisneros as Secretary of Housing and Urban Development, and Federico Pena as Secretary of Transportation. Clinton's initial cabinet also included three women—Janet Reno as Attorney General, Donna Shalala as Secretary of Health and Human Services, and Hazel O'Leary as Secretary of Energy. As his first nomination to the Supreme Court, Clinton chose Ruth Bader Ginsburg, only the second woman to sit on this nation's highest tribunal. And as representative to the United Nations, Clinton named Madeline Albright, who would also become the country's first female Secretary of State during his second term.

On social issues Clinton claimed several victories during his first term. He ended the Reagan era's ban on abortion counseling in family planning clinics; pushed through Congress a family leave program for working parents; established Americorps (reminiscent of LBJ's VISTA), which allowed students to repay college loans through community service; and secured passage of the Brady Bill, which instituted a five-day waiting period for the purchase of hand guns. In conjunction with the Brady Bill, Clinton also pushed through a crime bill that banned the manufacture, sale, or possession of nineteen different assault weapons. He also won new funding for police and prison modernization as well as for a youth-oriented job corps.

Without question, one of Clinton's boldest yet questionable accomplishments was his deficit reduction initiative, which he made a priority over the middle-class tax cuts and social investment programs in infrastructure, education, environmental technol-

Senator Dick Durbin (D-IL) talks at the podium on the issue of handgun control. In the wheelchair to his left is Jim Brady, who was hit by gunfire when John Hinkley shot at President Reagan. The Brady Act is a congressional law mandating that state law enforcement agencies conduct criminal background checks prior to allowing an individual to purchase a handgun.

ogy, and health care he had promised voters in the campaign. In retrospect, it appears Clinton was paying only lip-service to such endeavors during his run for the White House. Once in office, he dropped the fight for large-scale infrastructure spending and the jobs such a program would have created in favor of a more conservative/moderate-pleasing plan of deficit reduction. Indeed, we know today that from his administration's outset, addressing the deficit was Clinton's priority. Before Clinton introduced his plan and even before his inauguration, he did his "homework" thoroughly, bringing together in Little Rock industrial leaders, financiers, and academics to educate the American people and his own team of advisors about the appropriate combination of deficit reduction and stimulus in the economic agenda he would introduce once he became president. The result was a carefully crafted package that would cut in half the annual deficit as part of the total expenditures, raise taxes on the wealthy, and put in place a mechanism for sustained economic growth. To sweeten the proposal and help create new jobs, Clinton offered an economic stimulus program that would inject $30 billion into the economy through various federal programs and incentives.

Despite their own avowed commitment to deficit reduction, the Republicans refused any cooperation with Clinton. Senate minority leader Robert Dole told the president that he would not get a single Republican vote. The Republicans then successfully filibustered against the stimulus package, and to secure a one-vote victory in the Senate for the overall deficit-reduction bill, Clinton sacrificed an energy tax that he had insisted House Democrats must support as proof of their loyalty to him. In the end, the legislation turned out to be a great success—even if it did pass by only one vote. Indeed, the bill proved critical to ending the seemingly interminable round of huge federal deficits, while encouraging record-setting economic growth and prosperity. Perhaps no other

Clinton initiative better reflected the neo-liberal ethos than his deficit reduction measure, which revealed that the ideology's adherents were fiscal conservatives. As a result, Clintonian economic policies mollified Wall Street bond traders and generated the lower interest rates that Clinton's more orthodox advisers thought necessary for business investment and economic recovery.

"Don't Ask, Don't Tell"

Within months of his presidency, Clinton's tendency toward "political schizophrenia" became apparent. Although initially creating the expectation that his priority was deficit reduction and an economic stimulus package to promote job growth, Clinton quickly got "off message" soon after entering the White House. Rather than focusing on his fiscal agenda, Clinton decided that his first major objective would be to end discrimination against homosexuals in the military. No sooner did he announce such policy than he was lambasted from both sides of the aisle as well as from the military establishment. Indeed, he immediately incurred the disfavor of two of the most powerful men in the capital, General Colin Powell, Chairman of the Joint Chiefs, and fellow Democrat, Senator Sam Nunn of Georgia, who was chairman of the Armed Services Committee. Both Powell and Nunn vigorously opposed the initiative. Without question, Clinton believed personally in civil rights for gays, and he was right to condemn their being discriminated against in the armed services. In his mind, he was now delivering on his pledge made during the campaign to ensure gay rights.

However, regardless of how courageous such an initiative might have been, it was completely the wrong timing for such a measure to be introduced. Clinton simply had not done his political homework. He had built a consensus among middle-class Americans for his vision and agenda, and to maintain their support he needed to give them something immediately beneficial like tax reform or some other new neo-liberal entitlement. By advocating instead something the majority of middle-class Americans believed to be not only peripheral to their lives but "deviant" as well, Clinton alienated the very class of citizens upon whom he hoped to build a new Democratic Party. For someone who was allegedly one of the most politically savvy men to inhabit the Oval Office, Clinton's proposal to end homosexual discrimination in the military quickly degenerated into his own "Bay of Pigs" fiasco, occurring, like for his hero JFK, in the first three months of his presidency.

Once Clinton realized the blunder he had made, he hemmed and hawed and finally came up with a policy of "Don't ask, don't tell," which he believed would be acceptable to the gay community. For gays in the military or for those wanting to join, the words were a meaningless sop designed to mollify homophobic Americans while keeping gay folk in the closet. Suffice it to say, homosexuals felt betrayed by Clinton. His actions also profoundly alienated liberals, especially the "neos," who found Clinton's digression away from economic reform to be most disheartening and alarming. Many now perceived Clinton to be a "waffler," especially when it came to sensitive social issues like homosexuality. "It was the grimmest start of any presidency in generations," the New Republic declared in August 1993.

Health-care Reform

From the beginning, however, everyone knew that Clinton's presidency would rise or fall on his success in passing health-care reform, guaranteeing some form of basic, adequate coverage to every American citizen. By 1992, the United States was the only developed industrial nation in the world without such a system. All the European countries had long since instituted national health-care programs, some even before World War II. That is not to say that liberals had not tried before Clinton. Indeed, both FDR and Truman had put forth such an initiative, only to see their respective proposals shot down by right-wing opposition to such a "socialist" notion. Now, for the first time in almost 50 years, it seemed possible to resurrect the idea, for nearly 40 million Americans were totally without health-care coverage. To many "old time" liberals, the "right" to health care was as fundamental in a democracy as the right to vote. For neo-liberals like Clinton, economic reform and health-care reform were symbiotic: a permanent cure for huge deficits required harnessing the explosive rate of inflation in health-care costs. In Clinton and other liberals' view, health-care reform represented the most massive, important social legislation in all of twentieth century American history, making even Social Security pale in comparison. Clinton was also keenly aware of the future political benefits such reform could bring both him and his party. If he could tie the middle-class to the Democratic Party through providing universal national health insurance, Clinton could solidify at least for another generation his party's dominance, much the same way FDR had used New Deal legislation to create the various coalitions that had made the Democratic Party the majority party until the 1980s. The Republicans were aware of this possible reality, and from the moment Clinton introduced the measure, they were determined to defeat it.

There were a multitude of reasons why Clinton's health-care reform initiative ultimately went down to crushing defeat. One of the most important and fatal errors made by Clinton was to give responsibility for drafting the proposal to a task force headed by his wife Hillary and his old friend and fellow Rhodes Scholar, Ira Magaziner. Although by everyone's account Hillary Clinton was brilliant, hard driving, a master of detail and charismatic leader, she was also dogmatic, did not accept criticism easily nor tolerate dissenting views. Magazine possessed an equally overbearing and overwhelming personality: the quintessential "policy wonk," who believed that non-politically motivated experts could devise such legislation if left alone to do their work. The project became policy-making by secret, expert fiat, led by individuals who were often seen as arrogant, dismissive, riding roughshod over those whom they believed were less bright and competent.

Compounding the personality problems of the task force was the exclusion of Congress, especially the wheelers and dealers who were (and are) key in getting such controversial legislation such as health-care reform passed. Not only were important legislators left out of the process but also were equally vital members of the administration, such as Secretary of Health and Human Resources, Donna Shalala, and Secretary of the Treasury, Lloyd Bentsen, who also had been chair of the Senate Finance Committee. Both of these cabinet people had handled more health-care legislation than anyone on the task force. No doubt individuals such as Shalala and Bentsen, as well as members of Congress, resented being "snubbed." The Hillary-Magaziner operation seemed eerily similar to when "the best and the brightest"—the inside elite and supposed foreign policy experts of both the Kennedy and Johnson administrations—took over the planning of the Vietnam War. Like the health-care task force, the "Wise Men" of that era often met in secret, usurping the role of Congress and other individuals in the decision-making process, ultimately leading the nation to defeat and humiliation in the catastrophe known as Vietnam. Such was about to befall the Clinton administration's health-care initiative.

Not surprisingly, the measure produced by this process was extraordinarily complicated, sophisticated beyond belief—with a provision for any and every eventuality—and completely incomprehensible to the average citizen. Nearly 1350 pages in length, the Clinton health-care package arrived on the Hill almost a full year after the president had taken office. The initiative immediately incurred the venom of both Republicans and Democrats, with the former especially harsh in their criticisms. Utah Republican Senator Bob Bennett denounced the bill as "incredibly bloated, complex, unresponsive, and incomprehensible; symbolic of everything people hate about government." Even supporters expressed anxiety, and the lobbyist for America's senior citizens openly worried "about the complexity of this [plan] and the ability of people to feel comfortable with something that is so complicated. If you're explaining it, people's eyes glaze over."

There was little doubt Clinton could have avoided such attacks and concerns had he gone to the American people with broad outlines of a program and worked with congressional committees to draft the appropriate legislation. For a brief time, however, Clinton overcame the plan's cumbersomeness and inaccessibility. In a cogent speech before Congress and the nation in September 1993, he explained to the American people the measure's most salient points—quality care, savings, simplicity, and security. At that moment the president was clearly in his element, rising to the occasion with a memorable address that galvanized even his opponents in the audience. One Republican senator called Clinton's speech "the most comprehensive, brilliantly presented analytical dissection of everything that is wrong with the present health-care system" that he had ever heard. Yet, almost immediately, Clinton allowed the momentum he had created to dissipate. Other issues distracted him—NAFTA and a military crisis in Somalia, which ended in disaster for the United States. Meanwhile, the Magaziner task force labored away trying to produce a legislative draft—a process that would take two more months. Suddenly the wind in Clinton's health-care sails disappeared, to be replaced by inaction, confusion, and demoralization, especially among reform advocates who saw passing from their control the best chance they would ever have to secure success.

Into the vacuum strode the Republican opposition, who had been waiting to savage the president's plan precisely because of its gargantuan size, its incomprehensibility, and its apparent threat to small business and individual choice. Interestingly, however, the Republicans didn't get very far in their effort to destroy the proposal for Clinton rebounded once again toward the end of his first year with some notable legislative successes such as the ratification of NAFTA, the Brady Bill, passage of his deficit reduction package, creation of Americorps, and a new, more liberal voter registration bill, all of which helped Clinton regain momentum on his health-care initiative. Then Whitewater, sex scandals, and the suicide of White House aide Vincent Foster exploded in the national press, sending Clinton reeling for cover and crippling any chance his health-care proposal might have had. Notwithstanding a determined last-minute effort by Senate moderates to devise a compromise plan, the Clinton health-care initiative was doomed. As late as December 1993, Clinton enjoyed a 17-point margin of approval for his health-care proposal; by March 1994, all support had evaporated with a new majority now saying they opposed health-care legislation. Clinton had lost his moment to become another FDR and to redefine American politics.

To a large extent Clinton was responsible for the defeat of health care, and he openly admitted his culpability to reporters. "We made the error of trying to do too much, took too long, and ended up achieving nothing," he declared in an interview with Haynes Johnson and David Broder. Clinton had failed to "stay on message," as he had done during the campaign. Compounding his legislative dilatoriness and digressions was the fact that Clinton went outside "the system" with his task force approach, slighting and thus alienating key congressional leaders as well as vital members within his own administration, whose knowledge and experience in health-care matters would have been most valuable to his cause. Finally, he failed on the critical terrain of timing and momentum, which any politician will admit is perhaps the most important factor in determining a bill's success or failure.

THE 1994 REPUBLICAN COUNTER REVOLUTION

The Right's Momentary Triumph

Largely as a result of Clinton's failed health-care proposal, the Republican opposition seized the opportunity to initiate its counterrevolution against Clintonian liberalism. Indeed, the Republican right, led by such stalwarts as Newt Gingrich in the House and Texan Phil Gramm in the Senate, had been waiting since the first day of the Clinton's presidency to, as Gramm put it, "blow this train [Clinton's administration] up." After the health-care debacle, Gingrich insisted that Republicans unite in total opposition; even Senator Bob Dole of Kansas, certainly no hard right ideologue, joined with the hardliners not wanting to jeopardize his hopes for the 1996 Republican presidential nomination. The Republicans were simply "chomping at their bits" at the prospect of bringing the Clinton administration to its knees. Clinton faced an implacable opposition that brooked no dissent and set out from day one to demonize the president. If Clinton knew the stakes when he began his initiatives to finish the social revolution started by FDR, Newt Gingrich knew them better. The Georgia congressman was confident that

Clinton's failed health-care reform would be the coup de grace to the last vestiges of liberalism, as well as any future attempts by Democrats to revitalize the welfare state. Gingrich (who holds, interestingly, a Ph.D. in history) believed health-care reform would be the Democrats' "Stalingrad, their Gettysburg, their Waterloo." In short, "General" Gingrich would defeat Clinton, giving no quarter and proceed to lead a Republican counterrevolution that would attempt to destroy the liberal ramparts that the Democrats had built over the preceding six decades.

Fortunately for Bill Clinton, the United States did not have a parliamentary system of government, for if it had, Clinton's presidency would have been the shortest on record. Two years after *Time* magazine called him the "second chance" for the sixties generation, Clinton received a resounding vote of "no confidence" from the American people. Indeed, it was clearly a personal repudiation. The Republican Party gained 9 Senate seats, 52 House seats, and 11 governorships, winning control of both houses of Congress in the process. As one member of the Democratic Leadership Conference observed, "The New Deal is over; the nails are in the coffin; New Deal liberalism is dead and buried." All of Clinton's hopes of becoming the next FDR or LBJ were shattered; the Roosevelt coalition seemed finished, with even the Roosevelt social welfare legacy gravely imperiled. As another Democrat observed in the aftermath of the 1994 elections, "The Republicans enjoyed a double triumph, killing reform and then watching jurors—the American people—find the president guilty. It was the political equivalent of the perfect crime." It appeared that no matter how engaging and persuasive a speaker and politician Clinton had been, many Americans had turned against him personally as well as ideologically, and as a consequence, his presidency seemed doomed. As Democratic consultant Ted Van Dyke believed, "It's over. The president is done. He's finished. He's like the old cartoon where the guy has just had his head sliced off in a fencing match. He just hasn't noticed it yet, but as soon as he tried to turn or stand up, his head is going to topple right off his back."

Gingrich emerged as the main architect of his party's counterrevolutionary agenda, "Contract With America." The "contract" consisted of ten objectives, but the most immediate and urgent were cutting taxes, passing a balanced budget amendment, and reducing the bloated government bureaucracy and radical welfare reform—in short, to begin the dismantling of the New Deal state. From his position as the newly-elected Speaker of the House, Gingrich sought to whip his minions into a phalanx of united, disciplined zealots committed to enacting their own anti-Rooseveltian "hundred days" of reactionary policies, certain the American people wanted such reform. One after another, bills were brought to the floor for votes. There were no hearings; legislators did not even know what they were voting on. Clinton, of course, became an object of ridicule: an emasculated, irrelevant bystander, watching an unstoppable juggernaut tear to pieces not only his agenda but the last vestiges of New Deal liberalism as well. The counterrevolution appeared triumphant. "We are finally seeing where [the Republican contract has] been carrying us," Russell Baker acidly noted in the *New York Times*. "Dr. Kevorkian is now waiting in the parlor. He's about to be shown upstairs to finish off the government we have known for sixty years."

Contributing significantly to the resurgence of the Republican Party was the reappearance of re-energized conservative, evangelical religious sentiment and organization across the nation. The movement had somewhat abated during the Reagan-Bush years, largely because evangelical leaders believed both presidents supported at least tacitly their agenda (in reality and much to their credit, neither Reagan nor Bush pandered to the evangelicals, only occasionally in public forums paying lip service for political advantage to their rantings). However, with the allegedly "non-believing" Clintons and their liberal cohorts in charge of the government, the evangelicals believed it was time to resurrect their crusade against the "Godless" and all of their "sinful" policies and beliefs. Clinton's notorious philandering and his wife's aloof, often cold, personality, intellectualism, and feminism, only added fuel to the evangelical fire. In short, the Religious Right perceived the Clintons and their supporters as the most "un-Christian" administration to ever inhabit the White House. Indeed, so despised by these fanatics were the Clintons that the antipathy each had for the other helped to usher in the culture wars of the 1990s, which, as will be seen later in this chapter, made the beginning years of the twenty-first century one of the most polarized, intolerant, shrill, and inimical times in United States history.

The majority of the Religious Right continued advocating their beliefs and values through civic participation, often gaining control of important local institutions such as school boards, city councils, and other public forums. However, there also emerged within this potentially dangerous movement more extremist sects who sought to remove themselves entirely from the temptations, corruptions, and regulations of contemporary American society. One such group of dissidents was the Branch Davidian cult led by David Koresh, who established their "church" (a barracks-style compound) near Waco, Texas in the early 1990s. Federal officials had long suspected that Koresh and his followers were a potentially dangerous para-military organization who had been stockpiling illegal firearms. Equally attracted to the fundamentalist fringe were white-supremacist militia organizations, which also rejected contemporary America for such alleged weaknesses as "mongrelization," religious and ethnic pluralism, and a whole host of other "sins." This radical fringe of conservatism believed that the federal government represented the greatest threat to American freedom and in order to protect their "rights" they believed it essential to arm themselves to fend off oppressive authority. Such was the platform of groups like Aryan Nation, Posse Comitatus, and other self-proclaimed "Christian patriots." Such fanatics found safe havens for their withdrawal and fortresses in the more remote rural regions of the Far West and Rocky Mountain states.

In early 1993, U.S. Bureau of Alcohol, Tobacco, and Firearms (ATF) agents went to Waco to arrest Koresh and his followers for the illegal possession of firearms. Although that was the official reason, it had also been "leaked" to government officials that Koresh was forcing many people to stay in his compound who wanted to leave. When ATF agents approached the buildings, Koresh and his followers opened fire, and in the gun battle that followed, four ATF agents were shot and killed. After the initial skirmish, a 51-day stand-off ensued. Finally, Attorney General Janet Reno approved a new assault on the compound but instead of another firefight, government agents found a mass suicide a-la-Jim Jones that killed 86 people in the compound, including 25 children. Interestingly, post-melee investigations placed much of the blame on Reno's alleged overreaction and heavy-handedness in dealing with the crisis and thus by extension, the Clinton administration.

For far right extremists, the Waco debacle transformed Koresh into a martyr who had defended both gun ownership and Christian separatism. Tragically, it was only a matter of time before one of the militia groups noted above would seek revenge for "Brother Koresh's murder." The nation became acutely aware of the violent nature of such groups when, on April 19, 1995, precisely two years after the Waco incident, Timothy McVeigh and Terry Nichols, who had associated with right-wing militias, exploded a fertilizer truck bomb in front of the Murrah Federal Building in Oklahoma City, killing 168 people. At the time, it was the most deadly terrorist attack on U.S. soil. Interestingly, the initial news reports of the tragedy all claimed the attack to have been the handiwork of a Muslim terrorist organization! However, McVeigh was arrested within hours of the bombing on a misdemeanor traffic violation and charged in connection with the crime just three days later. After a trial in federal court and demonstrations both for and against the death penalty, McVeigh was executed for capital murder and conspiracy to overthrow the government in June 2001.

Domestic terrorism also assumed political and ideological manifestations. For example, medical clinics that provided abortion services to women became prime targets. Although the ratio of abortions to live pregnancies had been declining since the late 1970s, rabid right-to-lifers became even more bellicose in the 1990s. Opposition Rescue emerged as the vanguard of such fanaticism, which launched its crusade against abortion in a much-publicized blockade of three abortion clinics in Wichita, Kansas in September 1991. Although the "war in Wichita" ended peacefully after 46 days, antiabortion protests became increasingly violent in its aftermath. Several doctors and other medical providers were murdered outside their clinics in the early 1990s. In 1994, with Bill Clinton's support, Congress passed the Freedom of Access to Clinic Entrance Act, which provides protection to any abortion clinic requesting such service. Sadly, despite the passage of the act, the attacks on clinics continued throughout the rest of the decade, resulting in 19 bombings of abortion clinics and the murder of 42 doctors, nurses, and other medical providers.

Perhaps even more alarming than the fact that the killers at Oklahoma City were "home-grown" fanatics was the equally disturbing revelation that a blatantly racist and anti-Semitic novel called *The Turner Diaries* had inspired McVeigh and Nichols. Written by American Nazi Andrew MacDonald in 1978 and widely distributed via mail order and sales at gun shows, the book depicted in gruesome detail a white supremacist insurrection against the U.S. government, including the bombing of federal buildings in Washington, D.C. and Houston, Texas, and the extermination of the nation's Jewish population and people of color.

Although more benign than the militias, the Promise Keepers movement of predominantly male WASP evangelicals, nonetheless reflected the spirit and agenda of the Religious Right. A Promise Keepers gathering in June 1996 attracted 60,000 white males to the Charlotte Motor Speedway in Concord, North Carolina. During the late 1990s the organization filled scores of raceways and stadiums to preach the return of male authority (code for supremacy and chauvinism) and responsibility within the Christian family. Although the Keepers' message appeared to promote the idea of men (white) becoming more family-oriented and accountable, the movement's overall intent was to further the Religious Right's agenda of bringing to the evangelical fold wayward white males or to reinforce among those already committed, the Religious Right's fundamentalist doctrine.

Perhaps no where at the time did Gingrich Republicanism better resonate than in California, where voters in 1994 enacted a state ballot initiative—Proposition 187—that would halt illegal immigrant access to vital social services such as prenatal and childbirth care, child welfare, public education, and non-emergency health care. Interestingly, the measure's passage reflected the belated effect of the 1978 property tax revolt in California, which had frozen most property taxes, costing local government more than $200 billion in badly needed revenue. One of the most disastrous repercussions of this earlier conservative backlash was the end of California's reign for having the best public education system in the nation from the elementary school to the university. California had attained such status because its citizens willingly funded educational institutions. By the 1990s, California schools, particularly at the elementary and secondary levels, had deteriorated sharply, to quality levels that had historically been associated with the far poorer South.

Proposition 187's passing also reflected white Californians historical tendency toward nativism and racism. As they had in their bigotry toward Asians in the late nineteenth and early twentieth centuries, conservative white Californians (mostly concentrated in the suburbs of southern California, such as Orange County), displayed similar sentiment toward the non-white immigrants (mostly Mexican) currently inundating their state, for whom they blamed for California's economic declension. An infamous TV spot broadcast during the 1994 campaign showed illegal Mexican immigrants pouring through a San Diego border checkpoint, with the ominous background voice declaring "They keep coming." Although federal courts overturned the statute, the immigration controversy, as will be seen, will only intensify in the coming years, becoming one of the most divisive issues affecting the nation in the late twentieth and early twenty-first centuries.

The country's political polarization was matched by growing racial tensions, first displayed in the riots in south-central Los Angeles in the aftermath of the Rodney King court fiasco and then again in 1995 as tens of millions of Americans watched with rapt attention the murder trial of football legend O.J. Simpson for allegedly having killed his former white wife, Nicole, and her white male friend, Ronald Goldman. For nine months Simpson's televised trial saturated the airwaves and print media from the most respected publications to the tabloids, as well as dominating most topics of everyday conversation. The spectacle even captivated the international community. Simpson's high-powered defense team led by the now posthumously legendary trial lawyer, Johnny Cochran, exploited America's racial divide, charging detectives who investigated the murder with racism and portraying their clients as the victim of a racially tainted system of justice—the same prejudiced system that had acquitted four years earlier the police who had beaten Rodney King. Sixty percent of all African Americans believed Simpson innocent while 75 percent of white Americans believed him guilty. Simpson's acquittal in October 1995 by a jury of nine blacks, two whites, and one Hispanic revealed once again the racial biases that still constitute the diverging social and legal realities of white and black Americans. The news of Simpson's acquittal precipitated outpourings of jubilation in many African-American communities throughout the nation. Indeed, for many black Americans it was a righteous day of reckoning for decades of unequal justice.

The decade of the 1990s also witnessed the resurgence of black nationalism and separatism as the Black Muslim movement led by the frequently impolitic and inflammatory Louis Farrakhan attempted to attract alienated black males to his crusade for greater black solidarity. Answering Farrakhan's call for such a cause, hundreds of thousands of African-American men participated in a "Million Man March" in 1996 to the nation's capital where they peacefully assembled on the mall in Washington, D.C. to affirm their unity and dignity. Leaders of the march, the largest convocation of black people since Martin Luther King's March on Washington in 1963, made no demands on the government but implored black men to refrain from behaviors and lifestyles injurious not only to themselves but the black community as well and devote themselves to redeeming the black family and the African-American community, both of which had witnessed moral and economic declension since the 1980s. Although often shrill, white-baiting, and anti-Semitic in his speeches, Farrakhan nonetheless rightly believed that the black community was on a path of self-destruction if black men in particular did not assume greater responsibility for the African-American commonweal by embracing their role as fathers and caretakers and as the progenitors and propagators of black pride and solidarity.

Also in 1996, California once again showed its rightward drift by enacting the California Civil Rights Initiative, which banned affirmative action in the University of California system relative to student admissions criteria and in state agencies, further polarizing white and black Americans, especially in matters concerning educational and employment opportunities. Interestingly, since the late 1960s, most university administrators and corporate executives had supported affirmative action, for they saw diversity as a key to business success in a multiracial society. Despite reputable studies that demonstrated that African Americans who were admitted to mostly white universities as a result of affirmative action graduated as readily as any other group of students, they simply needed equal access to opportunity. Studies further showed that African-American graduates went on to careers in the professions, government, and in the private sector in numbers even greater than their white peers. Nonetheless, conservatives argued that affirmative action had become code for "reverse discrimination," and that African Americans, women, and other "minorities" received preferential treatment when it came to job opportunities and admission to universities. As a result, white males in particular had become the victims of prejudice. Conservatives further argued that affirmative action made a mockery of the sanctity of advancement by merit. It contravened the idea of a color-blind society, that the 1960s civil rights laws had successfully ended most racism, eliminating the necessity for such policies. The debate over affirmative action turned into an argument over the degree to which racism (and sexism) remained a reality in American society.

As Gingrich and his cohorts slashed and burned their way across the liberal landscape, they never stopped to think that perhaps they might be pushing the people too fast and too hard to accept their counterrevolution. Indeed, although "filled with vengeful glee" on election night, only 38 percent of eligible voters had turned out at the polls, perhaps reflecting that the American people did not embrace the Gingrich revolution and the Republican "contract" as enthusiastically as the party believed. In short, so drunk with power, the Gingrich Republicans ignored the reluctance of the American people to take radical leaps, either backward or forward, without adequate discussion and negotiation. Indeed, within a few months of what appeared to be the end of liberalism, the American people began questioning the wisdom of what was essentially being done to them by fiat. Were there not some government programs worth preserving, even expanding, such as those protecting the environment? Equally alarming to many Americans was the fact that a high percentage of the new Republicans had no prior elective experience and had won simply because of their ideological connection to powerful far right groups such as Ralph Reed's Christian Coalition. As a result, increasing numbers of Americans wondered whether the individuals they just elected were acting in their interests or were these people nothing more than the lackeys of extreme right special interest groups from whom they took their marching orders while disregarding their constituents' wishes. Moreover, to many Americans vilifying Clinton and destroying the welfare state seemed to be what motivated many of these Republicans rather than serving the nation. By September 1995, less than a year after their supposed mandate, the conservatives found themselves "on the run," as 58 percent of the American people disapproved of the job Congress was doing.

Although bruised and battered, Clinton, to the surprise of many (after all, he wasn't nicknamed "the comeback kid" for nothing) came out fighting, determined to triumph over the reactionaries who had tried to destroy his presidency. In the months between the Republicans' victory and his reemergence, Clinton developed a new strategy for reclaiming and redefining the vital center of American politics. The Democrats had lost the 1994 congressional elections because Clinton's health-care proposal and other measures, such as gays in the military, had alienated the white middle-class, who felt betrayed by the Arkansan because he had assured them in 1992 that he was a new Democrat with fresh ideas, especially about big government and a willingness to take a hard look at its excesses. In short, Clinton had promised voters that he was not a traditional liberal, devoted to old Democratic shibboleths. Yet, the Republicans succeeded in 1994 to paint him with that "old" Democratic brush, and he now had to escape that straightjacket and put the Republicans in one of their own. If Clinton hoped to once again "come back," he had to recast his image back into the new Democrat mold that brought him to the Oval Office in 1992.

In Clinton's venture to resurrect his presidency, he received help from an unexpected quarter: the Republicans, who began digging their own graves by arrogantly believing they could continue to wantonly dismantle even the most sacred programs of the welfare state like Medicare. They were wrong, and Clinton shrewdly exploited their hubris to regain momentum. The Republicans not only foolishly proposed major reductions to this program but simultaneously tried to ramrod through Congress a tax cut for the wealthy that would return to the rich almost exactly the same amount of money that was to be cut from Medicare. This was the opening Clinton had been waiting for to counterattack, which he promptly did by rightly accusing the reactionaries of taking money away from senior citizens, who needed it, and putting it in the pockets of the rich, who did not. Aiding Clinton were the impolitic comments of Newt Gingrich, who declared that Medicare would "wither on the vine" during his counterrevolution. Clinton "ran" with such comments, accusing the Republicans of "killing" the entitlement program of greatest importance to middle-class citizens over 65, while at the same time making the rich richer.

Taking a page from the Truman administration, which in 1947-48 had found itself in a similar confrontation with often venal Republicans, Clinton, in the summer of 1995, launched his counterattack. Like Truman, Clinton flooded Congress with an array of measures (many of which have already been discussed), ranging from a bill that put 100,000 new police on the streets to giving life sentences to criminals convicted three times of felonies to limiting to two years people "on the dole," to cutting the deficit, to even addressing the controversial issues of affirmative action, which he agreed the initiative's excesses had to be kept in check—"mend it, don't end it." Interestingly, unlike Truman's "bombardment" of Congress with programs that called for the expansion of traditional New Deal programs, Clinton's agenda reflected a retrenchment of such policies while simultaneously proposing legislation designed to demonstrate to moderate and conservative middle-class Americans that he understood their concerns, their priorities, and, of course, their "pain." Naturally, Clinton's legislative barrage went far toward bolstering and reinforcing his image as the harbinger of a "new Democrat." The strategy worked; by the end of 1995, Clinton's poll ratings were soaring while those of Gingrich and the Republican Congress plummeted.

However, it was not until Clinton's State of the Union Address in January 1996, did his counterattack become complete when he opened his peroration with the declaration that, "The era of big government is over." With that one line, Clinton took all the wind out of the Republican sails, for in effect, Clinton was declaring to the country that his party had finally shed its New Deal/Great Society shibboleths and in its place had emerged a new Democratic Party devoted to the interests and concerns of middle-class America. No longer could the Republicans criticize either Clinton or his party for being traditional liberals, advocates of big government, and still tied to the old New Deal coalitions. Indeed, no matter how hard Republicans tried to paint Clinton as a classic liberal the president could dismiss such charges, pointing to deficit reduction, a tough crime bill, the Family Leave Act, and a commitment to welfare reform as testimony writ large that he was a new Democrat devoted to the vital center.

Perhaps most important, less than a year earlier Republicans were certain they would obliterate Clinton and the Democrats in the 1996 presidential race. The opposite was about to occur, with Clinton and his fellow Democrats poised to send the Republicans reeling to one of their most embarrassing defeats in several decades. In many ways the Republicans brought such a calamity upon themselves, for they dreadfully miscalculated how long the public would tolerate their wanton arrogance and mean spiritedness directed not only at Clinton but often at the American people as well.

THE 1996 ELECTION: Clintonian Liberalism Vindicated and Triumphant

For many observers, the 1996 presidential election was over the day Bill Clinton gave his January 1996 State of the Union address. Yet, the Republicans continued to believe that Clinton's resurgence was momentary and fleeting, a fluke that would become readily apparent as the campaign year unfolded. With such confidence, the party chose the moderate senator from Kansas, Robert Dole, as their standard bearer. They wisely stayed away from Gingrich and other hard-right possibilities such as Jesse Helms! Although frequently vituperative in his attacks on Clinton, Dole was comparatively benign compared to his more rabid Republican colleagues. His criticism of Clinton was rarely personal or mean-spirited. He focused his assaults on Clintonian liberalism and the policies it had produced as well as on the Democratic Party's alleged excesses and wantonness. People trusted Dole (he had a 62 percent approval rating in 1995, compared to 35 percent for Gingrich and 45 percent for Clinton), and he appeared to put country over partisanship. On the downside, Dole was the oldest person ever to run for president—he was 73 at the time, a World War II "product,"—and despite his good health, he was of another generation and to many Americans, especially among the majority baby-boomers, he represented a step backward. Also undermining Dole's chances was the fact that extreme right groups, such as the Christian Coalition, still had overweening influence within his party. Clinton could thus portray Dole and the Republicans as a candidate and party of reaction and extremism. Never a person given to soaring rhetoric, Dole's unimpassioned speeches and phlegmatic personality created the image that the senator, although an individual of unimpeachable integrity and pragmatism, lacked vision and energy. As his own chief campaign strategist observed, "Dole's strength is [that] what you see is what you get. Dole's weakness is [that] what you see is what you get."

Within weeks it became clear that the younger, more energetic, more charismatic Clinton possessed the advantage. The Clinton staff brilliantly portrayed Dole as Gingrich's clone, always picturing the two together, intimating that by association Gingrich was Dole's running mate, not New York congressman and ex-Buffalo Bills quarterback, Jack Kemp, whom Dole chose before the Republican convention. By Election Day it was a foregone conclusion that Clinton would triumph in one of the most amazing political comebacks in modern American history. Winning 50 percent of the popular vote and 70.4 percent of the electoral college, Clinton succeeded in his fundamental strategy of presenting himself as a dynamic centrist running against an "older generation" captive of narrow interests and shrill partisanship. In contrast to 1992, independent candidate Ross Perot's impact was minimal in 1996 (he garnered only 8 percent of the popular vote compared to 19 percent four years earlier), and his presence hurt the Republicans more than the Democrats. Clinton without question benefited from a burgeoning economy. Typically Clinton ran particularly well among African Americans, women, and Hispanics, who came of age politically in the 1996 election. The Latino electorate, which had increased substantially, swung sharply to the Democrats, largely because of the Republicans' anti-immigrant politics. During the 1980s Latinos had given Ronald Reagan more than 40 percent of their vote, for neither Reagan nor the Republicans of that era were foolish enough to allow the immigration issue to affect or imbue their politics. However, their 1990s counterparts did not demonstrate such political savvy, and as a result, Latino voters began migrating to the Democratic Party. In both 1996 and 1998, their wholesale shift into the Democratic column locked up California for Clinton and his party, and in subsequent elections the Latino vote helped to turn the Golden State solidly "blue." In short, in a booming economy with a focused message dedicated to the middle-class, Clinton had done what he needed to do to recapture the support he had lost in 1994. Indeed, Clinton not only kept his job, winning by even greater numbers than he had four years earlier, but perhaps more important, progressivism (albeit a neo-liberal brand) had prevailed, demonstrating that when given a choice between a radical leap backward and completely dismantling the welfare state and positive government and preserving and even expanding what was good about liberalism, Americans wisely chose the latter. In many ways Clinton's reelection reflected the sufficient faith the majority of Americans still had in the ethos that had served and protected them for over sixty years from the vagaries and excesses of unbridled capitalism and reactionary Republican social policies.

Although soundly beating Dole, Clinton's victory was not a mandate. Despite some loss of seats in the House, the Republicans retained control of Congress, even gaining additional seats in the Senate and several new governorships. Democrats still held a majority of seats in state legislatures, a sign that many voters found ticket splitting (voting for both Democrats and Republicans at varying levels of office) to be a sensible course. Indeed, many experts concluded that voters had made a decision for "divided government," not for one party over another. To a good number of voters such had to be the case to prevent the nation from moving too far left or right. In the minds of many Americans, a "balanced" government was what was now needed. Reforms, yes, if targeted to specific problems and limited in expense and a leaner government, yes, but not if it meant jeopardizing the environment, entitlements such as Medicare, or government guarantees of fundamental rights. In essence, the American people seemed to be directing their political leaders to stay the middle course, which meant allowing the government the flexibility to intervene to maintain and expand, if necessary, the fundamentals of the welfare state but constrain as well those liberals wanting to use the government to enlarge the public sphere while curtailing or negating completely private sector participation and input. Over the course of the next four years, this new frame of reference that the voters had chosen would be strenuously tested, and in the end many concluded that it was not sufficient to deal with the ongoing problems challenging the nation's ability to survive and prosper.

BILL CLINTON AND THE WORLD: Clintonian Foreign Policy

In foreign affairs the Clinton administration made important inroads. Like his predecessor, Clinton too faced the task of reorienting U.S. foreign policy. For nearly half a century, anticommunism and rivalry with the Soviet Union determined much of the nation's policymaking agenda. However, with the breakup of the Soviet Union and the dissolution of the Eastern Bloc, the United State no longer had to worry about "monolithic" communism and thus needed to redefine national security to fit a multipolar world. Clinton (to the surprise of many who believed his understanding of foreign policy issues and real politique was marginal at best) understood this and promoted an expansive, internationalist vision of improving relations with the UN, reinforcing NATO, advancing human rights and democracy abroad, reducing nuclear threats, working on global environmental concerns, and advocating free-market policies. In essence Clinton believed the United States could replace the Cold War strategy of containment with a foreign policy that reflected the attainment of larger humanitarian goals in conjunction with an equally important objective of enlarging "the world's free community of market democracies" under U.S. leadership.

Interestingly, in many ways, Clinton shared the same foreign policy frame of reference and world view as Jimmy Carter. With the United States now indisputably the world's dominant power, Clinton, like Carter, believed he could settle long-standing international conflicts by moral suasion and bring about the end of totalitarians' repression and brutality by making the support for human rights the most important foundation in international relations. It was within this frame of reference that the "Clinton Doctrine" evolved.

Clinton Doctrine and The People's Republic of China

The first application of the Clinton Doctrine occurred during the president's first year in office in response to tensions that had emerged between the United States and the People's Republic of China (PRC). Clinton inherited a less than cordial relationship with the PRC from his predecessor, who had been pressured by Congress to impose economic sanctions on China in the aftermath of the Tiananmen Square massacres. That particularly violent oppression by China's totalitarian government resulted in the killing by government troops of some 3,000 prodemocracy demonstrators and the wounding of 10,000 more in the summer of 1989. International television news agencies broadcast the massacre and subsequent attacks live, provoking condemnation of the Chinese government around the world. The Bush administration was especially affected (embarrassed) by this crisis, for the president had recently negotiated a series of trade agreements with China, extending to the PRC Most Favored Nation status, which in effect would allow Chinese goods to enter U.S. markets after paying minimal to no tariffs.

During the 1992 election campaign, Clinton accused Bush of "coddling" China despite that nation's reputation for being one of the world's worst violators of human rights. However, no sooner was Clinton in the White House, than all such rhetoric ceased. Indeed, Clinton completely reversed his position, declaring that he believed China had seen the error of its ways and that the U.S. should now be looking for "hopeful seeds of change." Clinton thus recommended restoring China's MFN status, despite the PRC's continued religious and cultural persecution in Tibet. The PRC remained a formidable world power, with the planet's greatest number of human beings, the fastest growing economy, a substantial nuclear arsenal, and a veto in the UN Security Council. In short, Clinton believed his predecessor's economic sanctions to be too harsh of reprisals that could backfire on the United States by adversely affecting the nation's economy. In the new Clintonian foreign policy frame of reference the most effective way for the United States to advance democracy in totalitarian countries such as China was to promote free enterprise, which Clinton believed would ultimately force from within the collapse of politically oppressive regimes. Clinton used the same approach in other countries noted for their human rights repressions such as Turkey, Saudi Arabia, and Indonesia.

North Korea

Clinton also found himself embroiled with North Korea over the ongoing issue of that nation's development/acquisition of nuclear weapons. Clinton responded to North Korea's aggressive attempt to create a nuclear arsenal with a "carrot and stick" approach that proved effective during Clinton's tenure in preventing North Korea from going "nuclear" but unraveled after he left office. Clinton succeeded in getting North Korea to abandon its goal of building nuclear war-headed missiles in exchange for assistance

Prime Minister of Israel, Yitzhak Rabin, President Clinton, and Yasser Arafat, chairman of the Palestine Liberation Organization, shaking hands in an electrifying ceremony. September 1993
Photo credits:Clinton Presidential Materials Project

with its energy needs. However, as will be seen later in this chapter, in 2005 North Korea announced that it did in fact possess nuclear weapons, which despite earlier promises to Clinton had been secretly developing all along. Such a revelation not only portended new instability in East Asia but potentially dire consequences for the United States as well.

Middle East

Relative to the Middle East, Clinton strongly supported the Oslo (Norway) Accords, negotiated between Israel and the Palestine Liberation Organization in which Israel for the first time in its history recognized the PLO's legitimacy to speak and govern on behalf of the Palestinian people living in Israeli territory. The accords appeared to be a monumental step toward peace in the Middle East. Unfortunately, when it came time for their implementation, both sides retracted, with local Israeli officials expanding Jewish settlements on Palestinian land in the West Bank—a part of Jordan seized by Israel during the 1967 Six-Day War. Such action by the Israelis upset the Palestinians because the West Bank was the region they had hoped would become the new Palestinian state. Compounding the territorial issues was the corruption, powerlessness, and inability of the new Palestinian Authority, which became the PLO's governing body in the West Bank, to stop the rise of extremist groups from other Arab countries infiltrating into the area determined to bring about the violent destruction of Israel. Clinton, like virtually all his predecessors, worked assiduously to try to make the accords work, for he knew that one of the main keys to peace and stability in all the Middle East was the ending of the long-standing enmity between Israel and the PLO. By the end of his presidency Clinton had succeeded in bringing the two belligerents to Camp David to try to work out a final peace treaty, hoping to leave a legacy similar to that of Jimmy Carter's, who at the end of his tenure delivered the milestone Camp David Accords, which established what appears to have become a permanent peace between Egypt and Israel. Such good fortune was not in the cards for Clinton, whose attempt at rapprochement failed, and tragically violence once again became the order of the day between Israel and the PLO, which after Yasser Arafat's death saw the organization's leadership taken over by hard-line extremists bent on Israel's destruction.

Africa

Like Carter, Clinton found it difficult to balance concern for human rights with the nation's strategic and economic interests and to formulate clear guidelines for humanitarian intervention abroad. Perhaps nowhere during the Clinton years did this contradiction more tragically and graphically appear than in the central African nation of Rwanda, which in 1994 witnessed one of the worst tribal massacres in the history of the continent. Over 800,000 people were slaughtered while 2 million more fled the country while the Clinton administration did nothing but utter rhetorical condemnations. The UN and the French (Rwanda had once been a French colonial possession) ultimately intervened with troops but only after the killing had decimated the country. In retrospect it becomes clear that Clinton knew he tragically mishandled the Rwandan crisis and that his failure to intervene to stop the butchery will forever taint his legacy. Perhaps Bill Clinton's current devotion to his Global Initiative program is an attempt to atone for having so egregiously blundered in Rwanda. In the end, Clinton sacrificed his own inherent sense of humanity to appease the more callous, calculating, non-interventionist mentality of those advisers and citizens who believed that only those regions of the world of the most vital interest to the United States warranted American intervention to stop acts of brutal violence upon innocent people. Tragically, Rwanda did not fall into that category.

One of the most perplexing issues confronting Clinton involved revamping the U.S. military for the post-cold war world and under what exigencies should U.S. troops be sent abroad either as peacekeepers or to help restore order or to protect a legitimate government from revolutionary forces from either the right or the left wanting to overthrow it. Americans were torn on these issues, some believing it was time for retrenchment, or a new isolationism and "America first," while others maintained that the worst thing the United States could do was to turn its back on the world, for if the United States did then the fanatics would surely rise and threaten the planet with greater violence than the cold war ever portended. Typically, Clinton sought a middle ground between the isolationists and those wanting new, more expansive international commitments.

Clinton's policies were tested early in his first administration with several trouble spots sparking debate. In the African country of Somalia, ravaged by famine and civil war, which saw powerful, brutal warlords take over the country, Clinton ordered U.S. troops to the region under the umbrella of a UN humanitarian mission to help provide food and relief support. Clinton decided that the U.S. should take the initiative in trying to end the bloodshed and the warlord's oppression and ordered a "raid" to capture them. Unfortunately, the mission ended up disastrous for the United States as U.S. troops suffered well-publicized and graphically depicted casualties. Indeed, the public, more in an isolationist mood than a humanitarian disposition, pressured Clinton to pull American forces out, which he did in the spring of 1994. In retrospect it appeared Clinton had miscalculated the American public's readiness to deploy troops to liberate oppressed people, particularly those living in underdeveloped nations. Apparently, for many Americans, seeing on the news a dead U.S. soldier being dragged by a jubilant "tribal" people through the streets of a Somalian city was more than they could bear. They were no longer willing to sacrifice their young men to the savagery and barbarism of people who obviously were incapable of civilized behavior. In the minds of many Americans that was to be one of the lessons learned from Vietnam.

Other Crises

In Haiti, closer to home, U.S. interests seemed clearer, and Clinton vowed to help reestablish Haiti's elected president, Jean Bertrand Aristide (who, interestingly

Citizens with Serbian ties protest the bombing of Yugoslavia. On the other side of the street marched those with ties to the ethnic Albanians.

was deposed again in 2003). In September 1994, the first 3,000 of a projected 15,000 American troops landed in Haiti in cooperation with the UN, and last minute negotiations by former president Jimmy Carter persuaded the Haitian military to peacefully step aside. After six months with Aristide in power and political institutions functioning again, U.S.soldiers handed over the peacekeeping to UN forces.

In the former Yugoslavia, the United States also committed troops, under NATO auspices, to halt the massacre of Bosnian Muslims by Bosnian (Christian) Serbs and to oversee a cease-fire and peace building process that all parties to the conflict accepted in the 1995 U.S.-brokered Dayton (Ohio) Accords.

Beginning in 1998, the United States found itself once again in conflict with Iraqi president Saddam Hussein, who was now reneging on the agreements he had signed at the end of the Gulf War and refused to permit international inspectors to examine military sites in his country. Clinton responded by ordering a series of American bombing strikes at military targets inside Iraq.

In 1999 the president faced the most serious foreign policy crisis of his presidency, once again in the Balkans. This time the conflict involved a province of Serbian-dominated Yugoslavia—Kosovo—most of whose inhabitants were Albanian Muslims. Reminiscent of the Bosnian crisis, a savage civil war erupted in the region with Serbian forces accused once again of committing unspeakable atrocities on their "enemies." Clinton and the world knew that Yugoslav president, the Christian Serb Slobodan Milosevic, was nothing more than a brutal dictator, pursuing another ethnic cleansing of his country. Clinton tried negotiating a settlement, but all such efforts failed. Thus, the president decided he had no choice but to use force to stop the genocide. Clinton unleashed a bombing campaign against the Serbians, which was successful in stopping Milosevic from engaging in further acts of genocide. The intense bombing of Serbian forces and bases resulted in a cease-fire and eventual withdrawal of Serbian troops from Kosovo entirely. No doubt Clinton's resolve and his willingness to use force to stop the genocide were responsible for the Serbian withdrawal and the possibility of future peace in the Balkans.

As can be seen from the above crises, during the Clinton years, human rights played an increasingly important role in international affairs. By the 1990s hundreds of nongovernmental agencies had emerged throughout the world defining themselves as protectors of human rights. These various organizations ranged in focus from health care and women's issues to the rights of indigenous peoples like the Aborigines of Australia and the descendants of the original inhabitants of the Americas. Two of the most important were

Amnesty International and Human Rights Watch, for their "specialty" was monitoring how governments treated their citizens. The proliferation of these coalitions not only strongly influenced world public opinion but, perhaps more important, provided justification for interventions in matters once considered to be the internal affairs of sovereign nations. Also as a result of the human rights crusade, new institutions emerged for the purpose of finding and punishing those who had violated the rights of their citizens or those of another nation. The Rwandan genocide produced a UN-sponsored war crimes court that sentenced the country's former prime minister to life in prison. An international tribunal put Yugoslav president Slobodan Milosevic on trial for authorizing the massacre of thousands of Albanian civilians in Kosovo. Spanish and British Human Rights courts wanted to arrest and charge former Chilean dictator Augusto Pinochet with the murder of thousands of Chileans in the 1970s but unfortunately Pinochet was too old and too ill to stand trial, eventually dying while the tribunals debated. It remained to be seen whether these initiatives would evolve into an effective international system of protecting human rights across national boundaries. However, many governments only paid lip service at best to the idea, all the while continuing to persecute and even kill their own citizens or those of other nations or ethnicities in the name of national "purification" and "security."

During the 1990s and first years of the new century, anxiety about international terrorism escalated. Yet, Americans within their own borders felt safer from terrorist attacks than the citizens of many other countries. However, Americans' sense of security from such reprisals was shaken on February 6, 1993, when a small group associated with Osama bin Laden bombed the World Trade Center in New York City. The terrorists used a rented van loaded with explosives that they parked and then exploded in an underground parking area under the Trade Center. The blast killed six people and injured a thousand more. The bin Laden-associated terrorists declared that their action was one of retaliation for U.S. policies in the Middle East. The attack represented the most destructive act of terrorism committed on U.S. soil to that time. In response, Congress, with Clinton's wholehearted approval, passed the Antiterrorism and Effective Death Penalty Act of 1996, which greatly expanded the budget and powers of federal authorities to monitor likely terrorists. Despite increased surveillance of terrorist organizations, bin Laden's Al Qaeda cadre struck another lethal blow. On August 7, 1998, car bombings of U.S. embassies in Kenya and Tanzania injured more than 5,500 people and killed 225. Although in the aftermath of these attacks the Clinton administration put forth concerted efforts to track down the culprits and break up terrorists bands, such as Al Qaeda, bin Laden and his followers as well as other terrorist organizations, cells seemed to disappear or go so far "underground" that the Clinton administration could not find them. Unfortunately, Al Qaeda and its leader, Osama bin Laden, were regrouping and rearming and, most important, preparing to unleash upon the United States the most devastating external attack on American soil in the Republic's history.

Trade Agreements

One of Bill Clinton's principal foreign policy goals was to lower trade barriers, thus expanding U.S. global markets, which he believed essential to sustain the nation's economic boom and prosperity. (Out-sourcing of jobs, however, was not part of the Clinton initiative; American products, not American jobs, were to find greater outlets around the world). Building on the Reagan-Bush legacy, Clinton argued that such policies would not only boost prosperity but help promote democracy around the world as well. Consequently, his administration consummated several historic trade agreements, one of the most important of which was in the nation's own backyard. Despite opposition from labor unions (who feared a loss of jobs and perhaps now they were correct) and other groups that usually supported the Democratic Party, Clinton strongly backed the North American Free Trade Agreement (NAFTA), which called for cutting tariffs and eliminating other trade barriers between the United States, Canada, and Mexico over a 15-year period. After adding new provisions on labor and environmental issues in December 1993, Clinton muscled the bill through Congress in a close vote that depended on Republican support. NAFTA took effect on January 1, 1994. Then in early 1995, Mexico's severe debt crisis and a dramatic devaluation of its peso prompted Clinton to extend a $20 billion loan from America's Exchange Stabilization Fund, an unprecedented act that stabilized the Mexican economy. Clinton realized that economic chaos in Mexico could easily lead to political upheaval in that country, which in turn could impact the United States adversely, especially if violence erupted causing, as it did between 1910-1920, the massive exodus of Mexican nationals to the United States. Indeed, any U.S. president worth his salt must be cognizant at all times of the volatile nature of the Mexican economy and politics. Bill Clinton surely was.

In the same context as NAFTA, Clinton completed the "Uruguay Round" of the General Agreement on Tariffs and Trade (GATT) in late 1993, and in early 1994, GATT was replaced by a new World Trade Organization (WTO), a more powerful multilateral group created to enlarge world trade by implementing new agreements and mediating disputes. Clinton also reversed his election-year position on China, and as noted earlier, despite the PRC's dismal human rights record, returned China to a Most Favored Nation status. To justify this about-face, Clinton argued that increased trade with China would contribute to its democratization process. Similarly, in February 1994, the U.S. ended its 19-year-old trade embargo against Vietnam, and American businesses began establishing relations with a regime that had once been cast as a major threat to U.S. global interests. Surprisingly, Clinton did not make such an overture to Cuba, which, excluding the missile crisis of the early 1960s, had never been a threat in any capacity to the United States. Apparently Clinton concluded the island nation had no economic or even strategic value to the United States and that as long as Fidel Castro ruled, any gestures toward rapprochement would be rejected by Castro. Moreover, too many Americans still feared "communism," and since Fidel was a professed Marxist, the U.S. simply could not have relations with such a regime, even though that was precisely the type of government which ruled Vietnam. Perhaps a future president will see that it is time to reestablish relations with the most important island nation in the Caribbean and that such a gesture would go far toward helping the economies of both countries and especially the Cuban people, who have suffered great economic deprivation and hardship since the early 1960s. When Asian economies faltered during 1998, Clinton strongly supported acting with the International Monetary Funds to provide huge emergency credits to reform and restore financial systems from Korea to Indonesia.

THE CLINTON ECONOMY

Bill Clinton owed a great deal of his popularity to the booming economy he was fortunate to have presided over during his second term and thus benefit from politically. Indeed, the recession of 1990-91 which Clinton exploited to defeat George H.W. Bush was over by Clinton's second year in office and from that point on, economic expansion continued for the rest of the decade. By his last year in office, national unemployment was below 4 percent, a figure not seen since the mid-1960s. Many economists had insisted that if unemployment remained that low, inflation would inevitably occur, the result of excessive consumer spending because everyone had money because they had a job. However, much to these economists surprise, prices barely rose during the boom because rising world-wide oil production kept energy costs low and weak unions and increased global competition made it difficult for workers to demand significant pay raises and concomitantly, for corporations to raise prices. The "Clinton boom" became the longest uninterrupted period of economic growth and general prosperity in the nation's history. Clinton not only garnered great political capital from the boom but expansion also gave him the opportunity to address the massive budget deficits he inherited from Bush and Reagan. Clinton worked assiduously to balance the federal budget—usually an obsession or certainly the *raison d'etre* of the fiscal conservatives traditionally associated with the Republican Party. However, since protracted economic growth produced increased tax revenues, Clinton during his second term not only used such income to balance the budget but to actually produce budget surpluses—not only an anomalous accomplishment for a Democratic president but

President Clinton working at his desk in the Oval Office. Photo credits:Clinton Presidential Materials Project

a rare occurrence for the majority of post-World War II presidents.

THE LEWINSKY DEBACLE AND THE UNRAVELING OF THE CLINTON PRESIDENCY

No sooner was Bill Clinton reelected to his second term than his penchant for self-destruction began, ruining any chance of redeeming an already somewhat tarnished presidency and minimizing the significance of even Clinton's positive accomplishments in domestic and foreign affairs. Clinton's undoing began at the height of his confrontation with Gingrich over the national budget in 1995. The government, in effect, was shut down because Congress failed to pass a year-long appropriations measure. In a crisis-style-a-la-Kennedy, the White House was operating around the clock, staffers and politicians running in and out with the latest news and strategies. One night, a 23-year-old intern named Monica Lewinsky brought dinner (pizza) to the president. Long attracted to Clinton, Lewinsky by her own admission initiated what became a torrid mutual seduction that supposedly never escalated to intercourse but did involve repeated rendezvous for oral sex, which on one occasion resulted in a semen stain on the blue dress Lewinsky was wearing. After about a year Clinton abruptly ended the affair. However, phone calls, notes, and presents between the two continued for several more months. Most damaging to the president was Lewinsky's "sharing" of her affair with Linda Tripp, who, unbeknownst to Lewinsky, was tape-recording their conversations. Almost a year after Clinton's second inauguration, Americans, as well as the world, began to learn piece by piece all the lurid details of Bill Clinton's tryst with a White House intern barely older than his own daughter.

The Lewinsky story exploded into national (as well as world) headlines. Clinton's situation worsened as his affair with Paula Jones and his alleged shady involvement in a land speculation enterprise called Whitewater hit their full impact. Compounding Clinton's problems was the appointment of archconservative Kenneth Starr as special prosecutor for the Whitewater gambit. In the meantime, Paula Jones had filed a federal lawsuit against Clinton, and over the president's objections, the Supreme Court unanimously ruled in May 1997 that the Jones lawsuit should not be deferred until Clinton left office, arguing that it would not sufficiently preoccupy the president to prevent him from conducting his presidential duties. On January 17, 1998, in testimony under oath in the Paula Jones case, lawyers surprised the president by asking if he ever had sex with Monica Lewinsky. Clinton declared, without hesitation, he had not. At the same time, a federal appeals court granted Kenneth Starr's request that his investigative purview in Whitewater be expanded to include the Lewinsky case. On January 21, Clinton unfortunately dug his grave deeper when he flatly denied ever having an affair with Lewinsky. "There is no sexual relationship," he said before TV cameras and later said, "I never had sex with that woman." Hillary Clinton, as she had done in the past, "stood by her man," telling the press that the story had no validity and that it was simply another manifestation of a right-wing conspiracy to destroy her husband.

While Clinton swore "to the world and God Almighty" that no affair had taken place, evidence continued to mount that confirmed Clinton was lying. Clinton faithfuls wanted and needed to believe that the whole sordid business was a right wing concoction designed to vilify the president and bring down his administration. After all, the judges who appointed Starr were conservatives who had lunch with Jesse Helms just before naming Starr. There had always been an irrational hatred for the Clintons among the far right, as if their very presence in the White House symbolized a defamation of conservative values. Moreover, the leaks from Starr's office and Linda Tripp's tawdry behavior reinforced the hope among Clinton loyalists that their man was innocent, the victim of a reactionary plot to "get" the president. Although conservatives certainly relished all that was happening to Clinton, there was no conspiracy. Clinton flat out lied to everyone, for the now famous (or infamous) "blue dress" stain revealed via a DNA test that the semen did come from Bill Clinton. Such undeniable evidence put the last nail in Clinton's coffin, making even his most ardent defenders suspicious that once again the Republican caricature of "Slick Willie" had more truth than falseness to it.

Called to testify before a grand jury Starr had convened to consider the Whitewater-related allegations, Clinton finally admitted to what had now become a given, "I did have a relationship with Ms. Lewinsky that was not appropriate." Even this late in the game, had Clinton gone to the American people, confessed his transgression, and asked for forgiveness or understanding or compassion, he would have received a degree of absolution. Instead, he appeared on television, and while admitting he had dissembled, he offered a truculent and aggressive defense of himself, portraying Bill Clinton as the victim and Ken Starr and his conservative allies as the real perpetrators of wrongdoing. It was simply an awful, embarrassing, and unsuccessful attempt to displace the blame for his lying and cheating onto someone else. By September 1998, Starr told Congress that he had "substantial and credible information" that Clinton had committed offenses that constituted grounds for impeachment. For the next three months the nation watched as Congress heard and debated four different counts under which Starr wished Clinton indicted. On two of those four counts, most importantly that of perjury, the House of Representatives voted for impeachment. In the end, the U.S. Senate, acting as the jury of Clinton's guilt or innocence, acquitted him of the charges, allowing him to remain in office.

Why was Bill Clinton not impeached, let alone removed from office? There were many reasons such a potentially catastrophic act by Congress did not occur. Without question, as more of Clinton's immoral behavior was revealed, compounded by his bold-face lying, the more repulsed people became. Yet, for almost bizarre reasons, the American people continued to like Clinton's ideas and thus, by extension, Bill Clinton. Apparently, Clinton's sexual escapades no longer shocked and disgusted the American public sufficiently enough to turn them against either Clinton or his policies. No doubt the revelations of John Kennedy's notorious philandering made Clinton's womanizing seem not only mild by comparison but excusable as well. It was as if the public separated in their minds Clinton the president from Clinton the man or human being, who like any other normal person was going to make mistakes, and as long as those personal transgressions were not un-Constitutional (which they clearly were not) and did not adversely affect the country, all was to be forgiven. In short, it was as if Americans had come to understand or expect that people in power are physically attractive and that such appeal is simply for many, such as Clinton, too overwhelming to resist.

Moreover, fresh in the memory of many Americans, particularly baby-boomers, was the horrible disgrace and embarrassment of Watergate and the resignation of a president who definitely would have been removed from office for legitimate high crimes and misdemeanors. In 1986, during the Reagan administration, scandal again hit the Oval Office in the form of the Iran-Contra affair. Ronald Reagan, like Clinton, was a personally and extremely popular president who no doubt knew enough of the particulars of the operation to be guilty of complicity. Yet, the American public, wanting to avoid at all costs another humiliating Watergate with the possible impeachment or resignation of yet another chief executive so soon after the first one, were willing to look the other way, in effect exonerating Reagan of any "serious" wrongdoing.

Although Clinton lied about his affair with Monica Lewinsky and did commit adultery, his actions did not violate the Constitutional provisions of his office, nor did they at any time place the nation's welfare in jeopardy. Indeed, unlike either Nixon or Reagan, Clinton's activities, while perhaps morally reprehensible, paled in comparison to the clandestine, arrogant, illegal, and nefarious doings of his predecessors and their respective henchmen. Ironically, as the more conservative Republicans vilified Clinton, with many of their attacks reflecting an obsessive personal hatred, the more popular the president became with many Americans rushing to his defense. Clinton assumed an interesting celebrity or "star" status, like a box office matinee idol, especially among those Americans who responded positively to his vision and message. "Everything about such people is big," wrote one citizen who described Clinton as a classic hero, "their loves, their eagerness to do spectacular things, their deep understanding of how the world works and also their moral failings and their need to win. Clinton's enemies never grasped this; they measured him according to their own smallness."

Nonetheless, the impeachment process rendered immaterial whatever else Bill Clinton hoped to accomplish. He not only was a lame duck in the sense that he could not run again but also in his ability to push through any more meaningful legislation. Although many Americans continued to "like" Bill Clinton, more citizens were so disgusted by his questionable behavior, both sexual and financial, that they no longer had faith or confidence in his leadership. In the end, it was Clinton's moral failings that made tragic what might have been triumphant. Indeed, what in the end destroyed Clinton's possibility for greatness? Hubris, an arrogance that knows no bounds and whose ambitions almost always turn into excess and wanton self-destruction. In short, it was Clinton's character flaws and recklessness that killed his potential for greatness. Wasted opportunities, vicious partisanship, and failure to deal with domestic challenges defined the last two years of his second term. To punctuate this point, Clinton, as if to spite the American people and Congress for having the audacity to question his integrity and leadership, spent the remaining days of his administration issuing pardons to people who had supported him throughout his political career, many of whom had engaged in dubious behavior on his behalf. Among Clinton's "friends" and associates was a fugitive multi-millionaire whose ex-wife contributed substantial sums to the Clinton library in Little Rock. To many Americans, Clinton's eleventh-hour pardons were an appropriate end to a president who left office perhaps not in disgrace but surely not exalted—a "presidential paradox," who was the first chief executive to be impeached since 1868 while simultaneously credited with implementing fiscal policies that allowed him to preside over one of the greatest eras of sustained economic growth in the Republic's history.

However, despite Clinton leaving office with his popularity higher than it had been when he begun his presidency, his questionable moral behavior came back to haunt the Democratic Party and its candidate for the Oval Office in the 2000 election.

THE ELECTION OF 2000

As the 2000 election campaign began, the key issue seemed to be whether "Clinton fatigue," the disenchantment caused by the president's ethical lapses would outweigh the achievement of America's longest economic expansion. After rather bitter primary struggles, the two parties picked candidates one observer described as "a matched set of dauphins." The Democrats chose Vice President Al Gore, the son of a senator, who was described as a "policy wonk." The Republicans picked the Governor of Texas, George W. Bush, son of President George Bush and grandson of a senator from Connecticut. Despite his privileged background, Bush presented himself as a "regular guy." A less sympathetic commentator saw him as a "frat boy" who lacked seriousness. The public was faced with choosing between "a man who knew too much and one who knew too little." The media framed the public perception of the two candidates. Missteps by Gore were presented as further evidence of deception, while mistakes by Bush brought up questions about his preparedness. Gore's factually accurate boast that he had played a crucial role in the legislation that brought about the Internet was changed into the preposterous claim that he "invented" the Internet and continually repeated. Since lack of experience can be remedied while dishonesty cannot, two experts on media and public policy argued, "the dominant press frame in the 2000 election hurt Gore more than Bush."

Both candidates tried so hard to present themselves as centrists that much of the electorate found it hard to distinguish between them. As columnist Ellen Goodman opined it was, "a campaign by two self-described moderates aiming to the center of the center of the undecided center of the country as if they were both trying to straddle a two-lane blacktop." Bush proclaimed himself to be a "compassionate conservative," rather than an extreme right-wing ideologue. Gore declared himself to be a supporter of "fiscal responsibility" and ran on a platform that one writer noted, "sounds as if it was written by the GOP."

A series of three debates highlighted some differences between the two men along traditional Democratic/Republican lines. But many observers felt that the major impact of the debates was to prove that George W. Bush could hold his own and to convey the perception (whether justified or not) that Al Gore was arrogant and untrustworthy. People who watched the debates tended to remain unchanged in their opinions about Gore, but those who didn't came to describe him as less and less honest in the following days, showing the influence of the coverage of the debates rather than the debates themselves. Gore made history in the campaign by choosing Senator Joseph Lieberman of Connecticut as his running mate. Lieberman became the first Jewish American to be chosen for such a position in American history. Aside from attracting some interest for his Orthodox observances, this did not turn out to be much of a factor. Bush selected his father's Secretary of Defense, Dick Cheney as his running mate.

The actual election was extraordinary in many ways. It showed a nation so evenly divided that it was virtually at equilibrium. The two parties were very close in the House, with a slight Republican majority. The Senate was a dead heat: 50-50. This was due in part to the election of a dead Democrat from Missouri (his wife was picked to succeed him) and the extraordinary election of First Lady Hillary Rodham Clinton as Senator from New York.

The presidential election was even more of a cliffhanger in which the media played a key role. Early in the evening, based on erroneous poll results, the networks projected that Al Gore won the state of Florida, which would have given him the election. A few hours later they declared that Bush won Florida and declared him the new president. Millions went to bed assuming that Bush had won, but they awakened to a contested election. When Gore challenged the results, the Republicans were able to portray him as a "sore loser" who was trying to divide the country. The news media reinforced this assumption and created an atmosphere that may well have encouraged the Supreme Court to take the election in hand. In the end, the election was so close that it came down to a few hundred votes in Florida and the vagaries of confusing punch card ballots.

The election was still in doubt in December when the case was eventually brought to the Supreme

Court. Conservative justices on the court had long championed court "minimalism," criticizing judges who impose "their solutions to national problems on the popularly elected branches of government and on the people." Chief Justice Rehnquist had written, "the states are themselves sovereign entities with their own system of laws and courts, and the supreme court of a state is concededly the final authority in construing the meaning of its own constitution and laws." Despite this, Rehnquist led the conservative majority of the Court to vote 5-4 to overturn the Florida Supreme Court's order to recount the votes. The angry Court minority characterized the decision as "a self-inflicted wound."

Despite the controversy, the result was final and George W. Bush was declared president with 271 electoral votes to 267 for Gore. Gore won the popular vote by more than 500,000 votes. This had last happened in the 1888 presidential election. Despite the closeness of the election, there were clear differences that the election revealed in America. Liberals backed Gore with 80 percent of their vote, while a similar margin of conservatives voted for Bush. Abortion rights supporters voted overwhelmingly for Gore, as opponents of gun control did for Bush. Poor people, African-Americans, Jews, Hispanics, and women gave large majorities to Gore. Rich people, white Protestants, and men did the same for Bush. There was a rural/urban divide. *Newsweek* commented that American politics seemed to have crashed: "Voters were hopelessly Balkanized, as if two distinct countries voted, Gore controlling the coasts and the shores of the Great Lakes and Bush nearly everything else." It will take many years for scholars to explain why such sharp divisions led to a virtual dead heat.

THE BUSH PRESIDENCY

Bush began his presidency with a cabinet largely composed of people who had served in his father's or Gerald Ford's administration. He did make history by appointing two African-Americans to lead American foreign policy: General Colin Powell as Secretary of State and Condoleezza Rice as National Security Advisor. As he started his new administration, observers wondered if he could overcome the shadow over his victory and work with an evenly divided congress to achieve his goals in education, national security, and tax reduction.

The president's popularity declined as a result of worsening economic news. Some observers wondered if he would suffer the fate of the other four men who had been elected with fewer popular votes than their opponents and failed to win reelection. Bush was determined to avoid the mistakes that had made his father a one-term president.

The Impact of 9/11

The terrible events of September 11, 2001, when terrorists hijacked three planes and crashed them into the World Trade Center towers and the Pentagon, killing more than 3,000 people, completely transformed the political and social landscape. Initially, President Bush did not project an image of great strength. Americans speculated that he was fearful of returning to Washington as Air Force One bounced around the country in the hours after the attack. He was compared unfavorably to New York City's mayor, Rudolph Guiliani who had impressed the nation with his indomitable performance. However, the president had asserted himself by September 20 in a powerful speech to Congress, and his approval rating as commander in chief climbed to an astounding 90 percent.

The nation experienced a fear it had never known. Some commentators called it "a second day of infamy," comparing September 11 to December 7, 1941, the attack on Pearl Harbor. In both instances there was an unexpected attack preceded by a massive failure of intelligence. The enemy in the earlier assault, however, was an established nation with identifiable aims, and the attack took place on a military target (although many civilians also were killed). Now the enemy was a shadowy terrorist organization, Al Qaeda, whose cells could be anywhere and whose aims were unclear. The actions of these 19 Arab men (16 were from our ally, Saudi Arabia), forced Americans to recognize that there were people who detested the United States so intensely that they would commit "suicidal acts of massacre to make this hatred plain." American anxiety was compounded by

Historians will certainly view the destruction of the World Trade Center in New York City, on September 11, 2001, as a turning point in American foreign, as well as domestic, policy.©Danny C. Sze Photography

the discovery of the deadly anthrax in letters sent to media companies and political figures. No evidence was found to connect this possible bioterrorism to Al Qaeda, but the mere possibility left people even more apprehensive.

President Bush immediately declared war on terrorism, proclaiming that Osama bin Laden would be captured, "dead or alive." By October 7 bombers, fighter planes, and missiles pulverized Al Qaeda camps in Afghanistan and destroyed airfields and military strongholds of the Taliban, the extremist group that was protecting bin Laden and his followers. Within a few days the Afghan skies were under control. Shortly thereafter, the Taliban administration collapsed, and the United State was able to install a new friendly government. A more daunting task would be the rebuilding of an Afghanistan battered by years of conflict and the actions of Taliban zealots. Despite intensive efforts to root the terrorists out of their mountain cave hideaways, both Osama bin Laden and Mullah Muhammad Omar, the Taliban leader, thwarted American efforts to capture or kill them. Al Qaeda terrorist cells were responsible for attacks that killed more than 200 people in Indonesia and Kenya. Some Defense Department officials began to argue that America should launch a more sweeping campaign against other state sponsors of terrorism, particularly Iraq. As the attention of the American government turned elsewhere, the Taliban, who had fled across the border to Pakistan, began to drift back into a beleaguered Afghanistan.

A shaken public demanded answers about intelligence failures that had allowed Islamic radicals to enter the country, study at American flight schools, and launch an unimaginably successful terrorist suicide attack. Congressional investigation revealed vast collections of unanalyzed material and unheeded warnings. "We didn't know what we knew," a former FBI official lamented. After considerable agitation by the families of 9/11 victims, a reluctant administration agreed to the formation of a commission to examine what had gone wrong. The Commission eventually concluded that there had been a massive failure of intelligence agencies to share and coordinate information that they possessed. After much prodding by the commission's leaders and the families of 9/11 victims, the administration agreed to an intelligence overhaul that included the establishment of a new Director of Intelligence above all the agencies involved.

September 11 caused a substantial change in what had been a growing American concern with invasion of privacy. Strong public support developed for such domestic security measures as wiretaps approved by secret courts, delivery people as informants, and government surveillance of churches, mosques and rallies. All these became part of the October 2001 USA Patriot Act which modified the precarious balance between government and privacy. Federal appeals courts endorsed these changes. The public also tolerated closed immigration hearings and prisoners being held without benefit of attorneys. The government conducted sweeps arresting some 1200 Arab and South Asian men who has overstayed visas or entered the country illegally. Many had quietly lived in the United States for years, unmolested by immigration authorities. They were often held in solitary confinement for months and nearly 500 were deported. Although some people worried about profiling of Muslims, concerns about threats to civil liberties were muted. As a public policy expert noted, "One thing 9/11 did was to make Americans a little less reflexively supportive of civil liberty."

Right after 9/11 Democrats suggested the creation of a new cabinet department to combine all agencies involved with America's security. Initially, the administration resisted, but public opinion in favor of such an agency forced the Bush regime to embrace the concept. After some political infighting, a Department of Homeland Security was created to deter future terrorist attacks. It was designed to include border security, emergency preparedness, the Secret Service, and coordination of all intelligence gathered to find suspected terrorists. It would be the second largest agency in the federal government after the Pentagon.

The American economy was already somewhat wobbly when it was hit by the events of September 11, leading to further uncertainty and a steep decline in the stock market. There had seemed to be a tentative recovery, but on October 16, 2001, the Enron Corporation, listed as the seventh largest in the country with a reported $101 billion in revenue, was forced to disclose $1 billion in losses. This initiated a chain of events that annihilated Enron's stock price and propelled the company into bankruptcy, eliminating thousands of jobs and wiping out billions of dollars in savings.

The company, created in the 1980s in the wave of the deregulation of energy markets by the Reagan administration, had impressed Wall Street commentators as "the most innovative company in the nation." In reality, the ever-expanding profits were only an illusion. Enron had utilized the perplexing intricacy of its financial affairs to cover up its true nature. It was, as one observer noted, "a fundamentally self-destructive institution, a house of cards where human error and a culture of ambition, secrecy and greed made collapse inevitable." Its failure exposed the deficiencies of supposed watchdogs at all levels. These included a board of directors that neglected its oversight role, outside accountants who ignored the rules of their profession, lawyers who sanctioned deceptive deals, and regulators who were bewildered by Enron's complicated finances. Wall Street analysts recommended the stock at the same time that their firms secured gigantic banking fees from the company. The fall of Enron was followed by a series of business scandals enveloping such seemingly solid companies as WorldCom and Tyco International. These events destroyed investor faith and led to a multi-trillion dollar stock market slide. Many people believed that corporate reform was essential to restore public confidence, but the political clout of large corporations limited any steps the government would take in that direction.

President Bush had long favored tax cuts as the measure to solve any and all economic woes. He had succeeded in gaining the passage of tax cuts that were weighted so that more than a third of the money went to 1 percent of the taxpayers. It was assumed that "a rising tide lifts all boats." As the economy continued to falter and 1.4 million jobs were lost, the president suggested further cuts in taxes. These included the repeal of the inheritance tax, a significant source of revenue. It was dubbed the "death tax" by Republicans, even though only the top 2 percent of estates paid any tax at all and half of the tax was paid by estates over $5 million, 0.16 percent of the total. The president also argued for a complicated repeal of the tax on most dividends to rebuild the confidence of investors. Democrats argued that the $360 billion in revenue this would cost would worsen the federal deficit and do little to stimulate the economy. The combination of tax cuts and growing expenses as a result of 9/11 had turned the budget surplus of the Clinton years into a growing deficit that reached $300 billion by 2003.

Domestic Policies

Although George Bush had run as a centrist in his election campaign, he was well aware of the problems his father had faced when he appeared to ignore his conservative core constituency. He attempted to roll back many of the environmental initiatives of the Clinton administration. Shortly after taking office, he rejected the Kyoto Protocol, the global warming treaty negotiated by his predecessor. Believing that mandatory reductions in emissions linked to global warming would harm the economy, the president sent senior officials around the country to collect voluntary written promises from industries to curb such emissions. He also favored legislation to open part of the Arctic National Wildlife Refuge to oil drilling, although the Democrats blocked this effort.

President Bush continued to press for his Faith Based Initiative that would turn some federal welfare funds over to religious charitable organizations. While this had yet to pass Congress, the president was more successful in efforts to modify the historic 1973 *Roe v. Wade* decision that had established a woman's right to end her pregnancy. He attempted to fill the judiciary with individuals hostile to that decision. The status of a fetus or fertilized egg was elevated by the administration to that of a person with rights equivalent to that of women. Federal financing for research on all new embryonic stem-cell lines was prohibited, despite arguments that such research could be valuable in finding treatment for a variety of diseases. He favored the Abortion Non-Discrimination Act that would permit government-supported health-care providers to refuse to perform abortions or even prohibit their doctors from informing their female patients about the option of obtaining an abortion. On his first day in office the president reinstated the global "gag" rule that had been instituted by Ronald Reagan and then lifted by President Clinton. It barred any world health providers that received American assistance from counseling or even discussing abortion as an option with their clients. As a consequence, millions of dollars were frozen intended for programs to combat AIDS and improve reproductive health, sponsored by the World Health Organization and the United Nations Population Fund. In the summer of 2002 the president revoked support for Senate ratification of a women's rights treaty, barring nations from discriminating against women in such areas as health care and legal rights. American delegations at international conferences opposed endorsement of condom use to prevent AIDS and efforts to help female war crime rape victims, worrying that his might mean information about abortion.

Conservative Republicans had long fantasized about making Social Security more like a private pension system. In his post 2002 election news conference President Bush reiterated his commitment to that idea: "I still strongly believe that the best way to achieve security in Social Security for younger workers is to give them the option of managing their own money through a personal savings account." Democrats declared that they would welcome a fight on this issue in the 2004 election, but they didn't offer any plan of their own to solve the issue of the system running out of money when the baby boomers retired.

"The Axis of Evil"

In his 2002 State of the Union address President Bush spoke of an "axis of evil" in the world. He identified the nations in this axis as Iraq, Iran, and North Korea. World leaders worried that the heightening rhetoric was reminiscent of the Cold War campaign against Communism. Vice President Dick Cheney declared that the war was divided into the forces of darkness and light and that "the United States and only the United States can see this effort through to victory."

As the war on terrorism settled into a stalemate, officials in the Defense Department argued that the time was right to go to war with Iraq to oust Saddam

Hussein. They contended that Saddam was in the process of accumulating weapons of mass destruction and posed a "grave and growing danger." President Bush declared, "I will not wait on events while dangers gather. I will not stand by as peril draws closer and closer." In the following weeks Bush and his top aides invariably added warnings about the Iraqi threat in their speeches and interviews to bolster their argument for the necessity of "regime change."

Secretary of State Colin Powell and others in the State Department believed that it was important to gain support of a coalition of nations for any action by going to the United Nations and demanding a return of international weapons inspectors to Iraq. On September 12, 2002 the president appeared before the United Nations and challenged its members to act or risk rendering the world body "irrelevant." Powell was able to push through a Security Council resolution demanding that Saddam disarm and cooperate with arms inspectors or face "serious consequences." Although the resolution passed unanimously, its vague phrasing papered over serious division among the member nations. The administration expected Hussein to shuffle his weapons of mass destruction around the country, showing that he was hiding something. But conclusive evidence to convince undecided nations and people proved difficult to uncover. Secretary Powell attempted to break the deadlock by disclosing what he claimed was undeniable evidence of Iraq's weapons of mass destruction and ties to terrorism. Despite the backing of Britain's Tony Blair, the Europeans, particularly the French, Germans and Russians, were not convinced and opposed any new resolution that could lead to war. In the meantime American troop deployment in the Persian Gulf area escalated in early 2003 in preparation for war. Finally, on March 17, Bush addressed the nation. He issued an ultimatum: "Saddam Hussein and his sons must leave Iraq within 48 hours. Their refusal to do so will result in military conflict to commence at a time of our choosing."" Within two days the nation was at war.

At the same time that the Iraqi situation was worsening, North Korea announced that it was pulling out of a 1994 agreement under which it froze its nuclear reactor and renounced any development of nuclear weapons. The North Koreans acknowledged that they had cheated on that accord. It was difficult to understand whether the reclusive "Great Leader," Kim Jong II, an isolated tyrant, wanted a nuclear arsenal or a new relationship with the West. Administration hard-liners pressed the president to further isolate North Korea to increase pressure on Kim or lead to the collapse of his regime, even though it might intensify the crisis. As thousands of American troops were heading to the Persian Gulf, President Bush did not want to risk a military confrontation with North Korea and South Korea, usually a reliable American ally, opposed any punitive policy. The president declared that the problem could be "solved in a peaceful way" and that America might be willing to negotiate to reward "right behavior" by the North Koreans. Cynics noted that the lesson of the two nations was that it was better to already have nuclear weapons: blackmail was more effective.

The Elections of 2002

Historically, the post-World War II average loss by a president's party in the first midterm after his election was 22 House and two Senate seats. In the 2002 congressional elections the Republicans gained 6 seats in the House and 2 in the Senate. This unprecedented outcome came from careful planning by Karl Rove, the president's "political mastermind." Rove determined by early August to make security the overarching theme of the campaign and to rely on Bush's positive ratings as commander in chief and leader of the war on terror. Iraq would be the central story bolstered by congressional approval obtained before Election Day.

As usual, Republicans tended to be more disciplined and ideologically united than the Democrats, particularly in matters involving use of force. Polls showed that Americans, as Karl Rove informed party leaders, "trust the Republican Party to do a better job of protecting and strengthening America's military might and thereby protecting America."

A crucial moment at the end of September was the failure to reach a compromise with the Democrats on the homeland-security bill. Ironically, the creation of such a department had been a Democratic idea, initially resisted by Bush. But when the Democrats sought to protect their union constituency by opposing limitations on federal employee unions in the bill, Bush had gained an issue. In several "Red" States (states that had voted for Bush), Democrats were charged with being soft on tackling terrorism. Some ads showed their faces alongside Saddam Hussein and Osama bin Laden. The Democrats, the president charged, were more responsive to "special interests" than to the security of America. In Georgia these charges of lack of patriotism succeeded in causing the defeat of Senator Max Cleland who had lost three of his limbs fighting in his nation's armed forces. "The issue resonated, " Rove noted with some glee.

No sooner did the 2002 results come in, than Rove and his colleagues began planning for the presidential election of 2004. While the president's approval ratings remained high, by early 2003 they had fallen below 60 percent for the first time since September 11, 2001. A majority disapproved of his management of the economy, tax cuts, and even foreign policy. The author of several books about President Reagan once remarked, "Reagan invited us to underestimate him. He felt that gave him an advantage." The same often seemed true of President Bush.

THE 2004 ELECTION

The Democrats were heartened by polls that seemed to show declining approval ratings for the president. They chose Senator John Kerry of Massachusetts as their standard-bearer, ignoring warnings about the difficulties of electing long-term senators with substantial numbers of legislative votes that could be attacked. As his running mate, Kerry chose Senator John Edwards of North Carolina who balanced the ticket geographically and was attractive and charismatic. Kerry believed that his background as a decorated Vietnam War veteran would immunize him against any charges of softness in matters of national security. The Republicans were able to counter this by producing a television commercial by Swift Boat Veterans for Truth that disputed Kerry's claims to bravery. Although their charges were never proven, the Kerry campaign was slow to respond to them, and they were successful in confusing the public's understanding of the differences between the Kerry and Bush war record.

Despite the passage of a campaign finance reform law, the election revealed a loophole in allowing so-called "soft-money" contributions. As a result, an astounding $3.9 billion was spent on the campaign. Despite this, Kerry was unsuccessful in turning the campaign into a referendum on the economy or in articulating his vision for America. He was also harmed by the appearance on television on the weekend before the election of a tape by Osama bin Laden that seemed to urge the defeat of George Bush. Others argued that "moral issues" were the key, but later close analysis appears to contradict this view.

Whatever the reason, President Bush was able to accomplish what one Democrat called a "monumental achievement" of winning the election despite polls that showed concern with the direction of the country and unhappiness with his job performance and the public's clear belief that Kerry had won the presidential debates. This time George Bush won the popular vote with 51 percent of the vote, a margin of three and a half million votes. Few of the "red" or "blue" states switched their positions from 2000. (New Mexico and Iowa went for Bush this time, and New Hampshire moved to Kerry.) Bush did better in the states he had won the last time, and Kerry improved the Democratic totals in some showdown states. Despite the fact that this was a much clearer victory, a switch of less than 60,000 votes in Ohio would have changed the results. The nation continued to be closely and bitterly divided.

The results, however, were more clear-cut on the president's psyche. No longer would there hang over his administration the issue of whether he was the legitimate president. He could now feel free to argue that free market principles should prevail in environmental and social policies. It was not clear whether he could convince the country that he had a true conservative mandate on these and on moral issues.

There were substantial changes in the president's cabinet for his second term. The beleaguered and disillusioned Secretary of State Colin Powell resigned. Condoleezza Rice, who became the first African-American woman to reach such a high position in government, replaced him. The controversial Attorney General John Ashcroft also left office. Alberto Gonzalez, who took his place, was the first Hispanic American to hold that job. Donald Rumsfeld, however, despite public demands that he too should be removed, remained in his position as Secretary of Defense.

THE BUSH SECOND TERM

President Bush believed his reelection was a "mandate" for the direction he wanted to move the country both at home and abroad. Indeed, Bush was certain that his victory over the hapless and lackluster John Kerry was confirmation from the American people that they embraced his right-wing agenda. Bush believed there was no better place to start his final assault on what was left of the liberal ethos than the federal court system, especially the Supreme Court, should the long-expected vacancies become reality. Bush was determined to fill every open position at any and all levels with conservative jurists. He also wanted to make permanent the tax reductions Congress had passed during his first term, which had blatantly benefited the upper classes significantly more than the middle and lower classes. So confident was Bush of public support for his war on the last remnants of liberalism that he even believed he could "transform" Social Security from a public pension system into a privatized "401-K" form of retirement. Such an initiative reflected not only Bush's arrogance that he could destroy the "third rail" of American politics but his devotion as well to the supposed righteousness of free market principles. Bush of course sought to continue the Iraq war. He was certain that the United States would prevail and that victory over the insurgency would vindicate his ambitions for a "second American empire" realized by the Bush Doctrine of preemptive strikes against those nations he and his fellow neo-con hawks designated as "evil" entities out to destroy the United States. Bush also believed the United States had to persevere in Iraq until a regime amenable to U.S. influence and interests was securely in place.

Much to the right's and evangelical's joy Bush triumphed in his war on the alleged liberal court system. The president succeeded in moving the most important tribunal, the Supreme Court, decisively to the right on social and civil liberty issues. In 2005, Sandra Day O'Connor, the first woman to be appointed to the Supreme Court by Ronald Reagan, announced her retirement. O'Connor's decision to step down was followed shortly thereafter by the death of Chief Justice William Rehnquist. Bush now had the rare opportunity to appoint not just one but two justices to the most important bench in the nation. This was the moment Bush and conservatives had been waiting for; not since before the New Deal had the Court been dominated by conservatives. Bush wasted no time in filling the vacancies. He nominated and Congress confirmed two conservative jurists who he was confident would align themselves with justices Antonin Scalia and Clarence Thomas, the aggressive justices who had enthusiastically supported Bush's usurpation of expanded executive power. A 50-year old appellate jurist, John Roberts, who had once worked in the Reagan Justice Department, succeeded Rehnquist as Chief Justice. Roberts proved to be a qualified choice but such was not the case for Bush's other nominee, Harriet Miers, his long-time family friend and White House counsel. Even right-wing pundits were outraged by Bush's selection of Miers, for she possessed at best the most meager qualifications. Bush eventually retracted, removing Miers for consideration and quickly nominated in her place Samuel Alito, a staunch judicial conservative, who was confirmed in early 2006 after a hard-fought Senate battle.

Although successfully moving the Supreme Court to the right, the rest of Bush's political agenda fell far short of realization. Bush's attempt to privatize social security fortunately failed, for had such an initiative succeeded, it would have resulted in trillions of dollars ending up in the hands of many of the very Wall Street brokerage firms that collapsed completely in the fall of 2008 because much of the money these firms controlled had gone to egregiously bloated salaries and "incentives" for CEOs and short-sighted, speculative investments. Bush sought to "reform" the social security system by creating private investment accounts that would be paid for with money diverted from the Social Security trust fund itself. In other words, he wanted to turn the whole system over to private investment houses such as those named above. Since its inception in the late 1930s, conservatives had disliked Social Security for both practical and ideological reasons. It was an efficient government-run program that redistributed funds from the young to the old and from the affluent to the poor. To conservative, free-market capitalists, the program not only smacked of "socialism" but represented a huge source of potential funds and new investment opportunities that many Wall Street firms hoped to get their hands on and "manage" directly. So determined was Bush to see his plan prevail, that he unaccustomedly barnstormed the nation in 2005, but most Americans were rightly wary of the initiative, aware of the implications and turned decisively against this supposed "reform," dooming for the moment any large-scale effort to dismantle the last cornerstone of the welfare state initiated by FDR. Although meager, for millions of elderly Americans, their guaranteed monthly Social Security check determines whether they will eat, pay their utility bills, and keep a roof over their heads, at least for another month.

The Unraveling of the Bush Regime

Despite the Bush administration's hubris that their right-wing initiatives would eradicate forever the last vestiges of New Deal liberalism, it was that very arrogance that guaranteed the Bush presidency would soon implode. By the end of 2005, it had become clear that Bush and his Republican cohorts had overplayed their hand relative to the politics of terrorism and fear, which they had kept in the forefront of people's minds since 9/11 and which they had used to sustain the Bush regime in power. It also became increasingly apparent to many Americans that the entire Bush presidency had been sustained not by any real substance, vision, or commitment to governing but rather, from the beginning, had been an administration that simply had kept itself alive by perpetually "campaigning," exploiting one sensitive and divisive issue after another with a constant overlay of fear. Although able to parlay the "fear factor" of the 9/11 trauma through the 2004 election, by the close of 2005 the American people had grown tired of such empty and polarizing "politicking" and turned their attention to the conflicts and controversies that were part and parcel of the dramatic spread of the twenty-first century global market in goods, services, labor, and ideas. Equally important to the demise of the Bush presidency was the disastrous Iraq war, which appeared to have no end in sight. All of the president's and his colleagues' talk of how the U.S. was daily winning over the Iraqi people to "freedom and democracy," and how U.S. forces, especially after the so-called "surge" had been implemented (January 2007 with the addition of 30,000 more U.S. military forces spread across the country intended to quell the sectarian violence and prop up the weak civilian government), had the insurgents on the run if not on the verge of defeat, the American people grew increasingly weary of the president's platitudes and dissembling. Indeed, by the beginning of 2006 a new wave of antiwar sentiment had emerged, as well as a growing popular mistrust of the Bush administration and the GOP-controlled Congress. Not surprisingly, the surge failed to crush the insurgents, and there was no real decrease in the sectarian violence that continued to wrack the country. As of the writing of this chapter over 4,000 U.S. troops had been killed in Iraq and nearly 35,000 wounded, many of them gravely in the five years since the U.S. military led the invasion to overthrow Saddam Hussein who allegedly possessed hidden weapons of mass destruction who the Bush administration convinced Americans was going to unleash on the United States or at the very least provide them to other terrorist groups who would use them on the United States.

However, for most Americans, the war was peripheral in their daily lives; they were more concerned and affected by the ever-shifting exigencies of a capitalist economy that had become inextricably tied to a worldwide market, the dynamics of which they could not understand nor effectively change. "Outsourcing" of jobs and services became the order of the day, as increasing number of U.S. corporations, looking for greater profits and cheaper labor costs, moved many, if not all, of their company's components "overseas." Even when Americans called on the telephone about the balances on their credit cards, they spoke with someone living and working for the credit card company in a non-English speaking nation. Indeed, the nation of India in particular seemed to have benefited the most from the outsourcing of such services, but the voices of barely comprehensible spoken English of the people from many other "emerging" countries could also be heard over the telephone when Americans called other supposedly U.S.-headquartered companies for information or services that affected their daily lives. Such outsourcing greatly disturbed and angered Americans on a variety of levels, most important of which was the reality that tomorrow they could lose their job to a "foreigner" all because of the profiteering that had become the *raison d'etre* for many American corporations and that the Bush administration appeared to approve and bolster with its endorsement of the free-market mentality. Indeed, not since the days of the infamous Robber Barons of the late nineteenth century had there been an administration more supportive of the laissez faire ethos or demonstrate a willingness to look the other way as the freebooters of the early twenty-first century ran roughshod over the nation's economy than the Bush regime. Bush's complicity, or at the very least culpability for allowing such abuse and exploitation, helped to cause the worst financial collapse since the Great Depression. However, the disastrous affects of Bush's economic policies would not become reality until the end of his second administration.

Hurricane Katrina

Perhaps no natural disaster in the history of the United States revealed more of the inherent flaws of an administration than the aftermath of Hurricane Katrina that slammed into the Gulf Coast on the morning of August 29, 2005. The storm destroyed tens of billions of dollars in property from the Florida panhandle to the Texas state line. However, it was the havoc the storm surge wreaked on the levees of New Orleans built by the U.S. Army Corps of Engineers that caused the massive flooding of one of the nation's major metropolitan areas. It was that particular impact of Katrina that opened the eyes of many Americans to the incompetence and detachment, if not disregard, of the Bush presidency to the plight of thousands of citizens who were black, poor, and working class and who had no means to leave the city as the water rushed in from the levees that had failed to hold back the storm's surging water. The rapidly rising water stranded more than 100,000 residents, the majority of whom were African American, poor, or without cars, in their homes without electricity, water, or food. Interestingly, the majority of New Orleans' more affluent white residents had left the city days before the storm hit. Also revealed to Americans outside the South was not only how "black" of a city New Orleans was but how poor and desperate the city's "people of color" had been for generations. New Orleans had long been one of the nation's favorite cities to visit, attracting hundreds of thousands of tourists annually. Indeed, for decades tourism had been one of Louisiana's most important industries and thus revenue streams. Drawing people to the "Big Easy" was the city's fame and mystique of being the nation's most exotic, eclectic, and "carefree" urban environments, whose cuisine was unlike any other in the country and could only be found and enjoyed in New Orleans. However, the majority of visitors rarely ventured beyond the main tourists enclaves, and consequently they never saw the squalor, crime, and general destitution that was endemic among the city's majority black population. They were thus shocked at seeing such plight graphically covered by the television news camera that arrived in New Orleans days before the Bush administration responded to the calamity. Hundreds of the city's inhabitants died during and after Hurricane Katrina made landfall, most of them residents of low-income New Orleans neighborhoods. They not only drowned but fell victim as well to sickness, heat, and dehydration because of an inept evacuation plan and, perhaps most important, to an excruciatingly slow response from National Guard units and FEMA, now a subagency of the Department of Homeland Security. As a result of Katrina, more than 1.5 million Gulf Coast residents became homeless, eventually finding shelter in schools, sports arenas, hotels, and trailers in Houston, Baton Rouge, Memphis, and other neighboring Southern and even Northern cities. Images of the destitution and destruction of a major American city caused many Americans to wonder why the U.S. government was promising so much abroad but could deliver so little at home.

Not only did Katrina raise the environmental issue of global warming, which many scientists and meteorologists believed was increasing the frequency and intensity of Atlantic hurricanes, but for the Bush administration, the debacle made apparent the disparate and highly graphic racial and class divisions that still existed in American cities. The question that arose among many Americans, both black and white, was would the government's response have been more prompt and genuinely helpful had New Orleans been a majority white city? Such a query discredited the Bush administration's notion of a militarized ideology of homeland security and the president's concept of federalism. Bush's failure to respond swiftly and decisively resulted in the resignation of Michael Brown, FEMA's director, who in many ways became the scapegoat for the Bush administration's overall mishandling of the Katrina disaster. Politically, the Katrina debacle caused a sharp decline in Bush's overall approval rating. A year after Katrina, corruption and continued mismanagement of the reconstruction process pervaded practically every facet of the recovery program. Less than half the money ($70 billion) that had been appropriated to assist victims had been spent; $2 billion had been lost to fraud and waste; $900 million worth of mobile homes never got to individuals or went unused because they were inappropriate housing for a flood plain, and because of the overall political and financial shenanigans and boondoggling that ensued during reconstruction, only 35 percent of the city's population returned to the Crescent City; the other 65 percent decided that the New Orleans they had loved and that had been one of the nation's most famous and unique cities would never be the same again and thus chose to live permanently elsewhere.

The Politics of Immigration Citizenship

For the first time since the early 1920s, immigration politics once again became a national issue. Indeed, immigration dominated the public debate for the first several years of the twenty-first century. The immigration "problem" was not new to native-born Americans; they had witnessed throughout the nation's history immigrants coming from a variety of nations and continents whose legal status was questionable and who became competitors for jobs and a burden on schools, hospitals, and social services. However, what made the immigration issue so potentially explosive in the early years of the twenty-first century was the volume and composition of the majority of individuals pouring into the United States during this time. The overwhelming percentage of the immigrants were from "south of the border," mostly Mexico, but the number of individuals from other Central and South American countries had also increased significantly as well as people from south Asia and Africa. Such expanded numbers of "people of color" precipitated a nativism and ethnocentrism among the nation's WASP community not seen in such intensity since the turn of the last century. Much of the native-born bigotry and hostility was directed at the recent wave of Latino immigrants, most of whom were "illegal"—undocumented, who because of their numbers and willingness to work in any capacity even for the most meager wages had transformed the workforce in cities across the country, not just the urban areas of the Southwest. By the writing of this chapter (late fall 2008), sizeable Latino communities had emerged in Memphis, Cincinnati, and Pittsburg—cities that just a few years before had only a handful of Latino workers and residents. "I tell you that the area where I grew up now resembles Tijuana more than the U.S.," one white Nashville resident proclaimed. "My neighborhood is gone; I can't read the signs because I don't speak Spanish—in my native country!" A paramilitary-vigilante group called the "Minutemen" made highly publicized sojourns to the U.S.-Mexican border in order to stop the influx of "illegals" with force. In Congress, many politicians of both parties backed highly restrictive legislation that would criminalize illegal aliens and appropriate billions for a construction of a "Berlin Wall" type of edifice between the U.S. and Mexico. However, as many pundits and others opposed to such a harsh measure pointed out, the wall would never be built because the labor for such a project would not be allowed into the country!!! Indeed, the Mexican-American comedian George Lopez reminded Americans that the rebuilding of New Orleans was being done by "FEMA"—Find Every Mexican Available." Many business leaders, the

Democratic Party, and even the Bush administration realized the importance to the American economy and workplace Latino labor provided and thus advocated an expanded guest worker program that would put undocumented immigrants on the path toward citizenship. As of the writing of this chapter, such individuals living and working in the United States totaled around 12 million human beings.

The immigration issued divided both major political parties but also impacted the millions of Latinos, both citizens and non-citizens. Beginning in early spring 2006 and reaching a crescendo on May Day of that year, hundreds of thousands of Latinos marched in demonstrations against immigration restriction all across the country. Promising to boycott work and the spending of their money, Latinos declared May 1 as "Day Without Immigrants" to show Americans that if they were either deported or restricted from coming to the United States, the U.S. economy would suffer dire consequences; they were correct. As one participant declared immigrants deserved "not just green cards, not just visas, but citizenship." Because their non-union, largely Latino workforce participated in these marches, many Midwestern pork and poultry processing plants supported their Latino workers' position by closing their operations on May Day. Interestingly, these demonstrations reminded many Americans of the protest tradition and boycotts of the early twentieth century ethnic-proletarian movements, which had as their objective not only higher wages, better working conditions, stronger unions, and more political power for the working class but also a desire for citizenship and equal rights.

BUSH REPUBLICANS DIVIDED AND DEFEATED

Despite the Bush administration's protestations to the contrary, by the summer of 2006, there appeared to be no end in sight for the Iraq War. Indeed, the war had drained the Bush presidency of the remaining power and legitimacy it had won after 9/11. Compounding the president's war-related woes was the ongoing revelations of corruption and scandal that seemed to be rife within the administration and the Republican Party. So disillusioned and betrayed did the American people become with the Bush White House that in the November elections of 2006 they handed the president and his party a devastating blow, electing Democratic majorities to both houses of Congress for the first time since 1994.

Although the war's growing unpopularity was the central issue of the 2006 campaign, scandals and legal issues proved to be equally devastating to both the president and his party. In April 2006, Texan Tom DeLay, the powerful House Majority Leader, resigned amid indictment on campaign finance corruption charges. Other Republicans followed suit for similar malfeasance allegations, most notably those congressmen associated with Jack Abramoff, a notorious influence peddler and rabid Republican partisan. Sexual impropriety also scared the Republican Party as some of the party's evangelical supporters were revealed to have engaged in homosexual escapades. Most appalling was the abrupt resignation of Florida House member Mark Foley who had solicited former congressional pages for homosexual encounters. Such disclosures were especially damaging to the Republicans because during the Bush years the party had articulated an incredibly shrill, righteous, and intolerant position concerning such "deviancy" as homosexuality, and now some of the party's stalwart supporters and members proved to be just as aberrant in their behavior; such hypocrisy did not go unnoticed by voters. Finally, for all of the Bush administration's talk about the need for tighter national security, Vice-President Dick Cheney's office, through the agency of one of the vice-president's henchmen, I. Lewis "Scooter" Libby, was responsible for the vindictive "outing" of a covert CIA operative, Valerie Plame because Plame and her husband (who was also a former CIA agent) publicly disclosed many of the administration's clandestine and illegal operations ranging from attempts to overthrow foreign governments to lying about the presence of WMD's in Iraq. Libby was found guilty of perjury and obstruction of justice and sentenced to 30 months in prison in June 2007 but never served a single day's confinement because President Bush "exonerated" him two weeks later.

Perpetually plaguing the Bush White House was the Iraq War, which public opinion polls revealed by 2006 that more than two-thirds of the American people considered Bush's conduct of the war misguided. Among some of the conflict's chief critics were a sizable number from the military establishment—recently retired upper echelon officers who rightly fixed much of the blame for the war's debacle on Secretary of Defense Donald Rumsfeld, whom they charged with failing to provide an effective exit strategy for U.S. troops in that war-torn country. Two years earlier Secretary of State Colin Powell, a national hero in the eyes of many Americans and an individual known for his integrity, resigned. It was Colin Powell who had put his reputation and credibility on the line when he appeared before the United Nations just before the war began and declared to the world that the United States had clear evidence that Saddam Hussein had WMD's and that Hussein had supported Al Qaeda and other terrorist organizations. Powell later found out that he had been deceived by other members of the administration. Thus it should have surprised few Americans when Powell declared his support for Democratic nominee Barack Obama in October 2008.

Thus the 2006 midterm elections became a referendum on Iraq. President Bush and other Republican true-believers (including 2008 Republican nominee John McCain) declared that they would "stay the course" until the Iraqi insurgency had been crushed. Any other consideration, any contemplation of withdrawing before "mission accomplished" they said, was tantamount to surrender in the battle against Al-Qaeda. However, by November 2006, the majority of Americans no longer equated the conflict in Iraq with the war on terror, which a report from the CIA and other intelligence agencies concluded had contributed to the instability and protracted insurgency throughout the Middle East. In effect, such reports supported the assertion that continued American presence in Iraq had caused an increase in the ranks of terrorist organizations throughout the region and that all the U.S. invasion had "accomplished" was the overthrow of a brutal dictator but that in the end such an action had only served to further destabilize an already precarious balance of power. Meanwhile increasing numbers of initial supporters of the war within the Democratic Party moved decisively toward a rapid withdrawal policy of American troops from Iraq. As Americans went to the polls that November they vented their frustrations toward the Bush administration by delivering to the president and his party one of the most searing repudiations in American electoral history. The Democrats captured both houses of Congress and in an unprecedented move elected the first woman Speaker of the House, Nancy Pelosi of California. In a portent of what was to occur two years later, Republicans, in even some of the most secure "red states," lost their congressional seats largely the result of an unpopular president and his policies.

Further eroding the Bush administration's credibility relative to the war was the December 2006 bipartisan report of the Iraq Study Group, co-chaired by former George H.W. Bush Secretary of State, James Baker, and former Indiana Democratic House member Lee Hamilton. The report called for a massive reexamination and overhaul of U.S. military and diplomatic policy in Iraq and the Middle East in general. However, despite the moderate position of the overall recommendations and broad bipartisan support the committee generated, the Bush White House stubbornly refused to consider changes in its Iraq policy. As noted earlier the president did the opposite of what had been advocated—he ordered a "troop surge," which began in January 2007 and involved a U.S. forces escalation of nearly 30,000 to be placed in and around Baghdad.

Despite Bush's repeated calls for "patience," support for the Iraq war and the United States' continued presence in that country has weakened considerably since the "surge." Democrats, although sweeping to victory largely because of their criticism of Bush's Iraq war policies, have had trouble since their triumph in 2006 agreeing on an exit strategy from the quagmire. However, in 2007 and 2008 a number of Republican senators and representatives broke ranks with their colleagues and their president calling for a firm date for withdrawal of U.S. troops from Iraq or at the very least, implementation of the Iraq Study Group's recommendations. By the close of 2007, because of Iraq, President Bush had great difficulty holding together his own party, many of whose elected officials were concerned that the continued failure of "staying the course" in Iraq would have serious, negative consequences for Republican candidates in the 2008 election. Like Richard Nixon before him during the Vietnam War, George W. Bush had become increasingly isolated by the beginning of 2008, seemingly impervious to the growing political and economic crises the Iraq war had engendered both within the United States and throughout the world. And like Nixon, Bush's overall public approval ratings sank to historic lows for a sitting president, reaching 26 percent in several opinion polls by the beginning of 2008—a powerful measure of how isolated and unpopular the president and his war in Iraq had become.

CONCLUSION: The Bush Presidency in Retrospect

By the beginning of 2008, it had become clear to many Americans that the Bush administration was no longer capable of effectively governing the country. The president's mishandling of Katrina, the controversy over immigration issues, the war, and the repudiation of the conservative social and cultural agenda had given hope to many people that the reactionary ethos that had come to envelop and define both Bush and the Republican Party was at an end. Nonetheless, George W. Bush gave little heed to the arguments of those who disagreed with him. His strength as a leader came from this self-certainty, enabling him to triumph on issues as diverse as drastic tax cuts to how the United States should wage the war on terror. In the end, it had become clear that Bush's character proved to have been both his greatest strength and his most severe handicap. On the one hand, if his administration's policies in Iraq led to stability and the spread of democracy throughout the entire Middle East, which he was "certain" would be the result of his "war of liberation," then Bush's single-mindedness would deserve a large part of the credit. Conversely, if the Iraqi insurgency persists, which it appears to be currently doing, and the United States cannot defeat such opposition and ultimately withdraws without having brought democracy to Iraq or inspired other Middle Eastern nations to embrace change, then Iraq, represented a completely inappropriate target for the war on terrorism. In short, Bush's single-mindedness and Manichean worldview would be to blame for the calamity that would ensue when the United States finally withdrew. As the Bush administration came to an end, the one thing that seemed most clear was that profound divisions in the American polity were likely to persist and that the lessons provided both by the events in Iraq and by Katrina would have to be carefully learned if any successor hoped to overcome those divisions and restore a sense of "commonwealth" to the nation as a whole.

THE 2008 ELECTION: A Milestone in United States History

Few elections in the history of the United States have been as momentous as that of 2008, which ultimately saw victorious not only the Democratic Party and a resurrection of the liberal ethos but the election of the first African American as President of the United States. First-term Illinois Senator Barack Obama's overwhelming victory over his Republican rival (365-173 in the Electoral College while winning 53 percent of the popular vote), Arizona Senator John McCain, proved to be historic in many ways. Even the Democratic primary was unprecedented, for not only did Obama defeat a host of male party stalwarts, but from the beginning to the very end of the primary campaign, his main challenger was Senator Hillary Rodham Clinton, the first female in American history to run for the highest office in the land and almost take her party's nomination. However, after a hard-fought battle, which frequently saw acerbic exchanges between the candidates, Clinton finally acknowledged that Obama had won more delegates to win the party's nomination on the first ballot. Clinton's concession fortunately occurred before the party convention in Denver, Colorado. Such a gesture by Clinton avoided what could have easily become a party-dividing donnybrook at the Democratic convention, which no doubt would have hurt the party's chances of victory in November. In short, the Democrats realized the importance of party unity and solidarity among all of its leaders. In previous election years such had not been the case, and thus the party had gone down to defeat. Moreover, Obama's primary triumph and eventual presidential victory reflected one of the most organized, disciplined, grass-roots organizations ever put together by a presidential contender in either party. From the moment he announced his candidacy in January 2007 and over the course of the next year, Obama, his staff, and his legions of supporters throughout the country created a campaign strategy that not only raised the most money in the history of presidential campaigns but one that successfully garnered the support of Americans from all classes, regions, color, and even political affiliation; even moderate to liberal Republicans alienated by the Bush regime supported Obama. As mentioned earlier in this chapter, such was the endorsement that Obama received from Colin Powell in October 2008 as well as from Nebraska Senator Chuck Hagel, also a Republican.

Also ensuring victory for Obama was his message of "change," which after eight years of Republican rule and a president who had failed on many fronts to deliver what he had promised both at home and abroad, the American people heartily welcomed. Indeed, Obama wrapped himself in a definite liberal mantle but not one that harkened back to the liberalism of the Great Society years but rather a "fusion" liberalism of New Deal ideology tempered by an overlay of the centrist, neo-liberalism of the Bill Clinton years. Indeed, this has become the "new" liberalism of the twenty-first century and one that Obama brilliantly articulated to the American people and one that they embraced. To the surprise of many Democrats, especially Clinton supporters, Obama did not choose his former contender as his running mate, which many hoped would be the case and, if so, would have created the most unprecedented ticket ever in United States history—a white female and an African-American male, together, seeking the highest offices bestowed by the American people. No doubt such a combination would have engendered a very serious crisis of conscience for many Americans, particularly among the more conservative traditional members of the white middle/working class, regardless of gender, religion, or party affiliation. Although during the primary campaign, Hillary Clinton had great appeal among blue collar Americans, and, in fact, many Democratic strategists worried that without her presence on the ticket, Obama could easily lose this key Democratic voting bloc to his Republican opponent. However, such a possibility never materialized; Obama took the blue collar vote in key industrial working class states such as Pennsylvania and Ohio, which helped to ensure his victory. For his running mate, Obama turned to the veteran senator from Delaware, Joe Biden, who had been one of Obama's more pugnacious primary opponents. Obama's choice of Biden reflected the need to enhance his foreign policy portfolio as well as hopefully bring back the wayward blue collar vote, which Hillary had so overwhelmingly won. In both instances Biden proved to have been a wise choice.

On the Republican side, to the surprise of many, especially the conservative wing of the party, the moderate "maverick" Senator John McCain of Arizona came out of nowhere and easily won the Republican primary, dispensing relatively early in the season his two closest rivals, former Massachusetts Governor, the Mormon Mitt Romney, and the pro-Creationist, darling of the fundamentalist evangelical Right, Governor Mike Huckabee of Arkansas. As Clinton and Obama slugged it out from January to June, McCain moved ahead in the polls, regardless of who the Democratic nominee might be. However, the "Bush factor" had yet to come into play and the economy, showing signs of impending calamity, had yet to reach the crisis point. Indeed, McCain, much to his subsequent chagrin, continued to declare that the "economy was fundamentally sound." However, McCain's chances for victory diminished rapidly after his selection of first-term Alaska Governor Sarah Palin as his vice-presidential choice.

Although selecting her only a few days before the early September Republican convention, a good number of Republicans, especially the moderates, were shocked by such a choice. Yet, for a few weeks after the Republican ballyhoo in Minneapolis, the "Palin factor" appeared to have a positive affect for the McCain campaign. The Republican Right celebrated her selection, proclaiming her to be the fresh, new, young, attractive look they needed to win. Moreover, Palin expressed support for the hard Right agenda, which only endeared her more to that wing of the party. However, as the campaign rolled into the fall months, the economy continued its precipitous decline, forcing both candidates in October to return to Washington to vote on a $600 billion stimulus (bailout) package for all the banks and major Wall Street brokerage firms that had gone under. Such a financial calamity could not have been worse for McCain. The collapse of the Wall Street firms was only the beginning; the economy continued its decline and the more it plummeted, the worst it became for McCain. Obama brilliantly tied McCain in his every speech to George Bush, whether it was the economy or Iraq. McCain, Obama declared, was no different than George Bush in mentality and policy and thus responsible for the present crises both at home and abroad. Perhaps the biggest mistake McCain made was to allow the Republican Right to highjack his campaign. To his credit, McCain had indeed been a "maverick" within his party, a moderate to even a surprising liberal on many social issues such as immigration, election reform, and other concerns. Had he remained true to his own brand of Republicanism he might have given Obama a much closer election fight. However, for reasons that have yet to be revealed by McCain, he unfortunately allowed the right wing of his party to take control of his campaign, dictate the strategy, and even choose his running mate. Such a decision by McCain more than likely cost him the election. The American people had become so alienated and disillusioned with George Bush, with whom they had come to associate with the Republican Right, that if McCain expressed the same ideology he would only be uttering what the American public no longer wanted to hear nor believe to be right for the country.

Compounding McCain's woes was Sarah Palin, who, it seemed, every time she opened her mouth to speak, especially when she was not closely managed, monitored, and scripted, uttered the most inarticulate, unintelligible, inane, uninformed diatribe heard in quite some time by a vice-presidential candidate. Palin's repeated gaffes and general inability to put together a coherent sentence caused increasing numbers of Americans to genuinely fear that the governor could become president of the United States if a potential President McCain should die in office. No matter how hard the reactionary Right tried to the bitter end to bolster Palin as a viable running mate, their shrill and rabid promotion fell largely on deaf hears. Even the three debates between Obama and McCain, in which neither candidate proved to be exceptionally brilliant, failed to move the polls in McCain's favor. As the economy worsened and Sara Palin continued to say not only absurd but caustic denunciations of Obama, it was becoming increasingly clear as Election Day approached that Obama would win, as Bill Clinton declared on the Larry King Show after the August Democratic Convention, "handily." The "political soothsayer" Clinton was correct. Now it remains to be seen whether Barack Obama can deliver, as any president is expected to do, the proverbial "goods"—all the campaign promises about change; all the huzzahs about "yes we can"; and all the programs that will hopefully bring this country out of its worst economic downturn since the Great Depression, as well as end a disastrous war in Iraq. We will simply have to wait until January 20, 2008 and hope that after that date for the next four years, Barack Obama will indeed emerge to be the "messiah" as FDR had been in a similar time of crises over 70 years ago.

Chronology

1992 Bill Clinton elected president
Major race riot in Los Angeles follows "not guilty" verdict in Rodney King case

1993 Janet Reno becomes first female attorney general
Israel and the Palestine Liberation Organization sign Oslo peace accord
U. S. soldiers killed in humanitarian mission in Somalia
Congress approves North American Free Trade Agreement (NAFTA)
Gun control, anticrime and Family and Medical Leave laws passed
Toni Morrison becomes first African American to win Nobel Prize for Literature
Terrorist bomb explodes in World Trade Center in New York City

1994	U. S. troops intervene in Haiti to return democratic government to power Nelson Mandela elected president of South Africa Republicans win control of Congress after declaring "Contract with America"
1995	Bomb explodes in Federal Building in Oklahoma City, killing 169 Israeli Prime Minister Yitzhak Rabin assassinated by opponent of Oslo accords U. S. arranges Dayton accords to temporarily end conflict in former Yugoslavia
1996	Personal Responsibility and Work Opportunity Reconciliation Act seeks to end federal welfare Clinton re-elected president Comprehensive nuclear test ban treaty signed by leaders of nuclear powers
1997	Economy reaches new heights Madeleine Albright becomes first female secretary of state Supreme Court clears way for Paula Jones civil suit against President Clinton
1998	Monica Lewinsky case embroils Clinton presidency Democrats gain seats in Congress Clinton impeached, found not guilty in Senate trial.
1999	Nuclear Test Ban treaty rejected in Senate
2000	George W. Bush elected president Gore wins popular vote Senate divided 50-50
2002	Republicans gain 6 House and 2 Senate seats in election
2003	War with Iraq
2004	Bush re-elected for a second term
2008	Barack Obama elected first African American President of the United States

SUGGESTED READINGS

Richard Bernstein, *Out of the Blue: the Story of September 11* (2002).

Bryan Burroughs and John Helyar, *Barbarians at the Gate: The Fall of RJR Nabisco* (1990).

Greg Critser, *Fat Land: How Americans Became the Fattest People in the World* (2002).

Martin Duberman, *Stonewall* (1993).

Lawrence Freedman and Efraim Karsh, *The Gulf Conflict, 1990-1991* (1993).

Andrew Hacker, *Two Nations: Black and White, Separate, Hostile, Unequal* (1992).

Christopher Jencks, *The Homeless* (1994).

Haynes Johnson, *Divided We Fall: Gambling with History in the Nineties* (1994).

Michael Katz, *The Undeserving Poor: From the War on Poverty to the War on Welfare* (1989).

Joe Klein, *The Natural: The Misunderstood Presidency of Bill Clinton* (2002).

Alex Kotlowitz, *There Are No Children Here: The Story of Two Boys Growing Up in the Other America* (1991).

Nicholas Lemann, *The Promised Land: The Great Black Migration and How it Changed America* (1989).

Jere Longman, *Among the Heroes: United Flight 93* (2002).

Martin Lowy, *High Rollers: Inside the Savings and Loan Debacle* (1994).

David Mervin, *George Bush and the Guardianship Presidency* (1996).

Timothy Phelps and Helen Winternitz, *Capitol Games: Clarence Thomas, Anita Hill and the Story of a Supreme Court Nomination* (1992).

Kevin Phillips, *Wealth and Democracy* (2001).

Arthur M. Schlesinger Jr., *The Disuniting of America* (1991).

Randy Shilts, *And the Band Played On: Politics, People and the AIDS Epidemic* (1987).

James B. Stewart, *Den of Thieves* (1991).

Sanford J. Unger, *Fresh Blood: The New American Immigrants* (1995)

Gary Wills, *Under God: Religion and American Politics* (1990).

APPENDIX A

Declaration of Independence

Congress, July 4, 1776

When, in the course of human events, it becomes necessary for one people to dissolve the political bonds which have connected them with another, and to assume, among the powers of the earth, the separate and equal station to which the laws of nature and of nature's God entitle them, a decent respect to the opinions of mankind requires that they should declare the causes which impel them to the separation.

We hold these truths to be self-evident: That all men are created equal; that they are endowed by their Creator with certain unalienable rights; that among these are life, liberty and the pursuit of happiness; that, to secure these rights, governments are instituted among men, deriving their just powers from the consent of the governed; that whenever any form of government becomes destructive of these ends, it is the right of the people to alter or to abolish it, and to institute new government, laying its foundation on such principles, and organizing its powers in such form, as to them shall seem most likely to effect their safety and happiness. Prudence, indeed, will dictate that governments long established should not be changed for light and transient causes; and accordingly all experience hath shown that mankind are more disposed to suffer, while evils are sufferable, than to right themselves by abolishing the forms to which they are accustomed. But when a long train of abuses and usurpations, pursuing invariably the same object, evinces a design to reduce them under absolute despotism, it is their right, it is their duty, to throw off such government, and to provide new guards for their future security. Such has been the patient sufferance of these colonies; and such is now the necessity which constrains them to alter their former systems of government. The history of the present King of Great Britain is a history of repeated injuries and usurpations, all having in direct object the establishment of an absolute tyranny over these states. To prove this, let facts be submitted to a candid world.

He has refused his assent to laws, the most wholesome and necessary for the public good.

He has forbidden his governors to pass laws of immediate and pressing importance, unless suspended in their operation till his assent should be obtained; and, when so suspended, he has utterly neglected to attend to them.

He has refused to pass other laws for the accommodation of large districts of people, unless those people would relinquish the right of representation in the legislature, a right inestimable to them, and formidable to tyrants only.

He has called together legislative bodies at places unusual, uncomfortable, and distant from the depository of their public records, for the sole purpose of fatiguing them into compliance with his measures.

He has dissolved representative houses repeatedly, for opposing, with many firmness, his invasions on the rights of the people.

He has refused for a long time, after such dissolutions, to cause others to be elected; whereby the legislative powers, incapable of annihilation, have returned to the people at large for their exercise; the state remaining, in the mean time, exposed to all the dangers of invasions from without and convulsions within.

He has endeavored to prevent the population of these states; for that purpose obstructing the laws for naturalization of foreigners; refusing to pass others to encourage their migrations hither, and raising the conditions of new appropriations of lands.

He has obstructed the administration of justice, by refusing his assent to laws establishing judiciary powers.

He has made judges dependent on his will alone, for the tenure of their offices, and the amount and payment of their salaries.

He has erected a multitude of new offices, and sent hither swarms of officers to harass our people and eat out their substance.

He has kept among us, in times of peace, standing armies, without the consent of our legislatures.

He has affected to render the military independent of, and superior to, the civil power.

He has combined with others to subject us to jurisdiction foreign to our constitution, and unacknowledged by our laws, giving his assent to their acts of pretended legislation:

For quartering large bodies of armed troops among us;

For protecting them, by a mock trial, from punishment for any murder which they should commit on the inhabitants of these states;

For cutting off our trade with all parts of the world;

For imposing taxes on us without our consent;

For depriving us, in many cases, of the benefits of trial by jury;

For transporting us beyond seas, to be tried for pretended offenses;

For abolishing the free system of English laws in a neighboring province, establishing therein an arbitrary government, and enlarging its boundaries, so as to render it at once an example and fit instrument for introducing the same absolute rule into these colonies;

For taking away our charters, abolishing our most valuable laws, and altering fundamentally the forms of our governments;

For suspending our own legislatures, and declaring themselves invested with power to legislate for us in all cases whatsoever.

He has abdicated government here, by declaring us out of his protection and waging war against us.

He has plundered our seas, ravaged our coasts, burned our towns, and destroyed the lives of our people.

He is at this time transporting large armies of foreign mercenaries to complete the works of death, desolation and tyranny already begun with circumstances of cruelty and perfidy scarcely paralleled in the most barbarous ages, and totally unworthy the head of a civilized nation.

He has constrained our fellow-citizens, taken captive on the high seas, to bear arms against their country, to become the executioners of their friends and brethren, or to fall themselves by their hands.

He has excited domestic insurrections among us, and has endeavored to bring on the inhabitants of our frontiers the merciless Indian savages, whose known rule of warfare is an undistinguished destruction of all ages, sexes, and conditions.

In every stage of these oppressions we have petitioned for redress in the most humble terms; our repeated petitions have been answered only by repeated injury. A prince, whose character is thus marked by every act which may define a tyrant, is unfit to be the ruler of a free people.

Nor have we been wanting in our attentions to our British brethren. We have warned them, from time to time, of attempts by their legislature to extend an unwarrantable jurisdiction over us. We have reminded them of the circumstances of our emigration and settlement here. We have appealed to their native justice and magnanimity, and we have conjured them, by the ties of our common kindred, to disavow these usurpations, which would inevitably interrupt our connections and correspondence. They, too, have been deaf to the voice of justice and of consanguinity. We must, therefore, acquiesce in the necessity which denounces our separation, and hold them, as we hold the rest of mankind, enemies in war, in peace friends.

We, therefore, the representatives of the United States of America, in General Congress assembled, appealing to the Supreme Judge of the world for the rectitude of our intentions, do, in the name and by authority of the good people of these colonies, solemnly publish and declare, that these United Colonies are, and of right ought to be, FREE AND INDEPENDENT STATES; that they are absolved from all allegiance to the British crown, and that all political connection between them and the state of Great Britain is, and ought to be, totally dissolved; and that, as free and independent states, they have full power to levy war, conclude peace, contract alliances, establish commerce, and do all other acts and things which independent states may of right do. And for the support of this declaration, with a firm reliance on the protection of Divine Providence, we mutually pledge to each other our lives, our fortunes, and our sacred honor.

JOHN HANCOCK

BUTTON GWINNETT
LYMAN HALL
GEO. WALTON
WM. HOOPER
JOSEPH HEWES
JOHN PENN
EDWARD RUTLEDGE
THOS. HEYWARD, JUNR.
THOMAS LYNCH, JUNR.
ARTHUR MIDDLETON
SAMUEL CHASE
WM. PACA
THOS. STONE
CHARLES CARROLL OF CARROLLTON
GEORGE WYTHE
RICHARD HENRY LEE
TH. JEFFERSON
BENJ. HARRISON

THOS. NELSON, JR.
FRANCIS LIGHTFOOT LEE
CARTER BRAXTON
ROBT. MORRIS
BENJAMIN RUSH
BENJA. FRANKLIN
JOHN MORTON
GEO. CLYMER
JAS. SMITH
GEO. TAYLOR
JAMES WILSON
GEO. ROSS
CAESAR RODNEY
GEO READ
THO. M'KEAN
WM. FLOYD
PHIL. LIVINGSTON
FRANS. LEWIS
LEWIS MORRIS

RICHD. STOCKTON
JNO. WITHERSPOON
FRAS. HOPKINSON
JOHN HART
ABRA. CLARK
JOSIAH BARTLETT
WM. WHIPPLE
SAML. ADAMS
JOHN ADAMS
ROBT. TREAT PAINE
ELBRIDGE GERRY
STEP. HOPKINS
WILLIAM ELLERY
ROGER SHERMAN
SAM'EL HUNTINGTON
WM. WILLIAMS
OLIVER WOLCOTT
MATTHEW THORNTON

APPENDIX B

The Constitution of the United States of America

PREAMBLE

We the people of the United States, in order to form a more perfect union, establish justice, insure domestic tranquility, provide for the common defense, promote the general welfare, and secure the blessings of liberty to ourselves and our posterity, do ordain and establish this Constitution for the United States of America.

ARTICLE I.—THE LEGISLATIVE ARTICLE

Section 1. All legislative powers herein granted shall be vested in a Congress of the United States, which shall consist of a Senate and a House of Representatives.

House of Representatives: Composition, Qualification, Apportionment, Impeachment Power

Section 2. The House of Representatives shall be composed of members chosen every second year by the people of the several States, and the electors in each State shall have the qualifications requisite for electors of the most numerous branch of the State Legislature.

No person shall be a Representative who shall not have attained to the age of twenty-five years, and been seven years a citizen of the United States, and who shall not, when elected, be an inhabitant of that State in which he shall be chosen.

Representatives and direct taxes shall be apportioned among the several States which may be included within this Union, according to their respective numbers, *which shall be determined by adding to the whole number of free persons, including those bound to service for a term of years and excluding Indians not taxed, three-fifths of all other persons.* The actual enumeration shall be made within three years after the first meeting of the Congress of the United States, and within every subsequent term of ten years, in such manner as they shall by law direct. The number of Representatives shall not exceed one for every thirty thousand, but each State shall have at least one Representative; *and until each enumeration shall be made, the State of New Hampshire shall be entitled to choose three, Massachusetts eight, Rhode Island and Providence Plantations one, Connecticut five, New York six, New Jersey four, Pennsylvania eight, Delaware one, Maryland six, Virginia ten, North Carolina five, South Carolina five, and Georgia three.*

When vacancies happen in the representation from any State, the Executive authority thereof shall issue writs of election to fill such vacancies.

The House of Representatives shall choose their Speaker and other officers; and shall have the sole power of impeachment.

Passages no longer in effect are printed in italic type.

Senate Composition: Qualifications, Impeachment Trials

Section 3. The Senate of the United States shall be composed of two Senators from each State, *chosen by the legislature thereof,* for six years; and each Senator shall have one vote.

Immediately after they shall be assembled in consequence of the first election, they shall be divided as equally as may be into three classes. The seats of the Senators of the first class shall be vacated at the expiration of the second year, of the second class at the expiration of the fourth year, and of the third class at the expiration of the sixth year, so that one-third may be chosen every second year; and if vacancies happen by resignation or otherwise, during the recess of the legislature of any State, the Executive thereof may make temporary appointments until the next meeting of the legislature, which shall then fill such vacancies.

No person shall be a Senator who shall not have attained to the age of thirty years, and been nine years a citizen of the United States, and who shall not, when elected, be an inhabitant of that State for which he shall be chosen.

The Vice President of the United States shall be President of the Senate, but shall have no vote, unless they be equally divided.

The Senate shall choose their other officers, and also a President *pro tempore*, in the absence of the Vice President, or when he shall exercise the office of President of the United States.

The Senate shall have the sole power to try all impeachments. When sitting for that purpose, they shall be on oath or affirmation. When the President of the United States is tried, the Chief Justice shall preside: and no person shall be convicted without the concurrence of two-thirds of the members present.

Judgment in cases of impeachment shall not extend further than to removal from the office, and disqualification to hold and enjoy any office of honor, trust or profit under the United States; but the party convicted shall nevertheless be liable and subject to indictment, trial, judgment and punishment, according to law.

Congressional Elections: Time, Place, Manner

Section 4. The times, places and manner of holding elections for Senators and Representatives shall be prescribed in each State by the legislature thereof; but the Congress may at any time by law make or alter such regulations, except as to the places of choosing Senators.

The Congress shall assemble at least once in every year, and such meeting *shall be on the first Monday in December, unless they shall by law appoint a different day.*

Powers and Duties of the Houses

Section 5. Each house shall be the judge of the elections, returns and qualifications of its own members, and a majority of each shall constitute a quorum to do business; but a smaller number may adjourn from day to day, and may be authorized to compel the attendance of absent members, in such manner, and under such penalties, as each house may provide.

Each house may determine the rules of its proceedings, punish its members for disorderly behavior, and with the concurrence of two-thirds, expel a member.

Each house shall keep a journal of its proceedings, and from time to time publish the same, excepting such parts as may in their judgment require secrecy; and the yeas and nays of the members of either house on any question shall, at the desire of one-fifth of those present, be entered on the journal.

Neither house, during the session of Congress, shall, without the consent of the other, adjourn for more than three days, nor to any other place than that in which the two houses shall be sitting.

Rights of Members

Section 6. The Senators and Representatives shall receive a compensation for their services, to be ascertained by law and paid out of the treasury of the United States. They shall in all cases except treason, felony and breach of the peace, be privileged from arrest during their attendance at the session of their respective houses, and in going to and returning from the same; and for any speech or debate in either house, they shall not be questioned in any other place.

No Senator or Representative shall, during the time for which he was elected, be appointed to any civil office under the authority of the United States, which shall have been created, or the emoluments whereof shall have been increased, during such time; and no person holding any office under the United States shall be a member of either house during his continuance in office.

Legislative Powers: Bills and Resolutions

Section 7. All bills for raising revenue shall originate in the House of Representatives; but the Senate may propose or concur with amendments as on other bills.

Every bill which shall have passed the House of Representatives and the Senate, shall, before it become a law, be presented to the President of the United States; if he approve he shall sign it, but if not he shall return it with objections to that house in which it originated, who shall enter the objections at large on their journal, and proceed to reconsider it. If after such reconsideration two-thirds of that house shall agree to pass the bill, it shall be sent, together with the objections, to the other house, by which it shall likewise be reconsidered, and if approved by two-thirds of that house, it shall become a law. But in all such cases the votes of both houses shall be determined by yeas and nays, and the names of the persons voting for and against the bill shall be entered on the journal of each house respectively. If any bill shall not be returned by the President within ten days (Sundays excepted) after it shall have been presented to him, the same shall be a law, in like manner as if he had signed it, unless the Congress by their adjournment prevent its return, in which case it shall not be a law.

Every order, resolution, or vote to which the concurrence of the Senate and House of Representatives may be necessary (except on a question of adjournment) shall be presented to the President of the United States; and before the same shall take effect, shall be approved by him, or being disapproved by him, shall be repassed by two-thirds of the Senate and House of Representatives, according to the rules and limitations prescribed in the case of a bill.

Powers of Congress

Section 8. The Congress shall have power

To lay and collect taxes, duties, imposts and excises, to pay the debts and provide for the common defense and general welfare of the United States; but all duties, imposts and excises shall be uniform throughout the United States;

To borrow money on the credit of the United States;

To regulate commerce with foreign nations, and among the several States, and with the Indian tribes;

To establish an uniform rule of naturalization, and uniform laws on the subject of bankruptcies throughout the United States;

To coin money, regulate the value thereof, and of foreign coin, and fix the standard of weights and measures;

To provide for the punishment of counterfeiting the securities and current coin of the United States;

To establish post offices and post roads;

To promote the progress of science and useful arts by securing for limited times to authors and inventors the exclusive right to their respective writings and discoveries;

To constitute tribunals inferior to the Supreme Court;

To define and punish piracies and felonies committed on the high seas and offenses against the law of nations;

To declare war, grant letters of marque and reprisal, and make rules concerning captures on land and water;

To raise and support armies, but no appropriation of money to that use shall be for a longer term than two years;

To provide and maintain a navy;

To make rules for the government and regulation of the land and naval forces;

To provide for calling forth the militia to execute the laws of the Union, suppress insurrections, and repel invasions;

To provide for organizing, arming, and disciplining the militia, and for governing such part of them as may be employed in the service of the United States, reserving to the States respectively the appointment of the officers, and the authority of training the militia according to the discipline prescribed by Congress;

To exercise exclusive legislation in all cases whatsoever, over such district (not exceeding ten miles square) as may, by cession of particular States, and the acceptance of Congress, become the seat of the government of the United States, and to exercise like authority over all places purchased by the consent of the legislature of the State, in which the same shall be, for erection of forts, magazines, arsenals, dock-yards, and other needful buildings;—and

To make all laws which shall be necessary and proper for carrying into execution the foregoing powers, and all other powers vested by this Constitution in the government of the United States, or in any department or officer thereof.

Powers Denied to Congress

Section 9. *The migration or importation of such persons as any of the States now existing shall think proper to admit shall not be prohibited by the Congress prior to the year 1808; but a tax or duty may be imposed on such importation, not exceeding $10 for each person.*

The privilege of the writ of habeas corpus shall not be suspended, unless when in cases of rebellion or invasion the public safety may require it.

No bill of attainder or ex post facto law shall be passed.

No capitation, or other direct, tax shall be laid, unless in proportion to the census or enumeration herein before directed to be taken.

No tax or duty shall be laid on articles exported from any State.

No preference shall be given by any regulation of commerce or revenue to the ports of one State over those of another; nor shall vessels bound to, or from, one State, be obliged to enter, clear, or pay duties in another.

No money shall be drawn from the treasury, but in consequence of appropriations made by law; and a regular statement and account of the receipts and expenditures of all public money shall be published from time to time.

No title of nobility shall be granted by the United States; and no person holding any office of profit or trust under them, shall, without the consent of the Congress, accept of any present, emolument, office, or title, of any kind whatever, from any king, prince, or foreign state.

Powers Denied to the States

Section 10. No State shall enter into any treaty, alliance, or confederation; grant letters of marque and reprisal; coin money; emit bills of credit; make anything but gold and silver coin a tender in payment of debts; pass any bill of attainder, ex post facto law, or law impairing the obligation of contracts, or grant any title of nobility.

No State shall, without the consent of the Congress, lay any imposts or duties on imports or exports, except what may be absolutely necessary for executing its inspection laws: and the net produce of all duties and imposts, laid by any State on imports or exports, shall be for the use of the treasury of the United States; and all such laws shall be subject to the revision and control of the Congress.

No State shall, without the consent of Congress, lay any duty of tonnage, keep troops or ships of war in time of peace, enter into any agreement or compact with another State, or with a foreign power, or engage in war, unless actually invaded, or in such imminent danger as will not admit of delay.

ARTICLE II.—THE EXECUTIVE ARTICLE

Nature and Scope of Presidential Power

Section 1. The executive power shall be vested in a President of the United States of America. He shall hold his office during the term of four years, and, together with the Vice President, chosen for the same term, be elected, as follows:

Each State shall appoint, in such manner as the legislature thereof may direct, a number of electors, equal to the whole number of Senators and Representatives to which the State may be entitled in the Congress; but no Senator or Representative, or person holding an office of trust or profit under the United States, shall be appointed an elector.

The electors shall meet in their respective States, and vote by ballot for two persons, of whom one at least shall not be an inhabitant of the same State with themselves. And they shall make a list of all the persons voted for, and of the number of votes for each; which list they shall sign and certify, and transmit sealed to the seat of government of the United States, directed to the President of the Senate. The President of the Senate shall, in the presence of the Senate and House of Representatives, open all the certificates, and the votes shall then be counted. The person having the greatest number of votes shall be the President, if such number be a majority of the whole number of electors appointed; and if there be more than one who have such majority, and have an equal number of votes, then the House of Representatives shall immediately choose by ballot one of them for President; and if no person have a majority, then from the five highest on the list said house shall in like manner choose the President. But in choosing the President the votes shall be taken by States, the representation from each State having one vote; a quorum for this purpose shall consist of a member or members from two-thirds of the States, and a majority of all the States shall be necessary to a choice. In every case, after the choice of the President, the person having the greatest number of votes of the electors shall be the Vice President. But if there should remain two or more who have equal votes, the Senate shall choose from them by ballot the Vice President.

The Congress may determine the time of choosing the electors, and the day on which they shall give their votes; which day shall be the same throughout the United States.

No person except a natural-born citizen, *or a citizen of the United States at the time of the adoption of this Constitution*, shall be eligible to the office of President; neither shall any person be eligible to that office who shall not have attained to the age of thirty-five years, and been fourteen years a resident within the United States.

In case of the removal of the President from office or of his death, resignation, or inability to discharge the powers and duties of the said office, the same shall devolve on the Vice President, and the Congress may by law provide for the case of removal, death, resignation, or inability, both of the President and Vice President, declaring what officer shall then act as President, and such officer shall act accordingly, until the disability be removed, or a President shall be elected.

The President shall, at stated times, receive for his services a compensation, which shall neither be increased nor diminished during the period for which he shall have been elected, and he shall not receive within that period any other emolument from the United States, or any of them.

Before he enter on the execution of his office, he shall take the following oath or affirmation: —"I do solemnly swear (or affirm) that I will faithfully execute the office of President of the United States, and will to the best of my ability preserve, protect, and defend the Constitution of the United States."

Powers and Duties of the President

Section 2. The President shall be the commander in chief of the army and navy of the United States, and of the militia of the several States, when called into the actual service of the United States; he may require the opinion, in writing, of the principal officer in each of the executive departments, upon any subject relating to the duties of their respective offices, and he shall have power to grant reprieves and pardons for offenses against the United States, except in cases of impeachment.

He shall have power, by and with the advice and consent of the Senate, to make treaties, provided two-thirds of the Senators present concur; and he shall nominate, and by and with the advice and consent of the Senate, shall appoint ambassadors, other public ministers and consuls, judges of the Supreme Court, and all other officers of the United States, whose appointments are not herein otherwise provided for, and which shall be established by law: but the Congress may by law vest the appointment of such inferior officers, as they think proper, in the President alone, in the courts of law, or in the heads of departments.

The President shall have power to fill up all vacancies that may happen during the recess of the Senate, by granting commissions which shall expire at the end of their next session.

Section 3. He shall from time to time give to the Congress information of the state of the Union, and recommend to their consideration such measures as he shall judge necessary and expedient; he may, on extraordinary occasions, convene both houses, or either of them, and in case of disagreement between them, with respect to the time of adjournment, he may adjourn them to such time as he shall think proper; he shall receive ambassadors and other public ministers; he shall take care that the laws be faithfully executed, and shall commission all the officers of the United States.

Section 4. The President, Vice President and all civil officers of the United States shall be removed from office on impeachment for, and on conviction of, treason, bribery, or other high crimes and misdemeanor.

ARTICLE III.—THE JUDICIAL ARTICLE

Section 1. The judicial power of the United States shall be vested in one Supreme Court, and in such inferior courts as the Congress may from time to time ordain and establish. The judges, both of the Supreme and inferior courts, shall hold their offices during good behavior, and shall, at stated times, receive for their services a compensation which shall not be diminished during their continuance in office.

Jurisdiction

Section 2. The judicial power shall extend to all cases, in law and equity, arising under this Constitution, the laws of the United States, and treaties made, or which shall be made, under their authority;—to all cases affecting ambassadors, other public ministers and consuls;—to all cases of admiralty and maritime jurisdiction;—to controversies to which the United States shall be a party;—to controversies between two or more States;—*between a state and citizens of another state*;—between citizens of different States;—between citizens of the same State claiming lands under grants of different States, and between a State, or the citizens thereof, and foreign states, citizens or subjects.

In all cases affecting ambassadors, other public ministers and consuls, and those in which a State shall be party, the Supreme Court shall have original jurisdiction. In all the other cases before mentioned, the Supreme Court shall have appellate jurisdiction, both as to law and fact, with such exceptions, and under such regulations, as the Congress shall make.

The trial of all crimes, except in cases of impeachment, shall be by jury; and such trial shall be held in the State where said crimes shall have been committed; but when not committed within any State, the trial shall be at such place or places as the Congress may by law have directed.

Treason

Section 3. Treason against the United States shall consist only in levying war against them, or in adhering to their enemies, giving them aid and comfort. No person shall be convicted of treason unless on the testimony of two witnesses to the same overt act, or on confession in open court.

The Congress shall have power to declare the punishment of treason, but no attainder of treason shall work corruption of blood, or forfeiture except during the life of the person attained.

ARTICLE IV.—INTERSTATE RELATIONS

Full Faith and Credit Clause

Section 1. Full Faith and credit shall be given in each State to the public acts, records, and judicial proceedings of every other State. And the Congress may by general laws prescribe the manner in which such acts, records and proceedings shall be proved, and the effect thereof.

Privileges and Immunities; Interstate Extradition

Section 2. The citizens of each State shall be entitled to all privileges and immunities of citizens in the several States.

A person charged in any State with treason, felony or other crime, who shall flee from justice, and be found in another State, shall on demand of the executive authority of the State from which he fled, be delivered up, to be removed to the State having jurisdiction of the crime.

No person held to service or labor in one State, under the laws thereof, escaping into another, shall, in consequence of any law or regulation therein, be discharged from such service or labor, but shall be delivered up on claim of the party to whom such service or labor may be due.

Admission of States

Section 3. New States may be admitted by the Congress into this Union; but no new State shall be formed or erected within the jurisdiction of any other State; nor any State be formed by the junction of two or more States, or parts of States, without the consent of the legislatures of the States concerned as well as of the Congress.

The Congress shall have power to dispose of and make all needful rules and regulations respecting the territory or other property belonging to the United States; and nothing in this Constitution shall be so construed as to prejudice any claims of the United States, or of any particular State.

Republican Form of Government

Section 4. The United States shall guarantee to every State in this Union a republican form of government, and shall protect each of them against invasion; and on application of the legislature, or of the executive (when the legislature cannot be convened) against domestic violence.

ARTICLE V.—THE AMENDING POWER

The Congress, whenever two-thirds of both houses shall deem it necessary, shall propose amendments to this Constitution, or, on the application of the legislatures of two-thirds of the several States, shall call a convention for proposing amendments, which, in either case, shall be valid to all intents and purposes, as part of this Constitution, when ratified by the legislatures of three-fourths of the several States, or by conventions in three-fourths thereof, as the one or the other mode of ratification may be proposed by the Congress; *provided that no amendment which may be made prior to the year one thousand eight hundred and eight shall in any manner affect the first and fourth clauses in the ninth section of the first article*; and that no State, without its consent, shall be deprived of its equal suffrage in the Senate.

ARTICLE VI.—THE SUPREMACY ACT

All debts contracted and engagements entered into, before the adoption of this Constitution, shall be as valid against the United States under this Constitution, as under the Confederation.

This Constitution, and the laws of the United States which shall be made in pursuance thereof; and all treaties made, or which shall be made, under the authority of the United States, shall be the supreme law of the land; and the judges in every State shall be bound thereby, anything in the Constitution or laws of any State to the contrary notwithstanding.

The Senators and Representatives before mentioned, and the members of the several State legislatures, and all executive and judicial officers, both of the United States and of the several States, shall be bound by oath or affirmation to support this Constitution; but no religious test shall ever be required as a qualification to any office or public trust under the United States.

ARTICLE VII.—RATIFICATION

The ratification of the conventions of nine States shall be sufficient for the establishment of this Constitution between States so ratifying the same.

Done in Convention by the unanimous consent of the States present, the seventeenth day of September in the year of our Lord one thousand seven hundred and eighty-seven and of the Independence of the United States of America the twelfth. In witness whereof we have hereunto subscribed our names.

GEORGE WASHINGTON
President and Deputy from Virginia

New Hampshire
JOHN LANGDON
NICHOLAS GILMAN

Massachusetts
NATHANIEL GORHAM
RUFUS KING

Connecticut
WILLIAM S. JOHNSON
FER
ROGER SHERMAN

Virginia
JOHN BLAIR
JAMES MADISON, JR

South Carolina
J. RUTLEDGE
CHARLES G. PINCKNEY
PIERCE BUTLER

New York
ALEXANDER HAMILTON

New Jersey
WILLIAM LIVINGSTON
DAVID BREARLEY
WILLIAM PATERSON
JONATHAN DAYTON

Pennsylvania

BENJAMIN FRANKLIN
THOMAS MIFFLIN
ROBERT MORRIS
GEORGE CLYMER
THOMAS FITZSIMONS
JARED INGERSOLL
JAMES WILSON
GOUVERNEUR MORRIS

Delaware
GEORGE READ
GUNNING BEDFORD, JR.
JOHN DICKINSON
RICHARD BASSETT
JACOB BROOM

Maryland
JAMES MCHENRY
DANIEL OF ST. THOMAS JENI-

DANIEL CARROLL

North Carolina
WILLIAM BLOUNT
RICHARD DOBBS SPRAIGHT
HU WILLIAMSON

Georgia
WILLIAM FEW
ABRAHAM BALDWIN

THE BILL OF RIGHTS

The first ten Amendments (the Bill of Rights) were adopted in 1791.

AMENDMENT I.—RELIGION, SPEECH ASSEMBLY, AND PETITION

Congress shall make no law respecting an establishment of religion, or prohibiting the free exercise thereof; or abridging the freedom of speech, or of the press; or the right of the people peaceably to assemble, and to petition the government for a redress of grievances.

AMENDMENT II.—MILITIA AND THE RIGHT TO BEAR ARMS

A well-regulated militia being necessary to the security of a free State, the right of the people to keep and bear arms shall not be infringed.

AMENDMENT III.—QUARTERING OF SOLDIERS

No soldier shall, in time of peace, be quartered in any house without the consent of the owner, nor in time of war, but in a manner to be prescribed by law.

AMENDMENT IV.—SEARCHES AND SEIZURES

The right of the people to be secure in their persons, houses, papers, and effects, against unreasonable searches and seizures, shall not be violated, and no warrants shall issue but upon probable cause, supported by oath or affirmation, and particularly describing the place to be searched, and the persons or things to be seized.

AMENDMENT V.—GRAND JURIES, SELF-INCRIMINATION, DOUBLE JEOPARDY, DUE PROCESS, AND EMINENT DOMAIN

No person shall be held to answer for a capital, or otherwise infamous crime, unless on a presentment or indictment of a grand jury, except in cases arising in the land or naval forces, or in the militia, when in actual service in time of war or public danger; nor shall any person be subject for the same offense to be twice put in jeopardy of life or limb; nor shall be compelled in any criminal case to be a witness against himself, nor be deprived of life, liberty, or property, without due process of law; nor shall private property be taken for public use without just compensation.

AMENDMENT VI.—CRIMINAL COURT PROCEDURES

In all criminal prosecutions, the accused shall enjoy the right to a speedy and public trial, by an impartial jury of the State and district wherein the crime shall have been committed, which district shall have been previously ascertained by law, and to be informed of the nature and cause of the accusation; to be confronted with the witnesses against him; to have compulsory process for obtaining witnesses in his favor, and to have the assistance of counsel for his defense.

AMENDMENT VII.—TRIAL BY JURY IN COMMON LAW CASES

In suits at common law, where the value in controversy shall exceed twenty dollars, the right of trial by jury shall be preserved, and no fact tried by a jury shall be otherwise reexamined in any court of the United States, than according to the rules of the common law.

AMENDMENT VIII.—BAIL, CRUEL AND UNUSUAL PUNISHMENT

Excessive bail shall not be required, nor excessive fines imposed, nor cruel and unusual punishments inflicted.

AMENDMENT IX.—RIGHTS RETAINED BY THE PEOPLE

The enumeration in the Constitution, of certain rights, shall not be construed to deny or disparage others retained by the people.

AMENDMENT X.—RESERVED POWERS OF THE STATES

The powers not delegated to the United States by the Constitution, nor prohibited by it to the States, are reserved to the States respectively, or to the people.

PRE-CIVIL WAR AMENDMENTS

AMENDMENT XI.—SUITS AGAINST THE STATES
[Adopted 1798]

The judicial power of the United States shall not be construed to extend to any suit in law or equity, commenced or prosecuted against one of the United States by citizens of another State, or by citizens or subjects of any foreign state.

AMENDMENT XII.—ELECTION OF THE PRESIDENT
[Adopted 1804]

The electors shall meet in their respective *States*, and vote by ballot for President and Vice President, one of whom, at least, shall not be an inhabitant of the same State with themselves; they shall name in their ballots the person voted for as President, and in distinct ballots the person voted for as Vice President, and they shall make distinct lists of all persons voted for as President, and of all persons voted for as Vice President, and of the number of votes for each, which lists they shall sign and certify, and transmit sealed to the seat of the government of the United States, directed to the President of the Senate;—the President of the Senate shall, in the presence of the Senate and House of Representatives, open all the certificates and the votes shall then be counted;—the person having the greatest number of votes for President shall be the President, if such number be a majority of the whole number of electors appointed; and if no person have such majority, then from the persons having the highest numbers not exceeding three on the list of those voted for as President, the House of Representatives shall choose immediately, by ballot, the President. But in choosing the President, the votes shall be taken by States, the representation from each State having one vote; a quorum for this purpose shall consist of a member or members from two-thirds of the States, and a majority of all the States shall be necessary to a choice. And if the House of Representatives shall not choose a President whenever the right of choice shall devolve upon them, before *the fourth day of March* next following, then the Vice President shall act as President, as in the case of the death or other constitutional disability of the President.

The person having the greatest number of votes as Vice President shall be the Vice President, if such a number be a majority of the whole number of electors appointed; and if no person have a majority, then from the two highest numbers on the list the Senate shall choose the Vice President; a quorum for the purpose shall consist of two-thirds of the whole number of Senators, and a majority of the whole number shall be necessary to a choice. But no person constitutionally ineligible to the office of President shall be eligible to that of Vice President of the United States.

CIVIL WAR AMENDMENTS

AMENDMENT XIII.—PROHIBITION OF SLAVERY
[Adopted 1865]

Section 1. Neither slavery nor involuntary servitude, except as a punishment for crime whereof the party shall have been duly convicted, shall exist within the United States, or any place subject to their jurisdiction.

Section 2. Congress shall have power to enforce this article by appropriate legislation.

AMENDMENT XIV.—CITIZENSHIP, DUE PROCESS, AND EQUAL PROTECTION OF THE LAWS

[Adopted 1868]

Section 1. All persons born or naturalized in the United States, and subject to the jurisdiction thereof, are citizens of the United States and of the State wherein they reside. No State shall make or enforce any law which shall abridge **the privileges or immunities** of citizens of the United States; nor shall any State deprive any person of life, liberty, or property, without **due process of law**; nor deny to any person within its jurisdiction the **equal protection of the laws.**

Section 2. Representatives shall be apportioned among the several States according to their respective numbers, counting the whole number of persons in each State, excluding Indians not taxed. But when the right to vote at any election for the choice of Electors for President and Vice President of the United States, Representatives in Congress, the executive and judicial officers of a State, or the members of the legislature thereof, is denied to any of the male inhabitants of such State, being twenty-one years of age and citizens of the United States, or in any way abridged, except for participation in rebellion, or other crime, the basis of representation therein shall be reduced in the proportion which the number of such male citizens shall bear to the whole number of male citizens twenty-one years of age in such State.

Section 3. No person shall be a Senator or Representative in Congress, or Elector of President and Vice President, or hold any office, civil or military, under the United States, or under any State, who, having previously taken an oath, as a member of Congress, or as an officer of the United States, or as a member of any State legislature, or as an executive or judicial officer of any State, to support the Constitution of the United States, shall have engaged in insurrection or rebellion against the same, or given aid or comfort to the enemies thereof. Congress may, by a vote of two-thirds of each house, remove such disability.

Section 4. The validity of the public debt of the United States, authorized by law, including debts incurred for payment of pensions and bounties for services in suppressing insurrection or rebellion, shall not be questioned. But neither the United States nor any State shall assume or pay any debt or obligation incurred in aid of insurrection or rebellion against the United States, or any claim for the loss or emancipation of any slave; but all such debts, obligations and claims shall be held illegal and void.

Section 5. The Congress shall have power to enforce, by appropriate legislation, the provisions of this article.

AMENDMENT XV.—THE RIGHT TO VOTE

[Adopted 1870]

Section 1. The right of citizens of the United State to vote shall not be denied or abridged by the United States or by any State on account of race, color, or previous condition of servitude.

Section 2. The Congress shall have power to enforce this article by appropriate legislation.

AMENDMENT XVI.—INCOME TAXES

[Adopted 1913]

The Congress shall have power to lay and collect taxes on incomes, from whatever source derived, without apportionment among the several States, and without regard to any census or enumeration.

AMENDMENT XVII.—DIRECT ELECTION OF SENATORS

[Adopted 1913]

Section 1. The Senate of the United States shall be composed of two Senators from each State, elected by the people thereof, for six years; and each Senator shall have one vote. The electors in each State shall have the qualifications requisite for electors of (voters for) the most numerous branch of the State legislatures.

Section 2. When vacancies happen in the representation of any State in the Senate, the executive authority of such State shall issue writs of election to fill such vacancies: Provided, that the Legislature of any State may empower the executive thereof to make temporary appointments until the people fill the vacancies by election as the Legislature may direct.

Section 3. This amendment shall not be so construed as to affect the election or term of any Senator chosen before it becomes valid as part of the Constitution.

AMENDMENT XVIII.—PROHIBITION

[Adopted 1919; Repealed 1933]

Section 1. *After one year from the ratification of this article the manufacture, sale, or transportation of intoxicating liquors within, the importation thereof into, or the exportation thereof from the United State and all territory subject to the jurisdiction thereof, for beverage purposes, is hereby prohibited.*

Section 2. *The Congress and the several States shall have concurrent power to enforce this article by appropriate legislation.*

Section 3. *This article shall be inoperative unless it shall have been ratified as an amendment to the Constitution by the legislatures of the several States, as provided by the Constitution, within seven years from the date of the submission thereof to the States by the Congress.*

AMENDMENT XIX.—FOR WOMEN'S SUFFRAGE

[Adopted 1920]

Section 1. The right of citizens of the United States to vote shall not be denied or abridged by the United States or by any State on account of sex.

Section 2. The Congress shall have power to enforce this article by appropriate legislation.

AMENDMENT XX.—THE LAME DUCK AMENDMENT

[Adopted 1933]

Section 1. The terms of the President and Vice President shall end at noon on the 20th day of January, and the terms of the Senators and Representatives at noon on the 3rd day of January, of the years in which such terms would have ended if this article had not been ratified; and the terms of their successors shall then begin.

Section 2. The Congress shall assemble at least once in every year, and such meeting shall begin at noon on the 3rd day of January, unless they shall by law appoint a different day.

Section 3. If, at the time fixed for the beginning of the term of the President, the President-elect shall have died, the Vice President-elect shall become President. If a President shall not have been chosen before the time fixed for the beginning of his term, or if the President-elect shall have failed to qualify, then the Vice President-elect shall act as President until a President shall have qualified; and the Congress may by law provide for the case wherein neither a President-elect nor a Vice President-elect shall have qualified, declaring who shall then act as President, or the manner in which one who is to act shall be selected, and such persons shall act accordingly until a President or Vice President shall have qualified.

Section 4. The Congress may by law provide for the case of the death of any of the persons from whom the House of Representatives may choose a President whenever the right of choice shall have devolved upon them, and for the case of the death of any of the persons from whom the Senate may choose a Vice President whenever the right of choice shall have devolved upon them.

Section 5. Section 1 and 2 shall take effect on the 15th day of October following the ratification of this article.

Section 6. This article shall be inoperative unless it shall have been ratified as an amendment to the Constitution by the Legislatures of three-fourths of the several States within seven years from the date of its submission.

AMENDMENT XXI.—REPEAL OF PROHIBITION

[Adopted 1933]

Section 1. The eighteenth article of amendment to the Constitution of the United States is hereby repealed.

Section 2. The transportation or importation into any State, Territory, or Possession of the United States for delivery of use therein of intoxicating liquors, in violation of the laws thereof, is hereby prohibited.

Section 3. This article shall be inoperative unless it shall have been ratified as an amendment to the Constitution by conventions in the several States, as provided in the Constitution, within seven years from the date of submission thereof to the States by the Congress.

AMENDMENT XXII.—NUMBER OF PRESIDENTIAL TERMS
[Adopted 1951]

Section 1. No person shall be elected to the office of President more than twice, and no person who has held the office of President, or acted as President, for more than two years of a term to which some other person was elected President shall be elected to the office of President more than once. But this article shall not apply to any person holding the office of President when this article was proposed by the Congress, and shall not prevent any person who may be holding the office of President, or acting as President, during the term within which this article becomes operative from holding the office of President or acting as President during the remainder of such term.

Section 2. This article shall be inoperative unless it shall have been ratified as an amendment to the Constitution by the legislatures of three-fourths of the several States within seven years from the date of its submission to the States by the Congress.

AMENDMENT XXIII.—PRESIDENTIAL ELECTORS FOR THE DISTRICT OF COLUMBIA [Adopted 1961]

Section 1. The District constituting the seat of Government of the United States shall appoint in such manner as the Congress may direct:

A number of electors of President and Vice President equal to the whole number of Senators and Representatives in Congress to which the District would be entitled if it were a State, but in no event more than the least populous State; they shall be in addition to those appointed by the States, but they shall be considered for the purposes of the election of President and Vice President, to be electors appointed by a State; and they shall meet in the District and perform such duties as provided by the twelfth article of amendment.

Section 2. The Congress shall have power to enforce this article by appropriate legislation.

AMENDMENT XXIV.—THE ANTI-POLL TAX AMENDMENT
[Adopted 1964]

Section 1. The right of citizens of the United States to vote in any primary or other election for President or Vice President, for electors for President or Vice President, or for Senator or Representative in Congress, shall not be denied or abridged by the United States or any State by reason of failure to pay any poll tax or other tax.

Section 2. The Congress shall have power to enforce this article by appropriate legislation.

AMENDMENT XXV.—PRESIDENTIAL DISABILITY, VICE-PRESIDENTIAL VACANCIES
[Adopted 1967]

Section 1. In case of the removal of the President from office or his death or resignation, the Vice President shall become President.

Section 2. Whenever there is a vacancy in the office of the Vice President, the President shall nominate a Vice President who shall take office upon confirmation by a majority vote of both Houses of Congress.

Section 3. Whenever the President transmits to the President pro tempore of the Senate and the Speaker of the House of Representatives his written declaration that he is unable to discharge the powers and duties of his office, and until he transmits to them a written declaration to the contrary, such powers and duties shall be discharged by the Vice President as Acting President.

Section 4. Whenever the Vice President and a majority of either the principal officers of the executive departments or of such other body as Congress may by law provide, transmit to the President pro tempore of the Senate and the Speaker of the House of Representatives their written declaration that the President is unable to discharge the powers and duties of his office, the Vice President shall immediately assume the powers and duties of the office as Acting President.

Thereafter, when the President transmits to the President pro tempore of the Senate and the Speaker of the House of Representatives his written declaration that no inability exists, he shall resume the powers and duties of his office unless the Vice President and a majority of either the principal officers of the executive department{s} or of such other body as Congress may by law provide, transmit within four days to the President pro tempore of the Senate and the Speaker of the House of Representatives their written declaration that the President is unable to discharge the powers and duties of his office. Thereupon Congress shall decide the issue, assembling within forty-eight hours for that purpose if not in session. If the Congress, within twenty-one days after receipt of the latter written declaration, or, if Congress is not in session, within twenty-one days after Congress is required to assemble, determines by two-thirds vote of both Houses that the President is unable to discharge the powers and duties of his office, the Vice President shall continue to discharge the same as Acting President; otherwise, the President shall resume the powers and duties of his office.

AMENDMENT XXVI.—EIGHTEEN-YEAR-OLD VOTE

[Adopted 1971]

Section 1. The right of citizens of the United States, who are eighteen years of age or older, to vote shall not be denied or abridged by the United States or by any State on account of age.

Section 2. The Congress shall have power to enforce this article by appropriate legislation.

AMENDMENT XXVII.—VARYING CONGRESSIONAL COMPENSATION

[Adopted 1992]

No law varying the compensation for the service of the Senators and Representatives shall take effect until an election of Representatives shall have intervened.

APPENDIX C

PRESIDENTIAL ELECTIONS

Year	Name	Party	Popular Vote	Electoral College Vote
1789	George Washington	Federalist	—	69
1792	George Washington	Federalist	—	132
1796	John Adams	Federalist	—	71
	Thomas Jefferson	Democratic-Republican	—	68
1800	Thomas Jefferson	Democratic-Republican	—	73
	John Adams	Federalist	—	65
1804	Thomas Jefferson	Democratic-Republican	—	162
	Charles C. Pinckney	Federalist	—	14
1808	James Madison	Democratic-Republican	—	122
	Charles C. Pinckney	Federalist	—	47
1812	James Madison	Democratic-Republican	—	128
	George Clinton	Federalist	—	89
1816	James Monroe	Democratic-Republican	—	183
	Rufus King	Federalist	—	34
1820	James Monroe	Democratic-Republican	—	231
	John Quincy Adams	Democratic-Republican	—	1
1824	John Quincy Adams	Democratic-Republican	108,740	84
	Andrew Jackson	Democratic-Republican	153,544	99
	William Crawford	Democratic-Republican	46,618	41
	Henry Clay	Democratic-Republican	47,136	37
1828	Andrew Jackson	Democrat	647,286	178
	John Quincy Adams	National Republican	508,064	83
1832	Andrew Jackson	Democrat	687,502	219
	Henry Clay	National Republican	530,189	49
	Electoral votes not cast		2	
1836	Martin Van Buren	Democrat	765,483	170
	William Henry Harrison	Whig	550,816	73
	Hugh White	Whig	146,107	26
	Daniel Webster	Whig	41,201	14
	Total for the 3 Whigs		739,795	113
1840	William Henry Harrison	Whig	1,274,624	234
	Martin Van Buren	Democrat	1,127,781	60
1844	James K. Polk	Democrat	1,338,464	170
	Henry Clay	Whig	1,300,097	105
1848	Zachary Taylor	Whig	1,360,967	163
	Lewis Cass	Democrat	1,222,342	127

Year	Name	Party	Popular Vote	Electoral College Vote
	Martin Van Buren	Free-Soil	291,263	—
1852	Franklin Pierce	Democrat	1,601,117	254
	Winfield Scott	Whig	1,385,453	42
	John P. Hale	Free-Soil	155,825	—
1856	James Buchanan	Democrat	1,832,955	174
	John Frémont	Republican	1,339,932	114
	Millard Fillmore	Whig-American	871,731	8
1860	Abraham Lincoln	Republican	1,865,593	180
	John C. Breckinridge	Democratic	848,356	72
	Stephen Douglas	Democrat	1,382,713	12
	John Bell	Constitutional Union	592,906	39
1864	Abraham Lincoln	Unionist (Republican)	2,206,938	212
	George McClellan	Democrat	1,803,787	21
	Electoral votes not cast		81	
1868	Ulysses S. Grant	Republican	3,013,421	214
	Horatio Seymour	Democrat	2,706,829	80
	Electoral votes not cast		23	
1872	Ulysses S. Grant	Republican	3,596,745	286
	Horace Greeley	Democrat	2,843,446	
	Thomas Hendricks	Democrat	—	42
	Benjamin Brown	Democrat	—	18
	Charles Jenkins	Democrat	—	2
	David Davis	Democrat	—	1
1876	Rutherford B. Hayes	Republican	4,036,572	185
	Samuel Tilden	Democrat	4,284,020	184
	Peter Cooper	Greenback	81,737	—
1880	James A. Garfield	Republican	4,453,295	214
	Winfield S. Hancock	Democrat	4,414,082	155
	James B. Weaver	Greenback-Labor	308,578	—
1884	Grover Cleveland	Democrat	4,879,507	219
	James G. Blaine	Republican	4,850,293	182
	Benjamin Butler	Greenback-Labor	175,370	—
	John St. John	Prohibition	150,369	—
1888	Benjamin Harrison	Republican	5,447,129	233
	Grover Cleveland	Democrat	5,537,857	168
	Clinton Fisk	Prohibition	249,506	—
	Anson Streeter	Union Labor	146,935	—
1892	Grover Cleveland	Democrat	5,555,426	277
	Benjamin Harrison	Republican	5,182,690	145
	James B. Weaver	People's	1,029,846	22
	John Bidwell	Prohibition	264,133	—
1896	William McKinley	Republican	7,102,246	271
	William J. Bryan	Democrat	6,492,559	176
	John Palmer	National Democratic	133,148	—
	Joshua Levering	Prohibition	132,007	—
1900	William McKinley	Republican	7,218,491	292
	William J. Bryan	Democrat	6,356,734	155

Year	Name	Party	Popular Vote	Electoral College Vote
	John C. Wooley	Prohibition	208,914	—
	Eugene V. Debs	Socialist	87,814	—
1904	Theodore Roosevelt	Republican	7,628,461	336
	Alton B. Parker	Democrat	5,084,223	140
	Eugene V. Debs	Socialist	402,283	—
	Silas Swallow	Prohibition	258,536	—
	Thomas Watson	People's	117,183	—
1908	William Howard Taft	Republican	7,675,320	321
	William J. Bryan	Democrat	6,412,294	162
	Eugene V. Debs	Socialist	420,793	—
	Eugene Chafin	Prohibition	253,840	—
1912	Woodrow Wilson	Democrat	6,296,547	435
	William Howard Taft	Republican	3,486,720	8
	Theodore Roosevelt	Progressive	4,118,571	86
	Eugene V. Debs	Socialist	900,672	—
	Eugene Chafin	Prohibition	206,275	—
1916	Woodrow Wilson	Democrat	9,127,695	277
	Charles E. Hughes	Republican	8,533,507	254
	A. L. Benson	Socialist	585,113	—
	J. Frank Hanly	Prohibition	220,506	—
1920	Warren Harding	Republican	16,143,407	404
	James M. Cox	Democrat	9,130,328	127
	Eugene V. Debs	Socialist	919,799	—
	P. P. Christensen	Farmer-Labor	265,411	—
	Aaron Watkins	Prohibition	189,408	—
1924	Calvin Coolidge	Republican	15,718,211	382
	John W. Davis	Democrat	8,385,283	136
	Robert La Follette	Progressive	4,831,289	13
1928	Herbert C. Hoover	Republican	21,391,993	444
	Alfred E. Smith	Democrat	15,016,169	87
	Norman Thomas	Socialist	267,835	—
1932	Franklin D. Roosevelt	Democrat	22,809,638	472
	Herbert C. Hoover	Republican	15,758,901	59
	Norman Thomas	Socialist	881,951	—
	William Foster	Communist	102,785	—
1936	Franklin D. Roosevelt	Democrat	27,752,869	523
	Alfred M. Landon	Republican	16,674,665	8
	William Lemke	Union	882,479	—
	Norman Thomas	Socialist	187,720	—
1940	Franklin D. Roosevelt	Democrat	27,307,819	449
	Wendell Willkie	Republican	22,321,018	82
1944	Franklin D. Roosevelt	Democrat	25,606,585	432
	Thomas E. Dewey	Republican	22,014,745	99
1948	Harry S. Truman	Democrat	24,179,345	303
	Thomas E. Dewey	Republican	21,991,291	189
	Strom Thurmond	Dixiecrat	1,176,125	39
	Henry Wallace	Progressive	1,157,326	—
	Norman Thomas	Socialist	139,572	—
	Claude A. Watson	Prohibition	103,900	—

Year	Name	Party	Popular Vote	Electoral College Vote
1952	Dwight D. Eisenhower	Republican	33,936,234	442
	Adlai Stevenson II	Democrat	27,314,992	89
	Vincent Hallinan	Progressive	140,023	—
1956	Dwight D. Eisenhower	Republican	35,590,472	457
	Adlai Stevenson II	Democrat	26,022,752	73
	T. Coleman Andrews	States' Rights	111,178	—
	Walter B. Jones	Democrat	—	1
1960	John F. Kennedy	Democrat	34,226,731	303
	Richard M. Nixon	Republican	34,108,157	219
	Harry Byrd	Democrat	—	15
1964	Lyndon B. Johnson	Democrat	43,129,566	486
	Barry Goldwater	Republican	27,178,188	52
1968	Richard M. Nixon	Republican	31,785,480	301
	Hubert H. Humphrey	Democrat	31,275,166	191
	George Wallace	American Independent	9,906,473	46
1972	Richard M. Nixon	Republican	47,170,179	520
	George McGovern	Democrat	29,171,791	17
	John Hospers	Libertarian	—	1
1976	Jimmy Carter	Democrat	40,830,763	297
	Gerald R. Ford	Republican	39,147,793	240
	Ronald Reagan	Republican	—	1
1980	Ronald Reagan	Republican	43,904,153	489
	Jimmy Carter	Democrat	35,483,883	49
	John Anderson	Independent candidacy	5,719,437	—
1984	Ronald Reagan	Republican	54,455,074	525
	Walter F. Mondale	Democrat	37,577,137	13
1988	George Bush	Republican	48,881,278	426
	Michael Dukakis	Democrat	41,805,374	111
	Lloyd Bentsen	Democrat	—	1
1992	Bill Clinton	Democrat	43,727,625	370
	George Bush	Republican	38,165,180	168
	Ross Perot	Independent candidacy	19,236,411	0
1996	Bill Clinton	Democrat	45,628,667	379
	Bob Dole	Republican	37,869,435	159
	Ross Perot	Independent candidacy	7,874,283	0
2000	George W. Bush	Republican	49,820,518	271
	Albert Gore Jr.	Democrat	50,158,094	267
2004	George W. Bush	Republican	58,900,000	286
	John Kerry	Democrat	55,400,000	252
2008	Barack Obama	Democrat	66,882,230	365
	John McCain	Republican	58,343,671	173

APPENDIX D

Members of the Supreme Court of the United States

Chief Justices	State App't From	Appointed by President	Service
Jay, John	New York	Washington	1789-1795
Rutledge, John*	South Carolina	Washington	1795-1795
Ellsworth, Oliver	Connecticut	Washington	1796-1799
Marshall, John	Virginia	Adams, John	1801-1835
Taney, Roger Brooke	Maryland	Jackson	1836-1864
Chase, Salmon Portland	Ohio	Lincoln	1864-1873
Waite, Morrison Remick	Ohio	Grant	1874-1888
Fuller, Melville Weston	Illinois	Cleveland	1888-1910
White, Edward Douglass	Louisiana	Taft	1910-1921
Taft, William Howard	Connecticut	Harding	1921-1930
Hughes, Charles Evans	New York	Hoover	1930-1941
Stone, Harlan Fiske	New York	Roosevelt F.	1941-1946
Vinson, Fred Moore	Kentucky	Truman	1946-1953
Warren, Earl	California	Eisenhower	1953-1969
Burger, Warren Earl	Virginia	Nixon	1969-1986
Rehnquist, William H.	Virginia	Reagan	1986-2005
Roberts, John G., Jr.	Maryland	Bush, G. W.	2005-
Associate Justices			
Rutledge, John	South Carolina	Washington	1790-1791
Cushing, William	Massachusetts	Washington	1790-1810
Wilson, James	Pennsylvania	Washington	1789-1798
Blair, John	Virginia	Washington	1789-1796
Iredell, James	North Carolina	Washington	1790-1799
Johnson, Thomas	Maryland	Washington	1791-1793
Paterson, William	New Jersey	Washington	1793-1806
Chase, Samuel	Maryland	Washington	1796-1811
Washington, Bushrod	Virginia	Adams, John	1798-1829
Moore, Alfred	North Carolina	Adams, John	1799-1804
Johnson, William	South Carolina	Jefferson	1804-1834
Livingston, Henry Brockholst	New York	Jefferson	1806-1823
Todd, Thomas	Kentucky	Jefferson	1807-1826
Duvall, Gabriel	Maryland	Madison	1811-1836
Story, Joseph	Massachusetts	Madison	1811-1845
Thompson, Smith	New York	Monroe	1823-1843
Trimble, Robert	Kentucky	Adams, J. Q.	1826-1828

*ActingChief Justice; Senate refused to confirm appointment.

McLean, John	Ohio	Jackson	1829-1861
Baldwin, Henry	Pennsylvania	Jackson	1830-1844
Wayne, James Moore	Georgia	Jackson	1835-1867
Barbour, Philip Pendleton	Virginia	Jackson	1836-1841
Catron, John	Tennessee	Jackson	1837-1865
McKinley, John	Alabama	Van Buren	1837-1852
Daniel, Peter Vivian	Virginia	Van Buren	1841-1860
Nelson, Samuel	New York	Tyler	1845-1872
Woodbury, Levi	New Hampshire	Polk	1845-1851
Grier, Robert Cooper	Pennsylvania	Polk	1846-1870
Curtis, Benjamin Robbins	Massachusetts	Fillmore	1851-1857
Campbell, John Archibald	Alabama	Pierce	1853-1861
Clifford, Nathan	Maine	Buchanan	1858-1881
Swayne, Noah Haynes	Ohio	Lincoln	1862-1881
Miller, Samuel Freeman	Iowa	Lincoln	1862-1890
Davis, David	Illinois	Lincoln	1862-1877
Field, Stephen Johnson	California	Lincoln	1863-1897
Strong, William	Pennsylvania	Grant	1870-1880
Bradley, Joseph P.	New Jersey	Grant	1870-1892
Hunt, Ward	New York	Grant	1873-1882
Harlan, John Marshall	Kentucky	Hayes	1877-1911
Woods, William Burnham	Georgia	Hayes	1880-1887
Matthews, Stanley	Ohio	Garfield	1881-1889
Gray, Horace	Massachusetts	Arthur	1882-1902
Blatchford, Samuel	New York	Arthur	1882-1893
Lamar, Lucius Quintus C.	Mississippi	Cleveland	1888-1893
Brewer, David Josiah	Kansas	Harrison	1889-1910
Brown, Henry Billings	Michigan	Harrison	1890-1906
Shiras, George, Jr.	Pennsylvania	Harrison	1892-1903
Jackson, Howell Edmunds	Tennessee	Harrison	1893-1895
White, Edward Douglass	Louisiana	Cleveland	1894-1910
Peckham, Rufus Wheeler	New York	Cleveland	1896-1909
McKenna, Joseph	California	McKinley	1898-1925
Holmes, Oliver Wendell	Massachusetts	Roosevelt T.	1902-1932
Day, William Rufus	Ohio	Roosevelt T.	1903-1922
Moody, William Henry	Massachusetts	Roosevelt T.	1906-1910
Lurton, Horace Harmon	Tennessee	Taft	1910-1914
Hughes, Charles Evans	New York	Taft	1910-1916
Van Devanter, Willis	Wyoming	Taft	1910-1937
Lamar, Joseph Rucker	Georgia	Taft	1911-1916
Pitney, Mahlon	New Jersey	Taft	1912-1922
McReynolds, James Clark	Tennessee	Wilson	1914-1941
Brandeis, Louis Dembitz	Massachusetts	Wilson	1916-1939
Clarke, John Hessin	Ohio	Wilson	1916-1922
Sutherland, George	Utah	Harding	1922-1938
Butler, Pierce	Minnesota	Harding	1923-1939

Sanford, Edward Terry	Tennessee	Harding	1923-1930
Stone, Harlan Fiske	New York	Coolidge	1925-1941
Roberts, Owen Josephus	Pennsylvania	Hoover	1930-1945
Cardozo, Benjamin Nathan	New York	Hoover	1932-1938
Black, Hugo Lafayette	Alabama	Roosevelt F.	1937-1971
Reed, Stanley Forman	Kentucky	Roosevelt F.	1938-1957
Frankfurter, Felix	Massachusetts	Roosevelt F.	1939-1962
Douglas, William Orville	Connecticut	Roosevelt F.	1939-1975
Murphy, Frank	Michigan	Roosevelt F.	1940-1949
Byrnes, James Francis	South Carolina	Roosevelt F.	1941-1942
Jackson, Robert Houghwout	New York	Roosevelt F.	1941-1954
Rutledge, Wiley Blount	Iowa	Roosevelt F.	1943-1949
Burton, Harold Hitz	Ohio	Truman	1945-1958
Clark, Tom Campbell	Texas	Truman	1949-1967
Minton, Sherman	Indiana	Truman	1949-1956
Harlan, John Marshall	New York	Eisenhower	1955-1971
Brennan, William J., Jr.	New Jersey	Eisenhower	1956-1990
Whittaker, Charles Evans	Missouri	Eisenhower	1957-1962
Stewart, Potter	Ohio	Eisenhower	1958-1981
White, Byron Raymond	Colorado	Kennedy	1962-1993
Goldberg, Arthur Joseph	Illinois	Kennedy	1962-1965
Fortas, Abe	Tennessee	Johnson L.	1965-1969
Marshall, Thurgood	New York	Johnson L.	1967-1991
Blackmun, Harry A.	Minnesota	Nixon	1970-1994
Powell, Lewis F., Jr.	Virginia	Nixon	1972-1988
Rehnquist, William H.	Arizona	Nixon	1972-1986**
Stevens, John Paul	Illinois	Ford	1975-
O'Connor, Sandra Day	Arizona	Reagan	1981-2006
Scalia, Antonin	Virginia	Reagan	1986-
Kennedy, Anthony M.	California	Reagan	1988-
Souter, David H.	New Hampshire	Bush, G. H. W.	1990-
Thomas, Clarence	Georgia	Bush, G. H. W.	1991-
Ginsburg, Ruth Bader	New York	Clinton	1993-
Breyer, Stephen G.	Massachusetts	Clinton	1994-
Alito, Samuel A., Jr.	New Jersey	Bush, G. W.	2006-

Notes: The acceptance of the appointment and commission by the appointee, as evidenced by the taking of the prescribed oaths, is here implied; otherwise the individual is not carried on this list of the Members of the Court. Examples: Robert Hanson Harrison is not carried, as a letter from President Washington of February 9, 1790 states Harrison declined to serve. Neither is Edwin M. Stanton who died before he could take the necessary steps toward becoming a Member of the Court. *Chief Justice Rutledge is included because he took his oaths, presided over the August Term of 1795, and his name appears on two opinions of the Court for that Term.

[The foregoing was taken from a booklet prepared by the Supreme Court of the United States.]

**Elevated.

Index

A

B

D

E

G

I

J

K

L

N

O

S

U

V

Y

Z